STARTUP LAW AND FUNDRAISING

FOR ENTREPRENEURS AND STARTUP ADVISORS

D1602383

Paul A. Swegle

BLSG BUSINESS LAW
SEMINAR GROUP

Seattle, Washington

This book is intended to provide accurate and authoritative information, but the author and the publisher disclaim providing any legal advice or representation to its readers. If you require legal advice regarding specific facts and circumstances, retain the services of a qualified lawyer licensed in the appropriate jurisdiction.

No copyright is claimed or asserted in the excerpts of any court opinions or other materials from government sources or other third-party sources quoted within this work.
Request permission to copy or use material exceeding fair use,
17 U.S.C. § 107, by emailing Business Law Seminar Group, LLC at
businesslawseminargroup@gmail.com.

Library of Congress Control Number: 2018911095
ASIN# 0578236702
ISBN# 978-0-578-23670-4

I dedicate this book

to

my wife Serena and
our children Matthew and Stephanie
for their love and support,

and

to my father, Robert W. Swegle, Sr., for instilling in me a love of writing.

Special thanks to Serena Swegle for her incredible contributions to this book.
Thank you also to the following persons for their insightful feedback on the manuscript:
Thomas Reinhard
Aaron J. Dickinson
Patrick Schultheis
Geoff Entress
Stewart M. Landefeld
Sally Thompson
Chris Harvey
Robert Cumbow
Traci Carman

SUMMARY OF CONTENTS

Table of Contents

PART I – LEGAL AND REGULATORY FOUNDATION

CHAPTER ONE

Introduction

"Hi Paul, do you have a few minutes?" "Sure, what's up?"

"I'm advising a successful software startup that just hit a bump. The founders had promised each other they weren't subject to any non-competition or intellectual property agreements with prior employers. It turns out that one of them is. And everything he contributed to the startup's software belongs to the prior employer."

This book was inspired by a love of entrepreneurship. It was necessitated, though, by an endless stream of calls like that one about startups with dire self-inflicted wounds.

In that call from a fellow attorney, it was painfully clear an errant co-founder had made a mess of the startup's intellectual property ("IP"). The comic character "Pigpen" and the choking clouds of dust that envelop him instantly came to mind.

The Pigpen call was followed just days later by a completely separate startup implosion. A founder called lamenting that *"a very disagreeable man was claiming co-ownership"* of his startup. Sadly, the claim had merit. Before forming his company, the caller had invited that person to participate in early business plan discussions. Without signing a non-disclosure agreement ("NDA") or any other IP documentation, they brainstormed extensively about the startup's products, IP, and go-to-market strategy.

In the vacuum of informality, the two likely had formed an "accidental partnership."

That call was still on my mind when I awoke the next day.

'Why didn't he just form the damn company first and use an NDA?"

Helpless indignation gave way to a calming epiphany. I jumped out of bed and formed a company. I would develop an all-day talk called *Startup Law and Fundraising*, go on a speaking tour, and coach founders across the country on how to keep their startups out of trouble and raise money successfully and legally.

Wish I Knew This Sooner

The *Startup Law and Fundraising* 15-city tour of 2017 and 2018 produced an avalanche of additional evidence for a fundamental hypothesis:

Most startup legal and regulatory mistakes are predictable and avoidable.

1

In every city, founders, attorneys, CPAs, investors, and others confided about making or witnessing the same startup mistakes featured in my talk.

After most sessions, once the lighthearted greetings and banter tapered off, more somber queues would form — penitents and grievants waiting patiently to unburden themselves of mistakes and treacheries ruining their entrepreneurial dreams.

Countless conversations with seminar attendees ended with the sentiment, *"I wish I knew this sooner...."*

The Mission

The tour was rewarding but insufficient. How could I take these ideas to other founders destined to inadvertently sabotage their startups?

The answer to that question is this book, *Startup Law and Fundraising*.

Like the talk, it is for entrepreneurs and their advisors. Its purpose is to help entrepreneurs do three essential things:

- build their companies on a solid foundation,
- avoid costly and distracting legal and regulatory mistakes, and
- raise the money they need to succeed.

The Close Relationship Between Law and Fundraising

As distinct topics, law and fundraising may seem an odd pair, but they are inextricably related. Startups need resources to handle legal and regulatory matters. Successful fundraising can provide those resources. The relationship goes the other way, too - legal and regulatory mistakes can hurt fundraising and drain resources.

Many legal and regulatory mistakes result from resource constraints. Entrepreneurs often must launch their startups with little cash, leading to a certain amount of do-it-yourself legal work. Early mistakes and omissions can damage the very foundations of startups from the outset.

Well past formation, many startups continue to suffer from resource constraints due to ineffective fundraising. This is particularly true of startups led by founders reluctant to raise money because they do not want to *"give up equity."* I find myself repeating the same line to these entrepreneurs:

"You can own 90% of a company worth nothing, or you can own 60% of a company worth tens of millions, but you can't have it both ways."

Many founders simply don't understand the importance of fundraising or how to do it successfully.

Organizational Overview

This book is organized into three parts:

- Part I – Legal and Regulatory Foundation
- Part II – Fundraising
- Part III – Liquidity or Liquidation

This organization reflects the core concept of building from a strong foundation to create and protect value and to minimize costs and distractions that destroy value.

Part I, Legal and Regulatory Foundation, takes up the first ten chapters and covers virtually every legal, regulatory, and governance issue a startup will ever face. By the end of Part I, any reader should be able to use the General Counsel Audit to size up a company as a client, investment opportunity, or employer.

Part II devotes five chapters to startup finance and fundraising. All companies need working capital to succeed, but fundraising goals and methods are varied and flexible. Some founders pursue a high-growth, venture capital ("VC") track. Others pursue slower-growth strategies — bootstrapping and taking smaller investments in a drive to profitability at more modest revenue levels.

Other founders have high growth expectations but are unwilling or unable to tap into VC funding

These founders might explore alternatives like crowdfunding and Reg A+ "mini IPOs."

Whatever path is taken, designing and executing a fundraising plan requires focusing on these concepts and skills:

- how much to raise and when,
- what milestones are supported by each funding round,
- how to find large numbers of promising investors,
- how to connect with those investors,
- how to get investors to believe in your vision and mission,
- what investment instruments work best in different situations,
- how to negotiate reasonable terms in different types of funding rounds,
- how to close the deal, and
- how to work with investors after the deal to maintain their support of the company and avoid unnecessary friction.

Part III is about the endgame – liquidity or liquidation. Chapter 16 looks at strategies for guiding a company toward and through a successful initial public offering of its stock ("IPO") or a lucrative sale transaction.

Going public with an IPO or selling all or part of a company in a merger or sale are the two primary ways investors can realize a financial return on their investment. Either type of event is called an "exit," as in *exiting from the investment.*

Unfortunately, financial troubles can strike anywhere along a startup's journey. Chapter 17 is about dealing with financial distress and either escaping or navigating through the "zone of insolvency," the final chapter for many ventures.

Style

This book is intended for both academic and non-academic audiences. Non-academic target audiences include entrepreneurs and professional startup advisors like attorneys, investors, accountants, and finance professionals.

It also provides the framework for a complete course in entrepreneurial law, regulation, and finance at the law school, MBA, or advanced undergraduate level.

To make the material work across all of these audiences, I have made certain writing style decisions, including:

- Omission of Footnotes and Citations. With just a few clues, anyone can find laws, rules, cases, and administrative actions online. Footnotes and citations to those sources have been minimized here to reduce distractions and let readers get through the book more easily.

- Tone. Aside from stubborn adherence to the Oxford comma, the writing style here continues the informal style of the tour. All swearing has been omitted, but there remain sentence fragments, contractions, split infinitives, sentences that begin with the conjunctions "and" and "but," and other instances of questionable grammar. Informality is also intended to ease the book's production as an audiobook.

- Document Names are Capitalized. Although they are neither proper nouns nor literary titles, some document names are capitalized for emphasis and ease of location within the text.

- Defined Terms. As with most lawyers, I define terms along the way. For example, IP, NDA, and VC have already been defined. If you forget the meaning of a defined term or acronym, use the Index of Terms, Laws, Rules and Acronyms at the back to locate its first and later references. (Sorry, e-books do not support indexes, due to "reflowable" pagination.)

Case Studies

Law students learn by studying cases involving real facts and real disputes. Similarly, this book details 51 startup anecdotes that are intended to keep things interesting and reinforce key ideas and best practices. It is always better to learn from others' mistakes than suffer them ourselves.

Case Study #1 takes us back to our errant founder, "Pigpen."

Case Study #1 - Pigpen

Again, Pigpen was an errant founder who caused a company-threatening IP storm to swirl menacingly around himself and his new startup. The problems resulted from Pigpen's failure to disclose to his co-founder the Proprietary Information and Invention Agreement ("PIIA") Pigpen had signed with a prior employer. Because of the PIIA, that prior employer now had legitimate claims to substantial parts of the new startup's software-as-a-service ("SaaS") product offering. That product was in the market and selling well.

The caller and I unsuccessfully explored possibilities for pivoting around the clouded IP or invalidating the PIIA. Seeing no other good solution, I ultimately and reluctantly suggested working with the former employer to negotiate a "Settlement, Waiver, and Release." Alternatively, the solution could simply be called a "Licensing Agreement." Whatever the name, the resolution would almost certainly cost the startup.

Although it could not be compelled to do so, the former employer might grant a waiver and release of any legal claims against the startup in exchange for a royalty-bearing licensing agreement. The startup would likely have to share some percentage of its sales with the prior employer, possibly in perpetuity.

I also suggested seeking equity (ownership) and compensation reductions from Pigpen for recklessly pledging IP to the new startup that was owned by his former employer. Pigpen's mistake was a clear breach of his written representations and warranties to the startup and to the other co-founder.

Even though the prior employer was not yet aware of its potential ownership rights in the new company's software, not dealing with the issue was not one of the startup's options. The startup's liabilities to the prior employer would only grow. Also, any leverage to resolve the issue favorably could gradually decrease over time if the startup's successful trajectory continued.

Perhaps most importantly, the startup was about to raise funds from outside investors. Failing to disclose an IP cloud of this scale to new investors would constitute securities fraud under both state and federal statutes. That fraud would be attributable to *both* co-founders, as well as the startup itself.

> Lessons: New hires and founders themselves are often subject to one or more written "Confidentiality, Intellectual Property and Non-Competition Agreements," PIIAs, and other forms of agreements that govern IP ownership. Push to get those documents for each recent or otherwise significant role held by founders.

If a potential co-founder denies he or she signed one in a recent role, strongly consider requiring a confirming written statement from the founder's prior employer(s). As Pigpen's co-founder realized, written reps and warranties provide little actual protection.

BLSG Data Room

To see an example of a typical PIIA, plus examples of most of the other types of documents discussed in this book, request access to the Business Law Seminar Group ("BLSG") Data Room, a cloud-based document repository, by doing the following:

- Email businesslawseminargroup@gmail.com

- Use this email subject line: Request Access to BLSG Data Room

- Include the purchaser's (or owner's) first and last name, plus the purchaser's (or owner's) valid email address to be associated with the BLSG Data Room.

- Provide a copy of the receipt in or attached to the email.

Only one person will be granted access to the BLSG Data Room per purchased copy of the book. BLSG reserves the right to request additional information confirming the purchase.

Access to the BLSG Data Room is by invitation only and is offered solely as a gift at the discretion of BLSG.

Documents in the Data Room are "view only" and may not be printed, copied, or shared in any manner.

The Data Room is for purely educational purposes. No documents in the Data Room constitute legal advice, and they may not be used as or falsely held out as legal advice.

BLSG may terminate all access to the Data Room, or just your access, at any time. It may be hosted elsewhere, or even nowhere, in the future.

The BLSG Data Room is currently hosted and managed on the RR Donnelley "Venue" platform.

And as a reminder – none of the content of this book is legal advice. Working closely with experienced legal counsel is always recommended.

Reach out to me at businesslawseminargroup@gmail.com if you need a lawyer referral, and I will be happy to help.

Sources for Governance and Deal Templates

In addition to the BLSG Data Room, the following sources also offer excellent governance, finance, and legal templates for review and consideration.

Disclaimer: These links and others throughout the book are believed to be safe, but we disclaim any warranty of such safety. Use links at your discretion and risk.

- Wilson Sonsini Venture Term Sheet Generator

   https://www.wsgr.com/wsgr/Display.aspx?SectionName=practice/termsheet.htm

- The National Venture Capital Association

   https://nvca.org/resources/model-legal-documents/

- The Cooley law firm and Cooley Go

   https://www.cooleygo.com/documents/

- Y Combinator

  https://www.ycombinator.com/documents/

- The Orrick law firm

  https://www.orrick.com/Total-Access/Tool-Kit/Start-Up-Forms

- AskTheVC – Venture Deals

  https://www.venturedeals.com/resources

- Perkins Coie Startup Percolator

  https://www.startuppercolator.com/

Contract Drafting and Negotiation

Lastly, had I not already written "*Contract Drafting and Negotiation for Entrepreneurs and Business Professionals*," this book would have contained at least two other chapters – one on common contract mistakes and another on dispute resolution.

Readers who find this book useful may appreciate *Contract Drafting and Negotiation* as well. Find it on Amazon by searching for Paul Swegle or by going to https://www.amazon.com/dp/0692138307.

CHAPTER TWO

Overview of Legal and Regulatory Mistakes

In business, we have to learn by making mistakes. This is particularly true for startups innovating and developing business models in new areas of science, technology, and commerce.

"Fail fast" is the idea that entrepreneurs should experiment aggressively but also not be afraid to pull the plug quickly on poorly performing ideas.

In other words, take bold risks and pursue them aggressively, but do not prolong the death of losing ideas by wasting additional time and resources on them.

The ready acceptance of learning from mistakes speeds up scientific and technological innovation and the evolution of new business models.

But mistakes involving legal, regulatory, governance, and fundraising can produce more hardship than learning. The mantra *'It's better to get forgiveness than permission,"* has some validity in commercial relationships. With most laws and regulations, the better mantra is *"Measure twice and cut once."*

Business mistakes often show up quickly in a company's operational progress and financial results. Legal, governance, and regulatory mistakes can be more insidious. Some take their toll on a startup's resources gradually over time; others remain hidden, set to blow up at unfortunate junctures like financings or acquisitions.

This chapter provides an overview of common startup legal and regulatory mistakes, their root causes, how and when they usually come to light, and the various harms they cause.

The Most Harmful Legal and Regulatory Mistakes

The most harmful legal and regulatory mistakes by startups tend to involve:

- business entity formation issues,
- governance lapses,
- equity issuance issues,
- cap table errors and anomalies,
- gaps in financing documentation,
- unprotected IP,
- inadequate employment practices,
- poorly documented business arrangements, and
- regulatory non-compliance.

Most of these topics are the subject of their own chapter, but here are some short overviews for context.

Business Entity Formation

The term business entity refers to the type of legal structure established for a business. Virtually all startups are either corporations or limited liability companies formed under state law. Partnerships and sole proprietorships are also legal entities recognized under state law, but neither would provide a suitable foundation for a high-growth startup.

As we learn in chapters 5 and 6, there are numerous ways to err in forming a business entity, including selecting the wrong entity type, failing to complete the process for the chosen entity type, or negotiating inadequate or inappropriate governance and control provisions.

Founders sometimes set up corporations by selecting the default articles of incorporation offered by a secretary of state's online platform. These are usually silent on key issues like limiting director and officer liability.

Failing to appoint a board or key officers is another common mistake. Doing so clouds the validity of any actions purportedly taken by the company.

Founders forming a limited liability company ("LLC") often fail to timely negotiate and sign an Operating Agreement. Doing so muddies the respective owners' rights and obligations and often results in disputes.

Governance Lapses and Alter Ego Liability

When companies take important actions without proper approval, counsel for potential investors or acquirors sometimes later raise difficult questions regarding whether the action could be subject to challenge.

A very common mistake in this regard is the failure to obtain board approval for grants or sales of equity, including stock options. These issues are extremely common and can be tricky to clean up.

A key benefit of forming an entity is to shield the individuals involved from personal liability. Failure to observe governance formalities can jeopardize those shields and also render corporate acts and decisions invalid.

Founders and others need to avoid conduct that could lead to "piercing the corporate veil," also referred to as "alter ego" liability. Third parties can go after dominant shareholders personally when they have treated an entity (and its assets) as their own alter ego and ignored proper governance rules and processes.

Courts will find in favor of piercing the veil in situations where injustice would otherwise result. Alter ego liability can be applied against all shareholders but is generally sought against active shareholders who influence and govern a corporation or LLC.

Facts that can support piercing the veil include:

- insider fraud,
- failure to maintain separate identities of the corporation and its founders or shareholders,
- commingling corporate funds and founder funds,

- entering into agreements in the alter ego name,

- use of company funds for personal purposes,

- undercapitalizing an entity, and

- failure to observe corporate formalities, such as approving matters through appropriate board actions, keeping board minutes, and executing documents correctly in the name of the corporation.

While these issues are less common in more established startups, they are important to be aware of and to avoid. This is particularly true in light of the high failure rates for startups and the inability to walk away from alter ego liabilities in insolvency, including under Chapter 7 bankruptcy rules.

Equity Issuance Mistakes

In addition to the failure to obtain board approval for equity issuances, there are myriad other mistakes that can occur involving equity issuances. Again, in this context, the term equity refers to any type of *ownership interest* in a company - often meaning stock or stock options in corporations and membership units in LLCs.

Startups frequently delay following through on promised equity grants to employees, consultants, board members, and others. These delays can result in unnecessary tax issues, as will be discussed later, along with higher stock option exercise prices where the value of the company's shares increases before the delayed grant.

Cap Table Errors and Anomalies

A company's cap table describes who owns its shares or units and also who has potential future claims to shares or units. Promising equity grants in terms of percentages of ownership instead of specific share numbers is one of several types of mistakes that can lead to inaccurate or otherwise uncertain cap tables. Find examples of cap tables in the BLSG Data Room under *Finance > Cap Tables*.

Potential investors also do not like cap tables with too much "dead equity." Dead equity is stock acquired by a third party in exchange for little or no financial consideration and, thus, no longer available to the company for raising working capital or granting as equity compensation to current or future employees.

Some investors call all equity held by persons with no ongoing, active role dead equity, even interests of early investors and vested stock options held by departed employees.

These more extreme views are less common. But any time a founder with a sizable ownership stake is forced out and the company has no contractual recourse to claw back any of that equity, the result is dead equity of a size and nature that can drive away potential investors and harm future fundraising.

Dead equity in the hands of an antagonistic or irrational shareholder is even worse, particularly when that shareholder can withhold key votes for critical matters such as financings. Keeping equity out of potentially hostile hands is an awkward but important subject. Smart founders establish agreements, policies, and best practices at the outset to ensure control over all transactions in a company's equity.

The key tools for preventing dead equity are (i) vesting schedules that require ownership interests like stock and stock options to be earned over time and (ii) clawback provisions that permit a company to take back or buy back equity interests under appropriate circumstances.

Clawback provisions rarely go by that name and are more often couched in less obvious terms, like "company repurchase rights," "redemption," or "forfeiture."

We look further at preventing dead equity in Chapter 8 - *Structuring and Managing Key Relationships.*

Gaps in Financing Documentation

The earliest financing documentation mistakes usually have to do with poorly documented loans by founders or friends and family. Sometimes they are not documented at all. Other times, the first funding tranche is documented, but subsequent tranches are not.

These mistakes raise several potential issues for the company and the lenders themselves. Undocumented or poorly documented founder loans raise questions regarding whether the advances constituted repayable loans or capital contributions in exchange for grants of equity.

Founders making undocumented loans face additional questions involving tax treatment and whether or not they even have valid claims to repayment. The U.S. Internal Revenue Service ("IRS") often sees "equity" where others wanted to claim "debt."

Other early documentation gaps can raise very fundamental questions. Do investors actually own shares issued without proper board or shareholder approval? Can investors demand their money back in the absence of documentation showing compliance with the securities laws?

Documentation gaps can involve:

- the absence of board approval records for share issuances,

- incomplete or unsigned share issuance documentation,

- evidence of written or oral promises of equity interests not yet honored, and

- other gaps that raise questions of possible company liabilities under the securities laws.

Potential investors and acquirors will closely scrutinize any circumstances indicating a company's loose handling of equity issuances might trigger claims impacting the cap table or otherwise threatening unexpected and costly disputes.

We go through the steps and documentation required to prevent these concerns in Chapter 11, *State and Federal Securities Laws*, Chapter 12, *Startup Finance Overview* and Chapter 13, *Seed and Pre-Seed Fundraising.*

Intellectual Property Mistakes

Chapter 9, *Intellectual Property – Protecting Rights and Avoiding Liabilities,* discusses how to avoid many IP mistakes. These sometimes have to do with inadequate IP assignment documentation from founders, employees, contractors, and vendors. Other common mistakes involve failing to timely and competently protect trademarks, patentable inventions, copyrights, and trade secrets.

The Pigpen Case Study demonstrates the severity of IP mistakes.

Poorly Documented Business Arrangements

Startups sign lots of bad commercial deals. And startups make lots of mistakes in what might be called "contract administration" – ensuring commercial relationships are supervised and performing well.

Common mistakes include:

- allowing work to begin before a contract is in place,
- agreements that are unclear about the other party's obligations, and
- agreements without remedies for poor performance.

Contract Drafting and Negotiation for Entrepreneurs and Business Professionals is a business person's guide for maximizing value and limiting risks in commercial relationships. Find it on Amazon by searching "Swegle" or going to https://www.amazon.com/dp/0692138307.

Inadequate Employment Practices

Few areas of operational and administrative weakness cause more legal difficulties than those involving employees. Some examples:

- Claims of flaunting wage and hour laws and family and medical leave laws.
- The desire to avoid payroll taxes drives startups to improperly classify workers as contractors that states view as employees.
- Employees often claim that startups failed to honor compensation promises relating to equity grants, performance bonuses, and increases in pay.
- Companies with weak onboarding, orientation, evaluation, and management training processes can end up with costly wrongful discharge, harassment, and discrimination claims.

Employees terminated without proper performance documentation seem to sue or threaten to sue at least 20% of the time.

In many cases, employees and former employees don't even need to sue. They can simply file an administrative complaint with one or more state, local or federal agencies.

Employment practices claims are among the easiest to avoid and mitigate through basic best practices, including establishing clear expectations and regularly providing timely performance feedback. These best practices and other employment-related issues are covered in Chapter 8, *Structuring and Managing Key Relationships.*

Regulatory Mistakes

As discussed in Chapter 10, *Common Regulatory Mistakes*, misclassification of employees as independent contractors is perhaps the most pervasive startup regulatory mistake – or alleged mistake.

With the 2020 implementation in California of Assembly Bill 5, or "AB5," and the likely passage of similar legislation in other states effectively banning many kinds of freelancers and independent contractors, this issue will likely grow. Specifically, it is increasingly difficult to hire as an independent contractor anybody whose job is in the usual course of a company's business. We consider these issues in more detail in Chapter 10, under *Misclassifying Employees as Contractors*.

There is a fine and somewhat artificial distinction drawn in this book between legal mistakes and regulatory mistakes. Still, the term regulatory mistake seems to fit here because of the ability and willingness of both state and federal labor and tax authorities to bring actions and assess penalties for employee misclassification.

Other common regulatory mistakes by startups include violations of state and federal securities laws, unfair and deceptive advertising laws, unfair business practices laws, sweepstakes and contest laws, privacy and data security laws, and unsolicited call, text and email-related laws.

This summary highlights just a few of the many types of startup legal and regulatory mistakes. Some are obvious and easily avoided, others much less so. In the next section, we will briefly look at how most mistakes are caused, followed by when and how the harms from startup mistakes manifest themselves.

Causes of Legal and Regulatory Mistakes

Most startup legal and regulatory mistakes are inadvertent. They are often attributable to gaps in both sophistication and financial resources. Sometimes they arise unexpectedly out of poorly monitored legal, regulatory, or governance "loose ends." Other times, mistakes involve knowing gambles over not getting caught, or at least not being around when things go bad.

The term "loose ends" is used here as shorthand for a broad spectrum of neglect and procrastination concerning legal and regulatory matters common to startups.

Full-blown legal and regulatory mistakes often start as loose ends. Loose ends accumulate when a resource-strapped startup cuts corners and defers the proper handling of legal, governance, and regulatory matters.

Learning on the Job

Two primary causes of most startup legal and regulatory mistakes are inexperience and lack of knowledge. You don't know what you don't know. And if you can't afford to hire someone who does know, sometimes you have to learn on the job. Most startups face this dilemma to some degree.

Learning on the job generally works out fine when accompanied by a measure-twice, cut-once attitude. But when modest sophistication combines with high entrepreneurial speed and an "apologize-later" attitude, startups can find themselves plagued with problems.

Case Study 2 recounts a confluence of low sophistication and high confidence in action.

Case Study #2 – Bull in a China Shop

The fields of art and science have long provided examples of brilliant but eccentric creators and inventors who make terrible business decisions, take crazy risks, and make a bit of a mess. Vincent Van Gogh, Kurt Cobain, and Nikola Tesla are just a few eccentric creatives who come to mind.

We also find highly creative, poorly self-regulated individuals in business. Elon Musk of Tesla is a perfect example. Musk is a brilliant entrepreneur, but the U.S. Securities and Exchange Commission ("SEC") forced Tesla's board to remove him as board chair. His somewhat amusing online pot smoking incident triggered a federal review of Space X's workplace culture.

I have been asked to help with several situations involving wayward founders. One case involved a founder who could barely hold a meeting, send an email or talk on the phone without creating a legal or regulatory liability. Before finally being demoted from the CEO role, his mistakes included, among others:

- mishandling company trade secrets and third-party confidential information,
- negotiating and signing defective financing documents resulting in investor disputes,
- negotiating and signing unenforceable commercial agreements,
- casually violating governance requirements, and
- consistently rejecting the advice of outside experts.

In this case, the company was fortunate to have (i) three founders, (ii) a Shareholders Agreement that gave each founder a board seat, and (iii) the right to claw back, or forfeit, the shares of any founder terminated from an executive role "for cause."

The board terminated the errant founder from his executive role, clawed back his shares at fair market value, and removed him from the board. This ended the immediate crisis. But the financial costs and disruptions caused permanent harm.

> Lesson: As discussed in Chapter 5, under *Co-Founder Compatibility*, entrepreneurs should use care in selecting their co-founders and structuring their relationships with them. A founder typically wields power as an officer, director, and dominant voting shareholder. Few stakeholders can cause the scope of harm of a poorly selected and hard-to-remove founder. Self-awareness and good self-monitoring should be mandatory attributes for any co-founder.

Case Study #2 is revisited in Chapter 8, *Structuring and Managing Key Relationships*, under the discussion of Shareholders Agreements and Founder Employment Agreements.

Willful Misdeeds

While most mistakes result from simple negligence, oversights, and poorly calibrated entrepreneurial exuberance, some mistakes are more deliberate and sophisticated.

Consider a hypothetical marketing executive who might be tempted to engage in false or deceptive marketing to increase his near-term bonus based on current period sales. He may believe that any legal or regulatory action would come in the future after he is no longer an employee.

Similarly, some executives make bad legal or regulatory decisions in desperate bids to hit financing goals, hoping that raising lots of money will enable the company to hide the issues long enough to make them go away somehow. That strategy likely drove Elizabeth Holmes, CEO of Theranos, to hatch and perpetuate her shocking $700 million securities fraud.

Case Study #3 – Prime Time

One evening while preparing to leave the office of a successful startup, an advertising team member asked if I had time to quickly review a television ad he wanted to run that night.

A particular celebrity was appearing on late-night TV that evening. The proposed ad was intended to generate sales by appealing to fans of the celebrity, but it contained a message that was prohibited by applicable regulations.

This colleague was new to the team and came from a non-regulated environment. I told him I appreciated his enthusiasm but that it would be highly improper for us to run the ad. I rejected the ad, confirmed his agreement that it would not run, and said goodnight. I assumed that was the end of it.

Nonetheless, watching the celebrity that night seemed like a hot tip, given his recently elevated profile. Later that evening, I popped a beer and caught the show.

And then it happened. This celebrity was known for his tendency to shock, and I was shocked, but not by anything he said. It was seeing the ad on national TV that I had rejected just six hours earlier.

We called key federal regulators the next morning to notify them of the improper ad. We told them we had rejected it and assumed it would not air, and that we had terminated the individual responsible.

The regulators were understanding and appreciative of our no-nonsense response. Failure to have responded immediately could have resulted in a severe enforcement action, including a substantial fine.

Lessons. "Apologize later" is a real mindset among some in business. Case Study #3 highlights the importance of adopting and enforcing an Ethics Policy or Code of Conduct. They are sometimes the only tools available for immediately terminating scofflaws and other bad actors at any level within a company.

Even in this case of clear misconduct, the terminated employee hired counsel and threatened to sue. The existence of a robust Ethics Policy, and the terminated employee's up-front agreement to comply with it, enabled the company to ignore the terminated employee's threats. His lawyer likely told him it would be a difficult case.

Mistake Impacts - Timing and Materiality Matrix

Some legal mistakes have obvious and almost immediate consequences, like the example in Case Study #3. Others may be slightly less obvious and may take their toll over a longer time. And some mistakes can remain largely unknown or misunderstood for months or years, only to suddenly detonate unexpectedly like hidden landmines.

When working with non-attorneys, I occasionally use a "likelihood and materiality" matrix when discussing the range of possible consequences from a specific decision. As discussed below, we can also use that type of matrix to prioritize corrective actions for multiple legal or regulatory loose ends.

But let us first look at a slightly different "timing and materiality" matrix to highlight some other important facts about legal and regulatory mistakes.

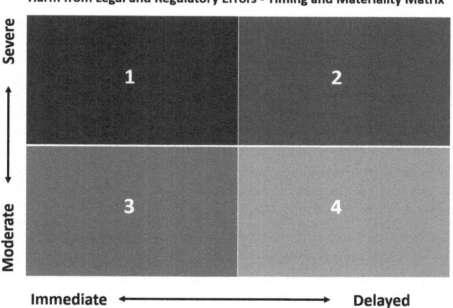

Harm from Legal and Regulatory Errors - Timing and Materiality Matrix

A few observations about certain correlations in this matrix:

- Some mistakes cause roughly the same harm, whether they come to light or cause harm quickly or slowly. The ones that cause the most harm the soonest, in box #1 above, are arguably most damaging. For one reason, newer companies are less likely to have resources to deal with their consequences.

- Some mistakes cause no harm if found and remedied soon. Those might belong in box #3.

- Some mistakes suddenly become extremely harmful months or years later, usually after a deadline or final corrective opportunity passes. These could be plotted anywhere near the top of boxes #1 or #2.

- Similarly, the harm caused by some mistakes steadily increases with time as opportunities for cure are gradually lost or as potential damages or penalties accrue. These mistakes also could fall anywhere within the upper regions of boxes #1 and #2.

Thinking back to Case Study #1, *Pigpen*, his IP mistake was identified relatively early in the company's history and likely had severe consequences for the company and its founders. Arguably, though, dealing with those consequences sooner prevented the harm from growing and spreading to new investors and other stakeholders.

This highlights the related fact that mistakes often cause different types and levels of harm to different actors and constituents as time passes. Thus, motivations to prevent, identify, or cure mistakes can vary by actor.

Most of us, for example, have witnessed individuals doing things they know they shouldn't be doing, perhaps motivated by an expectation that any negative consequences would be for others to address. As we discuss later, the tendency to cut corners and take chances is heightened in startups, due to the combination of low resources and high expectations.

In Chapter 4, we look at prioritizing the cleanup of legal mistakes and other loose ends. Most startups have to triage their remedial efforts, focusing on issues that are most likely to become problems sooner, and delaying efforts on those that seem less risky in the near term.

Discovery and Disclosure of Legal and Regulatory Mistakes

Willful mistakes, and mistakes committed through reckless indifference or casual negligence, are sometimes driven by a belief that the mistakes will go undiscovered forever or until there are resources to deal with or overshadow them.

In other cases, perpetrators of willful mistakes are likely betting they will have left the company before anybody discovers their malfeasance.

Such hopes may be misplaced. Startup legal and regulatory mistakes rarely remain benign or undiscovered for long. If not first flagged by current or former employees, customers, competitors, or regulators, due diligence almost invariably uncovers them.

Due Diligence

Due diligence is the process investors and acquirors use to determine whether to go forward with a transaction and, if so, on what terms.

When experienced lawyers, accountants, and other experts conduct due diligence, mistakes and loose ends have no place to hide.

Central to this process is a document called a "Due Diligence List." These usually go on for pages and often contain between 300 and 700 questions and requests for documents. Due Diligence Lists provide their users with a detailed and systematic approach to ferreting out all manner of legal and regulatory issues, big and small. Find a sample Due Diligence List in the BLSG Data Room under *Financing Documents > Due Diligence Lists.*

For companies that have their legal, governance, and regulatory acts together, and a robust virtual data room to prove it, getting through due diligence is no problem.

But even in clean deals, due diligence in mergers and acquisitions ("M&A") usually feels like a hunt for spurious concerns to lower the deal valuation and to shift risk, as discussed below.

This aspect of due diligence is made all the more annoying by the fact that deal "Term Sheets" usually require the company that is the subject of the due diligence to pay for all or part of the other party's due diligence costs.

Reps and Warranties and Schedules of Exceptions

In financings and M&A deals, Due Diligence Lists are often tied directly to the "Representations and Warranties" section of a Stock Purchase Agreement ("SPA") or Asset Purchase and Sale Agreement ("PSA"). These are commonly known by the abbreviated term "reps and warranties."

Find a sample Asset PSA in the BLSG Data Room under *Finance > Merger and Acquisition Documents.*

In any deal, reps and warranties are written assurances about the truth of myriad legal, governance, and regulatory matters and also about the absence of negative facts regarding specific legal, governance, and regulatory matters.

Signed reps and warranties provide investors and buyers with special rights in the event they prove untrue. These rights include financial damages for fraud and breach of contract and also "indemnification," which means legal and financial protection from third-party suits, governmental actions, and the like.

M&A deals frequently involve delayed payouts to the acquired company's shareholders that can be reduced or even eliminated if key reps and warranties turn out to be untrue or inaccurate.

As a result, written reps and warranties frequently include disclaimers that begin with language such as "Except as described in Section 13(f) of the Schedule of Exceptions…." A Schedule of Exceptions, also called a "Disclosure Schedule," is an exhibit or schedule frequently attached to a PSA, SPA, or other transaction document.

All of a company's legal and regulatory skeletons should be described in a Schedule of Exceptions or Disclosure Schedule to make any related reps and warranties in the main transaction document not false.

Unfortunately, there is no sample Schedule of Exceptions or Disclosure Schedule in the BLSG Data Room. These tend to consist almost exclusively of confidential information that is too difficult to anonymize.

Customers, Competitors, and Employees

In addition to due diligence, other common ways that legal and regulatory mistakes come to light include lawsuits or regulatory complaints by competitors, unhappy customers, or vindictive former employees.

- Unhappy customers are often quick to file regulatory complaints about false advertising, misleading product claims, product safety issues, and warranty claims.

- Competitors frequently raise similar advertising, product safety, and other regulatory issues with regulators. They also file civil suits for misleading product comparisons or intellectual property infringement. Regarding Case Study #3, I knew any competitors who saw the improper TV ad might quickly bring it to the regulators' attention.

- And few company secrets are safe with disgruntled former employees. Given any provocation, angry former employees will file claims involving alleged wage and hour violations and alert regulators to other perceived violations. They may also use social media to maliciously publicize alleged product or service shortcomings, legal or regulatory infractions, or other damaging information.

- Lastly, random opportunists also attack companies over perceived legal or regulatory vulnerabilities. A litigious couple from Wisconsin recently attempted to extort $20,000 from one of my clients. We reported the extortion to the Federal Bureau of Investigation.

Between the rigors of due diligence and the gauntlet of other actors prone to finding and reporting alleged malfeasance or misfeasance, never assume legal or regulatory mistakes will remain undiscovered for long.

Legal and Regulatory Risks

Assuming, then, that startup legal and regulatory mistakes will be ultimately discovered or otherwise blow up, what are some typical consequences, and how severe are they? Or in the often-used language of clients – *"What's the worst thing that could happen?"*

A Likelihood and Materiality Matrix ("L&M Matrix") is one way to start thinking about the fallout from startup legal and regulatory mistakes.

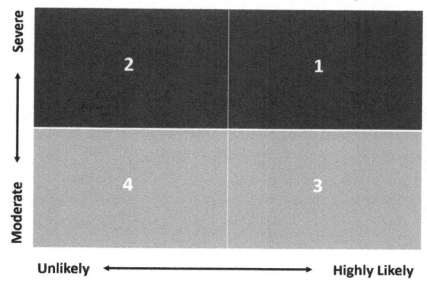

Legal and Regulatory Issues – Likelihood and Materiality Matrix

In this matrix, mistakes belonging in box #1 are ones most likely to come to fruition and to cause more severe harm if they do, while mistakes belonging in box #4 are the least likely to come to fruition or to cause substantial harm.

By way of example, Pigpen's mistake belongs in box #1. The potential harms from his error are both likely and severe. This is because (i) the former employer is almost certain to learn of the possible infringement, given that its former employee has launched a competitive product and (ii) an infringement suit by the former employer could potentially jeopardize the startup's continued existence or require burdensome royalty payments.

Direct and Indirect Risks

Legal and regulatory mistakes pose a wide range of direct and indirect risks:

- lawsuits by commercial partners, investors, employees, customers, and competitors,

- government agency civil suits, administrative actions, and criminal prosecutions, and

- costs and distractions related to the above.

- adverse impacts on operations and financial results caused by the diversion of resources and management's attention,

- negative impacts on reputation and employee morale,

- internal tensions, particularly between co-founders, and

- financing and M&A deal risks.

The risk of tensions between co-founders is very real. The co-founders in Case Study #2 were long-time friends but no longer speak to each other. The difficulties between them became an awkward and difficult disclosure matter in talks with potential investors.

And despite the existence of a non-disparagement clause in the parties' settlement agreement, the company has repeatedly heard that the ousted co-founder maligns and defames the business and the remaining co-founders.

Deal-Related Risks

Speaking of disclosable risks to investors, some of the greatest risks from legal and regulatory mistakes are the risks they pose to future financing and M&A deals.

Actual and even *perceived* risks can significantly undermine a startup's ability to (i) raise necessary funds on favorable terms and (ii) produce the best possible exit for its founders, employees, and investors.

A robust due diligence process will uncover virtually every type of potential risk of loss, liability, or other impairment that could hurt a company. These risks can be loosely called "contingent liabilities."

In accounting, a contingent liability is a potential liability that may occur depending on the outcome of an uncertain future event - things like lawsuits, regulatory investigations, product recalls, warranty claims, and environmental claims.

Capital Raising Difficulties

Companies with substantial contingent liabilities often have trouble attracting investors on any terms - a significant risk, given that running out of cash is one of the top reasons startups fail.

A closely related and more common risk is simply attracting fewer investors and less overall investor interest. Lower investor demand usually means a lower company valuation; a lower valuation means a higher cost of capital.

In equity-based financings, this means having to give away a greater percentage of equity to raise the same amount of money.

In debt-based financings, contingent liabilities can result in lower available funding, higher interest rates, shorter maturity dates, and larger conversion discounts, a concept discussed in Chapter 12 – *Startup Finance Overview.*

Risk Shifting

Contingent liabilities also reduce valuations in M&A transactions and increase "risk shifting." Acquirors shift risks to the sellers in acquisitions through larger and longer "earnouts," "holdbacks," or "escrows." These concepts are important for understanding how legal and regulatory mistakes can haunt a company for years.

- **Earnouts.** M&A transactions commonly include earn-out provisions that spread the deal payout, or consideration, over one or more years, usually based on revenue milestones and other benchmarks.

  While earnouts should be more directly related to valuation negotiations, they are also sometimes driven by risk. From a shareholder perspective, receiving the same amount of money in the sale of a company upfront is always better than receiving that same amount in installments over months or years.

  And failure to achieve any necessary milestones under an earnout clause can relieve the acquiror from making one or more contingent installment payments, thereby reducing total acquisition consideration and further harming the selling company's shareholders.

- **Escrows.** Escrow provisions withhold part of the acquisition consideration from the selling shareholders for months or years to cover known or unknown liabilities.

  Escrow provisions may call out specific escrow release triggers, like losses from lawsuits or regulatory actions, but often the escrow funds can be drawn down by the acquiror for any cost, expense, or liability related to a representation or warranty of the seller that turns out to be not true. Any claim of IP infringement during the escrow period, for example, can often result in a claim against the escrow fund by the acquiror.

- **Holdbacks.** A holdback is similar to an escrow, in that part of the sale proceeds are held back by the buyer for a period of time and based on specific provisions. A key difference is simply that the acquiror itself often holds onto the cash, rather than putting it into a formal escrow.

  A holdback is often used to true-up the "Final Purchase Price" in an M&A deal 60 or 90 days after closing. An acquiror might hold back $500,000, for example, in the event final payments for taxes, vendor obligations, employee bonuses and other such things turn out to be higher than estimated by the parties.

Deal Time Distractions

Even where problems uncovered during due diligence can be fixed before the closing date for a deal, time is usually tight, and there is usually a lot to do without having to fix mistakes that could have been fixed under less pressure and uncertainty.

Pressures to "close" often drive less-than-ideal solutions to problems that could have been fixed on better terms just weeks or months earlier. It is one thing to have to chase down a handful of state "good standing" certificates; it is quite another to try to resolve a thorny IP dispute on a deal timeline.

For a variety of reasons, deal time is the worst time for cleaning up loose ends.

- Deals with numerous or severe due diligence issues are said to "have a lot of hair" on them. That is not a compliment. "Clean" deals inspire investor and acquiror confidence and often move more quickly. Deals with "hair" are more likely to inspire skepticism, potentially resulting in a longer and more cautious approach to due diligence.

- A deal team focused on fixing deal "hair" is less able to focus on big-picture issues, key deal terms, and simply running the business.

- Cleaning up loose ends, whether litigation, IP, cap table, contractual, or governance, often involves negotiations with third parties. When these parties know a company needs help because of a pending transaction, the cost of cooperation usually rises.

- Acquirors willing to close despite some unresolved due diligence issues invariably shift those risks to the sellers (the company's existing shareholders) in the form of a lowered valuation or bigger, longer escrows, holdbacks, or earnouts.

- Deal hair can and does cause some investors and acquirors to walk away. Large, sophisticated investors and acquirors tend to be the most reluctant to get involved with companies beset by legal or regulatory matters, even if fixable. For a desperate seller, it is tragic to have a large, deep-pocketed potential acquiror walk from an acquisition based on things that could have been cleaned up earlier.

Specific Harms to Stakeholders

The following graphic illustrates those who can be harmed when founders and other startup actors err. The potential harms are greatest in the center and generally less severe toward the edges.

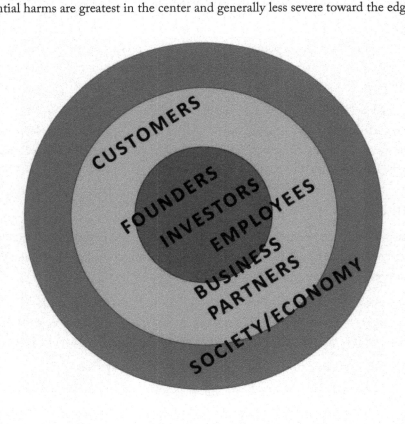

Investors. As indicated, shareholders bear much of the direct financial harm. These harms range from a minor reduction in the timing and amount of an investor's return on investment to the complete loss of the investment.

One all-too-common pattern is that companies with legal or regulatory problems have difficulty bringing in new equity investments. They end up having to raise more and more debt until their borrowing capacity is maxed out. Eventually, keeping up with the required debt payments can become impossible, forcing the company into a premature or even involuntary sale. As discussed in Chapters 16 and 17, lender-driven liquidations yield low sale proceeds, often leaving nothing for shareholders.

At a minimum, legal or regulatory turbulence can cause unnecessary delays and uncertainties in an investor's exit. In the financial world, where the "time value of money" is key, an exit delayed is less valuable than the same exit sooner.

Founders. Founders, as shareholders, share at least equally in such losses with other investors. And more often than not, they fare even worse. Founders almost always hold common stock. Sophisticated third-party investors, on the other hand, usually hold either Convertible Notes or preferred stock.

As discussed in Chapters 12 and 13, holders of both of these latter two types of interests generally come out ahead of common stockholders in less successful exits where a company's value has been impaired by poor financial performance or legal and regulatory issues.

Founders, as company officers and directors, are also exposed to civil lawsuits, regulatory actions, or even criminal prosecutions. Where the facts warrant, legal and regulatory mistakes can result in individual liabilities.

Others. As the diagram shows, others harmed by legal and regulatory mistakes include employees, business partners, customers, and the public.

- Employees receive less pay, sometimes lose their jobs, and generally receive less from any option grants whenever legal and regulatory mistakes diminish exit prospects.

- Business partners also often suffer when legal or regulatory mistakes reduce the value of a commercial relationship or, worse yet, cause the startup to default on its obligations to third-party business partners.

- Potential customers and society at large can also lose out when an otherwise promising startup is delayed or thwarted in its ability to provide an innovative new product, service, technology, or cure.

We will finish this chapter on the nature, causes, and impacts of legal and regulatory mistakes with four case studies that reinforce how these concepts and theories play out in the real world.

Case Study #4 – Dead Equity Dead End

It does not take much dead equity on a cap table to complicate the path forward. Three founders with an excellent idea for in-home sizing of online garment purchases learned this the hard way with an underperforming CEO.

The founders terminated the CEO after it was clear he was falling far short of expectations, particularly his fundraising abilities. The CEO's employment agreement, however, had no provision for clawing back any of his immediately-fully-vested equity grant – a total of 15% of the company's authorized common stock.

This 15% grant was unduly generous for an unproven CEO. Combined with too much other stock in the hands of other investors who proved unsupportive to the founders, the former CEO's dead equity made it impossible for the founders to obtain financing for the company on reasonable terms.

The combination of bad cap table planning and poorly selected early investors made it impossible for the founders to obtain the 51% shareholder vote needed to force a dilutive financing, or "cramdown," that would recapitalize the company and force out the obstructive influences on the cap table.

> Lessons: Founders need to plan out the evolution of their cap table through a company's anticipated financing rounds and avoid mistakes that will undermine those plans. The grant of 15% was too large. It also should have been subject to vesting based on milestones or to clawbacks in the event of his termination.
>
> Equity vesting, "cliffs," and clawback provisions should be included with every significant equity grant to avoid excessive dead equity. An equity vesting cliff establishes a timeframe, usually one year, before which no portion of an equity grant vests. A cliff is essentially a stock vesting "probation" period for new hires.
>
> As discussed in Chapter 8, *Structuring and Managing Key Relationships*, relationships with employees, officers, investors, and others must be documented much more carefully than was done here.
>
> Lastly, founders who lack fundraising skills and other CEO skills should try to acquire those skills rather than hoping that a "professional CEO" demanding founder-level equity grants will handle all of the company's fundraising needs. Founders should spread early equity grants across multiple key team members who will drive innovation and growth. They should not squander most of a startup's available equity on a narrowly focused, hired-gun CEO doing a founder's job.

Case Study #5 - Google It

In a spectacular but now forgotten example of issues surfacing at the 11th hour, Google's 2005 IPO hit regulatory turbulence because of issues involving its employee stock option plan.

Despite having excellent outside counsel, Google was called to account for a fairly common mistake in corporate America – failing to comply with the requirements of SEC Rule 701, the "exemption from registration" for stock options awarded as compensation.

We discuss SEC exemptions from registration further in Chapter 11, State and Federal Securities Law. For now, it's enough to understand that, where a company's total annual option grants exceed certain thresholds, "enhanced disclosures" must be provided to stock option recipients, including a stock option plan summary, financial statements, and a statement of risk factors.

According to the SEC's description, Google's failure to comply with Rule 701 was a calculated risk that went wrong. Reading between the lines, there may have been a math error. Google did not want to provide its optionees with the company's financials for competitive reasons and ended up violating a core prohibition of the securities laws.

In the end, Google and its general counsel David Drummond were hit with an SEC Cease and Desist Order. Google's IPO was allowed to go forward after significant delays and uncertainty. For more on this story, just Google it – specifically, SEC Rel. 33-8523.

https://www.sec.gov/litigation/admin/33-8523.htm

Lessons:

This is an L&M Matrix Box 1 issue. On the eve of an IPO, it caused huge risks and disruptions, including an SEC enforcement action. It made Wall Street Journal headlines. Had Drummond plotted this issue at the top of the severity axis for his board while they were weighing these risks, things might have been done differently. This was an unnecessary risk that turned out badly.

Case Study #6 – Total Recall

When legal mistakes and loose ends are part of a company's culture, the results can be catastrophic, particularly if multiple mistakes combine with other negative synergies.

One very promising company that raised $24 million committed just a few egregious legal and regulatory mistakes and was forced to forfeit virtually every dollar of revenue earned. It was also abandoned and left hanging by its VCs and angel investors, even after a new management team was brought in to impose greater legal, regulatory, and operational discipline.

In this case, inaccurate specifications provided in a contract with a manufacturer interacted badly with what regulators deemed false advertising about the quality and reliability of the company's products.

Absent the false advertising issues, the regulators might have agreed to something less than a crushing fine and product recall. And on the other hand, absent the product quality issues, the false advertising issues may have remained under the enforcement radar.

This founder probably thought he could stay out in front of the false advertising mistakes if he just raised enough money and sold enough products. Unfortunately, his success at selling served only to shine a brighter light on his errors and compound the ultimate scope of the liabilities.

Lessons: You never know what things are going to go wrong even when you are doing your best. Combining unknown but inevitable risks with intentional wrongdoing raises substantial risks that the known and unknown mistakes will amplify each other, possibly resulting in regulatory actions, fines, criminal penalties, and civil litigation.

Knowing violations of the law carry potentially catastrophic risks and are inherently breaches of the important fiduciary duties owed by company officers and directors. Startup founders should monitor themselves and their colleagues for above-the-law levels of hubris.

Case Study #7 – Bad Motor Scooter

Another sad example of indifference toward the law involved a potentially promising electric vehicle company and a founder whose marginal business judgment and managerial skills were further impaired by substance abuse. This error-prone scofflaw made every mistake in the book, killing any hope of commercial success for his electric scooters and utility carts. His many mistakes included:

- formed the wrong kind of entity,

- never finished forming the entity,

- promised way too much equity to entry-level employees,

- promised employee equity in vague percentages instead of fixed numbers of shares,

- never granted any of the promised employee equity,

- never obtained IP assignment agreements from any employees and refused to sign one himself,

- never produced proper financial statements or forecasts, even while soliciting investments,

- committed rampant violations of state and federal securities laws,

- sold equity in non-existent entities,

- offered and sold equity interests based on nonsensical formulas,

- lost important IP rights to a Chinese manufacturer,

- violated state and federal wage and hour laws,

- knowingly accepted stolen trade secrets,

- failed to supervise quality control over a key manufacturer, and

- ignored motorized vehicle import rules, resulting in severe product rollout delays.

State securities regulators moved quickly on the company and its founder and obtained a regulatory judgment detailing rampant securities fraud and imposing fines and other penalties.

Lessons: If you lie to investors and things do not go for them as promised, the securities regulators may still get you, even if your investors do not.

CHAPTER THREE

The General Counsel Audit

I call my high-level approach to uncovering and diagnosing an existing startup's legal and regulatory loose ends the General Counsel Audit.

It covers six areas:

- Governance foundation
- Ownership and control
- Protection of key business and IP assets
- Regulatory compliance
- Current or threatened disputes
- Ability to raise necessary capital

It is more interview and high-level document review than a deep-in-the-weeds audit. It's a bit like the game "20 Questions," but with more questions and less fun. These will all make more sense later. Read them now merely as a cognitive framework for organizing other information in the book. I also request copies of every type of document mentioned.

Governance Foundation

- What type of entity is the company, and when and where was it formed?
- Who set up the entity and was an attorney involved?
- Did you complete the process of setting up the entity?
- May I see all the company's formation documents?
- What factors drove the selection of that type of entity?
- Who are the entity's directors and key officers, and how were they appointed?
- Does the entity have its own bank account?
- Are all business and employment agreements signed in the name of the entity?

Ownership and Control

- After you formed the entity, what equity did you issue to the founders?

- What documentation is there for those issuances?

- Has an employee equity plan been established?

- Have you issued other equity?

- Are there any debt or loan agreements that are convertible into equity?

- Are there any other understandings with anyone else regarding future grants of equity in offer letters, consulting agreements, employment agreements, fundraising agreements, commercial agreements, or any other formal or informal documents or communications?

- Does the company have a current and accurate cap table?

Protection of Key Business and IP Assets

- Was a trademark search conducted to see if others are using the company's name or variations of it?

- Has the name been trademarked?

- Have any product names or other branding slogans been trademarked?

- What URLs has the company acquired?

- At formation, did the founders assign related IP and any other important assets to the company in exchange for their equity?

- Are any of the founders subject to agreements with prior employers regarding non-competition and IP assignment?

- What other assets does the company own, and how did it acquire those assets?

- Is there documentation for those asset contributions or acquisitions?

- Does the company require all employees to sign an Intellectual Property, Confidentiality, and Non-competition Agreement at the time of hire?

- Does the company require all independent contractors and consultants to assign to it all intellectual property invented or created in their work for the company?

- Does the company require its board members and other advisors to sign something like an Intellectual Property, Confidentiality, and Non-competition Agreement at the time of engagement?

- Does the company consistently use NDAs before discussing the company's trade secrets and other confidential or proprietary information with third parties?

- Has the company licensed the IP of any third party?

- Does the company maintain an accurate record of all open source software it uses?

- Has the company licensed any of its IP to any third party?

Regulatory Compliance

- What regulations apply to the company's products, services, and operations?

- Does the company share or sell any consumer information?

- What outside legal advice has the company paid for regarding regulatory compliance?

- Does the company stay on top of its annual state governance filings?

- Does the company file any state, local, and federal tax returns?

- Are all employees paid at least minimum wage?

- Describe the company's use of independent contractors instead of employees.

- In what states does the company operate, market goods or services, hire employees or contractors, or lease office space?

- In what foreign countries does the company operate, manufacture or market goods or services, hire employees or contractors, or lease office space?

- Has the company retained foreign counsel to ensure regulatory compliance in countries where the company has a presence?

- Has the company received any notices or other indications from state, federal, local, or foreign regulators concerning regulatory compliance issues?

- Describe any other known gaps or shortcomings in the company's regulatory compliance.

Current or Threatened Disputes

- Is the company involved in any active litigation or other disputes?

- Have any other third parties made any claims or threats against the company?

- Is the company aware of any claims or threats that might be made against it?

- Are there any existing disputes or issues between the company's founders concerning their respective roles, contributions, equity positions, or cash compensation, or concerning the company's direction, objectives, tactics, strategies, or financing plans?

- Describe the company's relations with its employees.

- Describe the company's relations with any independent contractors it uses.

- Describe the company's relations with its vendors and the nature and extent of any past-due financial obligations.

- Is the company in arrears on any other financial obligations or any other commitments to any person or other entity?

Ability to Raise Capital

- How much money does the company have in the bank, and how long will those funds last at the present burn rate?

- What fundraising has the company done so far?

- Is the company currently fundraising?

- What fundraising efforts does the company anticipate?

- Does the company have a current pitch deck or other offering documents that I can see?

- Have any fundraising efforts failed or fallen short?

- Describe the company's "balance sheet" – i.e., how much debt has the company incurred, to whom, and under what terms, and will that debt be viewed as risky to potential investors?

- Does the company have a virtual data room or similar place where the company's documents are organized and retrievable?

It is nearly impossible to get through that battery of questions with any company and not find issues. The next question usually then becomes, where to begin? Prioritizing loose ends cleanup is the subject of the next chapter.

CHAPTER FOUR

Cleaning up Loose Ends Where to Begin

As already discussed, even where an issue uncovered during due diligence can be fixed before closing a deal, easier and better alternatives for fixing it have usually passed.

Potential investors and acquirors often use due diligence issues to their advantage, but third parties that sense having any deal-related leverage over another often become downright extortionate. If you approach a third party to clean up an issue with them, whether contractual, IP, investment-related, or something else, any hint that your timeline is driven by a deal will almost always increase the cost of their cooperation.

Case Study #8 illustrates this well.

Case Study #8 – Taking On the Troll

Resolving a pending or potential third-party dispute is one of the more challenging assignments a deal team can face as a condition to closing a deal.

Once, during a significant M&A deal, my team was told we had to make a passively threatening patent troll go away. A patent troll is a person or entity that creates or acquires one or more patents and uses them to threaten others with litigation to extort exorbitant license payments. Trolls often do not use their patents to offer products and services but merely threaten others with them for financial gain. Patent trolls dislike being labeled as such, but they also don't seem to like their other name, "non-practicing entity," or "NPE."

Our team would have to pay all legal expenses, but the acquiror was willing to pay half the cost of any settlement necessary to resolve the patent troll's claims.

We had long-possessed nearly incontrovertible "prior art" that could have invalidated all of the troll's patents. Prior art is any evidence that an invention was not a new invention at the time of a patent's filing because the purported invention had already been known, described, or used. Only "novel" (new) inventions can be patented.

Before the M&A deal, our strategy had been to menace the troll with our prior art in response to the troll's demand letters, but not to waste money forcing the issue to resolution.

Under pressure to close the M&A deal, we quickly spent about $100,000 filing a Declaratory Judgment Action against the troll and preparing extensive regulatory challenges to each patent in the troll's patent portfolio. We met the troll's lawyers at their offices in Washington, D.C. and walked them through all of the evidence we intended to bring to bear in both our lawsuit and our administrative challenges to the patents in the U.S. Patent and Trademark Office ("USPTO").

We felt like we were making great progress in softening the patent troll's position and potentially reaching a low-cost resolution. Then an officer of the acquiring company unexpectedly telephoned the troll – theoretically to put pressure on him. Among other things, he let the troll know (i) his company was hoping to acquire our company by X date and (ii) they would not close the transaction with the troll's claims unresolved. The essence of this unfortunate call was, *"If you want to ever see any money from the company we are acquiring on XYZ date, this is your last, best chance."*

I liked the person who made this mistake, so I was charitable in my complaint to him about what he had done. I did tell him that, as a result, the price of resolving the dispute just went way up, and it would not be resolved until the day before the closing date he had just shared with the troll.

Both predictions came true, but the deal did close on time.

> Lessons. You never know what cleanup is going to be required by an acquiror or major investor. The cleanup assignment in this case study was extraordinary, and failure could have killed that $200 million deal. As I mentioned earlier, larger and more sophisticated investors and acquirors are particularly fussy about having loose ends cleaned up before closing.
>
> Fortunately, this company had few, if any, other significant loose ends and we were well-prepared to pick the fight with the troll. Nonetheless, it took some focus away from other parts of the M&A deal process. Had there been substantial other cleanup work required, the deal could have died.
>
> Another key takeaway from this example is the damage bad negotiating can cause. Calling our litigation opponent and advising him of our time frame and position harmed us. We settled the troll's meritless claims at the last minute for three times more than we would have otherwise.
>
> The following is an excerpt from my book, Contract Drafting and Negotiation for Entrepreneurs and Business Professionals:
>
> *If you negotiate on a team of two or more, try to make sure less experienced team members receive training also, since a negotiating team's weakest link often determines its success or failure. Once your less skilled colleague reveals your lack of viable alternatives, the importance of specific issues, your real or imagined timing constraints, or other weaknesses in your position, it is very difficult to re-set the talks. The other side naturally becomes more aggressive and inflexible. Good negotiation training can prevent rookie mistakes from ruining deals and careers.*

Prioritizing Pre-Deal Cleanup

As reinforced by that case study, cleaning up loose ends in the middle of a deal can be messy, distracting and dysfunctional – particularly if too many cooks invite themselves into the kitchen.

Consequently, pre-deal timeframes are almost always best for thoughtfully cleaning up mistakes and loose ends.

Many founders probably find it hard to predict when a significant financing or M&A transaction is coming. But for most startups, that timeframe is not usually more than a year or two away.

- Financings for rapidly growing startups tend to occur at 10 to 18-month intervals, give or take a few months.

- M&A opportunities often arise without warning. Competitors and other strategic buyers on the lookout for quick access to new technologies, markets and customers can "reach out" at any time.

Prioritizing legal and regulatory cleanup efforts sooner rather than later still usually requires judgments about which issues pose the greatest immediate risks and which can be allowed to simmer on a little longer.

Likelihood and Materiality Matrix

Legal and Regulatory Issues – Likelihood and Materiality Matrix

In Chapter 2, we used a *Timing and Materiality Matrix* to consider the nature of mistakes. We noted that an *L&M Matrix* (Likelihood and Materiality) could help assess and prioritize the correction of loose ends and mistakes.

Startups with a lot of legal and regulatory loose ends might consider working with a good business lawyer to plot them on a matrix to visually identify which ones are (i) most likely to become a problem and (ii) most likely to be severe if they do.

- Concerns highest and farthest right in box 1 are the most dangerous and warrant the highest priority.

- Concerns lowest and farthest left in box 4 are the least dangerous to the startup and warrant the lowest priority.

- Boxes 2 and 3 are more nuanced and might contain high priority matters, low priority matters, and a range of matters in between.

- We can generally assess and prioritize startup loose ends and mistakes using this scale:

  - Level 1 – highest danger/top priority

  - Level 2 – high danger/high priority

  - Level 3 – moderate danger/moderate priority

  - Level 4 – low danger/low priority

Another lesson from Taking on the Troll is that you may not be able to predict how an investor or acquiror will react to your company's particular loose ends. Before that M&A deal, my colleagues and I would have classified the patent troll's claims as Level 3 – likely to result in a dispute, but with only moderate-high materiality. The acquiror took a completely different view, effectively deeming it a Level 1 issue, primarily because of the acquiror's severe aversion to litigation.

As we discuss various types of loose ends and mistakes and some of the case studies used to illustrate them, we will refer back to see where they might be scored on the L&M Matrix. Many of the case studies are plotted on an L&A Matrix right before the Index.

Virtual Data Room

The final question of the General Counsel Audit was whether the company has a virtual data room. A virtual data room is an electronic filing system for a company's records. Cloud-based virtual data rooms provide easy access to company documents anytime, anyplace, by anyone with access credentials.

Having a well-organized and complete virtual data room is critical for any company that might soon be involved in a major financing or sale. A deal-ready data room gives an overview of the company's key records and makes it easy to find and retrieve important documents.

Creating one from scratch after deal talks have begun is no picnic, and a slow or imperfect end-product could put off sophisticated buyers or investors.

Even when a financing or sale is further off, establishing a virtual data room early always provides important operational, administrative, and risk management benefits.

> *Any company that is serious about getting organized and cleaning up its legal, governance, and regulatory loose ends should establish a virtual data room.*

In addition to providing ready access to all of a company's important documents, establishing a virtual data room provides a "gap analysis" of where a company is in terms of legal, governance, and regulatory matters, versus where it should be.

Below is a simplified data room org chart showing only two tiers of electronic folders. This template is one starting point for thinking about how to organize a data room. Additional top-line folders may be required, depending on the business, and any well-organized data room will also have third and fourth tiers of folders under the two tiers shown.

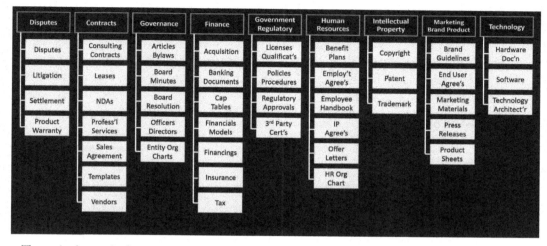

Disputes	Contracts	Governance	Finance	Government Regulatory	Human Resources	Intellectual Property	Marketing Brand Product	Technology
Disputes	Consulting Contracts	Articles Bylaws	Acquisition	Licenses Qualificat's	Benefit Plans	Copyright	Brand Guidelines	Hardware Doc'n
Litigation	Leases	Board Minutes	Banking Documents	Policies Procedures	Employ't Agree's	Patent	End User Agree's	Software
Settlement	NDAs	Board Resolution	Cap Tables	Regulatory Approvals	Employee Handbook	Trademark	Marketing Materials	Technology Architect'r
Product Warranty	Profess'l Services	Officers Directors	Financials Models	3rd Party Cert's	IP Agree's		Press Releases	
	Sales Agreement	Entity Org Charts	Financings		Offer Letters		Product Sheets	
	Templates		Insurance		HR Org Chart			
	Vendors		Tax					

The only firm rule for organizing a data room is that users should be able to find what they need without asking too many questions.

Here are some key considerations, besides cost, when choosing a data room platform:

- security, stability, and redundancy,

- capacity to quickly upload large documents,

- intuitive user interface,

- flexibility to create and organize folders and sub-folders,

- flexible administrator controls to smoothly add and remove users and to assign varying user access privileges for specific folders,

- advanced features such as allowing "view only" privileges, prohibiting printing or downloading, or allowing printing or downloading, but only with customizable watermarks on the documents, like *Company X – Confidential and Proprietary,*"

- oversight tools to see who is using the data room and what they are looking at and downloading, and

- auditing tools to track, retrieve, download, and store platform usage information.

Creating a comprehensive data room is like piecing together a big puzzle – one that creates a detailed picture of a company for a potential investor or buyer.

The biggest challenge in assembling the puzzle is the scavenger hunt that's inevitably required to find, fix, or create missing pieces – i.e., missing or deficient company records. These, in turn, often point to the need for new or improved processes or procedures.

Operating Data Room Versus Deal Data Room

Most companies have one or more virtual repositories where they keep all kinds of records for safe-keeping and easy access. These are usually organized according to the needs of the company and not third parties. When I tell a company they need a due diligence data room, they almost always resist and tell me they already have one. What they invariably mean is that they have a poorly organized document dumping ground on a non-deal-grade cloud platform.

There are several differences between an operating data room and a deal data room:

- A deal data room is logically organized to enable third parties to easily find what they are seeking.

- A deal data room contains every type of document identified in a typical M&A due diligence list.

- A deal data room should be on a state-of-the-art platform with robust administrative controls, including sophisticated access management tools down to the sub-folder level, activity notifications, and robust auditing features.

- A deal data room is not a dumping ground, but rather a curated repository containing only *required* documents, and not irrelevant documents.

That final point is critical. As we learn in Case Study #9, there should be no irrelevant documents in a data room.

Case Study #9 – Clean Your Room

Once, some non-M&A-savvy individuals inexplicably took the lead on setting up a deal data room when they should have left it to me. Before consulting me, they also granted access to a large, motivated acquiror - a $100+ billion multinational corporation.

In addition to uploading numerous unsigned and half-signed agreements into the data room, they also uploaded more than fifty long-terminated contracts from discontinued business lines. These included old vendor agreements, consulting agreements, manufacturing agreements, and minor IP licensing agreements.

Unfortunately, many of these agreements also had been sloppily terminated, with no actual written notice of termination or mutual agreement of termination.

I discovered this catastrophe in a screen-sharing video call with the CEO. We had previously sequestered the terminated contracts in a digital folder labeled "2015." Apparently, that was insufficient to keep these zombie documents at rest. I recognized them instantly in the new data room and spontaneously groaned, *"oh nooo...."*

As I feared, over the coming weeks, the acquiror's legions of attorneys spent countless hours and tens of thousands of dollars, reading and cataloging every document in the data room.

And when they were done, the myriad data room issues caused by my colleagues became my problem. I was forced to respond to an *extensive* list of questions about every long-dead agreement. The mistake resulted in a distracting waste of time for me and could have raised deal-threatening issues.

I was lucky the acquiror did not make me obtain confirmation of termination from the counterparties to all of these long-dead contracts.

Lessons: A deal data room is not a historical archive. Only documents required under a typical M&A due diligence list should be included in a data room – nothing more. A sloppy data room filled with garbage documents is no way to establish confidence that a management team knows what it is doing.

Also, every company should establish and maintain good contract management hygiene. Confirm in writing the expiration or termination of every contract. This can be a short friendly letter essentially saying:

> *"Please sign this letter below to confirm our mutual understanding that the XYZ Agreement between us has formally ended. We appreciate the opportunity to work with you and wish you great success."*

In any "stock deal," acquirors will be very focused on knowing everything they're getting, including any bad or otherwise unwanted contracts. Limiting the scope of those issues as much as possible allows everyone to focus on the important issues in a deal and reduces opportunities for the other party to fabricate issues as negotiating leverage.

The deal in this case study was delayed several weeks by the inclusion of confusing and irrelevant contracts in the data room. Time is the enemy of all deals.

Closing the Resources Gap

Startup founders who are merely resource-constrained, as opposed to ethics-constrained, should be as creative as possible to ensure competent and timely handling of critical legal and regulatory matters.

Here are several suggestions for prudently closing the legal and regulatory resources gap.

- Master the advice in Chapters 11 through 15 and raise funds, so your company has resources for administrative and legal needs.

- Look for attorneys who focus on startups and who can most efficiently meet needs like entity selection, formation and governance, issuing equity to founders and employees, protecting IP, properly onboarding employees and consultants, creating product or service terms and conditions, and supporting legally compliant fundraising.

- Many attorneys will consider lowering their hourly rates for startups or performing specific tasks for very reasonable "fixed fees," which can help to reduce uncertainty about costs. And some will even defer receipt of payment for a few months. It is always worth asking.

- Consider looking for an attorney who is willing to serve as part-time in-house counsel at a reasonable cost. Part-time employees, including in-house counsel, can agree to accept some (but not all) of their compensation in the form of equity grants.

- Local law schools frequently have business law or entrepreneurial law clinics or workshops where students work under supervision to help form companies, assist with governance processes, review contracts, and other legal tasks.

- Attorneys looking to work with startups often hold "office hours" at local startup incubators and shared workspaces and make themselves available to answer questions. While these sessions are generally limited in scope, they can be valuable and can provide the opportunity to discuss special billing arrangements. Call around to local incubators and shared workspaces to see who is holding office hours and when.

What Percentage for Legal?

While the "apologize later" culture plays a role in some legal and regulatory mistakes, the larger factor is simply that most startups are forced to make tough decisions with limited resources. Top priorities are usually market validation research, product development, engineering, and sales, not legal or regulatory matters.

There is certainly something to be said for not overspending on legal and regulatory at the expense of timely launching a product or service.

One of my former company's key competitors made that mistake. They spent millions of dollars on a large number of narrow patents. The competitor CEO's focus on patent applications instead of business execution was a vanity exercise, and it came at the expense of product improvement and marketing. My company handily beat that competitor in the market.

Unfortunately, there is no perfect answer to how much legal spend is optimal. Companies operating in largely unregulated fields can and should spend less on legal and compliance than companies in highly regulated fields.

But where a startup's spending on legal and regulatory is close to zero, almost no amount of business success will overcome the resulting problems.

Again, as noted in Chapter 2, the most harmful legal and regulatory mistakes by startups tend to involve:

- entity formation issues,
- governance lapses,
- equity issuance issues,
- cap table errors and anomalies,
- financing documentation gaps,
- unprotected IP,

- inadequate employment practices,

- poorly documented commercial arrangements, and

- regulatory non-compliance.

Whatever legal spend is necessary to avoid these mistakes is probably an appropriate guide, recognizing that some degree of triage is generally unavoidable. Early in a company's development, reasonably covering each of those areas might require a challenging percentage of available resources.

We have now finished introducing some foundational concepts around startup legal and regulatory loose ends and mistakes:

- how and why startups make them,

- when and how they might manifest themselves or come to light,

- the wide range of harms they can cause,

- ways to track them down,

- how to prioritize cleanup efforts, and

- the value of a strong financing plan to support appropriate spending.

Let's now start looking at how to build a company on a solid foundation that minimizes unnecessary friction and inspires investor confidence.

CHAPTER FIVE

Pre-Company Formation – Steps and Considerations

Chapters 5 - 7 are about building on a strong foundation. As with physical structures, startups built on weak foundations face problems.

Founders must navigate the period around *entity formation* with care and focus on these key goals:

- creating a governance structure that supports the business plan,

- marshaling and protecting IP rights,

- avoiding harmful governance, ownership, and control mistakes, and

- minimizing risks of co-founder disputes.

Those are the subjects of this chapter and the next.

Accidental Partnerships

A general partnership is a binding entity created (i) intentionally by a written Partnership Agreement, or (ii) by default, often accidentally, when individuals start working together before forming an actual entity.

"Accidental partnership" is another common name for the same default relationship. Again, a founder's call about an accidental partnership was a final catalyst for this book's publication.

Under the Uniform Partnership Act:

> *"The association of two or more persons to carry on as co-owners of a business for profit forms a partnership, whether or not the persons intend to form a partnership."*

An accidental partnership is generally a Level 1 or Level 2 mistake on the *L&M Matrix*. It's the opposite of a strong, thoughtfully-laid foundation, and likely to cause severe ownership, governance, and IP problems.

An accidental partnership might simply be an inadvertent passing phase that is cured quickly by the formation of an entity and documentation to re-establish everyone's rights and obligations. But ugly problems can quickly arise if less valuable and even disruptive purported co-owners claim an equal share of something to which they contributed little or nothing.

Even students collaborating on potentially viable science, technology, or engineering projects without proper documentation run the risk of clouding their IP rights and other legal rights and obligations through a general partnership.

Co-founders that form a general partnership are each deemed equal partners for purposes of voting and sharing in profits and losses. And all general partners are equally responsible individually for any liabilities of the partnership. In other words, a general partnership provides no liability protection for the individual partners.

Entrepreneurs can avoid entanglement in accidental partnerships by selecting and forming the correct type of entity as soon as the decision is made to create a business. Do so before bringing others into the discussions. For most startups, the correct entity is generally going to be either a corporation or an LLC, as discussed in Chapter 6.

Pre-Entity Formation IP Protection

Creating an entity allows the founders to marshal and protect key IP before bringing others into the venture.

Before forming an entity, follow these three guidelines:

- do not overshare about business ideas or other IP,

- do not seek input or feedback about a business idea or related IP, and

- do not attempt to negotiate potential roles or ownership splits with potential team members.

I have heard others give advice contrary to the above, suggesting that it's a good idea to bounce ideas off of others as early as possible, and even before forming an entity and protecting one's IP. That is advice from non-lawyers who haven't had to deal with its negative consequences.

An interesting IP issue worth highlighting is the fact that nobody "owns" a trademark until it has been used in association with the sale of goods or services in commerce. The first person who uses a mark in connection with goods or services is the owner.

Inventing a trademark or even filing to register it will not provide ownership rights or "priority" over the person or company that first uses a mark to identify and to distinguish goods or services in commerce in conjunction with the actual sale of those goods or services.

Trademarks are discussed in Chapter 9, but the first-user advantage is worth noting as just one of many reasons for using non-disclosure agreements with third parties whenever possible.

Invention patentability also can be lost by disclosures to third parties before a patent application is filed. As we discuss in Chapter 9, in many countries, including all of Europe, pre-filing disclosures end the "novelty" of an invention and make it unpatentable.

Use of Non-Disclosure Agreements

Protecting IP through customary NDAs before entity formation is tricky. Founders sharing information with potential co-founders or others need to sign in their personal capacities and not in the name of any yet-to-be-formed entity.

Any agreement signed in the name of a non-existent entity could be deemed unenforceable. Confidential information shared under unenforceable NDAs would be at risk, particularly under trade secret law.

Any NDA signed by individual founders before entity formation should include language permitting assignment of the founder's rights and responsibilities under the NDA to any subsequently formed entity.

After forming an entity and assigning their IP to it, a startup's founder or founders are then in a position, as official company officers, to negotiate with other potential co-founders or team members under NDAs signed in the name of the entity.

Find a sample "Mutual NDA" in the BLSG Document Data Room under *Intellectual Property > Mutual NDAs.*

NDA Benefits and Limitations

Regular and consistent use of NDAs is important in business. Properly drafted NDAs prohibit not only unauthorized disclosure of confidential information, but also the unauthorized misuse of confidential information. As discussed below, consistent NDA use is critical for protecting trade secrets.

But in reality, NDAs provide only modest assurance against confidential information theft and misuse. The only sure way to protect information is to not disclose it, which is not always practical.

In addition to the obvious fact that a party would have to file a lawsuit to protect its rights under an NDA, it can be very difficult to protect "ideas" that do not amount to actual "trade secrets." Most NDAs, by their terms, exclude protection for information that "is now or hereafter becomes generally known or available to the public."

Litigating to prove whether or not a business idea was "known or available to the public" would be an expensive and uncertain effort.

Trade secrets are discussed further in Chapter 9, *IP - Protecting Rights and Avoiding Liabilities.* The simple definition of a trade secret is anything that (i) is secret, (ii) has economic value because it is secret, and (iii) is the subject of reasonable efforts to protect its secrecy.

Despite difficulties enforcing NDAs, using them consistently is extremely important for protecting trade secrets. Sharing a trade secret even once without the protection of an NDA can destroy its trade secret status. That is how courts tend to interpret and apply the *"reasonable efforts to protect"* requirement.

Unfortunately, as is discussed in later chapters, VCs rarely sign NDAs. Other "professional investors" sometimes resist signing them as well, including some angel investors and angel investor groups.

Whenever any third party will not sign an NDA, it is very important to avoid sharing any trade secrets with that third party. Many investors do not need trade-secret-level technology, software or process information, so always avoid the temptation to share those things unnecessarily.

If trade secrets must be shared, require at least a limited non-disclosure agreement covering the specific trade secret information.

Founders Agreements

Another approach to pre-entity formation discussions among potential startup co-founders is a document variously called a Founders Agreement, Founders' Agreement, or Co-Founders Agreement. Find examples in the BLSG Data Room under *Company Formation > Founders Agreements*.

The idea of a Founders Agreement is to protect ideas and other IP while trying to work out how two or more individuals might come together as co-founders to establish a company. Issues addressed can include:

- confidentiality and other IP protections,
- the preferred type of entity,
- co-founder contributions to be made in cash or labor,
- relative ownership interests of the contributors,
- equity vesting or clawback provisions,
- individual titles, roles, and compensation,
- governance and decision-making principles,
- capital raising expectations,
- breakup/dispute resolution processes.

Interestingly, there seems to be more literature about Founders Agreements than examples of U.S. startup founders using them. The available commentary also seems to be largely by non-lawyers. It is somewhat inconclusive as to how they are used and their binding or non-binding nature, as evidenced by this characterization:

> *"First of all, we might define it as 'A clear agreement between founders on a number of key issues that their business might face.' So, in other words, it's not a legally binding contract—it's just a written agreement."*
>
> *—online commentator*

The word "Agreement" strongly implies a legally binding contract. In general, one should assume that, if someone proposes a Founders Agreement, it is intended to be legally binding certainly for purposes of protecting confidential information and IP.

Some Founders Agreements even spell out how they will be enforced, as illustrated by this paragraph from a template:

"If the Founders have not yet formed a Company within twelve (12) months of executing this Agreement, the Founders will have 30 additional days to take substantial steps toward forming the Company. If the Company has still not been formed after 30 days, the Founders will execute a separation agreement which divides rights to the Business Concept and any other assets accumulated by the Founders in pursuit of developing the Business Concept. The Founders will further define any and all confidentiality obligations related to the Business Concept within the separation agreement.

In the event that the Founders are not able to agree on a separation agreement, the Founders will submit to a binding confidential mediation to be held in and conducted by a mutually agreed to mediator. All provisions of this Agreement, including confidentiality provisions, will be binding up through the end of this mediation process. Costs of the mediation will be borne equally by all Founders."

These passages highlight some of the risks in even negotiating a Founders Agreement, let alone signing one.

In brainstorming about a business idea as a step toward signing a Founders Agreement, the individuals involved could be creating a general partnership. Always consider what the implications could be if no Founders Agreement is signed. Will IP be lost or clouded?

As with any contract, parties can write a Founders Agreement any way they wish. If the document ensures that each signor receives back all their IP if no entity is formed, that should reduce concerns about losing ownership and control over IP.

But if circumstances are such that "unscrambling the egg" will not be possible or easy because of the mixing of IP from several persons, then concerns around the loss or dilution of IP should be taken much more seriously by contributors of IP.

Any party presented with a Founders Agreement should think carefully before going down that path. Does that process make sense, or would it make more sense to first form an entity, establish its foundation, contribute personal IP, and then reach out to possible co-founders to talk under formal NDAs?

The latter approach seems better for founders who bring more to the table – particularly the core IP - and who want to ensure superior ownership, financial, and control rights.

Co-Founder Considerations

Many VCs and other sophisticated investors consider a startup's team to be its most important asset. And within any startup team, the founders are key.

The Single Founder

A startup with a strong co-founder team has some advantages over a startup headed by a single founder:

- Investor Concerns. Many sophisticated investors avoid investing in single founder startups. The founder could die or be incapacitated, leaving the company rudderless. Others believe the absence of co-founders might indicate that the founder is not a strong "team player," or that he or she may not be good at accepting constructive advice or criticism, including from investors. The absence of co-founders can also signal that a founder lacks a good teambuilding or fundraising network.

- The Power of Complementary Traits and Skills. The best co-founder teams have complementary backgrounds, skillsets, networks, and traits. The combined team is greater than the sum of its parts. A renowned scientist with no background in business operations or finance often needs a co-founder with those competencies to turn his or her ideas and vision into a well-funded, viable business. Conversely, the business and finance-oriented co-founder needs the scientist for his or her IP contributions, expertise, and credibility.

  Co-founder teams with at least one founder who has successfully raised money and taken a startup through a successful exit have an advantage over teams lacking those credentials. The single attribute most likely to correlate to successful fundraising is prior successful fundraising, especially when combined with impressive exits.

- Mutual Support and Cover. Starting, funding, and running a startup is one of the hardest endeavors one can undertake. As with any complex, challenging, and emotionally draining project, the difference between success and failure can come down to simply having a trusted teammate to serve as a sounding board, emotional supporter, reality checker, and dependable backup when things get overwhelming.

Co-Founder Ownership Percentages

One of the most important initial questions is often one of the most difficult to discuss in a thoughtful, rational manner – should the co-founder's ownership interests be equal or not?

When there are two founders, 50/50 ownership is often the default. The primary virtue of this approach is that it is usually the path of least resistance. Evenly divided interests demonstrate mutual trust, confidence, and respect. When all co-founders, however many, truly believe that each will be contributing equally in all respects, any answer but equal ownership can lead to ill feelings.

But equal ownership can also lead to problems, including serious voting deadlocks, absent a tie-breaking mechanism. In a startup with two founders, each owning 50% of the stock, critical board and shareholder decisions can be deadlocked by tie votes, and neither founder can force the other off of the board.

Possible tie-breaking mechanisms can involve a third board seat or a trusted, neutral third party required to cast tie-breaking votes in board or shareholder deadlocks.

These can be written into Shareholders Agreements or Voting Agreements, documents we discuss in Chapter 8, *Structuring and Managing Key Relationships.*

When equal ownership interests are agreed to, but the actual financial and sweat equity contributions of the founders are not equal, the result can be debilitating resentment and friction.

Co-founders should discuss questions like these openly and honestly:

- What financial and asset/IP contributions will we each make?

- Which of us is going to contribute full-time effort?

- What titles, and hence obligations, will each of us have?

- What roles will each of us play in the success of the business?

Discussions involving whose contributions are more valuable or important are inherently difficult. Consider seeking external guidance on these issues. Look online for resources on "how to split co-founder equity." Countless articles and online tools offer help guiding founders objectively and unemotionally through these difficult questions.

Co-Founder Compatibility

Disputes between co-founders can be extremely disruptive for a startup, if not catastrophic. According to one study, co-founder disputes cause approximately 13% of all startup failures. This study on startup failures can be found by searching "*CB Insights study on startup failures*" or by going to this link - https://www.cbinsights.com/research/startup-failure-reasons-top/.

Before going into business together, potential co-founders should have deep and candid conversations to confirm that they are a compatible team.

Doing so does not necessarily require a Founders Agreement, but the use of NDAs and cautious information sharing is important.

Even co-founders who start out as best friends can find themselves locked in conflict. When I hear co-founders snipping at each other, I look for opportunities to coach gentler inter-personal interactions – listening, empathizing, not overreacting, and reinforcing relationships. As in any relationship, slights, misunderstandings, and condescension can spell the beginning of the end for co-founders. Potential investors who see obvious co-founder tensions will pass on the opportunity.

Compatibility issues are particularly important where potential co-founders do not have any history of working together. This concern is one of several takeaways from Case Study #10, *Conniving Co-Founder*.

Case Study #10 – Conniving Co-Founder

An ambitious individual identified an opportunity to bring back a successful business but wanted someone else to join him as "*a second set of eyes and ears, someone I can bounce ideas off of.*" This person had the capital, the plan, and the ambition to take on the project, but he also thought it would be helpful to have a co-founder. He barely knew the person he selected for this role, but they seemed to hit it off. This second individual put in only $30,000, while the main founder put in over $250,000 and did all of the work.

The business was successful immediately and was generating lots of cash – an annualized run rate of more than $1 million within a couple of months. Almost instantly, the conniving co-founder demanded to receive distributions from the LLC. The majority founder replied that the cash reserves would be used to grow the business with new locations. Seven months after his investment of $30,000, the conniving co-founder demanded to be bought out for $1 million and threatened to sue.

The matter went through mediation, and the original founder agreed to pay the conniving co-founder $700,000.

> Lessons: Picking a bad co-founder is far worse than being a solo founder. Unwinding a poorly-conceived founder relationship can be difficult and expensive. Picking the wrong co-founder is a Level 1 mistake on the L&M Matrix – highly likely to cause very severe harm.
>
> We will discuss the conniving co-founder again in comparing LLCs and corporations and in looking at how LLC Operating Agreements can be written to prevent such disputes.

For purposes of this discussion, though, common areas of co-founder disagreement can be uncovered before it is too late by asking each other questions like these:

- What will our roles be, and how much time are we each going to give to the business?
- How are we going to make decisions, and how are we going to resolve differences of opinion in managing the company?
- What work styles and preferences does each of us have? Will we work remotely, or will we be working regular hours in the same space?
- How fast do we expect to grow a team? What positions do we need to fill first, and what types of persons are we seeking?
- If one of us is unable to work for the company as much as expected at any time within the next few years, will we be required to give back some of our equity?
- When and at what milestones will we draw pay, and how much?
- How do we intend to finance the company? Do we intend to take money from VCs, and thus be compelled to sell or go public within ten years?
- When and under what circumstances would each founder agree to sell the company?

There are plenty of other questions co-founders can ask themselves to determine compatibility. There is no single best approach. The important thing is honesty with each other about areas of agreement and areas of potential disagreement, and then assessing whether or not the areas of disagreement will be manageable or ultimately irreconcilable.

Case Study #11 – Trust but Verify

I was running errands in downtown Seattle and answered a call from an unknown number. The caller said he had been referred by another lawyer who described me as a "startup fixer." I jumped into a nearby coffee shop to hear the story.

The caller said he had founded an awesome arts platform that had big-name support, but that he had taken in a high-profile co-founder who had blown up the whole thing.

The alleged bad actor, we'll call him Goofus, had promised to competently handle all administrative, governance, and fundraising activities. The caller, Good Guy, would handle all other operations, development, and management.

The project had made great progress, including the coding and development of an innovative and potentially popular arts platform. Everything appeared to be going swimmingly until payroll checks started bouncing.

After a series of bounces and fixes, there came a point where fixes were no longer possible. Employees and others were holding worthless checks. Goofus then made an amazing, in-person mea culpa. He had lied about raising more than $1M. He had raised no money. He had merely spent more than $250K of his own money propping up the company while trying to raise money. And now he was out of money.

Based on his lies, individuals had left high-paying jobs to join the company, and some had sold belongings and moved from other cities to join the company. There was a large stack of unpaid vendor invoices, and, most importantly, there was about $100K of unmet payroll.

This situation got ugly quickly. Seeing a viable path through the mess was difficult.

I quickly wrote up a demand letter and settlement agreement requiring Goofus to (i) give up his entire interest in the company and assign it to Good Guy, (ii) come up with cash to pay off all of the unpaid employees and vendors immediately, and (iii) agree to indemnify and hold the company harmless from all claims resulting from his fraudulent conduct. In exchange, we offered that the company would issue him an unsecured promissory note for $250K, due in three years.

Goofus initially promised to do everything in his power to "make it right" and also to walk away from the company. Then he lawyered up, and his lawyer walked all of that back.

Weeks of negotiation ensued, during which employee wage theft claims escalated, employees and vendors abandoned the company, and other critical project supporters similarly faded away. The delays were killing any hope of putting Humpty Dumpty back together again.

Interestingly, Goofus' administrative skills and follow-through were so bad that he had never made Good Guy an officer or director of the company. In the end, following my advice, Good Guy simply walked away from the train wreck and left the entire mess to Goofus, including significant wage theft claims, breach of contract claims, and payment demands from contractors and vendors.

This was a sad outcome for Good Guy. Goofus destroyed his dream project by faking and lying the company into an impossible situation. He oversold himself and committed terrible misdeeds. But the ability for Good Guy to walk away with no liabilities and no reputational harm whatsoever was as good an outcome as he or I could have hoped for under the circumstances.

Lessons: It is not merely enough to know your co-founder and be compatible. Co-founders should interact meaningfully and not pass like ships. Co-founders should get regular updates and verification from each other to know that each is doing his or her job

Good Guy stayed in his own lane and placed too much trust in Goofus. He never examined any of the company's books and records, including basic documentation of claimed third-party investments.

As President Ronald Regan said during the Cold War, *"Trust, but verify."*

Naming Considerations

We discuss IP protection in greater detail in Chapter 9, *IP - Protecting Rights and Avoiding Liabilities*, but, at formation, some specific steps are recommended to vet and protect the company's name.

Checking for Name Availability

It is important to pick a company name that is not being used by others with stronger rights to it.

Start with a general Internet search to look for obvious matches.

Then check to see if the name is available for registration through the Office of the Secretary of State where the company will be formed. A state will reject any name too similar to a name in use by a business incorporated or registered there.

It is also smart to check name availability in all states where the company intends to actively conduct business. If the answer is "every state," take the hour or two necessary to check every state's Secretary of State website to see if the name is currently in use.

One of my companies failed to do this before my arrival. It had to use several "doing business as" (or "DBA") variations of its name in six states where its substantial business presence requires it to be "qualified to do business," i.e., a form of state business license.

After clearing the Secretary of State hurdle, search the name and variants in the United States Patent and Trademark Office's "Trademark Electronic Search System," or "TESS."

If you find others are using the name and you still want to use it, consult qualified trademark counsel.

Depending on various factors, it may or may not be an issue. Use of the name might be safe if (i) the companies are in different industries and (ii) the "likelihood of confusion" in the marketplace is low. Likelihood of confusion is the basis for trademark infringement claims.

As a general rule, using a name that is similar or identical to one or more other companies should be avoided. Not only will that create confusion for consumers and others who want to find you, but it also creates risks of trademark litigation – a risk that may not materialize until the company achieves a level of success and awareness following substantial investment in the name.

Trademark Strength

Some entrepreneurs are tempted to pick names that identify or describe their companies' products or services. While this is logical, these kinds of names are often deemed "generic" or "descriptive" by the USPTO. They hence may be difficult or impossible to register or protect.

Names that are more fanciful like Zippo, or arbitrary like Zoom, are stronger trademarks and easier to register.

Co-existence Agreements

If another company is using the desired trademark, a "Co-existence Agreement" might be a possible solution. These are negotiated agreements between companies, usually in different industries, in which the two companies agree they can reasonably prevent confusion if each party agrees to take certain described steps. Avoiding confusion often means (i) sticking to, or avoiding, specific colors and other branding cues, (ii) advertising in certain ways and places, and (iii) otherwise avoiding conduct that might contribute to confusion in the market.

Even though two parties may enter into a Co-existence Agreement, the USPTO can still prevent one of the parties from registering its preferred trademark. The USPTO will not register a mark if doing so would cause likelihood of confusion, despite the mitigating provisions of a Co-existence Agreement.

Co-existence Agreements are discussed again later in Chapter 9, under *Trademark Disputes*. Find an example of a Co-existence Agreement in the BLSG Data Room under *Intellectual Property > Trademark > Co-existence Agreements*.

Locking Down the Name

If the name clears the trademark search and is a good candidate for trademark protection, a next prudent step is to check the availability of the domain name for use in your website URL, or "Uniform Resource Locator," and grab it if it is available.

Even if you are not ready to form your entity, many Secretary of State online registration platforms allow founders to reserve and hold a name for a period of time. These periods vary by state but are often 120 days.

Quickly also file for trademark registration with the PTO. Trademark registration should be done by qualified trademark counsel whenever possible. It is easy to make harmful mistakes in drafting "class of goods" descriptions, as we discuss in Chapter 9.

If someone is "squatting" on the domain name in "bad faith," it may work to register the trademark and later file a UDRP (Uniform Domain-Name Dispute-Resolution Policy) action with ICANN (Internet Corporation for Assigned Names and Numbers). This is a way to force a transfer of the domain name(s) if negotiations do not work.

The "bad faith" hurdle can be difficult to get over in UDRP actions. We look more closely at the UDRP process in Chapter 9.

In addition to acquiring a new company's most obvious domain name using the ".com" "top-level" domain, the founders should consider acquiring:

- the same domain name across other common top-level domains, such as .net, .org, .co, and .us, and

- any likely variations or misspellings of the.com domain name that consumers may inadvertently enter.

Registering variations and misspellings of the desired domain name can prevent competitors or others with malicious intent, including "typosquatters," from redirecting, hijacking or "brandjacking" your Internet traffic to either a competitive website or to a website designed to commit identity theft or other crimes.

Given their relatively low cost, many companies lock up a large number of potentially valuable domain names early while they're available.

Case Study #12 – URLoser

As discussed above, the only 100% safe method for protecting confidential information is not sharing it.

Founders of a beer company learned this the hard way. Before finally settling on their name, they decided to hold an in-person focus group with friends and community members.

The proposed name was very popular. And then, promptly after the event, an attendee anonymously acquired the.com domain name for it. The domain name was now available for $2,500 instead of $30.

The founders consulted me. I told them they had a very strong case for a UDRP action given the bad faith involved, but that the cost of pursuing a UDRP action was just north of the $2,500 domain name purchase price, so not a perfect solution.

Rather than pay the domain name squatter's ransom, the founders picked a different name. They only shared that name after acquiring the.com domain name and securing the name with the Secretary of State.

Lessons: The best approach would have been to purchase the domain name before discussing the name.

NDAs might also have served as a deterrent.

CHAPTER SIX

Business Entity Selection

Forming a company should not be undertaken without a clear and complete understanding of the desired end-results in the areas of governance, control, finance, and tax.

Hiring legal help to select and form the correct entity should be a budget priority. Non-lawyers can make a terrible mess of things. Entity selection errors are generally Level 2 or 3 mistakes on the L&M Matrix. Many mistakes are fixable at some cost and distraction through what is called an entity conversion.

The Corporation versus LLC Dilemma

Given that startup founders have a 50/50 shot at picking the right entity for their new business, it is somewhat surprising how often founders get it wrong. Entity selection can have profound implications for governance, control, financing options, and incentivizing employees with equity compensation.

One common mistake seems to be forming an LLC because they are supposedly "easier." As discussed below, LLCs can be more expensive to set up and manage correctly than a corporation, and also more difficult to finance.

As a general rule, if your LLC formation was easy, you did it poorly.

On the other hand, a C corporation structure can lead to bad tax consequences for certain types of businesses, particularly where large asset sales are expected. Asset sales by corporations are usually subject to double taxation. The risk of double taxation is why, for example, the vast majority of property development projects are structured as LLCs.

We look at tax considerations below, including the differences between pass-through taxation and entity-level taxation, but tax issues, alone, should not drive choice of entity. As discussed below, a corporation can elect S corporation status to be treated like a partnership with "pass-through taxation," and an LLC can avoid being taxed as a partnership by electing to be taxed as a C corporation.

We will also discuss the pros and cons of starting with one type of entity and converting it to the other. Some founders intentionally start with an LLC to personally benefit from early "tax losses" and later convert to a corporation to facilitate fundraising and employee equity compensation.

Corporations

Startups that intend to raise money from angel investors, VC firms, strategic investors, and other third parties are generally better served forming a corporation than an LLC.

Some key advantages of corporations include:

- readily available corporate forms and templates,
- commonly understood governance principles,
- greater legal certainty under statutes and case law,
- commonly understood generic classes of equity,
- commonly understood equity compensation alternatives, including tax-advantaged incentive stock options,
- no investment restrictions on VCs and institutional investors
- the benefits of tax-free founder stock under Section 1202, and
- greater ability to retain earnings/accumulate capital.

On the other hand, closely-held small businesses that are not likely to seek substantial third-party investments may enjoy greater tax advantages and governance flexibility as an LLC.

In an LLC structure, a single owner or small group of founders can manage tax consequences more aggressively, allocate profits and losses with some freedom, and avoid double taxation on distributions to investors and asset sales.

For these reasons, as discussed more fully below, the LLC structure is often the better choice for many closely-held small businesses, including family businesses and those sometimes referred to as "lifestyle businesses."

A lifestyle business is a business formed by one or more persons who intend to grow it and operate it for themselves to provide income necessary to support a comfortable lifestyle.

But first, more on the pros and cons of incorporation.

Forms and Templates

Because modern corporations have been evolving since the late 1800s, standardized forms and templates are available. These include, among others:

- Bylaws
- Articles of Incorporation
- Stock Purchase Agreements
- Shareholders Agreements
- Voting Agreements
- Equity Compensation Plans
- Stock Option Agreements
- Restricted Stock Awards

The availability of corporate forms and templates contrasts sharply with the relative dearth of similar forms and templates for LLCs, first authorized by the Wyoming legislature in the 1970s.

Commonly Understood Governance Principles

Corporations are largely creatures of statute and case law. The corporate law statutes of all 50 states generally require every corporation to be governed by a board of directors and managed by officers bearing certain minimum titles, usually a president, a treasurer, a secretary, and any number of vice presidents desired.

This governance structure, as interpreted and defined through years of case law, is well-understood and quite predictable in its functioning.

As an example, while principles regarding officers' and directors' duties of care and loyalty have been tested and applied in the courts of most states for many years and are relatively fixed, case law in the partnership law world applicable to LLCs does not always provide the same degree of clarity or predictability.

The duties of care and loyalty are considered the twin pillars of corporate law and are referred to collectively as "fiduciary duties." Fiduciary duties arise in trust relationships and other legal relationships where one person is tasked with handling or managing the money or assets of another. Fiduciaries must exercise due care appropriate to the circumstances and may not act in their own self-interest to the detriment of the person for whom they are a fiduciary.

Fiduciary duties can be contractually waived or altered in an LLC Operating Agreement in ways that are not possible in the corporate context. Case Study 20 - Loyalty Not Required, in the next chapter, discusses how these differences can expose minority LLC members to greater risk of oppression by controlling LLC members.

In contrast to corporate governance, LLC governance is determined largely as a matter of contract law, based on what the LLC owners agree to in the LLC's Operating Agreement, and subject to any contract interpretation issues that might arise among the owners.

An LLC's contractual flexibility works well when all the players are sophisticated or sufficiently "lawyered-up." It can work less well in typical startup contexts where the participants are not sophisticated and not inclined or not able to pay legal fees to understand and protect their rights.

Legal Certainty

Corporations and their shareholder owners benefit from rich corporate case law, particularly in states with high concentrations of business activity like Delaware and New York. Courts of appeal have been adding to corporate case law for more than one hundred years, issuing opinions on matters of corporate governance, the powers of officers and directors, the rights of shareholders, and myriad other matters.

This rich corporate case law provides a level of certainty that many investors find reassuring. Rights and expectations are clearer. That presumably reduces the likelihood of disputes, corporate misconduct, and unexpected litigation outcomes.

LLCs, on the other hand, are still new and largely untested in the courts. Wyoming passed the first LLC statute in 1977, but most other states did not adopt LLC authorizing statutes until the 1990s. It is often difficult to find authoritative appellate decisions in any state on basic questions of LLC governance.

The absence of well-developed case law is important to many investors who may be concerned or even skeptical about LLC governance and the protection of LLC minority owners from majority-owner misconduct.

Generic Classes of Equity

Corporations also benefit from well-known and broadly understood classes of equity – common stock and preferred stock, both of which we explore in detail in Chapter 12, *Startup Finance Overview.*

As complex as preferred stock rights and privileges can be, the general parameters of these instruments are familiar to most sophisticated investors and, thus, fairly easily negotiated.

There are no widely recognized, standard analogues for equity interests in an LLC, other than that such interests are often called "member ownership interests" or ownership "units." As with other key aspects of LLCs, the rights and obligations associated with LLC units or other LLC equity interests are matters of negotiation and drafting.

Drafting contractual provisions of any kind can lead to differing interpretations and disputes. In the realm of LLCs, litigated issues involving Operating Agreement drafting questions are likely to be matters of first impression in most courts. Rarely does a lawyer researching a novel issue of LLC governance find case law from his or her jurisdiction directly on point with the question presented. Case law parallels and "precedent" tend to come from contract law and partnership law.

Well-Understood Equity Compensation Instruments

Corporate stock options, restricted stock awards, and other forms of stock-based compensation are ubiquitous in today's workplace. For the most part, employees understand, trust, and value stockbased compensation. The same cannot be said for LLC equity-based compensation, which has extremely low familiarity, particularly among typical startup employees.

Creating equity-based compensation plans for LLCs is certainly possible with some drafting and additional legal, tax advisory, and administrative expenses. Still, employees are less likely to understand, trust, or be motivated by such instruments compared to traditional stock-based instruments.

Additionally, the special tax treatment afforded "incentive stock options" under the Internal Revenue Code is limited exclusively to qualifying corporate stock option plans and grants. The Code contains no similar provisions for LLC equity compensation grants.

Many founders fail to understand the stark differences in using equity to compensate employees in an LLC structure and frequently misspeak about issuing "stock options." LLCs do not issue stock or grant stock options. When it comes to promises about compensation, language matters.

Case Study #16, *Not an Option*, goes into more detail regarding the specific challenges of issuing equity-based compensation in an LLC structure.

Case Study #13 – Forest of Confusion

Earlier in my career, I served as Director, Law for a publicly-traded timber company that was one of the largest private landowners in the United States. It was my first corporate job after working at the SEC.

Before we later converted the company into the world's first "Timber REIT" (Real Estate Investment Trust), the company was a master limited partnership, or MLP. An MLP is an odd duck for a publicly-traded company, much closer to an LLC than a corporation.

The company's "MLP Units" were traded on the New York Stock Exchange, and hence highly liquid. Despite this, all of the resources in the world could not help the company create an equity incentive plan with anywhere near the simplicity and clarity of a typical stock option plan.

Consequently, my 1996 Offer Letter vaguely referenced participation in the company's Long Term Incentive Plan, or "LTIP."

Despite the exceptional business sophistication and intellectual caliber of my colleagues, the open secret around the water cooler was that nobody understood completely how this plan actually worked or what kinds of payouts it would ultimately produce. It seemed to be equal parts math and magic when the Personnel Committee met behind closed doors to determine individual payment awards under the LTIP.

This uncertainty was a factor when I left in May 2000 to jump into the tail end of the ".com boom." My offer letter in that transition contained the attractive promise of "… *an incentive stock option grant of 85,000 options….*" I was quite happy to leave behind the opacity of my LTIP awards and my "MLP Tracking Units."

> <u>Lessons:</u> It is hard, if not impossible, for LLCs and other partnership-like structures to match the clarity, attractiveness, and ease of adoption and administration of corporation-based equity plans.

No Institutional Investor or VC Restrictions

A wide range of tax-exempt institutions, including pension funds, endowments, and foundations, cannot invest in LLCs. That is because those tax-exempt entities are prohibited under the Internal Revenue Code from receiving the "Unrelated Business Taxable Income," or "UBTI," that flows through an LLC to its owners.

The IRS defines UBTI this way:

> "… *unrelated business income is income from a trade or business, regularly carried on, that is not substantially related to the charitable, educational, or other purpose that is the basis of the organization's exemption.*"

Importantly, pension funds, endowments, and foundations invest as limited partners in virtually every VC fund. Consequently, VCs generally cannot and do not invest in LLCs.

Furthermore, other sophisticated investors have a strong preference for investments with no tax consequences prior to an eventual exit. This is the likely tax outcome for a successful investment in a corporation.

There are structural ways around the UBTI issue, but they are complex and imperfect. One approach is for an investment fund to establish a "blocker corporation" that essentially stands between the fund and the UBTI generating investment. The blocker corporation pays tax on the UBTI instead of the investment fund.

While a blocker corporation LLC structure is feasible, it is arguably not *desirable*. Most VCs seem to have little interest in investing in complex, uncertain structures, let alone creating or managing them for themselves to facilitate a single investment.

For a typical startup struggling to attract investors, any form of structural novelty or complexity is just another potential negative to overcome.

Section 1202 – Tax-Free Founders Stock.

Section 1202 of the Internal Revenue Code offers a less well-known advantage of incorporation. For investors (except other corporations), Sec. 1202 excludes from gross income up to 100% of the gain recognized on the sale or exchange of "qualified small business stock" ("QSBS") held more than five years.

For a company's stock to qualify for QSBS treatment, the company's assets must be valued at less than $50 million.

The gain eligible for exclusion is limited to the greater of $10 million or 10 times the investor's basis in the stock. Among other restrictions, QSBS means stock issued by a domestic (U.S.) C corporation. LLC equity interests are not eligible.

Again, Section 1202 allows purchasers (founders or other investors) of QSBS held five or more years to exclude from gross income up to 100% of the gain recognized on the sale of those shares.

This tax benefit was originally intended to be temporary, but it was made permanent in December 2015, with the passage of the Protecting Americans from Tax Hikes ("PATH") Act.

Retained Earnings/Capital Accumulation.

It is more tax efficient to accumulate capital in a corporation than in an LLC because of the higher tax rate for LLC's on retained earnings. If an LLC doesn't distribute all of its earnings to its shareholders in a given year, it could be liable for a supplemental corporation tax on any amount retained over $250,000. The tax rate on this excess accumulation is 39.6 percent, as of May 2020.

LLCs can avoid taxes on retained earnings if they can show there is a "business justification" for the retained earnings. They can do this by showing, for example, that the company is planning to expand in the next year or to increase staffing expenses or equipment purchases.

Doing so requires careful documentation, however, and tax advisors often default to recommending that LLCs pay out retained earnings to their unitholders.

As a result, accumulating capital for future uses, like strategic acquisitions, is generally easier for a corporation than for an LLC.

Double Taxation

As mentioned, one of the primary concerns about corporations is the possibility of "double taxation." Unlike an LLC, a corporation is a taxable entity under the Internal Revenue Code. LLCs are not subject to double taxation because they are "disregarded entities" for tax purposes. The taxation of disregarded entities is often referred to as "pass-through" or "flow-through" taxation. The tax obligations do not stay with the entity, but rather pass through directly to the owners themselves.

As a taxable entity, a corporation must pay tax on its profits. Additionally, corporate shareholders must also pay taxes on any corporate dividends, hence the risk of double taxation.

But even though almost 85% of companies included in the S&P 500 Index pay dividends, startups and smaller companies rarely pay dividends. Closely held corporations do not need to pay dividends to compensate their owners. Instead, they can avoid double taxation by paying salaries to their employee-owners. And those salaries are tax-deductible to the corporation.

The more likely double taxation risks for startups and other small businesses involve asset sales. The potential risk of double taxation in asset sales explains why most real property-intensive businesses are formed as LLCs. Asset sale tax risks are addressed further in the discussion of LLCs.

S Corporation Status

Another solution for avoiding double taxation is for the owners of a closely held corporation to elect "S corporation" status.

Contrary to a common misunderstanding, one does not "form" an S corporation or even a C corporation. Rather, an S corporation is merely a corporation that elects "small business" status on IRS Form 2553.

The source of these naming conventions is thus not state laws governing corporations, but rather the Internal Revenue Code, including 26 U.S. Code § 1361(a), which defines S and C corporations as follows:

(a) **S corporation defined**

  (1) In general

    For purposes of this title, the term "S corporation" means, with respect to any taxable year, a small business corporation for which an election under section 1362(a) is in effect for such year.

  (2) C corporation

    For purposes of this title, the term "C corporation" means, with respect to any taxable year, a corporation which is not an S corporation for such year.

In addition to preventing double taxation of dividends or asset sales, S corporation status allows a small business owner to:

(i) shift taxable income from a higher corporate tax rate to a lower individual rate, and

(ii) use business losses to reduce taxable income from certain other sources, but be sure to consult tax counsel to understand applicable risks and limitations.

To elect and to maintain S corporation status, a corporation may not:

(i) have more than 100 shareholders,

(ii) have any shareholders who are not real persons, except for certain estates and trusts,

(iii) have a nonresident alien as a shareholder, or

(iv) have more than 1 class of stock.

If any of these prohibitions are violated, S corporation status is immediately lost, whether the corporation's officers realize it or not.

Interestingly, concerning (iv) above, while the issuance of a single share of preferred stock terminates S corporation status, the addition of a non-voting common stock class does not violate the single class of stock requirement.

Limited Liability Companies

Notwithstanding the many benefits of incorporation, the tax attributes and flexibility of an LLC make it the right choice in many business contexts, particularly:

- businesses formed and operated by a single individual or small groups of individuals, including those thought of as lifestyle businesses,

- small businesses with little or no need for third-party investment, and

- any business that will acquire and eventually dispose of significant real property assets or other types of assets.

LLCs are appealing to many startup founders due to the *apparent* ease with which they can be set up and the minimal administrative burdens required to maintain them.

One key governance difference is that an LLC is not required to have a board of directors, just a "manager." That said, many LLCs end up having boards for governance reasons, and possibly to look less like LLCs to third parties.

Unlike S corporations, LLCs are not limited to domestic investors, a single class of security, or any specific number of investors.

Formation and Governance Challenges

As discussed earlier, the ownership, structure, and governance of corporations is more widely understood and more clearly defined by statute and case law. Founders and managers of corporations also benefit from the wealth of available corporate forms and templates.

In contrast, LLCs are governed and managed almost exclusively as a matter of contract law, based on what the LLC owners agree to in the LLC's Operating Agreement, sometimes also called a "Company Agreement."

For some, the *apparent* ease of setting up an LLC can be misleading. As discussed below, co-founders are strongly advised to execute a thoughtfully negotiated 35 to 40-page Operating Agreement simultaneously with the formation of an LLC.

Operating Agreements are inherently more complicated documents than any of the documents required to form a corporation and issue founder stock. Much of this complexity has to do with tax considerations, but an Operating Agreement also needs to spell out *every aspect* of governance, management, control, and economics.

Consequently, although LLCs *seem* easy to set up and they do not require a board of directors, governance mistakes and misunderstandings may be more likely with an LLC.

Additionally, legal expenses for drafting things like Operating Agreements, LLC equity compensation plans, and LLC financing documents are often significantly higher.

Regarding the possibility of misunderstandings, Case Study #10, *Conniving Co-Founder*, highlighted this risk all too well.

Three months into the business enterprise, the conniving co-founder claimed that the original founder and Manager of the LLC had no authority to establish and grow reserves for the expansion of the business. The conniving co-founder wanted cash, and he wanted lots of it immediately.

The LLC Operating Agreement had the following very typical language concerning distributions and reserves (underlining added):

> *"Distributable Cash" means all cash received by the Company in any calendar year <u>less the sum of the following</u> to the extent paid or set aside by the Company: (i) all principal and interest payments on indebtedness of the Company and other sums paid or payable to lenders; (ii) all cash expenditures incurred incident to the normal operation of the Company's business; <u>and (iii) Reserves established in the discretion of the Manager.</u>*

Since the business was a successful and easily replicated restaurant, expansion was in the best interests of the company and its owners. And subpart (iii) above clearly gave the original founder and Manager discretion to establish reserves nessary to support exapansion.

But the conniving co-founder somehow found room for disagreement in the relatively clear language of subpart (iii) above. The 39.6% tax on an LLC's retained earnings also might have bolstered his position, had he known to raise it.

Had the founder formed the business as a corporation, the Conniving Co-founder's demands for substantial distributions in the business's first months would have been laughable. No reasonable person would doubt the power of a board of directors to reserve cash for such expansion, and not many attorneys would have taken that case – certainly not on a contingent fee basis.

But because it was an LLC, and because there was little or no case law interpreting the phrase *"Reserves established in the discretion of the Manager,"* the Conniving Co-founder was able to hire an unscrupulous attorney, who promptly threatened to sue for $1 million.

Given the case law vacuum on LLC reserves, the litigation-averse founder was unable to get comfortable with the litigation risks and settled for $700,000.

Again, this happened just eight months after the Conniving Co-founder invested only $30,000.

Case Study #10 is an example of how the relative dearth of legal precedents regarding LLCs and their largely contractual nature can result in costly disputes between owners, particularly when less sophisticated parties are involved.

Pass-Through Taxation

As we know, an LLC itself doesn't pay any income taxes on its profits. Instead, LLCs are taxed like partnerships. All profits or losses pass through to the owners, or members, as they are called. The members then report those profits or losses on their individual tax returns.

And just as a corporation can make an S corporation election, an LLC can elect to be taxed like a C corporation.

Most states with income taxes respect an LLC's federal pass-through or entity-level tax election and impose their taxes on the individual owners or entity in the same manner, but not all states do so. Consult a competent tax advisor for an analysis of the applicable state tax laws before forming an LLC or making pass-through or entity-level tax elections.

Tax Risk

LLC members bear some risk that their taxable profit "allocations" in a given year may create tax obligations that exceed their cash distributions from the LLC. In other words, an LLC investor might not receive any cash from the LLC in a given year but could still have a substantial tax liability due on any profits of the LLC allocated to the investor.

In general, LLC Operating Agreements are drafted to require cash distributions sufficient to cover the owners' expected tax liabilities.

But superior debt repayment obligations or other claims on an LLC's cash can cause distributions to fall short of investors' tax liabilities.

Special Allocations of Profits and Losses

A unique feature of LLCs over corporations is the ability to allocate profits, losses, and ownership percentages with relative flexibility.

Under state law and IRS guidance, the default rule is that an LLC member's initial ownership interest should reflect the member's investment relative to the other LLC members' investments, or relative to the other members' current "capital account" percentages if the LLC has an operating history. The capital account of each member starts with their initial investment and adjusts over time based on additional contributions, cash distributions, and profit and loss allocations.

Similarly, the default rule is that profits and losses are allocated in the same ratio as each member's ownership interest, again, based on the member's capital account.

But LLC owners can also agree to alter the default rules by what are called "special allocations," provided they do not violate IRS requirements that allocations have "economic substance" and are not just intended to reduce member tax liabilities.

Special allocations commonly involve ownership interests or profit and loss allocations that are not based purely on financial contributions, but that also reflect agreements about deferred contributions, labor contributions ("sweat equity") or other facts and circumstances.

An example might involve an Operating Agreement granting 50/50 ownership between two co-founders where one is required to make a certain financial investment, and the other is required to contribute labor of equal financial value. The Operating Agreement might allocate 55% of all profits (and losses) to the member making the financial investment until that amount has been paid in the form of salary and distributions, after which the allocations would be 50%-50%.

Special allocations are subject to strict IRS rules. The IRS can review special allocations for what it calls "substantial economic effect," meaning that the allocations truly reflect the owners' actual economic circumstances and are not merely an attempt to shift income to reduce taxes. Allocations blatantly designed to allocate all of an LLC's losses to the owner with the highest tax rate, for example, would not pass scrutiny.

Asset Sale Tax Advantages

Advocates of LLCs point out correctly that risks of double taxation from asset sales may be greater than some realize. The possibilities for asset sales rise in real property-intensive businesses, such as property development, oil and gas, mining, chains, and other businesses with multiple physical locations, like restaurants.

But asset sales happen all the time in M&A transactions and are certainly not limited to cases involving real property. M&A transactions are structured in several ways, but, broadly speaking, they are either equity (stock or units) transactions or asset transactions. The risk of double taxation makes it important to understand the factors that might help predict a major asset sale in the future.

Many considerations go into deciding whether to structure an M&A transaction as an equity transaction or an asset transaction. And while complex tax considerations are often most important, many other factors can tip the deal one direction or the other.

Two common reasons for preferring an asset transaction over an equity transaction are an acquiror's desire to: (i) leave debts and other liabilities with the "target" company being acquired, and (ii) acquire only certain of the target's assets, like a specific product line or division.

In an M&A deal, all kinds of known or unknown liabilities or concerns can spook an aquiror away from a "stock deal," including potential personnel issues, environmental liabilities, IP concerns, regulatory problems, pending litigation, and so forth. An acquiror takes on all of those potential liabilities in a stock deal, albeit subject to remedies in the SPA, such as escrows, holdbacks, and indemnification.

Personnel issues can include active or potential litigation or simply just a desire to not keep all or any of the target's employees. Many asset deals are predicated on reaching agreement with the target regarding which employees will "come over" as part of the asset deal – perhaps the most desirable employees associated with the specific assets or division being acquired.

So, the question of whether or not a newly formed entity will one day be involved in an asset sale that could trigger double taxation is often trickier than just considering the importance of real property in the business.

Where real property is a prominent component, the likelihood of future asset sales is very high. But a company that intends to pursue multiple product lines or service offerings also could be a participant in future asset sales if lower-performing or less synergistic lines need to be sold off.

Asset sales may also be in the future for companies that are likely to incur potential environmental liabilities, or that might be involved in buying and selling IP or other types of assets.

Self-Employment Taxes

In addition to the tax considerations already considered, closely-held small businesses often use LLCs to implement other tax strategies, including (i) minimizing employment-related taxes and (ii) income shifting.

For many years there has been great uncertainty around when LLC "distributive income" should be subject to employment-related taxes as being more like self-employment income than investment income.

Characterizing all or part of a member's cash payments from an LLC as "distributions" shelters those payments from federal Social Security and Medicare taxes, state and federal workers' compensation taxes, and other types of payroll taxes.

Distributions are transfers of "Distributable Cash" or "Available Cash" by an LLC to its members in respect of the members' ownership interests, in contrast to payroll payments for the performance of labor or other services.

The application of self-employment tax rules to LLCs has been unclear since their inception in 1977, leading to a variety of practices that have been coming under greater IRS scrutiny in recent years. The IRS has recently won important Tax Court cases in this area. These decisions support the IRS's position that LLC distributions to a member constitute self-employment income subject to self-employment taxes when the LLC member actively participates in the business and has managerial decision-making authority, or "management control."

In 2018, the IRS announced that the under-reporting of self-employment income by members of LLCs, limited liability partnerships (LLPs) and professional limited liability companies (PLLCs) would become an enforcement priority.

Going forward, while non-participating, non-managerial LLC members should have no concerns about having to report LLC distributions as self-employment income, LLC members who participate in a business and who exercise any degree of managerial authority need to understand their self-employment tax obligations and may need to adopt a more conservative tax posture.

The IRS website as of April 2020 provided this information regarding Self-Employment taxes:

> *Self-Employment Tax Rate*
>
> *The self-employment tax rate is 15.3%. The rate consists of two parts: 12.4% for social security (old-age, survivors, and disability insurance) and 2.9% for Medicare (hospital insurance)....*

Income Shifting

Income shifting includes a variety of "wealth management" strategies that shift income from individuals in higher tax brackets to their dependents in lower tax brackets.

This can involve things as simple as gifting income-producing stocks or bonds to dependents in lower tax brackets, such as children, retired parents, or siblings.

In a small business context, income shifting can include giving jobs to dependents, or even granting ownership interests to the dependents, including LLC units, limited partnership interests, or other types of interests called family limited partnership interests. The LLC or other entity may hold the entire business or only certain assets contributed by the business, perhaps a building leased back to the business. LLC or limited partner distributions to those family members might then be used to fund things like housing, living expenses, medical expenses, and educational expenses.

The IRS carefully scrutinizes income shifting strategies and often disregards structures and transactions which it decides lack economic substance and are designed solely for tax avoidance.

Entity Conversions

As we know, one reason many startups begin as LLCs is the desire by one or more founders to use the startup's up-front expenses to lower the founders' taxable income from other sources. These founders often plan to convert to a corporation once the startup becomes profitable or when seeking third-party investments.

Conversions from corporations to LLCs also happen, but they are less common.

Some attorneys and tax advisors say it is no big deal to start as an LLC for tax reasons and convert later to a corporation.

Mark Zuckerberg's co-founder of Facebook, Eduardo Saverin, might beg to differ. It was during a Florida LLC-to-Delaware corporation conversion effected via merger that he was unwittingly diluted from 24% ownership to less than 10%.

The reality is that conversions are not always easy, and they are never free. Complexity and legal expenses can rise sharply if novel LLC equity interests or governance rights have been created or if other facts and circumstances have complicated the company's balance sheet.

Many startups struggle to form and govern a single entity properly. Doubling a startup's risks of formation and governance errors by building in a conversion should not be undertaken too lightly.

When LLC owners create "revenue participation interests" or assign preferential rights to profits and expenses between owners in ways that are not possible with corporate ownership interests like common or preferred stock, conversion to a corporation will require negotiations among the owners. Those negotiations may or may not go smoothly.

Lastly, like any other transaction, entity conversions need to be considered very carefully from a tax perspective. Depending on the assets involved, their tax basis (original cost plus any required adjustments), and any accumulated operating losses, there are likely several choices for structuring a conversion.

And almost any conversion of a corporation to an LLC is going to generate negative tax consequences, however structured, unless perhaps the existing corporation is an S corporation.

In summary, entrepreneurs should consider the source (and related financial interests) of any advice suggesting that it is easy to begin a startup as one type of entity and later change it to another. Projects always look easier when someone else is paying the bills, executing the project, and bearing the risks.

Domicile Considerations – Home State versus Delaware?

Where to form a company is an important early question. LLCs and corporations are all formed under the laws of a specific state called its "domicile." As discussed below, for most businesses, this means its home state of operations or Delaware.

Selecting the right domicile comes down to whether the additional costs and administrative burdens of forming in Delaware versus the company's home state are worth it for one or both of these reasons:

(i)   the founders appreciate the greater legal certainty Delaware provides, or

(ii) important third-party investors could be turned off by the company's non-Delaware legal status.

Why Delaware is So Popular

More than half of all publicly traded companies are Delaware corporations, as are more than 60% of Fortune 500 companies. How did the second smallest state in the U.S. pull this off?

In the early 1800s, only New York had enacted an "incorporating statute." By and large, individual corporations could still only be created in any state by legislative act. In 1896, in a bid to draw businesses (and tax revenues) from New York, New Jersey created what is considered the first modern incorporation act. Seeing New Jersey's success, Delaware quickly followed suit.

In 1913, New Jersey's governor, Woodrow Wilson, required that New Jersey's corporate laws be tightened up. After that, Delaware took the lead in new incorporations. Delaware has maintained that lead since by continuing to fine-tune its "General Corporation Law."

Delaware's early lead in business-friendly corporate laws attracted thousands of companies large and small. As a result, Delaware's trial and appellate courts have decided many thousands of disputes applying and interpreting the Delaware General Corporation Law ("DGCL").

The volume and complexity of cases decided in Delaware's court system over the decades have created a body of business and governance law that is richer and more comprehensive than that of any other state. This makes interpretations of Delaware's corporate laws more predictable.

Delaware corporate law is also the body of corporate statutory and case law with which the greatest number of lawyers and non-lawyers are familiar.

Because of this, companies, investors, and their attorneys all have greater confidence in how Delaware courts will address a wide range of business or governance disputes. Individual VCs who are expected to serve on multiple corporate boards also prefer the robustness and predictability of Delaware corporate law – particularly the standards applicable to officers and directors.

Nevada and Wyoming

But what about other states that advertise to lure businesses? States like Nevada and Wyoming, for example, both work hard to appeal to new businesses through claims like greater privacy, lower taxes, lower fees, and greater anonymity for founders. These enticements may be illusory at best for most startups, and potentially even harmful.

The emphases on asset protection and anonymity have a somewhat negative or evasive connotation. Asset protection and anonymity probably should not be driving factors for most businesses intending to comply with applicable laws and regulations and seeking to convey an upstanding image.

Additionally, the idea of protecting assets by incorporating in another state seems highly suspect if a company is not doing business or maintaining assets in that state. Neither Nevada nor Wyoming has any jurisdiction over the courts of any other state when it comes to assets outside of Nevada or Wyoming.

Likewise, the promises of lower taxes and fees seem misleading. First, a company will pay taxes wherever it does business, based on applicable state-by-state tax laws, including its home state.

Secondly, any annual registration fees paid to Nevada or Wyoming, however small, would be *in addition to* the fees required to qualify to do business in a company's home state. The best way to lower annual fees and administrative burdens is home-state formation.

In summary, picking a state, aside from Delaware, that has no discernable connection to the business, makes little sense and might raise red flags with sophisticated potential investors. Consequently, for many startups, the question of domicile is generally between the home state or Delaware.

Downsides to Delaware

There are several downsides to forming an entity in Delaware instead of a company's home state.

Dual Registration. First and foremost is simply the cost and administrative burden of dual registration. Any business forming under Delaware law but headquartered elsewhere will need to be "qualified to do business" in its home state. In Washington state, for example, this involves obtaining a Washington State Business License.

Dual registration requires paying annual fees to both states and making annual filings with both states.

Delaware Franchise Tax. Newly incorporated Delaware corporations invariably receive a shock in the form of a notice indicating that their "Delaware franchise tax" is some very large amount, often ranging between $32,000 and $75,000.

A brief online search of the phrase "Delaware franchise tax" highlights that Delaware's approach to sending out these notices causes unnecessary anxiety.

Unless certain mistakes have been made in setting up a company and managing its cap table, there is almost always an easy fix for an exorbitant Delaware franchise tax bill.

There are two ways of calculating a company's Delaware franchise tax, the Authorized Share Method and the Assumed Par Value Method. The latter of these tends to produce the lowest tax for most startups. You can learn more about these methods by searching "How to calculate Delaware Franchise Taxes" or by going here - https://corp.delaware.gov/frtaxcalc/.

The page at that link also has a downloadable franchise tax calculator spreadsheet.

Here's how the Delaware Secretary of State says franchise taxes are calculated under the two methods:

Authorized Shares Method

- *For corporations having no par value stock the authorized shares method will always result in the lesser tax.*

- *5,000 shares or less (minimum tax) $175.00.*

- *5,001 – 10,000 shares – $250.00,*

  - *each additional 10,000 shares or portion thereof, add $85.00*

  - *maximum annual tax is $200,000.00*

- *For Example*

  - *A corporation with 10,005 shares authorized pays $335.00 ($250.00 plus $85.00).*

  - *A corporation with 100,000 shares authorized pays $1,015.00 ($250.00 plus $765.00 [$85.00 x 9]).*

Assumed Par Value Capital Method

To use this method, you must give figures for all issued shares (including treasury shares) and total gross assets in the spaces provided in your Annual Franchise Tax Report. Total Gross Assets shall be those "total assets" reported on the U.S. Form 1120, Schedule L (Federal Return) relative to the company's fiscal year ending the calendar year of the report. The tax rate under this method is

$400.00 per million or portion of a million. If the assumed par value capital is less than

$1,000,000, the tax is calculated by dividing the assumed par value capital by $1,000,000 then

multiplying that result by $400.00.

Following that somewhat opaque description of what many simply call the Assumed Par Value Method, there are several relatively complex examples. Again, those are found here - https://corp.delaware.gov/frtaxcalc/

Any startup receiving an inflated Delaware franchise tax and needing help to figure out what went wrong can always call the Delaware Secretary of State Division of Corporations at (302) 739-3073.

There are several things companies can do to try to ensure the availability of the Assumed Par Value method to produce a lower tax bill.

Many are tempted to simply authorize a small number of shares. Under the Authorized Shares Method, any number 5,000 or fewer results in only $175.00 in annual franchise tax. But this generally doesn't work long for companies planning to raise substantial outside capital, or that may want to grant employee stock options. Many companies intending to go the VC funding route tend to authorize around 10 million shares from the outset.

For companies planning to seek VC funding and that want to issue option grants that are comparable in share numbers to those of other VC-funded companies, the following three steps should result in a modest franchise tax:

- In filing articles of incorporation, use a very low par value of either $.0001 per share or $.00001 per share.

- Do not authorize unreasonably large numbers of shares in the initial articles of incorporation – 10,000,000 shares seems to be a safe number.

- Lastly, promptly issue a substantial percentage of the company's initially authorized shares, perhaps 60% or more.

Following these steps results in an annual Delaware franchise tax of about $350 for most newer startups under the Assumed Par Value Method.

No-Par-Value Trap for the Unwary. Par value is the minimum amount that must be paid for each share of a company's stock. As with other states, the DGCL allows corporations to issue stock with no par value.

Doing so, however, prevents the company from using the Assumed Par Value Method for determining its franchise tax obligations and limits the company to using the Authorized Share Method. The inability to use the Assumed Par Value Method could result in very large franchise tax bills. Fortunately, there is a process for converting to a par value, but there are likely fees to pay and potential tax implications, so better to get it right the first time.

Risk of Suit in Delaware. Many Delaware companies are disappointed to remember that they can be sued in Delaware, even though they have a somewhat superficial relationship with the state.

Being sued in another state is administratively inconvenient for many companies and almost always means higher costs. In addition to travel costs, legal fees are often almost doubled. This is because companies frequently want their usual litigation counsel to lead the litigation. Unless those attorneys are licensed to practice law in Delaware, "local counsel" licensed in Delaware must be hired as well.

As one might imagine, Delaware litigation attorneys can be pricey given the strong, built-in demand for their services. As one might also imagine, Delaware's attorneys have protected their monopoly well, imposing a five-month in-Delaware "clerkship" as one of the requirements for admission to the Delaware Bar.

Another interesting consideration is the fact that Delaware's trial court system can be clogged, inefficient, and even dysfunctional sometimes, as we see in Case Study #15, *Sued in Delaware*.

We close out this chapter on business entity selection with three case studies.

Case Study #14 – Not So Easy

As discussed, entity conversions are trickier than some tax and legal professionals lead founders to believe. One of my companies recently decided to make the switch from an LLC to a corporation to raise capital more easily.

In the interest of efficiency, the company also decided to simultaneously re-domicile from Washington to Delaware to make it a more attractive investment to non-Washington residents.

This isn't a particularly interesting case study, but it provides a real-world example of the complexities required to accomplish these two objectives. And this example involved a one-owner cap table.

As mentioned earlier, conversions can be greatly complicated by the presence of substantial tax issues or novel investment interests, none of which existed in this example.

The following documents were required to accomplish this simultaneous LLC-to-corporation conversion and Washington-to-Delaware re-domiciling.

- Plan of Conversion of XYZ Co., LLC
- Unanimous Consent of LLC Members to Conversion
- Washington Secretary of State "Cover Sheet for Conversion of Entity"
- Articles of Conversion of XYC Co., LLC
- Delaware Certificate of Conversion from a Limited Liability Company to a Corporation
- Certificate of Incorporation of XYZ, Co., Inc.
- XYZ Co., Inc. Consent Resolutions in Lieu of Organizational Meeting of Board of Directors
- Bylaws of XYZ, Co. Inc.
- Stockholders Agreement of XYZ, Co., Inc.

The Plan of Conversion is a key document as it approves and details the overall transaction. The Plan of Conversion is approved by the company and by the Members and details the following:

- the company's name, entity type and domicile before the conversion,
- the conversion effectiveness date,
- that the entity continues as the same entity,
- how ownership interests from the LLC become shares of stock in the corporation, and
- other miscellaneous details of the conversion.

The Stockholders Agreement carries forward or changes certain understandings among the owners, including things like:

- restrictions on transfer,
- rights of first refusal,
- circumstances that trigger the rights of the company or other shareholders to acquire another shareholder's shares (death or impending involuntary transfers due to divorce or court orders),
- drag-along rights (discussed in Chapter 8), and
- other miscellaneous terms, such as certificate legends, termination provisions, and choice of law.

Getting the above documents right requires assistance of experienced counsel. Another equally important step in executing an entity conversion is obtaining advice regarding all tax implications of the transaction.

Obtaining a fair market valuation for the entity as of the date of conversion and also having current financials as of the most recent period (accountant verified, if not audited) are both additional important steps.

Entity conversion goes to the heart of a company's governance foundation, cap table, and tax status. An improperly executed conversion could be just as detrimental to a company as a defective initial formation.

Full records for any conversion will be requested for years to come by potential investors and acquirors, auditors, and possibly also taxing authorities, among others.

Case Study #15 – Sued in Delaware

Delaware's body of corporate law is the envy of all other states, and deservedly so. But the lower trial courts that produce the decisions feeding Delaware's appellate court system seem to struggle under the burden of Delaware's popularity.

One of my companies was sued in Delaware by a man with a history of filing unfounded lawsuits. My experiences with the Delaware court system left me desiring to never litigate in Delaware again.

Among other concerns, the system transferred our case to a total of three judges over two years. With each transfer, overworked judges seemed to struggle to get up to speed on the case and move it forward, adding delays and costs.

Worse yet, the Delaware court system's deference to "pro se" (unrepresented) litigants was extreme to the point of denying my company justice. The Delaware trial judges refused to entertain a motion to dismiss the case for "failure to state a claim upon which relief can be granted," simply because of the pro se status of the plaintiff.

As an experienced litigator, I knew that not only would any Washington State court have heard our motion to dismiss promptly, it would have also thrown the case out.

We ultimately won a $366,041.87 judgment against the plaintiff, to his disappointment. By then the plaintiff had filed three meritless lawsuits and the court finally took him to the woodshed. The decision and order are found at the link below. Among other things, the order demonstrates the power of robust customer-facing terms and conditions. The ones I wrote provided the basis for a sizable attorneys' fees award.

https://www.ded.uscourts.gov/sites/ded/files/opinions/09-340_0.pdf

Unfortunately, the additional costs to defend these meritless cases in Delaware versus Washington were around $300,000.

> Lesson: Delaware may have great case law, but its trial courts can be just as dysfunctional and inefficient as those in any other state if they're too busy. Fortunately, the Delaware courts seem to get things right in the end.

Case Study #16 – Not an Option

Two entrepreneurs approached me to help them structure an LLC for a new business. One of them was contributing labor as the full-time CEO, and the other was contributing $1.3 million of capital.

A tax accountant was already involved and had convinced them to go with an LLC based on tax considerations – primarily the personal deductibility of early expenses. The founders also confirmed that they would not need to raise any funds from outside parties.

Consequently, they were not interested in discussing the wider range of pros and cons of LLCs versus corporations discussed in this Chapter, and I did not force that conversation.

After weeks of working with the two entrepreneurs and another attorney to set up an LLC and negotiate the details of an Operating Agreement, I received the following question via email:

> "… we're now hiring three salespeople, and we want to offer stock options to the new hires as part of their compensation package. Are you able to advise us on how different class stock options work and how to set aside stock options for employees, the board of advisors, etc.?"

This email made me realize I need to create a one-page disclaimer for clients to sign, acknowledging the full range of issues related to founding any startup as an LLC. One of the top items on that one-pager will be <u>LLCs Do Not and Cannot Issue Stock Options</u>.

Below is the email I sent in response:

> "LLCs are, in my view, poorly suited to issuing equity to employees due to the administrative burdens, tax issues/uncertainties and potential costs of setting up and administering any such scheme.
>
> If issuing equity to employees is important, you should consider converting to a C Corporation.
>
> The ability to issue "options" to purchase LLC membership units is unsettled. Incentive Stock Options are certainly out of the question under the tax code, but "non-qualified" options to purchase LLC membership units may be possible – some say yes, and others seem to say no.
>
> Outright equity grants in an LLC are immediately taxable to employees and, by law, cause those persons to be converted from W-2 employees to Form K-1-receiving LLC partners/members.
>
> The tax implications can be softened but not eliminated by having any outright equity grants vest over time, which causes the taxable income to accrue over time. The problem with these taxes is that they must be paid in the year the grants are received, with no guarantee regarding if or when the employee will receive cash from an exit to recoup any of those taxes.
>
> Because of these types of complexities and uncertainties, "profits interests" seem to be the most common solution to the question of how to grant employee equity in an LLC. Profits interests represent an ownership interest in the future profits and future appreciation of the company, but not in its current value. Because these are "equity interests," recipients become members of the LLC, with all of the complications membership entails.
>
> By all accounts, "profits interests" are complex and will require assistance from tax counsel.

Needless to say, unfortunately, the client was not thrilled with this bad news about issuing LLC equity to employees.

Other considerations regarding profits interests from an LLC (or other entity taxed like a partnership) include:

- Profits interests can vest over time.

- Under detailed IRS safe harbor rules, recipients can avoid employment compensation tax consequences at grant and at vesting, but vested profits interests do generate flowthrough tax consequences based on the related allocations of the company's *future* profits and losses. Put another way, each recipient of LLC profits interests automatically converts from being a W-2 employee to a "partner" for tax purposes, and must then comply with burdensome "self-employment" quarterly tax reporting, and must also receive a Form K-1 annually.

- Unlike stock options, the company cannot take any compensation deduction for profits interests.

No doubt, some lawyers and accountants will say LLC profits interests are a great compensation alternative for startups. Experts who routinely structure and administer LLC equity compensation programs certainly have success stories they can point to and would likely downplay the costs and complexities.

But no expert can say with a straight face that structuring, granting, and administering LLC equity compensation plans is as simple, inexpensive, straight forward, and well-understood by typical recipients as either corporate stock options or restricted stock awards.

It is also hard to dispute that compensation that is more easily understood (and trusted) is more likely to advance the primary goal of equity compensation, which is to inspire value-creating effort.

If you thought Case Study #16, *Not an Option*, was the most tedious case study so far, don't blame the messenger. If you are an entrepreneur hoping to attract, retain, and inspire future employees, and you found the above discussion painful, absent compelling tax considerations, the LLC structure may not be your best choice.

CHAPTER SEVEN

Entity Formation

In Chapter 5, we looked at key pre-formation considerations – avoiding "accidental partnerships," taking other steps to protect a future entity's IP, confirming co-founder compatibility, and choosing, vetting, and locking down the best name.

In Chapter 6, we studied entity selection alternatives and considered the pros and cons of forming in the home state versus in Delaware.

Now we look at forming entities, and doing so with the following goals still in mind from Chapter 5:

- creating a governance structure that supports the business plan,

- marshaling and protecting IP rights,

- avoiding governance, ownership, and control mistakes, and

- minimizing risks of contentious co-founder disputes.

An entity is "formed" upon a Secretary of State's approval and acceptance of the company's formation documents. But this is just the beginning of the process. There are other documents to sign and other steps to take to achieve the above goals.

Corporations and Corporate Governance

A corporation is a legal entity that is separate and distinct from its owners. It can own property, sign contracts, employ others, and take many other types of actions that an individual can take.

To appreciate the steps required to form a corporation properly, it helps to understand some basic principles of corporate governance.

Corporate governance principles are grounded in state corporate law statutes, court decisions, and a company's Certificate of Incorporation and Bylaws. Serious students of corporate governance should read the DGCL. Again, that's the Delaware General Corporation Law. It is available online for free. https://delcode.delaware.gov/title8/c001/

But contract law principles also work their way into corporate governance. This happens through Stock Purchase Agreements, Shareholders Agreements, Voting Agreements, and documents by many other names, all of which we will consider.

From the top-down, a corporation is:
- owned by its shareholders,
- managed by or under the direction of a board of directors, and
- run by its officers.

Shareholders

Shareholders hold ultimate corporate power in that they elect a corporation's board. They also have powerful voting rights regarding certain types of actions, like issuing new stock or selling the company.

Obtaining Shareholder Approval or Consent. It is important to always obtain shareholder approval for all transactions requiring approval, and also to obtain what is called "shareholder consent(s)" for actions or transactions that would otherwise be forbidden under a company's Certificate of Incorporation and (ii) whenever a company wants its shareholders to waive specific rights.

Rights that are commonly waived include rights to participate pro rata in a current financing and what are called "anti-dilution" rights, which are discussed in Chapter 12 under *Preferred Stock Key Provisions*.

Taking any action or failing to observe any right for which shareholder approval, consent, or waiver was required results in a presumption that the act was *ultra vires*, or not authorized, and hence void. This can result in complex legal problems impacting the validity of equity issuances, cap table accuracy, the validity of M&A transactions, and the like. It is best to err on the side of obtaining shareholder approvals, consents, and waivers, when in doubt.

Find a sample Shareholder Consent in the BLSG Data Room at *Company Formation and Governance > Corporations > Shareholder Meetings and Resolutions > Shareholder Approvals, Consents and Waivers.*

Aside from their rights to approve and consent to specific types of corporate acts and transactions, Shareholders generally have very little say in how a corporation is managed, particularly regarding its day-to-day operations.

Board of Directors

The board oversees a corporation and sets its direction by, among other things, hiring and firing the CEO, reviewing and approving budgets and business plans, and approving many types of transactions.

Here is the statement of board powers from Section 141 of the *Delaware Corporate Law:*

> *The business and affairs of every corporation organized under this chapter shall be managed by or under the direction of a board of directors, except as may be otherwise provided in this chapter or in its certificate of incorporation. If any such provision is made in the certificate of incorporation, the powers and duties conferred or imposed upon the board of directors by this chapter shall be exercised or performed to such extent and by such person or persons as shall be provided in the certificate of incorporation.*

Well-functioning boards tend to stay out of a company's day-to-day affairs and instead rely on the CEO and other officers to handle operations and related matters. The Board's power to remove the CEO is a key source of leverage to ensure that the management team is executing on the business plan as expected.

But boards are not all-powerful. As noted above, shareholders have the right to vote on a variety of matters under both corporate statutes and under Certificates of Incorporation. Certain decisions require approval, or "consent," from both the board and the shareholders.

Shareholder voting rights tend to grow in scope and power as a company brings in large investments from sophisticated investors who demand a greater say – particularly over future financings, M&A transactions, and other significant decisions.

Officers

A corporation's board and Bylaws can establish officer positions very flexibly, but, under state law, every corporation generally must have a president, a treasurer, and a secretary – all of whom can be the same person.

Corporations act almost exclusively through their officers pursuant to decision-making hierarchies, with senior officers often taking their direction from, and reporting to, the CEO.

It is the officers and not board members, for example, who sign contracts, enter into leases, open bank accounts and otherwise handle the corporation's day-to-day actions necessary to execute the business plan.

That said, *authorization* for many significant actions must first come from the board before officers may act. Boards must approve, among other things, borrowing funds, issuing stock, granting stock options, and entering into substantial lease commitments.

Incorporator

As discussed below, the first step in forming a corporation is to file a Certificate of Incorporation. This generally involves an individual, often a founder, acting and signing in the capacity of "incorporator" or "initial incorporator."

The powers of the incorporator are akin to those of an agent or trustee, and they are limited and temporary.

Section 107 of the *Delaware Corporation Law* has this to say:

§ 107 Powers of incorporators.

> *If the persons who are to serve as directors until the first annual meeting of stockholders have not been named in the certificate of incorporation, the incorporator or incorporators, until the directors are elected, shall manage the affairs of the corporation and may do whatever is necessary and proper to perfect the organization of the corporation, including the adoption of the original bylaws of the corporation and the election of directors.*

As discussed below, this language is vague. The most common practice is for the initial incorporator to resign as a final official act after, or as part of, signing resolutions appointing the board and also possibly appointing officers and adopting the corporation's bylaws.

Certificate of Incorporation

In the hierarchy of corporate governance documents, the Certificate of Incorporation is most important. In many states, this same charter-type document is called the Articles of Incorporation.

A corporation's initial Certificate of Incorporation is a relatively short document that establishes, among other things:

- the name of the entity,
- the number, type, and par value of authorized shares of stock,
- the corporation's authorized activities,
- certain powers of the board,
- limitations of liability for board members,
- indemnification of officers and directors (legal and financial protections for lawsuits and other claims), and
- name and address of the registered agent.

Find a sample initial Certificate of Incorporation in the BLSG Data Room under *Company Formation and Governance > Corporations > Articles of Incorporation.*

Certificates of Incorporation become much longer and far more complicated as they are amended following successive financing rounds, as discussed in Chapter 14 - *VC Fundraising.* Find an example of a more complex *Amended and Restated Certificate of Incorporation* in the BLSG Data Room under *Company Formation and Governance > Corporations > Articles of Incorporation.*

Bylaws

Corporations also must adopt Bylaws. They provide the basic ground rules for how a corporation will be governed, including some areas that are covered by default state laws absent a contrary or supplemental Bylaw provision.

Bylaws tend to cover:

- time and manner of shareholder meetings,
- shareholder quorum and vote requirements,
- voting by proxies,
- board duties and authority,
- number and election of directors,
- when and how board meetings are called,
- board member compensation,
- names and functions of board committees,
- officer titles and duties,

- processes for issuing stock certificates,

- restrictions on stock transfers,

- payment of dividends, and

- indemnification of officers and directors and related insurance issues.

Find sample Bylaws in the BLSG Data Room under *Company Formation and Governance > Corporations > Bylaws.*

Case Study #17 - Who Owns My Business?

"Who owns my business?" was the actual subject line of a question posted online.

The individual stated that his mom had helped him start a corporation two years earlier, listing herself as registered agent and treasurer, and giving him the title of incorporator. He added:

> *"I am and have been pres/ceo, and own 100% of the stock. She is now trying to claim ownership of my business. She was only supposed to help me with articles of inc. so I could get started, since I had never started a business before."*

There may be some legal and governance mistakes and loose ends hiding between the lines here. The founder seems to have thought he only needed help with *"articles of inc."* Once mom filed the Articles of Incorporation, the founder appears to have assumed the boring stuff was done.

Importantly, there was no mention of a "board." The incorporator could have listed board members in the Articles of Incorporation, but that seems a rare practice and was not mentioned here.

If that's where his entity formation efforts ended, they formed no board, appointed no officers, and issued no stock. A company in that situation has no "owners." It still just has an initial incorporator.

As a peripheral issue, even though his mom was listed *somewhere* as treasurer, the absence of any clear appointment by the initial incorporator could mean that did not happen either. Simply listing her on the company's "first annual report" as treasurer is not sufficient to make her treasurer.

A key fact here is that the son is the incorporator - the only person empowered to appoint the initial board. He also has the power to remove mom as registered agent and treasurer, appoint all required officers, and adopt Bylaws.

The duly appointed board can then authorize the issuance of his shares of stock, and the officers can sign the documents to make that happen, establishing his ownership of the business.

Situations like these are common and raise other uncomfortable issues likely not appreciated by this founder. The actual powers of incorporators are unclear in some states. Can they enter into contracts, leases or other commitments with third parties? If not, could any such actions be challenged as *ultra vires* (done beyond legal power or authority)?

Lessons: Actions taken by improperly constituted entities are potentially *ultra vires* and open to challenge, leaving both parties to any tainted transactions exposed to possible harm.

Forming a Corporation and its Governance Structure

So now we know these things:

- shareholders have certain powers, boards have certain powers, and officers have certain powers,

- newly authorized corporations generally have no board, no officers, no bylaws, no shareholders and no assets,

- before a duly-appointed board issues shares of stock, a corporation also has no actual owners, and

- the incorporator's temporary and limited agent-like powers are considered to continue until the incorporator appoints a board.

Filing the Certificate of Incorporation

Filing a Certificate of Incorporation (or Articles of Incorporation) should not be taken lightly. It is a good juncture in the process to involve competent counsel, if that has not been done.

Every Secretary of State has helpful content online about their specific requirements. Any variances from their instructions can add substantial delays. The submission process usually must include a copy of the Certificate of Incorporation, signed by the incorporator, a cover letter explaining the filing and providing requested contact information, and a check in the correct amount and to the correct payee.

Read all language about fees carefully. If your check is short $.50, you will be in for delays.

If you are filing in Delaware or any other state other than your home state, first select and hire a registered agent. The registered agent's name and address generally must be included in the Certificate of Incorporation.

If you file in your home state, you can serve as registered agent, but there is a lot of value in hiring a professional registered agent if you can afford it. The primary role of a registered agent is to receive "service of process" (lawsuits and other claims) on behalf of the company, but professional registered agents also provide reminders about and assistance with filing annual reports and other administrative tasks.

Confirmation from Secretary of State

Important note – "filing" a Certificate of Incorporation does not mean the entity exists yet. Entity formation occurs *only when the Secretary of State says so*. Until then, no actions may be taken in the name of the entity, whether by the sole incorporator or any other persons.

In most cases, unless you pay rush fees, it can take a week or two to receive an official stamped copy of the filed Certificate of Incorporation evidencing that the entity exists and its formation date. The following language is typical of what the Delaware Secretary of State, Division of Corporations stamps into the upper left corner of a new corporation's Certificate of Incorporation:

State of Delaware
Secretary of State
Division of Corporations
Delivered 01:01 PM 08/05/2015
Filed 12:55 PM 08/05/2015
SRF 151136039 - 5787973

Resolutions of the Initial Incorporator

Once the Secretary of State confirms the existence of the new corporation, the initial incorporator can adopt resolutions like the following to appoint the board, appoint officers, adopt bylaws, and resign. These were the key steps missed in Case Study #17, *Who Owns My Business?*

[COMPANY], INC.

WRITTEN ACTIONS OF THE SOLE INCORPORATOR

THE UNDERSIGNED, being the sole incorporator of [COMPANY], Inc., a corporation organized and existing under the laws of the State of Delaware (the "Corporation"), hereby consents to the adoption of the following resolutions with the same force and effect as if such resolutions had been adopted at a duly convened meeting of the sole incorporator of the Corporation:

RESOLVED, that the Board of Directors of the Corporation consists of two (2) members; and

FURTHER RESOLVED, that [NAME OF DIRECTOR] and [NAME OF DIRECTOR] are elected as Directors of the Corporation effective as of the date hereof, to serve or hold office until the first annual meeting of shareholders or until their successors are elected and qualify; and

FURTHER RESOLVED, that [NAME OF CHAIR] be, and hereby is, appointed as the Chairman of the Board of Directors of the Company; and

FURTHER RESOLVED, that the following officers be, and hereby are, appointed as officers of the Corporation:

Name Office

[NAME] President and Secretary
[NAME] Treasurer

FURTHER RESOLVED, that the attached Bylaws of the Corporation be, and hereby are, approved and adopted.

FURTHER RESOLVED, the sole incorporator of the Company shall have no further rights, duties, or obligations in connection with the Company as incorporator thereof.

IN WITNESS WHEREOF, the undersigned Sole Incorporator has executed this Written Action on [MONTH]_____, 2020.

[NAME],
Sole Incorporator

Founders Equity, Asset Contributions

Once a corporation has a board, officers, and bylaws, the next step is marshaling assets into the entity and protecting its current and future claims to IP.

The first opportunity to do this involves the board-approved acceptance of capital contributions and IP assignments from the founders in exchange for their stock in the corporation, often called "founder stock." Note, founder stock is usually just regular common stock.

Immediately issuing founders their stock has other benefits as well. Perhaps most important of these is starting the 5-year clock under Section 1202 of the Internal Revenue Code, as discussed in Chapter 6, *Entity Selection*.

Founder Stock Issuance Board Resolutions. As discussed above, only the board can approve the issuance of stock. Therefore, the board of directors must approve resolutions along these lines:

ACTION BY WRITTEN CONSENT
OF THE BOARD OF DIRECTORS OF
[COMPANY], INC.

In accordance with Section 141 of the Delaware General Corporation Law and the Bylaws of [COMPANY], Inc. (the "Corporation"), the undersigned, constituting all of the members of the Board of Directors of the Corporation (the "Board"), hereby consent to the adoption of the following resolutions:

Issuance of Founder Shares

WHEREAS, the Board wishes to authorize and cause the issuance by the Corporation of shares of common stock to the Corporation's founders in exchange for the Corporation's initial assets, primarily intellectual property; and

NOW, THEREFORE, BE IT RESOLVED, that [6,000,000] common shares of the Corporation's authorized and unissued common stock, par value $.0001, be and hereby are allotted to and shall be issued to the individuals listed below and for the amounts indicated below upon the execution by such individuals of Subscription Agreements substantially in the form attached hereto as Exhibit A, along with any other documents required for each individual under the applicable Subscription Agreement, and the Corporation having received such amounts in respect of each such share, the shares are hereby declared to be issued as fully paid and non-assessable as follows:

SUBSCRIBER	NUMBER AND CLASS	SUBSCRIPTION PRICE
[FOUNDER 1 NAME]	3,000,000 Common	$300 + Contribution of IP
[FOUNDER 2 NAME]	3,000,000 Common	$300 + Contribution of IP

Omnibus Resolutions

RESOLVED FINALLY, that the officers of the Corporation be, and each hereby is, authorized and directed on behalf of the Corporation to make all such arrangement, to solicit appropriate consents and waivers from stockholders, to do and perform all such acts and things, to execute and deliver such instruments, documents and certificates as he may deem necessary and appropriate in order to effectuate fully the purpose of each and all of the foregoing resolutions (hereby ratifying and confirming any and all actions taken heretofore and hereafter to accomplish such purposes, all or singular).

IN WITNESS WHEREOF, the undersigned members of the Board of Directors of [COMPANY], Inc. have executed this Action by Written Consent effective as of [MONTH]_____, 2020.

Directors:

_____
[DIRECTOR NAME]

_____
[DIRECTOR NAME]

Note that, in exchange for their founder stock, each founder will pay $300 and contribute their IP to the entity. The company's common stock has a par value of $.0001. That is the minimum amount that must be paid for the stock, including by founders. That is how the $300 was calculated.

As discussed below, an underlying assumption here is that, while the founders' IP is important to the new company, it probably has little market value. In most cases, the IP is just the founders' collective ideas for the business model, possibly a trademarkable name, and maybe the beginnings of some software code.

On the other hand, a founder contributing IP or other assets with substantial value should consult with a tax advisor. That advisor may require that the founder obtain a fair market value appraisal of the IP, as that value becomes part of the founder's tax basis in the stock.

Founder Stock Purchase Agreement. The transactional document used to issue founder stock can be captioned in a variety of ways, including Founder Stock Purchase Agreement ("Founder SPA"), Stock Purchase and Sale Agreement, Founder Stock Subscription Agreement, or just Common Stock Subscription Agreement.

Find a template Founder Stock Subscription Agreement in the BLSG Data Room under *Finance Financings and Equity Issuance Docs > Founder Share Issuances*.

Asset Contribution and Assignment Agreement. As just described, the initial contribution of assets to a corporation often occurs in connection with each of its founders entering into a Founder SPA.

Whenever a founder contributes IP in consideration for his or her founder stock, instead of just cash, the Stock Purchase Agreement should contain a reference stating that the founder is simultaneously entering into an attached Asset (or Intellectual Property) Contribution and Assignment Agreement as full or partial consideration for the founder's stock in the company, depending on the facts.

This is different from a PIIA. An Asset Contribution and Assignment Agreement covers IP *already* owned by the founder; a PIIA, which each employee founder should also sign as a term of their *employment*, covers IP developed or obtained *during* their employment.

Capital Contributions. Because founders are often long on ideas but short on cash, it is common that the contributions a founder agrees to make in their Founder SPA is solely IP and not financial. By way of example, the relevant language might read:

EXHIBIT A

PURCHASE PRICE

In sole consideration for the Shares, hereby agrees to execute, enter into and deliver to the Company the following agreements:

- *The Intellectual Property and Related Assets Assignment and Contribution Agreement, a copy of which is attached hereto as Exhibit A-1.*

While it is better for a newly formed entity to also receive some operating cash in exchange for its stock, founders are not required to make cash contributions under corporate governance laws, provided the IP contributed is equal to or greater in value than the par value of the shares received.

One risk related to this is that a claim of "undercapitalizing" the entity might be combined with other facts to pierce the corporate veil to hold a corporation's officers and directors liability for debts or other liabilities of the corporation.

Undercapitalizing any company carries risks, but piercing the veil almost always requires a showing of additional mistakes or misconduct, as described in Chapter 2 – *Overview of Legal and Regulatory Mistakes.*

Vesting and Clawback Provisions

The term vesting is reasonably familiar to many in business because stock options are generally subject to vesting. Most stock option grants vest, for example, in equal monthly or quarterly amounts over four years, often subject to a one-year cliff, meaning no shares vest if employment ends in year one.

The term clawback is less well known because it is rarely used in legal documents. Clawback provisions can be cloaked in a variety of terminology, including *forfeiture, buyback,* and *repurchase.*

Essentially, any provision under which a company can force any shareholder to sell back their shares is a clawback. As discussed in other chapters, we find clawback clauses of various types in many types of documents: Stock Purchase Agreements, Stock Option Grant Agreements, Employment Agreements, Shareholders Agreements, Voting Agreements, and others.

Fair and reasonable clawbacks serve valuable purposes. They limit dead equity on the cap table, keep company stock out of unhelpful hands, and prevent co-founders from walking away and "free-riding" – benefiting from the hard work of co-founders who remain at the startup.

But clawbacks can also be unfair and unreasonable, as illustrated in the following case study.

Case Study #18 – Skyped!

Leading up to Microsoft's acquisition of Skype in May 2011, Skype employees with vested stock were likely looking forward to their big payday. But for some, the big payday never happened. That's because Skype fired some of its executives just before the $8.5 billion acquisition – ostensibly for performance reasons.

Some of them had very confusing and unfavorable clawback provisions, apparently giving the company the right to repurchase their shares and cutting them out of the larger payout from the then-imminent sale. These shares were acquired back by Skype at the original purchase price, completely erasing any upside value.

The following is the opaque paragraph that permitted these clawbacks:

> *"If, in connection with the termination of a Participant's Employment, the Ordinary Shares issued to such Participant pursuant to the exercise of the Option or issuable to such Participant pursuant to any portion of the Option that is then vested are to be repurchased, the Participant shall be required to exercise his or her vested Option and any Ordinary Shares issued in connection with such exercise shall be subject to the repurchase and other provisions in the Management Partnership agreement."*

Presumably, the Management Partnership Agreement contains language confirming the right to claw back the shares at the original purchase price.

In a letter to impacted employees, Skype's then Associate General Counsel sent out a letter detailing the operation of the above language and the related Management Partnership Agreement, and stating matter-of-factly:

> *"As explained in greater detail below, we are writing to inform you that you will not receive any value from the Options regardless of whether the Options were vested."*

Skype and the private equity firm that had control over it took heat in the press at the time, with one former worker quoted as saying, *"Seriously, how greedy do you have to be to make $5 billion and still try to screw the people who made that value possible?"*

Lessons: Although clawback provisions are reasonable tools for keeping equity out of adverse hands, limiting dead equity, and preventing founders from walking away prematurely, founders and others should protect themselves from being "Skyped."

Clawback provisions have the potential for preventing optionees and other equity holders from realizing all or any of the value of their shares in an exit.

Here is another example of an overreaching clawback provision that could unfairly harm founders and other early shareholders:

Where, in the case of an Employee Participant, Executive Participant or a Consultant Participant, an Optionee's employment, term of office or consultant agreement is terminated for any reason, such Optionee shall immediately offer to sell to the Company all of the Common Shares owned by the Optionee which have been or may be issued to the Optionee upon the exercise of Options at a price equal to the Exercise Price of such Common Shares. Such offer will be irrevocable until the day that is 120 days from the Termination Date. The Company shall have the option (but not the obligation) to purchase such Common Shares. If the offer to sell Common Shares is accepted by the Company, the Company shall purchase such Common Shares for cash consideration.

This provision requires a terminated individual to offer to sell back to the company at the exercise price all stock received from his or her hard-earned stock options, depriving the terminated individual of any financial benefit whatsoever.

Founders should be careful not to allow potentially abusive clawback provisions into their companies' documentation, whether at the advice of their own counsel or the urging of aggressive investors.

While it is helpful to be able to claw back equity in cases of misconduct, demonstrably poor performance, or other exceptional circumstances, unrestricted clawback rights can be harmful to morale and even to a company's reputation, as Skype learned. And those same unrestricted clawback rights can also be turned against founders themselves if control of a company shifts to others.

VC Vesting Concerns. Many VC firms are reluctant to invest in companies where the founders are fully vested in their shares. The VCs' concern is that if founders own their shares outright, what incentive do they have to continue to "pursue the dream" once VCs have put in millions of dollars.

One can easily argue that such founders have more incentive than ever to work hard after a major funding event because the "dream" is more viable than ever. Funding often follows years of struggle and enables exciting new phases of development, marketing, and distribution.

But that alone may not be sufficient to close a VC round without renegotiating the terms of founders' equity.

These discussions often depend on the relative negotiating leverage of the parties. Founders building the next big thing may be able to tell aggressive VCs to go pound sand. Founders in a more typical posture, slight-to-severe financial desperation, may have to negotiate more flexibly.

Clawback Versus Forfeiture and Re-grant. Founders should resist any compelled forfeiture and re-granting of their shares subject to a vesting schedule. That approach to locking in founders not only risks reducing a founder's shareholder voting rights, it also jeopardizes his or her potential Section 1202 capital gains benefits.

As we have learned, under Section 1202, Qualified Small Business Stock must be held longer than five years. Forfeiture and re-granting restart that five-year period.

Founders forced into tough discussions about their equity holdings are better off accepting new clawback provisions instead of equity forfeitures and re-grants subject to vesting.

As discussed in the next chapter, startups and co-founders alike can benefit from adopting *reasonable* clawback terms up front, as a way of dealing with co-founder misconduct or non-performance. Doing so can also take those issues off of the table before future VCs feel the need to explore them.

Founder Clawback Protections. As an example of what might be sufficient to prevent renegotiation by future VCs, co-founders might agree, at entity formation, to clawbacks of 50% of their equity in the event they depart voluntarily before an exit transaction or are terminated "for cause" before an exit.

Any clawback "for cause" should arguably include a clause unwinding the clawback if an exit transaction occurs within the following six months. This limits the ability of others to use such a clause to improperly remove a founder before an exit to steal their equity, as we saw in *Skyped!*.

In the next chapter, we will look at the pros and cons of different types of clawback provisions in documents such as Shareholders Agreements, Stockholders Agreements and similarly captioned documents. We will also look at why clawbacks requiring repurchases of stock by a corporation could be potentially unenforceable under corporate law statutes involving "capital impairment."

Equity Grants to Non-founder Team Members

Make Team Option Grants Quickly. In addition to promptly issuing founders their stock, it is important to issue any stock options promised to other team members promptly.

In addition to the importance of simply honoring commitments to those team members, promptly issuing their stock options has substantial financial benefits for them.

First, it is important to remember that a newly formed entity has a fairly readily ascertainable value of something close to $0. If the founders have contributed meaningful IP in connection with their share purchases, those assets might bump the company's value to between $10,000 and $50,000 at formation, but values above those near the time of formation are probably uncommon.

Consequently, stock options granted at or near formation almost invariably have the lowest "exercise price" among all options issued during a company's life – likely just a few cents per share.

Thus, granting options to key team members at or near formation gives those persons the best chances for realizing value in an exit.

As we discuss in later chapters, holders of common stock often fare poorly in exit transactions due to existing debt obligations and preferred stock liquidation preferences. Preferred stock liquidation preferences are debt-like features, as they set a floor amount the preferred shareholders receive in a sale or liquidation before the common shareholders receive anything. That floor amount of liquidation preference usually equals the price per share paid for the preferred shares in question.

We will go much deeper into liquidation preferences in Chapter 12, *Startup Finance Overview*.

Suffice it to say for now that delays in issuing option grants can exacerbate poor outcomes for team members if those delays result in higher exercise prices for their stock options.

Rule 409A Compliance. Additionally, the time near entity formation is generally the easiest time to accurately determine the "fair market value," or "FMV," of option grants under what is called Section 409A. This provision in the U.S. Internal Revenue Code requires that all stock options be granted at fair market value, meaning that the exercise price for all stock options must be equal to the fair market value of the underlying shares at the time of grant.

Companies that obtain valid "409A valuation reports" in conjunction with their stock option grants are doing themselves and their option grantees a huge favor. When a valid 409A valuation report supports an option grant, the burden of proving that the FMV was incorrect shifts to the IRS. Absent a 409A valuation report, that burden stays with the company and its option grantees. Shifting the burden of proof to the IRS is important, as the penalties associated with 409A can be severe.

The rule allows for a 409A valuation report to be used for as long as twelve months or until a "material event" indicates that the FMV of the company's shares has changed. It is probably prudent to not rely on 409A valuation reports older than six months.

VCs and potential acquirors focus closely on all aspects of option grants in due diligence, including compliance with 409A.

Companies like Encarta and Capshare both provide 409A valuation services, as do many smaller, independent valuation firms. Brand new startups seeking a 409A valuation report should expect to spend about $1,500. From start to finish, obtaining a 409A report usually takes several weeks.

LLC Governance Principles

As discussed in Chapter 6, *Business Entity Selection*, LLCs are essentially governed by principles of contract law. The contract that governs properly formed LLCs is generally called an Operating Agreement. Other common variations include Limited Liability Company Agreement, Company Operating Agreement, and LLC Operating Agreement.

For simplicity, we will use the term Operating Agreement.

Case Study #19 – We Don't Need No &*%$ Attorney!

A multi-member LLC without an Operating Agreement is like a ticking bomb. And the results can be just as bad whether one was never signed, only partially signed, or lost after being fully executed by the founders.

In one story of a missing Operating Agreement, an attorney described how, in her first meeting with a founder of a new client LLC, the co-founder burst in on them yelling, "we don't need no &*%$ attorney…." The attorney had asked for a copy of the Operating Agreement repeatedly and without success over several weeks.

Eventually, the friendlier of the two founders, "Jack," called to say that the other founder, "Bill," was leaving the company. Jack also said that while he was at the bank trying to remove Bill from the account, Bill was at another branch emptying the company's bank account of $21,000. Bill was still a signor on the account, so the bank was forced to oblige.

The attorney opined that, because there was no Operating Agreement to prohibit Bill from cleaning out the bank account, he was not in breach of any obligations not to do so. And because Bill withdrew the funds in cash, the withdrawal could not be prevented or reversed.

The above analysis is only partially correct. The bank was legally permitted to process Bill's withdrawals. But if Bill simply stole the funds, a court would ultimately find that Bill breached multiple obligations to the company and to Jack.

Under the "default rules" of most states, an LLC without an Operating Agreement is a "member-managed LLC." In a member-managed LLC, each member can unilaterally bind the LLC. That is certainly a license to cause chaos, but not to steal.

Jack's only recourse is to pursue a costly, time consuming, and uncertain lawsuit alleging theft, breach of fiduciary duties, breach of the duty of loyalty, and other claims.

> Lessons: The absence of an Operating Agreement not only creates legal, governance, and operational uncertainties, it can also lead to bad behavior by those who might take advantage of the absence of any governing document.
>
> Secondly, remove departing officers or members from any bank account authorizations without delay.
>
> Lastly, if your co-founder ever says, '*We don't need any &*%$ attorney,*' that might be a red flag.

Operating Agreement Basics

An Operating Agreement should provide clarity as to, among other things:

- members' ownership percentages,
- voting rights,
- powers and duties of members and managers,
- how the management team will be selected,
- distribution of profits and loses,
- admission of new members,
- meeting requirements,
- buyout and buy-sell rights and obligations, and
- what can trigger the disassociation of a member.

Below are excerpts of the Delaware Limited Liability Act provisions regarding Operating Agreements, found at § 18-101(7). Consider whether this degree of flexibility about what constitutes an Operating

Agreement might or might not help to resolve ambiguities involving an Operating Agreement's existence or enforceability (underlining added):

> *(7) "Limited liability company agreement" means any agreement (whether referred to as a limited liability company agreement, operating agreement or otherwise), <u>written, oral or implied</u>, of the member or members as to the affairs of a limited liability company and the conduct of its business. A member or manager of a limited liability company or an assignee of a limited liability company interest is bound by the limited liability company agreement <u>whether or not the member or manager or assignee executes the limited liability company agreement</u>. A limited liability company is not required to execute its limited liability company agreement. A limited liability company is bound by its limited liability company agreement <u>whether or not the limited liability company executes the limited liability company agreement</u>.... A limited liability company agreement is <u>not subject to any statute of frauds</u> (including § 2714 of this title).... A written limited liability company agreement or another written agreement or writing:*
>
> *a. May provide that a person shall be admitted as a member of a limited liability company...*
>
> *If such person... executes the limited liability company agreement or <u>any other writing evidencing the intent of such person to become a member or assignee</u>; or*
>
> *Without such execution, if such person... complies with the conditions for becoming a member or assignee as set forth in the limited liability company agreement or any other writing;....*

This extremely lenient statutory language no-doubt has its benefits and is intended to be helpful, but it also creates substantial uncertainty in situations where a draft Operating Agreement has been circulated, particularly if it has been signed by some but not all members.

Here are some questions that might be addressed differently by courts in different states:

- Can a single member sign an unfinished draft Operating Agreement and force it on the other member or members?

- Under what circumstances does a completely unsigned draft become enforceable?

- Given the complexity of most Operating Agreements, what would be deemed included in an oral or implied Operating Agreement?

It is unlikely that these questions have been resolved or clarified yet by case law in very many states.

The fact that no state requires or even allows the filing of an Operating Agreement results in many LLCs being formed without an Operating Agreement.

Interestingly, only five states require that an LLC have an Operating Agreement – Delaware, New York, California, Missouri, and Maine. And only New York requires that it be in writing. In the others, it can be oral, and in Delaware and Maine, it can even be "implied" – presumably created by the "actions" of the parties.

It is also worth noting again that veil piercing efforts are aided by the absence of an Operating Agreement or the failure to comply with an existing Operating Agreement. Both are considered evidence that an entity has not been run *like a real business."*

Waiver of Fiduciary Duties

Potential members of LLCs formed under Delaware law or New York law need to be alert for the existence and implications of "fiduciary waivers."

While shareholders and board members of a corporation cannot waive their fiduciary duties to minority shareholders, Courts in both Delaware and New York have held that members of LLCs can waive their fiduciary duties to minority interest members and act in their own self-interest.

Case Study #20 – Loyalty Not Required

The Delaware Court of Chancery decided a case in 2018 in which the plaintiffs alleged that the defendants, majority members in an LLC, favored themselves in a sale of the company to the detriment of minority members of the LLC. The plaintiffs knew their Operating Agreement, or "OA," contained complete waivers of all fiduciary duties, but nonetheless alleged that the defendants' conduct violated *"…the implied covenant of good faith and fair dealing inhering to an LLC operating agreement."*

The Court largely agreed with the facts as alleged by the plaintiffs, saying:

> *"It is true that the Complaint reflects a sales process that was tilted in favor of the Defendants' interests…. In fact, the 'perverse' incentive at the heart of this case—namely, the Defendants' interest in seeking a quick payout on their investment regardless of the effect on Trumpet's other members—is clear from the distribution waterfall itself."*

But the Court was wholly unreceptive to the plaintiffs' legal arguments, illustrating in stark terms the differences between legal duties in LLC governance versus corporate governance.

Concerning the vastly disparate treatment received by the minority LLC members in the sale of the Trumpet LLC, the Court said:

> *"… the OA waives any fiduciary duties that the Defendants otherwise would have owed to Trumpet's other members. The Plaintiffs seek to get around this contractual waiver by invoking the implied covenant. I reject the Plaintiffs' attempt to "re-introduce fiduciary review through the backdoor of the implied covenant.' As this Court has made clear, "[t]o use the implied covenant to replicate fiduciary review 'would vitiate the limited reach of the concept of the implied duty of good faith and fair dealing.'*
>
> *Finally, if the Plaintiffs had wanted protection from self-interested conduct by the Defendants, they could easily have drafted language requiring the Board to implement a sales process designed to achieve the highest value reasonably available for all of Trumpet's members. The Plaintiffs also could have sought other protections, such as a minimum sales price, a majority-of-the-minority sales*

provision, or a period during which sales were prohibited. Such a contract would, of course, have been less attractive to investors. Instead, the Plaintiffs struck an investor-friendly bargain with which they are now dissatisfied. But "[p]arties have a right to enter into good and bad contracts[;] the law enforces both." It does not fall to this Court to give the Plaintiffs what they failed to get at the bargaining table. Thus, the Complaint fails to state a claim for breach of the implied covenant of good faith and fair dealing."

Miller v. HCP & Co., 2018 WL 656378 (Del. Ct. Ch. Feb. 1, 2018)

https://courts.delaware.gov/Opinions/Download.aspx?id=268570

This is the state of the law for LLCs in Delaware and also in New York, and who knows what other states will ultimately follow their lead as similar issues arise in other jurisdictions.

Lessons: Again, LLCs have the reputation of being "easier," but this is somewhat misleading. They are creatures of contract, and the contractual principles and drafting challenges are both complex and critical. The statutory law and case law do not provide the kinds of "fiduciary" and "loyalty" safety nets found in basic principles of corporate governance.

Minority investors in LLCs would be wise to seek guidance from experienced counsel before investing in any LLC in which fiduciary duties are waived.

Default Rules in Lieu of Operating Agreement

When an LLC is formed without an Operating Agreement, it is governed by what are called the "default rules" of the LLC's state of formation. These default rules vary and are generally derived from the law of partnerships, not the law of corporations.

Because of the significant and not commonly appreciated differences between partnership law and the law of corporations, the failure to adopt a proper Operating Agreement can cause counter-intuitive results.

A focus in drafting any Operating Agreement should be to supplement or override any current or future state law default rules that are inconsistent with the members' intended governance and business arrangements.

The following are just a few examples of default rules that may be inconsistent with LLC member expectations.

Member-Managed. In general, an LLC can be managed by all of its members (member-managed) or by one or more "managers" (manager-managed). In most states, the default rule is member-managed. In a member-managed LLC, all members must agree on all the business decisions, and all members have the authority to bind the LLC by entering into contracts with third-parties.

One Member, One Vote. A default rule in some states entitles each member to one vote – regardless of contributions. Assume a situation in which one member contributes 70% of the capital, and two others contribute only 15%. Absent an Operating Agreement, the two members contributing only 30% of the capital would be entitled to 66% of the vote. As a result, they could vote to remove or otherwise oppress the larger contributor.

Equal Allocation of Profits. Similar to the preceding, the default rule in some states is to allocate profits and losses equally among members, regardless of respective contributions.

Decisions Requiring Unanimous Consent of Members. California's LLC Act was amended in 2014 to expand the number and breadth of default rules, including some that overrode provisions of existing Operating Agreements unless and until those Operating Agreements are amended to specifically override the new California default rules.

Possibly the most concerning of these new California default rules prohibits both member-managed and manager-managed LLCs from taking any action *"outside the ordinary course of business"* without obtaining the consent of all members.

Absent an Operating Agreement enumerating, and hence limiting, the types of decisions specifically requiring a supermajority vote of the members, any member of a California LLC who does not approve of an action undertaken by a manager could contest that action, claiming it was outside the ordinary course of business and that the member had not consented to it.

California's LLC Act contains many default rules worth considering in drafting Operating Agreements.

Limiting Liability of Members and Managers. Many states, including Georgia, have default rules providing that managers or members must act *"in a manner he or she believes in good faith to be in the best interest"* of the LLC and with the care *"an ordinarily prudent person in a like position would exercise under similar circumstances."*

This is a "simple negligence" or an "ordinary due care" standard. This is a low bar for potential liability as an officer or director.

Given the risks of litigation and other disputes under liability standards predicated on simple negligence, Operating Agreements frequently modify these default rules to protect managers, officers, and directors from unreasonable liability exposure. Georgia's LLC Act is fairly typical in allowing the following types of modifications to member and manager liability:

> *"The member's or manager's duties and liabilities may be expanded, restricted, or eliminated by provisions in the articles of organization or a written operating agreement; provided, however, that no such provision shall eliminate or limit the liability of a member or manager:*
>
> *For intentional misconduct or a knowing violation of law; or*
>
> *For any transaction for which the person received a personal benefit in violation or breach of any provision of a written operating agreement;…"*

Other state law default rules govern distributions, meeting requirements, member contributions, and other critical aspects of LLC governance, management, and membership. The only way to implement agreed-upon LLC member expectations is to describe them in an Operating Agreement.

Ownership

Just as the "initial incorporator" of a corporation is not an "owner" of the corporation and may never become one, the "organizer" of an LLC is also not automatically an owner or member of an LLC and may never become one.

Conversely, although LLC organizers are generally named in LLC formation documents, LLC's members may or may not be required to be identified. Some states' certificates of formation, such as Washington's, Delaware's and New York's, provide no place to identify members. Other certificates of formation templates, such as Texas's, only require the identification of "initial members" when the LLC is to be member-managed.

A common feature of all state certificate of formation templates is that they are extremely short — just one or two pages. In no case do they provide any detail regarding substantive aspects of LLC ownership, like ownership percentages.

The upshot of this is that LLC ownership and all attributes of ownership *must be* detailed in an Operating Agreement.

The certificate of formation (or articles of formation) templates for Washington, Texas, Delaware, and New York are all available in the BLSG Data Room under *Company Formation and Governance > Limited Liability Company.*

Management

As described, LLCs are either member-managed or manager-managed. A member-managed LLC is managed by *all* of its members. A manager-managed LLC is managed by one or more individuals appointed by the members.

In many states, an LLC manager can also be another LLC or a corporation. An LLC's manager or managers may or may not be members of the LLC.

Again, in many states, absent language in a signed Operating Agreement, the default rule is that an LLC is member-managed, meaning:

- every member has an equal say in the management and decisions of the LLC,
- every member is an "agent" of the LLC and can bind it in agreements with third parties, and
- as we saw in Case Study #19, every member who is a signatory on the LLC's bank account can probably clean it out, albeit, not without the possibility of litigation.

The following excerpt from the official Texas LLC certificate of formation template shows the organizer must identify whether the LLC will be member-managed or manager-managed, but no other details.

***

Article 3—Governing Authority

(Select and complete either A or B and provide the name and address of each governing person.)

A. The limited liability company will have managers. The name and address of each initial manager are set forth below.

B. The limited liability company will not have managers. The company will be governed by its members, and the name and address of each initial member are set forth below.

***

Article 3 of the Texas LLC formation template goes on to require the names and addresses of the managers, but nothing specific about management duties and authorities in the LLC.

Since those duties and authorities are not established by the Certificate of Formation, they must be established by the Operating Agreement.

An Operating Agreement could address LLC management duties and authorities with language like this, from a template in the BLSG Data Room:

> Section 5.7 Authority of the Manager. Subject to the limitations and restrictions set forth in the Act, the Certificate of Formation and this Agreement, the Manager shall have the sole and exclusive right to manage the business of the Company and shall have all of the rights and powers which may be possessed by Manager under the Act and the Certificate of Formation including, without limitation, the right and power, on behalf and in the name of the Company, to:
>
> (a) Conduct the Company business in the ordinary course, and exercise the powers granted by the Act, the Certificate of Formation and this Agreement; and
>
> (b) Transact any other lawful business not inconsistent with the Act, the Certificate of Formation and this Agreement.
>
> Section 5.8 Restrictions on Authority of the Manager.
>
> (a) A Manager shall not have the authority to do any of the following acts without the Major Decision Special Majority vote of the Class A Members:
>
> • Knowingly do any act in contravention of this Agreement or without the consent of the Class A Members as required by this Agreement;
>
> • Knowingly do any act which would make it impossible to carry on the ordinary business of the Company, except as otherwise provided in this Agreement;
>
> • Knowingly perform any act that would subject any Member to personal liability in any jurisdiction; and
>
> • Make any Major Decision.

This same Operating Agreement lists numerous types of transactions, acts, and decisions that each constitute a "Major Decision." The Operating Agreement then mandates that Major Decisions require approval by 66% of the LLC's member/ownership interests. That supermajority threshold of 66% could have been any percentage agreed to by the members in the Operating Agreement, including up to 100%.

As we discuss again later, high supermajority voting thresholds can limit flexibility to take important actions.

LLC Formation

So now we know what is required to <u>form an LLC properly</u>:

- An "organizer" must fill out and file a document usually called either a "Certificate of Formation" or "Articles of Formation," paying close attention to all instructions provided by the Secretary of State, including designating a "registered agent."

- Simultaneously, those who wish to be members of the LLC should promptly negotiate and sign an Operating Agreement.

The first of these tasks is extremely easy; the second, when done correctly, is far more complex and generally requires substantial assistance from qualified legal counsel for each initial member/founder.

Licensing, Registration and Nexus

Whether the founders of a new business enterprise have formed a corporation or an LLC, there are additional administrative tasks to handle before they are forgotten and cause problems later.

Home State Business License/Qualification to Do Business

As discussed in Chapter 6 under *Domicile Considerations – Home state versus Delaware*, many businesses incorporate in Delaware or in other states despite having no operations there. When founders incorporate in a state other than their headquarters state, they must also look into the specific registration requirements of their state.

Those registration requirements vary by state, but generally the process is handled by a state's Secretary of State and is called "Foreign Business Registration."

Qualification to Do Business in Other States

In addition to registering as a "foreign business" in a company's home state, a company domiciled in Delaware or elsewhere must also register, or "qualify to do business," in every state where it has a certain level of presence or activity.

Unfortunately, no state law contains a comprehensive definition of the term "doing business."

Factors requiring companies to qualify to do business vary by state statutes and case law. Many states, like Washington, have adopted some version of the Model Business Corporation Act, which takes the approach of listing activities that do *not* require a business to qualify to do business in Washington.

Washington's statute is reproduced in part here:

RCW 23.95.520

Activities not constituting doing business. (Effective January 1, 2016.)

(1) *Activities of a foreign entity that do not constitute doing business in this state under this chapter include, but are not limited to:*

   (a) *Maintaining, defending, mediating, arbitrating, or settling an action or proceeding, or settling claims or disputes;*

   (b) *Carrying on any activity concerning its internal affairs, including holding meetings of its interest holders or governors;*

   (c) *Maintaining accounts in financial institutions;*

   (d) *Maintaining offices or agencies for the transfer, exchange, and registration of securities of the entity or maintaining trustees or depositories with respect to those securities;*

   (e) *Selling through independent contractors;*

   (f) *Soliciting or obtaining orders by any means if the orders require acceptance outside this state before they become binding contracts and where the contracts do not involve any local performance other than delivery and installation;*

   (g) *Creating or acquiring indebtedness, mortgages, or security interests in property;*

   (h) *Securing or collecting debts or enforcing mortgages or security interests in property securing the debts;*

   (i) *Conducting an isolated transaction that is completed within thirty days and that is not in the course of repeated transactions of a like nature;*

   (j) *Owning, without more, property;*

   (k) *Doing business in interstate commerce;...*

Failure to qualify to do business in a state when required can have several consequences: (i) modest fines and penalties, (ii) inability to bring claims within the courts of the state, and (iii) delays in financing and M&A transactions while waiting for state filings to be processed.

The threshold to qualify to do business is always met where a company has active operations in a state, such as offices, stores, manufacturing facilities, or other similar business activities, but can be murkier when more temporary, transient or insubstantial activities are involved.

Given the low cost and ease of registering to qualify to do business, the best practice is to register when the question is close, particularly when there might be a financing or M&A transaction in the future.

Tax Nexus

Tax "nexus" is a constitutional question under what is called the "Commerce Clause" of the U.S. Constitution. Nexus is the name of the threshold for when a state can tax an out-of-state business based on its activities in that state.

In 2018, the U.S. Supreme Court revisited the question of taxing sales by online retailers. In doing so, it reversed its prior precedents requiring "physical presence" in a state to establish nexus, stating in part in the *South Dakota v. Wayfair, Inc.* case:

> *"...the first prong of the Complete Auto test simply asks whether the tax applies to an activity with a substantial nexus with the taxing State. 430 U. S., at 279. '[S]uch a nexus is established when the taxpayer [or collector] 'avails itself of the substantial privilege of carrying on business' in that jurisdiction.'"*

The prevailing view now is that, for example, a retailer delivering goods or services into a state will be availing themselves of the *"privilege of carrying on business"* in that jurisdiction. Companies with nexus with a taxing state must register with state taxing authorities to obtain what is often called a Business License in that state. The Washington State Business License Application is available in the BLSG Data Room under *Finance > Foreign Entity and Tax Registration*.

In general, the standard for tax nexus is a lower standard than the standard for qualification to do business. Resolving nuanced tax nexus questions requires consultation with specialized tax counsel or tax accountants.

Federal Tax Registration

A Federal Employer Identification Number ("EIN") is necessary for many business structures and activities, but not all. The IRS webpage captioned, "Do You Need an EIN?" (https://www.irs.gov/businesses/small-businesses-self-employed/do-you-need-an-ein) says you will need an EIN if you answer 'Yes' to any of the following questions:

- Do you have employees?
- Do you operate your business as a corporation or a partnership?
- Do you file any of these tax returns: Employment, Excise, or Alcohol, Tobacco and Firearms?
- Do you withhold taxes on income, other than wages, paid to a non-resident alien?
- Do you have a Keogh plan?
- Are you involved with any of the following types of organizations?
- Trusts, except certain grantor-owned revocable trusts, IRAs, Exempt Organization Business Income Tax Returns
- Estates
- Real estate mortgage investment conduits

- Non-profit organizations
- Farmers' cooperatives
- Plan administrators

From this list, most real businesses are going to need an EIN. An exception is a single-member LLC with no employees.

Even single-member LLCs with no employees might need to or wish to get an EIN for these reasons:

- it will probably be impossible to open a bank account or business credit line without an EIN,

- many state business license applications require them,

- having an EIN enables a company to hire its first employee, and

- an EIN might also be necessary to establish credibility with vendors and other third parties.

CHAPTER EIGHT

Structuring and Managing Key Relationships

Nature Abhors a Vacuum

Aristotle postulated the concept of *horror vacui* - or *"nature abhors a vacuum"* - more than two thousand years ago to express the notion that truly "empty space" is unnatural and violates the laws of physics. While scientists have successfully created perfect vacuums for an instant, they collapse into "quantum fluctuations."

The same applies in business law. Where there is empty space instead of proper legal structures and understandings, that vacuum will collapse into chaos and contention.

In the last two chapters, we studied entity selection and entity formation, with a view toward doing those things correctly.

This chapter looks at best practices for establishing and managing relationships involving:

- founders
- employees
- officers
- consultants
- board members

We start here with several caveats.

Variations in Practice. As in many areas of the law, there are no perfect or "right" answers or solutions to the concepts explored here and elsewhere in this book. Thoughtful decisions and careful reliance on common best practices are not guarantees against disputes and chaos. Even perfectly reasonable provisions in an agreement can be misused or misinterpreted, or just not effective.

The People Factor. The most important consideration in structuring and managing key relationships is not what or how, but <u>who</u> – i.e., not what documents we use, or what legalese we use when and how, *but with whom.*

Many of the case studies in this book colorfully illustrate why entrepreneurs must use great judgment in picking their co-founders, early team members, board members, and investors. A company's people are almost always its greatest asset. And often, they are its greatest liability.

Double-Edged Swords. Second, any provision that might help a founder prevent or remedy disruptive behavior by another founder, such as an aggressive equity clawback clause, can potentially be used for malicious purposes against a founder engaged in no bad conduct. It is always important to think carefully about how even a well-crafted clause might be misused by those with motives and means.

Beware High Voting Thresholds. Third, be wary of documents requiring unanimous or near-unanimous consent for amendment or termination. Keep in mind the possibility that departed co-founders or antagonistic early shareholders might be able later to hold up important financings or other transactions by declining to give consent.

LLCs Distinguished. Given the contractual nature of LLCs and the flexibility to concentrate or distribute management, control, and ownership in any way imaginable, concepts regarding officers and boards do not apply to all LLCs the way they apply to most corporations. The discussions concerning employees and contractors, however, apply to all types of companies.

Founders

Relationships between founders and between co-founders and their companies are critically important in every startup.

Successful startups usually owe their success to their co-founders.

And unfortunately, many failed startups owe their demise to disputes and friction between co-founders.

Below we discuss documents that frequently govern founder rights, roles, relationships, and responsibilities, including Stock Purchase Agreements, Shareholders Agreements, Voting Agreements, and Employment Agreements.

Different lawyers provide different advice on these types of documents and issues, depending on what they have learned or what has worked for them. Some lawyers favor detailed agreements with strong remedies, including broad clawbacks; others favor a lighter touch regarding founders.

Lawyers in the latter camp sometimes argue that general principles of corporate law and governance, including duties of care and loyalty, are sufficient to ensure smooth functioning and proper conduct by founders.

Any documents governing founders clearly need to strike a delicate balance. They should operate in the best interests of founders who are committed and performing well. They also must anticipate less-ideal possibilities, like founder misconduct, neglect of duties, or outright abandonment, and other company-threatening personal issues, including divorce, legal judgments, or other legal troubles.

Founder Stock Purchase Agreements

As discussed in Chapter 7, *Entity Formation*, issuing founders their stock is a key first step in forming a corporation because it establishes the corporation's initial ownership and also generally commences the process of marshaling cash, IP, and other assets into the company.

The operative document can be called many things, including either a Founder SPA or a Founder Shares Subscription Agreement.

A Founder SPA is a lot like a standard Stock Purchase Agreement, but it is worth treating a founder's stock purchase differently than others. A founder generally receives stock representing a large percentage of the company, and most co-founders want to be sure that stock is not going to end up in the wrong hands.

Relative Ownership Interests. As discussed in Chapter 5, under *Co-Founder Considerations*, one of the most important initial questions for a startup is the relative ownership interests of the co-founders. It is also central to completing Founder SPAs.

We noted that when there are two founders, 50/50 ownership is often the default. We also noted that equal ownership can lead to problems, including voting deadlocks.

Where 50/50 ownership is unavoidable, mandating that there always be three members of the board could help prevent certain types of deadlocks. Determining how to elect that third board member without the typical majority vote requires creative thinking and drafting.

Note, though, having a third board member doesn't prevent deadlocks on shareholder votes on decisions requiring shareholder approval or consent, like financings or M&A transactions.

Another tie-breaking approach is to provide for a trusted third party to vote to break ties or impasses involving two founders. These can be written into a Shareholders Agreement or a Voting Agreement.

A final approach that allows the primary founders to be equal while providing a tie-breaking vote at the shareholder level is to bring in a trusted third founder with an ownership interest as low as 2%.

Right of First Refusal. Right of First Refusal ("ROFR") refers to obligations and rights usually requiring a shareholder (including a founder) who wants to sell (or who is forced by law to transfer) their shares in any transaction to (i) first offer them back to the company and (ii) then offer them to one or more co-founders.

ROFRs are often found in Founder SPAs. As discussed later, they are also commonly found in Shareholders Agreements and, for many VC-backed companies, in stand-alone ROFR and Co-Sale Agreements.

At a minimum, a Founder SPA should have ROFRs to prevent "involuntary transfers" of stock resulting from a founder's death, disability, or divorce. Some Founder SPAs have ROFRs covering all voluntary and involuntary transactions.

A founder has a legitimate business interest in not allowing his co-founder's ownership stake to fall into unhelpful hands, like a former spouse, other family member, or almost anyone else who is not the co-founder. Broad ROFRs are key to controlling the disposition of founders' shares and the voting rights they carry.

Sometimes the purchase price under a ROFR is the price another purchaser has already offered, sometimes it is some nominal number like the original purchase price paid, and sometimes it is based on a process for determining fair market value. FMV-based ROFRs provide less protection to the company and its cap table, as the company may not be in a financial position to repurchase the shares, rendering the ROFR ineffective.

Fortunately, ROFR repurchases by a company are often permitted to be paid for over time. This commonly involves a small initial payment, often 20%, and issuance by the company of a promissory note to pay the remainder over several years.

Co-founders usually face only financial hurdles in exercising ROFR rights, but a *company's* contractual ROFR rights to buy back founder shares, or shares from any other shareholder, can run into other obstacles.

Common law fiduciary duties can restrict a company's flexibility to buy back shares. After all, any purchase from one shareholder might be viewed by another shareholder as providing preferential liquidity to the other. Any company that wants flexibility to exercise ROFR rights should include that flexibility in its Certificate of Incorporation so other shareholders cannot complain.

Also, once a company issues shares of preferred stock, its Certificate of Incorporation will likely include "protective provisions" (voting rights for a class of shares) prohibiting many types of repurchases of shares without first getting signed consents from a majority of the preferred stock shareholders, or from a supermajority. ROFRs can be explicitly carved out of protective provisions with language in the protective provisions saying such repurchases are permitted.

Equally important, state corporate laws often prohibit dividends or share repurchases by insolvent companies.

Section 160 of the DGCL, for example, prohibits a corporation from redeeming its shares when the capital of the corporation is "impaired," or when the redemption would cause any impairment of the capital. Delaware common law also prohibits a corporation from redeeming its shares when the corporation is insolvent or would be rendered insolvent by the redemption. As discussed in Chapter 17, *The Zone of Insolvency*, a company with debts exceeding the fair market value of its assets is technically "insolvent."

Lastly, any company that has outstanding loans or borrowings from a bank or other sophisticated lender has likely agreed to loan agreement covenants prohibiting stock repurchases without lender consent. Again, ROFR repurchases should be included as explicit exceptions in any loan covenants prohibiting stock repurchases.

In summary, ROFRs are standard tools for keeping shares out of unhelpful hands but intervening factors like insolvency may limit their effectiveness.

Find a stand-alone Right of First Refusal and Co-Sale Agreement in the BLSG Data Room at *Company Formation and Governance > ROFR and Co-Sale Agreements.*

Vesting or Clawback Provisions. As we know, vesting and clawback clauses reduce dead equity, keep equity out of unfriendly hands, and prevent departing co-founders from free-riding on the efforts of others.

Clawbacks are generally repurchase or forfeiture clauses. They can find their way into Shareholders Agreements, Offer Letters, Employment Agreements, Stock Option Plans, and other documents. They can require a founder who walks away or who is removed for cause to forfeit all or part of his or her shares, either with or without compensation for the shares.

Clawbacks seem less common than vesting clauses in Founder SPAs and are more commonly found in Shareholders Agreements, as discussed next. They are also common in founder Employment Agreements, if and when those come into play.

Restricted Stock Awards. A common approach to issuing founder equity in companies anticipating VC funding is the use of Restricted Stock Awards, versus allowing the founders to acquire their shares outright by means of a Founder SPA or similar document.

Vesting is a customary component of restricted stock. If a co-founder with unvested restricted stock leaves the company, he or she would be required to either forfeit the shares back or sell them back to the company, depending on the nature of the grant.

Restricted stock grantees can also likely take advantage of Section 83(b) of the Internal Revenue Code and elect (within 30 days of grant) to pay income tax on the entire restricted stock award based on the value of the shares at the time of the award versus paying potentially higher income taxes as the shares vest. An 83(b) election is an election to include in one's taxable income the value of property subject to a substantial risk of forfeiture – such as a grant of restricted stock under which the company can repurchase unvested shares.

Filing an 83(b) election makes particularly good sense if the restricted stock recipient had to pay full value at the time of grant, since that would mean there was no "compensation" and hence no income tax liability. Making an 83(b) election and paying tax on the value of a no-cost restricted stock grant can also be a rational choice if the restricted stock is likely to increase in value as it vests. In all cases, making an 83(b) election on a restricted stock award starts the recipient's capital gains holding period.

The gamble with an 83(b) election in the case of no-cost restricted stock grants is that the employee may be paying tax on shares that never vest, particularly if he or she is fired or takes another job.

Restricted stock also generally has full voting rights, unlike stock options.

If a VC firm were involved in forming a startup and establishing the founders' equity positions, it would probably choose to do so with restricted stock, subject to a four-year vesting schedule. Issuing restricted stock later in a company's development can create huge tax bills for recipients, but tax impacts are much lower with newly formed startups.

A restricted stock award recipient *must* file a timely (within 30 days) Section 83(b) election to start the five-year holding period for the capital gains tax benefits of Section 1202 of the Internal Revenue Code. Otherwise, the "issuance date" of those shares under Section 1202 is the first date on which the stock becomes either transferable or no longer subject to a substantial risk of forfeiture.

Shareholders Agreement/Stockholders Agreement

Shareholders Agreement and *Stockholders Agreement* are interchangeable terms for documents that vary from one to the next. Some open with "whereas" recitals stating their purposes along these lines:

> *"The Shareholders are entering into this Shareholders Agreement to provide for the management and control of the affairs of the Corporation, including management of the business, division of profits, disposition of shares, and distribution of assets on liquidation."*

The goal of most Shareholders Agreements early in a startup's existence is to ensure the continuity of control and management of the company for some time so the founders and initial shareholders can pursue their vision without interference or disruptive changes of direction.

They are commonly signed by all founders, all initial shareholders and also by the company. Many companies require later investors also to sign the Shareholders Agreement and to be bound by its terms and restrictions.

Shareholders Agreements vary in style, length, and complexity. The only way to appreciate their variability is to review a number of them. Examples are available in the BLSG Data Room under *Company Formation and Governance > Corporations > Shareholders Agreements/Stockholders Agreements*.

VC Shareholders Agreements Distinguished. As discussed in Chapter 14, *VC Fundraising*, when VC dollars come in, it is common for an entirely new Shareholders Agreement to be imposed on the company and its shareholders, along with a battery of other governance and transactional documents. Until the first VC investments in a company, Shareholders Agreements tend to be quite a bit simpler.

The decision of whether to establish a Shareholders Agreement and what terms to include in it is a founder and board-level decision. Early in a startup's existence, the board may consist of the initial founders, and the Shareholders Agreement may reflect that simplicity.

The following are descriptions of the most common types of provisions found in Shareholders Agreements, roughly in order from most common to least common.

Transfer Restrictions. Transfer restrictions are the most common type of provision found in Shareholders Agreements. Founders generally do not want their fellow co-founders selling their shares or having those shares transferred to others involuntarily in the event of death, divorce, bankruptcy, or legal judgments.

Transfer Restriction Legends. Virtually all Shareholders Agreements require a company's stock certificates to bear a legend saying that (i) the shares are subject to a Shareholders Agreement that can be viewed at the company's offices, (ii) the shares may only be transferred in compliance with the Shareholders Agreement, (iii) any non-compliant transfers are deemed invalid, and (iv) that any transferee of the shares agrees to sign the Shareholders Agreement and shall be deemed bound by its terms.

Many companies also decide not to issue actual stock certificates to avoid problems involving unauthorized transfers, since it is much harder to sell something not in a potential seller's physical possession.

Penalties for Shares Transferred in Violation. Shareholders Agreements can similarly include a range of provisions for dealing with shares transferred in violation of a Shareholders Agreement, including simply deeming the transfers invalid.

The following language represents another approach to dealing with unauthorized transfers:

*"**Right to Purchase Stock from Outside Party.** In addition to the other rights provided in this Agreement, if any Outside Party purports to acquire ownership of or an interest in any Stock from a Shareholder without having fully complied with the terms of this Agreement, Company has the right to purchase that Stock from the Outside Party at the price of $1 per share. This right of purchase exists for a period of five years after Company first receives actual notice of the Outside Party's claim of ownership or interest in any Stock.'*

ROFRs. ROFRs are common in Shareholders Agreements. Unlike Founder SPAs, signed only by the founder and the company, Shareholder Agreements involve multiple signatories, all of whom would have contractual rights to enforce ROFR clauses.

ROFRs are less susceptible to abuse than clawbacks, as they cannot be unilaterally triggered by the company. Because of this, it makes more sense to draft them in a company-friendly manner. It might be wise, for example, to allow the company to repurchase ROFR stock at the lesser of (i) the price offered by a third party or (ii) an FVM determined in the board's discretion. A ROFR should also allow the company to pay only 10% or 20% of the purchase price up front and the remainder over several years.

Board of Directors Composition and Voting Requirements. Although provisions governing board composition and requiring that shares be voted to place certain individuals on the board are commonly addressed in Voting Agreements, they are also commonly found in Shareholders Agreements, especially in the absence of a Voting Agreement.

The right of shareholders to elect directors is one of the most powerful rights in a corporation. When a Shareholders Agreement is in place, even if co-founders find themselves in a dispute, they may still be forced to keep each other on the board.

Influential early investors can also negotiate board seat rights into Shareholders Agreements.

Amendment Requirements. All Shareholders Agreements state a voting or consent threshold required for any amendment to the agreement. These can be as low as 51%, or they can require supermajority votes as high as 70%, 80%, and even 100%.

As noted earlier, founders should consider the potential implications of high consent thresholds that could interfere with desirable future transactions in the event of a falling out among the shareholders.

Rights of First Offer of New Securities. Some Shareholders Agreements also provide the signatories with "rights of first offer" or "preemptive rights" to buy into new offerings of securities by the company in order to allow existing shareholders to maintain their overall ownership percentages in the company and to own shares in any new classes of shares issued that might have superior financial or control rights.

As a general rule, companies should resist granting preemptive rights to third parties in early financings, since VCs frequently want the ability to take most or all of a round.

Right of Co-Sale. Co-sale rights, also called "tag-along rights," are less common in early Shareholders Agreements, but certainly not unheard of.

Co-sale rights are triggered when any shareholder encounters an opportunity to sell some or all of his or her shares. Where co-sale rights are present, that shareholder must give notice of the selling (liquidity) opportunity to all other signatories to the Shareholders Agreement and give those shareholders a period of time to consider whether or not to participate. Other shareholders can generally participate in the sale in an amount reflecting their pro rata ownership interest. A 10% owner of a company, for example, might have the ability to sell shares equal to 10% of the total shares sold in the liquidity opportunity, depending on the particular clause.

The presence of co-sale rights might serve to dissuade a co-founder from selling his or her shares, avoiding the need for the company or a co-founder to exercise expensive ROFR rights.

Drag-Along Provisions. Drag-along provisions generally impose an obligation on all signatories to vote in favor of a sale of a company if holders of a certain percentage of the voting shares favor the transaction or if the holders of a certain class of shares favor the transaction.

They can also force other shareholders to vote in favor of financing transactions that are favored by a requisite number and class(es) of other shareholders.

Drag-along clauses are less common in early Shareholders Agreements, but they are always imposed by VCs to ensure a timely exit from an investment. VCs insert drag-along rights into Shareholders Agreements, Voting Agreements, and even Certificates of Incorporation.

Founders of a company with substantial early investors might include drag-along provisions in their Shareholders Agreement to address the possibility of an early strategic exit opportunity. Even when founders have voting control, minority shareholders may still have state law rights to object to a sale.

We look closer at drag-along provisions in Chapter 12, under *Preferred Stock Key Provisions*.

Termination of Founder Employment. Founders of startups often serve in senior executive roles, commonly as Chief Executive Officer, Chief Technology Officer, Chief Operating Officer, Chief Product Officer, or Chief Marketing Officer.

Removing a poorly performing or disruptive founder from an executive role is usually almost impossible unless and until a company accepts VC money.

Remember back to Case Study #2, *Bull in a China Shop*. That situation involved disruptive behavior by one of three co-founders. The company's unusual Shareholders Agreement helped pave the way to a solution. Not only did it provide for a board seat for all three founders as long as they held their shares, it also contained a right in the company to claw back a founder's shares if the founder's employment with the company was terminated for "cause."

This rare provision provided a clear path for completely removing a disruptive and dysfunctional founder, although at a cost, as the co-founder's shares had to be purchased at fair market value in installment payments over three years. Those payments caused the company severe financial hardships.

Although governance documents vary considerably across startups, it seems rare that early-stage Shareholders Agreements provide effective mechanisms for terminating founders from their officer positions, let alone clawing back their shares and removing them from the board.

Case Study #2 proved the value of termination-based clawbacks. But those same provisions can be misused. Two founders, for example, could unfairly accuse a third of misconduct or neglect of duties merely to run him or her out of the business. A formula providing for a modest purchase price makes a clawback more viable against a bad co-founder, but higher pricing better protects innocent founders from oppression.

Voting Agreements

With that background on Shareholders Agreements, the discussion of Voting Agreements can be summed up to say that they typically include the same types of provisions discussed earlier: (i) board of directors composition and voting requirements and (ii) drag-along provisions.

Election of directors language might read like the following:

> *Election of Directors. On all matters relating to the election and removal of directors of the Company, the Common Share Holders and the Preferred Share Holders agree to vote all Common Shares and Preferred Shares held by them (including by voting by written consent, when applicable) so as to elect members of the board of directors of the Company (the "Board") as follows:…*
>
> *(b) At each election of directors in which the Common Share Holders and the Preferred Share Holders, whether voting together or as separate classes, are entitled to elect directors of the Company, they shall vote all of their respective Common Shares and Preferred Shares, as applicable, so as to elect: (i) one person designated by persons holding a majority of the Common Shares held by the Common Share Holders, (ii) one person designated by persons holding a majority of the Preferred Shares held by the Preferred Share Holders, and (iii) the person serving as Chief Executive Officer of the Company, which individual shall initially be Jim Smith.…*

Likewise, the signatories to the Voting Agreement would be required to vote in certain ways, or not vote, regarding the removal of one or more directors.

Similarly to drag-along provisions in Shareholders Agreements, drag-along provisions in Voting Agreements generally commit the signatories to vote in favor of variously described transactions that might be defined using terms like "Qualified Sale," "Qualified Transaction," "Approved Sale," "Approved Transaction," and the like.

Some Voting Agreements have "power of attorney" language appointing a specific person, like the CEO, to be the signors' "true and lawful proxy and attorney" and giving that person "the power to act alone and with full power of substitution" to vote the signors' shares in the event the signor fails to do so as required.

Founder Employment Agreements

At a minimum, every founder serving as an employee should sign an Offer Letter Agreement, as discussed next under *Employees*. Concurrently with that, a founder should sign every other document required for other employees, including a PIIA, Employee Handbook acknowledgment, and acceptance of the company's Ethics Policy or Code of Conduct.

It is hard to say, though, how common full-blown founder employment agreements are. Founder CEOs with plenty of leverage often have them, but they seem less common otherwise. If so, this might be because founders see no need for one while they hold more than 51% of the company's stock and control the board, and maybe they do not push for them later once major investors are involved since the terms might not be as appealing, as discussed below.

Nonetheless, founders frequently ask if they should have an employment agreement. I generally say yes, but might add that it is for different reasons than ones they may have in mind.

Founder Perspective. A founder might be most interested in locking down a multi-year employment agreement with no termination "without cause," or providing substantial severance payments in the event of early termination without cause. Other common employment agreement requests from founders include:

- board seat rights,

- favorable equity granting provisions, such as faster vesting, including potentially what's called "accelerated vesting in the event of a change of control" – meaning that in the event of an M&A sale, all unvested shares immediately vest,

- extended post-employment time frames to exercise vested options beyond the standard 90 days,

- rights to director and officer liability insurance coverage and related rights to indemnification from the company.

Company Perspective. As company counsel, on the other hand, I want an executive employment agreement to include the following elements:

- duties and obligations that are clear and measurable,

- clear definition of the executive's reporting relationship,

- the ability to remove a poorly performing executive by voiding any severance obligations in terminations "for cause,"

- "cause" defined for purposes of termination to include not just poor performance, but also failure to comply with duly issued commands or orders, failures to comply with internal policies and procedures, violations of ethics policies, and certain types of arrests and convictions,

- compensation incentives that are aligned with the company's objectives,

- mandatory board seat resignation for any terminated executive, and

- protections against post-termination theft or misuse of proprietary information, and, to the extent allowed under state law, reasonable non-compete provisions (no longer allowed in California).

Clawbacks Revisited. I usually also put the idea of clawback clauses on the table, acknowledging that they can have severe impacts and can be misused. Each member of a co-founder team needs to assess the risks of clawback misuse against the risks of possible freeriding, dead equity, or other adverse outcomes should their co-founder depart or engage in misconduct.

Two examples of situations where clawbacks can prove indisputably valuable are: (i) when an executive has committed a significant crime or was terminated for other serious malfeasance and (ii) when a founder executive is performing poorly in his or her role and is in irreparable conflict with the board, including any co-founders.

Unexpected situations involving errant founders can pose severe reputational risk to a company. An executive's conviction for fraud or other wrongdoing can threaten a company's survival. Many companies are extremely surprised when they cannot remove a convicted individual from their board or cap table without a written agreement saying so. We discuss some of those challenges later under *Dealing with Problem Directors.*

Redundancies and Conflicts. One risk of employment agreements is possible conflict with other documents.

As an example, every employee of a company from top to bottom should sign the same PIIA effective as of their hire date. As a result, provisions related to confidentiality, trade secret protection, and the assignment of IP created during employment should not be required in an employment agreement, but they often are. From a company's perspective, the key is to ensure that an employment agreement does not inadvertently conflict with and override more stringent confidentiality and IP provisions in a previously signed PIIA.

Conflicts also need to be avoided regarding things like equity grant provisions. If an employment agreement provides for accelerated vesting of options in the event of a change of control, the option grants approved by the board must also, or there will be a conflict.

Investor Perspectives. A final cautionary note about founder employment contracts – VCs do not like to see generous severance provisions in any senior officer employment agreement, including those with founders. Any severance exceeding six months of salary will be seen as excessive, possibly even shorter periods. Sophisticated investors will look unfavorably at any language that makes it difficult to terminate a poorly performing executive, particularly a CEO or CFO.

Severance provisions in founder employment agreements or other senior officer employment agreements can pose challenges for companies that need to downsize quickly to preserve cash.

A clause nullifying a company's obligation to pay severance in the event a defined insolvency threshold is triggered can address this concern. I once advised a financially desperate company caught in the dilemma of either continuing to pay an un-needed and very expensive CFO or biting the bullet and writing a huge 6-month severance check to cut its losses. In the end, it spent half of its cash in the bank to write that one check.

Founder Issues

The role of a startup founder is extremely challenging. For many first-time founders, it is the most significant role to date in their career, and there may be gaps in training, skills, and professional development.

Relentless pressures often bear down from all sides, including investor expectations, time and resource constraints, personnel management challenges, and personal financial stresses.

In companies with loosely structured relationships and expectations, this mix of inexperience and overwhelming demands can lead to founder mistakes and dysfunctions. These are sometimes discretely referred to by investors and other stakeholders as "founder issues."

Case Study #21 is about founder issues.

Case Study #21 – The Party is Over

In trying to "right the ship" at one nearly penniless startup, it soon became clear the founder was using the company as a private piggy bank. He had already been removed as CEO and his credit card was finally cut off. This belatedly stopped regular meal deliveries to his apartment, limousine rides, and $1,000 bottles of wine.

The accounting staff told of other excesses, including expensed strip club visits, lavish travel, and medics having once been called to the founder's hotel room due to poorly calibrated intoxicants.

The vacuum in this instance was not just documentary, but primarily loose board oversight. The board, mostly VC representatives, did not have the time or temperament to exercise close oversight over the flamboyant founder, particularly when the wheels were already falling off the company and hopes of any upside were evaporating.

> Lessons: Responsibilities for reigning in errant founders rest with the board. Educate and coach founders and other fiduciaries to be mindful of their fiduciary responsibilities before they raise piles of cash.
>
> Adopt travel and entertainment policies and a strong code of conduct from the earliest days to establish appropriate spending attitudes, oversight, and standards for "termination for cause."
>
> When lots of money is raised quickly, founder excesses and misconduct cannot always be prevented, particularly where a founder dominates or manipulates the board. Uber went through similar, highly public founder issues.

Boards can prevent a variety of problems by resisting founders' attempts to erect communication barriers between the board and other key officers and employees, including key accounting, finance, legal, and compliance personnel. Board members, particularly those serving on the audit committee, should routinely reach out privately to senior employees and ask sensitive questions about the integrity of internal controls, the absence of fraud or other misconduct, legal and regulatory compliance, and even the job performance of other senior personnel, including the CEO.

Employees

HR Best Practices

Relationships with founders, key executives, and investors may be more complex, but regular *employees* are far more likely to target their companies with lawsuits and regulatory complaints. While some employee complaints are legitimate, companies with weak employment practices are frequently targeted with baseless claims and have little choice but to pay substantial nuisance settlements to deal with them.

Fortunately, the same human resources ("HR") practices that help protect companies from baseless claims also improve employee productivity and morale. These best practices are based on four key principles:

- document the company's expectations of each employee,

- document employee performance against those expectations,

- document positive and negative performance feedback and employee acknowledgment of it, and

- provide appropriate rewards for positive performance, but also take appropriate disciplinary action when performance issues do not improve after written feedback and disciplinary warnings.

Two keys to success:

- careful documentation, and

- consistency.

Consult HR experts when possible in creating and implementing these processes, including manager training. Manager training is critical for ensuring consistency and fairness.

Many entrepreneurs feel like their startup of five to ten employees is too small to justify HR practices that feel so "corporate." Those feelings usually go away quickly after receiving the first demand letter on law firm letterhead inaccurately claiming that the company terminated an employee for improper reasons.

Case Study #22 is just such an example.

Case Study #22 – Not Fit for Work

A manager at a successful startup had been experiencing performance difficulties with an employee who was maxing out every conceivable form of leave to stay away from work. Her documentation was never sufficient, and her absences were unpredictable and disruptive. The only thing this employee seemed to do with total dedication was avoid work.

The employee had exceeded both her allowed paid time off and family medical leave, and things were coming to a head. The manager set up a meeting with the employee late one afternoon.

Just before the appointed time, he received an email from her that she was experiencing a medical condition and would not be in the office to meet him.

The exasperated manager notified another manager of the situation, saying the employee was out on leave again. The other manager looked surprised and said, *"Are you sure? I just talked to her, she's in the gym."* The shocked manager went to the gym downstairs and confronted the employee. Her most obvious medical condition was treadmill fatigue.

The supervisor terminated her the following day.

The employee retained counsel and threatened to sue the company for wrongful termination and wrongful denial of her medical leave rights.

After months of costly distraction, and despite substantial documentation that the employee had failed to meet performance expectations despite written performance warnings, (ii) abused the company's leave policies, and (iii) lied to her supervisor, the company still wrote a check for $80,000 to settle the matter rather than litigate.

This nuisance payout would have been even larger had the company not taken great care to document items (i) through (iii) and, equally importantly, had the manager not fortuitously discovered the employee in the gym enjoying a vigorous workout.

> Lessons: Without strong HR processes, well-trained managers, and a willingness to take decisive action, situations like this one can be extremely costly and disruptive.

The following are basic HR best practices.

Offer Letters

No employee should be allowed to begin employment without entering into an Offer Letter Agreement. A good Offer Letter Agreement can be just two or three pages, but it should cover the following:

- state that the employee's employment is "at will," and may be ended at any time by either the employee or the company,

- state the employee's job title, general duties, hourly rate or monthly salary, and reporting relationship,

- state that the Offer Letter is entered into concurrently with a PIIA and is contingent upon executing the PIIA,

- state that the employee is simultaneously being provided a copy of the company's employee handbook, ethics policy, and any applicable travel or expense policy, that the employee acknowledges receipt of said documents, and that the employee acknowledges that his or her continued employment requires compliance with them,

- state that the employee will not bring any IP of any other employer with him or her into their role or use such IP in any manner in connection with their employment, and

- recite any required state law notices.

To be enforceable, an Offer Letter Agreement must be signed by the employee and by the company.

A common Offer Letter mistake is promising stock options. Any reference to an option grant or other equity grant should be in the form of a statement that *"a recommendation of an option grant for [x number] of shares of the company's stock will be made to the board of directors as soon as reasonably possible."* Again, only a board of directors can issue options, not the CEO or any other officer.

Employee Onboarding

In employee onboarding, several things need to go correctly from the beginning. Employers need to timely obtain numerous legal, tax, and regulatory documents at the time employment begins.

Many companies use a check-the-box employee onboarding sheet to confirm that the key steps have been taken, which might include the following:

- fully executed Offer Letter Agreement,

- concurrently signed PIIA,

- concurrently signed Employee Handbook acknowledgment,

- completed Form I-9, Employment Eligibility Verification,

- completed IRS Form W-4, Employee's Withholding Allowance Certificate,

- completed payroll processing/direct deposit paperwork, and

- completed medical/dental benefits elections.

Obtaining all of those properly signed documents, initiating any orientation and training and, as applicable, providing new employees with a workspace, computer, telephone, any necessary security keycards, business cards or other work-related equipment and materials is called "onboarding."

Onboarding weaknesses are endemic in companies of all sizes, but particularly in startups.

Laypersons also often seem to believe, quite incorrectly, that being able to produce an email proving an Offer Letter Agreement, PIIA or other critical document was *presented* to an employee is almost as good as being able to produce fully executed copies of those documents.

Nothing could be further from the truth. Unsigned documents have no authoritative value whatsoever and may have negative proof value – i.e., the employee refused to sign, and the company accepted and agreed to that refusal.

Growing Use of Professional Employer Organizations

While many companies still handle critical HR functions on their own, startups are increasingly using "professional employer organizations," or "PEOs."

PEOs help to automate, streamline, and foolproof a number of critical HR functions in one place

- employee onboarding, electronic document signing, capture and preservation, payroll and payroll tax processing, medical and other benefits enrollment, leave processing and tracking, and more.

Competition in the PEO space has grown in recent years. This has been due to the convergence of cloud-based technologies, ever-increasing software sophistication, and greater acceptance of administrative task outsourcing. Strong competition has increased the quality of these services, while also reducing costs. And while these platforms aren't free, the errors they can help prevent are well worth the expense.

The best of these online platforms perform well in:

- ensuring managers follow detailed onboarding checklists,

- providing excellent, editable templates of employee handbooks, ethics policies, and travel and expense policies,

- ensuring that all necessary documents are properly presented, signed, and stored for later retrieval,

- ensuring that all tax and benefits elections are made timely,

- providing smooth and reliable payroll processing, and

- providing online document and information accessibility for both employer and employee, including former employee access to historical tax information.

Handling these critical HR tasks in-house using paper-based, human-error-prone processes and systems seems increasingly outdated. Once a startup has the financial resources to consider using a PEO service, it should consider doing so for risk management reasons, administrative efficiency, and improved employee onboarding.

Management Training

Few investments can provide a company greater benefits than ensuring that all managers receive training on (i) how to bring out the best performance from those who report to them, (ii) how to properly address performance deficiencies, and (iii) how to avoid making costly HR-related legal and regulatory mistakes.

Among other things, train managers in these areas:

- state, federal and local laws and regulations governing employment practices, employee rights, anti-harassment, and anti-discrimination,

- cultural differences sensitivity, implicit bias, and the value and necessity of fostering diversity and inclusion in the workplace,

- how to interview successfully, with a view toward helping interviewers represent the company well, identify the best candidates, and avoid saying or doing things that create legal liability,

- how to write and communicate job descriptions and performance objectives,

- how to interact effectively with employees in a manner that motivates and inspires them, gives direction and purpose to their work, and steers them back when they get off track,

- how to provide effective praise and rewards when things are going well, and

- how to effectively deal with performance issues through written performance evaluations and warnings.

Poorly trained managers can wreak havoc on companies of all sizes, causing poor morale, high employee turnover, loss of a company's best talent, and recruitment challenges.

These issues can cause immediate impacts to a company's ability to achieve its objectives by increasing costs while also impairing performance. They can also cause indirect impacts, like hurting fundraising efforts and business development efforts. Negative impacts are even more likely if a company's toxic culture spills out into social media, sites like www.glassdoor.com, or the news media at large.

As discussed in Chapter 14, *VC Fundraising*, most VCs and other sophisticated investors place high importance on a company's team. By this, they certainly mean the founders and their ideas, experiences, leadership qualities, and prior track records of success. But team also means the company's other key leaders and the company's overall ability to scale up to realize its mission and vision.

If the word on social media and elsewhere is that a company's environment is toxic, that its leaders do not know how to lead, that morale is low, or that turnover is high, those signals can be red flags to investors and potential customers.

Performance Evaluation Processes

The three-legged-stool analogy fits well with HR best practices. The first two legs of the stool are the ones we just discussed onboarding and management training. The third is performance evaluation.

Ideally, employee performance evaluation means a fair, consistently applied system of regular feedback between manager and employee on how the employee is doing, providing both praise for successful efforts and productive feedback for areas where improvement is needed.

A common approach is to supplement an annual review process with mid-year reviews and, as needed, interim performance warnings, including final warnings.

In support of better employee engagement, the process should encourage employees to make suggestions or requests. When asked, employees tend to ask for things like improved goal clarity, different communication processes or styles, additional training, or more support.

The benefits of well-designed and well-implemented performance feedback processes include:

- inspired and productive employees,

- high employee morale and engagement,

- achievement of company goals,

- low turnover, which results in greater accumulation of institutional knowledge and a stronger pipeline of future leaders,

- enhanced ability to quickly remove problem employees, and

- reduced exposure to HR litigation and regulatory risks.

The literature on *"what employees want"* offers mountains of great information for entrepreneurs interested in strengthening their teams. High on the list are things like:

- knowing how they fit into the big picture, so they know their work is meaningful,

- having the right tools and authority to do the job correctly, and

- being properly rewarded for a job well done.

But "communication" is also always very high on the list. Strong communication is critical for achieving the highest levels of employee engagement. The best employees are often the ones most interested in strong communication.

Managers must provide employees clear and logical expectations, opportunities to learn in their work, including from their mistakes, and also an understanding of how the employee's role supports the company's key objectives.

Case Study #23 – Termination Bonus

As often happens, an appointment was put on my calendar to meet with a technology team manager and the HR VP about a "personnel matter." From the title and attendees, I knew it was a meeting about an employee's performance issues. I knew the manager involved, but we had not worked on personnel issues before.

At the meeting, the manager detailed an employee's poor performance and insubordinate behavior, including months of specific warnings to the employee. The employee was hurting his team's productivity and morale, and the manager wanted to terminate him as soon as possible.

I asked how long the issues had been going on, and the manager said, *"Six months or so."*

Interested to see what written performance or behavioral warnings had been issued, I asked to see the file. The manager shifted uneasily, slid a thin manila folder across the conference table and said, *"there's not much there."*

In the folder, I found an (i) offer letter, (ii) a positive year-end evaluation and (iii) a bonus approval recommendation, all from this same manager.

Since starting 1.5 years earlier, the employee had received no written warnings of any kind and had recently received a bonus.

By definition, performance bonuses reward performance that at least *meets* expectations, if not exceeds them.

Our established practice was that we never fired anybody without strong documentation of their performance or behavioral issues, a written record of working with the employee to identify and correct the issues, and clear warnings about the potential for termination if the issues are not corrected.

These processes drove high morale across the company and, for many years, had enabled the company to terminate underperforming employees without a single employment-related lawsuit.

The manager admitted to handling all of his negative feedback orally and not putting anything in writing, but said they had met multiple times to discuss the performance problems and spoke very frankly.

The manager's approach to the situation represented a complete breakdown of the processes, and my disbelief was evident.

The fact that this manager had signed a "performance bonus" recommendation for the same employee after the performance issues had begun caused me almost dizzying dissonance. Removing the bonus form from the file and waving it incredulously, I asked, "*What is this? It has your signature!*"

The manager said he thought the performance bonuses were paid to anybody still on the team. The error of his logic came to him as he said this.

I liked this manager, but my disappointment was hard to suppress. I explained that terminating an employee with perfect written reviews and a recent performance bonus, and stating the reason as "poor performance," creates a reasonable inference that the stated reason is a "pretext" for another reason, potentially an illegal reason such as discrimination.

I slid the file back across the table and said something like:

> "*This employee cannot be terminated yet. The record is perfect for opposing counsel. We are stuck with a non-performing employee for another six months while we correctly re-do our performance feedback and improvement processes. Please tell me nothing like this will happen again.*"

The manager assured me and the HR VP that he would not mess up like this again. I asked the HR VP to work with the manager on the employee matter and also to launch performance evaluation training refreshers.

Epilogue: The subsequent written performance warnings and corrective measures brought the employee's performance into the range of "meets expectations." The manager in question became a model in handling performance reviews, and he later laughed with me about how much that meeting scared him.

Lessons: Do not give "performance bonuses" to poorly performing employees.

Performance issues must be identified in writing. Do not ignore performance issues for any reason during routine evaluation cycles. Between scheduled evaluation cycles, document performance issues in interim written warnings signed by the employee and the manager.

Judges and juries are generally biased in favor of employees and against employers. Call it the "underdog" effect. Or the "everybody hates bosses" effect. The result is that judges and juries often look for reasons to find in favor of employees. Consequently, they will assign no credibility to testimony about performance warnings given orally, *particularly* where company policy and practice is to put them in writing.

For these reasons, this would have been an unwinnable case for the company had the employee been terminated and later raised any colorable claim of discrimination.

Lastly, as in this case, written performance documentation can succeed in correcting problems where oral feedback might not. Writing feedback can force managers to communicate more clearly, and employees also take written warnings more seriously.

Case Study #24 – Missed Opportunity

This case study is also focused on employee discipline, and it reinforces the need to not only be in a position to take decisive action but to actually take decisive action.

A few years ago, a client called me about a problematic employee who was performing poorly and who also had stolen sales accounts (customers) from other colleagues by reassigning them to himself in a Customer Relationship Management ("CRM") system and then contacting those clients directly. These sales accounts were clearly outside of this employee's geographic account territory. The account thefts caused a high degree of tension within the small sales team.

The company did not have clear, written policies on account theft and, when confronted, the employee feigned ignorance that reassigning accounts outside his territory and working them was improper. The company also did not have in place any written system for annual reviews or progressive discipline, including the issuing of ad hoc performance warnings.

To its credit, the company did orally warn him not to commit any further account thefts, wrote up a summary of that conversation, shared it with him, and told him it was going into his personnel file.

Because the company was already aware that this employee was likely to be litigious in any employment-related disputes, I suggested that the company put the employee on a 60-day Performance Improvement Plan ("PIP"), outlining in detail his duties and the company's expectations, including that he not violate any company policies, such as stealing accounts. Failure to meet the obligations of the PIP within 60 days would warrant termination.

After the written warning, but before completing and presenting the PIP document, the company discovered that this same employee had again manipulated the CRM system, reassigned another colleague's sales account to himself, and contacted that account directly.

At this point, the company would have been well within its rights to promptly terminate the employee for violating a policy for which ignorance could no longer be claimed. Instead, the company insisted on him signing the 60-day PIP. In response, the employee made allusions to a "hostile work environment" (i.e., harassment or discrimination) and claimed to need Family Medical Leave Act ("FMLA") leave and possibly Americans with Disabilities Act ("ADA") accommodation.

These claims, however baseless, put the company in a difficult situation that could have been avoided entirely by promptly terminating the employee for the newest account thefts.

<u>Lessons:</u> When a problem employee provides you a clear and compelling opportunity to terminate them, take it without hesitation and be clear and consistent about the reason for the termination.

Multiple reasons to terminate are not required. When there is one very good reason to terminate, decide based on that one reason and do not cloud the decision by offering other reasons. Providing multiple reasons for a termination creates more opportunities for opposing counsel to attack the decision.

New Hire Probation

Many companies put new employees on probationary periods, commonly ranging from 30 days to 90 days. When managed consistently and thoughtfully, this is a smart practice. Although it is not a whole lot different than "employment at will," probation puts new hires on notice that the company takes performance and good conduct seriously.

Probation can be a good time to assess technical skills, teamwork strengths and weaknesses, and reliability in timely completing assigned projects.

During probationary periods, give new employees objective standards or tasks to perform against, and support them in succeeding. Terminations during probation should be well-documented, just like any other termination, as should any performance shortcomings that do not rise to the level of terminable issues.

Be Scrupulously Fair but Decisive

When all three legs of the stool are in place, particularly performance evaluation and feedback processes, chronically poorly performing employees can be terminated with relatively low risk of lawsuits or regulatory complaints.

There are huge rewards in promptly removing bad employees:

- removing a bad employee creates the opportunity to hire a good employee,

- team members negatively impacted by bad employees will be eternally grateful for their removal - morale is always improved by the removal of toxic colleagues, and

- the longer an employee's termination is delayed, the greater the legal challenges might be.

Summary

The three-legged-stool of what might be called *"good HR hygiene"* requires (i) consistent use of a strong Offer Letter Agreement template, (ii) military precision in onboarding to ensure everything is done correctly both in terms of documentation and employee orientation, and (iii) a well-conceived and well-executed program of employee performance evaluations.

Robust HR processes are usually too much for a typical group of businesspeople to divine, plan, and execute on their own. Dangerous gaps and errors are likely without expert assistance.

Key resources:

- PEOs provide automated, cloud-based onboarding, robust payroll and tax infrastructure, vetted HR templates, assistance complying with state, federal and local leave laws, and other HR technical guidance and support.

- Sophisticated HR consultants can help teams achieve their potential and avoid disastrous mistakes.

- Employment counsel in every city hold seminars on the latest employment law developments. Require managers to attend these.

Make the performance evaluation process as simple, informal, and positive as possible for managers and employees alike. Keep it focused. Include all appropriate praise. Use evaluations as tools for identifying opportunities for internal advancement. Do not avoid or downplay areas of needed improvement.

Do not let fears of frivolous litigation prevent decisive action in removing problem employees. And as we learned in Case Study #23, *A Termination Bonus?*, never award performance bonuses to poor performers.

Contractors and Consultants

Many companies use contractors and consultants to perform special projects, cover temporary staffing gaps, or to maintain staffing flexibility. This generally works well, but there are pitfalls to be avoided.

If you do not think that contractors and consultants can cause problems, then you missed the movie about Mark Zuckerberg and the Winklevoss brothers. That story is the subject of Case Study #25, later in this section.

Best practices with contractors and consultants include:

- signing NDAs before discussing anything substantive about prospective work,
- not confusing independent contractors with employees,
- ensuring all work is *"work made for hire,"*
- obtaining full IP assignments covering all works and inventions,
- obtaining IP representations and warranties, including non-infringement,
- imposing other appropriate contractual terms, including confidentiality, non-competition, non-solicitation, insurance, and indemnification, and
- requesting reasonable compensation formulas for converting contractor-agency employees to company employees.

Independent Contractors are Not Employees

As discussed more fully in Chapter 10, *Common Regulatory Mistakes*, in their zeal to run lean, startups frequently misclassify employees as "independent contractors."

Many state taxing authorities and a growing number of courts consider individuals working on projects in the usual course of a company's business to be employees, not independent contractors. It does not matter what documents, titles, or legalese a company uses to try to obscure the relationship.

The issue is taxes. States cannot easily collect payroll taxes, like social security, unemployment and worker compensation taxes, from independent contractors.

The law in this area is becoming increasingly restrictive, due in part to litigation and enforcement actions involving "gig economy" players like Uber.

A fairly certain route to regulatory trouble is to stand between a state and its tax revenues. Unhappy current or former contractors are well aware that they can cause serious trouble for startups by reporting that they were *"misclassified and deprived of worker protections, like overtime."*

Even if possible misclassification issues are not raised by regulatory authorities, latent tax and compensation liabilities relating to perceived over-reliance on independent contractors could be a red flag for potential investors or acquirors.

We will discuss the growing regulatory implications of these issues further in Chapter 10.

Work Made for Hire

There is a presumption under the law that IP created by non-employees, including independent contractors, is *not* owned by the company. This presumption must be overcome with contractual "work for hire" language.

As discussed in Chapter 9, *IP – Protecting Rights and Avoiding Liabilities*, "work made for hire," or "work for hire," is a core tenet of copyright law.

Fortunately, these issues are relatively easy to address through contractual language, but those provisions must be used consistently in all independent contractor agreements, consulting agreements, development agreements, and any other agreements under which any IP could be created.

Here is an example of work made for hire language from an independent contractor agreement:

> *Company shall own all right, title and interest (including patent rights, copyrights, trade secret rights, mask work rights, trademark rights, sui generis database rights and all other intellectual property rights of any sort throughout the world) relating to any and all inventions (whether or not patentable), works of authorship, mask works, designations, designs, know-how, ideas and information made or conceived or reduced to practice, in whole or in part, by or for or on behalf of Consultant during the term of this Agreement that relate to the subject matter of or arise out of or in connection with the Services or any Proprietary Information (as defined below) (collectively, "Inventions") and Consultant will promptly disclose and provide all Inventions to Company. All Inventions are work made for hire to the extent allowed by law....*

A common mistake worth avoiding involves allowing inconsistent contractual language indicating that the contractor or consultant has a right to withhold the transfer of IP until the payment of all fees.

Transferring IP rights after payment sounds reasonable, but such terms undermine any argument that any resulting IP was created as "work made for hire." Works made for hire can *never be owned* by the contractor or consultant who produces them.

It is best to resolve a contractor's or consultant's concerns about timely payment by other means, such as up-front deposits.

California Caveat. California Unemployment Insurance Code Section 686 dictates that "work for hire" language in an agreement means that the contractor is presumed to be an employee for purposes of state unemployment and disability taxes.

The California Employment Development Department routinely demands to see all of a company's independent contractor agreements in its audits and uses this provision to pursue unsuspecting companies for back unemployment and disability taxes.

Although IP assignment language versus work for hire language may largely resolve these issues, companies operating in California and hiring independent contractors have to carefully weigh whether to forgo work for hire IP protections or take the risk of unfair tax penalties if audited.

IP Assignment Language

Work for hire language in a contractor or consulting agreement protects copyrightable works, including software code. But non-copyrightable "inventions" also need to be protected. To secure its IP rights in patentable inventions, a company must have every inventor sign a written assignment document in favor of the company.

Although IP assignment language is often longer and even more jargon-filled, the following is an example of an excerpt from a typical clause:

> … *Consultant hereby makes all assignments necessary to accomplish the foregoing ownership as if Consultant was an employee of Company. Consultant shall assist Company, at Company's expense, to further evidence, record and perfect such assignments, and to perfect, obtain, maintain, enforce and defend any rights assigned. Consultant hereby irrevocably designates and appoints Company as its agent and attorney-in-fact, coupled with an interest, to act for and on Consultant's behalf to execute and file any document and to do all other lawfully permitted acts to further the foregoing with the same legal force and effect as if executed by Consultant and all other creators or owners of the applicable Invention.*

As discussed shortly, these concerns have been reduced under the AIA, which gives employers greater rights and flexibility to file and prosecute patent applications covering the inventions of employees and others when appropriate IP assignments are in place.

Non-Infringement Reps and Warranties

If a contractor or consultant incorporates infringing IP into their deliverables for a client company, it is usually the company that will become the target for any patent, trademark, copyright, or trade secret infringement lawsuits, not the contractor.

Including reps and warranties that the contractor will not use or incorporate any infringing IP is important for preventing and remedying potentially harmful infringements. They are often embedded with other important reps and warranties, like in this example:

> *Consultant represents, warrants and covenants that: (i) the Services will be performed in a professional and workmanlike manner and that none of such Services nor any part of this Agreement is or will be inconsistent with any obligation Consultant may have to others; (ii) all work under this Agreement shall be Consultant's original work and none of the Services or Inventions nor any development, use, production, distribution or exploitation thereof will infringe, misappropriate or violate any intellectual property or other right of any person or entity (including, without limitation, Consultant); (iii) Consultant has the full right to allow it to provide Company with the assignments and rights provided for herein (and has written enforceable agreements with all persons necessary to give it the rights to do the foregoing and otherwise fully perform this Agreement;...*

Indemnification and Insurance

Reps and warranties are the hooks for pulling a contractor into any IP infringement suit, but indemnification clauses provide the teeth, and insurance clauses guarantee a degree of financial responsibility.

In general, a contractor or consultant should agree to indemnify clients for suits and damages resulting from their performance and any breaches of the contractual commitments, including IP infringement. Writing these clauses as mutual, or two-way, makes them more palatable, as in this innocuous-looking example:

> *Each Party hereto agrees to indemnify and hold harmless the other Party for any and all costs (including reasonable legal fees) and damages incurred by the indemnified Party as a result of any claim by any other third party which relates to an alleged breach by the indemnifying Party of any Warranty made herein or other breach of this Agreement, or to the indemnifying Party's alleged willful misconduct or gross negligence.*

Insurance requirements are the final piece of the risk allocation puzzle when working with contractors and consultants.

Think carefully about the nature of the work to be done and what kind of insurance would be most appropriate. Data security and IP infringement coverages are some of the most expensive and difficult to obtain, but a contractor without appropriate coverages will otherwise be unable to honor the most important reps and warranties they are making.

A call to a qualified insurance agent can be very helpful in pinning down appropriate language.

The following is somewhat generic, but certainly better than nothing:

> *Insurance. Contractor shall maintain the following insurance policies with insurance companies carrying a Best's financial rating of A or better licensed in the state in which Contractor is providing Services: (a) workers' compensation insurance with statutory minimum amount if and as required to comply with applicable laws; (b) errors and omissions liability insurance with respect to the Services in an amount equal to or greater than $2,000,000 per occurrence and $5,000,000 aggregate; (c) intellectual property infringement defense coverage in an amount equal to or greater than $2,000,000 per occurrence and $5,000,000 aggregate, and (d) general liability coverage in an amount equal to or greater than $1,000,000 per occurrence and $1,000,000 aggregate.*

Consultants and contractors often claim that insurance is expensive and unreasonable to request. In fact, insurance is usually less expensive than expected and most businesses should carry insurance for their own benefit, so it is worth suggesting that quotes be obtained. Any consultant or contractor that cannot afford insurance almost certainly cannot honor indemnification obligations either.

Confidentiality and Non-Use

Even though a contractor or consultant may have already signed an NDA before signing an actual contractor or consulting agreement, it is still important for the latter to contain confidentiality and non-use clauses. This is because an NDA generally covers discussions and information sharing leading up to a business arrangement, but not the parties' ultimate business arrangement.

In fact, NDAs are generally superseded by specific language in a new agreement, so it is important to confirm that the new clauses are as protective as the superseded NDA protections.

Absent contractual confidentiality and non-use obligations being imposed on contractors or consultants, the law is unlikely to impose them. Courts are particularly loath to "write in" provisions missing in agreements between commercial parties.

A typical clause might look like this:

> *Contractor hereby acknowledges and agrees that in the course of activities under this Agreement Contractor may have access to confidential and/or proprietary information which relates to the Company's marketing, business, and technology development efforts (the "Confidential Information"). Contractor shall treat the terms of this Agreement as Confidential Information. Contractor agrees to: (a) preserve and protect the confidentiality of the Company's Confidential Information; (b) refrain from using the Company's Confidential Information except as contemplated herein; and (c) not disclose such Confidential Information to any third party....*

Non-Competition and Non-Solicitation

Although non-competition clauses for employees are under increasing legal and legislative assaults in recent years, including being banned completely in California and now mostly banned in Washington, non-competition and non-solicitation continue to be important considerations in structuring relationships with contractors and consultants.

Because the law is developing fast in this area on a state-by-state basis, companies should work closely with local counsel to use language that is up to date, tailored to the specific industry and applicable geographic region, and that includes valid justifications for the specific limitations imposed.

It may help, for example, to describe the types of information the contractor or consultant will be exposed to in the course of a project and to explain that the non-competition limitations are necessary for a period of time to ensure that trade secrets or other proprietary information are not used directly or indirectly to support the design, development, or marketing efforts of the company's direct competitors.

Case Study #25 – That Zucked

The complaint filed by the Winklevoss brothers against Facebook and Mark Zuckerberg in March of 2007 describes how the brothers and another plaintiff lost their business idea to Mark Zuckerberg, whom they hired without an NDA or Independent Contractor Agreement.

In June of 2002, the brothers and Divya Narendra, all students at Harvard, began to develop a website to be called harvardconnect.com. The idea was to provide students and alumni a place to meet, exchange information, network for employment opportunities, and make romantic connections. After launching first at Harvard, the platform would expand to other schools.

In November of 2003, the three engaged Harvard classmate Mark Zuckerberg to help complete the software code. Zuckerberg was given access to the software code for the website as it then existed. The complaint alleges that the three shared everything about the business model with Zuckerberg, including the website design, functionality, features, user interface and content, and information to be collected from users, as well as the business model and plan.

Zuckerberg repeatedly told them he would finish and deliver the code, saying as late as January 8, 2004, by email to Cameron Winklevoss, that he would do so.

On January 11, 2004, Zuckerberg registered the Internet domain, "TheFacebook.com." On January 14, 2004, Zuckerberg met with the three, without mentioning the thefacebook.com website.

Zuckerberg and others launched thefacebook.com website on February 4, 2004. The connectu. com website was launched four months later on May 21, 2004.

Among other allegations against Zuckerberg, the complaint accused him of (i) copyright infringement for taking copyright protected matter and creating unauthorized derivative works, (ii) misappropriation of trade secrets, (iii) breach of implied or actual contract under Massachusetts law, (iv) breach of the implied covenant of good faith and fair dealing under Massachusetts law, (v) unfair and deceptive acts and practices, (vi) breach of fiduciary duties, (vii) unjust enrichment, intentional interference with prospective contractual relationships, (ix) fraud, and (x) breach of confidence under California law.

In February of 2008, Facebook paid up to $65 million to settle the lawsuit, including $20 million in cash and 1.25 million shares of the company's stock.

> Lessons. The Winklevoss brothers probably wish they had required Zuckerberg to sign a proper Independent Contractor Agreement including all of the elements described in this section. Entrepreneurs should learn from these mistakes. Where IP is involved, "trust" should play no role.

Board Members

Overview

Fortunately, individual board members rarely present significant legal or regulatory issues for companies. As a body of co-equals, overall board effectiveness is paramount, and not necessarily the role of, or issues related to, any single director.

Board member education and training can help prevent inadvertent failings. Understanding a board's authority, responsibilities, and standards of conduct can help an inexperienced board avoid mistakes that could attract unnecessary litigation or regulatory scrutiny, or complicate a company's ability to raise capital or complete an exit.

Role, Authority, and Standards of Conduct

As noted in Chapter 7, *Entity Formation*, the board oversees a corporation and sets its direction by, among other things, hiring and firing the CEO, reviewing and approving budgets and business plans, and approving certain types of transactions.

While the board is not supposed to be involved in a company's day-to-day operations, it is ultimately responsible for the company's management.

Here again is the general statement of board powers from Section 141 of the Delaware Corporate Law:

> *The business and affairs of every corporation organized under this chapter shall be managed by or under the direction of a board of directors, except as may be otherwise provided in this chapter or in its certificate of incorporation....*

Section 8.30 of the Revised Model Business Corporation Act ("MBCA"), adopted by 24 states, includes the following additional gloss on these basic powers and duties:

§ 8.30 Standards of Conduct for Directors

(a) Each member of the board of directors, when discharging the duties of a director, shall act: (i) in good faith, and (ii) in a manner the director reasonably believes to be in the best interests of the corporation.

(b) The members of the board of directors or a board committee, when becoming informed in connection with their decision-making function or devoting attention to their oversight function, shall discharge their duties with the care that a person in a like position would reasonably believe appropriate under similar circumstances.

These MBCA "Standards of Conduct" are derived from case law. Whether or not specifically captured in a state's corporate governance statutes, case law across all states defines directors' fiduciary duties, including their duties of care, loyalty, and good faith, along similar lines:

- directors are fiduciaries and, as such, must act with "due care," as would a reasonable person under similar circumstances,

- due care, for a director, means being adequately informed about the business and making decisions in an informed manner with due deliberation,

- the "duty of loyalty" requires that directors not engage in self-dealing but act solely "in the interest of the corporation," which tends to mean in the interest of the company's shareholders, and

- the duty of "good faith" prohibits turning a blind eye to legal or regulatory violations.

"Self-dealing," as we will use that term, is defined by the Merriam-Webster Dictionary as "engagement in a transaction for the benefit of oneself rather than for the benefit of someone to whom one owes a fiduciary duty."

The Duty of Care and the Duty of Loyalty

As suggested by the above, directors meet their fiduciary duties by being informed and educated about the company's business and about the decisions they are asked to make, and by making decisions only after due deliberation.

Fulfilling fiduciary duties requires directors to attend meetings, review board materials, ask questions, and make decisions believed in "good faith" to be in the best interests of the company.

This last requirement requires avoiding self-interested decisions that are not in the company's best interests. Obtaining any personal gain or benefit to the detriment of the company's shareholders violates the duty of loyalty.

Business Judgment Rule. The "business judgment rule" provides directors with protection from being second-guessed, even in the event a particular decision turns out to be incorrect and harmful to the company.

Under the business judgment rule, a party wishing to challenge a board's action has the burden of proving that the board did not act with due care if the board (i) followed reasonable processes, including informing itself regarding an appropriate range of facts, (ii) considered all relevant facts in making its decision, and (iii) made its decision "in good faith."

Maintaining reasonably detailed meeting minutes that cover the nature and scope of important deliberations can help create an appropriate record under the business judgment rule. It is also important to (i) timely distribute relevant documents for board member review, (ii) always consider a full range of options and diverse opinions, (iii) seek input from outside experts, and (iv) observe "procedural fairness" at every opportunity, such as requiring directors to recuse themselves from voting on transactions in which they are, or might be perceived to be, financially interested.

The Entire Fairness Standard. The "entire fairness standard," sometimes called the "intrinsic fairness test," is triggered where a majority of a board's directors approving a transaction have a personal financial interest of some kind in the transaction. The entire fairness standard can also be triggered when a majority stockholder has interests on both sides of a transaction.

When the entire fairness standard is triggered, a board of directors has the burden of demonstrating that a proposed transaction is "inherently fair," or "intrinsically fair," to the shareholders by demonstrating both procedural fairness and substantive fairness.

Directors can also rely reasonably on management and outside experts, but they cannot ignore the obvious. Information gaps and contradictions should be cues for directors to ask more questions and to push for additional information or clarifications.

When considering a significant transaction that is subject to the entire fairness standard, companies often retain independent outside experts to render what is called a "fairness opinion," opining as to whether or not the proposed transaction is inherently and objectively fair to the company's shareholders.

Good Faith. Acting with due care and in good faith also requires not turning a blind eye to issues or concerns within the board's responsibilities, including potential legal or regulatory violations. Board members are advised to carefully inform themselves regarding legal and regulatory matters.

Regarding financings, for example, a board is responsible for ensuring the company does not violate state or federal securities laws by recklessly or negligently allowing company officers to make false or misleading statements or omissions to potential investors or otherwise violate securities offering requirements. A board must approve all proposed financing activities and exercise reasonable oversight.

The duty of good faith is different from the duty of loyalty. A decision or activity that benefits a corporation or its shareholders, and is hence "loyal" to the corporation, can still violate the duty of good faith if it violates the law.

A federal appeals court captured that distinction this way:

> *"... we find that a deliberate attempt to undermine the regulatory authority of a government agency cannot constitute good faith conduct, even if such actions benefit the corporation...."*

Director Documentation

The documentation used to onboard directors is often very limited. Some companies onboard directors with no paperwork whatsoever. Unlike other positions in a company, the roles and responsibilities of directors are governed almost entirely by the corporate law statutes and case law just described.

Additionally, directors are not "employees," so offer letters and employment agreements do not apply.

At a minimum, director documentation should include an NDA or PIIA.

Onboarding documentation should also include option grant paperwork or other documentation for any promised equity grants. If financial compensation is involved, which is rare for startups, there will be more paperwork.

Lastly, some companies also require their new directors to sign statements of expectations. These relatively informal documents cover things like the board's role, meeting attendance, preparation and diligence, training requirements, compliance with company policies and procedures, and other such matters. Although laudable for setting appropriate expectations, the use of such documents seems rare in startups.

Director Education and Training

The board is a company's top governing body. Bad boards can create bad companies. Conversely, excellent boards can help create excellent companies.

From a risk management perspective, it is also probably safe to say that most business and legal problems start at the top. This was true in Case Study #21, *The Party is Over*, where the board's lax oversight had enabled the founder's bad behavior.

Consequently, educating and training board members can have significant and lasting impacts on both risk management and business success.

Legal Basics for Startup Boards. Startup founders serving as their company's initial board members should read a good book or two on the role, authority, and standards of conduct for directors.

As discussed above, these largely involve case law principles on fiduciary duties, the duty of loyalty, the business judgment rule, conflicts of interest, the entire fairness standard, and related concepts.

Asking qualified counsel to give a presentation on those duties and responsibilities would also be beneficial. Attorneys are often willing to provide these and other types of training sessions free of charge to form or maintain a relationship.

Board Effectiveness for Startups. Beyond governance standards, it is also important for startup founders serving as new directors to learn different perspectives on creating highly effective boards and to put recommended ideas into practice. It is said that all early team members have significant and lasting impacts on a company. This can also be true for a company's first board of directors.

Board Performance Evaluations

Established boards often implement processes similar to the employee performance evaluations discussed earlier, but that are specifically designed to measure board member performance. These are often conducted as "360 reviews" in which board members rate their own performance and also receive ratings and evaluations from their colleagues.

While these processes are likely rarely put into place before a board has grown to five, seven, or more members, when done properly, they may have the potential for preventing dysfunctional behaviors and tendencies and directing a board's energies and efforts toward the highest value concerns, including budgeting and planning, strategic initiatives, management oversight, and financing needs.

Implementing board review processes can also be used as a tool for reforming an individual board member's poor performance or even pushing for his or her resignation under appropriate circumstances, as discussed later regarding *Dealing with Problem Directors*.

Procedural Formality

In general, startup boards tend to operate relatively informally until someone or something imposes a higher level of formality.

Early on, for boards of one or two persons, it makes sense to conduct most board business with a simple document called a "Unanimous Written Consent in Lieu of Meeting," or "UWC." Rather than hold a meeting, the directors sign a short document containing "Resolutions" in the form of a series of "Whereas" clauses and "Resolved" clauses outlining the decisions made and the basic reasons for them.

Meeting less often and conducting business with UWCs is generally sufficient for small startup boards. Founder board members are usually very close to every aspect of the business, have continuous access to important information about the company and its key decisions, and are likely already meeting regularly to discuss the company's business plan, strategic direction, and critical initiatives — all top priorities for any high functioning board.

One key to UWCs is implied in the name – it is generally a statutory requirement that *all* directors sign a UWC for it to be valid.

Once third-party investors join the board, or others who are not close to the business on a day-to-day basis, it makes sense to hold regular board meetings, generally every month or two.

Evolving boards can still handle routine items by UWC, but as companies grow out of their early one to three-person board phase, regular meetings help to ensure effectiveness.

Board Committees

Stock exchange "listing standards" and SEC rules require publicly traded companies to have certain board committees to ensure key duties and responsibilities are thoughtfully delegated and diligently discharged.

The three committees mandated by SEC and stock exchange rules include:

- Audit Committee
- Compensation Committee
- Nominating/Corporate Governance Committee

But non-public companies are not required by law to form any board committees. Thus, many startup founders and advisors wonder when and how to begin establishing a board committee structure and what the benefits of doing so might be.

These are subjective questions that depend largely on whether the issues facing a board are, or may soon become, so complex or numerous that it is no longer efficient for the entire board to handle all of the issues. Committees allow work to be delegated among board members depending on their skills, expertise, and interests.

Committees can also be used to address matters involving potential conflicts of interest, including executive compensation matters. Handling conflicts of interest responsibly and transparently can reduce risks of self-dealing and the appearance of self-dealing, and hence the risks of shareholder lawsuits.

Establishing committees before they are needed, on the other hand, can result in unnecessary effort and bureaucracy. For most startups, generating "traction" is key, not obsessing prematurely about elaborate governance structures.

Here are a few key attributes of board committees:

- committees do not have any special powers that are superior to those of an entire board,
- there is nothing a committee can do that a board cannot also do,
- committees have only those powers and responsibilities delegated to them by a board, and,
- ultimate authority always remains with the board, even when individual members must recuse themselves due to conflicts of interest.

Here is part of what the DGCL says about board committees and the limitations on their authority:

> *Any such committee, to the extent provided in the resolution of the board of directors, or in the bylaws of the corporation, shall have and may exercise all the powers and authority of the board of directors in the management of the business and affairs of the corporation, and may authorize the seal of the corporation to be affixed to all papers which may require it; but no such committee shall have the power or authority in reference to the following matter: (i) approving or adopting, or recommending to the stockholders, any action or matter (other than the election or removal of directors) expressly required by this chapter to be submitted to stockholders for approval or (ii) adopting, amending or repealing any bylaw of the corporation.*

While it should be obvious that it is generally unnecessary to create a committee structure for a board consisting of just two or three members, understanding common committee roles and considerations can help inform decisions on when and why to consider forming specific committees to improve board functioning or satisfy external expectations.

Compensation Committee. If a board adds a third member, and that new member is not a company officer, it might make sense to create a Compensation Committee consisting of that single "independent director" to study compensation survey data and other information to guide the board on appropriate executive compensation. Doing so adds a degree of independence and legitimacy to a company's compensation practices.

Audit Committee. And when might it be useful for a startup to create an Audit Committee? The answer to this question is likely tied to the company's fundraising activities.

An Audit Committee, also sometimes called a Budget and Audit Committee, or simply a Finance Committee, is primarily tasked with ensuring that (i) a company's accounting and financial reporting systems and processes provide accurate and detailed records and information concerning company revenues and expenses and (ii) its financial reports timely and accurately depict the company's financial results and provide a clear picture of the company's financial health.

Audit committees are also generally tasked with overseeing regulatory compliance and the implementation by management of fraud prevention processes and systems, as well as initiating and overseeing investigations into allegations of fraud or other misconduct.

Once a company reaches a point where outside investors insist upon the retention of an outside auditing firm to audit the company's financial statements, the Audit Committee plays a key role in recommending potential auditing firms, working with the chosen auditing firm to determine the scope of audits, coordinating the execution of audits with management and the auditors, receiving the preliminary and final results of any audits, and working with the auditors to report those results and any recommendations to the entire board.

VCs or other major investors will probably insist on the formation of an Audit Committee once more than $10 million has been raised. Those same investors might even insist on chairing or at least serving on it.

While airtight bookkeeping and accounting practices are important from day one of any startup's existence, there may be little practical need for an Audit Committee before significant infusions of outside capital.

Nominating and Governance Committee. A startup is also unlikely to need a Nominating and Governance Committee until it has grown to the point where it is seeking to add "independent directors" to its board or other directors beyond those put forward by investors with contractual "board designee" rights. An independent director is essentially any director who is not an officer or employee of the company or the designee of a major investor. This is a director with no other "pecuniary interest" (financial interest) in the company, aside from any fees received for serving as a director.

A primary function of a Nominating and Governance Committee is to assess the skills, backgrounds, strengths, and weaknesses of a board and to make recommendations on the skills and characteristics needed in future candidates to fill any gaps.

Any small group of two or three startup founders would generally be well-served by adding one, and possibly two, independent directors to their board for the expertise, skills, connections, and outside perspective they can bring to the board room.

Companies should have formal agreements with their advisory board members to ensure confidentiality and the assignment of any inventions conceived in their advisory board roles.

Advisory Boards. It is also worth noting, however, that many startups bring in outside perspectives by creating "advisory boards." These are non-decision-making bodies made up of independent outside advisors. In this way, a company can avail itself of invaluable outside expertise, guidance, and connections, while still maintaining the streamlined governance, decision-making and operational agility that startups often need to succeed.

In summary, a startup's decisions around board formality and structural complexity should be driven solely by what makes sense at the time, given the circumstances. Formality and structure can help companies establish and follow appropriate best practices.

On the other hand, calculated simplicity under the right circumstances can enable founders to focus on what they believe is most important for achieving traction in a company's early days.

As a final thought, the months leading up to VC board designees or others potentially joining their board might be an ideal time for founders to consider filling in any perceived gaps in board practices, routines, and structures, and even adding a strong independent director or two.

Doing so could appeal to investors by bolstering the company's image as established, sophisticated, and well-managed. It might also prevent opportunistic efforts by new investors to stack the board with unknown independent director candidates or otherwise engineer their own, less desirable notions of board governance and leadership.

Running Board Meetings

Running tight meetings can prevent them from being hijacked for unproductive purposes or derailed by dysfunctional behaviors. Again, nature abhors a vacuum, and vacuums in board room process and structure can make for unproductive and even counterproductive board meetings.

Some tips for good board meetings include:
- scheduling meetings with reasonable notice and always confirming attendance in advance to minimize absenteeism,
- timely distributing meeting documents, including agendas, financials, draft resolutions, and any management presentation materials,
- ensuring that management presentations are high quality, focused, and pertinent to important issues,
- establishing an expectation that directors will show up prepared,
- sticking to the agenda, whenever possible, and
- encouraging the exchanging of ideas by all directors on important strategic and tactical questions.

Board Chair Effectiveness. Every board needs to elect a board chair. Board chairs have actual powers when it comes to setting agendas, running meetings, and other matters.

Board chairs should be knowledgeable about board meeting best practices and should consider training with a coach. A good board chair maximizes board effectiveness by ensuring that meetings run smoothly, generate vibrant, focused discussions, and stay on the agenda unless there are good reasons for deviating.

In more evolved companies, this requires thoughtful preparation, a command of parliamentary procedure (e.g., *Robert's Rules of Order*), and, sometimes, a strong personality.

Without being overly confrontational, the chair must sometimes use procedure and firm diplomacy to prevent individual directors from hijacking meetings with irrelevant discussions and unimportant minutia.

Here are a few tricks of the trade for newer board chairs:

- If a director is stuck on an idea after the board has already moved on from the issue, the chair must know when to ask, *"Is this a concern for anyone else?"* If the answer is no, the chair should end the discussion and move to the next item.

- Rather than allowing a chronic naysayer to dominate and prolong a discussion, the chair must know when to solicit other opinions in the room by asking, *"Can we hear from someone who supports the proposal?"*

- Parliamentary procedure, even when imperfectly employed, can and should be used to timely cut off discussions, take votes, or table items as appropriate. The chair is empowered to run the meeting and must do so, lest others fill the vacuum.

Dealing with Problem Directors

If we define a good board member as one who is engaged, prepared, knowledgeable, and professional, what makes someone a bad board member? Certainly not just challenging management and pushing on issues with his or her colleagues. Board members are required to exercise independent judgment, which can require asking tough questions and challenging weak answers.

While opinions on proper board member conduct may differ, here are some commonly cited concerns:

- significant absenteeism or neglect of duties,
- an unusually difficult or divisive personality,
- an unsuitable background relative to the company's business,
- intellectual limitations that prevent meaningful participation,
- a propensity for getting stuck on or distracted by the wrong issues,
- integrity or character concerns involving civil, criminal, regulatory, or ethical allegations.

Online searches for "bad," "terrible," or "worst," and "board members" will produce colorful stories involving dominators, sleepers, and all types of characters in between.

But behind each of these anecdotes is a board that is probably holding its company back, if not also courting legal or regulatory risks.

The Quiet Conversation. In smaller companies, board dysfunctions are generally problems for the board chair or CEO to recognize and fix. In the spirit of maintaining harmony, a first step might involve the board chair or another board member pulling the problem board member aside privately for a talk about the offending behavior and the need to correct it:

- A board member who frequently dominates meetings with ideas not shared by the other members might be confronted with specific examples of the behavior and evidence that the ideas have little or no support among the group as a whole.
- A member who berates, interrupts, or insults managers or board peers should be told promptly that such behavior is troublesome and detrimental to the functioning of the board.

The Less Quiet Conversation. What if a director is severely disrupting a board's ability to function or alienating high-performing executive team members or fellow board members and continues to do so after coaching?

The board chair or CEO, or other designated board member, depending on the context, may need to confront the board member about the negative impact he or she is having and ask him or her to resign. Precede any such conversation with a reasonable investigation and seek the backing of other key board members.

Although these conversations are almost always difficult, they often achieve the desired result , especially if the CEO or board chair can say, *"I've spoken to several other board members and they also believe it would be best."*

Leveraging Board Evaluation Processes. If a problem director is a founder or other large shareholder, and the company doesn't already have a board member evaluation process, putting one in place may be the best way to convince that person that it's time to resign.

A board member evaluation process can take a while to implement, but confronting a director with a resoundingly negative 360 peer review can help produce the desired result in a *"We feel you should resign"* discussion.

Executive Committee or Special Operations Committee. A little known and rarely used approach for sidelining a difficult director is for the board to create an "executive committee" or "special operations committee" empowered to take most, but not all, actions that the entire board could take and to appoint several or all board members to the committee except for the problem director.

Under Delaware law, the excluded director is entitled to receive information about the activities and decisions of the committee.

I learned this master-level tactic from Stewart Landefeld of the Perkins Coie law firm and noted author on corporate law and governance. Any board considering this approach should first consult experienced counsel, as missteps regarding the scope of the committee's authority or other such matters could lead to more difficulties.

Involuntary Director Removal

The ease or difficulty of removing a director always depends on the facts.

Removal by Shareholder Vote. All states allow for all or some part of a board of directors to call a special meeting of shareholders, including to elect or remove directors. But without the votes to remove, calling such a meeting would be in vain.

Removal Through Share Clawback. As discussed previously, when board room problems involve a founder or executive officer, it is possible that an employment agreement with the individual, or even a Voting Agreement or Shareholders Agreement, may provide the solution.

Often this would be in the form of a right by the company to claw back the founder's or executive's shares, possibly following the individual's termination from an executive role "for cause." Once the individual's shares are clawed back, it may be possible for the other shareholders to vote him or her off the board.

This was exactly the course taken in Case Study #2, *Bull in a China Shop.* And despite the severity of that founder's misconduct, success in clawing back the shares and removing the founder from the board still required brief litigation.

Things get more complicated when investors holding new classes of stock have special rights to elect representatives to the board. In such cases, those investors also control the removal of persons from those board seats. Absent a clawback, and absent voting control over the shares of stock required to remove a problem director, alternatives for the involuntary removal of board designees are quite limited.

Judicial Removal. In limited circumstances involving fraud or other criminal behavior, some states allow a shareholder or board to seek judicial removal of a director.

These rules and procedures vary by state. Under Delaware law, for example, the Delaware Court of Chancery may remove a director if he or she has been convicted of a felony in connection with his or her duties as a director or has committed a breach of the duty of loyalty. The court must also find that:

- the director did not act in good faith regarding the act for which he or she was convicted, and

- it must remove the director to avoid irreparable harm to the corporation.

Under the Model Business Corporation Act, a court can remove a director in a suit filed by the corporation or by shareholders suing on behalf of the corporation. To remove the director, the court must find that the director:

- engaged in fraudulent conduct,

- grossly abused his or her position, or

- "intentionally inflicted harm" on the corporation.

For all practical purposes, judicial removal is only a viable option in extreme circumstances.

The challenges of reforming, working around, or ultimately removing dysfunctional or poorly performing directors again serve to highlight a recurring theme – the need for entrepreneurs to pick their co-founders, investors, and other team members, including directors, with great care.

Case Study #26 – Wait for Me!

Unsuitable backgrounds, poor interpersonal skills, and significant intellectual limitations can all lead to problems in the board room. These problems often come to the surface when a company's focus changes significantly, or its business becomes much more complex or sophisticated.

In one such case, a company started with a relatively simple business model with a low "regulatory profile," but then pivoted into a highly regulated space.

A CEO hired by the founder engineered this company-saving pivot. The pivot attracted substantial investment, and the company moved forward aggressively with its new business model.

The company's initial product and service offerings were put into "maintenance mode," meaning the company would serve existing customers for the foreseeable future, but no further development or marketing would be devoted to growing the "legacy" business. Additionally, customers using the legacy services were to be driven by persistent marketing efforts toward the new, vastly superior services.

The founder was initially enthusiastic about the successful funding rounds and the success and energy around the new business model, but he went through recurring and highly distracting episodes of trying to revert attention to the legacy business because of his attachment issues.

The founder continued to live in the past for almost two years, despite the company's decisive change toward a model that quickly developed strong traction in the market. As a director, he repeatedly distracted the board with pointless updates about the legacy business and potential initiatives to keep it alive. As an officer, he tried to divert internal resources and attention back to the legacy business, despite being warned repeatedly not to do so.

This continued through several funding rounds involving VCs and sophisticated strategic investors. The board eventually grew to nine persons to accommodate seats for multiple VCs and other major investors.

Patience grew thin for the founder's increasingly awkward "contributions" during board discussions. It was obvious to all that he was unable to keep pace with the board's discussions and decisions.

In consultation with other board members, and after attempts at quiet conversations with the founder about stepping down to make room for others on the board, the CEO pushed through a 360-style board member evaluation program.

A few months later, the 360 reviews of the founder turned out as expected. His glowing self-appraisal contrasted starkly with assessments by other board members that he was not contributing meaningfully, seemed unable to keep up intellectually, and was no longer a good fit.

At that point, the sole concession required in exchange for the founder's resignation from the board was honoring his request that the company's "About Us" descriptions continue to mention his role as the initial founder.

Lessons: Founders need to be flexible and self-aware about their role and the true scope, nature, and limitations of their abilities. Once third parties have invested, it's no longer about them, and it's no longer just about their dreams; it's about the good of the enterprise and all of its owners.

As mentioned earlier, VCs are concerned about single-founder companies, in part, for this very reason – the possibility that single founder status is a red flag about the founder's willingness to accept ideas, mentoring, and guidance from others with more experience.

A smart founder should hope and expect that their company will evolve in ways they never anticipated and that, one day, it might even outgrow their skills and abilities, such that they might be replaced by a more capable CEO. Possessing and demonstrating that humility, self-awareness, and openness is likely to make a founder more successful in business and in fundraising.

On the other hand, the longer highly-effective founder teams can grow and evolve in their roles and provide inspiring vision, leadership, and energy, the greater the prospects for success. The best founders know when and how to stay at the helm and do not allow themselves to be removed or replaced prematurely on the whims of misguided investors.

Examples of founders who stayed on through every phase of their companies' evolution, growing and evolving with their companies, include the founders of Microsoft, Amazon, Google, Tesla, and Facebook.

CHAPTER NINE

Intellectual Property – Protecting Rights and Avoiding Liabilities

Overview of IP Strategy

In this chapter, we look at identifying and protecting IP through the laws governing:

    (i)   trademarks,

    (ii) copyrights,

    (iii) trade secrets, and

    (iv) patents.

These four IP categories provide the framework for an IP strategy. Whether or not a strategy is formally adopted, understanding IP rights through this "four-legged stool" framework is critical.

A good IP strategy identifies and protects IP rights and deters infringements of others' rights across all four areas.

- **Trademark Law** protects company, product, and service names, logos, slogans, branding, visual appearance, and overall commercial impression.

- **Copyright Law** protects "works" – software code, websites, software-generated computer screens, mobile app user interfaces, video games, writings, pictures, videos, music, art, and all other "expressions" that are "fixed in a tangible medium."

- **Trade Secret Law**, like patent law, protects inventions; but unlike patent law, it also protects *ideas* that don't rise to the level of patentable inventions. Myriad other types of valuable business secrets can also constitute trade secrets. Trade secrets are protected from theft by state and federal statutes. Stealing trade secrets is "industrial espionage." But if others independently discover the same invention or idea, they are under no legal restrictions under trade secret law.

- **Patent Law** protects new and useful inventions and physical designs. Patent law does not protect mere ideas. An invention is generally defined as "a solution to a technical problem." A patent grants a 20-year monopoly to use and exploit an invention to the exclusion of others. The price for this monopoly is sharing the details of the invention with the world so that all may use and exploit the invention after the monopoly period.

We have already looked at many practices for marshaling and protecting IP and avoiding mistakes and disputes:

- protecting IP in the pre-entity-formation phase by strictly limiting discussions of sensitive information and ensuring proper NDAs are signed before such discussions, even with potential co-founders and independent contractors,

- ensuring proposed company, product, and service names will not conflict with existing trademark rights before committing to them,

- securing a company's entity name, key URLs, and primary trademarks at or before entity formation,

- requiring founders to make blanket contributions of all relevant IP in connection with receiving their founder shares or other ownership interests,

- requiring all employees, officers, founders, and independent contractors to sign PIIAs or equivalent documentation clarifying, among other things, the company's ownership rights to all works and all inventions created by them that are relevant to the company's business,

- receiving assurances from all employees, including founders, that they are not subject to PIIAs with prior employers that could result in trade secret, IP infringement, or non-competition claims,

- receiving assurances from all employees, officers, founders, and independent contractors that they will not bring to the company or in any way use in their work the IP of any third persons, and

- using NDAs before any potentially sensitive discussions with third parties, complying with the requirements of those NDAs, and not over-sharing IP, whether or not an NDA is in place.

Startups that take these steps are building on a strong IP foundation and reducing their exposure to common IP disputes and disappointments. Building on those concepts, we now look at how companies can actively and systematically identify and protect IP.

Trademarks and Service Marks

Overview

A trademark is a word, phrase, symbol, or design that identifies and distinguishes the source of the goods of one party from those of others. A service mark is a word, phrase, symbol, or design that identifies and distinguishes the source of a service instead of goods.

The terms "trademark" and "mark" refer to both trademarks and service marks.

The owner of a trademark has rights to prevent others from using the same or confusingly similar marks in connection with the sale of similar goods or services and may be entitled to damages for infringement.

Trademark registration does not create trademark ownership rights in a mark, but rather provides notice to the public of the trademark registrant's claim of ownership of the mark. But federal trademark registration does provide (i) a legal presumption of ownership of the mark nationwide by the registrant and (ii) the exclusive right to use the mark on or in connection with the goods or services listed in the trademark registration.

Federally registered trademarks can be identified as such by using the "®" symbol, whereas the "™" symbol can be used to signify unregistered, or common law, trademarks. These symbols provide notice to potential competitors of a mark's trademark status. Companies can use the ™ symbol after filing a federal registration until registration is granted. After that, they can switch to the ® symbol.

Seniority Equals Ownership

As noted in Chapter 5, being first to use a mark to identify and distinguish goods or services in commerce in conjunction with the actual sale of those goods or services is what establishes trademark ownership rights and priority over later, "junior" users of the same or confusingly similar marks.

Actual sales of goods and services in commerce is the ultimate standard for establishing first use and, hence, ownership, and what is referred to as seniority or priority.

This means that merely inventing a trademark, registering it with the USPTO, or even using it to advertise a product or service, will not provide priority over the person or company that first uses the mark to identify and to distinguish goods or services in commerce in conjunction with the actual sale of those goods or services.

Make Your Mark

Coming up with unique, strong trademarks, logos, and service marks and protecting them should be an absolute priority. They are a company's face to customers, investors, and the rest of the world.

Think back on, and maybe re-read, the discussions in Chapter 5 under *Naming Considerations, Checking for Name Availability, Trademark Strength, Locking Down the Name* and *Co-existence Agreements.*

Impactful marks that are federally registrable and legally protectable can be drivers of success. Poorly chosen marks, on the other hand, can be a curse. Weak marks cause conflicts, they can be used by and diluted by others, and they make it hard to stand out in the market.

Marks that are weak because they are "descriptive" or "generic" often perform poorly in online search advertising because so many others are using confusingly similar terms. It is nearly impossible to build defensible brand value with weak marks. Legally speaking, a generic term can never be a trademark.

The following excerpt from the *Trademark Strength* discussion in Chapter 5 goes to the heart of a common dilemma:

> Some entrepreneurs are tempted to pick names that identify or describe their companies' products or services. While this is logical, these kinds of names are often deemed 'generic' or 'descriptive' by the USPTO. They hence may be difficult or impossible to register or protect. Names that are more fanciful like Zippo, or arbitrary, like Zoom, are stronger trademarks and easier to register.

Marks that are potentially "confusingly similar" to others already in use regarding similar goods and services are also poor choices. As discussed next, not only might they be cited against the later-used junior mark in the USPTO registration process, holders of similar, earlier-used senior marks can file suit to enjoin (stop) further use of the junior mark and seek damages for infringement.

The costs, complexities, and uncertainties of seeking to later acquire the rights of senior mark holders should not be underestimated. They have absolutely no obligation to sell and stop using the mark for their own products and services, and the greater the commercial success associated with the junior mark, the greater the cost will be to acquire rights to the earlier mark.

The adoption of poorly-considered marks haunts many startups throughout their existence. Painful ripple effects can include:

- additional costs and resources in registering and defending weak or confusingly similar marks,

- poor or uncertain return on advertising and brand-building investments,

- the loss of customer goodwill and slowed marketing and sales traction if re-branding is required, and

- added difficulties in financing and M&A transactions, if others doubt the value and validity of weak, indefensible, or potentially infringing marks.

Federal Versus State Trademark Registration

Trademarks can be registered at the federal level with the USPTO and also at the state level.

Federal registration is available for any eligible mark that has been used in interstate commerce or that can be shown to have had an *"effect on interstate commerce."*

Any good or service being sold in more than one state meets the *"use in commerce"* requirement. Goods sold in just a single state, but to persons who regularly take those goods to other states, also pass the interstate commerce test.

Additionally, the USPTO allows for trademark registration on an "intent to use" basis. If a mark is deemed eligible for registration, the USPTO will issue a "Notice of Allowance," giving the applicant a period of time to file a "first use" specimen.

Although federal trademark registration is not required to own and defend a mark, federal registration provides important protections. As already noted, federal registration establishes a legal presumption of ownership of the mark nationwide by the registrant and the exclusive right to use the mark on or in connection with the goods or services listed in the trademark registration.

And while some state laws governing the protection of state-registered marks allow for more than just the right to stop infringements, including claims of damages like lost profits, federal registration provides those rights and more, including the ability to:

- file infringement claims in federal court,

- seek the defendant's profits,

- seek treble (3x) damages and attorneys' fees for willful infringement,

- seek "statutory damages" in cases of willful counterfeiting, and

- use USPTO registration to initiate registration in foreign countries through the "Madrid System," as discussed below under *Pursuing Foreign Trademark Registration Strategies.*

Threats of damages, defendants' profits, and attorneys' fees, let alone treble damages, are largely hollow in practice. But the ability to make those threats is often still powerful. Trademark damages and other remedies are discussed below.

For any mark that can be registered federally, state registration is probably a useless act. One reason given by some IP experts for filing at both levels is that state-level enforcement agencies are sometimes easier to engage in instances of counterfeit goods. State registration may also be useful while awaiting federal registration if use of the mark will be purely regional.

In summary, owners of important marks should promptly file for federal registration, but state trademark registrations are exceptionally rare. Completely unregistered marks, also called common law marks, are discussed below.

Eligibility for Federal Registration

The USPTO examines every application for trademark registration. The USPTO's most common reason for refusing registration is "likelihood of confusion" with a registered mark or one that is the subject of a prior, pending application. "Merely descriptive" is the second most common reason.

Likelihood of Confusion. Likelihood of confusion is said to exist when two conditions are met: (i) the marks are similar, and (2) the goods or services of the parties are related such that consumers would mistakenly believe they come from the same source.

In the event others are using a similar mark for unrelated goods or services, federal registration may still be possible, but probably only after responding to an official USPTO "office action" raising those concerns. Office actions by the USPTO are official decisions, both final and non-final, that are communicated by written correspondence to the individuals of record on a trademark registration application.

The USPTO's *Basic Facts about Trademarks* has this to say about likelihood of confusion:

> *"To determine whether a likelihood of confusion exists, the marks are first examined for their similarities and differences. Note that in order to find a likelihood of confusion, the marks do not have to be identical. When marks sound alike when spoken, are visually similar, have the same meaning (even if in translation), and/or create the same general commercial impression in the consuming public's mind, the marks may be considered confusingly similar. Similarity in sound, appearance, and/or meaning may be sufficient to support a finding of likelihood of confusion, depending on the relatedness of the goods and/or services."*

Relatedness. Concerning the "relatedness" of goods and services, the issue is not so much whether the actual goods or services, themselves, are likely to be confused, but rather the source of the goods or services.

This is more likely to be the case, for example, if the types of goods and how they are sold or marketed, and to whom, are similar, such as if two similar marks are both used for types of clothing, types of financial services, or types of software, for example.

Famous Marks. Courts have found an even greater likelihood of confusion when one party's mark is "famous." The Court of Appeals for the Federal Circuit has stated that the standard for a mark to be famous "… *requires a very distinct mark, enormous advertising investments and a product of lasting value.*"

In addition to increased risk of a successful infringement challenge, a company using a mark too similar to a famous mark can also be sued for claims of "trademark dilution" by the holder of the famous mark. These claims can be for either "dilution by blurring" or "dilution by tarnishment."

Other Grounds for Refusal. Other grounds for USPTO registration refusal include the mark being:

- a surname,
- geographically descriptive of the origin of the goods or services,
- disparaging or offensive,
- a foreign term that translates to a descriptive or generic term,
- an individual's name or likeness (without permission),
- the title of a single book or movie, or
- matter that is used in a purely ornamental manner.

Some objections to registration can be overcome, and some cannot. Some grounds for refusal constitute absolute bars. In other cases, smart trademark counsel can win the day with strong, or at least clever, "facts and circumstances" arguments.

For more on the USPTO's bases for refusing registration, see Chapter 1200 of the USPTO's *"Trademark Manual of Examining Procedure (TMEP)."* That publication and the USPTO's *Basic Facts about Trademarks* can be found at the USPTO's website (www.uspto.gov) or in the BLSG Data Room under *Intellectual Property > Trademarks.*

Foreign Language Considerations. We have noted that the USPTO will refuse registration of any mark that is a foreign term that translates to a descriptive or generic term.

Similarly, a mark that has a specific meaning in a foreign language, particularly a descriptive or generic meaning, may be ineligible for trademark registration in any country where that language is common. This could require, or at least warrant, adopting an alternate or modified mark in that country, a possibility worth considering up front.

Strong versus Weak Marks

As we know, some marks are not capable of serving as the basis for a legally supportable demand by the owner to stop others from using a similar mark for similar or related goods or services.

It is often tempting to use marks that are descriptive of the goods or services offered. The tradeoff is that such marks are legally weak and others can use the same or similar marks.

The USPTO's booklet, *Basic Facts about Trademarks*, offers this guidance regarding strong versus weak marks:

> *"Generally, marks fall into one of four categories: fanciful or arbitrary, suggestive, descriptive, or generic. The category your mark falls into will significantly impact both its registrability and your ability to enforce your rights in the mark.*
>
> *The strongest and most easily protectable types of marks are fanciful marks and arbitrary marks, because they are inherently distinctive. Fanciful marks are invented words with no dictionary or other known meaning. Arbitrary marks are actual words with a known meaning that have no association/relationship with the goods protected. Fanciful and arbitrary marks are registrable and, indeed, are more likely to get registered than are descriptive marks. Moreover, because these types of marks are creative and unusual, it is less likely that others are using them."*

Descriptive marks are words or designs that describe the goods or services. The USPTO's *Basic Facts about Trademarks* says this about descriptive marks:

> *"Such marks are generally considered "weaker" and therefore more difficult to protect than fanciful and arbitrary marks. If the USPTO determines that a mark is 'merely descriptive,' then it is not registrable or protectable on the Principal Register unless it acquires distinctiveness— generally through extensive use in commerce over a five-year period or longer. Descriptive marks are considered "weak" until they have acquired distinctiveness.'*

Generic words are the weakest type of mark. Etymologically speaking, a generic term simply refers to a genus, of which a particular product is a species. These are the everyday words used for particular goods and services that everyone has the right to use. They are neither registrable nor enforceable against third parties.

Legal Standards for Infringement

Likelihood of confusion is required to win a trademark infringement lawsuit under the federal trademark statute, called the "Lanham Act." Courts look at a variety of factors to determine likelihood of confusion.

The U.S. 9th Circuit has adopted what it calls the *"Sleekcraft 8 Factor Test."* All eight factors must be considered:

(1) strength of the mark,

(2) proximity of the goods,

(3) similarity of the marks,

(4) evidence of actual confusion,

(5) marketing channels used,

(6) type of goods and the degree of care likely to be exercised by the purchaser,

(7) defendant's intent in selecting the mark, and

(8) likelihood of expansion of the product lines.

Damages under the Lanham Act

A mark-owner plaintiff alleging trademark infringement can pursue several types of monetary relief under the Lanham Act, including :

- an accounting of defendant's profits (profits from infringement),

- actual damages sustained, like sales diverted from plaintiff to defendant,

- a reasonable royalty representing plaintiff's damages,

- attorneys' fees and costs (requires proof of willfulness), and

- treble damages for intentionally using a counterfeit mark.

Despite all of those potential remedies, the most commonly granted remedy by far in infringement cases is an "equitable remedy" called an "injunction." Equitable remedies are any form of court-ordered actions or prohibitions that are not financial damages. Courts have broad powers "in equity" to fashion relief beyond mere damages to make an injured party whole and to prevent future injury.

An injunction in a trademark case could prevent further infringement by prohibiting any further use of a mark. The court's injunctive order could also compel removal of the mark from all advertising materials, web pages, packaging, and physical products, essentially forcing the infringing company to completely re-brand the offending products or services.

Damage awards are described as rare and litigators often characterize the law of trademark damages as unpredictable.

Key issues in damages decisions include:

- Is injunctive relief available and to what extent does it restore the plaintiff ?

- Is "disgorgement"(forfeiting) of profits appropriate to prevent awarding the infringement?

- Damages cannot be "punitive."

- Was there intent to deceive?

- Were sales diverted?

- Did plaintiff unreasonably delay in asserting its rights?

The case law on damages in trademark cases is far beyond the scope of this book, but very interesting and worth exploring for any business attorney.

Other Trademark Claims under the Lanham Act

Beyond basic infringement claims, the Lanham Act also provides recourse for false or misleading advertising that harms the owner of a mark by false or misleading statements about or comparisons with a mark owner's products or services.

The Lanham Act's false advertising provisions read as follows:

(a) *Civil Action*

Any person who, on or in connection with any goods or services, or any container for goods, uses in commerce any word, term, name, symbol, or device, or any combination thereof, or any false designation of origin, false or misleading description of fact, or false or misleading representation of fact, which –

(A) *is likely to cause confusion, or to cause mistake, or to deceive as to the affiliation, connection, or association of such person with another person, or as to the origin, sponsorship, or approval of his or her goods, services, or commercial activities by another person, or*

(B) *in commercial advertising or promotion, misrepresents the nature, characteristics, qualities, or geographic origin of his or her or another person's goods, services, or commercial activities,*

shall be liable in a civil action by any person who believes that he or she is or is likely to be damaged by such act.

While the Lanham Act provides excellent protection against both infringement and unfair competition through false advertising, it is a double-edged sword. Startups and other companies need to be extremely careful to avoid false and misleading comparisons to the products and services of competitors.

All advertising or promotional comparisons must be strictly factual, indisputably accurate, and well documented, with records retained for at least several years following the use of any comparative advertising.

Common Law Trademark Rights

As noted earlier, the first use of a mark to identify and distinguish goods or services in commerce in conjunction with the actual sale of those goods or services is what establishes trademark ownership rights and priority over later, junior users of the same or confusingly similar marks.

Registration with the USPTO is the best protection for a mark, but unregistered trademarks enjoy protections under state case and statutory law, much of which evolved from common law concepts involving unfair business practices and unfair competition.

If a baker, for example, operates for years in a town under the name "The Crust Station," laws have evolved by different means in different jurisdictions to prevent a newcomer from creating another bakery nearby, also called The Crust Station, and stealing away the customers of the original business. This is considered unfair confusion in the market.

The result above would be the same even if the newcomer had already just received a federal trademark registration for The Crust Station. Federal trademark registration does not create rights senior to or that otherwise displace senior common law trademark rights.

This is why Burger King is unable to put one of its restaurants within 20 miles of Gene and Betty Hoots's Burger King restaurant in Mattoon, Illinois, which had already been a Burger King for a decade before the more famous, national brand was created.

Because of the origins of these concepts in case law, these are often called "common law trademarks," but they are also called "unregistered trademarks."

Common law or unregistered trademarks also lose protection to the extent they are descriptive or generic.

Geographic Limitations. Common law trademarks are limited in geographic scope. A restaurant operated for years in a specific city might be able to keep a newer national rival by the same name from opening in the city, but not in other cities.

Expanding the above example, if the common law mark is used across a state-wide chain of restaurants, the national competitor might be prevented from using the same name anywhere in the state.

In the case of products or services sold *solely online* with an unregistered mark not used previously by others in connection with other similar goods or services, that mark would have seniority over the same or confusingly similar marks for substantially similar goods and services in every state where sales of those products or services have been made.

Lapse of Registration. Because seniority or priority of a mark depends on first use in commerce, the lapse of a federal trademark registration does not defeat common law trademark rights, provided that, and to the extent that, the mark is still being used in commerce to distinguish particular goods and services.

Remedies. Common law trademark remedies include stopping infringing uses and, in some states, damages for infringement. As noted earlier, federal trademark registration is required to file infringement claims in federal court and pursue Lanham Act claims for treble damages and attorneys' fees for willful infringement or statutory damages for counterfeit goods.

Trademark Searching

Before filing any trademark application, conduct a thorough "trademark search," or trademark clearance, to identify all similar marks with (i) federal registration or application priority or (ii) common law rights.

The objective of a trademark search is to determine whether consumers would be likely to confuse a proposed mark with any earlier-filed or earlier-used mark(s) for goods or services that are similar in kind or nature to those for the proposed mark.

PTO Search Guidance. There is a surprising degree of nuance and complexity involved in identifying marks that the USPTO or a court might view as "similar" and likely to cause confusion. As the following insightful excerpts from the July 2010 edition of the USPTO's publication "Inventors Eye" explains, marks can be confusingly similar if they sound the same or have the same meaning, regardless of spelling:

> *"There are two main factors to consider when conducting your search: the mark and the goods or services. A complete search is one that will uncover ALL similar marks, NOT just those that are identical. For example, consider marks that sound the same (SEYCOS v. SEIKO), have the same meaning (TORO ROJO v. RED BULL), or even have a similar commercial impression (GAS CITY v. GAS TOWN). Be cautious in analyzing marks that have even one same or similar word as a word featured in your mark....*
>
> *In addition, you must also consider the goods or services to determine possible "relatedness" such as similarities in nature, use, and marketing. For example, if your mark is identical to another on the registry but your goods or services are completely different, then you may be in luck. It is unlikely that someone will be confused and think that your CANTANKEROUS shoes come from the same source as someone else's CANTANKEROUS legal services...."*

TESS. Searching for marks with priority evidenced by prior federal registration or prior application for registration is relatively easy. It involves using the USPTO's free search system called TESS (Trademark Electronic Search System). Explore TESS at http://www.uspto.gov/trademarks.

The TESS system is easy to use and offers instructions and sample searches to guide first-time users.

Common Law Searches. Searching for marks with common law priority is more difficult because they are, by definition, unregistered, meaning there is no single online repository. A mark can have common law priority with little or no online presence.

Common law searches require searching the Internet for advertisements, websites, and articles that reference marks that are similar to and that involve goods and services that are related to a proposed mark. Other resources for common law trademark research include:

* state trademark registers managed by each state
  (e.g., https://www.sos.wa.gov/corps/trademark-home.aspx),

* newspapers,

* cases and administrative materials,

* business databases, like Dun & Bradstreet,

* Yellow Pages and similar contact information repositories, and

* other government databases, such as the SEC's EDGAR system.

As the list above suggests, common law trademark searches involve accessing disparate sources and may require special skills, expertise, and resources.

The complexity and difficulty of common law searches alone should be sufficient reason in most cases for hiring trademark counsel to handle the entire matter of conducting a comprehensive trademark search and analysis.

Federal Trademark Registration

As the USPTO says on its *"Trademark Basics"* web page, *"The trademark application process is a legal proceeding governed by U.S. law."*

Benefits of Federal Registration. The USPTO lists the following benefits of federal trademark registration in *Basic Facts about Trademarks*:

- *A legal presumption of your ownership of the mark and your exclusive right to use the mark nationwide on or in connection with the goods/services listed in the registration (whereas a state registration only provides rights within the borders of that one state, and common law rights exist only for the specific area where the mark is used);*

- *Public notice of your claim of ownership of the mark;*

- *Listing in the USPTO's online databases;*

- *The ability to record the U.S. registration with U.S. Customs and Border Protection to prevent importation of infringing foreign goods;*

- *The right to use the federal registration symbol "®";*

- *The ability to bring an action concerning the mark in federal court; and*

- *The use of the U.S. registration as a basis to obtain registration in foreign countries.*

Qualified trademark counsel should prepare and file trademark applications. Trademark registration begins with an online application using the Trademark Electronic Application System (TEAS) at http://www.uspto.gov/teas.

Filing Date Priority. A trademark's application filing date is legally significant, in that it establishes priority over later-filed applications for the same or similar marks. Later-filed applications will not be processed until an earlier filing is abandoned or rejected.

If a trademark search reveals that you may be second in line to register a particular mark, all is not lost. A trademark owner that has been using a mark in commerce already may have stronger rights than a prior applicant and may be able to intervene with an "opposition proceeding" and prevent the prior application from registering. Trademark counsel can advise how to proceed in such cases.

Required Information. The information required in a trademark application includes:

- owner of the mark ("Applicant"),

- name and address for correspondence, email address optional,

- depiction of the mark ("the drawing"),

- goods/services description,

- basis for the filing ("use in commerce" versus "intent to use"), and

- specimen of actual use in commerce for use-based applications.

Classes of Goods and Services. Trademark classes and descriptions are slightly different things. A trademark is registered under one or more classes, with each class requiring a separate fee. The description of the particular goods or services associated with a mark will generally be more specific.

In 1973, the U.S. classification system was replaced by the "International Classification of Goods and Services for the Purposes of the Registration of Marks." Europe and the United States have used the same 45 "Nice Categories" of goods and services (named after the city of Nice, France) since 1973.

By way of example, Class 42 is:

> *Scientific and technological services and research and design relating thereto; industrial analysis and research services; design and development of computer hardware and software.*

Descriptions of Goods and Services. Once an applicant has determined the correct class or classes, getting the description of goods and services right can be tricky. In examining an application, the USPTO uses the description to assess whether the mark conflicts with any marks with registration or application priority.

Marks with more narrowly described goods and services are more likely to get through the examination process. Once the USPTO grants a mark, however, the USPTO will use that same narrow description of goods and services to assess later-filed marks of other applicants, which may be less likely to be found to conflict with a prior, narrowly described mark.

Furthermore, the description of goods and services, and not just the class or classes, determines the scope of rights arising under a registered trademark. A mark with narrowly described goods and services may be less protective in the marketplace.

On the other hand, a description that is too broad relative to the actual goods or services offered may be subject to a successful challenge by an alleged infringer.

Even if the USPTO does not question a broad "statement of use" in reviewing a trademark application, a third party can later point to an overly broad and inaccurate statement of use to defend its trademark application or to defend against a trademark infringement claim. In either case, that third party would seek to invalidate the prior trademark registration as having been obtained by fraud against the USPTO.

A trademark owner cannot later expand a description to protect goods and services not contemplated by the original descriptions without filing an entirely new application and losing the earlier filing date for priority purposes. Trademark applicants must think carefully about how a mark's use might evolve and include those uses in the original application.

The following excerpt from the USPTO's *Basic Facts about Trademarks* is instructive.

> *You must list the specific goods/services for which you want to register your mark. If you are filing based upon "use in commerce," you must be using the mark in commerce on all the goods/ services listed. If you are filing based upon a "bona fide intent to use the mark," you must have a good faith or bona fide intent to use the mark on all the goods/services listed.*
>
> *You should check the USPTO's Acceptable Identification of Goods and Services Manual (ID Manual) at https://tmidm.uspto.gov/, which contains a listing of acceptable identifications of goods and services. Any entry you choose must accurately describe your goods/services. A failure to correctly list the goods/ services with which you use the mark, or intend to use the mark, may prevent you from registering your mark. You will not be given a refund of any fees paid.*
>
> *If the ID Manual does not contain an accurate listing for your goods/services, do not merely select an entry that seems "close." Instead, you must create your own identification, describing your goods/ services using clear, concise terms that the general public easily understands. If you list vague terms, such as "miscellaneous services" or "company name," your application will be considered void and you must file a new application.*

Office Actions. Once a trademark application is filed, the next step is awaiting what is called an "office action," an official letter from an examining attorney at the USPTO. Trademark applications rarely sail through without any questions or comments.

Office actions can raise all kinds of issues, but often they either (i) require the applicant to make simple revisions, such as clarifying the scope or nature of goods or services covered, called "requirements," or (ii) raise larger issues, called "refusals," such as refusing an application because the chosen mark is likely to be confused with an existing registered trademark.

Some of the more common "requirement" or "refusal" office actions include:

- Requirement for a "definite" identification of goods or services.
- Requirement to "disclaim" a portion of a trademark.
- Specimen refusal.
- Section 2(d) "likelihood of confusion" refusal.
- Section 2(e)(1) "descriptiveness" refusal.

Depending on the nature of the issues noted, some office actions require a written response to fix a problem, while others suggest calling or emailing the examining attorney to talk through one or more issues.

Dealing with challenging office actions is just one of several points in the regisration process where top trademark counsel add immeasurable value. They can frequently save applications that seem irreversibly destined for rejection. They are masters at negotiating the most precise and least harmful modifications to descriptions of goods or services necessary to resolve the examiner's concerns.

In some cases, applications get through with just one or two office actions, while other marks may be the subject of multiple office actions before eventually being accepted or rejected.

Failing to timely respond to an office action can result in the application ultimately being abandoned.

Publication and Comment Period. If an application makes it through the review process, the examining attorney will approve the mark for publication in the "Official Gazette," a weekly publication of the USPTO. The USPTO will send a notice of publication to the applicant stating the date of publication.

This phase can be somewhat nerve-wracking for an applicant. After a mark is published, others have 30 days to file either an opposition to registration or a request to extend the time to oppose.

Comments in opposition can result in the examining attorney reopening their review in light of new information and can even result in rejection of the application.

One approach for saving an application in the face of an opposition is working directly with the third party behind the opposition to work out a Co-existence Agreement.

Co-existence Agreements

As already discussed, a Co-existence Agreement is a contract between two parties in which one or both of the parties make certain concessions and assurances as to how their mark(s) will appear, in what marketing channels and contexts, in connection with what goods and services and so forth, in order to minimize risks of consumer confusion.

The party in the weaker position may be required to do things like:

- only use the mark in combination with other words, such as the mark owner's company name,

- change the color, font style, or other visual attributes of a logo,

- refrain from using the mark in certain marketing channels, and

- agree not to apply to register new marks which might be confusingly similar to the mark claimed to have been infringed.

Co-existence Agreements can be short and to the point and they can be longer, more detailed, and more heavy-handed against one of the parties, depending on the relative strengths of the parties' positions and the potential likelihood and severity of any consumer confusion.

In the context of an opposition following the publication of a mark, the examining attorney will consider the concessions and assurances of the parties negotiating a Co-existence Agreement and make his or her own independent decision as to whether the likelihood of confusion has been sufficiently addressed.

Claims of trademark infringement are another context in which Co-existence Agreements can be used to address another party's concerns.

And lastly, they are also sometimes used in connection with attempts by competitors to bully another company into reducing the effectiveness of their advertising and branding. In this context, the bullying company might send a demand letter making baseless infringement claims in order to coerce the other company into signing a Co-existence Agreement forcing the other company to change its colors, mark wording, or other branding elements or to stay out of certain marketing channels.

The Madrid System and Foreign Trademark Registration

The "Madrid System" for the international registration of trademarks lets trademark owners seek protection for their marks in multiple countries through the filing of one application, in one language, with one set of fees, paid in one currency.

The Madrid System is administered by the World Intellectual Property Organization's ("WIPO") International Bureau, and is based primarily on a treaty called "The Protocol Relating to the Madrid Agreement Concerning the International Registration of Marks," or the "Madrid Protocol."

Even with the Madrid System, pursuing trademark protections beyond the U.S. can be challenging and often requires the coordinated assistance of multiple international law firms. This is because each country still reviews and determines eligibility for registration of a mark based on its own standards.

Pursuing a global trademark registration strategy usually requires hiring well-established U.S. trademark counsel with a global network of trusted foreign trademark counsel. The U.S. counsel takes responsibility for assigning, managing and tracking the work, and even the billings, of foreign counsel.

Execution of a global trademark strategy can be relatively smooth for extremely strong marks, but even moderately strong marks can encounter snags, particularly if the mark has an unexpected meaning or connotation in a foreign language.

It is also very important to keep in mind that while some countries, like the U.S. and England, award trademark protections based on first use of a mark, many countries award protection based on being first to file a trademark registration application.

The existence of first-to-file systems in other countries requires promptly executing on any foreign trademark registration strategies. Persons known as squatters can watch pending U.S. trademark registrations to file for those same trademarks in first-to-file countries, with the expectation of "squatting" on them and trying to sell them to the U.S. trademark applicants.

Trade Dress

The following excerpt is footnote 1 from a key 1992 U.S. Supreme Court case, captioned _Two Pesos, Inc. v. Taco Cabana, Inc._ It provides a good overview of trade dress protections under the Lanham Act:

> *[Footnote 1] The District Court instructed the jury: "[T]rade dress" is the total image of the business. Taco Cabana's trade dress may include the shape and general appearance of the exterior of the restaurant, the identifying sign, the interior kitchen floor plan, the decor, the menu, the equipment used to serve food, the servers' uniforms, and other features reflecting on the total image of the restaurant. 1 App. 83-84. The Court of Appeals accepted this definition and quoted from Blue Bell Bio-Medical v. Cin-Bad, Inc., 864 F.2d 1253, 1256 (CA5 1989): "The 'trade dress' of a product is essentially its total image and overall appearance." See 932 F.2d 1113, 1118 (CA5 1991). It*

"involves the total image of a product, and may include features such as size, shape, color or color combinations, texture, graphics, or even particular sales techniques."

John H. Harland Co. v. Clarke Checks, Inc., 711 F.2d 966, 980 (CA11 1983). Restatement (Third) of Unfair Competition 16, Comment a (Tent. Draft No. 2, Mar. 23, 1990).

Fortunately, most startups do not need to focus too much on trade dress, because it is, hands down, the fuzziest and quirkiest area of intellectual property. Some of those quirks include:

- trade dress cannot cover "functional" features,

- registering trade dress elements for trademark protection is notoriously difficult, with most applications drawing difficult-to-overcome objections based on "descriptiveness" and "functionality,"

- proving trade dress "distinctiveness" in competitive markets is fact-intensive and challenging, and

- all elements must be considered, both those that are distinctive and those that might be descriptive or generic; the entirety of what is sought to be protected must be distinctive or strongly associated with the source of the goods.

The present standard for determining whether a trade dress element(s) is "functional" or not is the not-so-bright-line test of whether it *is essential to the use or purpose of the article or affects the cost or quality of the article.*" Can a catchy website button or radial dial pass this test? Or a cool new trigger design on a game controller?

Beyond these hurdles, the ultimate test for whether all or part of a product's appearance constitutes protectable trade dress comes down to whether it is "inherently distinctive" or has acquired "secondary meaning." Secondary meaning in this context requires that the visual design elements in question have become associated in the mind of the public with the source of the goods.

Fortunately, many products can take a more certain route to the protection of visual elements beyond trademarkable words and logos by seeking product "design patents." These are discussed later under *Patents*. In short, design patents protect the "ornamental design" of functional items.

There are certainly cases where seeking to register trade dress elements for trademark protection makes sense, despite the potential difficulties and costs of doing so. More often, however, trade dress rights may be more successfully invoked defensively in cases of blatant infringement, as discussed below in Case Study #30, *Too Much Flattery*.

Trademarks and Domain Names

In Chapter 5, we discussed the importance of securing key domain names at the earliest opportunity, including a reasonable range of top-level domain variants, as well as likely variations and misspellings consumers might inadvertently use.

UDRP. As noted earlier, WIPO's UDRP process is a key legal tool for wrestling a domain name away from a cybersquatter sitting on it in bad faith. UDRP stands for Uniform Domain-Name Dispute-Resolution Policy.

Technically speaking, UDRP is a privately administered quasi-legal process trademark owners can use to cause WIPO to reassign a domain name to the holder of a trademark associated with that domain name.

Under the current domain name registration scheme, any registrant seeking to register a domain name must represent and warrant, among other things, that registering the name *"will not infringe upon or otherwise violate the rights of any third party,"* and agree to participate in an arbitration-like proceeding should any third party assert such a claim. This representation and warranty and related consent are the underpinnings of the UDRP process.

A claimant must prove three elements to prevail in a UDRP action:

- the domain name is identical or confusingly similar to a trademark or service mark in which the complainant has rights,

- the registrant does not have any rights or legitimate interests in the domain name, and

- the domain name has been registered and is being used in "bad faith."

Proving "bad faith" is the key to success in a UDRP action. The panel looking at the matter is required to consider the following in its assessment:

- whether the registrant registered the domain name primarily for selling, renting, or otherwise transferring the domain name registration to the complainant who is the owner of the trademark or service mark,

- whether the registrant registered the domain name to prevent the owner of the trademark or service mark from using the mark in a domain name,

- if the domain name owner has engaged in a pattern of such conduct,

- whether the registrant registered the domain name primarily for the purpose of disrupting the business of a competitor, and

- whether by using the domain name, the registrant has intentionally attempted to attract, for commercial gain, internet users to the registrant's website, by creating a likelihood of confusion with the complainant's mark.

While success in a UDRP generally results in re-assignment of the domain name in question and that is the end of the matter, UDRP decisions can be challenged in court and even overturned.

ACPA. The Anticybersquatting Consumer Protection Act ("ACPA") was enacted as new section 43(d) of the Lanham Act in 1999 to fight domain registration abuses. The ACPA provides a cause of action for registering, trafficking in, or using a domain name confusingly similar to, or dilutive of, a trademark or personal name, with bad faith intent to profit from that mark.

Again, bad faith is a required element, and a court may consider a variety of factors regarding the accused person's circumstances and conduct, including:

- the person's trademark or other IP rights, if any, in the domain name,

- the person's prior use, if any, of the domain name in connection with offering any goods or services,

- the person's bona fide noncommercial or fair use of the mark in a site using the domain name,

- the person's intent to divert consumers from the mark owner's online location to a site that could harm the goodwill represented by the mark, either for commercial gain or with the intent to tarnish or disparage the mark, by creating a likelihood of confusion as to the source, sponsorship, affiliation, or endorsement of the site,

- the person's offer to transfer, sell, or otherwise assign the domain name to the mark owner or any third party for financial gain without having used, or having an intent to use, the domain name to offer goods or services, or the person's prior conduct indicating a pattern of such conduct,

- the person's provision of misleading contact information when applying for the registration of the domain name or prior conduct indicating a pattern of such conduct,

- the person's registration or acquisition of multiple domain names which the person knows are identical or confusingly similar to marks of others that are distinctive at the time of registration of such domain names, or dilutive of famous marks of others that are famous at the time of registration of such domain names, and

- the extent to which the mark incorporated in the person's domain name registration is or is not distinctive and famous.

The ACPA also provides that bad faith intent *"...shall not be found in any case in which the court determines that the person believed and had reasonable grounds to believe that the use of the domain name was a fair use or otherwise lawful."*

The UDRP process is probably the more commonly chosen route for fighting garden-variety cyber-squatting, since it is both cheaper and faster than filing a lawsuit under the ACPA.

The ACPA, on the other hand, allows for damages, which are unavailable under the UDRP.

Likeness, Publicity and False Endorsement Rights

As exemplified by *Dave's Killer Bread's* branding, a person's name or likeness can develop into a trademark and be registered as a trademark.

Many celebrities register their names and likenesses as trademarks. The key requirement for trade-marking a name or likeness is that it be used in connection with branding a product or service.

Other rights protecting a person's name and likeness have evolved out of common law, and virtually all states now have statutory protections prohibiting the use of a person's name, photo, image, likeness, or voice for commercial purposes or financial gain without their permission.

These rights are often called "likeness rights" and "rights of publicity."

Remedies and penalties under these statutes generally include injunctive relief (stopping the conduct), damages, and recovery of profits from the violation. Some statutes also allow for punitive damages.

Washington State, for example, has codified name and likeness rights as property rights in RCW 63.60.010, which provides in part:

> *Property right—Use of name, voice, signature, photograph, or likeness.*
>
> *Every individual or personality has a property right in the use of his or her name, voice, signature, photograph, or likeness.*

Section 43(a) of the Lanham Act provides protection at the federal level in the form of rights against false endorsement, association, or affiliation, which are based in and arise out of unfair competition law.

Such claims are supported by Section 43(a)'s prohibition against the use of a name, a false designation of origin, or a false or misleading description or representation of fact which is likely to cause confusion or to deceive about the affiliation or association of a person with another person.

Trademark Disputes

Anecdotally, it seems like claims of trademark infringement are the most common form of IP dispute. Patent disputes are usually more expensive. Copyright disputes involving stolen riffs are usually more intriguing. And even trade secret theft allegations seem to make the headlines more often. But trademark disputes arise with remarkable frequency.

The biggest reasons for this are likely the obviousness of trademark infringements and the importance companies place on branding and advertising. When a third party's perceived trademark infringement thwarts a mark owner's expensive and carefully executed advertising strategies, this rarely goes unnoticed.

Trademark disputes can arise (i) before a trademark application is filed, (ii) while an application is pending, (iii) during the 30-day period after publication of an allowed mark in the Official Gazette, or (iv) years after a trademark has been registered and in regular use.

Sophisticated companies continually monitor for infringing marks and actively defend against them. Third parties provide these monitoring services at fairly reasonable costs, and the fees are usually worth paying. A monitoring service flagged the infringement described in Case Study #21, *Throwing Scissors.*

Demand Letters. Most trademark disputes begin with "demand letters" from IP counsel claiming that a company's entity name or product name is somehow improperly close to that of another company.

The following anonymized and redacted excerpt is from a demand letter initiating a dispute between two companies:

"As your client may be aware, Company X is a well-known enterprise software services provider specializing in…. Company X has been providing its services to customers nationwide, and adopted the iconic Company X logo in 2014. Over the past several years, Company X has developed common law rights in the Company X logo mark in connection with XYZ services. To protect its goodwill and investment, Company X diligently polices and enforces its trademark rights.

It has come to Company X's attention that Company Y has adopted a highly similar logo and filed an application to register the logo as part of the larger Company Y trademark with the United States Patent and Trademark Office ("USPTO") covering goods and services which directly overlap with those offered by Company X. From our initial research, it appears that your client offers services in the same channels of trade potentially marketing to the same customers as Company X…."

Counsel for larger or better-funded companies sometimes use demand letters like the above to bully less established companies into changing or abandoning their trademarks, service marks, and logos. They can be unnerving to receive, particularly when a company on the receiving end has invested resources in a mark that is performing well in the market.

Response Letters. Fortunately, many of these demand letters are sent with little conviction behind them.

While there is no single formula for making these issues go away, an excellent first step is to contact trusted trademark counsel and get their take on how to respond. Claims of infringement are often overstated and easily countered in a thoughtful response letter from counsel.

The initial response to any demand letter incorrectly claiming infringement should rebut the claims in detail, applying many of the concepts discussed above concerning "likelihood of confusion." A rebuttal letter might methodically address facts relating to the following, as applicable:

- the marks are spelled differently,

- the marks are pronounced differently,

- the words in the marks have different meanings,

- the overall "commercial impression" created by each mark is different,

- the marks are used in different commercial contexts – wholesale versus retail, business-to-business versus business-to-consumer,

- the marks are advertised in different ways and different marketing verticals,

- the marks are used to identify goods and services that are unrelated,

- the extent to which the accused mark is legally stronger than the other mark, with reference to the fanciful, arbitrary, generic, descriptive or suggestive classifications, and

- the absence of any known instances of consumer confusion between the two marks.

The response letter should raise every conceivable factual and legal argument disputing and disproving "likelihood of confusion" to make the issue go away. This is not a context where arguments should be held in reserve and revealed later for dramatic effect.

Additionally, it is always worth researching any weaknesses in the claimant's position.

- Who has been using the mark longer?

- Whose mark is more famous?

- Are there any inconsistencies with the claimant's mark's description of goods and services and how the claimant is using the mark?

- Does it appear that the claimant misrepresented anything to the USPTO in obtaining registration of the mark?

- Any other bases for attacking the claimant's trademark registration that might turn the tables and make the accusers think twice about picking a fight?

Coming back with a strong rebuttal to any claim of trademark infringement can sometimes dampen a mark owner's enthusiasm for pursuing the conflict.

Having seen this process from both sides, it is worth noting that infringement concerns often originate with non-lawyer marketing, brand, or product personnel in a company demanding that the law department take action.

An articulate, well-grounded rebuttal letter that threatens a viable counter-attack can give inhouse counsel the arguments they need to talk their marketing, brand, or product colleagues out of pursuing the conflict.

When a second or third demand letter continues to claim infringement after you have made your strongest rebuttal arguments, there are several courses of action to consider:

- writing up and proposing a Co-existence Agreement,

- doing nothing and hoping the other party loses interest in the issue,

- preparing a lawsuit called a "declaratory judgment action," sharing a courtesy copy of it with the other side, and possibly letting them know they have a brief window of time to settle the entire matter before the suit is filed.

Deciding which of these strategies to pursue depends entirely on the facts and circumstances. Others may have a different view, but Co-existence Agreements rarely seem to resolve aggressive infringement claims unless the claimed infringer agrees to make radical changes to their mark or how they use it.

Doing nothing, on the other hand, is often surprisingly effective. As two or three month pass and the other side starts to see actual legal bills from repeated back and forth legal correspondence, and as the full scope of issues in a potential lawsuit come into view more clearly, instigators of such claims sometimes lose their enthusiasm and allow the matter to die quietly. After responding to one or two demand letters, about half the time I adopt the *"do nothing"* approach, depending on the facts and circumstances.

Declaratory Judgment Action. A key risk of doing nothing, however, is being sued in an inconvenient and disadvantageous jurisdiction. Hence the reason for considering option three – threatening and then filing a declaratory judgment action.

The following is an excerpt on "DJ actions" from my book, *Contract Drafting and Negotiation for Entrepreneurs and Business Professionals.*

What is a DJ Action?

… A declaratory judgment action, or "DJ action," is a lawsuit that can be filed after one or both parties have begun "saber rattling" by sending notices of breach, demand letters or other communications evidencing a dispute.

In a DJ action, the plaintiff who files the suit will describe the dispute, including any unsuccessful efforts to resolve it, and request that the court issue a judgment "declaring the rights and obligations" of the parties and awarding appropriate damages. Contract disputes make up a meaningful percentage of DJ actions filed.

Courtesy Copy Prior to Filing

One element of the author's preferred strategy in using DJ actions involves sharing the draft lawsuit with the other side just hours before filing it. Again, this strategy is particularly effective when you can claim a hometown jurisdiction advantage by filing first, the facts and law are on your side, and you have a good litigator behind you.…

In the author's experience, once a courtesy copy of a well-drafted complaint has been received by opposing counsel, it usually is not long before requests to talk are received. If the parties can be brought together the same morning to try to resolve the dispute, the dispute can often be wrapped up the same day or within days.

Sometimes the other party's principals will be unavailable to weigh in on the emergency settlement talks and opposing counsel will ask for a delay in the lawsuit's filing. This can be agreed to, but only if the other party agrees in writing in a formal "standstill" agreement to not file its own lawsuit first.

In the event a standstill cannot be negotiated, the better approach is often to file the suit, while agreeing to hold off on serving the complaint for a few days while the parties negotiate. Although the lawsuit will still become a matter of public record, not formally serving the complaint gives the other party additional time to respond by not starting the 20 or 30 day clock for filing an answer.

This is definitely hardball, but where the facts warrant it, it is a tactic that often delivers excellent results very quickly. Of course, one always has to be prepared for the possibility that the other party is not going to back down. As a tactical matter, some recipients of a DJ action understand that they could improve their negotiating position by filing a formal answer and at least feigning interest in putting up a strong defense.

But if the facts and law are in your favor and you also have the hometown advantage, a prolonged, aggressive response to a DJ action is unlikely.

A significant factor in deciding whether to pursue a DJ action is whether the potential defendant's direct dealings with the potential plaintiff, or its business activities within the plaintiff's home state, are sufficient to subject the potential defendant to "personal jurisdiction" there. A DJ action in a defendant's home state can still be effective, but it is less likely to result in a quick settlement.

Case Study #27, *Throwing Scissors*, and Case Study #28, *Trolling for Trouble*, are both examples of Declaratory Judgment Actions being used to resolve trademark disputes.

International Trademark Registration Scams

Almost 100% of the time that companies file trademark registrations with the USPTO, those companies subsequently receive scam notices and invoices.

For information on these scams, search online for "Caution: misleading notices USPTO" and go to the USPTO webpage that comes up.

For numerous examples of these scam notices and invoices, search online for "Warning: Requests for Payment of Fees – WIPO" and go to the World Intellectual Property Organization page that comes up by that title.

Study these examples and share them with bookkeepers or others who might otherwise fall for these scams, as it would be impossible to recover money sent to these foreign criminal enterprises.

Case Study #27 – Throwing Scissors

This case study validates the importance of registering trademarks quickly, and it also illustrates the importance of conducting trademark searches before investing in expensive branding and marketing campaigns.

A mega "global communications agency headquartered in London" issued a press release announcing that it was launching a U.S. based subsidiary to offer a suite of marketing analytics services.

Great idea, except for one detail. The name for the new company and its services was identical to one of my companies' names, and it conflicted with our pending trademark registrations.

We promptly notified them of the direct conflict and the high likelihood of confusion and warned them to cease using the name immediately.

Communications with the other company were unusual from the outset. They stubbornly insisted on not involving lawyers. We told them that was unacceptable and that they would be dealing with me and other attorneys from two law firms.

It reminded me of a time when, as kids, my brother accidentally caused a large pair of scissors to impale me. In fairness, I did ask him to throw the scissors. I also expected him to say something like, "*Ok, catch.*"

Without warning, the scissors plunged through my right leg. Neither of us could pull them out. Several times he said, *'Don't tell mom and dad, we'll get in trouble.'*

I did not listen to my brother then, and we made it clear to these infringers that our side would communicate solely through counsel and they should as well.

They had spent millions of dollars preparing for this huge launch. It was a major strategic initiative. But had they really failed to perform a basic trademark clearance? In their correspondence, they put up a tough front, denying any likelihood of confusion and giving no signs of backing down.

We had at least five possible paths from which to choose , which I credit to my favorite trademark attorney, Robert Cumbow of Miller Nash Graham & Dunn LLP:

1. do nothing; accept their low-risk-of-confusion arguments, take a wait-and-see approach and renew our concerns later if circumstances warrant doing so,

2. write back and stick to our original position that they must immediately stop using the mark,

3. write back and suggest that they agree to use their mark always and only in conjunction with their parent company mark, never as a standalone mark,

4. write back and suggest that they file to register their mark and if the USPTO refuses them because of our mark, they'll abide by that and change their mark; but if the USPTO doesn't cite our mark against theirs, we'll abide by that and agree to coexist, or

5. write back and suggest that they provide us with specific terms of a proposed coexistence agreement, then see if we can negotiate something satisfactory.

We went with #2 and pushed back firmly. Our final correspondence, authored largely by Bob Cumbow, said, in part:

> *The founders of [Company X], Inc. invested considerable time, effort, cost, and creativity into naming their company and its principal product, and they did not do so in order to have a second-comer usurp from them the market distinctiveness of their chosen name and mark. They are embarking on a nationwide roll-out of their product, have a business presence in 33 U.S. states, and are already growing rapidly. They cannot afford to have to "share" their unique and distinctive mark with another company so likely to be perceived by consumers as operating in the same field as their own.*

They ignored our demands for weeks and continued their rollout, launching additional promotional materials that conflicted with our online marketing efforts. They eventually sent a final letter stating, among other things:

> *We have thoughtfully considered your letter. We respectfully decline to discontinue our use of*
>
> *[THE INFRINGING MARK] and will continue to use the term as a proposition to improve marketing communications for our clients.*

It seemed to us that, as a large multinational, they thought they could bully us into submission and steal our mark. But we had other plans. During their delays, we had begun drafting a lawsuit.

Just one week after their final letter, I sent them a courtesy copy of the lawsuit, with the following redacted email:

> *Hello Mr. Smith,*
>
> *Attached please find a complaint that we are in the process of filing today against your client [Company Y], Inc. in the U.S. District Court for the Western District of Washington here in Seattle.*
>
> *Please share this with your clients at your convenience and let me know if you have any questions. I will try to reach you by telephone to confirm your timely receipt of this courtesy notice.*
>
> *Mr. Bob C of [Law Firm A] is still very involved with this matter, and Mr. William K of [Law Firm B] will be handling the litigation, but for the time being, all inquiries by you or by other counsel for [Company Y], Inc. should be directed to me at this email address or the phone number below.*
>
> *If your client is willing to immediately agree to abide by our prior cease and desist notices before the suit is filed, please let me know. Time is very short, though, as we are essentially en route to the courthouse.*
>
> *Lastly, please advise your client that non-lawyer representatives of [Company Y] should not directly contact any of my colleagues at [Company X, Inc.].*
>
> *Sincerely,*
>
> *Paul Swegle*

They did not timely respond, and the complaint was filed. And it was a doozy:

- violations of the federal trademark statute, the Lanham Act, 15 U.S.C. §1125,
- common law trademark infringement,
- common law unfair competition, and
- violation of the Unfair Business Practices Act, RCW 19.86 (treble/3x damages).

Despite my requests that non-lawyers at the other company not contact me or my colleagues,

an officer sent me a cordial email expressing hope that the lawyers could work things out. He included this pseudo-Zen dig:

> *Apologies in advance, and at the risk of offending your profession, my experience of US law is that it's easy to create heat and not light. Once attorneys start sending letters or mails, nuance and sentiment can be lost.*

I remember thinking, *"The disconnect is strong."*

But just a couple weeks after the lawsuit was filed, the other side's tough talk spontaneously evaporated. It was replaced with anxious pleas to resolve the matter "before year-end." It was mid-December.

The lawsuit struck a nerve somewhere high in the organization. It was possibly going to become a distracting year-end reporting and disclosure matter.

Within a month of filing, we were able to force them to abandon any use of the mark in the U.S. and to grant us rights to use the mark in the EU. Total litigation costs on our side were around $6,000.

> <u>Lessons:</u> Sometimes where there is heat, there is light. We prevailed by turning up the heat to *"carpet of fire,"* a very reliable setting. The lawsuit elevated the matter to higher authorities who wanted nothing to do with a lopsided U.S. trademark infringement lawsuit.
>
> When a lawsuit is all-but-inevitable, filing first creates big tactical advantages. Our suit established our hometown advantage for venue and jurisdiction, and Washington law as the applicable state law. Had we delayed, they might have filed in California.
>
> Knowing local court rules and procedures without the need to rely on local counsel in another jurisdiction is another big advantage.
>
> This case study also validates registering trademarks as soon as possible and monitoring for infringements with online notification from services like Google Alerts.

Case Study #28 – Trolling for Trouble

We had merged our company with a larger company. The acquiror's branding was substantially different, so we knew changes were coming.

The federally registered mark for our primary service offering had, as its second half, a fairly common word. For the sake of anonymity, let us say the word was "maker."

There were other companies with this same word as the second half of their trademark, including one that was pretty well known.

Given that our two companies' services were completely different, the likelihood of confusion seemed low, and the companies co-existed in the market for years without concern.

It also probably helped that our logos looked quite a bit different. Before selling our company, our trademarked logo was green and gray. Their logo was two other colors – we'll call them "the Other Colors."

But the company that acquired us had a long tradition of using a logo prominently featuring one of the Other Colors. When the branding experts were finished working over our previously green and gray logo, they came up with a logo consisting of the Other Colors.

It looked nearly identical to the other company. Both companies had names composed of two words, the second of which was identical. Now, both marks would be displayed with the first word being one of the Other Colors and the other word being the second of the Other Colors.

I had been alerted to the issue somewhat early by colleagues who were concerned about the preliminary designs and asked me whether I was concerned about the similarities.

I kept my cards close but quickly approached the second in command at the acquiring company, where I was now also an officer. I pointed out the similarities and told him I was fairly certain the other company would bring a claim.

I asked him if we could at least switch the order of the colors from how the other company used them to lower our risk of a claim. He told me he would run the suggestion through the design committee and get back to me.

A couple of weeks later, the same officer informed me that the design committee had rejected my suggested change.

I took another run at the issue with the same officer, saying, with a simple color switch, we could probably save a couple hundred thousand in legal fees and have a more defensible brand.

He smiled and shrugged a bit and said, *"Let's see what happens."*

It did not take long. The first demand letter from the Chicago-based company arrived within a couple of months of the new branding rollout.

The other company had the appearance of being well-funded, based on its high profile in the market. A well-known media conglomerate had recently acquired it. The demand letter was on the letterhead of a very prominent IP law firm.

The arguments in our written response focused on the companies' entirely different markets and service offerings, the absence of any prior market confusion whatsoever, and the lack of distinctiveness to the second word of each mark, which was identical.

While we did not dispute the similarity of the colors, we maintained in good faith that there was no likelihood of confusion.

It was clear the other side was not backing down. Unable to convince our team to try to settle the matter by offering to switch the order of the colors, I urged that we should at least take the initiative and file a declaratory judgment action in federal court in Seattle before they sued us in Chicago.

We did so, and the other side seemed completely caught off guard. Because of our position in the Seattle area, they struggled to find strong local counsel willing to take a case against us.

Their defense of the case never seemed to get off the ground. They requested several extensions from the court and seemed to put little effort into the case.

Within about six months, we received a letter from the same high-end IP law firm that had started the fracas. They were waving the white flag and asking if we would enter into a Co-existence Agreement and drop the case.

We negotiated a very light Co-existence Agreement requiring the companies to simply be cautious about doing anything else that might create confusion in the market, but we did not have to change the logo.

While we never knew for sure exactly what was going on, we did know that the media conglomerate that owned the other company was experiencing financial challenges, and we assumed that those pressures caused the other company to lose interest in a potentially costly legal fight with us in Seattle.

Lessons: The lesson here is, do not take unnecessary risks with a logo that bears strong similarities to that of another prominent company. Our new leaders took us down a path that could have wasted a quarter million dollars with no guarantee of victory.

Another takeaway is the value of filing first in your hometown when faced with nearly certain litigation in a different jurisdiction. The added difficulty, cost, and inconvenience of dealing with federal litigation in Seattle seemed to have tipped the balance in our favor. When resources tightened, our jurisdictional advantages were likely key factors in forcing the other side's early surrender.

Case Study #29 – Dare to Compare

There are few better ways of attracting hostile attention from competing companies than by making unflattering advertising comparisons to their products. Virtually 100% of the time that my clients make such comparisons, whether fair and accurate or not, they receive a puffed up demand letter from the competitor's lawyers.

And in one instance, a competitor sent a federal regulator after a company where I was a senior officer to investigate complaints about an advertisement the regulator had previously reviewed and approved. The competitor's complaint and the regulator's new perspective against the comparative advertisement were both baseless, so I didn't tell my advertising team they *had* to pull it down. But I did tell them we'd likely be clobbered by the regulator if we didn't. My advertising team stood their ground and we were hit with an undeserved $240K fine. The regulators had started out at $1M, but a colleague and I negotiated it down to $240K.

With that scuffle in my background, it was interesting to counsel a client that wanted to compare their product in a detailed, feature-based comparison chart against several competitors. The client's CEO asked me to review their advertising mock-up. It was clear from the graphics and the underlying research that they had spent at least $30K on the project.

As with all comparative advertising proposals, I warned him of the risks that one or more of the competitors could come after them, likely first with demand letters to remove the comparisons, but potentially also with an unexpected lawsuit in a distant and unfavorable venue.

Unfazed, and perhaps skeptical, the CEO said:

> *"Why do you think they'll come after us? We're just telling the truth."*
>
> *"Because they can,"* I said, adding, *"If I were their attorney, I would tell them to do the same thing.*
>
> *It's easier and less expensive to threaten litigation than it is to quickly fix a product.'*

The CEO said:

"They have to tell me what's wrong with the ad before I'm changing it."

I replied:

"Although it might look better later to a court or jury for them to warn and guide you that way, they have absolutely no obligation to do so.'"

The company went forward with the advertising and the first demand letter came within two weeks. It was relatively short, seeking amicable resolution but threatening legal action based on the following basic claims:

"… the comparative advertising claims are literally false and constitute false advertising in violation of Section 43(a) of the Lanham Act, as well as state statutory and common law."

The CEO was busy at the time, so he decided to just remove that competitor from the comparison chart for the time being. After consultation with the client and trademark attorney Bob Cumbow, we wrote back the following, anonymized here:

"…Better Company denies that any of the comparisons made by it to Lesser Company's competitive products and services are false. Better Company stands by all of its advertising claims and is confident that each and every one of them is true.

As you are no-doubt aware, case law and U.S. regulatory policy strongly favor truthful, informative comparative advertising.

Notwithstanding the foregoing, and for reasons unrelated to the strength of our client's position in this matter, Better Company is voluntarily electing to cease running the advertisements cited in your letter. Better Company may very well run similar comparative advertising in the future and will vigorously defend its right to do so.…"

Only a few weeks passed before another demand letter arrived from the law firm of another competitor. Again, the alleged violations included:

1. *Trademark infringement under the Lanham Act 15 U.S.C. §1125(a)*

2. *Unfair competition and false advertising under Section 43(a) of the Lanham Act (15 U.S.C. §1125(a)*

3. *Unfair competition as per the common law of the United States and the state of Maryland*

4. *Unfair competition and false advertising under the statutory law of the state of Maryland*

5. *Tortious conduct under the statutory law of the state of Maryland, and*

6. *Other unlawful activity.*

We again reviewed every comparative element in the advertisement and made another set of revisions to remove all subjective marketing language, leaving only provable, factual, fair and accurate comparative elements.

We then responded to the demand letter asserting, among other things:

> "...As you may know, far from being "unfair competition," truthful and non-deceptive comparative advertising is encouraged as a means of providing consumers with information important to their purchasing decisions...."

We also added:

> "Better Company, LLC is revising its comparative advertising to provide the clearest, most concrete comparative points for customers, and is willing to revise any statement that you can demonstrate is false, if you provide us with a clear indication of why your client believes that statement to be false and what it believes to be a more accurate statement."

Concerning use of the competitor's logo in the advertisement, we made the following "nominative use" argument, which has been adopted in some, but not all, circuits:

> "...the doctrine of Nominative Fair Use allows an advertiser to use the trademark or trade name of a competitor in order to clearly identify the company whose products are being compared with its own...."

We cited two cases supporting nominative fair use-type arguments in the 4th Circuit, where the competitor was located: _Rosetta Stone Ltd. v. Google_, 676 F.3d 144, 155 (4th Cir. 2012) and _Radiance Found., Inc. v. NAACP_, 786 F.3d 316 (4th Cir. 2015).

Opposing counsel replied with one specific example of what the competitor viewed to be an inaccurate comparison. Counsel claimed there were still numerous others, but added that the competitor was under no obligation to guide Better Company, and again demanded that Better Company remove the competitor's logo, tacitly acknowledging no grounds for removing the competitor's name.

My client replaced the competitor's logo in the comparative chart with its non-stylized name and we reviewed the comparative chart again to ensure that we had removed all subjective comparisons, leaving only factually accurate and verifiable comparisons. Finally, the demand letters stopped coming.

My final advice to him on this matter was to research all of the comparative elements against all of the competitors monthly to ensure continued accuracy.

> Lessons: If you dare to compare, (i) be _completely_ fair, accurate, and purely factual, with no subjective marketing puffery, (ii) budget at least $10K to $20K in legal expenses for the inevitable back and forth of cease and desist letters and responses, and (iii) be reasonably certain that the financial and distraction risks of potential litigation, possibily in a distant venue, are worth the advertising benefits.

Copyrights

Copyrights and patents are both enshrined in Article 1, Section 8 of the U.S. Constitution, which includes the following regarding the powers of Congress:

> ...To promote the Progress of Science and useful Arts, by securing for limited Times to Authors and Inventors the exclusive Right to their respective Writings and Discoveries;...

Under that authority, Congress adopted the U.S. Copyright Act of 1976, or the Copyright Act for short. Every startup should make periodic assessments of opportunities and risks under copyright law.

- What "works" should be registered, and when and how?

- Where should copyright notices be used?

- Should potential infringements be monitored and, if so, how?

- What risks are there of accidental infringement of others' copyrights, and how should those risks be managed?

Copyright holders enjoy exclusive rights to modify, distribute, perform, display, and copy their protected works. For media companies, gaming companies, design companies, and others involved in creating, licensing, selling, and collaborating on content, having copyright counsel involved is a given.

Software as a service ("SaaS") companies, and other software-driven businesses often have more nuanced questions of when to rely on copyright law versus patent law or trade secret law.

For other types of businesses, a general understanding of copyright law is still necessary to ensure the proper identification and protection of copyrights and for avoiding expensive mistakes involving the copyrights of others.

Works of Authorship

The Copyright Act protects "original works of authorship fixed in any tangible medium of expression, now known or later developed, from which they can be perceived, reproduced, or otherwise communicated, either directly or with the aid of a machine or device." 17 U.S.C. § 102(a).

"Works of authorship" include, but are not limited to, literary works, musical works (including words or lyrics), dramatic works (including any accompanying music), pictures, drawings, graphics, sculptures, architectural works, motion pictures, sound recordings, computer software, video games, websites and other types of print or digital content or imagery.

Author as Owner. As we have discussed already, copyrights belong, by default, to the "author," or creator, of a work. Fortunately, works created by an employee within the scope of his or her employment are deemed to have been authored by the employer as "works made for hire."

But that is not the case with consultants or independent contractors. That is why agreements with effective "works made for hire" language should always be used when hiring consultants and independent contractors. That is the best approach for ensuring undisputed ownership of works produced by contractors and other third parties.

Original. Although works must be "original," works that are fortuitously similar, or even identical, may still each enjoy copyright protection. This clearly excludes works that are copies of other works, but the U.S. Copyright Office accepts as true an applicant's representations that a work is an "independent" creation.

Fixed in a Tangible Medium. Fixed in a "tangible medium," sometimes referred to as the "fixation requirement," means the work must be embodied in a copy that is sufficiently permanent to permit it to be perceived, reproduced, or otherwise communicated in more than a transitory way.

Changing technologies are anticipated by statutory language allowing the work to be "fixed in any tangible medium of expression, now known or later developed, from which [it] can be perceived, reproduced, or otherwise communicated, either directly or indirectly with the aid of a machine or device." 17 U.S.C. § 102(a).

Useful Articles. Useful articles, or things, are not copyrightable, but ornamentations or other artistic adornments of useful articles are copyrightable. The U.S. Copyright Office's *Circular 40* says the following on adornments:

> *"Copyright does not protect the mechanical or utilitarian aspects of such works of craftsmanship. It may, however, protect any pictorial, graphic, or sculptural authorship that can be identified separately from the utilitarian aspects of an object. Thus a useful article may have both copyrightable and uncopyrightable features. For example, a carving on the back of a chair or a floral relief design on silver flatware could be protected by copyright, but the design of the chair or flatware itself could not."*

Protection for product designs and other works involving "applied arts" (the use of design and artistic embellishments to make objects more visually pleasing) is generally accomplished through the use of design patents and, sometimes, the application of trade dress law. But only the "pictorial, graphic, or sculptural" elements of a useful article or thing are copyrightable.

Animals and Artificial Intelligence. Another interesting fact is that only works created by humans are eligible for copyright protection or registration. Although monkeys, elephants, and other animals have been involved in photographic and artistic creations, U.S. courts have repeatedly declined to extend copyright authorship and ownership to non-humans.

Of growing importance for many startups is the fact that works created through artificial intelligence ("AI") are also ineligible for copyright protections. The current general rule is that works created by AI are in the "public domain," not owned by anybody.

Ideas. Additionally, "ideas" are not copyrightable. The Copyright Act expressly precludes copyright protection for "any idea, procedure, process, system, method of operation, concept, principle, or discovery, regardless of the form in which it is described, explained, illustrated, or embodied in such work." 17 U.S.C. § 102(b). Ideas must be protected either through patents or trade secret law.

Automatic Rights

One of the most unique aspects of copyright law is that copyrightable works are automatically deemed copyrighted upon creation, whether a work is published or unpublished.

More specifically, works are copyrighted when "fixed" in a copy or "phonorecord" for the first time. The terms copy and phonorecord are interpreted very broadly under copyright law.

So, the correct but perhaps overly simplistic answer to the question *"How do I copyright my work?"* is often *"That already happened."*

In asking this question, many likely assume that some kind of filing or registration needs to be done to secure copyright protections. No filing or registration is required and most works go unregistered. As discussed next, however, registration is easy and has real benefits.

Duration of Copyrights

Copyright protections in the U.S. exist for a term beginning at the moment of a work's creation and lasting for the author's life plus an additional 70 years. For works made for hire and anonymous and pseudonymous works, the copyright term is 95 years from first publication or 120 years from creation, whichever is shorter.

Registration – Process and Benefits

Copyright registration fees vary by type of work, but they are very low, generally ranging between $35 and $85. See U.S. Copyright Office Circular 4 for all fees.

The U.S. Copyright Office is relatively flexible, offering both digital and paper application processes, and accepting a wide range of media to register different types of works.

The copyright registration process is probably a smidge more challenging for non-lawyers than registering a trademark and substantially easier than filing a patent application. That said, filing a copyright registration involving any degree of complexity should be done with the assistance of experienced counsel.

Registering software code raises some of the more unique and challenging issues under copyright law, including:

- protecting software trade secrets,
- registering multiple versions,
- registering screen displays,
- registering software documentation, and
- understanding the differing treatment of published versus unpublished software.

Those issues are discussed again under *Copyright Law and Software.*

In addition to the requirement that a copyright holder must register to bring a lawsuit for infringement of a work, there are important benefits to registration, including:

- registration within five years of a work's publication establishes prima facie evidence of the validity of the copyright and all facts in the registration certificate, including the copyright owner, all of which enhances the holder's position in any potential litigation,

- prevailing in an infringement suit regarding a registered work entitles the owner to "statutory damages," attorneys' fees and court costs, making infringement less likely and also providing strong leverage in settling infringement claims, and

- the U.S. Customs and Border Protection can be asked to seize and detain goods that violate U.S. intellectual property rights, including registered copyrights.

All of these benefits are important, but the availability of statutory damages, attorneys' fees, and court costs in successful infringement litigation may be paramount. The threat of getting hit with attorneys' fees can be enough to make an infringer back down from a protracted legal battle.

Statutory damages range between $750 to $30,000 per infringement, and up to $150,000 per willful infringement.

Proving the amount of damages from copyright infringement can be very difficult. The availability of statutory damages for registered works allows the holder to recover a specific amount for each infringed work, without presenting any proof of damages.

The threat of statutory damages, attorneys' fees, and court costs greatly enhances a registered copyright holder's leverage in resolving infringement claims, as highlighted in Case Study #27, *Throwing Scissors*, Case Study #30, *Too Much Flattery*, and Case Study #31, *Stop Thief!*

Copyright Notices

A copyright notice is a statement placed on a work to inform the public that a copyright owner is claiming ownership of it.

Until 1989, an owner's failure to consistently use proper copyright notices could result in the loss of copyrights. Copyright notices are now optional, but there are legal benefits to using them.

A copyright notice consists of three elements that generally appear as a single continuous statement:

- the copyright symbol © (or for phonorecords, the symbol ⊗), the word "copyright"; or the seldom-used abbreviation copr.,

- the year of first publication of the work, and

- the name of the copyright owner.

Example: © 2019 Business Law Seminar Group, LLC

The following excerpt on the benefits of copyright notices is from the U.S. Copyright Office's Circular 3:

Advantages to Using a Copyright Notice

Although notice is optional…, using a copyright notice carries the following benefits:

- *Notice makes potential users aware that copyright is claimed in the work.*

- *In the case of a published work, a notice may prevent a defendant in a copyright infringement action from attempting to limit his or her liability for damages or injunctive relief based on an innocent infringement defense.*

- *Notice identifies the copyright owner at the time the work was first published for parties seeking permission to use the work.*

- *Notice identifies the year of first publication, which may be used to determine the term of copyright protection in the case of an anonymous work, a pseudonymous work, or a work made for hire....*

For most startups, the first two of these reasons are most important, putting third parties on notice not to infringe and enhancing claims for damages for willful infringement.

Copyright Notice Updating. A common mistake with copyright notices is "updating" them with each new calendar year. Arbitrarily updating copyright notice dates is most common with websites and other online content.

Copyright notice dating principles:

- The correct date for a copyright notice is the year in which the content, or the "work," was created.

- When content is modified over time, state a date range in the notice like this: © 2017-2019 Business Law Seminar Group, LLC.

- When content is not modified in a given year, the copyright date should not be changed.

Webmasters and others responsible for online content understandably want to keep things "fresh," including copyright notice dates. The easy solution is to make some changes to the website or other copyrighted work, however small, so that a date range can be updated to reflect the changes.

Copyright owners should re-register copyrighted works that evolve. If annual re-registration is too burdensome or impractical, maintain records reflecting the changes made to a work and the years in which they were made.

Fair Use

As noted above, only the owner of a copyrighted work may legally reproduce, prepare derivative works, distribute copies to the public, or perform or display the copyrighted work publicly, including through digital transmission.

Others may generally engage in any such activities involving a copyrighted work only with the express authorization of the copyright holder, usually in the form of a license or other form of legally binding permission.

The only exceptions to these copyright restrictions are found in the very limited rules called "fair use."

Section 107 of the Copyright Act governs fair use, reproduced here in its entirety, with underling added for emphasis:

107. Limitations on exclusive rights: Fair use

Notwithstanding the provisions of sections 106 and 106A, the fair use of a copyrighted work, including such use by reproduction in copies or phonorecords or by any other means specified by that section, <u>for purposes such as criticism, comment, news reporting, teaching (including multiple copies for classroom use), scholarship, or research,</u> is not an infringement of copyright. In determining whether the use made of a work in any particular case is a fair use the factors to be considered shall include—

(1) *the purpose and character of the use, including whether such use is of a commercial nature or is for nonprofit educational purposes;*

(2) *the nature of the copyrighted work;*

(3) *the amount and substantiality of the portion used in relation to the copyrighted work as a whole; and*

(4) *the effect of the use upon the potential market for or value of the copyrighted work.*

The fact that a work is unpublished shall not itself bar a finding of fair use if such finding is made upon consideration of all the above factors.

Thus, the main categories of fair use include:

* criticism

* comment

* news reporting

* teaching

* scholarship

* research

In its webpage called "More Information on Fair Use," the U.S. Copyright Office makes these observations:

* *Courts look at how the party claiming fair use is using the copyrighted work, and are more likely to find that nonprofit educational and noncommercial uses are fair. This does not mean, however, that all nonprofit education and noncommercial uses are fair and all commercial uses are not fair; instead, courts will balance the purpose and character of the use against the other factors...*

* *Transformative uses are those that add something new, with a further purpose or different character, and do not substitute for the original use of the work.*

* *[Nature of the work]... analyzes the degree to which the work that was used relates to copyright's purpose of encouraging creative expression. Thus, using a more creative or imaginative work (such as a novel, movie, or song) is less likely to support a claim of a fair use than using a factual work (such as a technical article or news item).*

* *... courts review whether, and to what extent, the unlicensed use harms the existing or future market for the copyright owner's original work. In assessing this factor, courts consider whether*

the use is hurting the current market for the original work (for example, by displacing sales of the original) and/or whether the use could cause substantial harm if it were to become widespread.

Fair use always requires a very fact-dependent, case-by-case analysis. In general, startups should avoid relying on fair use as an excuse for borrowing or leveraging third-party content without permission.

Fortunately, works by the U.S. government are not subject to copyright protection, as described by the U.S. government itself on its "U.S. Government Works" web page:

> *U.S. government creative works are usually produced by government employees as part of their official duties. These works include writings, images, videos, and computer code. A government work is generally not subject to copyright in the U.S. Unless the work falls under an exception, anyone may, without restriction under U.S. copyright laws....*
>
> *(https://www.usa.gov/government-works)*

Copyright Law and Software

The benefits and limits of copyright protection for computer software are worth discussing, given several practical concerns and limitations.

This is, by necessity, a brief overview of these issues. Companies with software-driven business models need to understand what is and what is not protectable and must work with competent copyright counsel to stay on top of the evolving case law in this area.

A good starting point for understanding some of these issues is the U.S. Copyright Office's Circular 61, *Copyright Registration of Computer Programs*. The introductory paragraph of Circular 61 says:

> *A computer program is a set of statements or instructions to be used directly or indirectly in a computer to bring about a certain result. Copyright protection for a computer program extends to all of the copyrightable expression embodied in the program. The copyright law does not protect the functional aspects of a computer program, such as the program's algorithms, formatting, functions, logic, or system design.*

As this language says, while software code, as an "expression," is protectable, the ideas and functionalities underlying and produced by software are not.

To the extent those ideas or functionalities constitute patentable inventions, a combination of copyright and patent protections might resolve those concerns and provide relatively tight legal protection for computer software.

But as is discussed below, obtaining patent protection for software functions in the realms of "abstract ideas" or "business methods" has become more difficult.

A related concern is that both copyright registration and patent application processes require submission disclosures that could undercut protecting software merely as a trade secret or collection of interrelated trade secrets.

Fortunately, the U.S. Copyright Office does allow copyright owners to redact trade secrets from software copyright submissions, with certain limitations. Here are the options described in Circular 61:

Code with Trade Secret Material

If the source code does contain trade secrets, you must indicate in writing to the Office that the code contains trade secret material. Using one of the following options, submit a portion of the code for the specific version you want to register:

- *One copy of the first ten pages and last ten pages, blocking out none of the code;*

- *One copy of the first twenty-five pages and last twenty-five pages, blocking out the portions of the code containing trade secret material, provided the blocked out portions are less than fifty percent of the deposit;*

- *One copy of the first twenty-five pages and last twenty-five pages of the object code for the program, together with ten or more consecutive pages of source code, blocking out none of the source code (see subheading about object code below);*

- *If the source code for the entire program is fewer than fifty pages, one copy of the entire code, blocking out the portions of the code containing trade secret material, provided the blocked out portions represent less than fifty percent of the deposit; or*

- *If the source code does not have a precise beginning, middle, or end, twenty to fifty pages that reasonably represent the first and last portions of the code.*

Whether or not these alternatives for redacting trade secrets provide sufficient protection is likely a case-by-case analysis. Where they are insufficient, and where patentability of a software enabled invention is also an uncertain option, trade secret protections need to be carefully designed and executed, as discussed below.

Other software copyright nuances:

- Software copyright can extend to what are called "non-literal elements," including code sequence, structure and organization, screen displays, and user interfaces.

- Submitting object code instead of source code is highly discouraged and results in the U.S. Copyright Office applying what it ominously calls the "Rule of Doubt." Source code is code created by a programmer with a text editor or other programming tool. Object code means the output or compiled file produced from source code.

- The Copyright Office will not register HTML because HTML does not constitute source code created by a human, but instead is often generated by automated website design software. These issues can be overcome where HTML is created by a human and contains a sufficient amount of creative expression.

- There are special rules and considerations for registering later software versions, screen displays, user manuals and other forms of software documentation.

Software copyright registrations are inherently more complex than registrations of images or literary works and should be done with the assistance of experienced counsel.

Infringement Claims

Copyright infringement claims come in all shapes and sizes, from lifting a single photo for a blog post to larger claims regarding use of stolen software code in a commercially released product.

Big or small, all copyright infringement accusations are distracting and annoying — classic legal "gotchas." They should be consciously and actively avoided.

Infringement Elements. Key copyright infringement issues:

- Does the accuser really own the copyrights claimed?

- Did the accused have access to the original work and is the accused's work substantially similar to the accuser's copyrighted work?

- Alternatively, does the accused's work simply have a striking similarity to the accuser's copyrighted work?

- And are the allegedly copied sections of the work for sure protected by copyright?

- Is it fair use? Commercial uses are rarely fair uses, but even non-commercial uses can cross the line.

Companies that regularly create, manage, handle, or publish content are at greater risk for infringement claims. Many of the copyright cases that make headlines involve either (i) allegedly infringing songs, lyrics, works of art, or products or (ii) the unauthorized copying, distribution, display, or sale of copyrighted works. In this latter category, Spotify settled a $1.8 billion lawsuit at the end of 2018 with Wixen Music Publishing.

And while most companies not focused on riskier business models are able to stay out of copyright infringement trouble, news headlines only tell a small part of the story. The vast majority of infringement claims are settled out of court, and many involve IP mistakes that any company could make.

The following are a few key areas worthy of caution, based on recurring issues or evolving concerns.

Photos. The Internet provides endless rope for persons and companies to hang themselves. Right clicking has given new life to copyright law and lawyers.

Unlicensed or incorrectly licensed photos likely generate the most copyright infringement claims. Demands for a single unlicensed picture used in a blog can start at $8,000, even if the unlicensed use was well-intentioned and the image was taken down right away when notice of the infringement was received.

These claims are particularly distracting because they seem so unfair. But they also certainly serve to educate everyone about the toxicity of copyright violations.

Even if a license fee is paid, picture use licenses often allow only specific uses. Startups should restrict image procurement to persons with image licensing expertise to ensure that licenses cover the expected uses of a photograph.

Videos. Startups make a lot of videos. These often highlight companies as potential investment opportunities or showcase their products and services. Another video genre is the "explainer video." These are more focused on how a product or service works or should be used.

Videos generally incorporate music, images, background scenes, and other elements designed to generate interest. Care needs to be taken in shooting and producing videos to ensure that they do not infringe third-party trademarks, copyrights, or property rights known as rights of publicity and likeness rights discussed earlier under *Trademarks*.

In March of 2019, members of the National Music Publishers Association filed a lawsuit against fitness startup Peloton seeking more than $150 million in damages, claiming Peloton used their songs in its videos without proper licensing. This distracting and potentially costly lawsuit arrived at a time when Peloton was rumored to be working toward an IPO, potentially increasing the amount necessary to settle the matter.

Any video production should be handled by professionals who know how to avoid or "clear" any IP concerns. Contracts should put all burdens for doing so on the video production firm, along with all related liability and the obligation to defend and indemnify the client company. The video production firm's obligations should be backed by sufficient "media insurance" coverage. A smart client might also push to be a named insured on those insurance policies, a concession that is easier and less costly than one might expect.

Software. Software copyright disputes are alive and well, and recent cases are raising issues that are not expected to go away anytime soon.

In 2017, in *ZeniMax v. Oculus*, virtual reality video game publisher ZeniMax Media won a $500 million verdict against Oculus VR, based in part on the copying of software architecture.

This case is a lot like Case Study #1, *Pigpen*, in which one of two founders contributed IP owned by a prior employer. It highlights the importance of ensuring that no employee or contractor be permitted to intentionally or unintentionally incorporate software or other IP originally authored or conceived while employed by another.

In 2018, *Oracle v. Google* reminded us that you cannot take anything for granted in the world of IP. A Federal Court of Appeals found that Google's use of the Java API packages was not fair use as a matter of law. Google appealed to the U.S. Supreme Court. In November 2019, the Court said it would hear the case.

This decision overturned prior decisions finding that APIs were either not copyrightable or that their use by others to facilitate software interoperability constituted fair use.

Use of APIs and similar de minimis snippets of code allowing platforms and devices to communicate with each other is a common and longstanding practice. The case has raised concerns across the tech world about implications for other potential claims and for future software development, given the common use of APIs. A victory for Oracle would be considered by many a threat to future software interoperability.

International Copyright Considerations

Copyright laws vary by country, and a U.S. copyright registration is no guarantee against infringement in any other country.

But WIPO administers several international treaties that address copyright and related rights, including the *Berne Convention of 1888 for the Protection of Literary and Artistic Works* and the *WIPO Copyright Treaty* ("WCT"), a "special agreement" under the Berne Convention.

To date, 170 countries have signed the Berne Convention, including virtually all developed countries, providing relatively strong international protection for most copyrighted works. Key elements of the Berne Convention include:

- works originating in one of the Contracting States or from one of its nationals must be given the same protection in each of the other Contracting States as the latter grants to the works of its nationals,

- protection must not be conditional upon compliance with any formalities, but must be automatic,

- Contracting States must provide authors the following minimum, exclusive rights:

  - the right to translate,

  - the right to make adaptations and arrangements,

  - the right to perform in public dramatic and musical works,

  - the right to recite literary works in public,

  - the right to communicate to the public the performance of such works,

  - the right to broadcast,

  - the right to make reproductions in any manner or form, with some exceptions, and

  - the right to use the work as a basis for an audiovisual work, and the right to reproduce, distribute, perform in public or communicate that audiovisual work.

The Berne Convention also provides "moral rights," essentially the right to object to any mutilation, deformation, or other modification of, or other derogatory action regarding the work, prejudicial to the author's reputation.

The WCT provides for the protection of works and the rights of their authors in the digital environment and adds two subject matters for copyright protection: (i) computer programs, whatever the mode or form of their expression, and (ii) compilations of data or other material (databases), in any form, "which, by reason of the selection or arrangement of their contents, constitute intellectual creations."

In summary, copyrights may be protected in foreign countries either under that country's laws or under one of several international treaties and conventions, of which the Berne Convention is most significant.

Additionally, the U.S. IP Attaché program is ready to assist U.S. stakeholders with copyright infringement and other IP concerns. IP Attachés are posted at U.S. diplomatic missions around the world to address IP issues arising in their assigned regions.

U.S. authors and owners of other IP may locate IP Attachés and request other international IP infringement assistance at www.STOPfakes.gov. That is a website managed by the International Trade Administration of the U.S. Department of Commerce to assist U.S. businesses in protecting and enforcing their IP rights against counterfeits and pirated goods in the global marketplace.

Case Study #30 – Too Much Flattery

As Charles Caleb Colton wrote in 1820, *"Imitation is the sincerest of flattery."*

A product manager with a funny sense of humor once sent me an email with the subject line – *the sincerest form of flattery?*

The body of this cryptic email was a single website link. Clicking on the link was like being teleported to a parallel dimension. I was looking at my company's website, but with a different name and a different business model. Much of the text was identical or confusingly similar.

At this time, our website was a public-facing portal through which new customers opened large numbers of financial accounts each day. The brazen theft of our trade dress and written content was shocking but also somewhat amusing for its boldness.

Fortunately, a fine colleague in our finance department had dutifully followed our request to periodically download all several hundred pages of the website to a disc and send the disc to outside counsel for copyright registration.

Bingo. Because of this, we had indisputable claims to statutory damages instead of having to go through the difficult processes of factually demonstrating our actual financial damages. Not to mention having any attorneys' fees and court costs potentially covered.

We tracked down the owners through the domain registry "WhoIs" and sent them a demand letter, alleging both infringement of our registered copyrights in the website and our trade dress rights in the website under the Lanham Act.

In addition to the strong copyright claims, our letter made it clear that we were also confident in our ability to prove the three elements necessary for a trade dress claim: (i) our trade dress was inherently distinctive or had acquired a "secondary meaning," (ii) it was primarily non-functional, and (iii) their trade dress was confusingly similar.

The owner of the website futilely tried to pass off the blame and liability on an independent contractor who had done all the work. Unfortunately for them, that is not how either copyright law or trademark law works – *both* the website owner and the website creator were liable, and their counsel obviously advised them as such.

That was too much flattery, but we went easy on them. We settled for the very reasonable amount of $25,000 and used the money to fund Friday afternoon happy hours for a couple of years, advertised as jointly sponsored by the law and finance departments.

Lessons: Registering copyrights can pay off.

Case Study #31 – Stop Thief!

One of my companies accepted an investment from a strategic investor, an investor more interested in supporting a company for potential product or service synergies than for typical investment return considerations.

Things took a very strange turn with this investor when our company did a sharp pivot from the original business model to a new one that quickly proved to be much more successful.

Unfortunately for the strategic investor, the new model did not offer any of the service synergies of the original model.

The pivot involved maintaining a legacy transactional website for a few years to gracefully wind down that business and seek to persuade the customers on that platform to try the new service at an all-new website. During the wind-down period, we accepted no new customers at the legacy website.

The strategic investor in question was a large financial institution. We knew they were not happy with the pivot. We thought long and hard about their concerns, but there was nothing we could do differently that would not harm the company or our other investors.

Things seemed to calm down, and we thought the investor had come to accept the new paradigm.

Then we learned they had copied all of the code and all of the content from the legacy website and used it to launch a new version under their branding. As in Case Study #30, we had registered all of that website content with the Copyright Office.

This heist was shocking, but also amusing. The day of the discovery, several of us went out for beers, joking and laughing about it. How could a sophisticated company make such an unusual mistake?

We then promptly sent out a sternly worded demand letter requiring them to immediately shut down the copycat website and return all IP to the company, under threat of an action for copyright infringement, theft of trade secrets, breach of contractual non-disclosure and non-misuse of confidential information, and unfair competition.

They promptly complied, and the incident was over within days, but the relationship between the two companies never improved.

Lessons: The company had taken steps to register its copyrights in the legacy website periodically. Having done so subjected the thieving strategic investor to statutory damages, attorneys' fees, and court costs, had we decided to sue them.

The leverage provided by current copyright registrations was key to quickly and successfully resolving the matter.

Trade Secrets

Overview

Perhaps the most famous trade secret of all is the formula for Coca-Cola. It was invented in 1886 by pharmacist John Stith Pemberton in Atlanta, Georgia. Had Mr. Pemberton obtained a patent instead, it would have expired more than 100 years ago, and the formula for Coca-Cola would be in the public domain.

As we know, a trade secret is defined very broadly as any financial, business, scientific, technical, economic, or engineering information that (i) is secret, (ii) has economic value because it is secret, and (iii) is the subject of reasonable efforts to maintain its secrecy.

Number (iii) above is no throw-away element. Courts have held that the absence of reasonable efforts to maintain secrecy can invalidate trade secret legal protections – even where the information in question continued to be secret.

A court found in favor of an individual, for example, who exploited a company's trade secrets shared with him negligently under no enforceable confidentiality conditions, like an NDA. Thus, information can still meet criteria (i) and (ii) above, but still no longer qualify for trade secret status due to the failure to ensure its confidentiality by reasonable means, including a single failure to execute an NDA.

In 2018, an 11th Circuit case, *Yellowfin Yachts, Inc. v. Barker Boatworks, LLC*, rejected both trade secret claims and trade dress claims. The following excerpt from the case alludes to the types of failings that undermine arguments that information has been reasonably protected from disclosure:

> *"But Yellowfin compromised the efficacy of these [internal data security] measures by encouraging Barker to keep the Customer Information on his cellphone and personal laptop.... Indeed, Barker refused to sign an employment agreement which stated that he would, among other things, keep all Yellowfin trade secrets in confidence. Further, Yellowfin neither marked the Customer Information as confidential nor instructed Barker to secure the information on his personal devices.*
>
> *And when Barker left Yellowfin, the company did not request that Barker return or delete any of the information."*

The Trade Secret-Patent Dilemma

Inventors are sometimes distressed to learn they cannot simultaneously protect an invention under trade secret law and patent law.

We delve more deeply into that IP conundrum later, but the tensions stem from the facts that trade secrets require complete secrecy, while patents require complete disclosure.

A good understanding of the law and best practices in both areas is critical for evaluating the pros and cons of how each would work, or not work, in protecting specific items of IP under specific circumstances.

Pros and Cons of Trade Secret Protections

Trade secret protections are unique and valuable for many reasons:

- backed by robust state and federal statutes,

- broad protection for ideas, information and other IP assets that may not be protectable through trademark, copyright or patent law,

- no time limitations,

- no filing fees or government approvals required, and

- remedies can include treble damages, royalties, attorneys' fees, awards based on unjust enrichment, and even seizure of stolen trade secrets and any goods made from those stolen secrets.

But limitations on trade secret protections are also important, including:

- no protection from independent discovery by others, including the filing of patents by independent discoverers,

- reverse engineering is generally not prohibited under state or federal trade secret law,

- loss of secrecy, by whatever means, ends further protections,

- may be perceived as less valuable by investors or acquirors, and

- it is difficult to consistently maintain reasonable protections of trade secrets from disclosure.

Legal Framework

The law of trade secrets evolved from common law. As with other areas of IP law, the current legal framework for trade secret law is a combination of state and federal statutes and cases that have interpreted them.

State Uniform Trade Secrets Acts. All but two states, New York and Massachusetts, have adopted their own versions of what is called the Uniform Trade Secrets Act ("UTSA"). In those two states, trade secrets continue to be governed by common law.

The writers of the UTSA, amended most recently in 1985, sought to create uniform state-by-state trade secret laws that borrow heavily from what they saw as the best-reasoned trade secret principles from the common law.

Some general principles of the UTSA include:

- actual or threatened trade secret misappropriations can be enjoined,

- affirmative acts to protect a trade secret may be compelled by court order,

- in addition to or instead of injunctive relief, a complainant may recover damages for the actual loss caused by misappropriation, plus unjust enrichment caused by misappropriation above and beyond damages for actual loss,

- in cases of willful and malicious misappropriation, a court may award attorneys' fees and exemplary damages up to two times the amount of the underlying damages award,

- an injunction may condition future use upon payment of a reasonable royalty,

- more than one person can claim trade secret protection for the same subject matter,

- misappropriation includes acquisition of a trade secret by means that should be known to be improper and unauthorized disclosure or use of information that one should know is the trade secret of another,

- reverse engineering of a lawfully obtained product to discover a trade secret is permissible, and

- an action for misappropriation must be brought must be brought within three years after the misappropriation is discovered or should have been discovered by the exercise of reasonable diligence.

U.S. Economic Espionage Act of 1996. The first federal legislation involving trade secrets was the Economic Espionage Act of 1996 ("EEA"). Before this legislation, trade secret cases were prosecuted under federal mail fraud, wire fraud, and racketeering statutes, as well as state statutes based on the UTSA.

While combatting theft by state actors was a key motivation for the legislation, the EEA criminalizes trade secret theft by all actors in Section 1832:

Whoever, with intent to convert a trade secret... and intending or knowing that the offense will, injure any owner of that trade secret, knowingly—

(1) *steals, or without authorization appropriates, takes, carries away, or conceals, or by fraud, artifice, or deception obtains such information;*

(2) *without authorization copies, duplicates, sketches, draws, photographs, downloads, uploads, alters, destroys, photocopies, replicates, transmits, delivers, sends, mails, communicates, or conveys such information;*

(3) *receives, buys, or possesses such information, knowing the same to have been stolen or appropriated, obtained, or converted without authorization;...*

or

(5) *conspires with one or more other persons to commit any offense described in paragraphs (1) through (3), and one or more of such persons do any act to effect the object of the conspiracy, shall, except as provided in subsection (b), be fined under this title or imprisoned not more than 10 years, or both.*

Many of those convicted under the EEA have been employees caught stealing trade secrets from employers and attempting to sell them to competitors.

Companies that rely extensively on trade secret protections should consider ensuring one way or another that employees are aware of the potential criminal penalties for theft or misuse of company trade secrets.

U.S. Defend Trade Secrets Act. Trade secret law was given a significant boost in 2016 with the U.S. Defend Trade Secrets Act of 2016 ("DTSA"). Commenters have noted a significant rise in trade secret cases, based on both state and federal laws, following enactment of the DTSA.

The DTSA amended the federal criminal code to create a private civil cause of action in federal court for trade secret misappropriation related to a product or service in interstate or foreign commerce. The DTSA establishes remedies including injunctive relief, compensatory damages, and attorneys' fees. It sets a three-year statute of limitation from the date of discovery of the misappropriation.

The DTSA gives companies with national and international operations an important additional set of tools for trade secret enforcement. Like the state Uniform Trade Secret Acts, the DTSA defines trade secrets very broadly as follows:

> … *all forms and types of financial, business, scientific, technical, economic, or engineering information, including patterns, plans, compilations, program devices, formulas, designs, prototypes, methods, techniques, processes, procedures, programs, or codes, whether tangible or intangible, and whether or how stored, compiled, or memorialized physically, electronically, graphically, photographically, or in writing if (A) the owner thereof has taken reasonable measures to keep such information secret; and (B) the information derives independent economic value, actual or potential, from not being generally known to, and not being readily ascertainable through proper means by, another person….*

The DTSA provides powerful remedies, including allowing companies to request the seizure of misappropriated trade secrets. Like the UTSA, in cases of willful misappropriation, the DTSA allows for awards of "exemplary damages" up to two times direct damages, meaning 3x damages in total, or treble damages.

Courts may also award attorneys' fees when a trade secret is willfully and maliciously misappropriated, as well as under certain other circumstances.

Trade Secret Best Practices

The first step in protecting trade secrets is identifying them.

Trade Secret Inventory. Any company with trade secrets should prepare and maintain a trade secret inventory.

Make sure *key* employees are familiar with the inventory and the importance of not disclosing or otherwise compromising those secrets.

Another best practice would be to track on the trade secret inventory each instance in which trade secrets are shared, when, with whom, why, and in what manner.

Confidentiality Best Practices. Trade secret best practices are rooted in basic confidentiality best practices:

- careful and consistent use of NDAs and PIIAs with employees, consultants, vendors, investors, and others,

- limiting access to and disclosure of trade secrets to employees and third parties on a strict "need to know" basis,

- training employees to be cautious in their communications with others, including the NDA best practices discussed below,

- imposing strict prohibitions against disclosing any company trade secrets without explicit authorization from the company's CEO, general counsel, or other senior officer charged with protecting trade secrets,

- prohibiting storage of trade secrets on employees' or contractors' personal computers or other personal devices, and

- requiring departing employees and terminated contractors to return or delete all company confidential information and IP.

Avoiding NDA Mistakes. NDA mistakes are endemic in business. Here are the most common ones:

- exchanging confidential information without an NDA,

- exchanging confidential information with an unsigned or partially signed NDA,

- signing an NDA in the name of the wrong entity or in any other incorrect capacity that invalidates the NDA,

- not following an NDA's requirements to mark written information as confidential or provide written summaries of confidential information shared orally,

- exchanging confidential information under NDA, but then losing the NDA,

- signing NDAs with bad provisions:

    - overly restrictive language regarding what shared information is covered,

    - overly prescriptive requirements for obtaining protection of confidential information, such as requiring documents to be marked "Confidential" and requiring information shared orally to be memorialized in writing within a specified period of time,

    - short confidentiality period,

    - failure to explicitly prohibit information uses and misuses outside of typical NDA limitations,

    - failure to specifically protect all trade secrets for the life of the trade secrets, and

    - "residuals" language, essentially allowing the theft and misuse of anything that is "remembered" by a recipient of confidential or proprietary information.

Sloppy NDA processes and drafting are both common. All of the above mistakes happen. And the results can be painful, including the loss of confidentiality.

Any mishandling of a trade secret puts it permanently at risk. One provable instance of a trade secret shared sloppily can be the end of that trade secret.

Avoid NDA mistakes by:

- setting up good NDA policies and procedures,

- using strong NDA templates and having counsel review all third-party NDAs,

- emphasizing to the entire organization from the top down that the handling and protection of confidential information is an uncompromisable priority for everyone, and

- training employees on how to handle confidential information.

Employee training on handling confidential information should cover things like:

- company processes for ensuring the consistent use of NDAs <u>before</u> sharing any information with third parties,

- the importance of NDAs being properly drafted, fully executed/signed, safely stored, and reliably retrievable,

- the meaning of key provisions in the company's standard NDA template(s) and why they are important,

- the importance of having all third-party NDAs reviewed by counsel, including discussion of the types of unfavorable terms that might otherwise slip by,

- how to properly mark confidential information,

- complying with specific and possibly unique NDA requirements,

- not allowing the sharing of information to become too informal to track what is shared and how,

- not over-sharing information,

- being particularly mindful never to share trade secrets unnecessarily, and

- being alert for signs or signals that the other side might be mishandling or misusing information, or sharing it too broadly.

Other Contractual Restrictions. Consider the need to protect trade secrets in every type of agreement. Key trade secret contractual protection include confidentiality requirements and prohibitions against "reverse engineering."

Contractual prohibitions against reverse engineering close the hole in state and federal trade secret laws specifically allowing reverse engineering. Examples of agreements where this might be prudent include:

- commercial agreements for the purchase and sale of goods,

- customer terms and conditions, whether printed or electronic,

- licensing agreements,

- supply and distribution agreements,

- software agreements,

- independent contractor agreements, and

- any other agreements involving or potentially resulting in access to products.

Identify and Track Disclosed Trade Secrets. When trade secrets must be shared with vendors, suppliers, manufacturers, investors or others, identify those trade secrets as such, emphasize in writing that they are highly confidential and proprietary and their loss would be financially harmful. And as noted earlier regarding maintaining a trade secret inventory, keep a list of which trade secrets have been shared, when, why, how, and with whom.

Be Very Skeptical. Do not assume that trade secrets will in fact be protected by third parties, or even by employees.

Written agreements can be breached, intentionally or accidentally. A trade secret lost to unauthorized disclosure can rarely be recovered, whether or not there was an agreement that should have prevented its improper disclosure.

That is not to say, give up right away if a confidentiality breach happens. It might be possible to remedy a limited unprotected disclosure through negotiations or through legal action to restore the trade secret's secrecy. A court, for example, could order a party that has misappropriated a trade secret to take steps to protect its secrecy. But in the age of the Internet and electronic communication, valuable information can travel quickly and broadly.

A contractual claim for damages is rarely equal in value to the trade secret itself. Company culture should be that trade secrets are never shared beyond what is absolutely necessary, even when an NDA or other protective agreement is in place.

Trade Secret Litigation and Enforcement

Civil litigation and criminal enforcement actions to prevent, remedy, and punish trade secret thefts are common. While some cases involve highly organized criminal activities by "state actors," the most common fact pattern involves individuals stealing trade secrets from prior employers and sharing them with subsequent employers, where they are then incorporated into the later employer's products and services.

__Waymo v. Uber.__ In 2017, a company called Waymo sued Uber alleging theft of its self-driving car technology. Waymo alleged that one of its former engineers, Anthony Levandowski, stole confidential files full of trade secrets before leaving to form a new startup called Otto, which Uber acquired in 2016.

The matter went to trial, but on day five, as key witnesses were allegedly about to testify concerning the incorporation of stolen technology into Uber's systems, Uber settled for $245 million.

In August of 2019, the U.S. attorney's office indicted Anthony Levandowski for the trade secret thefts. Each of the 33 charges against him carried a potential penalty of 10 years and $250,000. In

March of 2020, Levandowski pleaded guilty to one count of trade secret theft and will serve at least 30 months in prison.

Tesla v. Zoox. In March of 2019, Tesla sued a company called Zoox and several former Tesla employees for stealing software used to develop and run warehousing, logistics, and inventory control operations.

Trade secret cases are invariably colorful, and this one is no exception. The departing employees allegedly wrote *"you sly dog you..."* and *"Good Stuff"* in emails shipping trade secrets out of Tesla and to their private email accounts. Even more damning is this allegation in the complaint:

> *"After Defendant Emigh joined Zoox, he mistakenly sent an email to Cooper's old Tesla email address, attaching a modified version of a Tesla proprietary document, freshly-emblazoned with the Zoox logo, yet still bearing the layout, design, and other vestiges of the Tesla version – showing, without doubt, that the Defendants are actively using the Tesla information they stole."*

The fact that there are so many cases of documented trade secret theft should provide all companies with motivation to better protect their own trade secrets and also take all reasonable precautions to prevent their employees, independent contractors, and others working on their behalf from stealing trade secrets of others – whether intentionally, negligently, or accidentally.

Patents

Patent Law Overview

As noted at the top of this chapter, Congress's authority to enact laws for patenting new inventions is enshrined in Article 1, Section 8 of the U.S. Constitution.

Under that authority, Congress has adopted the U.S. Patent Act. In addition to establishing the legal framework for patents, the Patent Act also established the USPTO.

35 U.S. Code Section 101 – "Inventions patentable," reads as follows:

> *Whoever invents or discovers any new and useful process, machine, manufacture, or composition of matter, or any new and useful improvement thereof, may obtain a patent therefor, subject to the conditions and requirements of this title.*

As discussed below regarding the 2014 *Alice* case, the U.S. Supreme Court has long held that the above language *"... contains an implicit exception for laws of nature, natural phenomena, and abstract ideas."*

As with most U.S. government agencies, the USPTO's website provides a wealth of useful information. Under a link caption "What Are Patents" on its homepage, the USPTO gives this overview of patents:

> *A patent for an invention is the grant of a property right to the inventor, issued by the United States Patent and Trademark Office. Generally, the term of a new patent is 20 years from the date*

on which the application for the patent was filed in the United States or, in special cases, from the date an earlier related application was filed, subject to the payment of maintenance fees.

U.S. patent grants are effective only within the United States, U.S. territories, and U.S. possessions. Under certain circumstances, patent term extensions or adjustments may be available.

The right conferred by the patent grant is, in the language of the statute and of the grant itself, "the right to exclude others from making, using, offering for sale, or selling" the invention in the United States or "importing" the invention into the United States. What is granted is not the right to make, use, offer for sale, sell or import, but the right to exclude others from making, using, offering for sale, selling or importing the invention. Once a patent is issued, the patentee must enforce the patent without aid of the USPTO.

There are three types of patents:

1. *Utility patents may be granted to anyone who invents or discovers any new and useful process, machine, article of manufacture, or composition of matter, or any new and useful improvement thereof;*

2. *Design patents may be granted to anyone who invents a new, original, and ornamental design for an article of manufacture; and*

3. *Plant patents may be granted to anyone who invents or discovers and asexually reproduces any distinct and new variety of plant.*

What the above does not mention is that the 20-year right to exclude others from making, using, offering, or selling an invention is given in exchange for the invention owner *fully disclosing how to practice the invention* so that others can use and exploit the invention as they wish after the 20-year monopoly expires.

As discussed later, this requires entrepreneurs to carefully weigh the pros and cons of protecting each of their innovations either through patenting or as trade secrets.

Patent law has undergone significant changes in recent years, both statutorily and through case law developments. Determining what is an "abstract idea" under Section 101 is the major issue of the day in patent law.

These statutory and case law changes have caused uncertainty around what is patentable and when and how granted patents can be invalidated.

Even so, patents are still critical offensive and defensive tools for inventive companies, often serving as both "sword and shield" to protect a company's core innovations.

Patent Eligibility

Below are some useful excerpts from the USPTO webpage under the caption *What Can Be Patented.*

In the language of the statute, any person who "invents or discovers any new and useful process, machine, manufacture, or composition of matter, or any new and useful improvement thereof, may obtain a patent," subject to the conditions and requirements of the law. The word "process" is defined by law as a process, act, or method, and primarily includes industrial or technical processes. The term "machine" used in the statute needs no explanation. The term "manufacture" refers to articles that are made, and includes all manufactured articles. The term "composition of matter" relates to chemical compositions and may include mixtures of ingredients as well as new chemical compounds. These classes of subject matter taken together include practically everything that is made by man and the processes for making the products....

The patent law specifies that the subject matter must be "useful." The term "useful" in this connection refers to the condition that the subject matter has a useful purpose and also includes operativeness, that is, a machine which will not operate to perform the intended purpose would not be called useful, and therefore would not be granted a patent.

Interpretations of the statute by the courts have defined the limits of the field of subject matter that can be patented, thus it has been held that the laws of nature, physical phenomena, and abstract ideas are not patentable subject matter.

A patent cannot be obtained upon a mere idea or suggestion. The patent is granted upon the new machine, manufacture, etc., as has been said, and not upon the idea or suggestion of the new machine. A complete description of the actual machine or other subject matter for which a patent is sought is required.

Novelty And Non-Obviousness. As reflected in the statutory language, an invention must be new. That means it cannot be the subject of a prior patent or application. It also must not have been previously described or disclosed by means of or as evidenced by any prior art.

The USPTO website addresses these requirements with the following excerpted text found under the caption *Novelty And Non-Obviousness, Conditions For Obtaining A Patent.*

In order for an invention to be patentable it must be new as defined in the patent law, which provides that an invention cannot be patented if:

"(1) the claimed invention was patented, described in a printed publication, or in public use, on sale, or otherwise available to the public before the effective filing date of the claimed invention" or

"(2) the claimed invention was described in a patent issued [by the U.S.] or in an application for patent published or deemed published [by the U.S.], in which the patent or application, as the case may be, names another inventor and was effectively filed before the effective filing date of the claimed invention."

There are certain limited patent law exceptions to patent prohibitions (1) and (2) above. Notably, an exception may apply to a "disclosure made 1 year or less before the effective filing date of the claimed invention," but only if "the disclosure was made by the inventor or joint inventor or by another who obtained the subject matter disclosed... from the inventor or a joint inventor."

In patent prohibition (1), the term "otherwise available to the public" refers to other types of disclosures of the claimed invention such as, for example, an oral presentation at a scientific meeting, a demonstration at a trade show, a lecture or speech, a statement made on a radio talk show, a YouTube™ video, or a website or other on-line material....

Even if the subject matter sought to be patented is not exactly shown by the prior art, and involves one or more differences over the most nearly similar thing already known, a patent may still be refused if the differences would be obvious. The subject matter sought to be patented must be sufficiently different from what has been used or described before that it may be said to be non-obvious to a person having ordinary skill in the area of technology related to the invention. For example, the substitution of one color for another, or changes in size, are ordinarily not patentable.

The *"1 year or less"* reference by the USPTO here is discussed more fully under *Public Disclosure and Patentability.*

Case Law Developments in Patent Law – Alice et al.

In 2014, the U.S. Supreme Court issued its decision in <u>Alice Corp. v. CLS Bank International</u>, declaring invalid what are often referred to as "business method" patents.

The *Alice* decision has created lots of uncertainty in the patent law field around what constitutes an unpatentable "abstract idea," the central defect inherent in all business method patents.

This is the Court's central holding in *Alice*:

> *The patents at issue in this case disclose a computer-implemented scheme for mitigating 'settlement risk" (i.e., the risk that only one party to a financial transaction will pay what it owes) by using a third-party intermediary. The question presented is whether these claims are patent eligible under 35 U. S. C. §101, or are instead drawn to a patent-ineligible abstract idea. We hold that the claims at issue are drawn to the abstract idea of intermediated settlement, and that merely requiring generic computer implementation fails to transform that abstract idea into a patent-eligible invention.*

Obviously this prose is a bit opaque to those who are not patent experts. It has also confounded countless experienced patent practitioners. The following excerpts from *Alice* provide a little more clarity:

> *… We have long held that this provision contains an important implicit exception: Laws of nature, natural phenomena, and abstract ideas are not patentable…..*

> *…Laws of nature, natural phenomena, and abstract ideas are… the basic tools of scientific and technological work…. [M]onopolization of those tools through the grant of a patent might tend to impede innovation more than it would tend to promote it,… thereby thwarting the primary object of the patent laws….*

> *…Accordingly, in applying the §101 exception, we must distinguish between patents that claim the "'buildin[g] block[s]'" of human ingenuity and those that integrate the building blocks into something more,… thereby "transform[ing]" them into a patent-eligible invention. The former "would risk disproportionately tying up the use of the underlying" ideas,… and are therefore ineligible for patent protection….*

> *…An instruction to apply the abstract idea of intermediated settlement using some unspecified, generic computer is not "enough" to transform the abstract idea into a patent-eligible invention….*

Abstract ideas are thus grouped with laws of nature and natural phenomena. They are *"building blocks of ingenuity"* that need to be integrated with each other to *"create something more,"* and be *"transformed"* into an invention.

The reasoning for the abstract idea disqualifier is similar to the disqualifier of "generic" terms for trademarks. Abstract ideas and generic terms are both things that everybody has a right to use – they cannot be monopolized.

The following examples of "abstract ideas" are sprinkled throughout the decision:

- an algorithm for converting binary-coded decimal numerals into pure binary form,
- an algorithm implemented on a general-purpose digital computer,
- a mathematical formula for computing "alarm limits" in a catalytic conversion process,
- a method for hedging against the financial risk of price fluctuations, and
- a method for measuring metabolites in the bloodstream to calibrate the appropriate dosage of thiopurine drugs in the treatment of autoimmune diseases.

And perhaps even more helpful is the decision's single example of the use of abstract ideas to create something truly inventive and patentable:

> *The invention in Diehr used a "thermocouple" to record constant temperature measurements inside the rubber mold—something "the industry ha[d] not been able to obtain." Id., at 178, and n. 3. The temperature measurements were then fed into a computer, which repeatedly recalculated the remaining cure time by using the mathematical equation…. These additional steps, we recently explained, "transformed the process into an inventive application of the formula."*

While it is difficult to predict what claims are going to get through the USPTO without a Section 101 rejection, practitioners agree that such rejections are less likely with inventions that:

- solve a technological problem,
- improve an industrial process,
- make a computer perform better, or
- improve technology.

A recurring theme in the *Alice* decision and other recent cases is that merely doing something already known and already done, but now doing it using a computer, is insufficient to transform the already known idea into an invention.

The European Union has long been stricter about not allowing business method patents. Article 52 of the European Patent Convention says the following, in part, about what is patentable and what is not:

Patentable inventions

- *European patents shall be granted for any inventions, in all fields of technology, provided that they are new, involve an inventive step and are susceptible of industrial application.*
- *The following in particular shall not be regarded as inventions within the meaning of paragraph 1:*

- *discoveries, scientific theories and mathematical methods;*

- *aesthetic creations;*

- *schemes, rules and methods for performing mental acts, playing games or doing business, and programs for computers;…*

Before *Alice*, many perceived an epidemic of vague, overly-broad patents governing business methods and processes. These vague and often poorly drafted patents were acquired wholesale by unscrupulous patent trolls and asserted broadly and unfairly against businesses.

Anyone doubting there was ever a problem need only realize that in the mid-1990s, the USPTO once granted a patent titled *"Method of Exercising a Cat,"* U.S. Patent US5443036A. The claims in this ridiculous and now-expired patent included:

What is claimed is:

1. *A method of inducing aerobic exercise in an unrestrained cat comprising the steps of:*

(a) *directing an intense coherent beam of invisible light produced by a hand-held laser apparatus to produce a bright highly-focused pattern of light at the intersection of the beam and an opaque surface, said pattern being of visual interest to a cat; and*

(b) *selectively redirecting said beam out of the cat's immediate reach to induce said cat to run and chase said beam and pattern of light around an exercise area.*

The dust is still settling following *Alice*. The USPTO's continuing high percentage of Section 101 rejections had practitioners rebelling and demanding guidance, which the USPTO provided in October of 2019.

That guidance document, captioned "October 2019 Update: Subject Matter Eligibility," can be found by searching that name or going to this link:

https://www.uspto.gov/sites/default/files/documents/peg_oct_2019_update.pdf.

The jury is still out on how helpful practitioners are finding the USPTO's new guidance, but it remains clear that, to avoid rejection, it is critical that *"…the claimed invention improves the functioning of a computer or other technology."* And on the other hand, processes or calculations that can be performed entirely in the human mind are *not* patentable.

Despite legitimate complaints regarding consistency in Section 101 rejections, *Alice* has produced positive changes by reducing the number of weak patents filed and improving the quality of patents getting through the USPTO review process.

Patent eligibility is discussed further below, but *Alice* and several subsequent cases have forced entrepreneurs and startups to focus their resources on pursuing truly useful and defensible patents.

Statutory Changes – America Invents Act of 2011

The America Invents Act ("AIA") was enacted into law in 2011. The AIA brought sweeping reforms to U.S. patent law, but the most significant change ushered in by the act involved moving the U.S. from the "first-to-invent" rule to the international standard, "first-to-file."

Under the new first-to-file standard, the patent for a new invention goes to the person who files a patent application first, not the person who claims to have first conceived the invention. The new law has been accused of setting up "a race to the patent office."

This change was the subject of much doom and gloom commentary predicting that it would favor larger, more sophisticated companies with well-designed IP protection strategies, to the detriment of smaller, less-well-funded and less sophisticated entrepreneurs. The naysayers argued that the change could dry up investments in startups due to concerns that entrepreneurs would be unable to compete in the race to the patent office.

Equally sophisticated commentators saw benefits for entrepreneurship in the first-to-file rule:

- eliminating the uncertainties involved with determining who first invented a patentable innovation,

- reducing the risk and uncertainties that prior invention claims might be asserted against an entrepreneur or startup after filing a patent application, and

- aligning the U.S. standard with international standards and thus providing greater certainty for global IP strategies.

It is still too early to say, but entrepreneurs seem to be adjusting to the first-to-file rule, and there is not much evidence of steamrolling by larger, better-funded companies in the race to the patent office.

At a subjective level, the rule generated substantial attention around timely protecting core innovations within entrepreneur and startup communities, possibly leading to improved IP protection practices.

Other significant changes ushered in by the AIA include:

Submission of Prior Art by Third Parties. Third parties can now submit prior art during the USPTO patent examination process to prevent a patent from being granted. This change arguably supports the work of the USPTO in granting only valid patents and seemed relatively uncontroversial.

Derivation Proceedings. A new process, opaquely called a derivation proceeding, allows an inventor/petitioner with a pending patent application to show that an inventor named in an earlier-filed application "derived" the claimed invention from an inventor named in the petitioner's application and filed the earlier application claiming the invention without authorization.

This process for contesting patent applications based on an allegedly misappropriated ("derived") invention, must be commenced within a year of the invention first being published.

Prior Use Infringement Defense. The AIA extended a "prior use" defense to infringement from business method patents to all patents. A party that can prove prior commercial use of an invention maintained as a trade secret before being patented by another can defend itself against a patent infringement claim by proving its prior commercial use based on the trade secret.

Challenges to Granted Patents. Third parties now have two new administrative alternatives for challenging the validity of granted patents: (i) inter partes review and (ii) post-grant-review or "PGR."

Without getting too deeply into these new processes for challenging granted patents, both are heard before the USPTO Patent Trial and Appeal Board, or PTAB, and both processes have resulted in high percentages of challenged patents being invalidated, primarily under Section 102 (novelty) or Section 103 (obviousness) of the U.S. Patent Act.

Commenters alarmed by the high rates of invalidations have referred to these processes as "patent death panels." Others point out that the rates of invalidations were initially high as a large number of weak patents were challenged, but that the invalidation rates have subsequently been coming down.

Public Disclosure and Patentability

It is important to understand that, in many countries, any prior "public disclosure" or commercial use or sale of an invention before the filing of a patent application can render the invention unpatentable.

In the U.S., inventors have an entire year to file for a patent following the first public disclosure or commercial use or sale. But the filing of a U.S. patent application during that one-year period will not cure any issues in foreign jurisdictions that require filing before any public disclosure.

Disclosures made under NDAs and other confidentiality restrictions do not constitute public disclosures, but participation in innovation competitions, joint projects with other students, or giving interviews to the media are all the types of disclosures that could undermine patent eligibility.

Patenting Software

Alice and later cases have complicated the question of when software may be patented. Software certainly may not be patented to execute a non-technical business method.

And as we saw regarding the EU's Article 35, the EU does not allow any software patents.

There is currently a two-part test in the U.S. for determining the eligibility of software patent claims. This *Alice/Mayo* test essentially asks: (i) are the claims directed to an abstract idea and (ii) if so, do the claims contain an "inventive concept" sufficient to "transform" the claimed abstract idea into "something more" than an abstract idea, a law of nature, or a natural phenomenon.

The Court of Appeals for the Federal Circuit found that an algorithm software invention that enabled the smooth display of numeric data on an oscilloscope was patentable. The Court found this to be the practical application of an abstract idea providing a "useful, concrete and tangible result."

This is consistent with the idea that, like other types of claims, software-based claims might not survive Section 101 rejection unless they solve a technological problem, improve technology, improve an industrial process, or make a computer perform better.

Copyright law is more commonly used to protect software than patent law. Copyright law has a key advantage in that it is for a longer term. In the U.S., copyrights are valid for the life of the author plus 80 years, compared to just 20 years for patents. Copyright registration is also much simpler than the patent application process.

But, as discussed, copyright protections extend only to expressions, not to inventions.

Invention Capture Process

One of the best ways to develop a patent strategy and to identify patentable inventions is to form a team to do so, have the team elect a leader, and find a good patent attorney who is willing to do some free work with a view toward hopefully getting some paid work. Many patent attorneys are very willing to play this role.

Invention Capture Team. A patenting team can go by any name, but my companies have called them invention teams, innovation teams, and invention capture teams.

We will call them invention capture teams here, since that clearly describes what they do:

- figure out everything the company is inventing as it creates products and solves problems,

- work with counsel to decide which of those inventions might be patentable, and

- work with counsel to file patent applications.

Invention capture teams should draw from almost every group in a company – certainly from technology, engineering, product, customer service, legal, compliance, and finance.

Role of Counsel. Picking the right outside patent counsel to help guide the team is key. Enthusiasm for entrepreneurship and invention and successful patenting experience in the industry are important qualities, as are strong group engagement and project management skills.

The patent attorney should be willing to put in some free time to train the team on what types of things are patentable and then facilitate a series of discussions about things like:

- current and future products,

- problems that the products solve,

- problems the team has solved or is solving in creating and offering the products,

- anything that made a computer perform better, and

- technologies and systems used, and how they were improved.

My favorite patent attorneys hold off on charging fees until patentable inventions are identified.

If no patentable ideas are identified, no fees are charged.

Here's a fee structure I sometimes request:

- $15,000 per submitted patent application, good through either patent grant or responding to two adverse USPTO office actions.

- That amount paid in equal installments over three milestones: (i) patent application filing, (ii) first response sent after first significant USPTO office action, and (iii) patent granted or response sent after second USPTO office action.

- After responding to two office actions, things tend to go hourly, so it's nice if the attorney's billing rate isn't sky high.

That's just one example of how patent legal fees might be negotiated. $15,000 per patent might seem low, but it works out well for counsel when a single core innovation spurs multiple related applications, called "a patent family."

Patent legal fees can get confusing and expensive quickly without a project-based, capped-fee structure. One way or another, make sure you and counsel are clear on budget limits and the need to defer any fees.

Identifying Inventions. Patent counsel should probe the team to learn about new or anticipated processes or procedures, new technical or design solutions, current technological or design problems or challenges, and any recent epiphanies team members have experienced in solving a problem or coming up with a better way to do something, or anything else that improved an industrial process or made a computer perform better.

Wherever and whenever problems are being solved, patentable inventions might be found.

For many, the possibility of being listed as an inventor on one or more patent applications can be very inspiring. Rarely does anyone turn down an invitation to join an invention capture team. As with most teams, there is always a spectrum of engagement and contribution among members, but teams ranging between 7 to 11 members seem to generate the most productive discussions and the best results.

Invention Capture Form. Design a simple "invention capture" form that isn't overly technical or intimidating and that members of the invention group can easily fill out to capture potential inventions for consideration by outside patent counsel.

Incentivize participants in the group with increasingly interesting rewards, monetary or otherwise, to submit ideas and to follow up as necessary through different phases of the process, including drafting patent applications with counsel.

Have outside counsel spend separate time with product managers, engineers, and other key managers. Do not assume outside counsel fully understands the business, as that is unlikely.

Prior Art Search. Deciding which patent applications to file can involve searching for prior art, including granted patents, published patent applications, and other documents that disclose the same invention. When this process is solely focused on finding patents or applications that could be cited against a proposed application it is sometimes referred to simply as a "patent search."

Patent counsel are divided on how exhaustively to search for patents, applications, or other prior art that might block a proposed patent application or patent family.

Some counsel urge a thorough search, while other urge a more minimalist approach. One reason given for a minimalist approch is "*The USPTO examiner will find any prior art, so it's really not necessary to go looking.*" Another stated concern is that finding potentially conflicting patents but then ignoring them increases risks of enhanced damages under willful infringement claims.

Fudging the prior art search is probably a minority position, so let's assume most companies will do at least basic prior art searching before paying counsel to start writing a particular patent application.

I begin most prior art searches on Google Patent and the USPTO website to identify and review potentially conflicting patents and patent applications.

Other search platforms can be used to look for similar products or services in the market that essentially disclose any proposed inventions. The ease of searching and reading patent abstracts makes prior art researching a little easier than one might expect.

Prior art research can help entrepreneurs fine-tune ideas discussed with patent counsel. Knowing the prior art facilitates the process of "writing around" any existing inventions, or possibly combining existing inventions in previously unknown ways to create "something more," as the post-Alice case law requires.

The USPTO website has a page with numerous resources relating to prior art searches, including tips for laypersons and more advanced discussions on how USPTO examiners conduct their prior art searches. That page can be found by searching online for "USPTO prior art search" or going to this link https://www.uspto.gov/patent/initiatives/prior-art-search.

Patent Application Requirements

Application. Every patent begins with an application. They are filed with the USPTO either electronically or by mail. A "non-provisional" patent application must include:

- "utility patent application transmittal form," or transmittal letter,
- title of the invention, a specification, including a description and a claim(s),
- drawings, when necessary (pro tip: always include them),
- an oath or declaration, and
- filing, search, and examination fees.

Non-Provisional versus Provisional Applications. For now, we are primarily discussing non-provisional applications.

Provisional applications are discussed below. At a high level, they allow applicants to hold their place in line for a year with a partially complete application. The USPTO does not review provisional applications, and it will continue to conduct no review of the application *unless and until* the applicant follows up with a non-provisional application.

Patent applications must provide extensive detail about an invention, but a provisional application will *never* be published (made public) if the applicant does not follow up with a non-provisional patent within twelve months.

Key advantages of provisional patents include: (i) locking in a priority date, (ii) delaying some legal expenses, (iii) being able to use the "patent pending" notice, and (iv) protecting an invention's confidentiality until a decision is made about filing a non-provisional application.

Specification. The heart of every patent is its "specification." In its online *"Nonprovisional (Utility) Patent Application Filing Guide,"* ("USPTO Filing Guide") the USPTO describes the specification, in part, as follows:

> *The specification is a written description of the invention and of the manner and process of making and using the invention that concludes with the claims to the invention, which must begin on a new page. The specification must be in clear, full, concise, and exact terms to enable any person skilled in the art or science to which the invention pertains to make and use the same.*

<u>Other Mandatory Elements of a Patent Application.</u> The USPTO Filing Guide describes other elements of an application, in part, as follows:

Background of the Invention

> *This section should include a statement of the field of endeavor to which the invention pertains. This section may also include a paraphrasing of the applicable U.S. patent classification definitions or the subject matter of the claimed invention.*

> *Also, it should contain a description of information known to you, including references to specific documents related to your invention. It should contain, if applicable, references to specific problems involved in the prior art (or state of technology) that your invention is drawn toward. See MPEP § 608.01(c) for more information.*

Brief Summary of the Invention

> *This section should present the substance or general idea of the claimed invention in summarized form. The summary can include the advantages of the invention and how it solves previously existing problems. Preferably, problems are identified in the Background of the Invention section. A statement of the object of the invention may also be included....*

Detailed Description of the Invention

> *In this section, the invention must be explained along with the process of making and using the invention in full, clear, concise, and exact terms. This section should distinguish the invention from other inventions and from what is old. It should also describe completely the process, machine,*

manufacture, composition of matter, or improvement invented. In the case of an improvement, the description should be confined to the specific improvement and to the parts that necessarily cooperate with it or that are necessary to completely understand the invention.

It is required that the description be sufficient so that any person of ordinary skill in the pertinent art, science, or area could make and use the invention without extensive experimentation. The best mode contemplated by the inventor of carrying out the invention must be set forth in the description....

Claim or Claims

The claim or claims must particularly point out and distinctly claim the subject matter that the inventor or inventors regard as the invention. The claims define the scope of the protection of the patent. Whether a patent will be granted is determined, in large measure, by the scope of the claims.

A nonprovisional application for a utility patent must contain at least one claim. The claim or claims section must begin on a separate physical sheet or electronic page. If there are several claims, they must be numbered consecutively in Arabic numerals.

One or more claims may be presented in dependent form, referring back to and further limiting another claim or claims in the same application. All dependent claims should be grouped together with the claim or claims to which they refer to the extent practicable. Any dependent claim that refers to more than one other claim (multiple dependent claim) shall refer to such other claims in the alternative only. Each claim should be a single sentence, and where a claim sets forth a number of elements or steps, each element or step of the claim should be separated by a line indentation.

Abstract of the Disclosure

The purpose of the abstract is to enable the USPTO and the public to quickly determine the nature of the technical disclosures of your invention. The abstract points out what is new in the art to which your invention pertains. It should be in narrative form and generally limited to a single paragraph, and it must begin on a separate page. An abstract should not be longer than 150 words. See MPEP § 608.01(b) for more information.

Drawings

A patent application is required to contain drawings if drawings are necessary to understand the subject matter to be patented. Most patent applications contain drawings. The drawings must show every feature of the invention as specified in the claims. A drawing necessary to understand the invention cannot be introduced into an application after the filing date of the application because of the prohibition against new matter....

Oath or Declaration

An oath or declaration is a formal statement that must be made by the inventor in a non-provisional application, including utility, design, plant and reissue applications. Either form PTO/ AIA/01 or PTO/AIA/08 may be used to make the required declaration in a utility application. It is preferred that applicants use form PTO/AIA/01, which must be filed together with an application data sheet. Each inventor must sign an oath or declaration that includes certain statements required by law and the USPTO rules, including the statement that he or she believes himself or herself to be the original inventor or an original joint inventor of a claimed invention in the application, and the statement that the application was made or authorized to be made by him or her. See 35 U.S.C 115 and 37 CFR § 1.63. An oath must be sworn to by the inventor before a notary public....

Dependent versus Independent Claims. A patent's claims are what the applicant is requesting protection for – i.e., the subject matter for which the applicant is seeking a 20-year monopoly. Things included in a patent's description but not in its claims are not protected. They do become "prior art" though, if not previously published or disclosed.

The difference between "dependent" claims and "independent claims" is very important. A claim that references and relies upon an earlier claim takes on its "limitations." This is called a "dependent" claim. A dependent claim is more limited in scope than the earlier independent claim. On the other hand, an independent claim is one that does not refer to any other claim.

Said another way, independent claims stand alone and have independent legal significance; dependent claims require the presence of the underlying independent claim. Infringement of the dependent claim only happens if both claims, independent and dependent, are infringed.

The following is an example of a dependent claim:

> *3. The fluid energy conversion system of claim 1, wherein said discs are axially spaced apart by resilient spacing elements.*

The independent claim is the fluid energy conversion system of claim 1. The dependent claim is claim 1, *plus* where certain described discs are axially spaced apart by resilient spacing elements.

Prioritizing and Drafting. The patent system is arcane, slow, anachronistic, and shrouded in obtuse jargon. It can be challenging for entrepreneurs to participate and stay in the game intellectually. But stay in the game they must.

This opacity and other challenges in obtaining patents require a close, trusted relationship with competent patent counsel.

Before filing any applications for a new client, the best patent attorneys will (i) participate in the company's invention capture processes and also (ii) spend quality time with its developers, engineers, and other technology team members understanding their work inside and out.

Immersion in a startup's business ensures the right applications are filed first and that they are well-drafted.

Omnibus Patent Application Strategy. Cash strapped startups often file an "omnibus" patent application, meaning a detailed "parent" application with enough disclosure and technical support in its specification to cover numerous inventions that are reasonably related to each other. Some also call this a "consolidated application."

Later, when it has more money, the company can slice off different "claim sets" into individual "continuation" or "continuing" applications. All of the continuation applications benefit from the earlier priority date of the omnibus application.

This cuts cost up front but preserves priority and flexibility down the road. As an added benefit, if a competitor comes along, it may be possible to file a continuation that "reads" right on top of what the competitor is doing.

Requesting Confidentiality/Nonpublication Request. There is a form that can be filed with a patent application to request that a patent application *never* be made public (published) unless and until a patent is granted. USPTO Form PTO/SB/35, *Nonpublication Request.*

Few seem to know about this, and it is surprisingly rarely discussed. It must be filed *with* the application – not later. Too late.

"Nonpublication" can only be requested if *no foreign applications* are ever expected to be filed. That is the only substantive requirement for requesting confidential information. If no foreign filings are contemplated, strongly consider including a Form PTO/SB/35.

The statutory authority for requesting "confidential status" is 35 U.S.C. 122(b)(2)(B)(i), which reads as follows:

> *If an applicant makes a request upon filing, certifying that the invention disclosed in the application has not and will not be the subject of an application filed in another country, or under a multilateral international agreement, that requires publication of applications 18 months after filing, the application shall not be published as provided in paragraph (1).*

The USPTO rule adopted under that statutory authority is "37 CFR 1.213 Nonpublication request." It reads, in part, as follows:

> (a) *If the invention disclosed in an application has not been and will not be the subject of an application filed in another country, or under a multilateral international agreement, that requires publication of applications eighteen months after filing, the application will not be published under 35 U.S.C. 122(b) and § 1.211 provided:*
>
> (1) *A request (nonpublication request) is submitted with the application upon filing;*
>
> (2) *The request states in a conspicuous manner that the application is not to be published under 35 U.S.C. 122(b);*
>
> (3) *The request contains a certification that the invention disclosed in the application has not been and will not be the subject of an application filed in another country, or under a multilateral international agreement, that requires publication at eighteen months after filing; and*
>
> (4) *The request is signed in compliance with § 1.33(b).*

Other trade secret strategies are discussed again below under *Strategies for Protecting Trade Secrets.*

Application Review and Office Actions

When filed with the USPTO, a non-provisional application is assigned for examination to the respective examining "technology center" with responsibility for the area of technology related to the invention. Applications are then assigned to an examiner.

On its website, under the caption, *General Information Concerning Patents*, the USPTO describes the examination process as follows:

> *The examination of the application consists of a study of the application for compliance with the legal requirements and a search through U.S. patents, publications of patent applications, foreign patent documents, and available literature, to see if the claimed invention is new, useful and non-obvious and if the application meets the requirements of the patent statute and rules of practice. If the examiner's decision on patentability is favorable, a patent is granted.*

Office Actions. Examiner decisions are communicated to applicants in writing using what is called an "Office action." Office actions provide the reasons for any adverse action or any objection or require-ment. An Office action also provides relevant information or references expected to help the applicant decide whether and how to continue prosecution of the application.

Again, under *General Information Concerning Patents*, the USPTO provides these insights about Office actions and applicant responses:

> *If the claimed invention is not directed to patentable subject matter, the claims will be rejected. If the examiner finds that the claimed invention lacks novelty or differs only in an obvious manner from what is found in the prior art, the claims may also be rejected. It is not uncommon for some or all of the claims to be rejected on the first Office action by the examiner; relatively few applications are allowed as filed.*
>
> *Applicant's Reply*
>
> *The applicant must request reconsideration in writing, and must distinctly and specifically point out the supposed errors in the examiner's Office action. The applicant must reply to every ground of objection and rejection in the prior Office action. The applicant's reply must appear throughout to be a bona fide attempt to advance the case to final action or allowance. The mere allegation that the examiner has erred will not be received as a proper reason for such reconsideration.*
>
> *In amending an application in reply to a rejection, the applicant must clearly point out why he or she thinks the amended claims are patentable in view of the state of the art disclosed by the prior references cited or the objections made. He or she must also show how the claims as amended avoid such references or objections. After reply by the applicant, the application will be reconsidered, and the applicant will be notified as to the status of the claims—that is, whether the claims are rejected, or objected to, or whether the claims are allowed, in the same manner as after the first examination. The second Office action usually will be made final.*

Interviews with examiners may be arranged, but an interview does not remove the necessity of replying to Office actions within the required time.

Provisional Patent Applications

As discussed, a provisional application allows an applicant to establish an early effective filing date for a later filed non-provisional application, while also allowing the applicant to omit substantial information, including:

- a formal patent claim(s),

- an oath or declaration, or

- information disclosure (prior art) statement.

There are many reasons for considering a provisional patent application over a non-provisional application, including but not limited to:

- funds are low but sufficient to cover the cost of a strong provisional patent to secure the earliest possible priority date for an invention, and to eliminate the risk of losing patent eligibility due to disclosure,

- securing a priority date while waiting for another year to see how the USPTO is dealing with certain types of claims or to see if USPTO policies become more favorable in some respect,

- saving cost on inventions that would be extensions of or variations of earlier-filed non-provisional patents to see how the earlier filings fair in the examination process,

- strategies discussed next relating to protecting the confidentiality of trade secrets or at least delaying their disclosure until a later-filed non-provisional application, and

- securing the right to use the "patent pending" notice for an entire year regarding an invention(s) the patentability of which may be uncertain.

As noted earlier, once a provisional application is filed, the applicant has an entire year to determine whether to proceed with a non-provisional application. Again, provisional applications never become public if a non-provisional patent application is not subsequently filed.

Given the ability to use the "patent pending" notice, even a provisional patent application might scare away a potential competitor – or its potential investors. I have heard VCs cite this concern to a startup during a pitch – i.e., *"Your competitor's website says patent pending. What do you know about that?"*

Another benefit of a provisional application is that it establishes an early effective filing date for an invention without triggering the beginning of the 20-year protection period if the patent is granted.

A provisional patent is only as good as it is drafted. It cannot be later expected to cover inventions not described. Entrepreneurs and their patent counsel must strive to disclose the company's core innovations and also the ways future competitors might try to design around them. This is a critical aspect of a provisional patent application that should not be viewed any differently than a non-provisional patent application.

Strategies for Protecting Trade Secrets

As we have discussed, patent protection and trade secret protection are largely binary alternatives to each other. There are, however, some gray areas around this general principle.

Publication Date. When a non-provisional patent application is filed, the USPTO provides a filing receipt that includes a "projected publication date," generally eighteen months later. That is the date the USPTO will publish the patent, which makes the patent application publicly available.

The publication date for an application is the Thursday after the date that is eighteen months after the earliest filing date claimed by the applicant.

If the application claims priority, such as priority to the filing date of a provisional application, then the projected publication date is the Thursday after the date that is eighteen months after the filing date of the provisional application.

Request for Nonpublication. As mentioned earlier, one often overlooked opportunity for protecting trade secrets involves the use of USPTO Form PTO/SB/35, captioned Nonpublication Request under 35 U.S.C. 122(b)(2)(B)(i).

Any inventor only seeking patent protection in the U.S. should consider submitting this form or otherwise making a nonpublication request in a "similarly conspicuous manner" in writing when filing the patent application.

If the patent is never granted, it will *never* be published, and all of its invention disclosures will remain confidential.

Most importantly, Form PTO/SB/35 (or similarly conspicuous language) must be submitted with the initial patent application. If the USPTO misses the request for nonpublication *for any reason*, it cannot be honored.

Form PTO/SB/35 requires the following (i) certification and (ii) undertaking to update:

> *I hereby certify that the invention disclosed in the attached application has not and will not be the subject of an application filed in another country, or under a multilateral international agreement, that requires publication at eighteen months after filing.*
>
> …..
>
> *If applicant subsequently files an application directed to the invention disclosed in the attached application in another country, or under a multilateral international agreement, that requires publication of applications eighteen months after filing, the applicant must notify the United States Patent and Trademark Office of such filing within forty-five (45) days after the date of the filing of such foreign or international application.* ***Failure to do so will result in abandonment of this application (35 U.S.C. 122(b)(2)(B)(iii)).***

If an applicant chooses not to use Form PTO/SB/35 in making its nonpublication request, all of the above language should be included conspicuously in the application.

See again the USPTO's *"Failure to do so..."* admonition. That warning represents the most significant risk in making a request for nonpublication. If a foreign filing is unexpectedly made later, failing to inform the USPTO will result in the USPTO administratively abandoning (rejecting) the application.

The USPTO posted the following answer in the Patent FAQ's, providing practice tips regarding both requests for nonpublication and abandoning patent applications before publication to, among other things, protect trade secrets:

> *A request for non-publication will not be recognized unless it is conspicuous. See 37 CFR 1.213(a)(2). Providing text as one paragraph among numerous other paragraphs with no highlighting of the request for non-publication is not conspicuous, and thus the Office's assignment of a publication date was appropriate. To avoid publication, you may expressly abandon the application, and file a new application under 37 CFR 1.53(b), claiming priority to the earlier-filed application, with a "Nonpublication Request under 35 U.S.C. 122(b)(2) (B)(i)" ([USPTO Form PTO/SB/35]) or make the request and certification in a similarly conspicuous manner when filing the patent application. If your application has been assigned a publication date within the next one to six months, you should consider filing a petition for express abandonment under 37 CFR 1.138(c). If your application has been assigned a publication date within the next four weeks, then it is too late to avoid publication of the application.... Applicant would have a similar remedy in other situations where the request is not conspicuous, for example, where the request is in the specification of the application, on a fee transmittal sheet, or buried in the transmittal letter.*

Petition for Express Abandonment. As indicated in the preceding guidance, an applicant can file a "petition for express abandonment" under 37 CFR 1.138(c) up to four weeks from its assigned publication date.

When done timely and correctly, this terminates a patent application and prevents it from being made public by the USPTO.

A petition for express abandonment could be a very helpful tactic in the event it becomes clear that (i) a patent is unlikely to be granted, (ii) the applicant has insufficient funds to pursue the patent, or (iii) the applicant decided the invention is better protected as a trade secret.

No specific reasons must be provided, but a petition for express abandonment will not be granted unless the petition and the fee (currently $130) are received at the USPTO by mail or fax (with authorization to charge the fee to a deposit account) more than four weeks prior to the projected date of publication.

Provisional Application as Trade Secret Strategy. As already discussed, if an applicant does not file a non-provisional application within one year of filing a provisional patent application, the application is abandoned and will never be published.

If the applicant does follow up with a non-provisional application, the date of publication by the USPTO is 18 months from the filing date of the provisional application.

The implications of this are that: (i) nothing needs to be done to abandon a provisional application to prevent it from being published and (ii) the filing of a provisional application does not extend the ultimate date of publication of an application when a non-provisional application is subsequently filed.

An applicant always has just under 17 months to decide whether or not to prevent the publication of a patent application if a non-provisional application has been filed.

Some have also made the case that a detailed provisional patent application that is allowed to lapse can then serve as a formal, time-stamped official document fully describing a trade secret, which then can be shared under NDA with potential investors or others. An expressly abandoned non-provisional patent application could be used similarly.

While this is not a whole lot different than maintaining a written inventory of a company's trade secrets, the official looking nature of a provisional patent application or abandoned non-provisional application might make the difference in convincing an investor to put up some money.

Inventor Assignment Documentation

As has already been emphasized, PIIAs with employees and Independent Contractor Agreements with contractors should include clear IP assignments in favor of the company. They should also include standard language explicitly making the company such persons' attorney in fact for the purposes of signing any IP assignment documentation necessary to effect such assignments in the event the person is unwilling, unable, or unavailable to sign them personally.

This is critical for establishing a company's ownership of inventions in the patent application process, which requires the listing of all inventors.

Before the AIA, all patent applications had to be filed in the name of the individual inventors, even if they were actual employees of the company that owned the inventions. Those individuals then had to sign assignment documentation in favor of the company to correct the official record as to ownership.

Where applications are signed in the names of the individual inventors and assignment documentation has not been timely obtained, companies can find themselves essentially extorted by former employees with little interest in cooperating to document such IP rights.

The assignment issue may be less problematic now that the AIA allows company-assignees to file patent applications in their names from the outset. Hopefully this option encourages companies to obtain assignments to specific inventions from all inventors before filing patent applications, thus leading to fewer IP concerns down the road.

Patent Search versus Patent Clearance or Freedom to Operate

Earlier we discussed prior art searches, or patent searches. These are searches conducted before filing a patent application to see if an idea is sufficiently novel to be eligible for a patent. Aside from searching for prior art to file its own patent applications, how much should a company do to find out if it might be infringing third-party patents?

Those efforts are called "patent clearance," or "freedom to operate" assessments – i.e., is there freedom to operate in an area without fear of infringing the patents of others? Patent clearance may reduce a company's risks of actually infringing third-party patents and it may help in designing around existing patents, but in some cases does it simply increase risks of larger penalties by providing evidence of knowing or willful infringement?

Facts and Circumstances. The answers to these questions are very fact specific. In areas like mobile phone technology where the top players are extremely litigious, patent clearance is probably more important. In areas less likely to be covered by highly enforceable patents held by litigious actors, patent clearance may be less important.

In most cases, it seems companies choose not to do much patent clearance research unless they are forced to by potential customers, investors, or acquirors.

Some of this is purely tied to resources and apathy, but there are clearly divergent views on how much to devote to patent clearance.

Reasons suggested for not conducting patent clearance research are (i) the cost and (ii) the possibility that knowledge of an allegedly infringed patent could lead to treble damages.

Regarding cost, patent firms can charge in the low thousands of dollars to conduct robust patent clearance research. If that research is to be backed up by a freedom to operate legal opinion, the cost can range between $10,000 and $30,000.

Some of those high fees are no-doubt used to cover the law firms' malpractice insurance premiums for issuing such high-risk opinions, but there is actually a big difference in the amount of time and effort that goes into a patent search to support a patent application versus to support a legal opinion. There is no legal liability for filing a poorly researched patent application, but issuing an erroneous freedom to operate legal opinion could result in substantial liability.

Treble Damages for Willful Infringement. The risk of treble damages for patent infringement was somewhat uncertain under the case law between 2007 and 2015, but in June of 2015 the U.S. Supreme Court threw out what it viewed as "unduly rigid" rules for determining whether or not a case of infringement warranted enhanced damages.

That case, *Halo Electronics, Inc. v. Pulse Electronics, Inc.*, gives U.S. district courts broad discretion to impose treble damages whenever warranted by the facts. In so finding, the Court said:

> In applying this discretion, district courts are "to be guided by [the] sound legal principles" developed over nearly two centuries of application and interpretation of the Patent Act. Martin, 546 U. S., at 139 (internal quotation marks omitted). Those principles channel the exercise of discretion, limiting the award of enhanced damages to egregious cases of misconduct beyond typical infringement.
>
> *Halo Electronics, Inc. v. Pulse Electronics, Inc.*, et al., 136 S.Ct. 1923 (2016)
> https://www.supremecourt.gov/opinions/15pdf/14-1513_db8e.pdf

It is a reasonable assumption that willful, knowing infringement might be equated with "egregious… misconduct." This *"careful what you know about"* concern drives many to avoid the cost of patent clearance efforts.

Third Party Demands for Freedom to Operate Opinions. Sometimes investors and acquirors raise freedom to operate questions. A company might want to assess the risks of finding conflicting patents before deciding how to respond.

On two occasions, I have refused a potential acquiror's demands that we obtain a freedom to operate legal opinion. In one case in particular, I knew an opinion would be costly and somewhat uncertain, but not unreasonably so. I also knew the opinion would then be used against my company to lower the valuation of the acquisition below what we were willing to accept.

In that case, I told the acquiror's counsel we were comfortable with our position and that if they needed greater comfort, they should pay for their own freedom to operate opinion concerning our business.

I also told them, if they did so, we did not want to be presented with the opinion or to be told anything about it, given the acquiror's inherent potential for bias toward lowering the acquisition valuation. Secretly, I also had in mind the risk of potential treble damages should I learn about any concerning patents.

That acquisition closed and no post-closing patent infringement issues ever arose. Obtaining a freedom to operate opinion might well have resulted in a different outcome.

That situation proved the adage that sometimes it's best to let a sleeping dog lie, likely a prevalent attitude when it comes to patent clearance.

The Rise and Fall of Patent Trolls

As noted earlier, patent trolls can be thought of as persons or entities that acquire portfolios of patents and use them to threaten others with litigation to extort exorbitant license payments.

Patent trolls seemed to have become a permanent burden on U.S. business in the 1990s and 2000s. All of my companies had to litigate with them during that period.

The problem appears to be abating due to several factors, including:

- the *Alice* case,

- the AIA's inter partes review and post grant review processes for challenging weak patents, and

- a 2017 U.S. Supreme Court case called *TC Heartland LLC v. Kraft Foods Group Brands LLC* that limited where patent owners can choose to file their lawsuits – either in the defendant's state of incorporation or anywhere the defendant has a regular place of business.

The *TC Heartland* case has made it harder for trolls to file cases in the much maligned, patent-troll friendly "Eastern District of Texas." In a sign of the importance of the *TC Heartland case,* in April of 2019, Apple closed both of its stores in the Eastern District of Texas – one in Plano and another in Frisco. Apple announced it did so to avoid patent trolls.

Comparison: Trademarks, Copyrights, Trade Secrets and Patents

We have looked at trademarks, copyrights, trade secrets, and patents individually and at some of their interrelationships. Understanding those interrelationships is helpful in developing a comprehensive IP strategy.

The graphic below represents which areas intersect, overlap, or complement each other. The arrows show types of IP that can be protected by one or more areas of IP law. Outside these four bubbles lies unprotectable IP – ideas and information in the public domain.

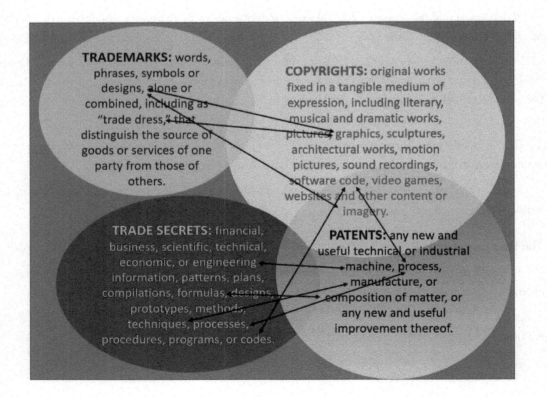

Overlap of Trademark and Copyright Law

Trademark and copyright law coverage often overlap for the same product. Both apply to IP assets that are represented visually, but with different legal protections.

A piece of clothing featuring a company logo is a good example. The logo is protected (i) under trademark law from being used by others in ways that cause confusion as to the source of goods and (ii) under copyright law as a visual design.

Copyright law protects the logo design from being reproduced in any manner that does not constitute "fair use."

Websites and similar properties also offer examples of trademark-copyright overlap. Where the "look and feel" of a website is copied by a third party, but not much of the text, copyright law might not provide a remedy. But if the theft of the website "trade dress" is sufficient to create confusion about the source of the goods or services, the Lanham Act can be invoked.

Overlap of Copyright Law and Patent Law

Similarly, copyright law and patent law overlap and provide complementary protections in industries where authored works and novel inventions are combined.

The best example might be the video game industry. All of the visual, textual, and musical aspects of a video game are protected under copyright law. Gaming software also constitutes a copyrighted work.

Patent law comes into play primarily to protect inventions embedded in gaming technology platforms, how ancillary hardware components interact, and potentially also in any related software innovations.

Game controllers, consoles, headsets, and other physical equipment can also be protected by design patents, not to mention trade dress protection.

Patents and Trade Secrets

Trade secret protection and patent law protection also intersect and overlap, but mostly as diametrically opposed alternatives.

If a company applies for a patent on an invention previously protected as a trade secret, all trade secret protections are immediately lost once the patent application is published by the USPTO 18 months from the date of filing.

That said, patents and trade secrets can and almost always do exist *side by side,* protecting different but related or complementary inventions, ideas, and information.

Aside from the role of copyright in protecting software code, the job of protecting ideas and inventions generally falls to patent law and trade secret law. Understanding their respective pros and cons is important.

Patent Advantages:

- the statutory right *"to exclude others from making, using, offering for sale, or selling"* the invention in the United States, or *"importing"* the invention into the United States,

- a patent is a government-issued *"sword and shield"* that empowers the owner to make, use, and sell the invention with relative peace of mind while preventing competitors from doing so,

- filing first under the "first-to-file" system provides valuable assurance against unknown claims by other inventors,

- U.S. patent applications can be leveraged internationally,

- patents provide a predictable time frame of protection, unless challenged and invalidated before expiration,

- patents have "slide value," meaning they can be listed in a slide deck and other materials shared with investors, potential customers and other stakeholders; trade secrets, on the other hand, can only be alluded to in vague terms, absent an NDA, and

- although patent valuations have come down in recent years, there is still a market for the purchase and sale of patents as stand-alone assets; no such corollary exists in the world of trade secrets, aside from asset-based M&A deals.

Trade Secret Advantages:

- trade secrets protect ideas and information that cannot be patented,

- protecting trade secrets involves nominal expense, no government filings, and few administrative burdens beyond adopting and observing confidentiality best practices,

- trade secrets have no expiration date, assuming the secret is kept, and

- trade secrets are essentially international in scope, particularly with the scope and reach of both the Economic Espionage Act and the Defend Trade Secrets Act; conversely, a U.S. patent application shares all of its disclosures globally without providing corresponding global protection.

Cost as a Key Factor. One of the biggest concerns in pursuing a patent-heavy strategy is cost. "Prosecuting" four to six patents through to grant can easily cost a startup $100,000 or more. The cost of failed patent applications is hardly any less.

Most startups, therefore, rightly consider cost as a significant factor in whether or not to apply for patents. Filing multiple patents is often simply beyond the means of many startups. Even for sophisticated companies with substantial resources, the high costs, administrative burdens, and uncertainties associated with pursuing patents can make trade secret protection more attractive for products expected to have a relatively short market life.

Lastly, the uncertainties caused by the *Alice* case, and its negative impacts on patent valuations, have caused some investors to send mixed signals on how much value they assign to costly patent strategies.

Protecting Core Innovations

Most startups begin as an idea – a new product or service that solves a problem or fills a need or want. Every startup needs at least one core innovation.

IP strategy should rightly focus on protecting these core innovations, but cost is always a factor, and some ideas are simply more protectable than others.

Unprotectable Ideas. In some cases, companies with largely unprotectable IP count on being first in the market and executing better than the competition, leveraging their "first mover advantage."

In any event, knowing what is protectable as IP and what is not helps prioritize resources. An unprotectable idea is one that is <u>not</u> (i) a patentable invention, (ii) a copyrightable "work," or (iii) an enforceable trade secret.

The competitive relationship between Uber and Lyft comes to mind. Both have patent portfolios. But their core innovation, a tech-enabled taxi service, is not protectable because it is too obvious, particularly following the demise of business method patents.

Copyright Law and Software. Software drives many innovative startup business models. Software is copyrighted when written, but it can be registered with the U.S. Copyright office for a fee of between $35 and $55.

As described earlier, software copyright registration rules allow for the protection of trade secrets through redaction. SaaS companies and others with software-driven business models should focus appropriate resources on both copyright and trade secret strategies.

The copyright strategies and expertise required in media-driven industries, such as publishing, broadcasting, cinema, news, video games, and music, are distinctly different from those of most other startups and are beyond the scope of this book.

Gaming companies, for example, devote substantial effort to clearing copyright issues for music, visual, and thematic elements, and also to negotiating revenue-producing licenses for advertising placements involving consumer products and brands.

Patent or Trade Secret – An Analytical Framework

Taking into account the respective advantages and disadvantages of patent protection versus trade secret protection, and assuming a budget for patent prosecution in the range of $150,000 to $200,000, (i.e., not unlimited), individual innovations might be selected for either patent protection or trade secret protection based on the following general criteria:

Consider patent protection for:

1. patentable innovations that are expected to be fully monetized within the 20-year life of a patent,

2. patentable innovations that are subject to the greatest risk of others patenting first, and

3. patentable innovations in fields where patents are actively used offensively and defensively against competitors.

Consider trade secret protection for:

1. ideas, innovations, and information that are clearly not patentable or subject to high risk of rejection by the USPTO,

2. patentable innovations that are unlikely to be patented by others,

3. patentable innovations that would provide greater value over a longer period as trade secrets than under the 20-year life of a patent,

4. innovations with international commercial potential but where the filing of a U.S. patent could result in copying by foreign competitors, particularly if funds for robust international patenting are unavailable, and

5. innovations that might or might not be patentable, but that are expected to have a very short product life cycle.

Protection of core innovations through the patent process is a "long game," as some experts describe it. The pendulum might swing back on what is patentable or enforceable. If you don't file an application now, you could lose that opportunity. Maybe hedge against that risk by filing an omnibus provisional application.

Investors may be a little more skeptical currently about the value of patents, but for most investors, patents still have slide value.

Current and prospective customers, especially B2B customers, may also take comfort in your company having broad patent protection. It could be a key differentiator against competitors with weaker patent protection. This is particularly true if the products or services in question will be embedded into the customer's critical business processes or systems, making the B2B customer a potential target for any infringement claims.

IP Summary

Trademarks

- Strong marks generally create more value and are easier to defend against infringers – be fanciful or arbitrary, and not generic or descriptive.

- Common law trademark protections are subject to geographic limitations.

- Rarely is there a good reason for delaying federal trademark registration of a company's key marks.

- The Lanham Act provides strong remedies against false and misleading product comparisons. All advertising involving comparisons to competitors' products or services must be factual, correct, and backed up by documentary support.

- Trademark disputes are common in business. Careful searching before naming companies, products, and services, and using fanciful names all serve to reduce litigation risks, improve chances of federal registration, and reduce risks of domain name-related difficulties.

- Individuals have strong state law rights protecting their likeness and personality from commercial exploitation.

Copyrights

- Copyright registration is the cheapest and easiest form of federal IP protection, and the availability of statutory damages is a powerful enforcement tool.

- Copyright registration rights include statutory damages and attorneys' fee awards against infringers – strong negotiating leverage for resolving infringement issues.

- Absent proper "work made for hire" language, independent contractors own the works they create, not their clients.

- Fair use of others' copyrighted works is limited to criticism, comment, news reporting, teaching, scholarship, or research. But other factors are also considered, including whether the use is commercial, how much of a work is used, and the extent to which the use impacts the commercial value of the work.

- Copyright registration is a powerful tool for protecting software code, particularly in light of the ability to redact trade secret information from software copyright registration submissions.

- Companies should train their employees about the potentially severe consequences of using pictures and other copyrighted works before trouble strikes.

Trade Secrets

- Strong confidentiality practices are critical, including the consistent use of PIIAs, NDAs, and tight independent contractor agreements.

- Trade secret protections can be lost when the information is, in fact, no longer secret, or simply when there is evidence of lax confidentiality protections.

- Limit all unnecessary sharing of sensitive information even when confidentiality documents are in place.

- Require departing employees to certify that they have turned over all confidential information.

- Creating an inventory of trade secrets can help others on the team know what to protect.

- Valuable inventions that can be reverse engineered or otherwise discovered are often best protected with patents, when that is an option.

- Companies should take appropriate precautions to ensure that the trade secrets of others are not incorporated into their products, services, or operations, as the criminal penalties and civil remedies for trade secret theft are severe.

- Working with NDAs can seem deceptively routine and simple, leading to costly mistakes. NDAs should be treated with the same care as any other contract, and employees should be trained to avoid all common mistakes.

Patents

- Patents offer some of the strongest IP protections available and, like trade secrets, they are used to protect ideas.

- Never release a new product or service without asking first whether it should be patented. The ability to obtain foreign patents can be lost permanently with a single disclosure before the filing of a patent application.

- Under the first-to-file system, it is more important than ever to consider protecting core innovations through patenting.

- Developing a close relationship with a great patent attorney with relevant industry expertise can mean the difference between a mediocre patent strategy and a game-changing patent strategy.

- Work with patent attorneys who are willing to give up some free effort and expertise defining a patent strategy and identifying patentable inventions.

- Use a team approach to identify and capture patentable ideas for counsel to convert into viable patent applications.

- Use a combination of non-provisional and provisional patent applications when necessary to manage resources.

- Provisional patent applications can be used to move quickly and cost-effectively to establish an early priority date and to take advantage of patent pending notices that might drive off competitors or their investors.

- Consider making a request for nonpublication when filing any patent application for an invention that is unlikely to be the subject of foreign patent applications.

- If a patent is doing poorly in the examination process and it contains important trade secrets, consider filing a petition for express abandonment within 17 months of initial filing to ensure those trade secrets are never published.

CHAPTER TEN

Common Regulatory Mistakes

This chapter looks at some of the most common startup regulatory mistakes. Each of these topics could easily be the subject of a complete chapter, and, in some cases, a complete book. The purpose here is simply to highlight recurring areas of risk and suggest some best practices for managing them.

Misclassifying Employees as Contractors

Misclassifying employees as independent contractors is probably the most common regulatory violation alleged against U.S. startups.

There is inherent tension between startups' interests in accessing flexible, less expensive labor and governmental interests in ensuring the protection of worker rights and the collection of payroll taxes and related contributions.

Payroll taxes include Social Security Tax, FICA (Federal Insurance Contribution Act), Federal Unemployment Tax, state unemployment, disability and workers compensation taxes, and local payroll taxes.

Beyond remitting payroll taxes, employers must also make contributions into workers' compensation and unemployment insurance funds for each employee to ensure their employees have access to those resources.

Independent Contractors Under the ABC Test and AB5

Independent contractors who are employees of firms that provide independent contractors to other companies raise few concerns. Those firms remit payroll taxes and other worker-based contributions on behalf of their employees and they also provide them with applicable worker protections, like overtime and leave.

Other persons can also properly be classified as independent contractors, but the tests under state and federal law seem to be increasingly tough to meet.

The ABC Test. A very strict test, called the "ABC Test," is used in varying forms in California, Washington, New Jersey, Connecticut, Delaware, Illinois, Indiana, Massachusetts, Nebraska, Nevada, and New Hampshire, with a growing list of other state legislatures looking at versions of the test.

The essence of the ABC Test is that any person doing work that is within the "*usual course of the hiring entity's business*" is deemed a statutory employee and not a contractor.

Thus, if a tech company hires an independent contractor to write code for its tech platform, a job that is in the usual course of the company's business, that person is probably a misclassified employee under the ABC Test.

The California Supreme Court described the ABC Test this way in April of 2018 in the <u>Dynamex</u> case:

> *"Under this test, a worker is properly considered an independent contractor to whom a wage order does not apply only if the hiring entity establishes: (A) that the worker is free from the control and direction of the hirer in connection with the performance of the work, both under the contract for the performance of such work and in fact; (B) that the worker performs work that is outside the usual course of the hiring entity's business; and (C) that the worker is customarily engaged in an independently established trade, occupation, or business of the same nature as the work performed for the hiring entity."*
>
> *<u>Dynamex Operations West, Inc. v. Superior Court</u>, 4 Cal.5th 903, 416 P.3d 1, 232 Cal.*
>
> *Rptr.3d 1 (2018)*
>
> *<u>http://www.courts.ca.gov/opinions/archive/S222732.PDF</u>*

Before the growing adoption of the ABC test, the factor described in (A) in the quoted excerpt was the most common test – i.e., a person was an independent contractor if he or she was free from the control and direction of the hirer.

Additional common guidance included ensuring that independent contractors use their own tools, work when and where they want, establish their own LLC or S corporation, carry applicable insurance and, when possible, perform similar work for other companies.

None of the above, however, is sufficient to overcome the ABC test as to independent contractors who perform work that is not *"outside the usual course of the hiring entity's business."*

AB5. Then, in 2019, the California legislature adopted a new law, Assembly Bill 5, called AB5 for short. AB5 outlaws all independent contractor or freelancing work except within a number of narrowly defined fields. In general, AB5 says that any person hired by a company to do work that is within the usual course of the hiring company's business must be hired as an employee, and not as an independent contractor.

AB5 became effective in early 2020 and turned California employment law upside down, forcing thousands of freelance workers out of work or forcing them to work illegally in fields such as journalism, acting, translating, copywriting, photography, music, and trucking, just to name a few.

Companies both inside and outside of California have been forced to immediately stop hiring independent contractors from California in order to avoid the risk of regulatory actions and steep fines and penalties.

AB5 is the subject of ongoing litigation to overturn it as unconstitutional and also legislative efforts to modify or rescind it. Startups inside and outside of California need to pay attention to these efforts and to developments in other states, like Washington, where similar legislative efforts are likely.

The policy arguments in favor of laws like AB5 resonate with many who fear the impacts of innovation on traditional work. But the vital role played by gig economy companies providing critical unmet transportation and home delivery needs during the global Covid-19 quarantines of 2020 also should not be ignored by policy makers.

Enforcement on the Rise

Complaints by correctly or incorrectly classified persons wanting to subsequently collect unemployment insurance are likely the largest source of regulatory actions, but state and federal regulators do not seem to be waiting for cases to come to them.

At the federal level, the Department of Labor ("DOL"), the IRS, and the Equal Employment Opportunity Commission ("EEOC") all have the ability to investigate and pursue claims involving misclassification. And many states have become very active in seeking to identify and take action against employee misclassification.

In one situation, the Washington Employment Security Department called a law firm regarding a potential case of misclassification. The agent said it involved a copy machine repair worker. True enough, the law firm had paid a local copy machine repair company to repair a copier recently.

The agency did not give up easily on the issue, but subsequently abandoned its claims that the worker from the repair company was the law firm's statutory employee.

Officer and Director Payroll Tax Liabilities

Unlike some types of legal or regulatory errors, company officers and directors cannot hide behind the entity in any case involving unpaid payroll taxes or contributions to worker insurance pools. Officers and directors are directly liable for those unpaid taxes.

Over several years those liabilities could grow into millions of dollars. If a company fails, as roughly 80% of startups do, employees can sue the officers and directors for any unpaid wages and state and federal regulators can sue the officers and directors for unpaid taxes.

Many startup founders and other small business managers are unaware of the dramatically evolving risks associated with employee misclassification. The numbers of enforcement cases and the amounts of judgments and penalties against companies in this area will certainly increase as state, local, and federal regulators seek to improve compliance and tax collections.

Misleading Advertising

False and misleading advertising may be the second most common startup regulatory mistake. All states have laws against false and deceptive advertising and 15 U.S. Code § 54 makes it a federal crime.

For many startup founders desperate for sales and market traction, exaggerated advertising claims and comparisons are extremely tempting. I have sat in countless meetings cajoling marketing and product teams away from false and misleading marketing and promotional schemes.

Traction-based bonus goals drive otherwise honest individuals to create marketing content they know is false and misleading, trying to dress it up as "mere puffery," and almost always justifying what they know to be wrong by saying, "*everybody's doing it,*" or "*look what our competitors are saying, that's way worse.*"

It is definitely true that, as consumers, we are bombarded almost constantly by false and misleading advertising. Many inexperienced marketing personnel have acted as though I was depriving them of a fundamental competitive tool by correcting questionable advertising proposals.

Many of these startup marketing and product managers simply have not seen the steady stream of false and deceptive advertising cases filed by state and federal regulators. Those are bread and butter cases for all 50 state attorney general offices in the U.S., as well as the U.S. Federal Trade Commission ("FTC").

What I often tell these marketing folks is that there are a lot of regulators out there looking to meet a quota and get a headline, and that false and deceptive advertising cases practically prove themselves.

It also never takes long to search the Internet and provide a handful of recent high-profile examples. Here are a just a few:

- In March of 2020, pain-therapy device company NeuroMetrix settled with the FTC and agreed to pay up to $8.5 million to settle a false advertising case. The FTC accused the company of falsely claiming its Quell device (i) reduces pain throughout the body when placed below the knee, (ii) is clinically proven to do so, and (iii) has been cleared by the FDA as doing so.

- Jessica Alba's ironically named company, "Honest Company, Inc.," has faced numerous claims of false advertising that appear to have stalled the company's growth and hampered its fundraising efforts.

- The FTC hit Lumosity with a $2 million fine in 2016, saying the company used "unfounded" advertising claims that playing its games could improve academic performance and prevent Alzheimer's disease.

- In 2017, the NY Attorney General's Office brought enforcement actions against three different makers (Cardiio, Runtastic, and Matis) of health-related smartphone applications regarding misleading claims and "*irresponsible privacy practices.*"

- In 2017, the CA Attorney General's Office sued Gatorade over its videogame Bolt!. California claimed Gatorade portrayed its products positively in Bolt!, while inaccurately and negatively depicting water as hindering athletic performance.

- In July of 2018, a class action lawsuit was filed against Dr Pepper Snapple for false advertising claiming that Canada Dry is "*Made from Real Ginger.*"

- In August of 2018, The Center for Science in the Public Interest filed a federal class action lawsuit against Jamba Juice alleging that the company engaged in deceptive marketing because its beverages are described as *"whole fruit and vegetable smoothies,"* when they often include sugary concentrates.

- In September of 2017, the Washington Attorney General's Office won a judgment of $4.3 million in penalties, attorneys' fees, and costs against the makers of 5-Hour ENERGY for false claims that the energy shots are superior to coffee, that doctors recommend 5-hour ENERGY, and that its decaffeinated formula provides energy, alertness, and focus that lasts for hours.

All advertising involving comparisons to competitors' products or services must be 100% accurate and backed up by irrefutable documentary support.

Unfair and Deceptive Business Practices

Just like false and misleading advertising, all states and the federal government have laws prohibiting unfair and deceptive business practices.

At the state level, these laws are commonly called either Unfair and Deceptive Trade Practice Acts or Consumer Protection Acts. Many are enforceable by citizens and government agencies, usually a state's attorney general. Many also authorize treble damages, penalties, and attorneys' fees.

Washington State's statute, for example, is captioned "Unfair Business Practices – Consumer Protection," but its short title is "Consumer Protection Act."

Approximately 25 states have Unfair and Deceptive Trade Practice Acts, or UDTPAs for short.

At the federal level, Section 5(a) of the Federal Trade Commission Act ("FTC Act") prohibits "unfair or deceptive acts or practices in or affecting commerce." Many state acts are modeled after the FTC Act.

Under the FTC Act, an act or practice is unfair if it:
- causes or is likely to cause substantial injury to consumers,
- cannot be reasonably avoided by consumers, and
- is not outweighed by countervailing benefits to consumers or to competition.

Under the FTC Act, an act or practice is deceptive where:
- a representation, omission, or practice misleads or is likely to mislead the consumer,
- a consumer's interpretation of the representation, omission, or practice is considered reasonable under the circumstances, and
- the misleading representation, omission, or practice is material.

Any kind of deceptive, unfair, or fraudulent business practice can trigger liability, but some common categories of misconduct include:
- false or misleading descriptions of goods or services,
- false or misleading free gifts or prizes,
- deceptive pricing, and
- bait and switch promotions.

Case Study #32 – Negative Option Subscription Plan

In 2016, the Washington State Attorney General sued startup Julep Beauty, Inc. and its founder, Jane Park, for unfair and deceptive business practices.

Julep sells nail polish and other beauty products. Julep was accused of tricking consumers out of their money with what has been referred to euphemistically as a "negative option subscription plan."

Juleps ads offered consumers "FREE" gifts and a free "Welcome Box." Many of these ads required consumers to enter credit or debit card information to pay for shipping and handling of the "FREE" gift or Welcome Box.

These ads neglected to tell consumers that paying for shipping and handling of the "FREE" gift or Welcome Box constituted enrollment in the "negative option" "Maven Plan," and that this would result in "subscription charges" against their cards until the consumer canceled the subscription.

To discover they were enrolling in a subscription plan, consumers would have had to read through Julep's terms and conditions, found at a different link.

Once customers were tricked into the negative option subscription plan, Julep then allegedly made it difficult to cancel their subscriptions.

A hidden negative option subscription plan is a poster child for "deceptive pricing." Julep's efforts to prevent customers from cancelling their subscriptions compounded the egregiousness of the misconduct.

Here is how the Washington State Attorney General described those efforts in its complaint against Julep and founder Jane Park:

> 3.7 *Defendants have typically only permitted consumers to cancel by contacting Julep by telephone. Defendants have at times employed an insufficient number of customer service representatives; a number that was woefully inadequate to handle the very high volume of consumers calling Julep to cancel their subscriptions and for other reasons. In some instances, Defendants' failed to answer consumers' calls. In other instances, consumers were put on hold for exceedingly long periods of time. On yet other occasions, consumers left 10 voicemails indicating a desire to cancel their subscriptions but Defendants failed to do so in a timely fashion (causing consumers to be charged for additional Maven Plan boxes). At times, the voicemail system was too full for consumers to even leave a message."*

> 3.8 *Defendants did allow consumers for a period of time to cancel their Maven Plan subscription by email. However, Defendants subsequently removed this as a cancellation method because Defendants believed it made it too easy for consumers to cancel; Defendants were losing too many subscribers by allowing email cancellation.*

228

Julep and Park settled with Washington in September 2016, agreeing to detailed injunctive relief, as well as:

- $1.5 million to be refunded to customers,

- $250,000 in attorneys' fees and costs,

- $250,000 suspended penalty,

- $250,000 of hygiene product contributions to shelters.

In the days following the settlement, Park was publicly combative with the Washington AG and appeared to lack any contrition. For more on that, search online for "Julep CEO disputes AG's claim of 'deceptive' marketing."

> Lessons: Pressures to grow quickly and meet investor expectations, when combined with an ask-for-forgiveness-later attitude, can lead to poor judgment in advertising and business practices. Julep's enforcement action shows that these are risky mistakes with severe consequences.
>
> When customers complain, regulators listen, and sometimes they bring the hammer down.
>
> Another lesson from this case is that Park's attitude toward the state may have harmed Julip's case. The fact that she was named personally is clear proof that the regulators saw her role and her attitude as central problems in the case. It also seems they sought to make an example of her as a warning to others.
>
> Antagonistic or defensive conduct in the face of a regulatory enforcement action is rarely constructive and usually backfires. Startup founders serving in officer or director roles have fiduciary duties that obligate them to set their egos and personal considerations aside and deal with regulatory inquiries in a manner that produces the best possible result for the company at the least cost. Antagonizing regulators rarely serves those ends.

Contests, Sweepstakes, and Lotteries

The marketing realm of contests and sweepstakes is another area where inexperienced marketers often naively stumble into state and federal violations. Contests and sweepstakes are appealing to marketers as low-cost and potentially "viral" strategies for generating product awareness and excitement.

Many seem to assume that giving things away is unregulated and low-risk. Nothing could be further from the truth.

Contests and sweepstakes have been used to abuse consumers since the beginning of marketing. These abuses have led to heavy state and federal regulation, as reflected by the extensive rules that are always used in connection with properly conducted contests and sweepstakes.

Another concern with contests and sweepstakes is that private "lotteries" are illegal under state and federal law. Only states can legally hold lotteries. Most states also have exemptions that allow non-profits to conduct "raffles," but those are not relevant for startups.

Avoiding Illegal Lotteries

An illegal lottery has three elements: (i) a prize, (ii) an element of chance, and (iii) consideration of some kind. A contest must eliminate one of these elements in order to not constitute an illegal lottery. Consideration simply means *any* exchange of value.

To complicate matters, virtually anything can constitute either a prize or consideration. A prize can be something of very nominal value and consideration to enter a contest can be monetary or non-monetary, including simply visiting a website, registering for a meeting or demonstration, or being "present to win."

The most common method for avoiding an illegal lottery is to eliminate the "consideration" requirement by providing an alternative means of entry, such as sending in an entry form – the classic "3 x 5 card."

Another common method for avoiding the lottery prohibition is to make a contest a game of skill, such as a contest for the best picture or essay. A game of skill has no "element of chance."

State Contest and Sweepstakes Laws

In addition to the general prohibition against lotteries, most states have extensive laws governing contests and sweepstakes that are intended to protect the public from unfair and deceptive practices. These laws impose requirements and restrictions regarding:

- sponsor name and contact information,
- disclosure requirements, including "no purchase necessary,"
- registration and bonding requirements,
- the posting of contest rules and regulations,
- prize notification,
- posting winners' names,
- requirements that all prizes be awarded, and
- requirements to retain contest records.

Contest Rules

The requirements for contest and sweepstakes rules vary by state, but minimum elements generally include:

- description of the contest or sweepstakes,
- approximate value of all prizes,
- chances of winning,
- methods of entry,
- eligibility to participate,

- beginning and end dates,

- applicable taxes,

- how winners will be selected, and

- how to obtain a list of winners.

Other common elements included in contest and sweepstakes rules:

- disqualification for tampering, cheating, fraud, and disruption,

- releases, conditions, limitations of liability, and indemnification provisions,

- sponsor rights to modify or cancel a contest or sweepstakes,

- participant consent to publicity and media rights,

- binding arbitration, and

- compliance with law, governing law, and venue.

Unexpected Outcomes

Contests, sweepstakes, and giveaways frequently result in unexpected turmoil and disappointments. The winner of ShareBuilder's PT Cruiser promotion was a non-customer who won by submitting a 3 x 5 card.

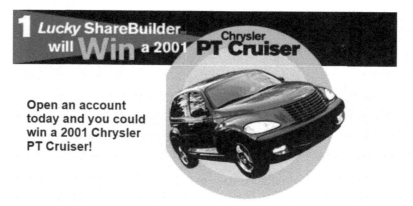

This was a huge disappointment to the marketing team that designed the promotion. The company was unable to capitalize on the awarding of that expensive prize for any meaningful PR purposes. The outcome was expensive and awkward.

Beyond simple return-on-investment disappointments, large contests and promotions can backfire in other ways. Poorly executed contests can generate negative social media attention. Some contests are plagued by scammers attempting to game the rules. Sometimes contest outcomes are challenged.

It is worth noting that there are quirky individuals who focus on finding and participating in contests and sweepstakes. These persons are rarely ideal customers. More often, they are nettlesome troublemakers who will pounce on any perceived ambiguities or unfairnesses. Contests that attract too many of these folks can quickly prove disappointing.

Contests and sweepstakes are sometimes championed by marketing persons whose compensation is driven not by the quality of new customers or accounts, but merely by quantity. Consider this dynamic when weighing the pros and cons of a potential contest.

Contest and Sweepstakes Vendors

Because of the complexity of complying with the laws of fifty states and the potential downsides of mistakes, it is worth considering working with a reputable vendor to structure and execute any major contest or sweepstakes.

The best of these vendors have internal counsel who specialize in complying with these laws. Reputable contest vendors can help structure and execute compliant promotions, draft appropriate and compliant rules, and ensure that contest execution, prize awarding, and recordkeeping are all done by the book.

Among other tasks, they can handle the receipt and tracking of alternative methods of entry, rule enforcement, the selection of winners, the awarding of prizes, and post-contest recordkeeping.

Endorsements and Testimonials

Testimonials and endorsements are an FTC enforcement priority. The focus has been on celebrities and other social media influencers, but the same concerns apply to all types of experts.

Protecting consumers and preventing "unfair methods of competition" are two overarching FTC mandates, and both are implicated by false and misleading endorsements and testimonials. The FTC's efforts in these areas focus on (i) requiring full disclosure of any advertiser compensation to, or relationship with, an endorser, and (ii) endorsement honesty and integrity.

Endorsement Enforcement

The FTC has made headlines in recent years with enforcement actions against high profile companies, advertisers, and influencers. FTC enforcement targets in 2015 and 2016 included big names like Lord & Taylor, Deutsch LA, Inc., Machinima, Inc., and Warner Brothers.

On April 17, 2017, the FTC issued a press release that contained this warning to advertisers and social media influencers:

> *After reviewing numerous Instagram posts by celebrities, athletes, and other influencers, Federal Trade Commission staff recently sent out more than 90 letters reminding influencers and marketers that influencers should clearly and conspicuously disclose their relationships to brands when promoting or endorsing products through social media.*

On September 7, 2017, the FTC announced the settlement of an enforcement action against CSGOLotto, Inc. and its principals and simultaneously sent out 20 follow-up letters to other influencers and marketers.

Deceptive endorsements are just another form of false advertising and, in certain contexts, even fraud. As such, they are actionable by any number of agencies or private litigants.

Floyd Mayweather and music producer DJ Khaled both settled with the SEC in 2018 for endorsing bitcoin offerings without disclosing they were paid hundreds of thousands of dollars. Mayweather and Khaled were also targeted in a class action securities lawsuit for the same endorsements.

An organization called Truth in Advertising, Inc. is also currently waging its own campaign against influencer scofflaws, sending a formal complaint to the FTC on March 9, 2019, which included this excerpted text (footnote references omitted):

> *It has now been almost two years since the FTC initially notified these influencers of their obligation to refrain from actively deceiving their social media followers yet all but one of them have continued to mislead their fan base, which range in size from just over 750,000 followers on Instagram to more than 32 million followers, by refusing to consistently and appropriately disclose their material connections to the brands they are promoting.*

While the FTC's financial penalties in these actions seem relatively modest, the costs and distractions of responding to any regulatory enforcement action are significant, as are the operational and reputational repercussions.

Settling companies could also find their advertising activities under very close and constricting FTC supervision for many years. I have resolved FTC matters. IRS audits are a walk in the park, by comparison.

FTC Endorsement Guides

The FTC's positions on endorsements and testimonials are stated and illustrated in what it calls its "Endorsement Guides," which the FTC announced in February 2020 it was again reviewing.

The Endorsement Guides address the application of Section 5 of the FTC Act to the use of endorsements and testimonials in advertising. They can be found at:

https://www.ftc.gov/sites/default/files/attachments/press-releases/ftc-publishes-final-guides-governing-endorsements-testimonials/091005revisedendorsementguides.pdf

The following key principles have been excerpted and paraphrased from the FTC's Endorsement Guides:

- An endorsement means any advertising message (including verbal statements, demonstrations, or depictions of the name, signature, likeness or other identifying personal characteristics of an individual or the name or seal of an organization) that consumers are likely to believe reflects the opinions, beliefs, findings, or experiences of a party other than the sponsoring advertiser.

- Endorsements must reflect the honest opinions, findings, beliefs, or experience of the endorser. An endorsement may not convey any express or implied representation that would be deceptive if made directly by the advertiser.

- An endorsement may not be presented out of context or reworded so as to distort in any way the endorser's opinion or experience with the product. An advertiser may use an endorsement of an expert or celebrity only so long as it has good reason to believe that the endorser continues to subscribe to the views presented.

- When an advertisement represents that the endorser uses the endorsed product, the endorser must have been a bona fide user of it at the time the endorsement was given.

- Advertisers are subject to liability for false or unsubstantiated statements made through endorsements, or for failing to disclose material connections between themselves and their endorsers. Endorsers also may be liable for statements made in the course of their endorsements.

- An advertisement employing endorsements by one or more consumers about the performance of an advertised product or service will be interpreted as representing that the product or service is effective for the purpose depicted in the advertisement. The advertiser must possess and rely upon adequate substantiation, including, when appropriate, competent and reliable scientific evidence, to support such claims made through endorsements in the same manner the advertiser would be required to do if it had made the representation directly.

Advertorials

Very similar concerns are raised by what is known as "native advertising," or "advertorials. This is promotional content designed and intended to look like news, feature articles, entertainment, or other non-promotional online content. Whether or not a specific endorsement or testimonial is involved, the use of native advertising should not be considered an opportunity to deceive consumers.

Privacy and Data Protection

Privacy and data protection is a challenging regulatory area for all companies, as evidenced by the never-ending news stories about data breaches and alleged privacy abuses. The challenges can be substantially greater for startups, which often must handle these formidable challenges with cutting-edge products and services, new and evolving systems, less experienced teams, and insufficient resources.

And unlike advertising and independent contractor regulatory issues, following reasonable privacy and security best practices is still no guarantee against catastrophe.

The direct financial costs of privacy violations and data breaches are so substantial that insurance coverage for such claims is among the most expensive available. Violators and data breach victims alike can find themselves facing both private lawsuits and regulatory actions.

The reputation and goodwill costs of privacy and data protection lapses are often more devastating than the costs of the lawsuits, judgments, and fines and would likely be sufficient to shut down most seed-stage or series A stage companies.

GDPR and CCPA

The rapidly tightening regulatory landscape is only making a difficult situation worse for smaller, modestly-funded companies. In May of 2018, the EU's General Data Protection Regulation ("GDPR") became law and in June 2018, California adopted the nation's strictest privacy rules, called the California Consumer Privacy Act ("CCPA"), which became effective in January 2020.

The CCPA contains many provisions that are similar to the GDPR, but the scope, penalties, and methods of enforcement of the GDPR are significantly more severe, with even modest privacy violations supporting potential claims and penalties in the tens of millions of dollars.

As an example of their different scope, the CCPA covers only California residents, while the GDPR covers "data subjects" regardless of their citizenship, residency or location, and applies to any company that sells goods in the EU or monitors the behavior of persons in the EU.

No company should consider doing any business in the EU without engaging qualified GDPR counsel many months in advance.

Among other things, the CCPA:

- provides consumers the right to request a business to disclose:

    - the categories and specific pieces of personal information that it collects about the consumer,

    - the categories of sources from which that information is collected,

    - the business purposes for collecting or selling the information, and

    - the categories of third parties with which the information is shared.

- requires businesses to make disclosures about information collected and the purposes for which it is used,

- grants consumers the right to make businesses delete personal information,

- grants consumers the right to request that a business that sells the consumer's personal information, or discloses it for a business purpose, disclose the categories of information that it collects and the identity of third parties to which the information was sold or disclosed,

- requires businesses to post a "Do Not Sell My Information" link on their website homepages,

- authorizes consumers to opt out of the sale of personal information and prohibits discriminating against consumers for exercising the right, including by charging those who opt out a different price or providing them a different quality of goods or services, unless the differences are reasonably related to value provided by the consumer's data.

Deep discussion of the GDPR and the CCPA are both outside the scope of this overview, which is intended to serve only as a warning of the nature and breadth of these laws and the need for companies to understand and comply with them when engaging in business in either the EU or California.

Privacy Policies

In general, most existing state and federal privacy rules and regulations require every consumer-facing business to conspicuously post privacy policies that disclose what information a business collects, how it collects it, how it uses it, how it protects information from unauthorized disclosure, with whom it shares the information, to whom it sells or rents the information, and pursuant to what opt-in or opt-out standards and mechanisms.

Companies are also required under many states' laws to timely report data breaches to impacted consumers.

Having been in place for more than a decade in their modern forms, these statutes and rules are relatively well understood. For most companies, writing up and posting a privacy policy is not the hard part. Most lawsuits and enforcement actions tend to arise out of alleged instances of companies not complying with the requirements of their own privacy policies.

The most common of these include allegations of sharing or selling data in ways that were not disclosed. In September of 2019, the video platform company Vimeo was hit with a class action lawsuit claiming that it was collecting, storing, and using user's facial biometric data without disclosing that collection and usage and without providing any means of opting out.

Data Protection

State and federal privacy laws all require businesses to reasonably protect consumer information from unauthorized access or disclosure, and many states require businesses to promptly disclose data breaches.

Startups are frequently victims of data breaches. In March of 2020, startup Social Bluebook, which matches advertisers and social media influencers, was hit with a breach impacting 117,000 influencers. In 2018, "sales engagement" startup Apollo was attacked in a breach involving its prospect database of 200 million contacts involving 10 million companies.

Failing to provide timely notice of data breaches is an increasingly common regulatory claim. In 2018, the SEC fined Yahoo $35 million for waiting months to disclose one of the largest data breaches to date.

For businesses with nationwide consumer reach, the CCPA will essentially become the standard around which privacy and data policies and procedures will be built. For businesses with reach into the EU, the GDPR will set the privacy and data protection bar.

Startups need to devote substantial resources and attention to complying with all applicable privacy and security requirements, and minimizing the risk of violations and breaches to the maximum extent possible.

CAN-SPAM and TCPA/DNC

CAN-SPAM. CAN-SPAM stands for "Controlling the Assault of Non-Solicited Pornography And Marketing," a 2003 U.S. federal law prohibiting unsolicited commercial email.

The Act covers all commercial email messages, not just bulk email. It covers "any electronic mail message the primary purpose of which is the commercial advertisement or promotion of a commercial product or service." Somewhat uncharacteristically of such legislation, CAN-SPAM makes no exception for business-to-business email or for communications to former customers.

Each separate violative email is subject to penalties of up to $42,530, making compliance a good investment. Key requirements and prohibitions of the Act include: (i) do not use false or misleading header or email origin information, (ii) do not use deceptive subject lines, (iii) identify the message as an ad, (iv) the message must include the company's valid physical address, (v) tell recipients how to opt out of receiving future email, and (vi) honor opt-out requests promptly.

Companies should closely monitor all advertising vendors and others sending marketing emails on their behalf and require those vendors to fully indemnify them for violations.

Fortunately, CAN-SPAM cases against startups seem few and far between and the act has mainly been used by government regulators to go after very large spam generators.

TCPA. The TCPA is the Telephone Consumer Protection Act. The TCPA was adopted as U.S. federal law in 1991 and is administered by both the FCC and the FTC. The TCPA is directed toward stopping unwanted "robocalls," pre-recorded messages, and unwanted *automated* texts to consumer (non-business) phone numbers.

Under the TCPA, consumers must explicitly consent to receiving such automated communications. Penalties under the TCPA are severe, particularly given the potential for class action lawsuits involving large numbers of consumers. Aggrieved consumers can recover up to $500 per phone call that violates the TCPA and up to $1,500 per phone call if the consumer can prove the caller violated the TCPA knowingly and willfully.

DNC. DNC stands for "Do Not Call" and refers to the U.S. federal registry mandated by the TCPA and operated by the FTC. The DNC registry lets consumers register specific phone numbers to prohibit unsolicited commercial phone calls. Marketers are required to have written policies and procedures for maintaining their own internal do-not-call lists and for utilizing versions of the federal DNC list that are no older than three months. The Do Not Call registry is found at this link: https://www.donotcall.gov/register.html.

TRACED. U.S. anti-robocall laws were given even sharper teeth on December 30, 2019, when the Pallone-Thune Telephone Robocall Abuse Criminal Enforcement and Deterrence ("TRACED") Act became law. TRACED authorizes the FTC to impose civil penalties of up to $10,000 per call for intentional TCPA violations and extends the FTC's time for enforcement action to four years. These new penalties are in addition to all other penalties for TCPA violations.

Professional TCPA/DNC plaintiffs and their counsel have built lucrative business models around filing TCPA lawsuits and forcing companies into relatively high-dollar lawsuits.

If that sounds like hyperbole, consider the case of James Everett Shelton. Mr. Shelton has filed at least 29 TCPA lawsuits, apparently mostly as a pro se litigant. According to at least one litigation pleading involving Mr. Shelton, his debt collection business website used to include the following:

> *"If you are reading this website, you are most likely a telemarketer that has illegally called my phone. You are going to be sued. I played along with your telemarketer script in order to find out who you really are. Put [Shelton's cell number] on your do not call list. Hire a really good lawyer."*

I settled one TCPA claim in 2019 in which the client agreed to pay $20,000 for a single alleged infraction rather than risk certification of a class action that might involve additional alleged violations.

I have also seen at least one company hounded into insolvency by multiple TCPA cases, many of which had no merit.

Companies that use mass-email and automated text or telephone marketing should understand these laws well and budget for pro-active compliance guidance and also for dealing with allegations of non-compliance.

The case law is still evolving, but some U.S. courts take the position that any automated assistance with dialing or texting constitutes automation. This could include any type of speed-dial technology, including clicking on a phone number in a CRM system instead of dialing the number manually. Currently, a key case in this area is *Marks v. Crunch San Diego, LLC*, 904 F.3d 1041, 1050 (9th Cir. 2018), in which the U.S. 9th Circuit Court of Appeals held:

> *"…the statutory definition of ATDS is not limited to devices with the capacity to call numbers produced by a 'random or sequential number generator,' but also includes devices with the capacity to dial stored numbers automatically."*

These marketing techniques are rarely used by SaaS or other technology companies, but they are critical for what might be called "marketplace" companies. These are businesses built around buying, selling, and sharing valid customer leads for requested services.

A good example of this is when a consumer requests loan quotes online. In so doing, the consumer will click "I Agree" to terms and conditions consenting to having third-party loan providers contact the consumer by email, phone, or text to provide individual loan quotes.

Marketplace lead generators and businesses that rely on legitimate consumer leads share and respond to hundreds of thousands, if not millions, of leads per month. These marketing activities invariably result in consumer claims, mostly alleging lack of consent to contact a consumer, lack of consent to share or sell a consumer lead, or failure to timely process a consumer's requests to revoke their consent.

Even companies with rigorous compliance systems can find themselves facing nuisance suits, including class action lawsuits, when the scale of these types of marketing efforts is significant.

Privacy and Data Security Insurance Coverage

Like IP infringement insurance, privacy and data security insurance coverage can be expensive. But it is still certainly worth buying in whatever amounts and coverages can be reasonably obtained and afforded.

Data breach insurance does not cover damaged goodwill or lost customers, but it can help cover costs associated with:

- restoring systems and networks,

- hiring consultants to identify the cause of a data breach,

- suits or regulatory actions,

- customer notification,

- public relations expenses,

- other legal fees, and

- credit monitoring and identity protection services for impacted customers.

Risk Disclosure to Investors

Startups should inform all potential investors of their particular privacy and data security risk exposure, including any prior breaches. As already mentioned, Yahoo agreed to pay the SEC a $35 million penalty to settle charges that it misled investors by failing to disclose one of the world's largest data breaches.

The same anti-fraud rules that drove that settlement carry equal force in the smallest of securities transactions. Material data security issues need to be disclosed.

Employment and Labor Law Issues

The frenetic, work-around-the-clock, sleep-in-the-office culture espoused at many startups can be challenging to reconcile with modern wage and hour rules, leave requirements, and other employment laws.

Workplace Posters Continue to Grow

State, local, and federal laws all tend to require that every employer receive and conspicuously post one or more handy posters each year that outline all of these obligations.

The poster for Seattle employers is now so packed with newly-adopted rules that it may soon take up an entire wall.

Here are all of the state, federal and city employment laws and standards applicable in Seattle, including Seattle's newest employee right, Safe Time Leave:

Federal Posting Requirements:

- EEOC Equal Employment Opportunity is the Law
- Fed-OSHA "It's the Law" Notice
- Federal Minimum Wage Notice
- Employee Polygraph Protection Notice
- Family and Medical Leave Act (FMLA) Notice
- USERRA Rights and Benefits Notice
- Payday Notice
- IRS EITC / Notice 797 / W-4 Notice

Washington State Posting Requirements:

- WA Discrimination in Employment
- WA Job Safety and Health Protection
- WA Minimum Wage
- WA Your Rights as a Non-Agricultural Worker/Family Leave
- WA Unemployment Insurance Benefits
- WA Workers' Compensation Notice

City of Seattle Posting Requirements:

- Seattle Minimum Wage Notice
- Seattle Wage Theft Statute Notice
- Fair Chance Employment (limits use of conviction and arrest records)
- Paid Sick and Safe Time Leave Notice

The U.S. Department of Labor ("DOL") maintains a list of the labor agencies for all fifty states here: https://www.dol.gov/whd/contacts/state_of.htm

In addition to the misclassification issues already discussed and the harassment and discrimination issues discussed a little later, the following are some employment regulations startups commonly trip over.

Wage and Hour

Minimum Wage. In the beginning, most startups have no cash. But they need some traction before they can raise money. Faced with this dilemma, founders frequently try to get team members to work for free.

Allowing employees to work for free is illegal about 99.99% of the time. Don't do it. *Always pay at least minimum wage.*

At the federal level the Fair Labor Standards Act ("FLSA") requires all employees to be paid at least minimum wage.

Under the FLSA, the only persons who don't have to be paid minimum wage are 20%-or-greater owners of a company, and then only if there isn't an even more restrictive state law, like in Washington state, where every employee must be paid at least $250 per week.

Companies that don't pay their employees are breaking laws with serious claws. Wage violations are among the surest routes to legal trouble, often with a state Department of Labor.

And again, officers and directors can be held liable for wage violations. For more on federal wage rules for executives, search online for the DOL publication, "*Fact Sheet #17B: Exemption for Executive Employees Under the Fair Labor Standards Act (FLSA)*."

https://www.dol.gov/sites/dolgov/files/WHD/legacy/files/fs17b_executive.pdf

Overtime. The terms "exempt employee" and "non-exempt employee" relate to whether overtime must be paid. Non-exempt employees must receive 1.5x overtime pay after 40 hours worked in a week. The rules for which employees are exempt vary by state, but they are generally based on minimum salary amounts and the nature of an employee's duties and level of responsibility.

State and City Minimum Wages. State and city minimum wage laws are frequently more restrictive for employers and more favorable for employees. When federal, state, or city wage and hour laws conflict, the most employee-favorable provisions apply.

A key question under state law is how the "officer exemption" is defined. When can a company officer be asked to, or even be allowed to, not be paid minimum wage and overtime?

Washington state's officer exemption, WAC 296-128-510, requires several elements, including:

- minimum salary of $250 per week,
- employee's primary duty must be managing the company or a recognized department or subdivision,
- employee must direct the work of two or more employees, and
- employee must customarily and regularly exercise discretion.

Even under this formula, every employee in Washington must be paid, even founders, at least $250 per week.

Another requirement that cannot be evaded is timely payment of wages. Wages must be paid regularly and on time. Employees cannot be forced, or even asked, to defer receipt of minimum wage payments.

Wage Theft Enforcement. When employees don't get paid, it's called "wage theft." Regulators can step in and force companies to pay current and former employees. In a handful of states, criminal authorities can seek fines and jail sentences.

The following wage and hour claims hit startups regularly:

- not paying a worker at all,

- not paying minimum wage,

- not paying overtime,

- not paying for all hours worked,

- not giving a worker their final check after leaving a job, and

- not paying out all accrued vacation or leave on termination of employment.

Wage claims are among the easiest of all claims to make and claimants often benefit from agency bias that tips in their favor and against employers. In Washington state, employees can receive 2x the amount of wages not paid, along with costs and attorneys' fees in pursuing the wage claim.

Hiring employees as contractors to avoid paying minimum wage and overtime or to defer paying compensation will work only until those persons have a falling out with the company and decide to dispute their classification.

Any startup that cuts the line close on wage and hour laws will eventually be called to account.

Equity in Lieu of Cash. Just as founders sometimes try to avoid paying minimum wage, founders sometimes cajole employees to take only stock and no wages for a period of time.

This is not legal. "Wages" require a paycheck. Anecdotally, arrangements to pay only in equity seem to be a prominent source of wage claims. An agreement to pay an employee only in stock is illegal and unenforceable against the employee.

Similarly, misclassifying someone as a contractor in order to pay them solely with company stock only works until the worker is deemed an employee, after which the company and its officers could be accused of wage theft.

Interestingly, in situations where someone has been promised equity instead of cash wages, the wage theft violation is frequently compounded by the company's failure to authorize, issue, and deliver any of the promised equity. That is another "bad fact" that can add to regulatory woes.

Family and Medical Leave

Any company with more than 50 employees is subject to the Family and Medical Leave Act (FMLA). The U.S. Department of Labor summarizes the key provisions of the FMLA as follows:

The FMLA entitles eligible employees of covered employers to take unpaid, job-protected leave for specified family and medical reasons with continuation of group health insurance coverage under the same terms and conditions as if the employee had not taken leave. Eligible employees are entitled to:

Twelve workweeks of leave in a 12-month period for:

- *the birth of a child and to care for the newborn child within one year of birth;*

- *the placement with the employee of a child for adoption or foster care and to care for the newly placed child within one year of placement;*

- *to care for the employee's spouse, child, or parent who has a serious health condition;*

- *a serious health condition that makes the employee unable to perform the essential functions of his or her job;*

- *any qualifying exigency arising out of the fact that the employee's spouse, son, daughter, or parent is a covered military member on "covered active duty;" or*

Twenty-six workweeks of leave during a single 12-month period to care for a covered servicemember with a serious injury or illness if the eligible employee is the servicemember's spouse, son, daughter, parent, or next of kin (military caregiver leave).

In addition to the FMLA, cities and states have their own patchworks of paid and unpaid leave requirements. San Francisco's Paid Parental Leave Ordinance, for example, requires all companies with more than 20 employees globally to pay 8 weeks of full pay to bond with a new child.

Suffice it to say, every company with employees needs to have legally compliant approaches for responding to lawful requests for leave and for not tripping over obvious landmines. In general, companies that want to get these issues right, can and do. Others that want to take aggressive or cavalier positions usually end up in messy fights.

Fair Credit Reporting Act

Businesses also need to be aware of and observe all Fair Credit Reporting Act ("FCRA") rules and restrictions on when and how credit report information can be used in the hiring process and what disclosures are required.

The U.S. Consumer Financial Protection Bureau says this to consumers in its notice, *A Summary of Your Rights Under the Fair Credit Reporting Act*:

> *"You must give your consent for reports to be provided to employers. A consumer reporting agency may not give out information about you to your employer, or a potential employer, without your written consent given to the employer....*
>
> *For more information, go to www.consumerfinance.gov/learnmore."*

Under FCRA, employers who decide not to hire a person because of their credit report must give the applicant a "pre-adverse action disclosure," along with a copy of the report and a notice of FCRA rights, including how to contact the Consumer Reporting Agency and dispute the report.

Officer and Director Liabilities in Insolvency

Just as with worker misclassification claims, officers and directors can be held personally liable for employee claims of unpaid wages, overtime, or leave if a company becomes insolvent.

When companies go under, employees report any unpaid wages to regulators almost every time. A single complaint can trigger a broader investigation and usually causes other employees to come forward. These issues are explored again in Chapter 17, *The Zone of Insolvency*.

PEOs

Once a startup is on a healthy growth trajectory with ten or fifteen employees, tripping over the ever-growing list of employee rights and protections becomes almost inevitable without careful oversight by in-house or external HR experts.

As mentioned in Chapter 8, *Structuring and Managing Key Relationships,* PEOs (Professional Employer Organizations) offer cost-effective process controls and de-risking across most HR functions.

Among other things, PEOs:

- provide locally and nationally compliant employee onboarding platforms that timely collect all required records and present all legally required notices about rights and benefits,

- incorporate all federal, state, and local wage, hour, and leave requirements into their payroll processing systems,

- handle all state, local, and federal tax compliance, and

- handle health insurance benefits administration.

Few areas of law and regulation are more complex than wage and hour rules and today's employee rights and protections. And few areas of law generate more actual legal and regulatory problems for businesses of all sizes.

Startups do not get a "pass" for being startups. They must comply fully, and if they do not, the founders may end up paying the tab. Use of PEOs can reduce these risks.

Discrimination and Harassment

Anti-discrimination and anti-harassment laws are arguably less complex than the employment topics discussed above, but the penalties for mistakes or lax oversight can be even more expensive.

While the rules against discrimination vary somewhat by locality, the message within and across any business needs to be that no forms of discrimination or harassment are permissible at any time or for any reason.

HR Best Practices

Strong HR practices, including consistent onboarding with strong anti-discrimination and anti-harassment policy statements in an employee handbook and ethics policy, combined with robust management training, can help keep a lid on the types of poor behavior that get companies into trouble.

Companies need to tread lightly in sensitive areas, like enforcing dress codes or no-dating policies, but need to be firmer in areas like prohibiting profane or sexually suggestive language or jokes and not allowing dating between supervisors and subordinates.

The nature of litigation and damages in discrimination and harassment cases is such that companies should consider adopting zero tolerance policies – i.e., immediate termination of any officer or employee found to have engaged in any form of discrimination or any form of harassment.

This is because the only way to win such cases is to not have them in the first place. Prompt, effective action against alleged violators is the best antidote against discrimination and harassment claims.

The following excerpt reinforces this advice. It is from a page on the U.S. Equal Employment Opportunity Commission's website captioned *"BEST PRACTICES FOR EMPLOYERS AND HUMAN RESOURCES/EEO PROFESSIONALS"*

"Adopt a strong anti-harassment policy, periodically train each employee on its contents, and vigorously follow and enforce it. The policy should include:...

- *Assurance that the employer will take immediate and appropriate corrective action when it determines that harassment has occurred."*

When in doubt about anti-discrimination or anti-harassment issues or potential claims, consult with counsel who specialize in those areas.

Theft of Trade Secrets

As discussed, opportunities for inadvertent, negligent, and willful theft of trade secrets abound in startups. The vast majority of cases involve thefts by employees.

Trade secret theft risk factors for startups include:

- hiring lots of new personnel quickly,

- weak HR practices,

- managers who are unaware of trade secret law,

- substantial positive and negative incentives to grow and innovate quickly,

- financial distress,

- ego, hubris, and greed, and

- an apologize-later culture.

In Chapter 9, we learned that all but two states, New York and Massachusetts, have adopted their own versions of what is called the Uniform Trade Secrets Act, or UTSA. We also learned that the U.S. Defend Trade Secrets Act, or DTSA, became law in 2016.

The UTSA provides these remedies and penalties:

- injunctive relief,

- damages for the actual loss caused by misappropriation,

- unjust enrichment caused by misappropriation, above and beyond damages for actual loss,

- in cases of willful and malicious misappropriation, possible awards of attorneys' fees and exemplary damages up to two times the amount of the underlying damages award, and

- payment of a reasonable royalty for any permitted future use.

At the federal level, the DTSA allows for all of the same, plus the seizure of misappropriated trade secrets.

One of the HR best practices discussed earlier involves including an affirmative statement in all new employee Offer Letter Agreements that the new employee will not bring any IP of prior employers with him or her and will not incorporate any such IP into any of the hiring company's products or services.

This is the first opportunity to set the tone for avoiding potentially catastrophic trade secret liability. The importance of this rule should be emphasized by a company's management at reasonable intervals.

Violations of the trade secret rights of others should be addressed swiftly and severely. Any employee that will misuse the trade secrets of a prior employer will also misuse the trade secrets of a current employer. This is an area where "zero tolerance" is a very reasonable default rule.

Anti-Trust

Anti-trust laws prohibit a range of business activities that reduce competition in the marketplace. These "anti-competitive activities" harm consumers by unfairly increasing prices of goods and services.

The U.S. anti-trust laws, called the Sherman Act and the Clayton Act, are enforced by the FTC, the Justice Department, all fifty state attorneys general, and private litigants.

In recent years there have been repeated calls to break up big players in tech on anti-trust grounds, including Google, Amazon, Microsoft, and Facebook. When most businesspersons hear "anti-trust," they think of large companies with monopoly-like "market power." Market power is essentially the ability to raise prices without losing sales, due to monopolistic dominance in the market.

But much of anti-trust law is focused on conduct that many companies might engage in without realizing the potential for serious federal anti-trust violations. Conduct among competitors is generally the most concerning, as explained by this excerpt from an online post by the FTC captioned *Dealing with Competitors:*

> *In today's marketplace, competitors interact in many ways, through trade associations, professional groups, joint ventures, standard-setting organizations, and other industry groups. Such dealings often are not only competitively benign but procompetitive. But there are antitrust risks when competitors interact to such a degree that they are no longer acting independently, or when collaborating gives competitors the ability to wield market power together.*
>
> *For the most blatant agreements not to compete, such as price fixing, big rigging, and market division, the rules are clear. The courts decided many years ago that these practices are so inherently harmful to consumers that they are always illegal, so-called per se violations. For other dealings among competitors, the rules are not as clear-cut and often require fact-intensive inquiry into the purpose and effect of the collaboration, including any business justifications. Enforcers must ask: what*

is the purpose and effect of dealings among competitors? Do they restrict competition or promote efficiency?

Essentially, any cooperation between competitors that restrains competition is prohibited and should be avoided. The following are common examples.

Price Fixing

Any agreement between competitors that establishes an agreed price or price boundaries, or that otherwise determines how the price will be set among the competitors, violates the prohibition against price fixing.

Market Division/Allocation

Market division or allocation refers to any agreement to not compete regarding specific products, customers, or geographical areas.

There are complex exceptions for non-competition and market allocation when one company buys another and the parties agree for a reasonable time to restrict competition as necessary to provide the purchaser with the benefit of their acquisition. But noncompetition restrictions in an M&A deal cannot be excessive.

New York courts have said that M&A non-competition restrictions cannot be "*…more extensive, in terms of time and space, than is reasonably necessary to the buyer for the protection of his legitimate interest in the enjoyment of the asset bought.*"

Tying

Tying is when a seller with market power with one product will only sell that product to buyers who agree to also buy a different product from the seller. Tying coerces buyers into purchasing the tied product from the seller rather than a competitor.

Startups should understand the boundaries of anti-trust law before having any communications with competitors or getting involved in any industry collaboration activities that might inadvertently trigger anti-trust concerns.

Laws Protecting Worker Organizing Activities

Most startups are unlikely to face union organizing activities, but those that do should quickly consult with experts, as they are otherwise likely to make costly mistakes.

Layperson attempts to thwart unionization frequently draw enforcement actions from the National Labor Relations Board ("NLRB"). The NLRB is charged with enforcing the National Labor Relations Act ("NLRA").

A December 2019 study by the Economic Policy Institute found that companies were hit with NLRA penalties in 41.5% of all union election campaigns.

As just one example, a startup called Lanetix, Inc. fired 15 technology engineers in 2018, allegedly in response to unionizing activities. The terminated engineers complained to a union they were working with, and that union brought a formal NLRB action against Lanetix.

Based on that complaint, the NLRB brought an enforcement action against Lanetix, seeking reinstatement of all fired engineers with back pay.

Just prior to the hearing in the matter before an administrative law judge, Lanetix settled. The company agreed to pay the fired engineers a total of $775,000 – a huge sum for the small company.

The NLRB complaint against Lanetix provides an excellent example of the troubles a company can suffer for missteps under the NLRA, both in terms of the charges to expect, as well as the NLRB's quasi-judicial administrative powers and processes.

The complaint against Lanetix can be found in the BLSG Data Room under *Employment Law and HR > National Labor Relations Act.* That version of the complaint also includes NLRB guidance about the formal administrative law process in such cases.

Rights to Unionize

Under the NLRA, employees have broad rights to engage in union organizing activities. Employees can also engage in non-union-related activities to try to improve wages and working conditions.

The NLRB lists a few key permitted unionizing activities as follows:

- *forming, or attempting to form, a union in your workplace,*

- *joining a union whether the union is recognized by your employer or not,*

- *assisting a union in organizing your fellow employees,*

- *refusing to do any or all of these things.*

Rights to Engage in Protected Concerted Activities

The NLRB's website also includes extensive information regarding permitted employee activities "outside of a union" to improve wages or workplace conditions, which are known as "protected concerted activity":

Activity Outside a Union

Employees who are not represented by a union also have rights under the NLRA. Specifically, the National Labor Relations Board protects the rights of employees to engage in "concerted activity", which is when two or more employees take action for their mutual aid or protection regarding terms and conditions of employment. A single employee may also engage in protected concerted activity if he or she is acting on the authority of other employees, bringing group complaints to the employer's attention, trying to induce group action, or seeking to prepare for group action.

A few examples of protected concerted activities are:

- *Two or more employees addressing their employer about improving their pay.*

- *Two or more employees discussing work-related issues beyond pay, such as safety concerns, with each other.*

- *An employee speaking to an employer on behalf of one or more co-workers about improving workplace conditions.*

Employer Prohibited Activities

There are certain limited steps employers might be able take to resist unionization and we discuss those next. But there are many actions that employers cannot take to discourage or interfere with unionization efforts or protected concerted activity without provoking the wrath of the NLRB.

Prohibited employer actions include, but are not limited to:

- firing or threatening to fire workers for union organizing activities or other protected activities, or even telling them that such activities are not permitted or inappropriate,

- taking adverse employment action or threatening such action against employees for discussing their wages or other compensation with other employees,

- engaging in, attempting to engage in, or threatening to engage in surveillance of employees engaging in protected activities, including forcing employees to divulge the identities of other employee engaging in protected activities,

- taking adverse employment action against employees for circulating or presenting petitions or other demands regarding wages or working conditions,

- taking adverse employment action against employees for posting complaints or concerns online about wages or working conditions,

- discriminating against unionizing employees' efforts by (i) forcing those efforts to occur during non-work hours, while conversations and meetings against unionization are permitted during work hours, (ii) preventing union postings on company bulletin boards but allowing other employee posts, or (iii) prohibiting visits to the company by union officials when the company is generally open to the public,

- coercing employees to vote against unionization, or

- promising benefits or anything of value to employees if they vote against unionization.

Permitted Company Responses

Any company planning to resist unionization efforts should immediately seek expert legal counsel, as the chances of mistakes with significant consequences are high. Additionally, companies can also hire professional organizations to help respond legally and effectively to a unionization effort.

With appropriate guidance from experts, here are *some* of the types of activities company managers may be able to engage in safely if they wish to discourage a drive for unionization:

- proactively increase wages and benefits and improve working conditions *before* a unionization drive begins,

- improve grievance intake and response processes *before* a unionization drive begins,

- talk to employees about the competitive nature of the company's wages, benefits, and working conditions,

- correct any inaccurate statements made by union organizers,

- make the point that unionization will not necessarily improve wages, benefits, and working conditions,

- make the point that union membership is expensive and that union dues, fees, and assessments will come out of employees' paychecks,

- provide other factual information about a union and union officials, including high union salaries, union dues, and any other union fees, fines, and assessments,

- provide factual information that unionization can lead to strikes, and the true financial implications of strikes,

- tell employees they are not required to support the union effort, sign a union authorization card, vote in favor of a union, or even speak to union representatives,

- describe personal experiences, either good or bad, as members of unions, or

- point out potentially adverse impacts of unionization on a company, including how it might make the company less competitive.

Again, this is a highly specialized area of law and regulation. Any company attempting to resist an active unionization drive without guidance from experts is likely to make expensive mistakes.

Industry-Specific Regulation

Startups generally operate in one or more overarching regulatory paradigms. Some are very challenging and others less so. Here are some examples, primarily at the federal level.

- Food and beverage products are regulated for safety and labeling by the Food and Drug Administration ("FDA") and the U.S. Department of Agriculture ("USDA").

- Drugs, health and medical devices, and health data platforms are regulated by the FDA.

- Fintech and other financial products or services are regulated by:

  - Federal Deposit Insurance Corporation ("FDIC"),

  - Office of the Comptroller of the Currency ("OCC"),

  - SEC,

  - Financial Industry Regulatory Authority ("FINRA"),

  - Consumer Financial Protection Bureau ("CFPB"), and

- State banking agencies.

- Money transmitters, payment processors, and other money services businesses ("MSBs") are licensed and regulated by state financial institution regulators and by the Financial Crimes Enforcement Network ("FinCEN") of the U.S. Treasury Department.

- The Department of the Treasury's Alcohol and Tobacco Tax and Trade Bureau ("TTB") regulates aspects of alcohol production, importation, wholesale distribution, labeling, and advertising.

- Biotech and pharmaceutical companies are regulated by the FDA, USDA, and Environmental Protection Agency ("EPA").

- Products and services with potential defense applications are subject to "Export Administration Regulations" administered by the Bureau of Industry and Security ("BIS") of the Department of Commerce.

- Transportation-related services are regulated by the National Transportation Safety Board ("NTSB") and the Department of Transportation's ("DOT") National Highway Safety Administration ("NHTSA"),

- The Federal Communications Commission ("FCC") regulates the radio, television, and phone industries, and all interstate communications, including wire, satellite, and cable, and international communications originating or terminating in the United States.

- Insurance Tech (or InsurTech) companies involved in the sale or processing of insurance products are regulated by state insurance commissioners in each state where they operate. Links to all of these state commissions can be found at: https://www.naic.org/state_web_map.htm

- State and local councils, commissions, departments, and other regulatory bodies regulate innovation that interacts with the built environment and state and local regulatory schemes, as Uber, Lyft, Airbnb, electric scooter companies, and other startups have discovered.

Regulatory Research Resources

Each of the agencies just mentioned has a website with educational resources concerning the agency's mission, processes, regulatory framework, policy documents, and regulatory decisions.

Most of these websites also include news releases regarding enforcement actions and priorities and mechanisms to sign up for regulatory updates.

The SEC's EDGAR ("Electronic Data, Gathering, Analysis, and Retrieval") system is another excellent source of information for industry-specific regulation.

Using EDGAR's vast and searchable electronic archive containing detailed information and records from every public company, one only needs to find a publicly traded company in the same industry and read the "Government Regulation" section in its most recent Annual Report on Form 10-K. In the case of a newer company, that information can be found in its IPO registration statement on Form S-1.

These documents can be found easily by entering the company's name in EDGAR's company search box:

https://www.sec.gov/edgar/searchedgar/companysearch.html

A company's regulatory discussions in its SEC filings often outline the company's entire legal and regulatory framework. Once you have all of the names of the statutes, rules, and codes, you can retrieve them from agency websites and other online sources. Researching and mapping regulatory requirements has never been easier for lawyers and non-lawyers alike.

Case Study #33 – Self-Disrupting Unicorn

Most startups seeking to disrupt highly regulated industries use technology to bring efficiencies in both product delivery and regulatory compliance. In one of the biggest regulatory fails in startup history, the founder of Zenefits instead used technology to facilitate non-compliance, costing investors billions of dollars in value and costing the company and the founder himself millions in fines across multiple state and federal regulators.

Zenefits was focused on disrupting the massive employee health insurance benefits space and enjoyed substantial financial backing. Launched in 2013 through startup accelerator Y Combinator, Zenefits raised $580 million in three fundraising rounds and became one of VC Andreessen Horowitz's larger investments. By 2015 it was valued at $4.5 billion.

The idea behind Zenefits was to simplify the process of presenting and selecting health plans and coverages for both employers and employees alike, essentially automating the highly regulated role played by health insurance brokers.

While Zenefits seemed to get off to a solid start, quickly growing recurring revenue to more than

$1 million in the first year, Zenefits's VC-minders pushed for much more rapid growth, particularly in the hiring of sales reps.

VC-driven growth pressures pushed the company's visionary and generally very capable founder, Parker Conrad, to run the company at a faster and faster pace, apparently ever in fear that he would be fired for not making the unrealistic numbers being forced on him. These pressures clearly did not bring out the best in Mr. Conrad.

Problems began to emerge. Rapid growth was not allowing for adjustments in processes to accommodate existing industry regulations and best practices. Quality control and customer service issues also emerged.

On November 25, 2015, the magazine *Buzzfeed* published an article captioned *"Startup Zenefits Under Scrutiny For Flouting Insurance Laws,"* which included the byline, *"The $4.5 billion startup allowed salespeople to act as insurance brokers in at least seven states despite lacking the licenses to do so."*

The article reported that Washington State's insurance commissioner had begun an investigation into insurance sales by unlicensed brokers in early 2015. In Washington law, it is a class B felony to knowingly sell, solicit, or negotiate insurance without proper state licensing. Violators face prison sentences of up to 10 years and civil penalties of up to $25,000 for each violation.

This *Buzzfeed* article detailed rampant violations across numerous states by persons knowingly engaged in unlicensed insurance sales.

Following this article, while the company claimed publicly to be getting a handle on its licensing issues, the board ordered an internal investigation, hiring both the Cooley law firm and PwC, one of the big four accounting firms. This investigation revealed pervasive regulatory violations.

The most stunning revelation of all though was that the founder, Mr. Conrad, had developed an app, a Chrome "extension," that allowed Zenefits employees to cheat on state online insurance licensing exams by creating the false appearance that the employees had logged the required 53 hours of study required to receive a state insurance brokerage license.

Ultimately, Washington, California and other states brought actions against Zenefits for unlawful insurance sales and the SEC brought an anti-fraud enforcement action against the company and Mr. Conrad. Zenefits paid $11 million to settle the state charges and $450,000 to the SEC. Mr. Conrad personally paid $534,000 to settle SEC charges.

In its press release on the settlement, the SEC stated, in part:

> *"A San Francisco-based software company whose insurance business has accounted for 90 percent of its revenues has agreed to settle SEC charges that it misled investors in a pair of private offerings by making false statements about whether its employees were properly licensed to sell insurance....*
>
> *Although Zenefits recognized that it operated in a highly regulated industry, it did not take sufficient steps to ensure its growing workforce was properly licensed to sell insurance. Unbeknownst to investors, the company allowed employees to use a computer script created by Conrad to enable them to spend less time on pre-licensing education than required by California law...."*

https://www.sec.gov/litigation/admin/2017/33-10429-s.pdf

Zenefits still exists, albeit at a much reduced scale. It is no longer in the lucrative business of selling insurance directly, but instead licenses out its previously free technology platform for selecting insurance to the same types of small business clients to which it previously sold insurance.

Lessons: Founders need to push back on unreasonable growth expectations from VCs and other investors. The company's investors, employees, and customers were harmed significantly by a "ready, shoot, aim" approach to regulatory compliance in the name of hitting unrealistic revenue targets.

This case study also teaches the related lesson that regulatory violations and penalties can rarely be isolated. In this case, the known but concealed insurance regulatory violations soon became equally serious securities law violations, which are covered in the next chapter.

Case Study #34 – Uber-Important Dilemma

The idea that laws and regulations don't always keep pace with technology and innovation first entered my consciousness in 1989. That year I worked as a summer associate in the corporate law department of Burlington Northern, Inc. in Seattle.

In a passing conversation that summer, I learned that federal regulations still required all trains to have a caboose staffed by two railroad workers. By then, however, all of the functions served by a caboose and its crew, primarily braking and signaling, had been rendered obsolete by new technologies already in use – i.e., airbrakes, electronic signaling, and various computer-enabled systems.

Still today, many life-improving innovations struggle to survive the stranglehold of laws and regulations written for a different era.

Tesla faced just such a threat from state laws, aggressively defended by dominant car manufacturers, that effectively prohibited Tesla or any other company from selling new cars online instead of through traditional dealerships.

Of countless startups forced to operate in regulatory gray zones, or even red zones, Uber is one of the clearest examples of a company that consciously chose to challenge and even violate obsolete taxi laws and regulations in the interest of innovation.

Following a performance review of her by Uber founder Travis Kalanick, Uber's first general counsel gave an interview in February of 2017 in which she said the following :

> *What I'm hearing from this is I actually don't have to do things like any other legal department. I don't have to go to best practices, I have to go to what is best for my company, what is best for my legal department and I should view this as actually freedom to do things the way that I think should be done rather than the way that other people do it.*

While we don't know everything that was said in her performance review, beyond an admonition that the Uber law department needed to be more "innovative," it seems she was possibly told that she needed to allow the company to operate more "flexibly" in the face of laws and regulations that effectively outlawed the company's ride sharing services.

Talk about being caught between a professional rock-and-a-hard-place. *"Allow us to break the law or lose your job"* seemed to be the message.

For founders and startup advisors, distinguishing between socially valuable disruption and willful civil or criminal misconduct is not always easy.

Navigating the intersection between innovation and regulation is a topic for an entire book, but here are some key considerations founders and startup advisors must take into account when innovation hits legal or regulatory roadblocks:

- Can you successfully advocate for legal or regulatory change, or at least relief, in a cost-effective and timely manner? If so, that is generally the best course, especially if you can tailor that relief to your own innovations, while keeping in place regulatory barriers for competitors.

- If some form of legal or regulatory violation is unavoidable, can you leverage a viable constitutional argument or other challenge to negotiate a compromise resolution?

- Can you claim the "moral high ground" in a PR campaign? Do the human, social, and economic benefits of the innovation in question outweigh the original policy justifications for the regulations in question?

- Strong public policy arguments often support a two-pronged approach of skirting regulations to the minimum extent necessary, while simultaneously pursuing political and regulatory changes. Uber's playbook seems to involve a similar dual-track strategy.

- What is the worst thing that could happen? Any decision to act in a manner that is or may be deemed contrary to a law, rule, or regulation must take into account the nature of the possible violations. Specifically, where do they lie on the spectrum between "minor local infraction" at the low risk end and "serious criminal conduct" at the high risk end. Is the true risk a light administrative penalty or censure, or could officers face prison time?

- What is the degree of regulatory, societal, political, or industry support for or resistance to changing or working around an existing rule or regulation? There are literally thousands of federal, state, and local laws on the books that are wholly-ignored and unenforced, having been forgotten or accepted as obsolete or even unconstitutional.

- Skirting unenforced laws with little or no social or political support poses little risk to entrepreneurs. On the other hand, skirting laws serving valuable public interests, or those that protect powerful political or economic interests, poses high risk of conflict and enforcement activity.

- Charging ahead in the face of known legal or regulatory risks frequently comes down to naked calculations of risk versus reward. When the sole consideration is simply, how much can be made by violating the law versus how much will the fines and penalties cost, the risks of a harsh outcome grow.

While companies do get away with pure cost-benefit gambles, Volkswagen knows it miscalculated badly in "emissionsgate," given the more than $30 billion in fines and penalties to date, and the prison sentences handed down so far.

More nuanced calculations led to the explosion of "initial coin offerings" discussed later, in which blockchain and cryptocurrency innovators went headlong into newly created methods for funding cutting-edge technologies and business models, some legitimate, and some not.

This gamble on the federal definition of a "security" paid off for some early players, as state and federal securities regulators spent several years getting their bearings. But the legal and regulatory consequences escalated rapidly and severely once the SEC decided that virtually all digital tokens were securities and, as such, fully subject to federal securities registration and anti-fraud laws.

<u>Lessons</u>. Innovators face difficult calculations when their business models collide with existing legal and regulatory frameworks. Work to remove barriers proactively whenever possible.

Knowingly flaunting any law always comes with risks. While a variety of factors can be considered to gauge and weigh that risk against corresponding opportunities, such evaluations are frequently more like art than science. When violations are unavoidable, risks may be reduced to the extent of any moral or public policy high ground. And always avoid violating any law or regulation backed by criminal penalties, versus less significant civil or administrative penalties.

Legal counsel asked to opine on or assist with business conduct that risks legal or regulatory violations walk a particularly delicate line. Under the rules of professional conduct in all states, lawyers are prohibited from *assisting* criminal conduct.

Washington's applicable rule of professional conduct is RPC 1.2(d), which states:

"A lawyer shall not counsel a client to engage, or assist a client, in conduct that the lawyer knows is criminal or fraudulent, but a lawyer may discuss the legal consequences of any proposed course of conduct with a client and may counsel or assist a client to make a good faith effort to determine the validity, scope, meaning or application of the law."

While this might seem clear to many non-lawyers, many types of conduct can violate a law or regulation and still not be "criminal" or "fraudulent." This is because only certain types of laws and regulations are part of a state's or locality's criminal code, and fraudulent conduct is even more narrowly defined. In most jurisdictions, for example, violating taxi licensing regulations is *not* a crime, but rather subjects a person or company to civil or administrative penalties and sanctions.

Such matters are defined by statute and case law and are outside our scope here. Suffice it to say that lawyers need to exercise great care when it comes to advising clients on activities that may violate any law or regulation.

From an entrepreneur's perspective, it is worth noting that external counsel are likely to be more conservative than a sophisticated in-house counsel, given the more limited role of outside counsel and given the practical reality that a company is more likely to make a claim of malpractice against outside counsel than against in-house counsel.

In-house counsel involved in high-level risk assessments are likely to be company officers and may also wear different "hats" regarding different matters – sometimes more of a legal hat, other times more of a business hat.

PART II - FUNDRAISING

CHAPTER ELEVEN

State and Federal Securities Laws

In this chapter, we are finally talking about fundraising, or at least the laws and rules of fundraising – the securities laws.

The securities laws govern the purchase and sale of securities of all kinds. Most of us are familiar with securities like stocks, bonds, options, mutual funds, exchange traded funds, and maybe even more exotic securities like variable annuities.

But the securities laws reach even further, covering "investment contracts." Investment contracts are generally defined as any (i) investment (ii) in a common enterprise (iii) with an expectation of profits (iv) from the efforts of others. An interest in an Armadillo ranch can be an investment contract.

This overview of the securities laws will be focused exclusively on concepts and issues of relevance to startups and startup advisors, including:

- state and federal anti-fraud rules,

- registration requirements for securities offerings and the key "private offering" exemptions from registration,

- restrictions on trading privately issued securities,

- restrictions on paying "finders fees" to persons who are not registered broker-dealers, and

- recent legislation and rule changes intended to help small companies raise money.

Some of the more dramatic and significant recent changes in the federal securities laws include crowdfunding, the "Mini IPO" rules, and the lifting of the 80+ year ban on publicly advertising private securities offerings.

Anti-Fraud Rules

Virtually all entrepreneurs need to raise money to fund their companies. The most experienced and successful among them know that a transparent, low-pressure, low-hype approach to pitching investors is the best way to raise money.

Most sophisticated investors have sat through countless pitches, and they tend to know when something sounds too good to be true. Entrepreneurs must gain the trust and confidence of potential investors to raise funds successfully, and overstating the opportunity while understating the risks rarely succeeds with the types of investors that a company should want.

A fundamental, universal truth underlies the psychology of successful pitching – those that play it cool and a little "hard to get" are inherently more attractive, whereas desperation, telegraphed by flash and hype, is less attractive.

Unfortunately, not all entrepreneurs succeed at pitching investors in a balanced, candid, truthful manner. Greed, financial desperation, and lack of sophistication all play roles in pitching that paints a distorted picture.

Entrepreneurs who succeed at raising funds through deception, however, can later find themselves in hot water if things go badly. Given that roughly 80% of startups fail, investor disappointment is not rare. And some percentage of disappointed investors, however small, will explore recourse under the securities laws.

Daily press releases and news stories serve as constant, colorful reminders of the effectiveness of state and federal securities anti-fraud rules at responding to investor abuse.

The SEC's daily press release webpage, found by searching online for "press releases – sec.gov," or at https://www.sec.gov/news/pressreleases, provides regular examples of things not to do, like this fraudulent digital token scam:

> *Washington, D.C., March 20, 2020 —*
>
> *The Securities and Exchange Commission today announced that it has obtained an asset freeze and other emergency relief to halt an ongoing securities fraud perpetrated by a former state senator and two others who bilked investors in and outside the U.S.*
>
> *The SEC's complaint alleges that Florida residents Robert Dunlap and Nicole Bowdler worked with former Washington state senator David Schmidt to market and sell a purported digital asset called the "Meta 1 Coin" in an unregistered securities offering conducted through the Meta 1 Coin Trust. The complaint alleges that the defendants made numerous false and misleading statements to potential and actual investors, including claims that the Meta 1 Coin was backed by a $1 billion art collection or $2 billion of gold, and that an accounting firm was auditing the gold assets.*
>
> *The defendants also allegedly told investors that the Meta 1 Coin was risk-free, would never lose value and could return up to 224,923%. According to the complaint, the defendants never distributed the Meta 1 Coins and instead used investor funds to pay personal expenses and funnel proceeds to two others, Pramana Capital Inc. and Peter K. Shamoun.*
>
> *…In all, the complaint alleges the defendants raised more than $4.3 million from more than 150 investors in and outside the U.S.*

State and federal securities anti-fraud rules and principles are well established, so we do not need to belabor their rich history. The basic federal rule is Rule 10b-5, adopted by the SEC under the Securities Exchange Act of 1934 (the "Exchange Act" or the "1934 Act").

Rule 10b-5

Rule 10b-5 is located in the Code of Federal Regulations at 17 CFR § 240.10b-5. It says:

Employment of manipulative and deceptive devices.

It shall be unlawful for any person, directly or indirectly, by the use of any means or instrumentality of interstate commerce, or of the mails or of any facility of any national securities exchange,

    (a) *To employ any device, scheme, or artifice to defraud,*

    (b) *To make any untrue statement of a material fact or to omit to state a material fact necessary in order to make the statements made, in the light of the circumstances under which they were made, not misleading, or*

    (c) *To engage in any act, practice, or course of business which operates or would operate as a fraud or deceit upon any person, in connection with the purchase or sale of any security.*

State and federal anti-fraud securities laws are essentially the same and are interpreted very similarly, sharing these common characteristics:

- they apply to *every* securities transaction,

- they are violated by any "false or misleading statement or omission" in connection with the "purchase or sale" of a security,

- they can be enforced through "rights of private action" by wronged individuals who can file lawsuits for damages, and

- they can be enforced by civil, administrative, or even criminal enforcement actions by state or federal regulators or criminal prosecutors.

Every state has its own securities enforcement division to enforce its own state securities laws, often called blue sky laws. Combined with the SEC's federal jurisdiction and resources, U.S. securities enforcement is effective.

Private Right of Action

Case law long ago clarified that private individuals may sue for damages under SEC Rule 10b-5. This right of private enforcement, or "private right of action," plays a big role in the overall enforcement of the federal securities laws.

Private plaintiffs seeking damages for fraud under Rule 10b-5 must prove six elements:

    (i)   a material misrepresentation or omission by the defendant,

    (ii) made with scienter, and

    (iii) made in connection with the purchase or sale of a security,

    (iv) upon which the plaintiff relied in making the purchase and sale,

    (v) and suffered economic harm,

    (vi) which harm was caused by the misrepresentation or omission.

Materiality and Scienter Standards

The 2010 9th Circuit Court of Appeals case captioned *SEC v. Platforms Wireless Int'l Corp.* provides a nice summary of the materiality and scienter (knowledge/intent) standards required under Rule 10b-5, not to mention several of the other topics covered in this chapter, such as Section 5, exemptions from registration, and trading in privately issued securities.

Search the caption online to read the full decision, or go to: http://cdn.ca9.uscourts.gov/datastore/opinions/2010/07/27/07-56542.pdf.

The Court in *SEC v. Platforms Wireless* summarized the relevant case law on materiality and scienter, in part, in the following passages:

> An omitted fact is material "if there is a substantial likelihood that the disclosure of the omitted fact would have been viewed by the reasonable investor as having significantly altered the total mix of information made available.' Id. at 908 (quotation marks omitted). Scienter can be established by intent, knowledge, or in some cases "recklessness." Hollinger v. Titan Capital Corp., 914 F.2d 1564, 1568-69 (9th Cir. 1990) (en banc).

> ***

> Reckless conduct may be defined as a highly unreasonable omission, involving not merely simple, or even inexcusable negligence, but an extreme departure from the standards of ordinary care, and which presents a danger of misleading buyers or sellers that is either known to the defendant or is so obvious that the actor must have been aware of it.... [T]he danger of misleading buyers must be actually known or so obvious that any reasonable man would be legally bound as knowing, and the omission must derive from something more egregious than even 'white heart/empty head' good faith.

> Hollinger, 914 F.2d at 1569 (citations omitted).

> ***

> Our definition of recklessness, as taken from Sundstrand, strongly suggests that we continued to view it as a form of intentional or knowing misconduct. We used the words "known" and "must have been aware," which suggest consciousness or deliberateness. Indeed, we expressly acknowledged our own prior statement that "recklessness is a form of intent rather than a greater degree of negligence." Id. at 976-77 (citing Hollinger, 914 F.2d at 1569).

> ***

> In Gebhart v. SEC, 595 F.3d 1034 (9th Cir. 2010), our most recent case to address the issue of reckless scienter, we concluded that scienter requires "either knowledge of falsity or conscious recklessness." Id. at 1041 n.10. "Scienter... is a subjective inquiry. It turns on the defendant's actual state of mind." Id. at 1042. Thus, "although we may consider the objective unreasonableness of the

defendant's conduct to raise an inference of scienter, the ultimate question is whether the defendant knew his or her statements were false, or was consciously reckless as to their truth or falsity." Id.

False and Misleading Statements or Omissions

Applying these materiality and scienter standards in everyday fundraising is highly subjective. One person's "puffery" or absent-minded omission might very well look like "conscious recklessness" to the SEC, a state regulator, or plaintiff's counsel.

Founders involved in fundraising should steer very wide of any form of puffery or "selective disclosure." That can be particularly difficult for enthusiastic founders or for virtually anyone who comes from a marketing or business development background, where standards of candor are more flexible.

The glowing and almost breathless adjectives and superlatives used in advertising have no place in fundraising materials.

As to every potentially exaggerated claim or prediction proposed for inclusion in a pitch deck, a founder should ask, "*If this investment does not work out, is this the type of claim, statement, or omission that a reasonable person might have considered important in deciding to invest?*"

If the answer is yes, it is potential fodder for a lawsuit or enforcement action. The following is just a partial list of the types of misstatements and omissions that could support an anti-fraud claim if later proved false or misleading:

- the product or service is ready for the market,
- the product or service produces certain results,
- the product or service has passed certain tests or approvals,
- the product or service can be easily and cost-effectively scaled up,
- there is little or no competition for the product or service,
- the product or service meets all regulatory requirements,
- the product or service is safe,
- we have sourced all of the materials and suppliers necessary to produce and market the product or service,
- we own all of the intellectual property for the product or service,
- we are aware of no actual or potential claims against the company that could hurt its ability to produce and sell the product or service.

It is particularly worth noting that the SEC considers it *prima facie* (accepted as correct until proven otherwise) securities fraud to promise investors a rate of return of any kind.

Promising an interest rate on debt or preferred stock is ok, but any promised return on investment, or "ROI," is fraudulent.

Rookie entrepreneurs make this glaring mistake often, claiming investors will double or triple their investment. All promises about returns should be assiduously avoided.

Candor, Transparency, and Other Anti-fraud Inoculations

The anti-fraud rules require a balancing act. Founders are expected to be tireless and enthusiastic promoters of their companies. Founders who are not passionate find it very difficult to raise any money.

But sophisticated and even very passionate founders know this dance well. They are comfortable with explaining "risk factors" and using hedging language:

- "if we can pull this off it will revolutionize transportation as we know it,"

- "yes, there are competitors, but I believe we have the team to get a better product to market faster,"

- "the first prototype had some issues, but we think we have figured them out and the team is hard at work on the next version, which we hope to have in hand within the next few weeks,"

- "yes, we know there are regulatory gray areas, and we're talking with counsel and regulators to look for solutions or workarounds."

Founders who identify issues head-on and discuss them openly are inherently more trustworthy and may have an easier time raising funds from smart investors. Sophisticated investors know that the greatest innovations are almost always the products of taking big risks and solving very difficult problems. If something sounds too easy, it probably is.

In addition to avoiding negligent, reckless, or willful misstatements and omissions, three types of "disclosures" can help to ward off anti-fraud claims when used in connection with other offering materials.

- Forward-Looking Statements Disclaimers

- Statements of Risk Factors

- Disclosure Schedules/Schedules of Exceptions

Forward-Looking Statements

The formalization of what are now called forward-looking statements happened under the Private Securities Litigation Reform Act of 1995 ("PSLRA").

These disclaimer-type statements, also called "safe harbor statements," are said to provide a "safe harbor" for certain types of written disclosures, predictions, forecasts, or estimates – i.e., statements by a company about what might or might not happen in the future concerning their business, prospects for success, market conditions, and the like.

A Forward-looking statement is essentially a disclaimer stating that (i) the company is making some predictions or assumptions that might or might not turn out to be true, (ii) they were believed to be true at the time made, but (iii) the company also is under no obligation to update those statements.

Here is a typical forward-looking statement from a private offering memorandum:

This Offering Memorandum and the Investment Documents include forward-looking statements and projections into the future, which, in most cases, include words like "projected," "estimated," "anticipated," "intended," "targeted," "predicted," "believed," "planned," "may," "could," "will" or "should", their negative, or other comparable terms. The Company has made every attempt to ensure that these forward-looking statements and projections are based on reasonable assumptions. However, they are typically subject to the influences of one or more of the risk factors discussed in this Offering Memorandum and the Disclosure Documents, or currently unknown risk factors, all of which are uncertain and unpredictable and could adversely affect the Company's actual performance results.

Projections concerning the Company's future results of operations are based on management's assumptions and estimates. These concern, among other things, the timely availability of capital on acceptable terms, the Company's ability to continue to develop and operate its proposed business in a timely and efficient manner, the ability to employ and train suitably skilled employees, the costs and expenses involved in the establishment of new facilities and operations, and other future events and conditions. Management's plans, strategies, and intentions may change based on increased experience with the Company's business model, as well as in response to competition, general economic trends or perceived opportunities, risks or other developments. As a result, the Company's actual results or activities, or actual events or conditions, could differ materially from the Company's projections and forward-looking statements, and the Company does not certify or assume responsibility for them.

Some forward-looking statements are very generic, like that example. Others include more specific language regarding unique issues or concerns the company wishes to highlight. Specific disclosures tend to provide better inoculation than generic disclosures.

To provide protection under the PSLRA, a company's forecasts, predictions, or other forward-looking statements and disclosures cannot be knowingly false or misleading, and the forward-looking statement disclaimer must be tailored, substantive, and meaningful, and not simply copied boilerplate.

The *Harmon International Industries* securities litigation involving the Harmon electronics company helps to define the protective limitations of the forward-looking statement safe harbor. Again, the safe harbor provides no protection for knowingly false statements. The *Harmon* court emphasized this point in stating, "*...those statements were not entitled to safe harbor protection because the accompanying cautionary statements were misleading insofar as they failed to account for historical facts... that would have been important to a reasonable investor.*" *In re: Harman International Industries, Inc. Securities Litigation* (No. 14-7017) (D.C. Cir. June 23, 2015).

https://www.cadc.uscourts.gov/internet/opinions.nsf/1B7208ADC298E6C985257E6D00539C76/$file/14-7017-1559106.pdf

Forward-looking statements are often just one to three paragraphs long and can be added to the front of executive summaries, pitch decks, and other offering documents discussed later. They should be used liberally.

Risk Factors

Most readers have probably encountered risk factor disclosures if they have ever seen or reviewed any investment offering materials. If not, an online search of the term will provide plenty of examples. Every IPO prospectus has risk factors within the first pages.

Risk factor disclosures are very common in offerings where a formal offering memorandum, prospectus, or other such investor disclosure document is required or prepared voluntarily.

They are required for offerings under Reg A, which we look at soon. The SEC form for those offerings, Form 1-A, says this at Section 3(b):

> *Immediately following the Table of Contents required by Item 2 or the Summary, there must be set forth under an appropriate caption, a carefully organized series of short, concise paragraphs, summarizing the most significant factors that make the offering speculative or substantially risky. Issuers should avoid generalized statements and include only factors that are specific to the issuer.*

The SEC's crowdfunding Form C asks similarly:

> *Discuss the material factors that make an investment in the issuer speculative or risky.*

Risk factors are most common in offerings involving a formal disclosure document. Offerings involving any non-accredited investors generally require a formal disclosure document containing risk factors. We discuss non-accredited investors next, but note here that their presence in any offering substantially ratchets up formal disclosure requirements.

On the other hand, very large offerings can be conducted with exclusively wealthy investors without any formal disclosure document.

As a rule of thumb for startups, risk factors are commonly found in offerings involving non-accredited investors and less often in offerings involving only accredited investors. One exception is if investment bankers are involved. They prefer to have a formal offering document.

Risk factor disclosures are very rare in VC led financings, where Disclosure Schedules are used to provide more precise information about specific risks.

When risk factor disclosures are required, it is important to ensure they are not simply generic descriptions of issues that any business could face, but that they are the issues the specific business in question could face.

Some founders are reluctant to lay out all of the potential risks they face for fear that they might drive away investors, but many investors are used to seeing them, so their negative impact is somewhat muted.

In short, risk factor disclosures are sometimes a necessary evil, so the best thing to do is take full advantage of their inoculating potential by providing thoughtful, detailed, and insightful risk factors. If litigation strikes, the risk factors risk factors you have to worry about are the ones you missed.

Disclosure Schedule/Schedule of Exceptions

In financing and M&A transactions, the SPA or PSA will almost always include a Disclosure Schedule or Schedule of Exceptions. I think of them as the closet where all of a company's skeletons, or dirty laundry, can be found.

Although the name Disclosure Schedule is more common and we'll use that here mostly, Schedule of Exceptions is more descriptive of these documents. They largely contain statements of facts that are "exceptions" to the representations and warranties made in the SPA or PSA.

As an over-simplified example, there might be a statement in the representations and warranties that says, "*The company is aware of no claims of IP infringement against it by third parties, except as disclosed in the Disclosure Schedule.*" If there are no claims of IP infringement, there's nothing to add to the Disclosure Schedule.

If the representation about no infringement claims isn't true, the company will be required to provide detailed disclosures about any specific claims or threats of claims about IP infringement.

Disclosure Schedules track the section and sub-section numbering of the reps and warranties from an associated SPA or PSA. If the rep about IP infringement is Section 3.12(e) in the SPA, responsive disclosures will be found at Section 3.12(e) of the Disclosure Schedule.

Even in less well-documented financings without lengthy reps and warranties, it is helpful to put together a Disclosure Schedule that lists out all IP concerns, pending or threatened litigation, regulatory matters, significant HR matters, key customer risks, and any other negative information the company does not want coming back to it in the form of an investor's anti-fraud claim.

Due to the sensitive information found in Disclosure Schedules, not every potential investor should see them, only serious investors who have been presented the purchase and sale agreement.

The Registration Requirement

Section 5 of the Securities Act

If the anti-fraud rules are the first pillar of securities law, the registration requirement and related "exemptions from registration" are the second. The federal securities offering registration requirement is found in Section 5 of the Securities Act of 1933 (the "Securities Act").

Under the Securities Act, it is not companies that are registered, but securities offerings.

The anti-fraud laws prohibit deception. But the registration requirements compel specific disclosures deemed material to investors. Registration means registration of a public securities offering. Registration also requires preparing and presenting to potential investors a "prospectus" that meets the substantial disclosure requirements of Section 10 of the Securities Act.

An IPO is the most familiar type of offering registration. IPOs are registered on SEC Form S-1. https://www.sec.gov/Archives/edgar/data/1288776/000119312504073639/ds1.htm#toc16167

As an overarching prohibition, Section 5 makes it illegal to use the means of interstate commerce to offer or sell unregistered securities.

Exemptions from Registration

Fortunately, other sections of the Securities Act, and various rules adopted thereunder, contain "exemptions" from Section 5's blanket prohibition and also from each state's corresponding registration requirements.

The term exemption is essentially shorthand for the idea - "private offering exemption from the registration requirements applicable to public offerings."

Interestingly, the term "exemption" is also used to describe certain types of offerings that are actually *registered and reviewed* – either by the SEC or state regulators – or in the case of Reg A offerings, possibly by both the SEC *and* by state regulators.

Other examples of "exempt" offering types discussed below that are actually registered and reviewed include federal and state-regulated crowdfunding offerings and state-based "SCOR" offerings. SCOR stands for Small Company Offering Registration.

There are several state and federal exemptions, but only a small handful are used by startups with sufficient frequency to warrant discussion:

- Rule 506(b)
- Rule 506(c)
- Rule 504
- Regulation A – Tier 1 and II
- Regulation Crowdfunding – Reg CF
- Miscellaneous intrastate exemptions, including state-based Reg D analogs, small offering registration forms, and intrastate crowdfunding.

Even the simplest of these state and federal exemptions for private offerings are tricky for all but the most experienced securities lawyers to navigate safely.

Minor technical non-compliance can constitute engaging in an "unregistered offering in violation of Section 5," potentially creating substantial legal, financial, and regulatory risk for all involved.

The SEC can bring enforcement actions for Section 5 violations, but it usually only pursues Section 5 claims when there are also anti-fraud violations.

In most cases, the larger legal and financial threat from a blown registration exemption may be that of "rescission," and the shadow that threat can cast over future financings and M&A deals.

Rescission

The right of rescission under the securities laws allows investors to get all of their money back. It is essentially a one-year right for investors to "put" the stock back to the company for a full refund.

The right of rescission for Section 5 violations is found in Sections 12(a)(1) and 13 of the Securities Act.

For its part, the SEC has broad latitude in enforcing Section 5 and is not constrained by the one-year period in ordering rescission.

The risk that a financing transaction could be unwound years later due to an alleged Section 5 violation is an extremely serious threat.

For companies considering going public, having private offerings in their past with blown exemptions is a huge risk. As an SEC examiner in the Division of Corporation Finance back in the mid-1990s, on two separate occasions I forced questionable issuers (companies issuing securities) to make full rescission offers simultaneously with their IPOs.

As discussed, during Google's 2004 IPO registration, the SEC determined the company had blown the SEC Rule 701 exemption in connection with its stock option plan and the SEC required Google to make rescission offers to 1,320 individuals involving more than 23 million shares. A rescission offer and related SEC enforcement action could easily derail a less successful company's IPO.

Here's how Google had to describe the mistake and the rescission offer in its IPO under Risk Factors:

Shares issued, and option grants made, under our stock plans exceeded limitations in the federal and state securities laws.

> *Shares issued and options granted under our 1998 Stock Plan and our 2003 Stock Plan were not exempt from registration or qualification under federal and state securities laws and we did not obtain the required registrations or qualifications.... As a result, we intend to make a rescission offer to the holders of these shares and options beginning approximately 30 days after the effective date of this registration statement. If this rescission is accepted, we could be required to make aggregate payments to the holders of these shares and options of up to $34 million plus statutory interest. Federal securities laws do not expressly provide that a rescission offer will terminate a purchaser's right to rescind a sale of stock that was not registered as required. If any or all of the offerees reject the rescission offer, we may continue to be liable under federal and state securities laws for up to an aggregate amount of approximately $34 million plus statutory interest. See "Rescission Offer."*

https://www.sec.gov/Archives/edgar/data/1288776/000119312504073639/ds1.htm#toc16167

Bad Actor Exemption Prohibitions

All state and federal securities exemptions prohibit the participation of what are called "bad actors," including simply as officers, directors, promoters, or controlling shareholders.

The provisions defining what makes a person or entity a bad actor vary subtly by exemption, as do the nature and length of applicable "look back" periods relating to bad conduct, but most bad actor provisions are similar to the definitions found in SEC Reg D.

Rule 506(d) of Reg D details certain "disqualifying events" that make one a "bad actor," including these:

- *Criminal convictions, court injunctions and restraining orders in connection with:*
    - *the purchase or sale of a security, or*
    - *making a false filing with the SEC,*
- *Final orders of state regulators of securities, insurance, banking, savings associations or credit unions; federal banking agencies; the Commodity Futures Trading Commission... that:*
    - *bar the person from associating with a regulated entity, engaging in the business of securities, insurance or banking, or engaging in savings association or credit union activities or,*
    - *are based on fraudulent, manipulative, or deceptive conduct and were issued within 10 years of the proposed sale of securities.*
- *SEC orders to cease and desist from violations and future violations of the scienter-based anti-fraud provisions of the federal securities laws*

Interestingly, securities exemption bad actor rules do not cover more common blemishes like personal bankruptcies and non-financial industry convictions.

Accredited and Non-Accredited Investors

Before diving into specific exemptions, it is worth highlighting the important distinction under state and federal securities laws regarding "accredited" versus "non-accredited" investors.

Section 5 is predicated on the notion of protecting the investing public by providing them information about investments before they invest. Since the adoption of the securities laws, there has been an evolving consensus that very wealthy, sophisticated investors do not need all of these protections, particularly in private transactions between themselves and issuers, in which they can negotiate for themselves and demand whatever information they desire before investing.

The definition of "accredited investor" is intended to draw a line at which individuals (and certain entities) are deemed capable of taking care of themselves and bearing the risk of investment losses. All of the exemptions below are structured in varying ways around these ideas.

Here is the two-part test to determine whether an individual is accredited:

- Income in the most recent two years equal to or greater than $200,000, with a reasonable expectation of earning the same or more in the current year (or $300,000 for married couples);

-OR-

- Net assets (all assets minus all liabilities) of $1 million or greater, not including primary residence (or amounts owed thereon below FMV).

Most entities, including trusts and LLCs, need to have at least $5 million of assets to qualify as accredited; alternatively, all of the owners of the entity must be accredited as individuals.

Under Rule 506(b), issuers must have a reasonable belief that an investor is accredited, but, as we will discuss, Rule 506(c) requires actual verification of accredited status.

In Rule 506(b) private placements, including virtually all VC-led financings, this reasonable belief is usually achieved, in part, by collecting Investor Questionnaires from every investor. The investors must attest to their accredited investor status and disclaim any "bad actor" disqualifiers.

Federal Preemption

Another important concept relating to Section 5 and offering exemptions is that of "preemption." Some federal offering exemptions, including Rule 506(b), 506(c), Reg A+, and Reg CF, preempt state regulation of those offerings. Other federal exemptions do not preempt state regulation, including Rule 504, Reg A (Tier 1), and Rule 147.

Federal preemption under Section 5 is primarily significant because of the differences discussed below between state "merit regulation" and federal "disclosure regulation."

Where state review of an offering is preempted, any required review of offering documents or other materials to *approve the offering* would be conducted solely by the SEC. State regulators are entitled to require "notice" filings by issuers conducting such offerings in their states and to charge fees in connection with those notice filings, but substantive offering regulation is not permitted.

The state regulators can even take it upon themselves to review those filings and any other related materials or activities. But such offerings do not require state approval to go forward and issuers are not required to change their disclosure documents in response to comments by state regulators.

Preemption does not, however, prevent state regulators from investigating and taking action against securities fraud, whether involving exempt or non-exempt transactions of any kind.

Merit Regulation versus Disclosure Regulation. Although regulatory policies vary by state, securities regulators in many states engage in what is known as "merit regulation," or "merit review." For more than 100 years, regulators with merit review authority have disapproved securities offerings if, in their judgment, the offering would be or could be unfair to investors or simply too risky.

As discussed later, because Reg A historically did not preempt state review, difficulties in getting Reg A offerings approved in merit regulation states over the years have rendered the exemption largely unused for capital formation.

The SEC, on the other hand, is a disclosure-based regulator. It reviews offerings for the completeness and accuracy of issuers' disclosures based on applicable disclosure standards. If the SEC believes the business plan is doomed to fail, it can make the issuer disclose that probability, but the SEC theoretically will not otherwise prevent the offering from going forward.

As a former SEC staffer, however, I can say with certainty that SEC staffers have achieved the same result, killing bad offerings, with heavy-handed application of the disclosure comment process.

Although regulating based on the quality of disclosure versus the quality of the business model might seem a subtle distinction, the insertion of business judgment into the regulatory process leads to a greater percentage of deals not passing regulatory muster under merit review.

This is a key reason that many issuers decide, on the advice of counsel, to avoid all securities exemptions that do not preempt state review.

Form D

Even though Reg D private offerings are not registered with the SEC, issuers conducting offerings under Reg D must file a Form D with the SEC within 15 days of the first sale.

Simultaneously with that filing, issuers must comply with state laws requiring similar notice filings in any state where any of the investors in the offering reside. This is what many refer to as blue sky registration. State Reg D notice filings have been greatly simplified in recent years, following the creation of what is called the Electronic Filing Depository, operated by the North American Securities Administrators Association, or NASAA.

Because the initial Form D filing with the SEC has to be done electronically through EDGAR, a somewhat quirky system, it is best to pay trained professionals to assist in the preparation and filing of Form Ds and any required state notice filings.

Apart from the cost of professional assistance, filing the Form D through EDGAR is free, but each state sets its own notice filing fees. Filing in ten or more states might cost two or three thousand dollars.

EDGAR Historical Note: my spouse and favorite proof-reader, Serena Swegle, was one of several SEC staffers tasked with launching and rolling out EDGAR between 1994 and 1996 to all issuers, SEC staff, and to the investing public. Search online for *"Serena Swegle EDGAR"* to review early EDGAR rule releases and the SEC's early guidance co-authored by Serena.

Rule 506(b)

With that background on Section 5, rescission, bad actors, accredited and non-accredited investors, federal preemption, and Form D, we will now study the main federal and state offering exemptions, starting with perhaps the most significant one, Rule 506(b).

Rule 506(b) is the king of exemptions for startups. Almost all fundraising involving VCs and angel investors is conducted under 506(b).

Section 4(a)(2) of the Securities Act exempts from registration transactions by an issuer not involving any public offering. Rule 506(b) of Regulation D is a "safe harbor" rule under Section 4(a) (2). Offerings in compliance with it are deemed to meet the requirements of the Section 4(a)(2) exemption.

No general solicitation is allowed under Rule 506(b), which means:

- no advertising,
- no pitching in public meetings to any non-accredited investors,
- no social media posts,
- no media stories or interviews, and
- no pitching accredited investors you do not know without an introduction from someone who does.

As noted above, Rule 506(b) is one of the federal exemptions that preempt state regulation.

Under 506(b) a company can raise unlimited dollars from unlimited "accredited investors" without producing any disclosure document.

That is a very important point. Under 506(b), if only accredited investors are solicited, the issuer has no obligation to produce a private placement memorandum, offering circular, offering memorandum, prospectus, business plan or any other kind of disclosure document.

That is not to say that some investors might want to see one. But the rule does not require one, and virtually no VC deals involve a substantial disclosure document. Reliance on 506(b) and sticking to accredited investors can save a company countless hours preparing a disclosure document and at least $10,000 to $20,000 in legal expenses reviewing and improving it.

That is why 506(b) is king of the offering exemptions.

But disclosure obligations change dramatically if a *single* non-accredited investor participates in a 506(b) offering. The rule allows up to 35 non-accredited investors in a single offering, provided they are also financially sophisticated.

But once there are any non-accredited investors participating in the offering, the company must:

- provide those non-accredited investors very substantial disclosures that are roughly equivalent to the information required in registered offerings (on SEC Form 1-A or Form S-1), along with certain detailed financial statement information specified in Rule 506, and

- make company officers available to answer questions from those non-accredited investors.

This is the key reason that most investors do not want *any* non-accredited investors involved in a financing – failure to provide fully compliant disclosure materials can then blow the entire exemption.

Excluding Non-Accredited Investors. Again, this is a key reason why allowing *any* non-accredited investors in a 506(b) offering significantly increases cost, complexity, and risk.

And unfortunately, allowing non-accredited investors into offerings has other negative consequences. Chief among these is that less wealthy individuals are more likely to be difficult or "needy" investors.

At the more benign end of the spectrum, the less wealthy an investor is, the more likely they seem to be to contact management more frequently for special updates or information.

Unaccredited investors may also be more likely to experience adverse changes in financial condition that could accelerate their time horizon for wanting their money back.

And lastly, less wealthy investors are correspondingly less able to absorb investment losses if things do not work out and, as a result, may also be more inclined to sue or complain to regulators when that happens.

Keeping in mind the fact that about 80% of startups fail, there are compelling arguments for not accepting investments from non-accredited investors. I advise all of my companies to avoid soliciting any non-accredited investors for the above reasons and, as discussed in chapters 12 and 13, because adding them to the cap table can jeopardize a company's ability to obtain VC funding.

The idea of excluding non-accredited investors is heresy for many who wish to see a more level playing field in the world of high-risk and potentially high-reward private investments.

This is a valid concern and also a noble one. In advising my clients, however, the equally valid maxim *"no good deed goes unpunished"* generally prevails and I consistently recommend only soliciting and accepting investments from accredited investors.

Finding Accredited Investors without General Solicitation

Under Rule 506(b), a company may not engage in "general solicitation."

General solicitation means any form of advertising or promotion, whether by TV, radio, newspaper, mail, email, online, public meetings, or otherwise, but also by simply reaching out to strangers in any manner whatsoever.

As discussed later, Rule 506(c) and certain types of registered exempt offerings permit general solicitation according to specific rules, including Reg A+, state and federal crowdfunding, and state-based SCOR offerings.

Pre-existing Substantive Relationship. So how does one find investors under Rule 506(b) without engaging in general solicitation? First of all, a company can solicit investments from persons with whom the company has a "pre-existing substantive relationship." A pre-existing substantive relationship is one that the issuer, through its officers, employees or agents, has formed with an offeree before the commencement of the offering.

A "substantive" relationship is one in which the issuer (or a person acting on its behalf) has sufficient information to evaluate, and does evaluate, a prospective offeree's financial circumstances and sophistication in determining his or her status as an accredited or sophisticated investor.

SEC guidance suggests that the existence of such a pre-existing, substantive relationship is one means, but not the exclusive means, of demonstrating the absence of a general solicitation in a Regulation D offering.

Brokers, Investment Advisors, Investor Groups, and Platforms. SEC guidance also says a pre-existing, substantive relationship can be established indirectly through registered broker-dealers or registered investment advisers, and also through groups of experienced, sophisticated investors who share information about private offerings through their networks.

Members of such groups who have a relationship with a particular issuer may introduce that issuer to the network without the issuer's request for the introduction being deemed a general solicitation. This guidance underlies the growth of angel investor groups.

The SEC has also issued guidance that allows crowdfunding platforms to establish password-protected sections for accredited investors where offerings can be made pursuant to Rule 506(b) without engaging in general solicitation. The platforms need to first satisfy themselves that an investor is accredited and sophisticated before allowing the investor to see 506(b) offerings.

Companies making 506(b) offerings on such a platform must be careful not to otherwise engage in general solicitation on social media or in other forms of advertising or public gatherings.

The key guidance in this area is the <u>Citizen VC, Inc.</u> SEC No Action Letter, dated August 6, 2015, which can be found by searching online or at this link:

http://www.sec.gov/divisions/corpfin/cf-noaction/2015/citizen-vc-inc-080615-502.htm. (Note, click on "Incoming Letter," where most of the factual recitations are found.)

Fundable (www.fundable.com) is a good example of an online platform that seems to emphasize 506(b) deals. Very little is presented about investment opportunities on the public-facing section of the website. Clicking on a company profile takes the user to a webpage with this message:

Private Fundraise

This company may be interested in raising funds from accredited investors.
You must Request Access to see more information about this company.

Request Access >

Fundable's approach to cordoning off Rule 506(b) investments to avoid general solicitation seems very consistent with the available SEC guidance.

Rule 506(c) and General Solicitation

The Jumpstart Our Business Startups Act of 2012, or the JOBS Act, spurred big changes in the federal securities laws, with ripple effects impacting state securities regulation as well. The most highly publicized change was the legalization of equity crowdfunding, discussed later. Less high profile, but equally interesting to many securities practitioners, was the sea change involving general solicitation.

The JOBS Act required the SEC to write rules allowing companies to generally solicit accredited investors in private placements. The congressional mandate to permit public advertising for private offerings overturned an 80-year prohibition and core SEC principle.

Previously, it has always been a point of concern as to whether a company or its officers, employees, or agents must have a "pre-existing substantive relationship" before approaching an investor, no matter how wealthy. And the rules and related guidance have always prohibited public statements or advertisements about offerings, including in the press, at meetings, on websites, in blogs, or any other context.

Startup founders, among others, often stumble badly over this prohibition. Traps for the unwary abound. It also seems the financial media are forever trying to trip founders by asking about their current or future financing plans and then publishing responses like "*we're just starting a series A round*" for all the world to see, including securities regulators. This leads to concerns around blown exemptions, investor rescission rights, and other legal and regulatory issues.

Rule 506(c) changes all of this for companies willing to only accept accredited investors and to take "reasonable steps to verify" such status. By simply collecting copies of W-2s, 1099s, tax returns, or attestations from personal bankers, accountants, brokers or lawyers as described in Rule 506(c), companies can now advertise their private offerings all they want and essentially "crowdfund" for accredited investors.

Rule 506(c) also helps to mitigate concerns about errant founder statements to the press or to fellow attendees in tech meetups.

And like Rule 506(b), Rule 506(c) also preempts state regulation.

As simple and potentially attractive as this sounds, relatively few companies use Rule 506(c). Most avoid general solicitation and rely on the old version of Rule 506, which is now Rule 506(b).

A review of the Form D filings streaming into the SEC's EDGAR system (https://www.sec.gov/edgar/searchedgar/webusers.htm) shows that 506(b) is claimed in Form D Item 6 at least ten times more often than Rule 506(c).

Informally surveying securities law practitioners on the reasons for Rule 506(c)'s low usage rates yielded these responses:

> *"My clients do not use 506(c) for several reasons. First, the process of verifying accredited status is more time consuming and more costly – the company must either use a verifying firm, or spend additional legal fees to ensure that the standards are met. Second, investors are reluctant to provide the backup needed to verify, and so there is a segment of potential investors that are not available. Third, the clients do not feel a need to undertake general solicitation – they believe they have a pool of potential investors needed to raise the funds."*

***

> *"Why would you spend more time gathering additional information and prying into the personal finances of investors unless you really have to? Most of my startup clients want to limit the hassle for their investors as much as possible (and limit the ways an investor could choose to back out of the investment)."*

Other respondents raised different concerns, such as these:

> *"Beyond the administrative and legal issues associated with using 506(c), I think that using it can be viewed as a "tell" that the offering isn't a particularly attractive one. Relying on it essentially signals to the investing public that the offering isn't expected to be appealing to the most desirable sources of funding, for whom a general solicitation isn't necessary."*

***

> *"If the 506(c) exemption fails, due to an inadvertent unaccredited investor, there is no fallback provision. 4(a)(2) is not available due to the general solicitation."*

Lastly, a staff member in the SEC's Office of Small Business Policy acknowledged in a phone conversation that the SEC staff has also been surprised by the low usage of 506(c).

The staffer speculated that some issuers are likely concerned about not having the ability to fall back to a 506(b) offering if a 506(c) offering fails to get traction after general solicitation efforts. The staffer's point alluded to here is explained below under *Integration of Exempt Offerings.*

But some issuers are using Rule 506(c). Many 506(c) offerings are posted on websites like SeedInvest (www.seedinvest.com) and Crowdfunder (www.crowdfunder.com).

A review of Form D filings suggests that Rule 506(c) has become somewhat popular for financing commercial real estate, consumer products, regional banks, and even oil and gas projects.

So how are these issuers meeting the investor verification requirements? And how difficult, intrusive, or expensive are the issuers or investors finding 506(c) compliance?

Interestingly, survey responses from counsel who have successfully used Rule 506(c) indicate fewer concerns about cost, difficulty, and investor reluctance, as evidenced by these representative responses:

> *"For the one 506(c) offering I did, the company used a combination of internal verification based on tax returns for those investors who were comfortable with this (about one-half of them) and having the other investors' CPAs or brokerage firms provide letters verifying accredited investor status."*

***

> *"For verification of accredited status we have the investor engage a 3rd party accounting firm to review their assets and liabilities and provide certification of accredited status based on net worth."*

***

> *"We've done a couple 506(c) deals. We have done some of the investor verifications in house, reviewing docs to fit within the safe harbor (W2s for the income test; or brokerage statements, credit reports under the net assets test). We also have a client who runs a fund with a 506(c) offering and since he's usually these folks' investment advisor, he generally has plenty of info about their financial situation to make a determination, and often they have $1mm+ with him."*

***

> *"For the 506(c) offerings I have done, the clients contracted with their placement agents (registered brokers) to handle the accredited investor screening. I think this is ideal because investors sometimes balk at providing that much personal information to the offeror directly and because engaging a professional bolsters the argument that the offeror has taken reasonable measures."*

In summary, usage of Rule 506(c) is off to a slow start, and only time will tell whether or not its popularity will grow. Investors may well get used to being verified, especially through services like www.verifyinvestor.com, and if enough big deals succeed on the larger fundraising portals and angel investing platforms, attitudes about general solicitation could become more positive.

For startups outside of metropolitan areas or founders who are less well connected to wealthy individuals, angels, or VCs, 506(c) may offer the best opportunity for reaching potential investors to fund new businesses – a central goal of the JOBS Act.

Startups with consumer-facing goods and services may also find marketing synergies in being able to use general solicitation, even if the eligible investor pool is limited to accredited investors.

Tactically, though, for most strong companies with good access to capital, it probably makes sense to start a funding round under 506(b) and then switch to 506(c) if the dollars don't come in.

Rule 504

Rule 504, a rarely used exemption under Reg D, allows a company to raise up to $5 million within a twelve-month period from an unlimited number of investors, both accredited and non-accredited.

A theoretical advantage of Rule 504 over 506(b) and 506(c) is that there are no specifically mandated disclosures, even to non-accredited investors. The theory behind this is that the $5 million cap limits risks to non-accredited investors.

Unlike Rule 506(b) or Rule 506(c), however, Rule 504 does not preempt state regulation, and that explains its low usage.

Figuring out the securities laws of multiple states to raise $5 million, or less, as may be the case under applicable, non-preempted state laws, is not generally considered "the path of least resistance" for most startups that can otherwise avail themselves of Rule 506(b) or other exemptions with federal preemption like Reg A+ or Reg CF.

Due to the lack of pre-emption, states are free to determine the disclosure required for Rule 504 offerings and impose other restrictions as well. In enacting its requirements for Rule 504-like small offerings (WAC 460-44A-504), Washington limited the maximum offering amount to $1,000,000 and the number of non-accredited investors to twenty.

Companies should be very cautious about relying on Rule 504 without first carefully considering the laws of each state where the offering might be conducted.

And lastly, somewhat recent amendments to Rule 504 allow for general solicitation if certain fairly onerous rules are followed, including that the company offers and sells the securities only in states that require registration, public filing, and delivery to investors of a substantive disclosure document before any sale of a security.

In Washington and other states, as discussed below, those "registration, public filing, and substantive disclosure document requirements" are the NASAA-developed Small Company Offering Registration, or "SCOR," disclosure form and related policies.

In many states, offerings under Rule 504 go through merit review. State securities regulators can and do refuse to approve offerings that they believe are simply too risky for the residents of their state. Merit review and regulation is a significant deterrent to use of Rule 504 and other exemptions lacking preemption.

Regulation A

The JOBS Act brought big changes to Regulation A. It boosted the traditional Reg A offering limit from $5 million to $20 million for what are now called Reg A Tier 1 offerings.

More importantly, the JOBS Act created a second type of Reg A offering for up to $50 million, variously called "Tier 2," "Reg A+," and "Mini IPOs." The JOBS Act preempted state regulation of Tier 2 Reg A offerings.

Before studying these changes, let us first look at the history of Regulation A, with an eye toward interpreting the present and predicting the future.

Sleepy Reg A. From 1988 to 1993, I worked in the SEC's Division of Enforcement in a Regional Office. My enforcement colleagues and I had lots of challenging work. The broker-dealer and investment advisor examination teams also seemed busy.

And then there was the two-person corporate finance team - an attorney and an accountant. Their job was to respond to inquiries about "Reg A" offerings and to review the very occasional Reg A filing that came in.

Issuers could use Reg A to raise up to $5 million by filing a Form 1-A with the SEC, which filing would also be reviewed by state securities regulators in states where the shares would be sold. Form 1-A requires a company to provide detailed disclosures about its business, risk factors, management, and financial position.

Most days, this talented duo had nothing to do. Most months, they had nothing to do.

But they would spring to life whenever a call or filing came in. They spared no effort assisting anyone wanting to register a Reg A offering. For days after a call with a prospective filer, they could be heard re-hashing the call and the advice they had given and wondering aloud if the company might proceed.

The finance attorney's office was next to mine. He was a charming, knowledgeable older gentleman. When I passed by, he was usually asleep.

One day I heard a loud crash, followed by a muted *"help."* I rushed next door. The man's old leather chair was on its back, wedged between a classic wood government desk and the wall. The legs of the chair faced me at the doorway, as did the soles of his shoes. He looked like a turtle on its back.

I helped my friend up. Thankfully he was uninjured, aside from his pride perhaps. We kept the incident between ourselves.

The turtle episode still defines my view of Reg A. It has been a seldom-used offering exemption that makes me sleepy just thinking about it. The numbers tell the story. The most Reg A filings nationwide in any year was 116 in 1997. Many years, fewer than 20 are filed.

By contrast, there are thousands of Rule 506 notice filings every year.

Despite low usage, Reg A has its advocates – particularly those who want to "democratize" investing. In contrast to Reg D's cap of 35 non-accredited investors in a Rule 506(b) offering, anyone can invest in a Reg A offering.

Another purported benefit of Reg A has been that investors can immediately resell their shares, whereas Reg D shares are "restricted," and cannot be sold for at least one year.

Although pre-JOBS Act Reg A registration was never anything like an IPO, Reg A has always actually been a type of "registered" small offering requiring SEC and state review and "qualification." As a result, Reg A shares are generally freely tradeable, except by "affiliates" of the issuer, who have to comply with the resale restrictions of Rule 144, discussed later.

Securities Act Rule 405 defines "affiliate" as a "person that directly, or indirectly through one or more intermediaries, controls, is controlled by, or is under common control with," an issuer. This definition generally includes any officer, director or shareholder owning 10% or more of the issuer.

A related benefit of the registration process is that general solicitation is also allowed.

The "Freely Tradeable" Double-Edged Sword. Is issuing non-restricted stock under Reg A really a benefit for a startup? The potential liquidity benefits for shareholders, which are limited for affiliates, need to be weighed against the loss of control over who owns the company's shares.

In our discussion of cap tables in the next chapter we learn that many founders tightly control who gets on the company's cap table. A clean cap table composed mostly of professional investors is always an advantage in financings and M&A discussions.

For these reasons, as discussed later under *Restrictions on Trading Privately Issued Stock,* most companies use governance and contractual restrictions to impose strict transfer restrictions on their stock.

Cap table control concerns probably outweigh the value many founders might otherwise see in issuing non-restricted stock.

Accidental Public Company. Another concern non-restricted stock might raise is called the "accidental public company" issue.

An accidental public company is one that inadvertently trips the requirements for becoming a public reporting company without doing an IPO – most of the pain, but none of the gain.

Under current SEC rules, this can happen when a company has 2,000 or more shareholders.

Why is it so bad? Because publicly reporting companies are required to file regular reports with the SEC. These include annual reports, quarterly reports, and current reports on Forms 10-K, 10-Q, and 8-K, respectively, and also proxy statements.

Before the JOBs Act, the threshold that triggered public reporting status was 500 or more shareholders.

The JOBs Act increased that number to 2,000 (or 500 non-accredited investors) and made other changes to reduce risks to issuers.

Here is how the SEC paraphrases the current thresholds for public company registration on its website. Note that the "exceptions" allow companies to exclude many investors from the shareholder counts:

Exchange Act Registration

Even if your company does not have an effective registration statement for a public offering, it could still be required to file a registration statement and become a reporting company under Section 12 of the Exchange Act if:

- *it has more than $10 million in total assets and a class of equity securities, like common stock, that is held of record by either (1) 2,000 or more persons or (2) 500 or more persons who are not accredited investors*

  or

- *it lists the securities on a U.S. exchange*

Exceptions to Exchange Act Registration

In calculating the number of holders of record for purposes of determining whether Exchange Act registration is required, your company may exclude persons who acquired their securities in an exempt offering:

- *under an employee compensation plan,*

- *under Regulation Crowdfunding if the issuer*

  - *is current in its ongoing annual reports required pursuant to Rule 202 of Regulation Crowdfunding*

  - *has total assets as of the end of its last fiscal year not in excess of $25 million and*

  - *has engaged the services of a transfer agent registered with the Commission pursuant to Section 17A of the Exchange Act, or*

- *as a Tier 2 offering under Regulation A if the issuer:*

  - *is required to file and is current in filing annual, semiannual and special financial reports under Securities Act Rule 257(b)*

  - *had a public float of less than $75 million as of the end of its last semiannual period, or if it cannot calculate its public float, had less than $50 million in annual revenue as of the end of its last fiscal year and engaged a transfer agent registered pursuant to Section 17A of the Exchange Act.*

Thus, the triggers for accidental public company status are now $10 million in assets, *plus* 2,000 shareholders *or* 500 non-accredited shareholders.

And the company can generally exclude from the 2,000 and 500 counts all shares:

- issued under employee equity compensation plans,

- issued in a Regulation Crowdfunding offering, and

- issued in a Regulation A Tier 2 offering (Tier 2 created a new reporting regime, as discussed later).

These thresholds are far less concerning than the previous bright-line rule of 500 shareholders.

The previous threshold tripped a few companies badly.

Tully's Coffee was a prominent case. Its founder issued too much stock to employees, contractors, and vendors. The costs and administrative burdens of public reporting hobbled the company. In 2007, Tully's made a good run at an IPO, but shelved it in 2008, citing the tough market conditions.

These days, the likelihood of tripping over the accidental public company triggers is greatly reduced, due to the increased thresholds and the carveouts for employee option plan participants and Reg A and Reg CF purchasers.

But again, most startup founders are concerned about managing their cap tables and have little interest in allowing third parties to actively trade their shares. Reg A's non-restricted stock feature is not important to those founders.

Reg A's Two Tiers after the JOBS Act. The JOBS Act sought to breathe new life into Reg A by increasing the amount that issuers can raise and by creating the new two-tiered offering scheme:

- Tier 1 for offerings up to $20 million and Tier 2 for offerings up to $50 million, and

- Tier 2 offerings require more complete disclosures from issuers, but they are reviewed *solely by the SEC*, with state regulation being completely preempted.

Another difference between the two tiers is that the financial statements disclosed in a Tier 1 offering do not have to be audited, whereas an independent accountant must audit the financial statements in a Tier 2 offering. Financial audits can be surprisingly challenging for companies with any operating history, however de minimis, and generally cost upwards of $30,000 at the low end.

Lastly, following a Tier 2 offering, the issuer company is required to file periodic reports with the SEC that are essentially lighter versions of reports required by 1934 Act reporting companies, as discussed shortly.

In speaking with a state regulator who is a top national expert on intrastate exemptions and small offering registration alternatives, Tier 2 offerings have completely eclipsed Tier 1 offerings.

This regulator said, in the early months following enactment of the JOBS Act Reg A amendments, filings were about equally split between Tier 1 and Tier 2. In her view, however, as soon as issuers and issuers' counsel realized that the SEC was taking a light approach to reviewing Tier 2 offerings, virtually all Reg A filings shifted to Tier 2 to avoid more rigorous state regulatory review.

As evidence of this shift, the regulator said that, despite a good number of Tier 1 filings in the early months following adoption of the two-tier system, her office had seen zero Tier 1 filings over the last twelve months. During that period, however, her state received "notice" filings indicating that 28 Tier 2 offerings were being conducted in her state.

Additionally, although state regulators are preempted from reviewing and commenting on Tier 2 offerings, my regulator friend was candid in disclosing that her staff obtains the documentation for *all* Tier 2 offerings occurring in their jurisdiction and reviews them for potential enforcement concerns.

She stated that they frequently find what they view to be problematic disclosures and that her staff had made "enforcement referrals" within her office based on concerns about false or misleading disclosures in Tier 2 offerings.

This highlights an important nuance of preemption. Under the securities laws, federal preemption regarding *offering registration requirements* does not limit states' *antifraud enforcement authorities* in any way. State regulators are free to investigate any securities offerings occurring within their borders for *antifraud* violations, even offerings relying on registration exemptions with state preemption. If state securities regulators discover fraud within their jurisdiction, they can always take action.

In summary, the JOBS Act changes have breathed new life into a formerly very sleepy small offering registration option. Between the two tiers, Tier 2 has come out on top, as issuers seek to raise larger amounts and avoid state-level review.

With that background, let us take a closer look at Tier 2 offerings, also commonly referred to as Reg A+ offerings and Mini IPOs.

Mini IPOs under Reg A+

Reg A Tier 2 offerings are called mini IPOs because the shares issued are freely tradeable and may be listed. Both tiers require completing SEC Form 1-A, but as already noted, Tier 2 offerings require audited financial statements, a significant burden for most startups.

The term mini IPO likely reflects the fact that shares issued in a Tier 2 offering can be registered to trade freely on national securities exchanges.

The expectation was that this would be the Nasdaq, an efficient and reputable securities trading market. But then problems arose. Reg A+ deals performed poorly in secondary markets. Virtually all have plummeted well into penny stock territory, some already declaring bankruptcy, as in the case of iPic, which we will look at soon.

And then there was a huge fraud called Longfin that changed everything. The SEC's <u>Longfin</u> case sheds additional light on Reg A+ concerns, including the ability of fraudsters to lie their way through the SEC's purportedly lenient Reg A+ registration process.

Search "SEC versus Longfin," or go here:

https://www.sec.gov/litigation/complaints/2019/comp24492.pdf

Nasdaq said enough is enough and proposed a rule change. The release announcing the rule proposal provides interesting insights and concerns about Reg A offerings from Nasdaq's perspective. The following excerpt (footnotes omitted) is illustrative of those concerns:

> *"The Exchange has observed problems with certain Regulation A companies. Most significantly, the Exchange believes that companies seeking to list in conjunction with a Regulation A offering are generally less mature companies with less developed business plans than other companies seeking to list. In addition, the Exchange believes that the Regulation A offering process may not adequately prepare companies for the rigors of operating a public company and satisfying the SEC and Exchange's reporting and corporate governance requirements. The Exchange also notes that the financial press, Congress (prior to the adoption of Regulation A) and others have raised concerns about the potential for fraud by companies conducting offerings under Regulation A."*
>
> *https://www.sec.gov/rules/sro/nasdaq/2019/34-85687.pdf.*

The SEC quickly approved Nasdaq's proposed rule. Companies must now have <u>two years of operating history</u> to list on the Nasdaq Exchange.

"Unlisted" companies can still trade in the far less liquid "over the counter" or "OTC" market, in which individual broker-dealers agree to be market makers in individual securities.

The OTC market is managed by the OTC Markets Group (https://www.otcmarkets.com/) and the Financial Industry Regulation Authority, or FINRA.

Regulatory Costs and Obligations. The legal and accounting costs of Reg A+ offerings are way higher than for a typical Rule 506(b) offering. Reg A+ expenses generally range between $100,000 and $250,000, while many Rule 506(b) offerings are completed for less than $20,000.

Upfront offering costs are just the beginning. Tier 2 triggers SEC reporting. Tier 2 reporting is less onerous than full-blown 1934 Act reporting, but issuers still have to file annual and semiannual reports, as well as what are called "current reports," which disclose events such as officer resignations and M&A transactions. Becoming a publicly reporting company can add tens or hundreds of thousands of dollars per year in new expenses, even under Reg A+.

Test the Waters. Tier 2 also allows companies to do something new called "test the waters." These rules allow a company to assess potential investor demand by publicly soliciting "indications of interest" before spending money on a financial audit, filing anything with the SEC, or taking other steps necessary to fully commit to an offering. Companies that decide to not go forward can simply abandon the offering without making any costly SEC filings.

The Reality of Customers as Investors. One argument offered by proponents of what became Reg A+ is that many companies want to be able to raise capital from customers and other fans.

Fatburger and a theater-restaurant company called iPic, along with a few other companies, jumped into the Mini IPO waters early, hoping to turn customers and fans into investors.

Both Fatburger and iPic successfully raised their rounds and achieved listing on NASDAQ. Since their Mini IPO debuts, their stock prices have declined from $12.00 to $3.45 and $18.50 to $0.00, respectively, as of May 17, 2020. iPic emerged from bankruptcy with new owners in November of 2019.

Virtually every other Reg A+ stock has tanked in the secondary markets, except for a small handful of regional banks, which trade based on their relatively stable book values.

While hundreds of companies have started the Mini IPO process, the completion rate for the SEC registration process seems to be in the 15% range, with perhaps a quarter of those achieving Nasdaq listing before the July 2019 Nasdaq rule change requiring two years of operating history.

Reg A+ Utilization. In summary, while Reg A Tier 2 offerings have certainly breathed new life into Reg A, poor results in secondary trading markets, the burdens of continuing reporting obligations, the availability of easier and cheaper private capital, and the potential for future regulatory changes are likely to confine Tier 2 to a relatively narrow niche of potential issuers, compared to Rule 506(b)'s far greater popularity.

Tier 2 is most likely to appeal to issuers in these situations:

(i) lack of access to substantial angel or VC capital under Rule 506(b) and perceived need for general solicitation,

(ii) strong focus on deepening customer relationships by making them investors, or

(iii) strong interest in a path to liquidity for founders and other current or prospective investors.

The first of these, lack of access to capital under 506(b), may be a key driver of Reg A+ deals.

The vast majority of capital raised under 506(b) comes from VC-led rounds. As will be discussed in chapter 14, VCs are focused on specific types of companies, sectors, and company profiles.

The following have not traditionally been strong candidates for VC funding:

- companies that are unlikely to grow revenues quickly enough to provide a 10x return within 7 to 10 years,

- companies with complicated cap tables showing lots of unaccredited investors from financing rounds conducted under Reg A, Reg CF, or even Reg D offerings, and

- companies in traditional, non-tech, or non-high-growth industries, including natural resources and property development.

In short, companies that do not fit VCs' preferred profiles are more likely to pursue, by choice or necessity, alternative financing strategies, including Reg A+ and, as discussed next, crowdfunding. We look closer at successfully conducting Reg A+ Mini IPOs in Chapter 15, *Venture Capital Alternatives*.

Crowdfunding - Regulation CF

A handful of diehard crowdfunding advocates worked tirelessly to ensure the SEC adopted reasonable rules after the JOBS Act authorized startup investing for the masses.

These individuals were driven to democratize early-stage investing. Their main points were that companies need more funding opportunities and also that non-accredited investors were unfairly deprived of opportunities to invest in the next Apple, Google, or Facebook.

After years of delays, the SEC's final rules, "Regulation Crowdfunding", or "Reg CF" for short, took effect in May of 2016.

As the numbers below show, Reg CF crowdfunding has been reasonably successful, especially compared to other offering exemptions, like Rule 504 and Pre-JOBS Act Reg A.

Every month companies are raising the maximum annual amount of $1.07 million under Reg CF, and many companies are doing repeat offerings of various sizes within the annual maximum.

Unless otherwise noted, the term crowdfunding here refers to "equity crowdfunding," meaning the solicitation of investments in securities, not Kickstarter-type donations in exchange for a discount on an upcoming game, album, consumer product, or new technology. Non-equity crowdfunding is also commonly called "rewards-based crowdfunding" and "product crowdfunding."

Many companies are using product crowdfunding to support early development and production expenses and to build consumer interest and support. The potential marketing benefits alone make this a strategy worth considering for many consumer products companies.

Reg CF Requirements. But equity crowdfunding under Reg CF involves substantially greater regulation. The key Reg CF requirements and limitations include:

- offerings must be conducted through SEC-registered, FINRA-regulated portals,
- maximum offering amount of $1.07 million within a 12-month period,
- must complete SEC Form C (https://www.sec.gov/files/formc.pdf),
- all issuers must provide financials prepared in accordance with GAAP and reviewed by a CPA, but audited financials are required for issuers that have previously raised more than $500K under CF,
- non-accredited investors are limited in how much they can invest in Reg CF offerings per twelve-month period at the higher of (i) $2,200 or (ii) 5% of net worth or annual income,
- securities purchased by investors generally cannot be transferred by them for one year, and
- issuers that complete a Reg CF offering must file annual reports with the SEC and post them on their websites within 120 days of financial year-end.

Reporting Obligations. The annual report required to be filed with the SEC and posted on the issuer's website within 120 days of an issuer's year-end must contain substantially the same (but updated) information required in the original Form C.

An issuer can file a Form CT-R giving its notice to terminate its annual report filing obligation when: (i) it has filed at least one annual report and has fewer than 300 holders of record, (ii) it has filed at least three annual reports and has total assets less than $10 million, (iii) it becomes a publicly reporting company under the 1934 Act, or (iv) it ceases to do business.

FINRA Portals. All fundraising under Reg CF must be conducted through portals registered with the SEC and regulated by FINRA.

There are currently 51 FINRA regulated crowdfunding portals, all of which can be accessed by searching "FINRA portals."

https://www.finra.org/about/funding-portals-we-regulate.

As of this publication, the top six Reg CF crowdfunding portals in terms of numbers of offerings and amounts raised are StartEngine, Wefunder, Republic, SeedInvest, Net Capital Funding, and MicroVentures.

Available data for these sites is not complete and, to some extent, not entirely reliable. StartEngine publishes a blog called the "StartEngine Index" that runs monthly statistical reports captioned "Equity Crowdfunding in Review." Go to StartEngine's blog to find these and other interesting resources - https://www.startengine.com/blog/.

These reports provide stats on amounts raised by month and year, often broken out by industry, geography, and platform.

Reg CF Statistics. Funding trends in Reg CF offerings seem to have remained in a positive trajectory from inception. The StartEngine Index opened its QI 2020 report with this assessment.

> *"In the first quarter of 2020, companies raised $33.3M via Regulation Crowdfunding, bringing the all-time total raised via Reg CF to $314.9M.*
>
> *223 companies launched Reg CF offerings in Q1, close to the 233 offerings launched in the final quarter of 2019. Since Regulation Crowdfunding began, there have been 2,322 offerings from companies all over the US."*

The following are some other approximated statistics for Reg CF offerings based on data collected by the SEC and others:

- number of offerings: 474 in 2017, 680 in 2018, 735 in 2019,

- amount raised: $71.2 million in 2017, $109.3 million in 2018, $137 million in 2019,

- average Reg CF raise per offering in 2019 - $270,000,

- campaigns last 3 to 4 months, or around 113 days, and

- about 60% of fundraising efforts are deemed successful, meaning they achieved their stated minimum fundraising goal.

Offering Expenses. Issuers are probably spending between 15% and 20% of the amounts ultimately raised in Reg CF offerings on legal, accounting, marketing expenses and platform expenses. That percentage could be higher for issuers that achieve only their minimum stated fundraising goal. An area of expense that might surprise some founders is the need to create a video and other expensive promotional content highlighting the company, its product or service, and its team. A review of offerings posted on the top crowdfunding portals shows that these materials need to be high quality to present well next to the others.

Marketing and content expenses generally run over $10,000, and they occur early in the process, well before any money is raised. Legal and accounting expenses can also easily be in the range of $10,000.

Platform fees can also be significant. Fortunately, some are charged only upon disbursement of funds following successful fundraising. These fees vary widely, so founders need to investigate carefully before committing to any particular platform. We will look at platform fees more closely in Chapter 15, *Venture Capital Alternatives*.

Crowdfunding Considerations. Crowdfunding is working well for many companies, and the number of deals and the amounts raised seem to be increasing steadily. It is also serving to "democratize" investing in new and emerging companies.

As with any means of fundraising, however, some pros and cons should be considered.

In the pros column, at least several companies per month appear to be raising the full amount of $1.07 million, which is relatively impressive. Crowdfunding has already proven to be a better way of raising funds than pre-JOBS Act Reg A.

As discussed below, crowdfunding numbers under Reg CF may also exceed the total of all fundraising efforts under the intrastate exemptions of every state combined.

In addition to successful fundraisings under Reg CF, many companies believe their business models and financial results are helped by turning customers into investors and investors into customers. Crowdfunding can be a great form of advertising and promotion for many types of consumer-facing companies and even for B2B companies.

As a form of advertising, crowdfunding may be cost-competitive relative to traditional media such as newspapers, radio, and television.

Crowdfunding Downsides. How about the downsides of crowdfunding? The first and biggest one for most companies is in the name – "crowd." There are few good things about having a crowd on one's cap table – crowds of non-accredited investors in particular.

While some platforms try to obscure this fact by having investors invest through various types of consolidating entities or instruments, a crowdfunding history may still spook both VCs and potential acquirors. Later we look at various techniques used for blunting cap table optics and other adverse impacts from crowdfunding, and the pros and cons of those techniques.

Right or wrong, sophisticated investors and acquirors are known for avoiding risks and unfamiliar complexity. Every person represented on a cap table, directly or indirectly, is a point of risk, as someone who could sue, file regulatory complaints, or otherwise become difficult. Those risks generally worsen in the case of non-accredited investors.

Additionally, all persons with direct equity interests in a company have rights under state law. These can include voting rights and rights to approve or not approve various types of transactions, or at least to dissent.

Because crowdfunding is still only a few years old, it remains unclear how reluctant VCs will be to fund or potential acquirors will be to acquire companies with evidence of crowdfunding on their cap tables. For now, it remains an uncertainty and a risk, whether or not most VCs would admit to their biases.

Another downside to crowdfunding is the related risks of upfront costs and uncertainty of success. Upfront costs can range between $10,000 and $20,000, given the legal and accounting expenses required to complete Form C with its required financials, and the costs necessary to create a flashy video and other promotional content.

All of that must be spent before the first dollar comes in.

Based on the stats shown above, if roughly 60% of deals are succeeding, 40% of them are not – meaning that some of those upfront costs have been wasted. Additionally, success is a relative term. Given that the average amount raised under Reg CF recently is under $300K, it seems possible that most "successful" raises fall well short of their fundraising goal.

Despite these low numbers, though, some companies are doing repeat Reg CF offerings over several years. That was something I did not foresee – companies raising fairly large amounts of capital in repeated Reg CF offerings over several years.

Deceptive Advertising. Having used two of these platforms, it seems clear that the dollar amounts shown for currently pending deals on some of the platforms are inflated. "Committed" dollar amounts are mere "indications of interest." Investors have the right to back out, and they do.

This flexibility for investors means that some of the money announced and touted on these websites as reflecting committed investor interest is illusory. A FINRA or SEC study of that issue would be interesting.

More concerning yet, there is nothing to prevent unscrupulous founders from manipulating the level of perceived interest in their deals by encouraging others to submit fake indications of interest.

The presentation of clearly inflated numbers with no obvious caveats or disclaimers is arguably misleading – both to potential investors and to potential issuers thinking about crowdfunding.

Rewards-Based Crowdfunding. Some companies are either supplementing equity crowdfunding with rewards-based crowdfunding or simply going the rewards-based crowdfunding route exclusively.

This potential alternative to equity crowdfunding is most popular with companies that have an exciting product or service consumers want to support and be first in line to receive.

Examples of companies that seem to be succeeding with this form of funding can be found at the Kickstarter website under the "Design and Tech" pages.

Most of these companies are seeking funding to complete design, development, and manufacture of products expected to be delivered within the next six to twelve months. While every page offers an opportunity to *"Make a pledge without a reward,"* most also offer various types of discounts and rewards for what are advance purchases of products that may or may not make it out the door.

Although this is a potentially exciting means of fundraising, success is in no way guaranteed. At the bottom of the Kickstarter website is a link to "stats" that might be worth digging into as an initial investigative step. The first page has a "see categories" link, with more detailed information by category.

As of this writing, *Games, Design and Technology* projects each had purported "Success" rates of 40.64%, 38.13%, and 20.66%, respectively. This also indicates that between 60% and 80% of campaigns are unsuccessful, and no doubt, even higher percentages are less successful than hoped.

By comparison, as noted earlier, Reg CF offerings meet their minimum fundraising goals approximately 60% of the time.

Do those success rates warrant the types of upfront marketing and promotion costs that a company would spend on a rewards-based crowdfunding campaign? That is a question each startup needs to answer for itself.

For the right company and the right product, getting a few hundred thousand dollars or more to support design and development without giving up any equity to non-accredited investors or signing any Convertible Notes could be a smart financial move.

Intrastate Offerings under SEC Rules 147 and 147A

As has been discussed, every state has its own securities laws. In many respects, states have been preempted by federal law from regulating many types of securities transactions. But preemption does not apply to certain offerings conducted wholly within the borders of a single state – called "intrastate offerings."

In 2016, the SEC updated its "Intrastate Offerings" exemption under Rule 147 to provide additional flexibility for issuers wishing to confine their offerings to a single state and comply with the securities laws of that state. In doing so, it amended 147 and created a new exemption called 147A.

Rule 147 and 147A. First, new Rule 147A permits issuers to make intrastate offerings *accessible to* out-of-state residents so long as all actual purchasers reside in a single state. The purpose of this was to allow issuers to use the Internet and other forms of interstate communication in making intrastate offerings, where permitted by state law, without concern that the exemption would be lost due to the Internet's or other modes of communications' *interstate* reach.

Rule 147A also allows intrastate offerings by companies incorporated in another state, like Delaware. This accommodates the reality that many companies truly "doing business" primarily in a single state may nonetheless be incorporated in another state for purely corporate law reasons.

Under the other amendments to Rule 147 and Rule 147A, issuers are deemed to be "doing business" in a single state and eligible for the intrastate offering exemptions if they satisfy at least one of the following requirements:

- the issuer derived at least 80% of its consolidated gross revenues from the operation of a business or of real property located in-state or from the rendering of services in-state,

- the issuer had at least 80% of its consolidated assets located in-state,

- the issuer intends to use and uses at least 80% of the net proceeds from the offering towards the operation of a business or of real property in-state, the purchase of real property located in-state, or the rendering of services in-state, or

- a majority of the issuer's employees are based in-state.

Keenly interested in remaining helpful and relevant, securities regulators in many states have worked with their legislatures to create intrastate offering exemptions.

These efforts have been focused primarily in two areas – intrastate limited offering exemptions analogous to Reg D and intrastate crowdfunding.

The Rule 147 and 147A limited offering exemptions have been used very little, but they are more popular than state-level crowdfunding. Very few companies are using state crowdfunding. This result is somewhat surprising, given that 34 states and the District of Columbia have gone to significant effort to adopt and promote intrastate crowdfunding statutes, rules, and processes.

Intrastate Crowdfunding. According to research performed by the Washington Securities Division, as of March 2019, across the 35 states with crowdfunding rules, there were a total of 347 crowdfunding offering filings. 57% of these were concentrated in six states – Georgia, Texas, Oregon, Michigan, Vermont, and Montana. These states all had high offering approval rates and have generally demonstrated a high level of commitment to helping entrepreneurs fund their businesses.

In Washington state, in the four years since adopting its first crowdfunding rules, *no* companies have successfully raised any money under those rules.

According to staff members of the Washington Securities Division, there have been two crowdfunding filings. In one case, the company never completed the registration process. In the second case, the company completed the registration process and then pivoted to a Rule 506(b) offering instead.

Given the Washington state example, particularly in light of the strength of the Seattle startup ecosystem and the commendable efforts of the Washington Securities Division to support intrastate crowdfunding, intrastate crowdfunding will continue to have a limited impact on startup funding.

Any exceptions to this prediction would occur only in states that go to extraordinary efforts to promote and support homegrown crowdfunding.

Rule 701 – Stock Options, Other Equity Compensation

Every security issuance must be registered or exempt. This includes employee equity compensation, like stock options and restricted stock awards.

SEC Rule 701 is the federal exemption from registration for issuances of equity as compensation by *issuers* to their employees, directors, advisors, and consultants.

Here's a summary of Rule 701 from the SEC's website:

> *Rule 701 exempts certain sales of securities made to compensate employees, consultants and advisors. This exemption is not available to Exchange Act reporting companies. A company can sell at least $1 million of securities under this exemption, regardless of its size. A company can sell even more if it satisfies certain formulas based on its assets or on the number of its outstanding securities. If a company sells more than $10 million in securities in a 12-month period, it is required to provide certain financial and other disclosure to the persons that received securities in that period. Securities issued under Rule 701 are "restricted securities" and may not be freely traded unless the securities are registered or the holders can rely on an exemption.*

No Exemption from Anti-fraud Rules. As with all exemptions – Rule 701 explicitly disclaims any exemption from the anti-fraud rules. As I tell over-zealous recruiters, hyping the value of company stock to job applicants is not a protected activity.

No State Preemption. Rule 701 also does not preempt state regulation. In California, this means complying with California's Corporations Code section 25102(o).

Non-Exclusive. Rule 701 is not exclusive. If necessary, for example, equity grants to senior officers or others can be made under Rule 506(b).

Non-compliance Risks. Blowing the Rule 701 exemption by exceeding the dollar/percentage caps or falling short on document delivery raises a rescission risk under Section 5 of the Securities Act.

At a minimum, a blown Rule 701 exemption is a potential due diligence problem. Investors and acquirors will always focus on potential rescission risks in a deal.

Basic compliance with Rule 701 involves providing equity compensation recipients the correct documents and staying within the grant caps.

- Recipients of equity compensation grants must receive certain equity plan documents. For stock option recipients, this means (i) a copy of the approved Equity Compensation Plan, (ii) a signed copy of their Option Agreement and any related Notice of Grant, and the Form of Exercise.

- Nothing else is required if equity compensation grants of a given type under Rule 701 do not exceed more than $1 million in a twelve-month period.

- If equity compensation grants exceed $1 million in a twelve-month period, they cannot exceed 15% of the value of the company's assets, nor may they constitute more than 15% of the class of securities involved.

- In any twelve-month period in which total grants exceed $10 million, the company must also provide recipients enhanced disclosures, including company financial statements and a plan summary. Proper compliance with these enhanced disclosure requirements trips up many companies.

Google's problem was that it issued too many options without providing optionees the required "enhanced disclosures," namely the company's financial statements. Rule 701 is not exclusive. This means concurrent grants to accredited investors under Rule 506(b), i.e., senior officers, can be excluded from the Rule 701 calculations. Google's option grants to non-accredited employees still exceeded the $5 million per-12-month threshold. That threshold is now $10 million.

It's always smart to retain the services of an experienced equity plan administrator and make sure any equity plan is tightly buttoned up.

Integration of Exempt Offerings

Companies that wish to raise funds in two exempt securities offerings simultaneously or in close time to each other must analyze certain rules and SEC policy statements on when the conduct of one of them might conflict with and invalidate the exemption for another.

This is known as offering "integration." When two offerings are integrated, they are viewed as a single offering for purposes of meeting or exceeding the requirements of the applicable exemption.

As noted below, Reg D offerings conducted six months apart are never integrated, and it is virtually impossible to "blow" the Rule 506(b) offering exemption (no cap on dollars or investors), through integration or otherwise, provided only accredited investors participate. Another reason why Rule 506(b) is the king of exemptions.

Five-Factor Test

There has long been a five-factor "integration test" that focused on the following facts to determine whether offerings should be integrated:

1. are the offerings part of the same plan of financing,

2. do the offerings involve the same class of securities,

3. are the offerings close in time to each other,

4. do the offerings involve the same type of consideration, and

5. are the offerings for the same general purpose.

Relationship Between Integration and General Solicitation

In recent years, the SEC has issued guidance supplementing and even superseding the five-factor test for certain combinations of offerings, while leaving other areas less clear.

The loosening of general solicitation restrictions for Rule 506(c), Reg A, Reg CF, and Rule 147A offerings is driving an evolving regulatory framework of not integrating offerings where:

- offerings are conducted under different exemptions that both allow general solicitation, or

- offerings are conducted under different exemptions, and any permitted general solicitation in one offering does not influence or attract offerees (condition the market) in an offering where general solicitation is prohibited.

The seeds of this evolving integration philosophy are evident in the following language from a 2007 release discussing various exploratory rule proposals (Release No. 33-8828):

> *For example, if a company files a registration statement and then seeks to offer and sell securities without registration to an investor that became interested in the purportedly private offering by means of the [IPO] registration statement, then the Section 4(2) exemption would not be available for that offering. On the other hand, if the prospective private placement investor became interested in the concurrent private placement through some means other than the registration statement that did not involve a general solicitation and otherwise was consistent with Section 4(2), such as through a substantive, pre-existing relationship with the company or direct contact by the company or its agents outside of the public offering effort, then the prior filing of the registration statement generally would not impact the potential availability of the Section 4(2) exemption for that private placement....*

Integration Relief – Rule Releases and Staff Interpretations

The following integration blurbs and pronouncements come from rule releases on Reg A, Reg D, and Reg CF, and also from the SEC's "Compliance and Disclosure Interpretations," or "C&DIs."

The SEC's C&DIs can be cut and pasted into a searchable document. They are found at: https://www.sec.gov/divisions/corpfin/guidance/securitiesactrules-interps.htm.

Some of the top integration takeaways from these rule release and staff guidance excerpts are:

- Only six months of no offers and sales is required between Reg D offerings,

- Rule 506(b) offerings solely involving accredited investors are never integrated with each other since 506(b) has no caps,

- a Rule 506(c) offering can occur right after a Rule 506(b) offering, provided all Rule 506(b) offers and sales occur prior to any 506(c) general solicitation,

- Reg A offerings and exempt offerings are not integrated, but exempt offering offerees must not have been exposed to general solicitation from the Reg A offering, and

- Reg CF crowdfunding offerings and exempt offerings are not integrated.

Here are excerpts from the SEC staff's key announcements regarding integration:

- **Reg D Six Month Rule.** Rule 502 provides this important "safe harbor" for Reg D offerings:

  ...Offers and sales that are made more than six months before the start of a Regulation D offering or are made more than six months after completion of a Regulation D offering will not be considered part of that Regulation D offering, so long as during those six month periods there are no offers or sales of securities by or for the issuer that are of the same or a similar class as those offered or sold under Regulation D, other than those offers or sales of securities under an employee benefit plan....

- **Rule 506(b) Offering followed by Rule 506(c) Offering.** SEC C&DI 256.34 says, in part:

  "... offers and sales of securities made in reliance on Rule 506(b) prior to the general solicitation would not be integrated with subsequent offers and sales of securities pursuant to Rule 506(c). So long as all of the applicable requirements of Rule 506(b) were met for offers and sales that occurred prior to the general solicitation, they would be exempt from registration and the issuer would be able to make offers and sales pursuant to Rule 506(c)."

- **Reg A Offerings and Other Concurrent Offerings.** In its final rules adopting release for Reg A in March of 2015 (Release No. 33-9741), the SEC said this at page 53 about non-integration of Reg A offerings and exempt offerings that do not permit general solicitation:

  As noted in the Proposing Release, we believe that an offering made in reliance on Regulation A should not be integrated with another exempt offering made by the issuer, provided that each offering complies with the requirements of the exemption that is being relied upon for the particular offering. For example, an issuer conducting a concurrent exempt offering for which general solicitation is not permitted will need to be satisfied that purchasers in that offering were not solicited by means of the offering made in reliance on Regulation A, including without limitation any "testing the waters" communications.

- **Reg CF and Other Concurrent Offerings.** In its 2015 adopting release for Regulation Crowdfunding (Release No. 33-9974) under "new Section 4(a) (6)," the SEC said this at page 19 about non-integration of Reg CF offerings and exempt offerings that do not permit general solicitation:

    Further, …we continue to believe that an offering made in reliance on Section 4(a)(6) should not be integrated with another exempt offering made by the issuer, provided that each offering complies with the requirements of the applicable exemption that is being relied upon for the particular offering. For example, an issuer conducting a concurrent exempt offering for which general solicitation is not permitted will need to be satisfied that purchasers in that offering were not solicited by means of the offering made in reliance on Section 4(a)(6).

Offering combinations for which the SEC has not provided relief from the five-factor test include where a Rule 506(b) offering follows, or is conducted concurrently with, a Reg A offering and (ii) where a Rule 506(b) offering follows or is conducted concurrently with a Rule 506(c) offering.

In these situations, the five-factor test still applies, except that the Rule 502 safe harbor would apply to any 506(b) offering following a Rule 506(c) offering by more than six months. Readers should not despair if the above discussion was difficult. Fortunately, many offerings are not at risk of integration. Rule 502 protects exempt offerings conducted more than six months apart, and compliant 506(b) offerings are always safe from integration when only accredited investors are involved.

Restrictions on Trading Privately Issued Stock

Securities sold in exempt private offerings under Rules 506(b), 506(c), 504, and 147, as well as Reg CF, are "restricted" securities.

Shares of an issuer acquired from a "control person" of the issuer are also always restricted securities – even if they were not restricted securities in the control person's hands. A control person is anyone who has the power to direct the management and policies of the issuing company.

As discussed earlier, securities sold under certain other "exemptions" are not restricted, but rather freely tradable. While technically called exemptions because they are not IPOs, offerings under Reg A, Reg A+, and the intrastate exemption called SCOR, are actually forms of small offering registration, and the securities issued in those offerings are not restricted.

We will look at regulatory transfer restrictions first. Then we will look at contractual transfer restrictions issuing companies often impose to control who can become a shareholder.

Rule 144

Rule 144 is like an exemption from registration, but it is technically a "safe harbor." If you comply with the specific terms of a safe harbor, you are safe from claims of wrongdoing.

Holders of restricted securities must meet the requirements of a registration exemption in order to sell them. Rule 144 is not the exclusive means for selling restricted or control securities, but it provides a "safe harbor" exemption to sellers.

One Year Holding Period. Rule 144's safe harbor requires compliance with a one-year holding period, during which restricted securities acquired directly from an issuer or a control person of an issuer cannot be transferred.

The holding period for restricted securities of issuers subject to the public company reporting requirements is only six months.

Public Information Requirement Applicable to Affiliates. Affiliates of issuers must follow certain other restrictions after the one-year holding period to stay within Rule 144's safe harbor. Affiliates can only sell their shares, or "control securities," if certain information about the company is publicly available. For a non-1934 Act company, this requires that information regarding the nature of its business, the identity of its officers and directors, and its financial statements be publicly available.

Time and Volume Limitations Applicable to Affiliates. Affiliates must also sell subject to restrictions on the numbers of shares that can be sold over time. These are called the Rule 144 time and volume limitations. In general, affiliates may not sell more than 1% of the class of securities over any three-month period, or, if listed on a stock exchange, more than 1% of the average reported weekly trading volume during the four weeks preceding the filing of a notice of sale on Form 144.

Section 4(a)(1-1/2)

Sales of restricted securities by affiliates outside of the Rule 144 safe harbor are risky and should only be done in close consultation with sophisticated securities counsel.

That is because, at least until 2015 when Section 4(a)(7) was adopted, there was no explicit statute or rule exempting such transactions from registration under Section 5.

Sales of restricted securities by issuer affiliates and control persons fall between the statutory exemptions in Section 4(a)(1) for transactions "by a person other than an issuer, underwriter, or dealer" and Section 4(a)(2) for transactions by an issuer not involving a public offering.

Section 4(a)(1) was essentially created to exempt "ordinary trading" between persons not affiliated with the issuer and not an "underwriter." An underwriter is anyone who takes shares with a view toward further distributing them.

The SEC and case law have made it clear that an affiliate cannot rely on Section 4(a)(1) or on the issuer exemption in Section 4(a)(2).

Despite this gap in the statutes for resales of restricted securities by insiders, practitioners have become somewhat comfortable with a legal fiction commonly referred to as the "Section 4(a)(1-1/2)" exemption, or the "Section 4(1-1/2)" exemption. Section 4(1-1/2) is a non-existent "statute" deemed by practitioners, or hoped by them, to reside between the two statutes. Although the SEC has seemed to passively tolerate this fiction for many years, obtaining a Legal Opinion covering transactions under Section 4(1-1/2) is likely difficult.

That said, risk-tolerant securities attorneys nonetheless handle such transactions discretely for insiders. The informal requirements likely imposed by competent securities counsel would include:

- the restricted shares have been held for at least six months, but preferably a year or more, reducing the appearance that the affiliate purchased them not with "investment intent" but with a view toward their further distribution,

- the sales are conducted with no advertising or other general solicitation, but rather in very private, discrete transactions,

- the number of purchasers should be very limited - the fewer, the better to avoid the appearance of a "distribution" by the affiliate,

- the purchasers are either accredited or at least sufficiently sophisticated to evaluate the risks of the purchase,

- the affiliate makes a reasonable effort to provide the purchasers with accurate and relevant information about the issuer company, to the extent he or she has the ability to do so, and

- the purchasers should represent and warrant that they are purchasing them for investment and not for further resale.

Section 4(a)(7)

In December of 2015, President Obama signed the Fixing America's Surface Transportation Act (the "FAST Act"). Given the nature of the legislation's main purposes, it was somewhat unusual that it offered a revolutionary new exemption for sales of restricted securities providing greater certainty than Section 4(1-1/2).

Section 4(a)(7) now provides affiliates (but not issuers) a safe harbor to sell restricted securities if the following requirements are met:

- all purchasers must be accredited investors,

- no general solicitation,

- the issuer company must be engaged in business and cannot be a shell company,

- no "bad actor" sellers,

- the securities must have been authorized and issued for at least 90 days and cannot constitute any unsold part of an "underwritten" offering, and

- the seller must provide the purchasers with certain information about the company and the securities, including current financial statements covering two years if the company has been in business that long, and the company's cap table.

Note that the last requirement, providing company information, requires the cooperation of the issuer company, which it is not legally required to provide.

Issuer-Imposed Transfer Restrictions

Restricted securities are supposed to bear a legend stating that they may not be sold unless registered or pursuant to an exemption from registration.

Privately issued securities also generally have legends warning that they may not be transferred under any circumstances except in compliance with the requirements of other identified documents.

The following is an example of a restriction tied to a Shareholders Agreement:

> *"THE VOTING AND TRANSFER OF THE SECURITIES REPRESENTED BY THIS CERTIFICATE ARE SUBJECT TO THE PROVISIONS OF THE SHAREHOLDERS AGREEMENT DATED AS OF AUGUST 15, 2019, AS AMENDED AND IN EFFECT FROM TIME TO TIME, AMONG THE COMPANY AND THE SHAREHOLDERS NAMED THEREIN, A COPY OF WHICH IS ON FILE AT THE OFFICES OF THE COMPANY."*

Here is a second example:

> *"THESE SECURITIES MAY BE TRANSFERRED ONLY IN ACCORDANCE WITH THE TERMS OF AN AGREEMENT BETWEEN THE COMPANY AND ITS SHAREHOLDERS, A COPY OF WHICH IS ON FILE WITH AND MAY BE OBTAINED FROM THE SECRETARY OF THE COMPANY AT NO CHARGE."*

Contractual restrictions on transfer, evidenced by legends such as these, help prevent transfers of shares to unknown investors. They are also helpful for imposing restrictions requiring all shareholders to sign a company's Shareholders Agreement, Voting Agreement, or other documents.

As noted earlier, most companies do not want to see their shares end up in the hands of numerous unknown investors any sooner than necessary, given the voting, control, and administrative implications.

As discussed in the coming chapters, there are many reasons for keeping tight control over a company's cap table. Transfer restrictions play an important role in cap table management.

Case Study #35 – Whose Ride?

Many years ago, in a meeting with the VP of finance at a company I had recently joined, I asked about a particularly flashy car in the lot. She told me it was the founder's and said, *"There's a story about that."*

I raised it later with the CEO. *"Biff has a pretty flashy ride…."* He replied, with a hint of consternation, *"Yes, he does."*

I dragged it out of the CEO that the founder had sold some of his founder shares to purchase it. The founder was a nice person but fairly unsophisticated and naïve, and more likely than most to get the company into trouble accidentally.

In general, it's a bad look for founders to raise money for themselves by selling company stock. Investors might ask:

- *Didn't the company need that capital?*
- *De-risking from your own company?*
- *Is there anything else I should know about why you're getting out?*

Beyond the bad optics, founder sales can raise serious regulatory questions, as we have discussed. In due diligence, those questions might take centerstage.

When I hear a founder or other insider has sold shares, I like to find out these things:

- How many shares, how many investors, and for how much?
- Accredited investors or unsophisticated friends and family?
- Were there efforts to document compliance with the "Section 4(1-1/2)" exemption or Section 4(a)(7) from the FAST Act?
- Did he work with counsel?
- Had he entangled the company by requiring it to provide the investors disclosure information, and if so, what did he provide?
- Did he disclose that these were his shares and that the company would not benefit from the proceeds?
- How did he value the shares, and was that disclosed?
- Were those sales considered in valuing the company's later stock option grants?
- Did the company issue certificates, and, if so, did they bear proper legends?

I found an opportunity to meet with the founder. He was evasive about the sales, saying only that the company's outside law firm had represented him individually in the sales and that everything was fine. The law firm was large and sophisticated.

At that, I did not want to know more. It was not my problem, and I did not want it to become my problem or the company's problem.

I told the founder that the company would disavow any involvement with the sales and that they were strictly between him and his purchasers. I also told him he should not sell any more shares. He said that was fine.

I also contacted the relationship partner at the law firm in question and told him there should be no more insider sales. He essentially said, *"Thank you,"* obviously sharing my concerns without directly saying so.

> Lessons: Startup founders should resist the temptation to sell stock. It certainly sends mixed signals about the founder's belief in the mission, not to mention possibly depriving the company of financing opportunities. The regulatory and due diligence risks are also very real.
>
> Boards should prohibit, if not at least actively discourage, stock sales by founders, officers, and other insiders.

Finders Fees and Section 15

At least once or twice a year, I am required to deliver the news that a startup's plans to pay referral fees or finders fees to a person or company helping solicit investors would not be legal.

The objections are roughly the same every time. *"But everyone is doing it."* *"This is their business, I doubt it would be illegal. Can you get on a call with them?"*

In general, state and federal securities laws prohibit the payment of fees to non-broker-dealers in securities transactions. It doesn't matter if those payments are called finders fees, referral fees, consulting fees, or success fees.

This is because registered broker-dealers play highly regulated gatekeeping functions between sellers of securities and purchasers of securities.

These statutory gatekeeping functions are in place to prevent fraud and other predatory behaviors, and they apply to all transactions involving securities, including financings and even mergers and acquisitions.

Section 15

At the federal level, Section 15(a) of the 1934 Act requires persons engaged in broker or dealer activity to register with the SEC under Section 15(b) of the Exchange Act.

The SEC and other state regulators take an "expansive" view of what constitutes "broker-dealer" activity. It certainly encompasses:

- soliciting investors,
- assisting in structuring securities transactions,
- participating in deal negotiations, and
- handling investment funds or securities.

Transaction-Based Compensation

The SEC and state regulators are particularly focused on the nature of any compensation paid to *"non-registered"* persons.

A concept etched into my mind from years as an SEC Enforcement lawyer is that *"transaction-based compensation is a hallmark of broker-dealer activity."*

What the frequent use of this phrase by the SEC means is that, regardless of the degree to which a person engages in the bulleted activities above or not, payment of either *"transaction-based"* or *"success-based"* compensation alone can trigger a violation of Section 15.

Common examples of transaction-based or success-based compensation include payments based on amounts invested or on closing above a certain amount.

SEC Guidance and the Myth of a Finders Exemption

Guidance from the SEC on these issues is limited and not encouraging, despite efforts over the years by the American Bar Association and numerous law firms to push the SEC for greater clarity.

In 1991, the SEC issued what's known as the Paul Anka No Action Letter, which permitted Mr. Anka to introduce prospective investors to an issuer, and nothing more, and receive success-based or transaction-based compensation without triggering broker registration under the Exchange Act.

The Paul Anka No Action Letter was relied on by finders for many years and appears to be the source of the widely held but erroneous belief in a "finders exemption" from the broker-dealer registration requirements.

Years after issuing it, the SEC distanced itself from the Paul Anka No Action Letter and doubled down with a series of no action relief denials. Paul Anka's popular songs live on, but his No Action Letter is dead.

Perhaps most importantly, in 2010, the SEC denied a no-action request from law firm Brumberg, Mackey & Wall, P.L.C., which wanted to introduce prospective investors to issuers for success-based fees. The SEC responded that *"the Staff believes that the receipt of compensation directly tied to successful investments in [issuer's] securities by investors introduced… would require broker-dealer registration."*

The only positive no-action relief at present is limited to the M&A realm and only covers finders who help identify potential buyers of companies who intend to be actively involved in running the acquired companies. See M&A Brokers No Action Letter, January 31, 2014.

https://www.sec.gov/divisions/marketreg/mr-noaction/2014/ma-brokers-013114.pdf

Potential Legal and Regulatory Risks

Violations of Section 15 can result in direct liability for finders in the form of injunctive actions, fines, and even criminal prosecution in the case of willful violations.

Companies paying finders can also find themselves in hot water, both in the form of aiding and abetting liability under Section 21 of the 1934 Act and also for directly causing violations of Section 15(a), as Ranieri Partners LLC learned in 2013.

Ranieri Partners paid a fine of $375,000 based on SEC findings that:

> "...*Ranieri Partners caused [finder] Stephens' violations of Section 15(a) of the Exchange Act, which requires persons engaged in the business of effecting transactions in securities to be registered as a broker or dealer or associated with a registered broker or dealer.*"

Ranieri also highlights that individual officers of issuers can be named as aiders and abetters. The SEC's Order found that Ranieri's Senior Managing Partner, William Phillips, "*willfully aided and abetted and caused Stephens' violations of Section 15(a) of the Exchange Act.*" The Order fined Philips $75,000.

Lastly, Section 15 violations also create potential rights of rescission in favor of the purchasers of securities. This is because Section 29(b) of the Exchange Act says every contract made in violation of the Exchange Act, including contracts where performance violates the Exchange Act, are void as to "*any persons who, in violation of any such provision, rule or regulation, shall have made or engaged in the performance of any such contract.*"

The payment of finders fees is a tough secret to keep since the payments can receive regulatory attention in several ways.

As noted above, companies that raise capital under Reg D, or that file a registration statement with the SEC for an IPO, must disclose payments to third parties in connection with financings. See Item 15 on SEC Form D, "Sales Commissions and Finders' Fees Expenses," and Item 15 in Part II of SEC Form S-1, "Recent Sales of Unregistered Securities."

Intentionally omitting these finders fee disclosures on Form D or Form S-1 is a felony under 18 U.S. Code § 1001, which prohibits any knowing or willful false statement on a federal form.

Unfortunately for a once-promising startup called Neogenix Oncology, Inc., finders fee disclosures from its IPO registration statement later became its undoing. Interestingly, this happened years later when SEC staffers dug into the earlier filings and forced the issue at a time when the company was struggling financially. The financial implications of the rescission issue prevented the company from being able to attract new capital.

The following disclosures from page 9 of Neogenix's 2011 Form 10-K spelled the beginning of the end:

> "*Certain shares of our common stock were sold through finders who were paid fees in spite of not being licensed as broker dealers. The Company has concluded that finders' fees were paid to certain individuals who were not registered as broker-dealers or otherwise licensed under applicable state law. Accordingly, it is possible that at least some investors who purchased shares of common stock in transactions in which finders' fees were paid may have the right to rescind their purchases of shares, depending on applicable federal and state laws and subject to applicable defenses, if any. In addition, the Company may be subject to additional liability under state and/or federal laws in connection with the use of unlicensed broker-dealers. If the Company is forced to rescind a significant number of share purchases and/or pay substantial damages, it will impact the ability of the Company*

to continue operations; therefore management believes that there is substantial doubt about the Company's ability to continue as a going concern."

Well before SEC staffers or state regulators start asking questions, however, potential rescission rights could be a powerful incentive for existing investors to raise "finders" issues if investors believe a company is not doing well and might be vulnerable to rescission demands.

Illegal Finders Fee Arrangements are Common. Despite the many risks to finders, companies, and company officers, the payment of questionable finders fees seems common. In most cases, this is due to lack of sophistication, particularly where the violation is simply due to the type of compensation involved and not the nature of the finder's involvement, which might be very limited. As noted above, the myth of a "finders exemption" is widespread.

In many other cases, calculated risks are taken to get deals done. Finders with networks of rich investors naturally want to make money referring those investors. And companies paying for referrals naturally only want to pay for ones that are "successful." The more difficult a deal is to complete, the greater the risks a company might be willing to take to get it done, particularly where a company's very existence depends on bringing in funds.

Deal dynamics, including financial desperation, simply drive some companies and individuals to gamble on the assumption that finders fee enforcement actions or litigation are unlikely.

More often than not, this seems to be a somewhat safe, albeit inappropriate, gamble. Finders fee issues are probably most often "add-on" issues where the primary claims involve allegations of securities fraud or unregistered securities offerings. Pursuing actions based solely on finders fee violations does not seem to be an enforcement priority for either state or federal regulators.

How to Use Finders without Violating Section 15

Again, the best way to ensure compliance with Section 15 is to use registered broker-dealers as finders. But relying on registered broker-dealers isn't always practical or desirable.

When non-broker-dealer finders are used, Section 15 issues can be largely eliminated by doing two things:

- Avoiding any compensation arrangements tied to deal success, investment amounts, or other deal-related factors.
- Ensuring that finders do nothing more than make initial introductions.

Any fees should be "flat fees," earned simply by providing access to the finder's wealthy contacts, along with a vague but warm introduction – *"Susan, I would like to introduce you to my friend, Beth. She is an entrepreneur with an opportunity she wishes to discuss with you. I hope you two can get together."*

Finders should not:

- attend meetings with the company and investors,
- attempt to explain or discuss the company, investment opportunity, or deal terms with the investors,

- aid in preparation or dissemination of deal materials, or

- handle securities, cash, or any other aspects of securities transactions.

The "anecdotal evidence" seems to indicate that many companies and finders are not content to work within these strict confines.

Based on the many finder proposals I have personally rejected, it seems many finders are accustomed to receiving success-based fees, and hence some companies must be paying them.

Whenever success-based compensation is involved, it becomes even more important to not trip over the above-bulleted no-no's. Participants in such arrangements are running afoul of the regulatory guidance. Preserving arguments that the compensation was a one-time arrangement and didn't involve any other aggravating circumstances might help limit, but not eliminate overall risk exposure.

In other cases, finders receiving flat fee compensation not tied to deal success metrics end up doing more than they should, sitting in on meetings with investors, helping structure the deal, trafficking in deal materials, or cajoling investors to get in.

These types of finder activities, depending on the facts, probably raise the greatest risks. When deals go bad, and investors are aggrieved, an overly active finder is more likely to be identified and caught up in any legal or regulatory aftermath than a finder who merely made a simple introduction and bowed out of the process.

Case Study #36 – Finders Weepers

Again, I receive several requests per year to review proposed finders fee agreements.

These projects go fine when the finder is a registered broker-dealer. If so, the issues are mainly business and financial. I focus on things like whether the client might be paying too much for too little. I also bolster warranties and indemnification language regarding the finders' compliance with the securities laws.

I also usually explore why the company feels the need to work with a finder. Strong founder teams pursuing a great idea often don't need to work with a finder. It is sometimes inexperienced teams that want to work with finders.

When the proposed finder is not a registered broker-dealer, the discussions rarely go well. As the messenger bearing bad news – i.e., that success-based fees to non-broker-dealer finders are illegal – I receive the proverbial slings and arrows.

The clients are disappointed and generally seem skeptical of the advice. Over and over, I hear "… *but everybody does it.*" The proposed finders, eager to earn fees, usually feed into this, acting like I am being overly cautious.

In a surprising number of cases, these finders live outside of the U.S. Where so, I point out that the finder may feel comfortably out of the SEC's reach – an advantage the company doesn't share.

In one such case, I told a client that two proposed finders arrangements were not legal and could result in concerns under Section 15 of the 1934 Act and Section 5 of the Securities Act. As always, I described the risk of rescission claims.

I specifically advised them not to sign the agreements and said further, "*I never let any of my own companies sign agreements like those.*"

A few weeks later, I received a call from my contact at the client, the CFO. He was freaking out. He said they had signed the finders fee agreements, and now the arrangements were jeopardizing the financing. In a tone that struck me as accusatory, he said a "*securities law expert*" at a top law firm doing due diligence had flagged both of the agreements as illegal.

I reminded him gently that another securities law expert had already provided him with the same information and urged against signing the agreements. He quickly back-peddled and acknowledged my prior advice, but added maybe he "*just didn't fully understand it.*"

Following that incident, I take an extremely firm position on all finder's agreements involving non-broker-dealers – they can get flat, non-success-based fees for making introductions, but they can't do much more.

CHAPTER TWELVE

Startup Finance Overview

Successfully financing a startup usually requires funding progressive stages of development.

Whether the end goal is an IPO, a sale, or achieving profitable independence, startup founders should be careful at each stage to use the right funding tools, raise the right amounts of money, do so on the best terms, and with the best investors.

The right money, on the right terms, from the right investors.

At every stage, founders face countless challenges, some external, but others self-inflicted. Meanwhile, the risk of running out of money looms continually for many companies.

In Chapter 11, we studied some of the rules of startup finance. In Chapter 12, we learn more about basic terminology, instruments, and mechanics of startup finance.

- What/who are VCs, angels, and strategic investors?

- What are typical funding stages for startups?

- What factors drive the timing and size of financings?

- What is a cap table, and why is it important?

- How is my company's valuation determined, and what role does valuation play in financing rounds?

- What are the differences between common stock and preferred stock?

- What are the differences between preferred stock and debt?

- What is a Convertible Note, and how is it similar to and different from a Simple Agreement for Future Equity, or SAFE?

- How do preferred stock liquidation preferences work?

- What is series seed preferred stock?

- What early financing activities might later turn away VCs?

Angels, VCs, Strategics, and Corporate VCs

We have used the terms angel investor, VC, and strategic investor, but we have not yet explored their meaning. We will do that now.

Angel Investors

Angel investors are primarily wealthy individuals who make early investments in new companies.

Any wealthy person can become an angel investor. Most are inspired by the idea of supporting innovation. Some focus on supporting advances in areas they believe are beneficial to society.

One advantage of working with an individual angel investor on an early financing round is their ability to make quick decisions without a lot of due diligence and legal expense.

Most angel investments are made through Convertible Notes, SAFEs, or series seed preferred stock, all of which are discussed later under *Types of Financing Instruments*.

Amounts. Angels tend to spread their investments, and hence their risks, among multiple companies, so the amounts of individual angel investments tend not to be large, mostly between $25,000 and $300,000, with perhaps larger average angel investments in Silicon Valley.

Angels who write checks of $500,000 and above are sometimes called "super angels."

Successful Entrepreneur Angels. Many angels are also entrepreneurs who received nice exit payouts from sales of their startups.

An angel investor with prior entrepreneurial experience and lots of investor connections could bring a lot to the table as a startup mentor and goodwill ambassador.

Angel Investment Groups. Since the 1990s, angel investing groups have sprouted up everywhere. We will discuss options for working with angel investor groups, like Seattle's Alliance of Angels.

Family Offices. Family offices are another potential source of angel investments. These are entities that perform investment and financial management services for wealthy families. The number of family offices has grown substantially in the last two decades.

As a reality check for entrepreneurs, family offices managing the largest fortunes simply have too much capital to manage to bother with making direct investments in startups. They tend to invest solely in the public markets, but some also periodically invest as limited partners in VC funds. In talking with the head of one of the largest family offices in the world, I learned that even investing in large VC funds is tricky for major family offices, as the family office ends up being the dominant investor in any such fund, something they prefer to avoid.

Smaller family offices, though, might be a potential source of capital for startups, particularly where there is a close relationship with particular entrepreneurs or where members of the wealthy family are very interested in a startup's business focus.

Family offices are selective and secretive organizations. Getting in front of them requires research and connections. The networking ideas discussed in Chapter 13 under *Developing Fundraising Connections* are a good starting point for identifying potential family office investors.

Venture Capital Firms and Funds

The term VC is used loosely to refer both to venture capital firms and also VC firm managers. We use the term in this section to refer to VC firms.

VCs create "funds" generally ranging in size between about $25 million and $800 million, depending on the fund's investment objectives. The investors in these funds are "limited partners."

These VC fund limited partners tend to be institutional investors like pension funds, insurance companies, banks, hedge funds, private equity firms, and university endowments, as well as very wealthy individuals and family offices.

Each VC fund has stated investment objectives or criteria that include a specific sector or sectors, preferred stage or stages of investment (seed, series A, late-stage), and usually also geographical limitations, such as Silicon Valley, or the Northwest.

Each VC fund has a ten-year "life," meaning that, after ten years, it should be liquidated and the proceeds distributed to the limited partners. There are two very important implications to this. First is that any startup taking VC money needs to realize that they must exit within the 10-year life of the fund.

Second, taking money from a VC fund that has been around for several years means that the time-frame to exit is shortened by that same number of years.

Another important thing for entrepreneurs to know about VCs is that the VC fund model is based on providing big returns. The fact that many companies in their portfolio will completely fail means that the other companies will invariably experience pressure to grow very quickly – likely involving substantial pressure to raise "growth money." This means a series B financing, a series C, and perhaps further into the fundraising alphabet.

Some companies successfully manage these huge infusions of cash and the growth it is intended to drive. Other companies flame out spectacularly, as even mountains of cash are not able to drive the revenues and profit margins necessary to support an IPO or attractive sale.

Many entrepreneurs have lamented taking VC funding after the fact, claiming that the pressure to grow at an unnaturally rapid pace destroyed an otherwise good business model that just needed more time to mature. That was the story of Zenefits discussed in Case Study #33.

Private Equity Versus Venture Capital. Many hear the term "private equity" and wonder what role it might play in startup fundraising. The answer is, likely "none." The term "private equity" has a fairly specific meaning in the finance world. It refers to firms like the Blackstone Group, the Carlyle Group, Bain Capital, and Warburg Pincus.

Without getting too deeply distracted, private equity firms like these are completely different than VCs and angels in their approach to investing. Instead of focusing on newer, tech-oriented companies, and making lots of investments, private equity firms concentrate their investments in amounts of $100 million or more in mature businesses that span a much wider range of industries, generally taking a controlling interest of 51% or better. They are more likely to be encountered at an exit, if at all, but rarely in a series A round.

Strategic Investors and Corporate VC

Strategic investors are frequently, but not always, the investing subsidiaries or affiliates of operating companies, many of which are extremely well known. While there's no strict dividing line, bigname strategics that make larger numbers of investments are referred to as "Corporate VC."

Some of the larger Corporate VCs include Google Ventures, Salesforce Ventures, Intel Capital, Qualcomm Ventures, Comcast Ventures, Samsung Ventures, Amazon Alexa Fund, Dell Technologies Capital, Microsoft Ventures, Unilever Ventures, Merck Ventures, Novartis Venture Fund, Rakuten Ventures, and the Sony Innovation Fund.

And those are just some of the bigger names. There are hundreds of other active strategic investors, large and small, pumping cash into startups.

Strategic investors make investments in companies focused on products or services that have strategic value to the investor or that offer other potential benefits, apart from a purely financial return on investment. For this reason, they are also sometimes described as "non-financial investors."

Some smaller strategics make one or two investments to fill a very specific need. Others create large funds and make many investments each year. Intel Capital, for example, invests in lots of companies it sees as potential chip customers.

More commonly, strategic investors are interested in acquiring access to technologies that would complement their own offerings, or to a service that might be combined with a product or service to make it more appealing in the market.

A large marketing firm, for example, might invest in one or more startups developing AI technologies for the marketing sector, or a large car manufacturer might invest in companies creating new battery or driverless vehicle technologies.

Strategic investors focus less on a company's profitability, which entrepreneurs often appreciate. Strategics do, however, sometimes seek to play a larger role in product development or prioritization than may be helpful or desired.

As part of many strategic investments, the parties will simultaneously enter into another agreement. The nature of that agreement will depend entirely on the circumstances, but a good example might be a Strategic Development, Licensing and Royalty Agreement. That agreement might require, for example, that the startup devote certain resources to developing a particular technology or service and grant the investor a license to use the technology or service for a stated period, either for free or at an agreed royalty rate.

Strategics can be great investors. They can add to a company's industry credibility, they can help make introductions, and they are usually less focused on near-term financial performance than are financial investors.

In some cases, they present a real, or at least perceived, exit possibility for a company – a future potential acquiror. This alone might help quietly bid up a company's perceived value with other potential investors.

There are also potential risks associated with strategics. They can sometimes try to impose their priorities too firmly on their portfolio companies. Founders must consider this carefully and try to avoid misunderstandings. What is best for the strategic might not always be best for the startup.

Another significant downside to consider before taking money from a strategic is how potential customers might react. If a strategic investor would be considered a direct competitor to many of your customers, that funding could be a double-edged sword.

And related to exit possibilities, potential investors seeking longer-term investments with bigger payouts might be wary that a strategic already on a company's cap table could try to acquire the company in an early exit at a modest valuation. Given the desire of many founders for liquidity and the lure of post-exit employment following a strategic buyout, this is a legitimate concern for VCs and other investors playing a longer game for a larger return.

Bearing in mind all potential pros and cons, every entrepreneur should identify and try to get to know interesting potential strategics.

As a final concern, watch out for IP slip-ups while courting strategics. Later we will discuss the fact that VCs will not sign NDAs. The same does not apply to strategics – they must sign NDAs.

Development Stages and Milestones

While some lucky startups strike it rich quickly by launching hot products or services into receptive markets using minimal outside investment, many need to raise money through a series of funding rounds as they work their way through multiple stages of growth and development.

These development stages are different for every company, but they might include some or all of the following:

- idea development,
- market validation,
- prototype/minimum viable product,
- product/service launch,
- market development/sales growth,
- scaling up operational capacity,
- seeking domestic market dominance, and
- seeking international market dominance through organic growth or acquisitions.

When done thoughtfully, these funding rounds, or financings, are used to fund the achievement of specific milestones within each development stage. These milestones could be product or service versions, new features, new markets, sales thresholds, or any other steps along the way to whatever has been defined as success.

For some companies, this means raising money every twelve to eighteen months, while others might find themselves raising more often, at six to ten-month intervals.

Early-Stage, Growth-Stage, and Late-Stage

Targeting potential investors requires understanding how those potential investors target their investments. Investors target not only by industry and sector but also by development stage. Virtually all startup investors, whether angels, VCs, or strategics, tend to view themselves as "early-stage" investors, "late-stage" investors, or something in between, often called "growth-stage."

While helpful, these labels are not fixed, nor are they sufficiently granular to completely understand a specific investor's investment strategy.

Some early-stage investors, for example, focus solely on writing a startup's "first check," while other early-stage investors are willing to make "pre-seed," "seed," and even series A investments.

Likewise, a VC that describes itself as a growth investor might commonly participate in series A, B, and C rounds.

Nonetheless, it is still helpful to understand how these stages are often viewed and described, in order to assess and communicate with potential investors. These four bullets represent early-stage pretty well:

- idea development,
- market validation,
- prototype/minimum viable product, and
- product/service launch.

These early-stage activities correspond to pre-seed and seed investments. Risks of product viability and market acceptance are still very high.

Series A investments can straddle early-stage and early growth-stage. In general, the early risks around product viability and market acceptance have been resolved, and the company has traction, including customers and growing revenues.

Correspondingly, investors focused on making series A investments tend to focus on companies that have launched and have traction, but that need funding for things like the fifth and six bullets above, *market development/sales growth* and *scaling up operational capacity*.

Series B investments are more clearly growth-stage investments, often funding further progress on similar types of growth objectives and milestones as series A rounds.

Late-stage tends to imply companies that often have strong revenues, may already be profitable, and are focused on scaling up operational capacity and pursuing market dominance.

Late-stage companies are also sometimes well on their way to an IPO or sale, and thus more likely to provide a quick investment return. Late-stage investing generally corresponds to series C investments and beyond.

As a general rule, early-stage investments are the most risky, and late-stage investments are least risky.

Angel investors tend to be at the more risk-tolerant end of the spectrum, series A investors are in the middle, and VC funds focused on late-stage investments are the least risk-tolerant, attracting limited partners that include entities like university endowments, pension funds, insurance companies, and banks.

Pre-Seed through Series C

Here again are the names of the primary startup funding rounds and the development stages they tend to fund:

- **Pre-seed.** Pre-seed funding might be viewed as a substitute for founder bootstrapping. It is used to assess demand for a company's products and services ("product-market fit") and to fund early steps to build and distribute a product or service prototype.

- **Seed.** Seed funding has evolved in recent years to fill the gap between bootstrapping and series A rounds. Seed funding supports product design and development, market research, hiring critical staff, and gaining sales and revenue traction for series A funding.

- **Series A.** Series A rounds are often a company's first round of VC funding, but not always. As discussed earlier, many VCs are now funding seed rounds as a pipeline for future series A deals. Series A funds are used to improve an existing product or service, scale up operations, add staffing and administrative infrastructure, and build upon existing traction in the market.

- **Series B.** Series B funds are often used for achieving "revenue at scale," building an already defined and successful business, and adding to teams in business development, sales, advertising, tech, and support. Series B rounds often involve VCs and other institutional investors that describe themselves as later-stage investors.

- **Series C.** Series C funds are often used in scaling a profitable business to achieve greater profitability and better unit economics, possibly through acquisitions and international expansion. Investors in C rounds tend to include larger, later-stage investors, including institutional investors that will not invest at earlier, riskier stages.

As will be explained in greater detail later, the letters A, B, and C correspond to sequentially authorized and issued series of preferred stock – all of which have superior economic and control rights compared to common stock. The rights and preferences of preferred stock are hard-coded into a company's Certificate (or Articles) of Incorporation.

Grow Fast or Perish

Whatever a company's particular milestones, many modern startups need to grow quickly to develop and commercialize a new technology, to create and launch a new product or service, or to revolutionize an existing product or service.

Why should startups grow quickly? While rapid growth is certainly not ideal for all businesses, it can offer two important benefits: (i) dominating a space before others move in creates a variety of "first mover" advantages and (ii) impressive early "key performance indicators" make it easier to raise money quickly, on better terms, and from better investors.

For these reasons, and simply because of the rapid pace of technological change, modern startups often strive for rapid growth.

Rapid growth strategies almost always require external funding since early revenue streams in most tech startups are rarely sufficient to support development, marketing, staffing, and other operational expenses.

For many startups, external funding means eventually working with VCs. As discussed earlier, startups that take VC funds are generally forced onto a rapid growth trajectory.

Ideally, that rapid growth is timely funded in the right amounts and on terms that reward investors for the risks assumed but without hindering the company's ability to raise the next round of funding.

Just-in-Time Finance

I use the phrase *"Just-in-Time Finance"* with founders largely to guide them away from two painful extremes:

- raising too much money too early, which can result in giving too much of a company away at too low of a valuation, and

- raising too little money too late, which often means missed business opportunities and also the possibility of raising money at fire-sale prices and on other bad terms.

Ideally, a startup only raises money at *necessary* intervals to fund specific milestones at successively higher valuations and on the best possible terms for the type of funding in question.

And in a perfect world, this means fully scaling up and achieving all of the company's objectives with the least amount of investment possible and, again, on the best possible terms.

A very rough benchmark to keep in mind is that it usually takes at least six months of diligent effort to complete a financing round. And it is almost always more difficult to raise money than founders expect it to be.

To optimize timing, founders need to know at all times exactly how many months of "financial runway" they have left and always allow a cushion of at least eight months to close the next round. A company's financial runway is current cash ÷ monthly burn rate, with monthly burn rate being the average amount by which monthly expenses exceed monthly revenues.

When all goes well, a company's ownership structure will change gradually and thoughtfully, with successive investment rounds bringing in new business advisors, mentors, and even new board members. In a perfect world, these individuals offer fresh insights, complement management's strengths and weaknesses, and lead to new and helpful business connections.

With these changes, investors often obtain greater say over the management of the company, including when and how it raises money and the strategic transactions it pursues.

Strong startup founders following a well-executed, thoughtful financing strategy can influence these changes for the better by increasing the likelihood that (i) each financing brings in talented, thoughtful, insightful investors to serve as partners in moving the venture forward and (ii) the amount of control that is given up in each financing round is logical and balanced.

An underlying assumption here is that, at least early on, a startup's founders are the individuals best positioned to lead their company to success. After all, it is their vision, and they have spent the most time shaping it and testing strategies for achieving it.

Thus, for many startups, thoughtful, measured changes in control should be the objective.

But fundraising is hard and often unpredictable. Most startups struggle to raise funds and have to go through multiple fundraising rounds involving less-than-ideal financial and non-financial terms.

The next several chapters offer ideas for how entrepreneurs can tip the odds of fundraising success in their favor, and positively influence the economics and control changes that inevitably occur with each round of funding.

Bootstrapping

Bootstrapping means founders funding their companies in the earliest days with their personal resources. Bootstrapping can involve tapping personal cash flows, savings and retirement accounts, credit cards, home equity lines of credit, and other types of personal loans.

Provided the terms of any borrowings are reasonable and not overly risky, bootstrapping is almost always an important part of initial funding.

Build Value Before Selling Equity

A key advantage of bootstrapping is its direct relationship to the idea of Just-in-Time Finance. It reduces the need to sell equity to third parties at fire-sale prices when a business plan is usually the least well-developed, and when risks and uncertainties are at their greatest.

If an idea is a big one, it often makes little sense to give away anywhere between 10% and 20% of the company for as little as $50,000 to $100,000 just to get incorporated, perform some initial market research, begin prototype development, and gain other early traction. Savvy founders try to cover those early costs themselves through properly documented personal loans to the company.

Later potential investors generally respond favorably to founders who have made personal financial sacrifices to launch their companies and demonstrated basic technical and administrative skills to achieve early research and development milestones.

Substantial early self-funding is a strong point of validation – i.e., the person who knows the most about the company and its prospects for success has invested their own money, sometimes at great personal financial sacrifice and risk.

The amount and nature of any bootstrapping is a very personal decision and one that requires careful consideration. If potential investors are eager to invest on very reasonable terms, it makes less sense for a founder to jeopardize personal finances instead of giving up a little equity to a supportive seed investor.

But any time it is not unduly risky to bootstrap, being able to tell investors you "*maxed out some credit cards*" or made some other meaningful financial sacrifice always plays well.

Founder Loans

Again, lending by founders to their startups is a form of bootstrapping. In a situation where two founders have received their founder shares solely in exchange for contributed IP, one or both of the founders might also agree to provide initial funding in the form of a loan.

Founders should carefully document any loans they make to their companies and charge a reasonable interest rate. Randomly advancing funds to the company or covering company expenses without proper loan documentation and without a stated interest rate can result in those advances being deemed equity investments.

If funds are going to be advanced at specific intervals or simply as needed, the loan documentation should specify processes under which (i) the company specifically requests advances, (ii) the founder advances the requested funds, and (iii) the loan documentation between the parties is updated to reflect (usually on a schedule or exhibit) the date and amount of the new funding tranche.

Poorly documented loans run the risk of significant disputes and the possibility of being recharacterized by the IRS as equity investments under Internal Revenue Code Section 385.

In the event of the startup's insolvency, instead of having the superior claims (and leverage) of a debt obligation, poorly documented loans can be deemed worthless equity. A proper debt instrument must generally be for a sum certain, with a specific due date, and a commercially reasonable interest rate.

The interest rate should be at least as high as the IRS's "applicable federal rate," or "AFR," to avoid interest being imputed and treated as a gift, capital contribution, or compensation. The AFR is usually less than the current market rate. The IRS provides AFRs for three loan categories: short-term (3 years or less), mid-term (3 to 9 years), and long-term (9 years or greater, or indefinite).

https://apps.irs.gov/app/picklist/list/federalRates.html

As a cautionary note, VCs and other sophisticated investors are often reluctant to see their investments used to pay off earlier founder loans or similar types of debts. Entrepreneurs should assume any unpaid founder loans might have to be rolled into equity to close a financing. Debt-to-equity conversions can raise minor tax questions for the company and the lender.

Founders might try structuring any loans to the company as longer-term Convertible Notes in anticipation of these types of issues. In any case, robust documentation will provide a stronger negotiating position with future investors than poorly-documented, ad hoc advances.

Shareholder Equity

The term "equity" is worth touching on briefly because it has at least two subtly different meanings for our purposes.

In more casual conversation, equity can be used to refer to an ownership interest in a company. Many stock option plans, for example are called "equity compensation plans." Participants are said to receive "equity grants."

In finance, equity, or shareholder equity, has a slightly more specific meaning. It is the amount of money a company's shareholders would receive if all of the assets were sold off, but after all of the company's debt has been paid off.

The formula for shareholder equity is total assets - total liabilities, or "total assets minus total liabilities."

Total shareholder equity is a key financial metric that is found on a company's balance sheet.

Without a reliable cap table, it is impossible to determine the "book value" per share of a company's stock, because that number is determined by this formula: shareholder equity ÷ total shares outstanding.

Book value per share is just one component of the actual fair market value of a company's shares, but it is an important one.

Many causes contribute to companies having unreliable cap tables, a significant impediment to successful fundraising. Under *Cap Table Fails* below, we will discuss a variety of mistakes that cause cap table chaos and confusion and how to avoid those mistakes.

Capitalization Tables

A capitalization table, or "cap table" as they are known, is a visual representation in the form of a spreadsheet or other interactive table reflecting a company's equity ownership – i.e., who owns what percentages of a company and through what types or classes of shares or other ownership interests.

Cap tables are depicted in many ways and varying degrees of detail. Sometimes individual investors are listed out by name, and sometimes they are grouped by share classes or other ownership interests.

Sometimes cap tables are simple, static documents, sometimes they are presented and maintained in the form of spreadsheets with embedded formulas, and, increasingly, they are managed and maintained in online platforms that also process option grants, stock issuances, and other transactions. The market for online, cloud-based cap table platforms has a steady stream of new entrants and is worth studying carefully before deciding how to proceed. The two top platforms are Carta and Shareworks (formerly, Capshare). Other top platforms include Eqvista, EquityEffect, and Captable.io.

The best way to appreciate the wide range of variation in cap table structure and content is to do an online search for "cap table examples" and look through the images and other information presented. Although patterns and commonalities will be obvious, it will also be clear that there is simply no single way to create a cap table. Here is a very basic example:

High Growth, Inc. Capitalization Overview as of August 15, 2019				
Authorized Shares:	13,000,000			
Outstanding Shares:	9,000,000			
Shares Reserved for Option Pool:	1,500,000			
Remaining Unissued Shares:	2,500,000			
Investor/Optionee	**Common Stock**	**Stock Options**	**Fully Diluted Shares**	**Percentage of Fully Diluted Shares**
Andy Hawkins	4,000,000		4,000,000	38.09%
Beth Sayer	3,000,000		3,000,000	28.57%
Brenda Frankefield	2,000,000		2,000,000	19.05%
Chip Johnson		400,000	400,000	3.81%
Remaining Option Pool		1,100,000	1,100,000	10.48%
Total	9,000,000	1,500,000	10,500,000	100%
Percentage Ownership	85.71%	14.29%	100%	100%

Study the example carefully, including the math.

Note that the "Fully Diluted" total includes the granted and ungranted shares in the option pool. When a company sets aside shares in an option pool, potential investors include those shares in calculating the fair market value, or FMV, they are willing to pay on a per-share basis. The bigger the option pool, the lower the price per share.

Some common data points that are missing from this example include the price per share that Andy, Beth, and Brenda each paid for their shares, along with a row showing the company's "total capitalization" – i.e., the amount founders and investors have put into the company.

Although rarely correlated to a company's total current value and FMV per share, potential investors are always interested in knowing how much earlier investors paid for their shares.

Cap Table Evolution Through Financing Rounds

Founder Dilution. When two founders form a company, they generally start out owning 100% of its issued stock.

As other investors come in, that percentage naturally declines. By the time of an exit, whether sale or IPO, founder equity is generally between 10% to 20%. This decline is commonly referred to as "founder dilution."

Managing the rate of founder dilution responsibly is part of what we discussed earlier regarding *Just-in-Time Finance.* Giving away 50% of the company to raise $10,000 in pre-seed capital is irresponsible and shortsighted. If possible, it would be better to use $10,000 in personal credit card cash advances to get the company to a stage where an investor is willing to provide at least $100,000 for a 10% stake.

On the flip side, founders who are obsessed with not giving away any equity often starve their companies of capital. It is better to own less of a well-capitalized company on a solid growth trajectory than to own a higher percentage of a company plummeting into insolvency.

Another common result of equity stinginess is being forced to accept "venture debt" term loans or receivable financing loans with high interest rates, company-betting security interests (rights to take the assets upon default), and, ironically, warrant coverage (dilutive equity) as high as 20% of the value of the loan. We will discuss venture debt later.

Financing Rounds and Equity Percentages. In early financing rounds, it is generally possible to raise pre-seed and seed capital without giving up more than 10% of the company's equity per financing round.

Once VCs enter the scene, though, larger numbers come into play. Series A rounds are usually for 20% to 25% of a company's equity. This is because VCs need to make meaningful investments and have meaningful ownership stakes in their portfolio companies to justify their time, attention, and mentorship. These ownership stakes are also intended to remain meaningful through future financing rounds.

Series B rounds used to be for even higher percentages, even up to 30% to 35%, but they also now tend to be in the 20% to 25% range.

Later stage financings are somewhat less predictable. Series C and D financings can range more widely, but most probably stay within a 15% to 20% range.

"Fully-diluted, as-Converted." As we have discussed, series A, B, and C rounds are financings involving the issuance of newly created series of preferred stock – series A preferred stock, series B preferred stock, series C preferred stock, and so forth.

To understand how cap tables work, it is important to realize that preferred stock is always convertible into common stock, initially on a one-share-for-one-share basis. Conversion at any time is generally an option of a preferred stockholder - called "voluntary conversion." Likewise, every series of preferred stock also generally has involuntarily conversion triggers. Virtually all series of preferred stock convert to common stock in an IPO, for example.

Thus, near the bottom right-hand side of most cap tables, you can find the total number of shares issued or issuable by a company "on a fully-diluted, as-converted basis." This number includes all shares of common stock, all shares of common stock issuable upon the conversion of outstanding preferred stock (and other convertible instruments), and the full number of shares of common stock underlying issued stock options and options still available for issuance under the option pool.

So when a VC is interested in investing, and it wants to own 20% of the company, the number of new shares that need to be created and authorized by the company must be sufficient so that the VC's total ownership, *post-closing*, will be 20% of the *new total number of shares* calculated on a fully-diluted, as-converted basis.

Series A Hypothetical. Thus, if a company has 10,000,000 shares of common stock outstanding and VCs are coming in with $XYZ ($ amount not relevant yet) for 20% of the company, the company's board and shareholders must approve the creation of a new class of series A preferred stock and authorize the issuance of at least 2,500,000 shares of series A preferred stock.

Here's the math for coming up with that 2,500,000 number of "additional shares" by first finding the number of total authorized shares post-closing or "PCS" – total Post Closing Shares:

Step 1: (formula) 10,000,000 + 20%(PCS) = PCS

Step 2: (convert to decimal equivalent) 10,000,000 + .2PCS = PCS

Step 3: (subtract .2PCS from each side):

$$10,000,000 + .2PCS = PCS$$
$$- .2PCS - .2 PCS$$
$$10,000,000 + 0 = .8PCS$$

Step 4: (solve for PCS by dividing each side by .8):

$$\frac{10,000,000}{.8} = \frac{.8PCS}{.8}$$

Step 5: right side cancels out, leaving 10,000,000/.8 = 12,500,000 PCS

Step 6: (to find the additional shares) 12,500,000 x 20% = 2,500,000

Therefore, when the series A financing closes, the cap table will show 10,000,000 shares of common stock and 2,500,000 shares of series A preferred, for a total number of shares on a fully-diluted, as-converted basis of 12,500,000.

Series B Hypothetical. Say a different VC leads the same company's series B financing but wants to put in a much larger amount for a 33% ownership stake.

Here is the math showing how to calculate how many shares of series B preferred need to be authorized by first finding the total shares post-closing.

Step 1: (formula) 12,500,000 + 33%(PCS) = PCS

Step 2: (convert to decimal equivalent) 12,500,000 + .33PCS = PCS

Step 3: (subtract .33PCS from each side):

$$12,500,000 + .33PCS = PCS$$
$$-.33PCS \quad -.33\,PCS$$
$$12,500,000 + 0 = .67PCS$$

Step 4: (solve for PCS by dividing each side by .67):

$$\frac{12,500,000}{.67} = \frac{.67PCS}{.67}$$

Step 5: right side cancels out, leaving 12,500,000/.67 = 18,656,716 PCS

Step 6: (to find the additional shares) 18,656,716 x 33% = 6,156,716

Therefore, granting the series B investors a 33% stake will require authorizing the issuance of 6,156,716 shares of series B preferred stock.

Impacts on Earlier Holdings. As the graphic below shows, after these series A and series B financings, the holders of Common stock end up with approximately 54% of the company's total equity and the ownership percentage of the series A shareholders was reduced from 20% to approximately 13%.

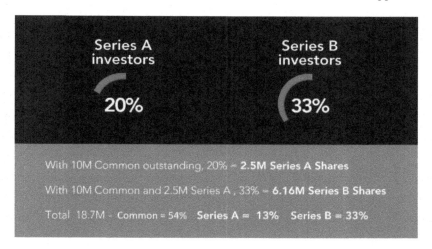

Series A investors 20%

Series B investors 33%

With 10M Common outstanding, 20% = **2.5M Series A Shares**

With 10M Common and 2.5M Series A , 33% = **6.16M Series B Shares**

Total 18.7M - Common = 54% **Series A = 13%   Series B = 33%**

Changing Control Dynamics. The 33% figure used in this example is high relative to most series B financings, but, for the vast majority of startups, gradually giving up equity to fund growth is a natural part of the development process. In many cases, say after the series B or C round, founders will find themselves no longer in control.

Hopefully they have chosen their investors wisely and they have managed the company well so that the views and objectives of the founders and investors are aligned.

In some cases, though, founders perform poorly as business managers and are jettisoned from management once other investors have sufficient voting authority to remove them.

More often, probably, there are differences and tensions between founders and dominant shareholders, but the board members still work together well enough to chart a course and approve plans, budgets, and financing strategies, and the board accepts many of the founders' proposals without modifications, but not all.

One point of this section is to highlight the importance of every percentage point of equity ownership. Metaphorically, this means *"keeping your powder dry"* – using every share of stock prudently and strategically. Founders need to be pragmatic about giving up equity to the right investors in the right amounts at the right time. And founders need to be extremely cautious about not committing *any* of the cap table fails below. Cap table fails (i) cause premature loss of control, (ii) squander the company's future ability to sell shares to finance operations, and (iii) raise doubts about the accuracy of a company's cap table, potentially hindering financings and exits.

Cap Table Hygiene and Maintenance

Managing a cap table by making timely, accurate entries for every equity issuance, stock option grant, convertible instrument, stock option vesting milestone, and stock option exercise is an administratively tedious task that many companies fail at miserably. One of the top platforms uses the advertising tagline – *"Most cap tables are wrong."* Sadly, this is not false advertising.

At a technical level, and in terms of time commitment, it is not difficult to set up a cap table as a spreadsheet, create the right fields and formulas, or even to make proper entries for each new equity event. Searching online for "cap table template" generally yields several acceptable templates for the price of a name and email address.

Managing a cap table is simply one of those tedious chores that is easy to fall behind on and then feel overwhelmed trying to get caught up.

For companies that cannot afford to use a subscription online cap table platform, the best approach is to add cap table management to the list of outsourced activities handled by a competent bookkeeper. Those folks are also usually good at handling annual corporate filings with secretaries of state – another genre of administrative task that often falls through the cracks.

This can be a good solution at least until a major financing like a series A round is coming up. At that time, however, it would be very worthwhile to migrate the cap table to a reputable online cap table platform in anticipation of VC expectations.

While there are some established and robust platforms that handle a wide variety of tasks very well, including issuing equity, processing option grants and exercises, and tracking option vesting and expiration schedules, these platforms can be quite expensive.

Fortunately, the basic requirements for cap table management are relatively simple, and new cloud-based cap table platforms are entering the market all the time. Shopping and comparing in this market, as with PEOs, could be worthwhile.

When pricing these platforms, be sure to ask what support is provided to migrate off of the platform in the event of pricing changes. A few years back, the then-leading platform raised its prices almost 500% and I had to move two companies to another platform.

Cap Table Fails

There are numerous ways to create cap table problems. Failing to keep up with option grants is a common but relatively fixable problem. Inexperienced entrepreneurs are prone to bigger blunders, unfortunately - mistakes that result in disputes, bloated cap tables, inaccurate cap tables, and even tax issues.

The following mistakes are harmful, difficult to fix, and should be avoided:

1. giving away equity like candy early in a company's development rather than raising funds correctly and paying basic wages,

2. making large equity grants to founders or officers without vesting or clawback provisions, resulting in substantial dead equity,

3. issuing equity in percentage terms or vague formulas instead of fixed numbers of shares or units,

4. issuing founder or officer equity grants with anti-dilution provisions,

5. allowing founders to sell their founder shares in poorly-controlled transactions to non-accredited investors,

6. promising equity issuances or option grants but not following through,

7. purporting to issue equity or option grants, but doing so in a manner that is improper and *ultra vires* (acts done without legal authority),

8. promising the wrong kind of equity, like LLCs offering common stock or stock options,

9. issuing equity or option grants from multiple entities, such as from a parent company and from one or more of its operating companies, and

10. issuing Convertible Notes or SAFEs in large dollar amounts relative to the anticipated equity financing round in which they will convert.

<u>Overly Generous Grants.</u> Fails #1 – #4 above are simply irresponsible and poorly considered uses of equity compensation. Regarding #1, before issuing any equity, founders and officers should be familiar with standard equity compensation practices. Equity should not be used as a *substitute* for compensation but as an enhancement to compensation designed to "align" officer and employee interests with the success of the enterprise.

Well-run companies establish tiers of equity compensation for various levels of responsibility within an organization, and they exercise discipline in keeping their grants within those tiers.

Clawbacks to Prevent Dead Equity. Regarding #2, we have already discussed the importance of vesting periods and clawbacks to prevent large equity positions from becoming dead equity on the cap table.

Vague or "Non-Dilutable" Grants. Regarding #3 and #4, all equity grants should be for fixed numbers of shares and otherwise precise in their terms. This means no formulas, no promises to be kept at a certain percentage of ownership through future financing rounds, and no other anti-dilution provisions directed toward similar ends.

When an early investor or officer asks for a percentage-based "non-dilutable" ownership interest, they are likely doing so out of a lack of sophistication. They do not understand how equity financings work, and they are likely mistrustful – concerned that they will be cheated.

Push back firmly against such demands, using the following points, as necessary:

- Granting non-dilutable interests could prevent the company from raising any additional funds, particularly from sophisticated angels or VCs.

- Equity investments need to reflect the fair market value of the shares issued at the time; a company cannot be burdened with the requirement to continually issue free shares to an early investor or employee to maintain their original ownership percentage.

- Early-stage "non-dilutable" interests should not be confused with the anti-dilution terms that VCs negotiate in exchange for *substantial investments* in a company that provide protection *only* in the case of subsequent down (lower-priced) rounds.

Founder Equity Sales. Regarding #5, founders often find themselves in difficult financial circumstances from working without pay. This often leads them to think about selling some of their equity stake to raise cash.

As discussed in Chapter 11, founder stock sales are problematic for many reasons, including (i) anti-fraud risks and potential offering registration risks for the officer and the company, (ii) the addition of dead equity to the cap table, (iii) the potential addition of non-accredited or unsophisticated investors to the cap table, (iv) depriving the company of a financing opportunity for personal gain, (v) adverse impacts to the pricing of stock option grants for employees and others, (vi) possible violations of "rights of first refusal" or similar investor rights to acquire any founders shares offered for sale, and (vii) the negative impression suggesting a lack of commitment by selling founders.

Granting and Issuance Errors. Regarding #6 and #7, these are blatant equity issuance errors that cast legal clouds over a cap table. Unmet obligations to issue equity can be difficult if not impossible to correct years later when the mistakes are discovered, resulting in certain liabilities.

Do not attempt to issue stock or options without documented board approvals. Such issuances are invalid and cannot be simply corrected by the board later. Always hire competent securities counsel to handle equity issuances.

LLCs Cannot Issue Stock. Regarding #8, entrepreneurs often promise grants of equity that make no sense, elevating the risk of disputes involving the cap table. It seems virtually every CEO of an LLC falsely believes the LLC can issue common stock or stock options.

Similarly, equity cannot be granted by non-existent entities. When it comes to issuing equity in the name of a company, *close* is not good enough.

Misaligned Option Grants. Regarding #9, this may be just a matter of opinion formed by bad facts, but issuing equity from more than one entity raises risks that divided loyalties may be alleged if and when business, financing, or M&A opportunities are pursued at one entity versus the other. Future potential investors will almost certainly raise such concerns and perhaps be driven off by them.

Too Much Convertible Note or SAFE Overhang. Fail #10 is an easy one to make when a Convertible Note round attracts a lot of positive interest. As an example, if a company intends to raise $7 million in a series A preferred stock round in a year or two, that effort could be harmed or complicated by raising $3 million before then in a Convertible Note round involving a 20% discount.

We discuss Convertible Note discounts later, under *Types of Financing Instruments*, but Convertible Notes generally convert from debt to equity in the next financing round, and those noteholders receive their equity at a "discount" to what the new investors pay.

In the example above, let's assume a series A financing happens one year later. The $3 million of debt will grow over one year to $3,150,000 of principal and interest, assuming 5% simple interest. Because of the 20% discount, those noteholders will receive $3.15 million of the series A shares at a 20% per-share discount to what the "new-money" investors pay.

Investors in a preferred stock round generally do not mind a reasonable percentage of the round going to noteholders with a 20% discount, but when the percentage of shares to be issued at a discount gets too large, the investment opportunity can look less attractive.

It is also natural for new investors to want to see more new cash in a financing round versus simply the conversion of old debts into equity.

The same concerns can be amplified by Convertible Note rounds with low "valuation caps," which are discussed below.

In any event, caution should be exercised to ensure that Convertible Note rounds are not excessively large relative to the equity round into which they are expected to convert. As discussed later, SAFEs (Simple Agreements for Future Equity) pose the same issues, in that they usually convert into a series A round at a 20% discount and sometimes also contain valuation caps that can increase that discount well beyond 20%.

Case Study #37 – Co-Founder Cash Crunch

An inexperienced founder thrust into the CEO role of a promising startup found himself in a cash crunch just months after co-founding the startup and walking away from a substantial salary. So, he did what all-too-many financially strapped founders do – he quietly sold some of his stock in the startup.

This founder's actions were particularly concerning because he was legally obligated under a Shareholders Agreement to first offer those shares to other existing shareholders, which he did not do.

The initial blowback from this decision occurred when the founder asked company counsel to process the share transfers. At this point, his co-founder learned of the sales and was furious. She was more sophisticated and very concerned about many of the issues mentioned earlier – inadvertent securities fraud, securities registration issues, dead equity on the cap table, the loss of a financing opportunity for the company, and violation of other investors' rights of first refusal.

She advised him to speak with the company's major investors and let them know but did not press the issue further or follow up with other investors or board members.

A year later, the board and its audit committee were meeting in San Francisco. The board included certain major investor representatives, as well as the founders. Outside auditors and legal advisors attended the meeting.

In one session, outside counsel went into a discussion on how the company needed to "establish better processes and controls for sales of insider shares." After a minute or two, one of the board members said:

> *"Why are we wasting our time talking about this? Who here would be stupid enough to sell any of their shares? Can we move on from this topic?"*

After 15 or 20 seconds of awkward silence, the founder who had sold shares sheepishly chimed in.

> *"I did…, I sold some of my shares."*

In front of the auditors and outside counsel, board members expressed disappointment about the founder's judgment, touching on issues of trust, sophistication, and leadership, and reinforcing the obvious – no insiders should sell shares without explicit, prior board approval.

> Lesson: Do not sell founder shares without first reviewing all potential documents where applicable restrictions on such sales might be found, and then consulting with any co-founders or key investors, as well as legal counsel. Failing to honor rights of first refusal to co-founders or other investors is not only an actionable contractual breach but also a serious breach of trust.

Even if approved, consider how founder sales will look to potential future investors and how they might impact future financings. The first question future investors might ask is:

"Who are these other people on the cap table?"

The second question might be:

"Why should I invest in a company if the founders are bailing out?

The hidden costs of founder sales may be much higher than simply taking out a home equity line of credit or finding cash elsewhere.

Outside counsel practice tip: Delicate situations need to be handled delicately. When a client's senior officers make mistakes, consider working behind the scenes to help them correct their mistakes.

Case Study #38 – Twenty-Four Hours

Days before a major M&A deal closed, a founder approached me and said:

"Say, there was this contractor who did some work for us way back in the beginning and we promised to issue him 20,000 shares of stock. We need to issue those shares to him before the deal closes this week."

Had I not known this individual pretty well, I would not have believed my ears. The company in question had gone through multiple VC-led financing rounds. In each of those rounds, we had issued representations and warranties regarding the accuracy of the cap table.

In none of these highly negotiated and meticulously documented financing rounds was there ever any disclosure of an obligation to issue 20,000 common shares to the contractor in question. Consequently, there was no possibility of legally issuing those shares.

Had that contractor received those shares as the founder had promised, they would have been worth about $40,000 in the deal.

The company had no record whatsoever regarding this independent contractor or the promise of 20,000 shares. This mistake was the founder's fault, and he was trying to fix it surreptitiously at the last minute. Issuing the shares was out of the question.

Knowing all of this instantly, I quietly told the founder that he would have to deal with this on his own. I told him I would write up a "waiver and release agreement" and that he would essentially have to negotiate a dollar amount to compensate the independent contractor sufficiently to get his signature on the agreement and go away. I told the founder that he would have to fund whatever amount was necessary – that it would be improper for the company to pay.

I did my best to arm him with some arguments for minimizing the price for the waiver and release – most importantly, the fact that neither party could produce a signed copy of the contractor agreement in question.

I also told the founder I needed the fully executed document within 24 hours.

To my relief, I received it. The founder had to write a personal check for $10,000 to make the problem go away. I thanked him for resolving it and told him I felt bad. He smiled and said, *"No problem."*

Lessons: Never make unauthorized promises to issue equity to anyone.

Whenever promises are made to provide equity compensation, follow through on those grants immediately – authorize them, grant/issue them, document them, and record them in the cap table.

Valuation

A company's valuation represents the amount someone would pay for the company, taking into account its assets, liabilities, and prospects for future profits.

Valuation is critical to investors. Without a valuation (and an accurate cap table), it is impossible to determine how much a particular ownership percentage should cost an investor.

This is why equity rounds are also referred to as "priced" rounds – a price per share is always established.

Valuation of publicly traded companies is relatively easy, given the constant availability of a bid and ask price. Public companies also tend to have long operating histories and lots of publicly available information mandated by the SEC, all of which reduce uncertainty in valuation.

Privately held startups are much harder to value, particularly startups with little or no revenue. Early valuations are often simply leaps of faith that investors are willing to take with small amounts of money.

Pre-revenue Valuation

How does one value a pre-seed or seed company?

Founders usually seem to work backward from what might be called a "minimally viable valuation" to get what they need for the ownership percentage they're willing to sell. The founders then argue for that valuation by talking up the idea, the opportunity, and the team. This results-oriented valuation approach probably happens to some extent in most financings, but it's more obvious with pre-revenue companies.

A minimally viable valuation in a seed round essentially means, *"we have to demonstrate that the company is worth XYZ amount,"* with XYZ amount being a function of two questions:

- how much cash does the company need for the next 12 to 18 months of milestones, and
- what percentage equity stake are the founders willing to give up?

Founders should consider targeting a pre-money valuation for a pre-seed or seed round that is no less than $2 million and hopefully closer to $4 million. Valuations of $2 million or less produce relatively small investment amounts for equity interests of between 10% and 20%.

As we will see, a 10% interest in a company valued at $2 million will only bring in $222K of cash, a small amount, even for a pre-seed round.

The following examples show how to calculate how much money can be raised for specific ownership percentages at specific pre-money valuations. The ownership positions in the examples, 10% and 20%, represent <u>post-closing</u> ownership interests of the new investor(s).

In other words, the math in the following graphic explains why:

- A 10% post-closing interest in a company with a $4.5M pre-money valuation costs the investor $500K,

- A 10% post-closing interest in a company with a $2M pre-money valuation costs the investor $222K,

- A 20% post-closing interest in a company with a $2M pre-money valuation costs the investor $500K, and

- A 20% post-closing interest in a company with a $4M pre-money valuation costs the investor $1M.

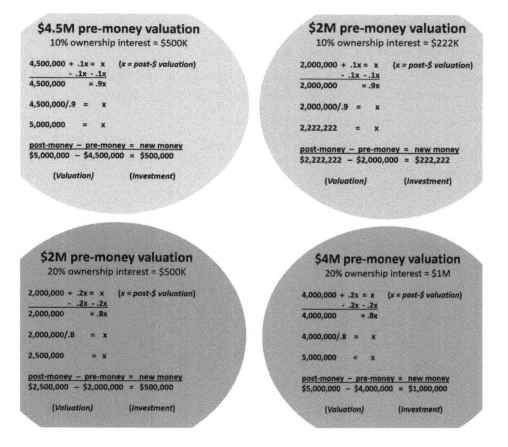

The transaction in the fourth example would be described as having *"a $4 million pre-money valuation and a $5 million post-money valuation."*

Pre-revenue valuations in the $3M to $5M range and higher are common in many parts of the country for startups with good ideas and demonstrable traction.

Many founders struggle with picking a valuation. They would rather have one suggested to them. And some early investors have relatively fixed ideas about the ownership percentage they want post-closing in exchange for a fixed investment amount. He or she may simply say, *"I'll put in $500,000 for 10% of the company."*

Conveniently, that fixed-investment, equity-percentage-driven investor perspective gets us to the same place as one of our examples – a $5,000,000 post-money valuation.

In this case, the math question is simply - *"$500,000 is 10% of what post-money valuation?"* The steps for this calculation are:

Step 1: $500,000 = 10% of x

Step 2: $500,000 =.1(x)

Step 3: $500,000/.1 =.1(x)/.1

Step 4: $500,000/.1 = x

Step 5: $500,000/.1 = $5,000,000

Answer: $500K is 10% of a $5M post-money valuation

Founders should think very hard before selling more than 20% in a seed or pre-seed round. It might be better to bootstrap a little longer instead and establish more valuation support.

Basic founder tools for negotiating valuation include:

- financial models to show the business's potential,

- product demos or prototypes,

- "comps" - terms of recently priced, comparable deals, and

- hyping the team and their individual past accomplishments.

Founders should be prepared to show traction on "key performance indicators," or "KPIs." KPIs vary by business model and sector, but some common ones include:

- launch of a basic product or service,

- number of users or beta testers,

- daily and monthly active users,

- customer "activation rate,"

- customer acquisition cost,

- customer attrition rates,

- lifetime value of a customer,

- burn rate/runway, and

- revenue growth.

Valuation from Revenue

Companies with one or more years of operating history can often start to peg their valuation to their revenues and revenue growth rates.

A successful e-commerce company, for example, might be valued at three to five times its current annual revenue run rate – i.e., an annualized revenue figure based on the most recent months' revenue performance.

For example, if a company is generating about $70,000 per month and climbing quickly, that company could have a fair claim to a pre-money valuation of at least $4.2M – i.e., $70,000 x 12 (months) x 5 (revenue multiple) = $4,200,000.

This is a common benchmarking valuation methodology in the startup world - estimate a company's revenues over the next twelve months based on the current run rate and then try to figure out what "multiple" to apply, based on the industry and the company's revenue growth curve.

Companies with flat revenue growth curves generally sell for around one times, or 1x, their 12-month (revenue) run rate.

On the other hand, companies with steep revenue growth trajectories can sell for high multiples, with SaaS companies often commanding multiples in the 7x to 10x range. A company with a steep revenue trajectory and a revenue run rate of $10 million in the next twelve months, therefore, could be valued as high as $100 million.

Of course, looking solely at revenue trends doesn't work as well if a company is burdened by substantial debt or has a broken business model with terrible unit economics.

Initial Valuation Deferral

Given the estimate that approximately 80% of startups fail, the most reliable thing that can be said about valuations of pre-revenue startups is that they are almost always wrong.

For this reason, many early investors prefer to structure their investments in ways that defer the need for a valuation. By doing so, they not only improve the chances that the eventual valuation of their interest will be more accurate, they can also lock in a discount on that valuation. More on this later under *Types of Financing Instruments.*

Valuation Moderation

Founders instinctively believe they should push for the highest valuation possible. This is short-sighted. In my view, in priced rounds, founders should accept a valuation that accurately reflects the company's current status and its *actual* prospects for financial success.

While selling equity at a very high price and being flush with cash can make for a fantastic deal closing party, the hangover from an unrealistically high valuation can be unpleasant.

We will discuss the concept of "down rounds" in detail below, but a down round is essentially any equity offering at a price per share that is lower than a prior offering's price per share.

Not only are down rounds arguably evidence of failure at some level, they also frequently trigger anti-dilution rights of earlier investors, diluting the ownership interests of common stockholders and complicating the cap table.

Investor perception is another important reason for avoiding artificially high valuations. When a company's performance does not ultimately justify an earlier valuation, that can harm the company's credibility and financing prospects. Investors assess risk. Any down round in a company's past is a red flag on the management team. Founders with a track record of missing their numbers by wide margins might be viewed by potential investors as untrustworthy or unreliable.

From an internal perspective, the stress on a management team missing artificially high revenue and profit targets can be demoralizing. Management teams under impossible pressures may be prone to short-term, risky decision making, at the expense of executing on longer-term strategic initiatives.

A final point about valuation is that founders should strive toward ensuring that all of their investors make money. As in most aspects of life and business, an entrepreneur's reputation is his or her most important asset. Entrepreneurs that provide positive returns to the angels, VCs, and other investors make those investors look good by validating their judgment in business and in people.

There is little long term value in fooling investors in the near term with an inflated valuation.

Valuation between Rounds

Once a company has taken equity investments, it always works out best when those funds are used successfully to quickly grow revenues and, hence, the company's valuation.

Revenue growth is required to support a series of equity investments on positive, non-dilutive terms. Once VC money comes in, failure to meet financial targets for two or three years can cause a company's existing investors to cut off further funding. When existing VC investors will not invest, getting others to invest can become extremely difficult.

While there are no hard and fast rules, various rules of thumb are sometimes cited, like these two aspirational guidelines:

(i)   a current financing round is generally 5x the company's prior financing round and should carry the company for 12 to 18 months; and

(ii) a company's current valuation is generally 3x to 4x the size of its current financing round.

Note regarding the first guideline: In applying the 5x formula to a company's "prior financing round," consider excluding any Convertible Note or SAFE conversions that occurred during that recent round. Those conversion amounts relate to an even earlier financing round and have little bearing on the company's actual cash needs at the time of the more recent round. Counting only new money investments in the 5x calculation provides a more accurate baseline for predicting a company's cash needs 12 to 18 months later.

The first of these two guides, raising 5x more each round than the last round, has to do with growth expectations, particularly those of VCs and sophisticated angel investors. Raising funds at those amounts and intervals pre-supposes that a company is gaining substantial traction month-over-month and year-over-year.

For many companies, unfortunately, achieving this funding rate is elusive. Many companies bog down in sequential seed rounds at similar or only slightly larger dollar amounts. When this occurs over several years, attracting VC interest can get increasingly difficult, even if the story is good. It is said that fewer than 50% of companies that obtain seed funding end up completing a series A financing.

The second of these two rules, that a company's current valuation should be about 3x to 4x the size of its current financing round, has to do with the fact that, in each round, investors tend to expect to receive a 20% or greater ownership interest. Thus, stated differently, the amount raised should not be much more than 1/5th of the company's post-money valuation.

Using these guides, if a company raised $1.5M in a Convertible Note seed round 12 months earlier, its series A round should be at least $7.5M ($1.5M x 5), thus suggesting a pre-money valuation of approximately $22.5M to $30M (3x to 4x $7.5M).

These numbers are perfectly reasonable, particularly if the company in question currently has an annual revenue run rate of between $5M and $6M and revenue growth warranting a 5x multiple or better – i.e., $5M x 5 = $25M and $6M x 5 = $30M.

Taking these numbers to the next financing round, VCs looking at the same Company for a series B financing might expect the company to be raising around $37.5M (5 x $7.5M of new money) and they would probably also expect to see that the company's financial performance and forecasts support a pre-money valuation of between $112.5M and $150M (3x to 4x $37.5M).

Again, these numbers also seem fairly reasonable and correlate to typical series B rounds, if perhaps on the high side in many markets outside of Silicon Valley or New York.

Valuation, Ownership Percentages, and Exits

Assuming things are going well, this same company's series C round might be a raise of $187.5M or so (5 x $37.5M) on a pre-money valuation of between $562.5M and $750M (3x to 4x $187.5M).

Instead of raising funds at this stage, assume the company exits for $500M. A company of that size is likely to have at least $40M+ of debt. Additionally, let's also assume investment banking, legal and accounting fees equal to about 3% in the exit transaction.

Using that math, the $500M is reduced by $40M for debt and becomes $460M. Taking out the 3% investment banking fees, or $15M, we end up with sale proceeds distributable to shareholders of $445M.

Let's assume that, like our earlier cap table example, management, employees, and some pre-seed common stockholders hold a total of 54% of the company's total fully-diluted, as-converted shares at the time of exit.

This exit is large enough that the series A and B preferred shareholders will not elect to take their "non-participating 1x liquidation preferences" but will instead elect to have all preferred shares convert into common stock on a one-for-one basis in the exit – concepts discussed later in this chapter.

Multiplying $445M by .54 (54%) tells us the holders of common stock will receive $240.3M, and the holders of preferred stock will receive $204.7M.

Let's back into the split between series A and series B by assuming that the series B hold 20% of the total outstanding shares. This leaves the series A shareholders with 26% - i.e., 100% - 54% - 20% = 26%.

Thus, the series A investors would receive total proceeds of $115.7M and the series B investors would receive $89M.

Return on Investment ("ROI"). An investor's ROI, or return on investment, is calculated using this formula: Net Profit/Total Investment, with Net Profit equaling Total Return – Total Investment. The entire formula can be stated as (Total Return – Total Investment)/Total Investment.

For the new-money series A investors, this is an exit ROI of approximately 14.4x ($115.7M-$7.5M/$7.5M). The noteholders that converted into the series A round did even better, because of their 20% discount.

The series B investors' ROI would be 1.37x ($89M – 37.5M/$37.5M). This is much smaller, but still a 137% return. And it was earned over a much shorter period than the series A investors - a *"time value of money"* benefit - and likely during a less risky stage of the company's development.

Thus, while the two rules of thumb are probably more realistic for bigger financial centers like Silicon Valley and New York than they are for Portland or Phoenix, we can see that they pencil out to and align with VC exit expectations, particularly the notion that VCs depend on having at least 2 or 3 10x winners in each of their funds.

Perhaps the biggest winners in this example, though, are the common stockholders. Their 54% ownership was preserved by not selling too much equity at low valuations, while still raising the right amounts of money at the right times to support the growth necessary for a $500M exit.

More on exits in Chapter 16, *The Exit*.

Types of Financing Instruments

This section provides an overview of the four most common types of equity and debt instruments used in startup financings. These are the building blocks of financing transactions, from seed rounds to VC-led rounds.

Common Stock

Common stock is the most basic ownership interest in a corporation. A corporation needs to have at least one owner, and hence, it needs to issue at least one share of stock.

Common stock generally has none of the "bells and whistles" of preferred stock, discussed later. Each share generally has a single vote and represents a pro rata interest in the corporation, based on the total number authorized and issued. The rights of common stockholders are rarely discussed in a company's certificate of incorporation because they are essentially defined by statute and case law.

As discussed below, the rights and privileges associated with owning preferred stock are more complicated and are written into a company's Certificate of Incorporation, and also in other financing deal documents discussed later.

Par Value. We have already talked about par value in Chapter 7, *Entity Formation*. Par value is stated in a company's Certificate of Incorporation, and it's the minimum amount the company should receive for a share of its stock.

Par value for a Delaware corporation should be $.0001 or less for favorable application of the Assumed Par Value Method for calculating Delaware Franchise Tax.

And not having a par value is also a mistake for Delaware corporations, since it removes the Assumed Par Value Method as an option for determining the company's tax obligation.

Common Stock Financing Considerations. Founders, employees, directors, and consultants tend to receive common stock, but sophisticated outside investors are increasingly reluctant to take common stock. In general, sophisticated investors prefer the security of Convertible Notes, discussed next, or the economic and control rights associated with preferred stock.

A less obvious consideration regarding the use of common stock in early financing rounds is that doing so can have the negative effect of "pricing" a company's common stock higher for purposes of employee stock option grants.

As discussed earlier, Rule 409A requires every option grant to be issued at FMV. When a company only uses instruments like Convertible Notes, SAFEs, series seed preferred, and later series of preferred stock in its financings, it is easier for valuation experts to legitimately assign the company's common stock a lower FMV, since those instruments have superior control and economic rights over common stock, including liquidation preferences.

When a company sells common stock to investors in arm's length transactions, it may be challenging to argue that options issued later should have an exercise price lower than the price paid in the financing. Interestingly, 409A valuation reports frequently disregard this logic, assigning an FMV to a company's common lower than what third-party investors paid for the common stock in prior financings. This is particularly true where the company has subsequently issued preferred stock.

As we learned first in Chapter 7, preferred stock liquidation preferences are debt-like features, as they set a floor amount that preferred shareholders receive in a sale or liquidation of the company before the common shareholders receive anything. That floor amount of liquidation preference usually equals the price per share paid for the preferred shares in question.

Notwithstanding the downsides, whenever investors are willing to take common stock for their investment, it is well worth considering. Common stock financings are generally the most founder-friendly.

Convertible Notes

A Convertible Note is a *debt instrument* that automatically converts to equity upon the happening of certain defined occurrences – most commonly an upcoming series A preferred stock financing. And they almost always convert at a discount to what the new investors pay.

Convertible notes are common in early financing rounds because they defer the need for valuation and they are popular with wealthy angel investors and other sophisticated investors. Convertible notes combine the protections of debt with the greater potential upside of equity investments.

Maturity Date and Potential Default Issues. Unlike equity, debt has a "maturity date" by which it is supposed to be paid back. And even though few Convertible Notes are issued by startups with the idea that they *will be* paid back, they do have maturity dates, ranging from 12 months to 36 months.

The shorter the maturity date, the greater the risk that the issuing company might find itself in "default" if a conversion event (financing or sale) has not yet occurred.

Holders of notes that are in default are often willing to waive the default and avoid causing trouble for the company, but not always.

Noteholders often use this leverage to extract additional terms and concessions, like warrants, which can further complicate a struggling company's situation.

A note in default can also provide the basis for forcing a company into bankruptcy, among other harsh and potentially disruptive remedies.

Interest. All Convertible notes have an interest rate, generally ranging from 2% to 8%. If the notes mature and are paid off before converting into equity, the amount owed will include interest at the stated rate. If the notes convert, all accrued interest will be added to the amount invested (the principal) to determine the total dollar amount to be converted into equity, taking into account the notes conversion discount and valuation cap.

Interest can be either compounded or simple. When interest is compounded, it is added to principal on a regular basis, gradually increasing the amount of principle that is accruing interest.

Conversion Discount. Convertible notes commonly convert at a discount of 20%.

Thus, Convertible Noteholders expect to benefit from future investors' negotiating acumen regarding valuation and also from a discount on top of those negotiations. If a series of notes with a 20% discount converts into a series A round priced at $10 per share, the noteholders' 20% discount means they get their series A shares at $8 per share.

The discount is a reward for the greater risks they took funding the company at an earlier and less certain stage of development.

Valuation Caps. Many Convertible Notes also have a "valuation cap."

Valuation caps are a bit more complex than discounts. If a company's valuation runs up unexpectedly high between the Convertible Note issuance and the closing of a series A round, a valuation cap can create an even steeper percentage discount for the noteholders.

The table below shows different scenarios for investor Bob depending on whether his Convertible Note has a $15 million valuation cap, versus a lower, and more investor-favorable $12 million valuation cap.

The row where the number 33% is highlighted shows how the lower cap would provide a 33% discount at conversion instead of a 20% discount in the case of an $18 million pre-money valuation. In this case, Bob only "pays" $1.33 per share of series A preferred, while the other investors in that round pay $1.99 per share.

	A	B	C	D	E	F	G
	Bob's Convertible Note Valuation Cap	Series A Pre-$ Valuation	VC's Series-A Investment	VC's Series-A Share Price	Bob's Series-A Shares Issued	Bob's Series-A Share Price	Bob's Series-A Effective Discount
2	$ 15,000,000	$ 18,000,000	$ 4,500,000	$ 1.99	128,272.88	$ 1.59	20%
3	$ 15,000,000	$ 15,000,000	$ 3,750,000	$ 1.66	153,927.46	$ 1.33	20%
4	$ 15,000,000	$ 12,000,000	$ 3,000,000	$ 1.33	192,409.32	$ 1.06	20%
5	$ 12,000,000	$ 18,000,000	$ 4,500,000	$ 1.99	153,927.46	$ 1.33	33%
6	$ 12,000,000	$ 15,000,000	$ 3,750,000	$ 1.66	153,927.46	$ 1.33	20%
7	$ 12,000,000	$ 12,000,000	$ 3,000,000	$ 1.33	192,409.32	$ 1.06	20%

The justification for valuation caps is that the noteholders would not otherwise be rewarded adequately for the risks they took in supporting a company in its early stages if they end up with an unexpectedly small ownership interest following a conversion event.

In reality, the noteholders would only be converting at a higher share price and getting a smaller stake because the company unexpectedly grew to be worth much more, but that is the theory for valuation caps.

Readers who find themselves negotiating valuation caps will need to wrestle with and master those mathematical difficulties for themselves.

I worked with a startup recently that was just preparing to close a $1.4 million Convertible Note round with a shockingly low $4.5 million valuation cap. Despite being represented by a major law firm, the founder-CEO did not understand the role or implications of a valuation cap.

In explaining why I thought that cap needed to be raised to at least $8 million, if not $10 million, I asked the founder to consider several questions:

> "If the company's series A round is priced at $9 million, these noteholders would be entitled to a 50% discount. Will sophisticated investors want to invest in a round where $1.4M of the round is for half-priced shares? Won't that low cap put negative pressure on the valuation for the series A round? What ripple effects might a low series A round valuation then have on the cap table and on future rounds?"

Founders should also realize that a note's valuation cap can send a key signal to future investors on how to value a company.

Consequently, in negotiating a valuation cap with investors in a Convertible Note round, a good argument for pushing back on an artificially low valuation cap is the fact that it could significantly harm the company's ability to obtain an appropriate valuation in a later financing, thus harming the Convertible Note investor as well.

In practical terms, a $4.5 million cap could prevent the company from raising funds on a valuation giving those noteholders more than a 30% or 35% discount, potentially capping the company's valuation in the next round at a $6 million to $7 million.

We have learned about the negative ripple effects low valuations in financings can have on a cap table and on future financings. Following *Just-in-Time Finance*, the goal is to consistently raise the right amount of money at the right times and on the right terms. Valuation is key. Care should always be taken to avoid harming valuation in a future rounds.

In the case of the $4.5 million valuation cap, I suggested strongly that the CEO, "*Go back and tell the investors that a financial advisor has said the company needs to raise the valuation cap so that it doesn't harm the company's ability to bring in future investments, and that doing so is in everybody's best interests.*"

Interplay of Valuation Caps and Liquidation Preferences. Another important point to make about valuation caps is that they can result in noteholders receiving outsized liquidation preferences upon conversion.

Because Convertible Notes convert into preferred stock, upon conversion the noteholders receive liquidation preferences equal to the initial value of their preferred stock on a price-per-share basis.

By way of example, let's say the actual price per share in a series A round was $4.00. Let's say further that, because of a low valuation cap, noteholders converted into that series A round at a 50% discount, or $2.00 per share. The amount of the liquidation preference per share is $4.00, which is 100% greater than $2.00. Thus, while the conversion discount was only 50%, the liquidation preference benefit to the noteholders is 100% in this example. This paradoxical result is a function of the simple facts that, while 2 is only half (50%) of 4, 4 is twice as large as 2, or 100% larger.

Some experts suggest adding language to valuation cap clauses capping the amount of any eventual liquidation preferences. In appropriate situations, this is probably the right approach, but it raises its own complications. Liquidation preferences are defined in a company's Certificate of Incorporation. Capping them would seem to require converting those noteholders into a completely different class of preferred with a different liquidation preference formula – perhaps a series A-1 preferred.

The more direct and better course for all of the reasons already discussed, is to ensure that valuation caps are set high enough to anticipate actual valuation increases before the series A round.

The challenges posed by modeling the impacts of varying valuation caps and preferred stock liquidation preferences are another selling point for the top cap table management tools, which have excellent built-in modeling capabilities.

Acquisition Instead of Financing. A final area of complexity regarding Convertible Notes worth mentioning here is that they should address what happens in the event of a sale of the company before a series A financing.

While there are several different approaches for addressing a possible sale in lieu of a financing, a common and logical approach is to mirror the same discounts and valuation caps in the note payout formula, meaning a noteholder would receive their full investment back, plus the greater of a 20% return or any larger percentage triggered by an M&A valuation cap mechanism.

Some Convertible Notes provide substantially greater payouts upon an acquisition, as much as 1.5x or even 2x the amount of the note. Notes with such terms can severely complicate the ability to sell a company, particularly in a distressed sale.

Founders should try to avoid or negotiate down high acquisition payout clauses, as they will be much harder to negotiate down at the time of an acquisition.

A "Note" of Caution. Again, startups should be cautious about raising too much money with Convertible Notes relative to the amount they expect to raise in the financing into which the notes are likely to convert.

VCs and other sophisticated investors are generally fine with a reasonable amount of their financing round going to noteholders at a discount. But, as already discussed, a substantial amount of convertible debt at a 20% discount, or even a lesser amount with a low valuation cap, could cause VCs or others to pass on the deal or require that the company renegotiate its terms with the noteholders.

Raising $500,000 under Convertible Notes using a relatively high valuation cap should not cause issues for most strong startups, but raising more than $1 million in Convertible Notes with a potentially low valuation cap should be approached with caution.

Valuation caps can also become problematic when there is a substantial gap in time between the issuance of Convertible Notes and consummation of a series A. A big run-up in the company's valuation could theoretically entitle the noteholders to a windfall.

But smart, new money might not go along with such a windfall. Smart money might instead first require the company to renegotiate the notes to a higher cap before the smart money is willing to invest.

This is because ownership interests are essentially a "zero-sum game." One investor's equity windfall is another investor's loss, in the form of equity dilution.

As discussed later, valuation caps also appear in SAFEs, or Simple Agreements for Future Equity.

Before closing any financing round involving a valuation cap, founders should prepare a "pro forma cap table" that shows the potential impacts of the valuation cap at different pre and post-money valuations in the future to fully comprehend the potential for dilution and also the potential for disrupting future financings.

Sample Convertible Notes. The Cooley law firm offers an excellent free "Convertible Note generator" through its Cooley Go website. It can be found as of this writing by searching online for "Cooley Series Seed Convertible Note Financing Package."

An example of a Convertible Note produced by the generator with customized inputs regarding both a valuation cap and a similar M&A mechanism can be found in the BLSG Data Room under *Finance > Debt Instruments > Convertible Notes.*

SAFEs

In Silicon Valley, "Simple Agreements for Future Equity," or "SAFEs," have overtaken Convertible Notes in popularity for seed rounds. The SAFE was invented in 2013 for use by the influential startup accelerator "Y Combinator." The SAFE seems to be the instrument of choice for seed rounds now in Silicon Valley, driven in part by its exclusive use by Y Combinator.

Y Combinator offers open-source access to four versions of its SAFE financing documents at - https://www.ycombinator.com/documents/#safe

Examples of SAFEs can also be found in the BLSG Data Room at *Finance > Equity Financing Documents – Simple Agreement for Future Equity (SAFE).*

Benefits. SAFEs offer multiple advantages for companies. As proponents like to say, one advantage is in the name – "simple." Since SAFEs are simpler than preferred stock or Convertible Notes, financing legal expenses are lower.

The second most-often touted benefit is the deferral of valuation, a benefit of Convertible Notes too.

But SAFEs have other, more substantive, company-friendly attributes, such as no maturity date, no interest, and no investor voting rights. We discuss these later.

Conversion at a Discount. Like Convertible Notes, SAFEs convert to equity following specified triggering events, generally a financing or change of control, and often at a discount.

In a "qualifying" (conversion-triggering) financing, for example, if new investors are paying $1.00 per share, a SAFE with a 20% discount would allow the SAFE holder to convert at $.80 per share.

Discount rates range between 5% and 30%, with 20% being seemingly the most common rate.

Many investors also push for valuation caps in SAFEs, which work as they do in Convertible Notes, including providing investors with potentially problematic liquidation preference windfalls.

As mentioned earlier regarding Convertible Notes, given the concerns that future possible investors might raise about the relative percentage of discounted shares in a deal, companies should be careful about (i) raising too much money with SAFEs and (ii) offering SAFE investors unreasonably low valuation caps.

No Interest Rate or Maturity Date. Unlike Convertible Notes, SAFEs have no interest rate or maturity date. A Convertible Note's interest rate results in more shares on conversion or more cash in a liquidation, and a maturity date establishes a firm deadline by which the note must be paid back, absent an earlier conversion event.

If a Convertible Note is not paid or converted by the maturity date, noteholders have special rights to declare the notes in "default" and demand their repayment, rights which can be enforced through litigation or even forced bankruptcy.

Despite not having a maturity date, SAFEs generally provide contractual rights of repayment in the event of a bankruptcy or winding up that are supposedly on par with holders of common stock, although these are questions that have not been thoroughly tested.

Company-Friendly, Not Investor-Friendly. Although SAFEs have become very popular due to the influence of Y Combinator and those associated with it, the use of SAFEs is not without controversy.

Because of the absence of an interest rate or a maturity date, and because SAFEs are also not "equity," they are more "company-friendly," and, conversely, less investor-friendly.

Unlike noteholders, SAFE holders have no leverage in negotiating with companies in financial distress. As discussed in Chapter 17, *The Zone of Insolvency*, boards of insolvent companies owe special duties to creditors such as noteholders.

And unlike equity holders, SAFE holders have no voting rights or state law shareholder fiduciary protections.

Both the SEC and FINRA have issued formal statements warning investors of these concerns regarding SAFEs. Search for these regulatory advisories online or go to these links:.

https://www.sec.gov/oiea/investor-alerts-and-bulletins/ib_safes

https://www.finra.org/investors/insights/safe-securities

No Case Law. Lastly, unlike Convertible Notes, stock, and other investment instruments, SAFEs and the contractual rights they embody have yet to be tested and analyzed in any published court cases. This fact suggests greater uncertainty in the event of drafting errors and omissions, failure to close a financing triggering conversion, or insolvency.

Context Matters. In my personal view, SAFEs are a reasonable substitute for stock or debt in contexts where VC financing, and hence conversion to actual equity, is a fairly sure thing. Companies graduating from the Y Combinator program in San Francisco likely fit this description.

In contexts where VC funding is far less certain, SAFEs can expose investors to risks and downsides that may or may not be clear to them from the language of the SAFE documentation.

As discussed in Chapter 15, *Venture Capital Alternatives*, certain crowdfunding platforms have also weakened the rights of investors by substituting direct equity ownership with "Crowd SAFEs" and other investor-aggregating approaches.

Preferred Stock Overview

This discussion of preferred stock is limited to terms and practices common in startups. Publicly traded companies sometimes issue dividend-paying preferred shares. The considerations for issuing and investing in preferred shares in other contexts are significantly different than in the startup context.

VC Term Sheets and the Role of Preferred Stock. A VC Term Sheet outlines a particular VC's terms of investment in a particular deal – both "economic" and "control" terms.

Upon the closing of any VC-led financing, certain economic and control rights and privileges are coded into a new series of preferred stock by means of an amendment to a company's Certificate of Incorporation. Other economic and control rights are coded into other deal documents, like Shareholders Agreements, Voting Agreements, and Investor Rights Agreements.

The explanations of preferred stock concepts in this section are brief. We will discuss VC term sheets and preferred stock bells and whistles again, along with the full range of other VC deal documents, in Chapter 14, *VC Fundraising*.

For now, note that VC term sheets are written using many of the same headings used below, and with brief descriptions regarding each applicable economic and control provision. Sample VC term sheets like those in the BLSG Data Room offer great examples of how preferred stock provisions vary by deal.

Board and Shareholder Approval. As already mentioned, the rights and privileges of any series of preferred stock are mostly baked into a company's Articles (or Certificate) of Incorporation.

Any issuance of preferred stock must be approved by a company's board and its existing shareholders, including the specific amendments to the Certificate of Incorporation.

After an initial preferred stock issuance, subsequent preferred stock issuances must be approved by all classes of preferred, sometimes voting separately as classes, sometimes voting in groups of classes, and sometimes voting together with all shareholders, depending on what a company's Certificate of Incorporation requires at the time.

Each subsequent preferred class generally has certain rights that build upon and that are often superior in some respects to the prior classes, liquidation preferences in particular. But existing preferred shareholders voting as a class can sometimes use the leverage of their veto or blocking rights to ensure that subsequent shareholders do not get a substantially better deal than earlier classes.

As discussed below, existing shareholders also usually have protections called "preemptive" or "pro rata" rights. These rights, in varying degrees, allow investors to participate in future financings and, thus, to maintain their relative ownership position and also to share in any newly created or enhanced rights.

Amending the Certificate of Incorporation. With each new class of preferred, the company must file an "Amended and Restated Certificate of Incorporation" with the secretary of state of its state of incorporation.

With the first issuance of preferred stock, a company's Certificate of Incorporation goes from one or two pages to as many as twenty pages. Each subsequent new class of preferred stock causes a company's Certificate of Incorporation to grow in complexity.

When companies file with the SEC to go public, they must include their Certificate of Incorporation as one of many exhibits. Lyft, Inc. filed to go public in 2018. Its initial Certificate of Incorporation and its Amended and Restated Certificate of Incorporation from its IPO can be found in the BLSG Data Room at *Company Formation and Governance > Corporations > Articles of Incorporation*.

Before going public, Lyft issued A, B, C, D, E, F, G, H, and I series preferred stock. Lyft's initial 2007 Certificate of Incorporation was just a half page long. By the time of its IPO filing, it had grown to 24 pages – in small type.

Preferred Stock Key Provisions

With that overview, let's look at some of the key preferred stock rights and privileges.

<u>**Dividends.**</u> Preferred stock dividends in typical startup financings should essentially serve no purpose but to ensure that common stockholders do not receive dividends ahead of the preferred stockholders.

Earlier, we noted that startups rarely, if ever, declare or pay dividends. Startup investors are interested in major exits, not periodic dividends that impair growth. A startup's available cash is expected to be devoted to scaling up toward an IPO or sale.

Therefore, even though all preferred shares always have a stated dividend rate, they are also generally "non-cumulative." Cumulative dividends "accumulate" and must eventually be paid, whereas non-cumulative dividends are not owed to shareholders if not "declared" to be paid by a company's board.

Despite dividend clauses being irrelevant for most startups, the obligatory clauses in a Certificate of Incorporation are nonetheless somewhat wordy, as in this example:

> *<u>Non-Cumulative Preferred Stock Dividend Preference.</u> The Corporation shall not declare, pay or set aside any dividends on shares of any other class or series of capital stock of the Corporation (other than dividends on shares of Common Stock payable in shares of Common Stock) in any calendar year unless, in addition to obtaining any consents required elsewhere in this Restated Certificate, the holders of the Preferred Stock then outstanding shall first receive, or simultaneously receive, out of funds legally available therefor, a dividend on each outstanding share of Preferred Stock in an amount equal to 8% of the Original Issue Price (as defined below) per share of such series of Preferred Stock. The foregoing dividends shall not be cumulative and shall be paid only when, as and if declared by the Board of Directors of the Corporation (the "Board").*

<u>**Liquidation Preference.**</u> Two preferred stock attributes we cover again later in this section are "liquidation preferences" and "participating versus non-participating preferred." Although these are separate concepts in a company's Certificate of Incorporation, they operate together and often result in preferred shareholders receiving more money in an exit.

Consequently, for ease of discussion, we will refer to both liquidation preferences and participation rights as "liquidation preferences." These economic rights generally put all preferred stockholders in front of all common stockholders in any exit transaction that is not substantially greater than the amount of capital raised by a company.

In a modest exit, after debt holders, employees and creditors have been paid, liquidation preferences cause preferred stockholders to be paid out before the common stockholders – even if that means the common stockholders receive nothing.

Liquidation preference "seniority" can either be standard or *pari passu*. Standard simply means that holders of later-issued series of preferred (B, C, D, etc.) have seniority and are paid in sequence before the holders of earlier series of preferred. *Pari passu* means "equal footing" and results in multiple classes of preferred stock being paid pro rata from the same pool of proceeds if it is insufficient to cover a company's entire "liquidation stack," or "preference stack," in an exit. Preferred stock seniority is only an issue among preferred stockholders and normally does not impact founders directly.

As previously mentioned, liquidation preferences are generally eliminated in an IPO. In the event of a "qualified IPO" (usually over a minimum valuation or net fundraising amount), all of a company's preferred stock automatically converts to common stock.

Later in the chapter, we will use a series of nine short scenarios to illustrate the range of outcomes produced by different liquidation preferences in small, medium, and large exit transactions.

Redemption. Redemption is a right to have a company buy back one's preferred stock after a certain period of time, such as five years. The company normally also has the right to make redemption payments in installments over several years.

Redemption rights are certainly not founder-friendly or company-friendly, as they can theoretically pull the financial rug out from under a company, particularly by impairing its ability to pursue further financings.

For practical purposes, company boards face fiduciary challenges in actually honoring redemption rights when cash on hand is insufficient to do so and also operate the company in the best interests of all shareholders.

A 2017 Delaware case provides helpful guidance on these issues and the conflicts that can be set up when a VC, especially one with a board seat, seeks to force a redemption.

In that case, _Frederick Hsu Living Trust v. ODN Holding Corp._, the DE Court of Chancery took exception to the actions of a controlling VC shareholder enforcing its redemption rights, finding among other things that:

> *"The allegations of the Complaint support a reasonable inference that Oak Hill used its power as a controlling stockholder to cause the Company to sell assets and stockpile cash so that funds would be available when the Redemption Right ripened, when a loyal fiduciary would have deployed those funds for the benefit of the Company and its residual claimants. Through the Redemption Right, Oak Hill was able to extract the cash to the exclusion of the Company's other stockholders, thereby receiving a non-ratable benefit."*

Find the *ODN Holding Corp.* case by searching online or going here:
https://courts.delaware.gov/Opinions/Download.aspx?id=255860

In addition to common law fiduciary standards, state corporate laws can also restrict the exercise of redemption rights. Section 160 of the DGCL prohibits a corporation from redeeming its shares when the capital of the corporation is "impaired," or when the redemption would cause any impairment of the capital.

Delaware common law also prohibits a corporation from redeeming its shares when the corporation is insolvent or would be rendered insolvent by the redemption. As discussed in Chapter 17, *The Zone of Insolvency*, a company that is unable to pay all of its debts is technically "insolvent."

Redemption rights should be resisted by companies with leverage to push back. Even if frequently unenforceable, their existence can potentially limit or interfere with a company's financing options.

A provision disallowing redemption could read something like this:

> *Neither this Corporation nor the holders of Preferred Stock shall have the unilateral right to call or redeem or cause to have called or redeemed any shares of the Preferred Stock.*

Or it might be even simpler, like this:

> *Redemption. The Preferred Stock is not redeemable at the option of the holder.*

Voluntary Conversion. Preferred stockholders always have the right to voluntarily convert their preferred stock to common stock at any time. Conversion from preferred to common is subject to what is called a "conversion ratio."

The following example adopts the common practice of basing the conversion ratio on what is called an "Original Issue Price" and a "Conversion Price." The Conversion Price is subject to adjustment for dividends and anti-dilution, both discussed later.

> *Each share of Preferred Stock shall be convertible, at the option of the holder thereof, at any time after the date of issuance of such share at the office of this Corporation or any transfer agent for such stock, into such number of fully paid and nonassessable shares of Common Stock as is determined by dividing the Original Issue Price for each such series of Preferred Stock by the Conversion Price applicable to such share, determined as hereafter provided, in effect on the date the certificate is surrendered for conversion.*

When would preferred shareholders want to voluntarily convert their preferred to common? Voluntary conversion is always exercised in exits where doing so results in a greater financial gain than the applicable liquidation preference.

Preferred shareholders also sometimes convert to common when doing so helps them achieve the necessary margin of voting control in a particular common stockholder vote, say, to approve (or force) a financing or sale of the company.

Mandatory/Automatic Conversion. The primary trigger for mandatory, or automatic, conversion of preferred shares into common shares is an IPO. That language can look like this:

> *Automatic Conversion. Each share of Preferred Stock shall automatically be converted into shares of Common Stock at the Conversion Price then in effect for such series of Preferred Stock as adjusted pursuant to Article IV.B.4(d)(ii)(C), if applicable, immediately prior to the closing of this Corporation's sale of its Common Stock in a firm commitment underwritten public offering*

pursuant to an effective registration statement under the Securities Act of 1933, as amended (the "Act"), resulting in gross proceeds to the Corporation (before deducting underwriter discounts and commissions) of at least $150,000,000....

Automatic conversion can often also be forced by the vote of a percentage of the holders of the specific class of preferred. Voting thresholds for automatic conversion range from a majority of the shares voted to supermajorities like 66% or 75%.

Anti-dilution. In Articles of Incorporation, anti-dilution provisions are often captioned along the lines of "Conversion Price Adjustments of Preferred Stock." Anti-dilution clauses consist mostly of dry mathematical formulas that are too boring to add here.

Despite their mathematical complexity, anti-dilution provisions fall into two relatively intuitive categories: (i) full-ratchet and (ii) weighted-average.

Full-ratchet anti-dilution has been described by at least one writer as a complete "do-over." If an investor with full-ratchet anti-dilution protection paid $2.00 per share and investors in a later preferred stock down round only paid $1.00 per share, the earlier investor's conversion ratio would be adjusted to reflect an original purchase price of $1 per share.

This adjustment to the original purchase price increases the number of shares of common stock the investor will receive for her preferred stock upon conversion.

Under weighted-average anti-dilution, in the event of a later down round, the conversion ratio of the earlier preferred shareholders would also be adjusted, but not on a linear, dollar-for-dollar basis tied exclusively to price per share. Rather, weighted-average anti-dilution accounts for the amount of shares sold in the down round relative to the total shares outstanding and adjusts the conversion price of the existing preferred shares to a new weighted-average price.

Weighted-average anti-dilution can also be "broad-based," which includes in the calculation of total shares outstanding all options, warrants, and shares issuable under convertible securities, or "narrow-based," which excludes those interests from the calculation. Broad-based, weighted-average anti-dilution is more company-favorable than narrow-based, as it will generally produce less severe conversion price adjustments.

Anti-dilution can often be negotiated away by founders in seed and pre-seed rounds since anti-dilution is less common when smaller investments are involved. In series A rounds and later, anti-dilution is a common fact of life. Founders should avoid unwinnable battles with prospective investors. On the other hand, it is usually quite appropriate to hold the line at weighted-average anti-dilution instead of full-ratchet.

Voting Rights. A Certificate of Incorporation will often have a general provision concerning votes per share (usually one) and provisions for when and how the common and preferred vote separately or together. The following clause is typical:

General. On any matter presented to the stockholders of the Corporation for their action or consideration at any meeting of stockholders of the Corporation (or by written consent of stockholders in lieu of a meeting), the holder of each share of Preferred Stock shall have the right to one vote for each share of Common Stock into which such share of Preferred Stock could then be converted. With respect to such vote, and except as otherwise expressly provided herein or as required by applicable law, such holder shall have full voting rights and powers equal to the voting rights and powers of the holders of Common Stock, and shall be entitled, notwithstanding any provision hereof, to notice of any stockholders' meeting in accordance with the Bylaws of this Corporation, and shall be entitled to vote, together with holders of Common Stock as a single class, with respect to any matter upon which holders of Common Stock have the right to vote....

Following these general provisions, it is common to next see clauses concerning how directors are to be elected by the common stockholders separately, by the preferred stockholders separately, or by the common and preferred stockholders voting together. A typical clause might look like this:

Election. For so long as at least 7,730,536 shares of Preferred Stock remains outstanding (as such number is adjusted for stock splits and combinations of shares and for dividends paid on the Preferred Stock in shares of such stock), the holders of record of the shares of Preferred Stock, exclusively and as a separate class, shall be entitled to elect two (2) directors of the Corporation (the "Preferred Directors"). The holders of record of the shares of Common Stock, exclusively and as a separate class, shall be entitled to elect two (2) directors of the Corporation (the "Common Directors"). The holders of record of the shares of Common Stock and of every other class or series of voting stock (including the Preferred Stock), voting together as a single class on an as-converted basis, shall be entitled to elect the remaining number of directors of the Corporation (the "Remaining Directors"). For administrative convenience, the initial Preferred Directors may also be appointed by the Board in connection with the approval of the initial issuance of Series A Preferred Stock without a separate action by the holders of a majority of the Preferred Stock.

Protective Provisions. Protective provisions are another genre of voting right. These rights are also informally referred to as "blocking rights," or "veto rights."

Protective provisions empower preferred stockholders, voting separately as a whole from common stockholders, or as individual preferred stock classes, to block or veto transactions, including issuances of new shares, asset sales, and even IPOs that do not meet certain minimum dollar amount requirements.

Existing preferred holders sometimes use their blocking rights to push for higher valuations in future financings, particularly if they are not participating in the financings.

Blocking rights also come into play when a company is struggling financially and wants to conduct a down round financing with potentially harsh impacts on prior preferred investors.

Many cramdown financings (severe down rounds) are blocked by existing preferred holders who have no interest in putting more cash into a struggling company but who also don't want their ownership interest to be diluted. Cramdowns are discussed in Chapter 17, *The Zone of Insolvency.*

Blocking rights also come into play when a struggling company is unable to attract new investors. Some of the company's later investors might want to sell it for whatever can be obtained and move on. In a situation where liquidation preferences are not *pari passu*, the holders of an earlier series of preferred with their own protective provisions might use them to block the transaction in order to negotiate concessions from the senior preferred series – perhaps to negotiate for *pari passu* treatment in any sale.

As a company goes through multiple preferred stock financings, the investors in each new round, say a series B round, will usually push for separate protective provisions allowing them to vote as a distinct share class on financings, exit transactions, and other similar events.

Founders with leverage should consider pushing back. Forcing all series of preferred stock to vote together on significant transactions can provide critical flexibility for a company and its board and limit the effects of self-interested gamesmanship between and among share classes.

A good compromise for getting investors in a new class of preferred to go along with voting together with all preferred classes on future financings and exits is to allow the new class to vote individually on any changes to its own class rights and privileges. The following sample protective rights provisions do just that – force all preferred classes to vote together on most things, but allow the series B holders to vote separately to protect their specific rights.

> *3.3 Preferred Stock Protective Provisions. For so long as at least 7,730,536 shares of Preferred Stock remain outstanding (as such number is adjusted for stock splits and combinations of shares and for dividends paid on the Preferred Stock in shares of such stock), the Corporation shall not, either directly or indirectly by amendment, merger, consolidation or otherwise, do any of the following without (in addition to any other vote required by law or this Restated Certificate) the written consent, or affirmative vote at a meeting or evidenced in writing, of the holders of a majority of the then outstanding shares of Preferred Stock, consenting or voting together as a single class on an as-converted basis:*
>
> > *(a) alter, waive or change the rights, powers or preferences of the Preferred Stock set forth in the certificate of incorporation or bylaws of the Corporation, as then in effect, in a way that adversely affects the Preferred Stock;*
> >
> > *(b) increase or decrease the authorized number of shares of Common Stock or Preferred Stock (or any series thereof);*
> >
> > *(c) authorize or create (by reclassification or otherwise), or obligate itself to issue, any new class or series of capital stock having rights, powers or preferences set forth in the Restated Certificate, as then in effect, that are senior to or on a parity with any series of Preferred Stock or authorize or create (by reclassification or otherwise), or obligate itself to issue, any security convertible into or exercisable for any such new class or series of capital stock;*
> >
> > *(d) redeem or repurchase any shares of Common Stock, Preferred Stock or Options, other than (i) pursuant to an agreement with an employee, consultant, director or other service provider to the Corporation or any of its wholly owned subsidiaries (collectively, "Service Providers") giving the Corporation the right to repurchase shares at no greater than the original cost*

thereof upon the termination of services, (ii) an exercise of a right of first refusal in favor of the Corporation pursuant to an agreement with any Service Provider, which exercise has been approved by the Board or (iii) as approved by the Board;

(e) *declare or pay any dividend or otherwise make a distribution to holders of Preferred Stock or Common Stock, other than a dividend on the Common Stock payable in shares of Common Stock;*

(f) *liquidate, dissolve or wind-up the business and affairs of the Corporation, effect any Deemed Liquidation Event, effect any reclassification or recapitalization of the outstanding capital stock of the Corporation or consent, agree or commit to any of the foregoing without conditioning such consent, agreement or commitment upon obtaining the approval required by this Section 3.3;*

(g) *constituting the Board; increase or decrease the authorized number of directors*

(h) *otherwise amend, alter, restate, or repeal any provision of this Restated Certificate or the bylaws of the Corporation; or*

(i) *amend this Section 3.3.*

3.4 Series B Preferred Stock Protective Provisions. For so long as at least 5,000,000 shares of Series B Preferred Stock remain outstanding (as such number is adjusted for stock splits and combinations of shares and for dividends paid on the Preferred Stock in shares of such stock), the Corporation shall not, either directly or indirectly by amendment, merger, consolidation or otherwise, do any of the following without (in addition to any other vote required by law or this Restated Certificate) the written consent, or affirmative vote at a meeting and evidenced in writing, of the holders of a majority of the then outstanding shares of Series B Preferred Stock, consenting or voting together as a single class on an as-converted basis:

(a) *increase or decrease the authorized number of shares of Series B Preferred Stock; or*

(b) *alter, waive or change the rights, powers or preferences of the Series B Preferred Stock set forth in the certificate of incorporation or bylaws of the Corporation, as then in effect, in a way that adversely affects the Series B Preferred Stock but that does not so affect all of the other series of Preferred Stock (provided that the authorization or issuance of a new series of preferred stock, on its own, is not deemed to have an adverse effect).*

Preemptive Rights. Preemptive rights, also called "pro rata rights," "rights of first offer," and "subscription rights," are rights to participate in future equity offerings, generally on a pro rata basis.

Preemptive rights are effectively a form of "anti-dilution" protection. They enable an investor to maintain the same ownership percentage and also benefit from the rights and privileges of the new class of securities, including, among others, the right to vote with that new class.

Shareholders with preemptive rights are generally entitled to notice of future offerings and given a period of time to decide whether to exercise their rights to participate in the offering.

Preemptive rights can be granted in any equity financing – common or preferred – but founders should be cautious about offering earlier investors preemptive rights. VCs sometimes frown on allowing smaller investors into their rounds.

As such, it is common for a Certificate of Incorporation to specifically disallow preemptive rights except pursuant to a separate written agreement between the company and a specific stockholder, as in this sample clause:

> *No stockholder of the Corporation shall have a right to purchase shares of capital stock of the Corporation sold or issued by the Corporation except to the extent that such a right may from time to time be set forth in a written agreement between the Corporation and any stockholder.*

Sample term sheet language for preemptive rights:

> *Each Major Investor, as defined herein, shall have preemptive rights to purchase their pro-rata share of new securities issued by the Company, subject to customary exceptions.*

Preemptive rights can be written into the Certificate of Incorporation, but they are also commonly addressed in Shareholders Agreements.

Drag-Along. Drag-along provisions, sometimes called "bring-along" provisions, are more likely to be inserted into a Shareholders Agreement or a Voting Agreement, and are less commonly found in a company's Certificate of Incorporation.

Drag-along rights give a defined group of shareholders, say, for example, a majority of the holders of the series A preferred, the right to force other shareholders, usually other preferred and common holders, to go along with certain types of transactions approved by the shareholders holding the drag-along rights.

Drag-along rights generally allow VCs to force the sale of a company, even against the wishes of the founders or other shareholders.

Drag-along rights also prevent minority shareholders from demanding what are called "appraisal rights" under state corporate law. Also called "dissenter's rights," appraisal rights are statutory rights of minority shareholders to dissent to a proposed transaction and have a court determine the value of their stock. Drag-along clauses are contractual waivers of those rights.

Given the finite life of a VC fund, VCs need the ability to force liquidity events to timely provide returns to their limited partners. That's a key part of the bargain in taking VC investments.

Drag-along rights also generally enable a defined group of stockholders to force financings. As discussed already, VCs want their portfolio companies on high-growth trajectories. This can require successive financings that founders might otherwise vote against to avoid dilution.

An abbreviated drag-along provision in a Certificate of Incorporation might look like this example:

> *Drag-Along Transactions. (i) In the event that one or more holders of the Corporation's Series A Preferred Stock holding a majority of the then-issued and outstanding shares of all classes of the Series A Preferred Stock (the "Selling Holders") determine to take any action that would cause*

a Sale Transaction (as defined in Section 7.5) to occur, the Corporation or the Selling Holders (or a designated representative acting on behalf of the Selling Holders) will have the right to deliver written notice thereof to all other holders of the Corporation's Series A Preferred Stock and Common Stock (the "Dragged Holders"). Such written notice shall contain a description of the material terms and conditions of the Sale Transaction, including without limitation the identity of the Third Party Purchaser and the amount and form of per share consideration to be paid by the Third Party Purchaser.

(ii) In the event notice of a Sale Transaction is given by the Corporation or by or on behalf of the Selling Holders to the Dragged Holders in accordance with the preceding paragraph, all shares of Series A Preferred Stock and Common Stock held by the Dragged Holders (or the applicable portion of such shares as set forth in the next sentence) shall be sold or transferred to the Third Party Purchaser, for the same type and amount of per share consideration and on the same terms as the Selling Holders, upon consummation of the Sale Transaction (free and clear of any liens and duly endorsed for transfer, or accompanied by duly endorsed stock powers). In the case of a Sale Transaction involving less than 100% of the then-issued and outstanding shares of the Corporation's Series A Preferred Stock and Common Stock, a portion of the shares of Series A Preferred and Common Stock held by the Dragged Holders shall be sold or transferred in the Sale Transaction, which portion shall correspond to the portion of such shares held by the Selling Holders (in the aggregate) that are proposed to be included in such Sale Transaction.

Tag-Along Rights. Preferred shareholders with "tag-along" rights, also called co-sale rights, have the right to participate in any sales of stock by certain other shareholders, sometimes defined as "Major Shareholders" or "Key Holders." In a startup, these are usually the founders and maybe other significant, specifically-identified shareholders.

A shareholder's right to participate in a sale of shares, a liquidity opportunity, is generally limited by a formula reflecting their overall equity ownership percentage. As an example, a shareholder with a 5% interest in a company might have the right to sell an amount equal to 5% of the amount of the overall liquidity event.

Like drag-along rights, tag-along rights are more likely to be covered in a Shareholders Agreement or a Voting Agreement than in a company's Certificate of Incorporation. This is partly because Shareholders Agreements and Voting Agreements are private documents that are not filed with a secretary of state, so they are more discreet, and they are also easier to amend (change).

A Tag-Along provision might read like this one:

Tag-Along Rights. Other than Permitted Transfers (as defined below), if a holder or holders of Common Stock (collectively referred to as the "Transferring Shareholder(s)") propose(s) to sell, transfer or otherwise dispose of (a "Transfer") a number of shares of Common Stock representing twenty percent (20%) or more of the Common Stock then outstanding, then the Transferring Shareholder shall give written notice (the "Tag-Along Sale Notice") to the Corporation and the other holders of Common Stock at least twenty (20) Business Days (as defined below) prior to the closing of such Transfer and the other holders of Common Stock shall have the right (but not the obligation) to include in such sale up to all of the shares of Common Stock held by such holder (the "Tag-Along Right"). If the proposed purchaser elects to purchase less than all of the shares of Common Stock offered for sale as a result of the holders' exercise of their respective Tag-Along Rights, the Transferring Shareholder(s) and each holder exercising its Tag-Along Right will have the right to include its Pro Rata Portion of the Common Stock to be Transferred to the proposed purchaser on the same terms and conditions and for the same price (the "Tag-Along Price") as the Transferring Shareholder(s) including without limitation in exchange for a pro rata share of all consideration received by the Transferring Shareholder(s).

Tag-along rights in LLCs sometimes have a different purpose than merely allowing partial participation in a liquidity opportunity. In LLCs, tag-along rights sometimes prevent a founder from selling his or her shares to a third party unless the purchaser is also willing to purchase all of the co-founder's shares too. The purpose is to force a buyout of a co-founder in the event his or her co-founder wants to bail out. This prevents a non-selling co-founder from being forced to be business partners with a stranger.

Pay-to-Play. Pay-to-play provisions are the least common of the preferred stock provisions discussed in this section. They are usually only introduced in difficult down round financings and can have very negative repercussions for earlier preferred round investors.

By "difficult down round financing," I mean a financing where the company is having trouble putting together a round at a price higher than or equal to the prior round. The lack of support from existing investors in such cases is often taken as a bad sign by potential new investors.

Companies in this position are usually struggling to achieve previously forecasted financial and operational objectives.

Some existing investors might be secretly weighing cutting their losses or pushing the founders and other investors to consider other options, like a fire sale or other M&A transaction to salvage a partial return on amounts invested.

But the board and management, honoring their fiduciary duties to maximize enterprise value, may believe a down round financing is necessary. They and other key investors may also believe a "pay-to-play" clause is critical for bringing earlier investors to the company's support, especially if new investors are unlikely.

Pay-to-play schemes vary widely, but the essential idea is always the same: existing investors who do not participate in a current financing or in future financings, will lose rights. Pay-to-play terms can apply only to a single, currently proposed transaction, or to a current transaction and to future transactions, or they can apply only to future transactions.

Sometimes the loss of rights under a pay-to-play scheme involves only losing anti-dilution rights or certain voting rights.

In more extreme cases, pay-to-play provisions can force the conversion of non-players' preferred stock to common stock, causing the loss of all preferred stock rights and privileges, including liquidation preferences.

When a company is doing great and investors are clamoring to get in, pay-to-play clauses are unnecessary. When a company is struggling, influential existing or potential investors will impose them as a hammer to encourage pro rata participation by existing investors and, arguably, to punish existing investors who stay on the sidelines while others risk more capital to keep a company alive.

Transactions called cramdowns anchor the extreme end of the "difficult financing" spectrum. In cramdown financings, a company's valuation will be lowered substantially from earlier rounds, necessitating the issuance of very large numbers of shares of a new class of preferred.

Investors who are unwilling or unable to participate in the round will not only be substantially diluted by the issuance of large numbers of shares at lower prices, they may also potentially lose key rights as a result of pay-to-play provisions.

Completing a cramdown financing usually requires getting a majority of the existing preferred shareholders to vote to waive anti-dilution provisions. Anti-dilution provisions can defeat the purpose of a cramdown. Cramdowns are structured to be highly dilutive – play or pay dearly.

These and other harsh aspects of difficult financings are often facilitated by or forced through by existing drag-along provisions.

A typical pay-to-play clause in a VC term sheet for a series B financing might look like this (brackets indicate alternative provisions in the template):

> *Unless the holders of 50% of the Series B elect otherwise, on any subsequent down round all Major Investors are required to purchase their pro rata share of the securities set aside by the Board for purchase by the Major Investors. All Preferred Shares of any Major Investor failing to do so will automatically [lose anti-dilution rights] [lose liquidation preferences] [lose the right to participate in future rounds] [convert to Common Stock and lose the right to a Board seat, if applicable].*

Liquidation Preferences

As noted earlier, no preferred stock attribute is more important than liquidation preferences. They put preferred shareholders ahead of common shareholders in a sale of the company if it's not a home run.

Consequently, we will give liquidation preferences special attention, including several examples that support three principles founders should follow:

- delay granting liquidation preferences as long as good judgment allows,
- when they cannot be avoided (series A financings and beyond), "1x, non-participating" is a reasonable position in most situations and should be the goal, and
- capped-participating with a low cap (1.5x) is the next best alternative.

Preference or Pro Rata? As explained in detail below, preferred shareholders make a choice in any exit: (i) take the liquidation preference or (ii) convert to common and receive the value of their "pro rata" ownership interest.

In small liquidity events, preferred shareholders tend to take their liquidity preference; in bigger liquidity events, they tend to take their pro rata payout. Basic math and economic self-interest always govern, and preferred shareholders always choose the larger payout.

Preference Multiplier. All liquidity preferences are stated in terms of a "1x" preference, a "2x" preference, or some other number, including numbers with a decimal, such as a "1.5x" preference.

In the case of a series A share class with a 1x liquidation preference, the liquidation preference is equal to the amount raised in the series A round. In mathematical terms, "1x" means "1 x the amount raised."

If that series A round raised $10 million, the amount of the series A liquidation preference would be $10 million. If the series A shares had a 1.5x liquidation preference, it would equal $15 million, or 1.5 x $10 million.

As will be reinforced elsewhere, 1x is by far the most common multiple across all VC deals, whether A round or H round.

Participating, Non-Participating, and Capped Participating. Every liquidation multiplier is supplemented by another term – whether the preferred stock in question is "participating," "non-participating," or "capped participating." Participation rights are very closely related to liquidation preferences and generally discussed together, but technically they are separate rights.

"Participating," also called "fully participating," means that, after receiving their liquidation preference, participating preferred shareholders also receive a pro rata share of the remaining sale proceeds with common shareholders.

In contrast, non-participating means that, after receiving their liquidation preference, those shareholders receive none of the remaining sale proceeds, which are allocated to the common stockholders on a pro rata basis.

Capped participating means the preferred holders receive a pro rata share of the remaining proceeds, but their total payments are capped, often at 1.5x, 2x, or 3x their initial investment.

Liquidation Preference Examples. It is difficult to understand liquidation preferences and participation rights without thinking through some examples showing how different multipliers and participation rights interact across various funding rounds and exit amounts.

The following are three funding round and exit scenarios, each analyzed against three different liquidation preference formulas: (i) 1x non-participating, (ii) 1x participating, and (iii) 1x participating with a 3x cap.

As a reminder, under *Preference or Pro Rata?*, we learned this:

> *"… preferred shareholders make a choice in any liquidity event: (i) take the liquidation preference or (ii) convert to common and receive the value of their "pro rata" ownership interest.*
>
> *In small liquidity events, preferred shareholders tend to take their liquidity preference; in big liquidity events, they tend to take their pro rata payout. Basic math and economic self-interest always govern; preferred shareholders always choose the larger payout."*

In the following examples, "Founders" really means "all of the common stockholders," and "Investors" means the series A investors.

Study the following infographics before looking at the *"Case Explanations"* below them. As to each of the 9 Cases, figure out (i) whether the series A shareholders would choose *preference* or *pro rata* and (ii) why that choice resulted in the financial outcomes shown.

Scenario 1 and Cases 1 – 3

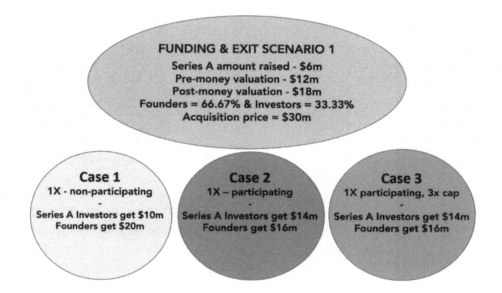

- **Case 1:** The series A investors choose *pro rata*. Their 33.33% pro rata interest yields a $10 million payout. That is $4 million more than their $6 million (1x non-participating) liquidation preference would have yielded.

- **Case 2:** The series A investors chose *preference*. They received $6 million plus $8 million ($30 million – $6 million x .3333 = $8 million), or $14 million. $14 million is $4 million more than the $10 million they received in Case 1 when they chose *pro rata*.

  The series A's 1x liquidation preference of $6 million left $24 million ($30 million - $6 million) to be shared 33.33% (fully participating) with the series A holders and 66.67% with the common stockholders. In this case, 33.33% of $24 million added $8 million to the payout.

- **Case 3:** Case 3 is the same outcome as Case 2. The 3x cap would only limit payouts above 3 x $6 million, or $18 million. The payout of $14 million falls under that cap and is not limited by it.

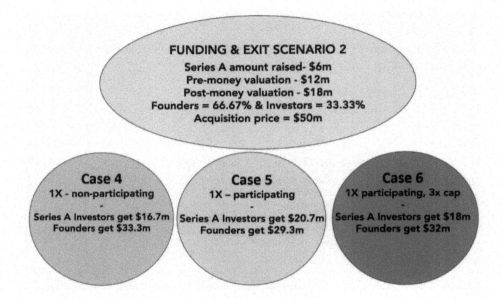

- **Case 4:** The series A investors chose *pro rata*. Their 33.33% pro rata interest yields a $16.7 million payout. That is $10.7 million more than their $6 million liquidation preference would have yielded.

- **Case 5:** The series A investors chose *preference*. They received $6 million plus $14.7 million, or $20.7 million total. $20.7 million is $4 million more than the $16.7 million they received in Case 4 when they chose pro rata.

  The series A's 1x liquidation preference of $6 million left $44 million ($50 million - $6 million) to be shared 33.33% (fully participating) with the series A holders and 66.67% with the common stockholders. In this case, 33.33% of $44 million added $14.7 million to the series A investors' payout.

- **Case 6:** The series A investors chose *preference*, but the 3x cap limited the payout to $18 million, or 3 x $6 million. In this case, the payout falls between the payouts in Cases 4 and 5. It is $1.3 million more than their pro rata interest would have yielded, but the 3x cap limited the fully-participating payout from Case 5 by $2.7 million.

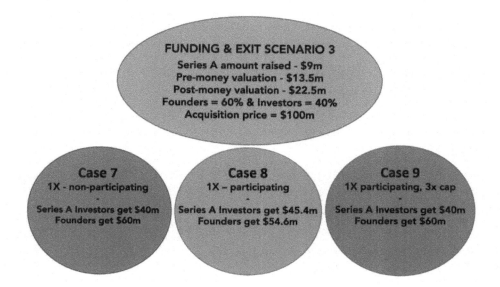

- **Case 7:** The series A investors chose *pro rata*. Their 40% pro rata interest yields a $40 million payout from the $100 million exit. That is $31 million more than their $9 million (1x non-participating) liquidation preference would have yielded.

- **Case 8:** The series A investors chose preference. They received $9 million plus $36.4 million, or $45.4 million. That payout is $5.4 million more than the $40 million they received in Case 7 when they chose pro rata.

  The series A's 1x liquidation preference of $9 million left $91 million ($100 million - $9 million) to be shared 40% (fully participating) with the series A holders and 60% with the common stockholders. In this case, 40% of $91 million added $36.4 million to the series A investors' payout.

- **Case 9:** The series A investors chose *pro rata* as they did in Case 7 because the 3x cap would have limited their payout to $27 million, or 3 x $9 million. In this case, the 3x cap made the liquidation preference far less advantageous than *pro rata*.

A few summary observations about preferred stock liquidation preferences:

- They become less material as exit consideration increases, except in the case of uncapped, fully participating preferred.

- Founders and their fellow common stockholders always do better in bigger exits, but this is even more true in the context of a large liquidation preference stack, or "liquidation preference overhang."

- As noted at the beginning of this section, founders should consider following these three tips:

- Avoid agreeing to liquidation preferences as long as prudence allows, particularly before an A round.

- When liquidation preferences cannot be avoided, "1x, non-participating" is a reasonable position in most situations, even VC-led rounds, and should be the goal.

- Capped-participating with a low cap is the next best alternative, with a 1.5x cap being a reasonable negotiating goal.

Liquidation Waterfall – Standard Seniority Versus Pari Passu. Multiple VC-led rounds invariably lead to highly complex cap tables with extraordinarily complex "liquidation waterfalls" – the term used to describe how liquidation preferences operate across multiple classes of preferred.

Any founder or startup advisor who has been through both an A round and a B round will start to understand how these preference waterfalls work. It is unnecessary for our purposes in this book to go too deeply into the subject, but at a high level, liquidation preferences generally operate one of two ways – *pari passu* or standard seniority.

As we learned earlier, *pari passu* is Latin for "equal footing." It is the less common approach, but it seems very common among big "unicorn" startups ($1+ billion valuation) with well-known founders and powerful VC backers.

In a *pari passu* structure, each class of preferred is paid out pro rata with the other preferred classes. In an exit where there is not enough money to pay off the entire preference overhang, each class receives a share of the sale proceeds pro rata to that class's share of the company's overall preferred stock funding.

When *pari passu* is not the agreed methodology, standard seniority rules come into play. This means that the most recent classes receive their liquidation preferences ahead of each class in front of them, with the series A paid last, followed by the common stockholders.

This very common approach to paying out liquidation preferences is consistent with another general theme of successive financing rounds – that they tend to build on each other. Overreaching terms in early rounds are likely to be amplified in later rounds, to the potential detriment of those earlier investors who initially overreached.

When early investors overreach in term sheet negotiations, it sometimes helps to explain how overly aggressive terms in early financings can backfire in later financings, particularly under standard seniority.

Series Seed Preferred Stock

Series seed preferred stock is a form of preferred with only some of the above preferred stock rights and privileges.

Find an example of a Series Seed term sheet in the BLSG Archive under *Finance > Equity Financing Documents > Series Seed Documents*.

While series seed templates differ, they generally include, among other provisions:

- 1x non-participating liquidation preference,

- 1:1 voluntary and mandatory conversion to common stock,

- preemptive rights to participate in future financings,

- separate class voting rights to approve changes to the series seed shares, a sale of the company and certain other transactions,

- a board seat,

- weighted-average anti-dilution, and

- information rights regarding company progress and financial results.

Another common feature of series seed term sheets is a clause that says the series seed investors "will be given the same rights as the next series of Preferred Stock."

Rights and privileges that are candidates for exclusion in series seed deals include:

- registration rights,

- anti-dilution,

- board seat (observation rights instead),

- full protective provisions,

- drag-along rights, and

- co-sale rights.

Given the growing popularity of SAFEs in seed rounds and the continuing popularity of Convertible Notes with certain investors, use of series seed preferred stock in seed rounds is likely somewhat limited.

A key distinction between series seed preferred on the one hand, and SAFEs and Convertible Notes on the other, is that a series seed preferred round is "priced." The company and the investors must come up with a valuation.

Series seed preferred, versus Convertible Notes or SAFEs, is probably most often used in certain VC-funded seed rounds as a matter of VC firm preference.

Series seed preferred may also be a good choice in a second or third seed financing round, where offering more instruments with discounts on future preferred issuances would be imprudent.

In fact, some series seed preferred financings might be purposely structured as such to constitute "qualifying transactions" that trigger the conversion of outstanding Convertible Notes and SAFEs at a lower valuation than in a later series A financing.

Warrants

Overview. Warrants and stock options are almost identical. They are both contracts for the future purchase of stock at a fixed price.

For our purposes, options are used for equity compensation and warrants are financing instruments that companies sometimes issue to "sweeten" financings.

Warrants are more common in later financings, particularly difficult later financings, but investors sometimes ask for them in early financings.

Most angel investors, strategics, VC seed funds, and friends and family investors do not ask for warrants. They are usually required, though, by venture debt lenders, certain institutional angel investor groups, and sometimes by other professional investors.

For a variety of reasons, requests for warrants should generally be resisted before a company's series A round. The cleaner way to make an offering more attractive is to lower the valuation and per-share price in a round.

Warrants on an early-stage or growth-stage company's cap table can be a sign of financial difficulties. Their presence in an offering can also be seen as a red flag since they are often associated with financings that are struggling due to lack of investor interest.

The issuance of warrants to early investors often prompts future investors to demand them too, compounding dilution and cap table complexity problems.

Warrant Overhang. The issuance of warrants in a seed round can complicate future financing rounds, particularly if they were priced well below the valuation in a later round. In those situations, warrants might dampen new investor interest just like dilutive Convertible Note discounts and valuation caps

Warrant Accounting and Cap Table Complexity Issues. Warrants can also raise complex accounting classification issues. While these accounting concerns are worse for publicly traded companies, private company CFOs also usually lament accounting for warrants.

The presence of warrants on a cap table also adds to its complexity. In situations where multiple investors receive warrants with different exercise prices and expiration dates, it becomes increasingly difficult for potential investors to understand the cap table and the company's true valuation.

Accounting complexities also arise for the holders of warrants. Companies that issue warrants can expect to receive regular communications from the warrant holders' accounting and finance departments asking for detailed financial and cap table information to meet their internal obligations to regularly establish a value for the warrants. These requests for information will continue for as many years as the warrants remain outstanding, no matter how "underwater" (worthless) the warrants may be.

Bridge Loans. Warrants are common in VC bridge loans. Companies that run out of money between VC financing rounds are often forced to seek a bridge loan from existing investors. These short-term notes usually come with high interest, harsh default provisions, and severely discounted warrants, including "penny warrants," which are warrants to purchase shares of stock a $.01 per share.

Unreasonable Warrant Provisions. When issuing warrants cannot be avoided, keep an eye for several onerous and unfair terms. In general, it is best to keep the warrant exercise period as short as possible, preferably two to five years. Ten years is a common but arguably unreasonable ask.

Cashless exercise is another area to push back. The holder of the warrant should be forced to pay cash to exercise the warrant, not merely forfeit a certain number of them equal to the exercise price.

The analogy of cashless exercise warrants to employee options is inapt. Employees have worked for their options, and those options were not intended as "financing" tools. Warrants are invariably granted in connection with financings – which means paying for them.

The third and most overreaching warrant provision gives the holder the right to either exercise the warrant or demand cash for its value or some artificial dollar figure. The following is from an actual warrant. Be alert for and reject any provision like this:

> *1.8 Purchase Right. At any time after the earliest to occur of (i) the Term Loan Maturity Date (as defined in that certain Loan and Security Agreement dated as of September 13, 2019 between Company and Overreaching Bank, as amended (the "Loan Agreement")), (ii) the date Company repays all Obligations (as defined in the Loan Agreement), (iii) an initial public offering of the Company's securities, and (iv) a merger or acquisition of Company in which Company is not the surviving entity, at the election of Holder, Company shall pay Holder an amount equal to Two Hundred Thousand Dollars ($200,000). Upon such payment, this Warrant shall be deemed cancelled and of no further force or effect.*

Traditional Lenders and the SBA

Local and regional banks advertise business-friendly lending, but the reception most startups receive from bankers rarely matches the advertising hype. These are generally not promising options for most startups with no revenues and no financial history.

It is generally far easier for a founder with good credit to simply rack up some credit card debt or even take out a home equity line of credit than it is for the founder or the business to take out a business loan at a traditional bank with strict credit standards.

When newer founders are running out of bootstrapping options, they sometimes explore taking out U.S. Small Business Administration ("SBA") loans.

The SBA route sometimes works well for startups but the process can be time-consuming, document-intensive, and uncertain. Founders should also be prepared to personally guarantee any SBA loan and to secure it against their home.

The SBA loan route is probably a better option for solo founder lifestyle businesses involving franchises and other opportunities with near term and relatively predictable revenue streams, versus more risky tech startup business models.

That said, SBA loan officers are always eager to connect prospective borrowers with SCORE ("Service Corp of Retired Executives") mentors who can readily explain SBA loan funding opportunities and processes. SCORE describes itself on its website as follows:

> *SCORE is a nonprofit association dedicated to educating entrepreneurs and helping small businesses start, grow, and succeed nationwide. SCORE is a resource partner with the U.S. Small Business Administration (SBA), and has been mentoring small business owners for more than forty years.*

Venture Debt

Venture debt, also called "venture lending," refers to lending to startups by certain types of banks and non-bank institutions. These can be term loans for general working capital purposes, loans based on and secured against receivables, and loans for equipment purchases.

Venture debt borrowings are often secured against most or all of a company's assets, including its IP.

As a general rule, companies need to have already raised substantial equity financing and be in pretty good shape to be eligible for venture lending, particularly from more reputable lenders. Venture debt is generally not available to struggling startups, nor would it be a good idea for them.

The best tactical use of venture debt is to cover business expenses like inventory or equipment at a tolerable cost without giving up additional equity.

Equipment loans and receivable loans seem to be the most common forms of venture debt.

Receivable loans are based on the value of a company's receivables – amounts owed by customers that have 30 or more days to pay the company's invoices. Some receivable financing companies focus exclusively on SaaS companies due to their relatively simple expense and revenue models.

Searching online for "venture debt" or "receivable financing" will yield a wealth of information about venture lenders and their loan products.

Revenue-Sharing Agreements

In addition to a stated interest rate, some of these specialized, startup-focused lenders require companies to pay some percentage of revenues to the lender, ranging anywhere between 6% and 20% according to recent advertisements. These forms of loans are sometimes called "Revenue Sharing Agreements" or "Revenue Participation Agreements."

Warrant Coverage

The oft-stated advantage of venture debt and receivables financing is that it is a "non-dilutive" form of financing, suggesting that these lenders do not take equity in their clients but require only the repayment of principal plus interest.

Even though venture debt is described as non-dilutive, most venture debt lenders require warrants as part of the deal. Warrants are equity. These warrants then sit on the cap table, lowering the company's fully-diluted per-share value. They will be exercised by the lender in a sale of the company, entitling the lender to sale proceeds that otherwise would have gone to the stockholders. Again, warrants are dilutive.

Venture debt loans also generally carry high interest rates of 12%, 15%, and higher. When combined with fees and warrants, the effective interest rate for venture debt can be well over 20%, with default interest rates sometimes exceeding 40%.

Default-Related Risks

While there are circumstances in which venture debt and receivables financing can be logical components of a startup's overall financing strategy, certain other risks need to be considered.

First, these types of lenders might respond severely in the event of a default, whether the default is material or not. Institutional lenders can be the toughest creditors to deal with in a financial crisis, and one shouldn't expect venture debt lenders to be any less difficult.

Like other lenders, venture debt lenders are likely to take advantage of every opportunity to exact additional fees, warrants, or other consideration if a borrower is late or violates a covenant. This is how they make money. Do not expect them to pass on any opportunity to charge fees or extract other value whenever possible, even at the risk of seeming non-supportive, or even greedy.

Before taking on any venture debt, be sure to understand all of the deal's legal and financial terms. Assume every potentially adverse term will be used against the company to the fullest extent.

Case Study #39 – Venture Debt Extortion

One of my startups had a very experienced CFO. This person sought to strategically balance the company's uses of equity and debt financing to optimize its overall "capital structure."

Consequently, the company took out a $1 million venture debt line of credit with a very wellknown lender in the startup finance space. This relationship worked very well until the confluence of three things.

First, a larger bank acquired the original lender. This seemed fine at first, given that our key personal relationships with the lender did not change.

Second, the CFO made a relatively innocuous decision to change one of the company's accounting principles regarding the treatment of certain expenses.

Third, the company found itself closing a series D financing round.

This sequence of events brought out the worst in the lender and in the fundamental DNA commonly associated with such lenders. The CFO's thoughtful but perhaps poorly timed decision to change an accounting principle caused the company to fall ever-so-slightly below one of the "financial ratios" required in the venture debt loan covenants.

Without belaboring the details, this was merely a technical change with no adverse impact on the company's otherwise healthy financial condition. The accounting change certainly did nothing to increase the lender's risk regarding the loan.

Nonetheless, the accounting change caused the company to violate the loan covenant at a technical and superficial level. In any financing, a company needs to represent and warrant that it is in full compliance with all loan covenants or that it has waivers for any non-compliance. Consequently, the company needed a written acknowledgment and waiver of the covenant violation from the lender before the investors in the series D financing would close.

When the company approached the lender for what should have been a routine, ordinary course waiver, the lender, led by its outside counsel, took advantage of the situation to demand fees of $24,000 from the company and additional warrants worth approximately $170,000 at the time.

At first, thinking this was a misguided position by lower-level personnel, we assured the lender in writing that, if the covenant breach waiver was granted, the series D would close immediately and the entire outstanding balance of the venture loan would be paid immediately. The lender's waiver was the only thing standing in the way of closing the $15 million deal, delaying the closing by more than two weeks.

Our established relationship managers at the lender, persons well-known to several of us on the senior management team, were unable to loosen the lender's position in any way. So much for the promise of "personal banking."

The company's management and board were vehemently opposed to granting this additional compensation to the lender, which we all viewed as extortion. Influential board members contacted highly-placed acquaintances at the lender and complained, but to no avail.

Several major VCs and strategics were involved, and all were shocked by the lender's behavior. All discussed the issue in their internal meetings, and there was unanimous agreement that none of their portfolio companies should work with this lender in the future.

In the end, the lender never relented, despite knowing how much damage the episode had done to its reputation. We paid $24,000 in "waiver fees," $17,000 for their external legal fees as required under the agreement, and issued the lender preferred stock warrants that were then worth $168,000.

This lender still comes up high in search results for venture debt or venture lending.

> Lessons: The above situation and several similar situations have caused me to have a bias against venture debt or any other kinds of institutional borrowing by any startup that might struggle to make the loan payments on time or maintain the required covenants. Even though borrowing can be a logical and rational part of any company's capitalization, startups are prone to the types of mistakes that put them at severe risk in relationships with aggressive, secured lenders.

Case Study #40 – Buzzard Removal

As outside counsel to numerous companies, I accept any and every invitation to meet with my clients' boards of directors. In the corporate world, that's often where you'll find the action – usually a financing, M&A deal, or some other interesting project.

Unsurprisingly then, I was happy to receive an invite captioned "Strategy Session - Draft Term Sheet," with a note requesting my attendance at a board meeting at a board member's residence. I was a little puzzled by the absence of any attachment to review but didn't think too much of it.

At the meeting the next day, I immediately detected a somber and agitated mood, the reasons for which were soon revealed. The company's Founder/CEO had been trying to pull together a financing for several months and had come up short, but for a single, incredibly bad term sheet.

This term sheet was one of the worst I have ever seen. It offered a Convertible Note of $800,000 with an extremely low valuation cap, and the investment funds would be provided to the company in three tranches, each months apart, and each at the sole discretion of the investor. Additionally, for a period of one year, the company would be locked up from doing any other financings unless the investor approved, and the investor would also have a right to buy the company for an amount that was lower than the company's valuation in its most recent financing.

In short, the company was running out of cash, and buzzards were circling.

The investor's terms seemed calculated to only weaken the company over the coming months and then force it into a fire sale to the investor. This particular vulture was seeking to cheaply "roll up" a group of similar companies into a single dominant player in the industry.

I splashed cold water on the deal and laid out a series of counter proposals. The board liked them and asked me to write them up.

I provided a full term sheet the next day that involved three components:

1. A Convertible Note with a 20% discount requiring $400,000 of funding now and $400,000 three months later.

2. Assuming the $800,000 investment came through, the investor could lead a series A round, taking a substantial interest in the company on these terms: (a) must invest at least $4 million, (b) in a round totaling at least $8 million, (c) with a pre-money valuation of at least $15 million, and (d) with at least 50% of the $8 million closing within five months from the current date and the remainder closing within two months after that.

3. Assuming completion of the above, the company would engage in good faith discussions about an acquisition but would make no promises about the outcome of those discussions.

Days later I was traveling and called the CEO for a report on how the terms had been received. He told me they were still playing hardball, hadn't budged much, but were still very interested and trying to talk him into the deal.

Prior to calling the CEO, I had had a bit of an epiphany. Sensing his possibly failing resolve to fight the buzzards amid the company's cash crunch, and feeling some righteous indignation toward the buzzards, I said,

> *"Look, I know an angel who is interested in your space; my guess is that he'd take that whole $800,000 convertible note in one installment, without any of the rest of the nonsense they're demanding. Should I call him and see?"*

The CEO liked that idea and asked me to call the potential investor. Within days, the investor signed a basic Convertible Note and provided funding of $800,000. Board members sent me smiley emoji texts. The CEO sent me a bottle of single malt Scotch. The buzzards flew.

> Lessons: This founder's fundraising efforts were sporadic, inconsistent, and insufficiently forward-looking. Laying the foundation for future financing successes takes time, a strategy, and consistent effort, and running out of money as this founder did can undo much previous hard work.

> Most founders should probably spend at least twenty minutes a day working on their fundraising strategies and identifying and cultivating key relationships.

VC-Unfriendly Funding Choices

For every new startup, there are a range of possible financing paths and alternatives. Sometimes it is easy to "pivot" from one path to another.

But there are limits on flexibility. In certain cases, going down one path can complicate or even cut off other funding paths. This is particularly true on the path to VC funding.

VC Pattern Recognition

Because of the large number of companies and deals they have to decide about quickly, VCs seem to rely on pattern recognition. They look for things they recognize, understand, and trust, and avoid things they don't recognize or trust.

Seeing that other reputable VCs are in a deal, for example, is a good sign. A simple, clean cap table with a small number of investors, all accredited and sophisticated, builds confidence that smart money is supporting the company and that no surprises are lurking in the cap table.

The simpler, cleaner, and more recognizable things are, the easier it is for VCs to quickly assess and trust what they are seeing.

VCs are always interested in a company's prior fundraising rounds and the instruments used, and the implications of those instruments for the company and future investors. Those implications are easier to understand in the case of common, template-based financing instruments.

As an extreme example of this, a VC in a meeting with one of my companies was a bit taken aback by the fact that the company had sold common stock to early accredited investors. He said, *"that's fine, but we prefer to see early investments as Convertible Notes on NAVC's (National Association of Venture Capital) template."*

It is hard to imagine any early investment instrument more benign than common stock for a company or its future investors, but VC reliance on pattern recognition is so profound that this VC preferred to see a familiar but less favorable instrument over common stock.

Another likely preference of most VCs is for early-stage rounds to have been solicited discretely under Rule 506(b) of Reg D. Use of general solicitation under Rule 506(c) probably would not turn off all VCs, but it could raise questions or concerns requiring extra scrutiny.

Crowded Cap Tables

VC concerns about crowded cap tables might seem snobbish and elitist, but they are perfectly rational. Notwithstanding the understandable push to allow smaller investors into private company investments behind the JOBS Act and equity crowdfunding, cap tables crowded with non-accredited investors are inherently dangerous and troublesome for many startups.

The following are all nine reasons for preferring fewer investors on a cap table and for preferring accredited investors over non-accredited investors:

1. The costs and difficulties of maintaining accurate shareholder records, as required by law, increase directly in proportion to the number of shareholders.

2. The costs and difficulties of obtaining necessary shareholder votes and consents increase directly in proportion to the number of shareholders.

3. The costs and difficulties of distributing proceeds after a company sale increase directly in proportion to the number of shareholders.

4. Management distractions from investor inquiries increase directly in proportion to the number of shareholders.

5. Shareholder litigation risks increase directly in proportion to the number of shareholders.

6. Risks of management distractions are higher with non-accredited investors than with accredited investors, given their greater concerns over potential investment losses.

7. Risks of shareholder litigation are generally greater with non-accredited investors.

8. Risks of regulatory complaints are generally greater with non-accredited investors.

9. Courts and regulators are more sympathetic toward non-accredited investors, resulting in potentially worse outcomes in litigation or regulatory matters.

So, any type of financing that attracts more investors and that involves any non-accredited investors could make the already difficult job of attracting VC investments more difficult.

General Solicitation

Another potential concern for some VCs might be the use of general solicitation in an earlier round. As discussed in Chapter 11, *State and Federal Securities Laws*, general solicitation includes all forms of open communication about an offering, including mass advertising, but it also includes emailing or otherwise communicating with potential investors with whom the company has no prior, substantive relationship.

The ability to legally use general solicitation to raise money is a recent development in the world of startup finance. It is the polar opposite of how private securities offerings have been conducted for more than 80 years - generally through discreet, private communications between previously acquainted individuals.

General solicitation may or may not lead to large numbers of investors coming into a round, and depending on the exemption used, it may or may not result in non-accredited investors joining a cap table.

Regardless, many VCs and securities counsel still view general solicitation in a negative light. Potential concerns could include needing to track down and vet all of the public disclosures made by the company across all media for anti-fraud concerns, the company's compliance with all applicable requirements for the exemption relied upon, and, more subjectively, whether the use of general solicitation had harmed the company's reputation.

Debt-Heavy Balance Sheet

Excessive debt can accumulate on a balance sheet when founders hold unrealistic views of a company's valuation for an extended period of time. When VCs and other investors don't queue up to invest at or above a valuation founders are fixed on, it can be tempting to keep the company alive with borrowed funds until equity investors come to their senses about the company's valuation.

After several rounds of debt financing with little or no equity financing, though, a company's bloated balance sheet, itself, can become a concern for equity investors who would stand in line behind the debt. Founders sometimes seem to forget that their stock also stands behind debt.

Working with Investment Bankers

Startups should only engage investment bankers to raise funds if they absolutely have to. One exception to this rule might be working with a banker on a Reg A+ mini-IPO. We discuss mini-IPOs in Chapter 15, *Venture Capital Alternatives*.

In general, though, only later-stage startups hire investment bankers to help find cash or a buyer. And, in the case of financings, these are often distressed startups that have been cut off from funding by their VCs.

I personally like investment bankers. My wife was a banker. They play invaluable roles in IPOs and big M&A transactions.

But their fees are too high and too complicated for most lower-level transactions. And VCs have little interest in seeing their investment dollars go to bankers.

Hiring bankers is also no cure-all for startups that are unable to raise funds due to major challenges in their business model, cap table, or balance sheet. On several occasions, I have seen investment bankers work diligently for more than six months without bringing in a single dollar for a struggling company.

Fee Tails. In addition to requiring warrants, retainer fees, transaction fees, and expense reimbursements, bankers *always* demand what is called a "fee tail."

A fee tail entitles an investment banking firm to receive substantial fees on future transactions, including transactions the bankers had nothing to do with. Fee tails last from 12 and 24 months after the relationship and often must be paid on every dollar that comes into the company, whether investment or M&A.

Banker fee tails can kill any remaining hope a struggling startup might have had to close a scrappy, company-saving financing. Potential investors in a nearly-doomed company rarely agree to let 5% of their investment go to investment bankers who had nothing to do with the deal.

Whenever a board deems it necessary to retain investment bankers, it is critical to limit the fee tail as much as possible. An aspirational target might be to cap it at six months. Try to also limit the fees to money from investors and acquirors introduced by the bankers. Even these simple restrictions will be resisted by most investment bankers.

The Goldilocks Rule

In this and prior chapters, we have considered the idea of *Just-in-Time Finance*. The *Goldilocks Rule* is a corollary to this principle that provides a segue into fundraising strategy and execution.

As a general rule, founders who achieve their entrepreneurial vision and financial objectives through fewer investment rounds, less outside investment, and fewer investors are happier than those who spent more time on the fundraising treadmill and gave up more of their equity.

Fewer investment rounds also usually means focusing more on business and less on fundraising, lower debt and, as we have just learned, smaller liquidation preference stacks ahead of the common stockholders.

Conversely, founders who are overly concerned about accepting third-party money sometimes starve their companies of cash and fall well short of meeting their entrepreneurial vision.

For any company with a very large addressable market, like Lyft or Uber, multiple preferred stock rounds that support continued growth and a strong exit serve all stakeholders' interests well. Even very large preference stacks become irrelevant in an IPO or major acquisition.

The *Goldilocks Rule* in this context means that a company should bring in *the "right" amount* of third-party capital to meet its needs. It goes hand-in-hand with the principle of *Just-in-Time Finance* - bringing in those funds *at the right time* when they can be used to create the most value at the lowest cost.

KISS

KISS (keep it simple stupid) is another principle worth bearing in mind in designing and implementing a financing plan. Founders should strive to keep things as simple as possible in each funding round.

It is also usually advantageous to stay on or near the most-traveled path whenever possible.

The reason for this is to preserve the greatest range of options in future financings. If founders accept onerous or exotic terms in an early financing, later investors may either find those terms objectionable and walk away, or they may demand their own onerous or exotic terms to one-up the earlier terms. Anything but plain vanilla deal terms can also create unacceptable uncertainty in the minds of future investors.

Let's now look at how to design and execute a fundraising strategy tailored to the needs of a specific startup.

CHAPTER THIRTEEN

Seed and Pre-Seed Fundraising

This chapter covers seed and pre seed-stage fundraising and focuses mostly on pre-series A fundraising strategies. Seed-stage funding covers a wide range of transaction sizes, up to and beyond what used to be considered series A financings.

They also include a wide range of investors, including friends and family, angels, angel investor groups, VCs, seed funds, and startup accelerators.

Many pre-series A companies raise more than a million dollars in seed money, and rounds as high as $5 million are not uncommon.

These larger numbers are being supported and even promoted by seed funds, including VC seed funds. Many VCs that previously only invested in series A and later rounds, now have investment funds focused on seed rounds. These seed funds serve as pipelines for potential series A investments.

Seed funds are a relatively new phenomenon that some thought would pass, but they have continued to grow.

The line that separates large seed rounds and small series A rounds is increasingly blurry. Even so, the distinction between them is still meaningful.

Seed versus Series A

Companies on a VC funding track can benefit from taking any seed money necessary to position the company for successful rapid growth following a series A round.

As discussed, VCs have high growth and revenue expectations during the 18 months following an A round. On the other hand, the expectations of seed investors, even VC seed investors, are not as severe.

Seed investors want to see good work on market validation, product design and launch, refining the business plan and revenue model, and hiring key team members.

For this reason, going straight from bootstrapping to a series A round can be unwise. Failure to meet VC expectations can be extremely detrimental.

Seed rounds can play an important role in a carefully developed financing strategy. Well-utilized seed funds can produce traction that drives up a company's series A valuation. Justifiably high valuations are always good for founders.

A properly timed, sized, and utilized seed round that produces strong growth leading into a series A round is a great example of *Just-in-Time Finance*.

Investment Instrument Alternatives

Most seed rounds these days are done with Convertible Notes, SAFEs, or series seed preferred stock, roughly in that order of popularity, likely followed in popularity by sales of common stock.

Founders will not always be able to dictate the structure of a seed transaction. Investors often have their preferences and are likely to impose them.

The best way to control the types of instruments and the specific terms used in funding rounds is to successfully develop lots of investor relationships and generate strong traction.

Successful negotiation in any fundraising situation requires understanding one's relative leverage and knowing what is negotiable relative to similar recent, comparable deals.

Developing a Fundraising Strategy

A fundraising strategy or plan is an overall plan for raising the funds necessary to support a specific entrepreneurial vision *in the right amounts, at the right intervals, and from the right investors.*

We ended Chapter 12 considering three interrelated principles: *Just-in-Time Finance*, the *Goldilocks Rule*, and *KISS*. We will keep them in mind this chapter and in Chapter 14, *VC Fundraising.*

Defining the Goal

Like any project, devising a fundraising strategy requires founders to think through their goals, personal preferences, and options:

- How much early-stage capital do we need to get a minimally viable product or service to market?

- Does the scale of our total addressable market warrant raising large amounts of funding?

- Do we require large amounts of funding to move fast into a new or potentially crowded market?

- What is our desired outcome – independent profitability, IPO, or sale?

- Could early revenues be sufficient to support an acceptable pace of growth at a burn rate that can be supported through non-VC financing alternatives?

- What timing/amount of profitability, or size of IPO or sale, seems reasonable?

- Would we be happy to exit in two years, or do we want to enjoy the experience of building the company to something much larger and more meaningful over eight or nine years?

With answers to those questions in mind, founders can begin to think about exactly how much money they need to raise in total, at what intervals, how, and from whom.

Deciding Whether to Accept Venture Capital

Some early-stage founders have no idea whether or not they want to ultimately accept VC funding and may take a wait-and-see approach to the question.

Other founders are dead-set against taking VC funding for a variety of reasons, but the most common two seem to be reluctance to be forced to grow at what is seen as an unreasonable pace or to give up control over fundamental decision making, including the ultimate decision of whether or when to IPO or sell.

As already mentioned, the first VC dollar sets a company on a nearly irreversible path to an IPO or a sale. I say "nearly irreversible" because I know of one case where a founder bought his company back from his VC investors for $200 million.

Founders who eventually want to seek VC funding may want to limit themselves to the more "conventional" early-stage financing instruments discussed below, while founders with no interest in VC funding have more latitude to use both conventional fundraising tools and more novel fundraising alternatives like those discussed in Chapter 15, *Venture Capital Alternatives*.

Different Paths for Different Goals

Many sophisticated founders, no doubt, start thinking about financing strategies from the first days of a new entrepreneurial vision.

There is always more than one way to fund a company, but it is also true that some paths are likely to work out better than others.

Want to develop and launch a SaaS product? Need to pay expensive developers with credible stock options? The following might be a logical series of financings to meet that goal:

- bootstrapping,
- seed round with SAFE, Convertible Note, or series seed preferred, and
- series A preferred round.

The series A just might be an optional round, depending on how quickly revenues scale up.

Once an A round is completed, though, the optionality of any future offerings may be up to the series A VCs. VC pressures might require a follow-on series B round. And maybe a C round, D round, E round, and so on.

Or perhaps the new SaaS company will only involve a team of three founders for the foreseeable future who do not want to be forced to exit after seven to ten years or grow according to the dictates of VC overlords.

In that case, it might be possible to form an LLC, split ownership evenly three ways, and bootstrap until there is a revenue stream to pay for additional employees.

Once there are revenues, future growth could be funded through venture debt or by offering what are called revenue participation interests.

As noted earlier, an LLC would generally be a non-VC-friendly governance structure. But if that structure and approach best accommodates the company's optimal fundraising strategy, then it is the right structure.

Entrepreneurs focused on the food and beverage industry instead of technology might feel that VC funding is too remote a possibility. Companies in those sectors might consider financing plans that look more like this:

- bootstrapping,
- crowdfunding under Reg CF,
- Regulation A+.

Companies with more modest fundraising needs may have a broader range of fundraising vehicles to consider, including borrowing against revenue streams or receivables. Where possible and not unduly expensive or risky, borrowing offers the advantage of not sharing ownership/equity.

Beyond venture debt and receivable financing, borrowing is generally not an option for most startups, but companies with cash in the bank and steady revenues can tap more traditional lending sources and terms.

Entity Considerations

To reinforce a point made in the SaaS example above, founders contemplating lower levels of outside, non-VC fundraising, should carefully consider their choice of entity.

A typical C corporation may not be the best choice because of the taxation of dividends, and making an S corporation election might not work either, particularly if the founders want to issue a different class of equity to third parties. As noted in Chapter 5, *Entity Selection*, an S corporation automatically converts to a C corporation if a second class of equity is issued.

Because of the ability to offer different classes of equity and to make distributions without double taxation concerns, LLCs may offer the greatest flexibility for providing small business entrepreneurs and third-party, non-VC investors a good ROI without having to do an IPO or sell the company.

LLC member units can function like common stock or preferred stock, but with the benefit mentioned earlier of investor distributions not being subject to double taxation.

Flexibility

Devising and executing a thoughtful fundraising plan is like any other kind of project, but arguably one with many unknowns and uncertainties.

Fundraising is harder, more time consuming, and more uncertain than many entrepreneurs expect. Your company's product can be great, but your timing or ability to make connections might not be, or vice versa.

Because of these uncertainties, most fundraising plans need to be flexible. When markets are tight, a struggling series A round may need to be substituted in the near term with more bootstrapping or a second seed round.

As discussed next, having more investor connections can serve as an insurance policy when circumstances require flexibility.

Building Fundraising Connections

Successful fundraising requires connections. We touched on this issue briefly in Chapter 5, under *Co-Founder Considerations*, with the following statement:

Every entrepreneur expecting to fundraise needs to put substantial effort into developing relationships with other entrepreneurs, angel investors, VCs, potential strategic investors, and others in their geographic and industry-specific startup ecosystems.

Fundraising is difficult even with lots of connections, but founders with few connections struggle the most. Early efforts to create a strong network of potential investors provide an entrepreneur numerous invaluable benefits:

- confidence to develop and execute on an optimized long-term fundraising plan,

- time to get to know potential investors and focus cultivation efforts on those who will provide the most value in the form of mentoring and additional connections,

- latitude to choose from among multiple potential investors,

- faster, easier financing rounds, and

- ability to push back on overreaching terms.

The laws of supply and demand apply to financing efforts. The more investors who know about a promising startup, the greater the demand will be for its shares.

Strong investor demand makes the entire fundraising process faster, easier, less distracting, and less expensive and drives better outcomes all around.

Some entrepreneurs try to develop fundraising connections solely by attending and mingling at startup or entrepreneur-focused talks, meetups, and pitch contests. All networking is good and can lead to important investor connections.

But this kind of networking has to be combined with more focused research and relationship building.

Social Proof

Establishing a network also helps with what is called "social proof." An investor who does not know you or your startup is more likely to find you interesting and trustworthy if you are introduced to that investor by someone the investor trusts and admires. That is because some of the introducing person's trustworthiness and credibility rubs off on you through the introduction.

Leveraging social proof is a key to successful fundraising.

Focus on Key Founders, Potential Investors

Based on the value of social proof and warm introductions, entrepreneurs should try to identify and connect with investors through founders and other investors.

Here are some steps for making those connections and building a list of investor prospects:

Research. Get familiar with www.crunchbase.com or www.pitchbook.com. Here are some searches you can run on Crunchbase:

- See "Search for:" and click on "Companies." Type your company's category in the "Industry" search box. Also try any category variations suggested by Crunchbase.

- Searching an industry generates a long list of funded companies. There should be columns showing each company's location, alternative industry categories for the company, and other information.

- Click on a company then on "Total Funding Amount" for: (i) all of the company's financing rounds, which VC, angel, seed fund, or strategic led each round and (iii) who else invested.

- Searching the name of each of these investors displays for each: (i) other startups funded, (ii) when and how much, (iii) the investor's funding categories by percentage, and (iv) information about each VC's investment funds, including date established, and size.

Crunchbase and PitchBook are both powerful fundraising research tools. Next, use either platform to find fellow founders and well-targeted investor prospects.

- **Find Founders.** Identify twenty or more non-competitive companies in your space or in an adjacent space that have received seed, VC, or strategic investor funding, especially any in your city. The goal is to find fellow founders who will network with you.

- **Find Investors.** Identify *all* angels, VCs, seed funds, strategics, and other institutional investors regionally and nationally funding those startups and other startups in or adjacent to your space.

- **Create Lists.** While doing this research, create two spreadsheets, each organized from highest to lowest relevance/promise. These lists should be adjusted *constantly* as new information comes in.
  - **List #1: 80 targeted investor prospects.** This is a list of 80 angels, VCs, seed funds, and strategics regionally and nationally funding startups in or adjacent to your space.
  - **List #2: 20 startup founder networking prospects.** This is a list of 20 founders of companies in your space or adjacent spaces that have received angel, VC, seed fund, and strategic investor funding.

- **Rank and Prioritize.** List #1 should be further segmented. Separate, if just by a blank line on the spreadsheet, your top 20 investor prospects. Do the same with your top 5 investor prospects. Your top 5 should always be the investors currently most likely to lead your next round.

Perform deeper research on your top 20 targeted investors to learn more about their focus, vision, investing philosophy, and check-writing tendencies. This research causes some investors to rise on the list and others to fall, or drop off completely. Constantly revise the ranking of your top 5, top 20, and top 80 investor prospects through research, networking, and by reaching out to those targeted investors for informational meetings.

Investor prospects that fall off the list must be replaced with new viable prospects. List #1 must *always* have 80 viable potential investors. Fundraising is a numbers game. These are minimum figures for success. Others might say have a total of 150 or 200 potential investors on the list instead of just 80, but that seems unmanageable for most founders, in my experience.

Regarding List #2, try to create strong relationships with these founders. Move positive, productive, interesting relationships higher on the list, lower and drop others. These relationships could result in very important introductions. A single, well-placed introduction can make all of the difference in the life of a company.

Networking Techniques and Objectives

The first phase of networking under this approach is meeting fellow founders and potential investors without asking for any money.

These efforts need to be sincere and thoughtfully executed. If winning friends and influencing others is not a personal strength, study up on the psychology of human relationships and time-tested techniques for developing relationships to make these efforts successful.

Early communications with fellow founders or potential angels or VCs should not go straight to fundraising. A better approach is to ask for feedback or advice. "*I know you also had to build a two-sided marketplace with XYC company. We are doing the same thing and I would love your feedback on our strategy.*"

The advice or feedback could be about anything important and interesting – a pitch deck, revenue model, go-to-market strategy, or even connections to talent.

Once a relationship has been established, ask fellow founders about their connections with your top priority angels, VCs, and other potential investors.

Build up relationships with potential investors slowly too. Desperation is a turnoff. Allowing relationships time to develop naturally always works out better. Look for opportunities to reciprocate.

Fundraising Mentor-Advisors

Finding a well-connected fundraising mentor-advisor can also be invaluable. Advisors with lots of experience and connections with angels and VCs can open doors and coach inexperienced founders on how to be more focused, confident, and effective in their fundraising.

Advisors cannot be paid "finders fees" to help secure investments, but incentivizing a good advisor with an appropriate stock option grant not tied to fundraising success is perfectly acceptable and can make the advisor feel appreciated and like part of the team.

Shifting from Networking to Fundraising

Founders should be very deliberate and intentional when shifting from networking to fundraising. The conversation needs to go from, "*Hoping we can meet to talk about what we're up to,*" to "*We just launched our series A round and we want you to lead it. We plan to close on $8 million by the middle of November before the holidays.*"

From a securities law perspective, this is important because knowing when an offering began and ended, and how each of the solicitations was conducted, is critical for ensuring (and proving) an offering's compliance with the claimed exemption(s) from registration.

But equally importantly, the mindset that is appropriate for networking is not usually the right mindset for fundraising. The former is arguably more casual, informational, and social, and the latter is more about sales and "closing."

Successful Fundraising Mindset

Founders who are more successful at fundraising make it their top priority. They focus on it relentlessly and exert a high degree of will on others to make it happen. They impose deadlines, overcome objections, focus on the positives and the bigger picture, cajole higher commitments, and take command of the process.

These founders set the tone and the schedule. They can be downright pushy, but with a positive *"let's get this done"* attitude.

Founders in active fundraising mode should have check-in or update meetings or calls two or three times a week with any others on the fundraising team. These half-hour check-ins are used to report progress, identify new investor prospects, prioritize and assign follow-up actions, and drive toward closing.

Some founders struggle to make the transition from networking and socializing to "closing." Rather than leading and forcing a deal to completion, they fail to create a sense of urgency, staying in a passive, and even submissive, follower mentality.

Breaking through an overly deferential, unconfident mindset is hard for many, and particularly daunting for newcomers to the game of convincing sophisticated, wealthy investors to part with their money.

Founders need to develop some of the traits and confidence of great poker players and business deal closers.

A great story with some compelling metrics can help build that confidence and urgency naturally, but so can putting in the work to develop a large network of engaged potential investors. Nothing beats strong investor interest for boosting founder confidence.

An experienced mentor-advisor can also help a struggling founder find their more assertive inner self.

Pre-Seed and Seed Rounds

The most common names for pre-series A financing rounds these days are pre-seed and seed. As we have learned, the range of financing transactions covered by these terms has become very broad, encompassing all financing rounds between bootstrapping and series A rounds.

We will focus on them by looking at:

- common seed round sizes and the activities typically funded,
- common participants in seed rounds,

- common instruments used in seed rounds,

- how to pitch seed round investments, and

- other key seed round considerations.

Pre-Seed Amounts and Uses of Proceeds

As mentioned in Chapter 12, pre-seed rounds are used to fund early activities in a company's life. Pre-seed rounds range anywhere from between $25,000 to $500,000+.

The stated uses of proceeds for these rounds are typically product-market fit research, product design, development and launch, fine-tuning the business plan and revenue model, hiring early team members, and purchasing necessary technology.

Pre-seed funding can also cover needs like legal work for entity formation and issuance of founder stock, acquiring URLs, and maybe even registering trademarks or copyrights.

By its nature, a pre-seed round follows, supplements, or substitutes for bootstrapping.

Seed Round Amounts and Uses of Proceeds

Seed rounds used to be $10,000 to $250,000, give or take.

Now they range from $50,000 into the millions of dollars. VCs, angels, seed funds, family offices, and other investors are leading a constant flow of $1 million to $3 million seed rounds.

In general, at least theoretically, even these larger rounds are still focused on developing and creating the product, building team and infrastructure, and otherwise preparing and testing go-to-market strategies.

The trend toward calling larger and larger funding rounds seed rounds undoubtedly began in Silicon Valley, then spread to larger markets like New York and Boston, and has now spread to medium-sized markets like Seattle.

Common Participants in Seed Rounds

When seed rounds were previously limited to smaller amounts, the participants were almost exclusively friends, family, and angel investors.

Depending on who the investors were, the participants might have called it a friends and family round or an angel round. The most common term these days is seed round, but the other names are still used.

Friends and Family. A large portion of early-stage startup funding still comes from friends and family.

This highlights the importance of remembering the distinction discussed in Chapter 11 regarding accredited and non-accredited investors.

Taking investments from non-accredited investors generally requires substantially more complex disclosure documents and correlates to greater legal or regulatory risk if things don't work out, even if they're friends or family.

On the issue of disclosure, recall that Rule 506(b) allows up to 35 non-accredited investors to participate in an offering, but the issuer then must provide extensive (and expensive) disclosure documents to all of the investors.

For these reasons, even companies that want to solicit friends and family should limit those solicitations to accredited investors and require all investors in any round, big or small, to complete an Investor Questionnaire attesting to their accredited status.

Angel Investors. As noted in Chapter 12, individual angel investors invest their own money, enabling them to make investment decisions more quickly than investors requiring committee approvals.

While individual angel investors are still active in most major cities, cities the size of Portland, Oregon may be lucky to have more than four or five high-profile angels. Even a city the size of Seattle may not have more than ten or fifteen individual angels who are actively investing at any given time.

In addition to their small numbers in most cities, anecdotally, they seem to work within circles of individuals with whom they are familiar or have a connection.

As a final caveat, before wasting time trying to get the attention of any specific, individual angel investor, try to confirm that the person is making investments currently. Some individuals falsely hold themselves out as angel investors on social media and elsewhere simply to boost their status and attract followers.

Use the process described above under *Developing Fundraising Connections* to discover and to ultimately connect with potential angel investors active in your region and industry sector.

In addition to Crunchbase, AngelList is another platform for making connections with angels.

Angel Investor Groups. Starting in the 1990s, angel investors began investing as groups. In some cases, they would invest as individuals in the same companies, but increasingly they began to pool their resources to become what might be called mini VCs, or early-stage venture funds, which we discuss later.

Almost all of these groups have been formed around common mission statements that include sharing knowledge and pooling resources to support innovation and establishing standards for angel investments. The growth of angel investment groups has added greater formality and structure to angel investments.

The Alliance of Angels says it invests $10 million across 20 startups yearly. (https://www.allianceofangels.com/)

The Angel Capital Association claims on its website (www.angelcapitalassociation.org) to have 260 angel group members. Use the ACA's handy online Member Directory to find angel groups by region.

As mentioned earlier, AngelList (https://angel.co) is a platform for connecting with both individual angels and what AngelList calls "syndicates," which it describes as *"Private single-deal VC funds led by top angels."*

For more on AngelList syndicates, go to https://angel.co/syndicates/for-founders. You can also look at individual syndicates by going to https://angel.co/ and entering "syndicates" in the search box. We discuss AngelList again in Chapter 15, *Venture Capital Alternatives*.

While it would be unfair to make sweeping generalizations, the investing terms of some angel groups can be less than angelic, skewing too far in favor of the investors. Founders considering working with angel groups should be alert for the following:

- **Too Much Equity for Too Little Cash**. Angel groups have been accused by some founders of pushing low valuations, resulting in modest investment amounts in exchange for unreasonably large ownership percentages.

- **Premature Issuance of Series A Preferred Stock**. Angels sometimes push for series A preferred stock in transactions where the amount of investment does not warrant those terms. As discussed later, series seed preferred is the better choice, versus series A preferred, for rounds of roughly $4 million or less. The rights and privileges that come with a series A round are significant and are intended to induce more substantial investments. Misnaming small rounds as A rounds and providing inappropriately generous terms to investors in early rounds can permanently impair a startup's ability to raise future rounds on reasonable terms.

- **Demands for Board Seat Rights**. Unless a startup's founders are already looking for a new board member and the angel group has a candidate that would be a great fit, requiring a board seat for an investment of less than $1.5 million seems unreasonable.

  At that level, investors should be happy with information rights in the form of quarterly and annual updates and possibly board observer rights. Board observer rights allow an investor delegate to receive most board materials and attend most board meetings, but not to vote.

- **Demands for Warrants**. Angel group sometimes require warrants. As discussed at length in Chapter 12 under *Types of Financing Instruments*, warrants are a bad idea in early rounds and should be avoided. Warrants violate the KISS principle.

- **Demands to Increase Option Pool**. Some angel groups require that a company's option pool be increased to as high as 25% of the company's issued and outstanding stock.

  The intention is for the founders and existing shareholders to experience the dilution of increasing the option pool, so that the angel investors pay less per share, *whether or not the options are ever actually issued or exercised*. This is a valuation game that VCs are entitled to play, but an overreach in most angel rounds.

Seed Stage Venture Funds. Seed-stage venture funds, or seed funds, are essentially VC funds that are focused on seed-stage investments. Similarly, there are also pre-seed funds.

Seed funds took off in the early 2000s. Their proliferation coincided with steep declines in costs associated with launching startups, particularly with the rise in cloud computing ushered in by Amazon's AWS cloud services.

One illustrative example of a seed fund is Founders' Co-op, which currently says it has invested in more than 100 startups since its founding in 2008. Founders' Co-op describes itself on its website (https://www.founderscoop.com/) this way:

The Pacific Northwest's Seed-Stage Venture Fund
Built by founders, funded by founders, and designed to put founders first.

Founders' Co-op says on its website that it *"typically invests $250K-$750K in the first fundraise of software startups based in the pacific northwest."*

Strategic Investors. As discussed earlier, there are both pros and cons in taking money from strategics. They often invest in early rounds and can provide helpful expertise, contacts, and industry credibility without being overly concerned about near-term financial performance.

On the other hand, strategics might also want to impose their priorities on the development of specific technologies, products, or services. Their presence on the cap table might also be a turn-off for potential customers who consider them competitors, and also for certain investors, including VCs, wary that they may seek to acquire the company before its value has risen sufficiently to support a home run exit.

On balance, strategics are increasingly important players in early-stage funding, and founders should focus substantial effort toward developing well-targeted relationships and seeing how they play out.

VCs. In recent years, many VCs have started investing in smaller rounds. Overall, the benefits of getting VC money in a seed round probably trump the downsides. The validation and attention that comes with any VC investment has value. Any VC investment is social proof that a startup and its team should be taken seriously.

VCs are known to be a talkative community, though, and there is a herd mentality that can be both positive and negative. If a VC considered to be "smart money" invests in a startup, other VCs are likely to follow.

On the other hand, if a VC makes a seed investment in a company but declines to participate in its series A round, that can send a damaging signal to the VC community. That signal might negate the value of the VC's seed round participation.

Before taking any seed investment from a VC, founders should talk about the likelihood of the VC's series A round participation and what that would require. Founders might also consider asking about the VC's track record for participating in the A rounds of its seed investment portfolio companies.

Startup Accelerators. The world of startup accelerators is a world unto itself. Accelerators are a bit like sport skills camps, but for startups. They provide instruction, mentoring, business model coaching, industry and fundraising contacts, a modest amount of funding, and, in some cases, temporary office space or other facilities.

On average, accelerators take between 7% and 15% for investment amounts ranging between $25,000 to $150,000.

The top three U.S. accelerators are Y Combinator, TechStars, and 500 Startups.

Y Combinator, or "YC," has an incredible track record. It takes on more than 200 companies per year and has provided seed funding to almost 2,000 companies. More than 200 of those companies have achieved meaningful exits. Y Combinator has backed countless famous companies, including Airbnb, Dropbox, Stripe, Reddit, Twitch, Coinbase, and Weebly.

Y Combinator invented and exclusively uses SAFEs in seed rounds. Y Combinator provides $150,000 of capital for a 7% investment and twelve weeks of mentoring that culminate in every startup giving a pitch at YC's Demo Days to all of Silicon Valley's top VCs.

For many, accelerators provide an invaluable mix of capital, mentoring, and connections. Unfortunately, not every founder or startup is located near Y Combinator, 500 Startups, or TechStars. And immersion in an accelerator program is costly and probably unnecessary for any founder who already has a promising idea in development and a strong fundraising plan.

Family Offices. Depending on the circumstances, a supportive, smaller family office might be a perfect seed investor for a startup. Entrepreneurs should always be interested in "patient money," and family office money would generally fit that description. As noted in Chapter 12, though, family offices with larger fortunes are generally not interested in investing at levels below participating as limited partners in VC funds. Any investment from a family office will probably require a pre-existing relationship or strong interest by the family office or its family members in a startup's technology or business focus.

Pitching Pre-Seed and Seed Rounds

Pitching angel investors and other seed round investors is generally less formal than pitching VCs because fewer decision-makers are involved and the amounts and terms are smaller and less complex. But founders still must be ready with some basics:

- an elevator pitch,
- an executive summary,
- a pitch deck,
- a financial model, and
- a cap table.

Elevator pitches, executive summaries and pitch decks are discussed in greater detail in the next chapter, but here are abbreviated descriptions:

- An elevator pitch is a memorable and impactful description of a startup that can be given in 20 or 30 seconds.

- An executive summary is a 1 to 3 page distillation of a company's pitch deck.

- A pitch deck is generally a 10 to 13 slide deck that usually covers the following:

  - the problem a company solves,

  - how it solves the problem,

- the size of the problem and market opportunity,

- the company's go-to-market strategy for the solution,

- the team that will execute the strategy,

- what competitors are providing other solutions, and

- summary financial forecasts.

When pitching any investor, it is important to listen carefully and answer questions directly, thoughtfully, and candidly. Founders should not get caught off guard by questions about the cap table, financial forecasts, size of the market and opportunity, competitors, or other fundamentals.

Founders also should not get defensive. I have seen VCs and angels ask questions designed to test founders' patience and thoughtfulness. Many investors want to know that they can ask difficult and sometimes annoying questions without provoking knee-jerk, poorly considered, or evasive responses.

Founders should always demonstrate patience, candor, and sincere interest in understanding and learning from investors' concerns.

Preparation is key. Practicing a pitch with fellow founders, friendly investors, and mentor-advisors is always helpful. Encourage them to ask difficult questions.

It's also important to realize that it is a good sign if an investor wants to take control of the conversation. Founders shouldn't be so myopically focused on finishing their slide deck that they miss cues about what an investor wants to talk about.

But the most important thing about pitching early investors is pitching the right investors. As persons and firms move up a company's lists of target investors, founders should increase their diligence and learn more about how the investors work with the companies they invest in. Have other founders had good experiences or bad experiences with them? Were they constructive and supportive, or at least professional, in difficult situations?

Look for investors who are genuinely interested in the company, its mission, and the team.

The techniques for pitching VCs, covered in the next chapter, are also applicable to pitching pre-seed and seed investors.

Negotiating Seed and Pre-Seed Rounds

Negotiations involving a seed round or pre-seed round will depend largely on the investors. In a friends and family round, the company will likely be in a position to dictate the form of the investment, whether SAFE, Convertible Note, series seed preferred, or even common stock.

If a VC or seed fund is leading the round, they will likely dictate the instrument used. Presumably, it will be a trusted template for one of the more common instruments – either a SAFE or Convertible Note. That said, I have heard at least one story of an investor proposing substantial, non-market revisions to a standard SAFE template.

Term Sheet

Whatever documentation is proposed, it will first be outlined in a term sheet. Receiving a term sheet from a serious, well-regarded potential investor is an important development for many first-time founders. While not binding, when a startup and an investor sign a term sheet, the prospects for a deal are very high, unless either the startup or the investor does something wrong.

Some of the things that might kill a deal after a term sheet has been signed include a founder backtracking on a term already agreed to in the term sheet, or an investor discovering negative information about the company that should have been disclosed before signing the term sheet.

Trust is extremely important and needs to be a two-way street in all fundraising activities. Backtracking on a term in a term sheet is considered a breach of trust. So is failing to disclose material information.

In the category of things founders might want to avoid, shopping an unsigned term sheet to other investors to get an auction going can cause an investor to pull the term sheet back, sometimes leaving a startup with nothing.

A smart first step for a startup that has received a term sheet is to get together with sophisticated deal counsel to assess the term sheet for unusual or out-of-market terms, and to develop a strategy for either declining the term sheet, accepting it as is, or negotiating the terms.

Prioritizing any issues for negotiation will depend on the nature of the proposed investment instrument. The following is a summary of some key issues to consider in negotiating seed round or pre-seed round term sheets involving SAFEs, Convertible Notes, series seed preferred stock, or common stock.

SAFEs

Because they are "simple" by design, there is very little to negotiate with a SAFE, primarily the discount rate and any valuation cap. A 20% discount is likely "market" in most situations and should not be negotiated aggressively unless the company is in a strong position.

More effort should be focused on either removing any valuation cap or setting it high enough so that it is not triggered.

Founders sometimes accept low valuation caps when they believe a series A round will be closed within the near future. Founders should always assume that they may be living on seed round funding for as long as two years before they can close an A round, and set any valuation caps according to that time horizon.

The best argument for eliminating a valuation cap in a SAFE or for setting it high is that it could hurt the company's chances for successfully closing a series A round with the right investors.

A second argument against a low valuation cap is that some VCs will peg a company's series A round valuation to the cap. Doing so gives the VC a lower valuation and protects the VC from dilutive share issuances under the cap. In other words, a low valuation cap is a perverse incentive that causes unintended consequences.

Convertible Notes

There is generally more to negotiate with Convertible Notes, as discussed in Chapter 12. Here are some terms that merit prioritization:

Maturity Date. The further out the maturity date of a Convertible Note, the better for the company. Twelve months is generally too short, but thirty-six months might be an overly-aggressive ask in most situations. Eighteen or twenty-four months are both reasonable time frames, and one or the other is likely to work for both sides.

Mandatory/Automatic Conversion Threshold. Every Convertible Note automatically and involuntarily converts into stock upon one or more specified events.

Most startups want and need their Convertible Notes to convert before maturity. Conversion takes the notes off the balance sheet. Conversion also means not having to pay off the notes.

In a seed round note, the type of transaction that will trigger conversion, a "Qualified Financing," might be described like this:

> *…an equity financing with total proceeds to the Company of not less than $2,000,000 (excluding the conversion of the Notes or other convertible securities issued for capital raising purposes (a "Qualified Financing")….*

As company counsel, I push for a low "Qualified Financing" bar. The $2M number in this example is fine, and probably even on the low side, but getting it down to $1M would be even better for the company.

Investors will resist low conversion thresholds. They do not want to lose debt holder priority until the company's solvency is more certain. Converting at lower dollar amounts provides less certainty.

Founders should also avoid conversion language that is too specific. In the example, any "equity financing" over $2M triggers conversion. Avoid language that specifies a "Series A financing," for example. The next financing is statistically more likely to be a second seed round.

Interest Rate. The interest on a Convertible Note is either converted into additional shares in a financing or paid out as cash in a sale of the company. Convertible note rates currently range between 2% and 9%, depending on the specific market and the direction of interest rates in general.

A rate of 5% or lower is best, but negotiate the lowest interest rate possible, without going below the AFR.

Rates lower than the federal rate can trigger an issue referred to as "original issue discount," resulting in unnecessary tax questions. See IRC Section 1272(a), captioned "*Current inclusion in income of original issue discount.*"

https://www.law.cornell.edu/uscode/text/26/1272

Discount. The most common discount for Convertible Notes is 20%. Anything higher is excessive unless the company's risk profile is even worse than a typical startup.

Valuation Cap. The comments above regarding SAFE valuation caps apply here. Again, new money won't always agree to fund a windfall.

Exit Payout Terms. As noted in Chapter 12, Some notes provide substantially greater payouts upon an acquisition, as much as 1.5x or even 2x the amount of the note. Notes with such terms can severely complicate the ability to sell a company, particularly a distressed sale.

Determine what is market for any such provision based on comparable deals, and be careful about agreeing to anything that puts noteholders in a position to effectively block or kill an important sale.

Note Amendment Provisions. Founders should try to avoid signing multiple notes that cannot be amended without a unanimous vote by all noteholders.

A common approach seems to be that each noteholder has the power to approve any changes to their note terms.

Creating a "Promissory Note Agreement" under which several individual Promissory Notes are issued allows the company to impose common terms across all of the individual notes. As company counsel, I always insist on a provision permitting amendment of most of the note terms by a majority of the noteholders, or even a supermajority.

Having the ability to amend a term like a mandatory conversion threshold with the majority vote of the noteholders can be very helpful in closing difficult transactions.

Amount. Another key point to remember about Convertible Notes and SAFEs is that the amounts raised under such instruments should not be excessive relative to the amount of the future series A round into which they will convert.

Given that the amount of a future series A round is generally difficult to predict accurately, it may be worth avoiding raising more than $1 million to $1.5 million *in total* under convertible instruments unless the anticipated series A round will be at least $8 million or higher. As a general guide, investors in a round probably do not want to see more than 20% of the round represented by note or SAFE conversions.

In a recent situation, a client's Convertible Note offering was significantly oversubscribed, and they ended up taking in $7.5 million.

During the offering, I reminded the CFO a couple times that their series A round would need to be substantial to absorb the conversion of so much discounted debt. Ten months later they closed a $30 million series A round.

This example demonstrates the difficulty of drawing hard lines in startup finance.

Series Seed Preferred

Series seed preferred stock deals are rare compared to SAFE and Convertible Note deals. They are generally less company-favorable, more complex, and more expensive due to legal fees. And, of course, any equity round requires coming up with a valuation.

Selling common stock instead of preferred stock would be more consistent with KISS.

But some seed round investors do prefer series seed preferred. These investors could be VCs, other seed funds, or angel groups with specific motivations. A desire for preferred stock likely reflects an expectation of greater control rights, including a board seat, blocking rights, preemptive rights, and other voting and control rights not found in SAFEs or Convertible Notes.

The following are some of the key term sheet items in a series seed preferred stock financing.

Liquidation Preference. Resist any liquidation preference more favorable to the investor than 1x, non-participating. Such terms are not just non-market, but they also generally backfire on early-stage investors who impose them, given that later stage rounds will only get more severe and may have liquidation preference priority over those earlier rounds.

Twice now, I have seen companies become insolvent because 2x financing instruments from early rounds caused subsequent sophisticated investors to take a "hard pass" on the opportunity.

Valuation. The earlier warnings about valuation should always be weighed carefully to avoid a valuation that is too low, and hence unfair to the company, or too high and potentially setting up a future down round.

Some investors, possibly VCs, might suggest a higher than anticipated valuation with the expectation that they will later just drive the founders hard to earn the valuation – a "stretch goal" of sorts for the founder team.

Founders in that situation may want to diplomatically re-calibrate the discussions. An example of that might be, *"Susan and I appreciate your confidence, but we are more comfortable with the lower number we suggested yesterday. There are still some unknowns in the revenue model, and we would rather delight than disappoint."*

Protective Rights/Blocking Rights. Another area where series seed term sheets probably differ from VC term sheets is in the types of blocking rights they afford investors. Series seed term sheets should probably only allow investors to vote separately on the following matters:

- adversely changing the rights of the series seed preferred stock,
- redeeming or repurchasing any shares (other than pursuant to employee or consultant agreements),
- declaring or paying any dividend,
- changing the number of directors, or
- liquidating or dissolving the company, including any change of control.

Blocking rights beyond these would be fair targets for negotiation, like the ability to block any future financing. It might also be wise to include language stating that, following any future preferred stock financings, the holders of series seed preferred will vote on such matters not as a separate class but together with all other preferred holders.

That clause may or may not be possible to impose when negotiating future financings, but adding it in the seed round documents at least takes the issue off the table with the seed investors. As we will discuss again in Chapter 14, *VC Fundraising*, limiting the number of separate "class votes" prevents smaller shareholders from holding up financings, M&A transactions, and other important matters.

Anti-Dilution. While early series seed preferred templates did not provide anti-dilution protections, the inclusion of weighted average anti-dilution seems to be the norm currently. That said, if the valuation in a specific seed or pre-seed deal is low, that could provide leverage and logic for eliminating any anti-dilution provisions. Anti-dilution provisions tend to complicate future fundraising conversations and documentation, so the longer those provisions can be avoided, the better.

Common Stock

In the somewhat rare instances when seed or pre-seed investors are willing to take common stock, and the founders believe it is a good choice, the only matter to negotiate will be valuation.

Because common stock is so basic and lacks most of the bells and whistles associated with preferred stock, negotiating and closing a common stock seed round can be very simple.

The lack of liquidation preferences, anti-dilution provisions, blocking rights, and board seat rights makes common stock the most founder-friendly seed round investment vehicle.

It is still a viable option for friends and family rounds, but with due caution for the issues highlighted previously. The most important of these is understanding the impacts of a common stock round on a company's ability to issue low-priced stock options to employees. Again, if a company raises money by selling common stock to investors at one price, it could become harder to later justify pricing common stock options at a lower price.

This concern warrants having a thoughtful discussion with the company's outside 409A valuation expert before using common stock in any financing. Interestingly, 409A valuation experts often assign common stock a low FMV even after a recent common stock round. When questioned about this one expert said:

> *"That was a negotiated price. The company was not willing to take less and the investor was willing to pay that price. Arm's length purchases are considered, but they are just one factor in the 409A analysis."*

Another 409A valuation expert told me that, no matter how a company's common stock was priced in an early round, once that company conducts a preferred share offering, its common stock will generally be valued at about 10% of the preferred shares, due to the preferred shares' liquidation preferences.

Another closely related concern is that, because common stockholders come at the end of the line behind debt holders and preferred stock liquidation preferences, it is important to price common stock fairly in a seed round to ensure that those investors have a chance of a reasonable return in any exit.

A high-priced common stock round is no way to treat friends and family.

As one data point to prove that the use of common stock in financings is not completely over, one of the top crowdfunding sites, StartEngine, recently sold common stock in a successful Reg A+ financing.

Common stock-based seed rounds might also be making somewhat of a resurgence on a few of the crowdfunding portals described in Chapter 15, *Venture Capital Alternatives*.

Closing Seed and Pre-Seed Deals

Conducting and closing any type of financing always requires documentation. Financing documentation is highly specialized and should only be handled by qualified legal counsel familiar with the type of financing in question. Otherwise, the possibility of errors is high, and the potential consequences significant.

Chapter 1 included a list of helpful online resources. Those links are included again here, as a reminder that the linked websites offer versions of many of the deal documents discussed.

- Wilson Sonsini Venture Term Sheet Generator

    https://www.wsgr.com/wsgr/Display.aspx?SectionName=practice/termsheet.htm
- The National Venture Capital Association

    https://nvca.org/resources/model-legal-documents/
- The Cooley law firm and Cooley Go

    https://www.cooleygo.com/documents/
- Y Combinator

    https://www.ycombinator.com/documents/
- The Orrick law firm

    https://www.orrick.com/Total-Access/Tool-Kit/Start-Up-Forms
- AskTheVC – Venture Deals

    https://www.venturedeals.com/resources

Purposes and Functions of Deal Documentation

Attorneys often refer to the final documentation in a deal as "the closing documents." The shorthand terms "closing docs" and "deal docs" are also common.

There are several important purposes and functions behind closing documents, whether the deal is a small friends and family round or a series C round with highly sophisticated institutional investors. Understanding those functions helps in understanding the documents themselves.

Small, earlier-stage financings definitely require fewer, shorter documents. But closing *any* financing with inadequate documentation is a mistake that leads to unpleasant consequences, including difficulties raising additional capital or achieving a successful exit.

<u>Anti-fraud Inoculation/Disclosure Compliance.</u> Issuer *disclosures* serve to advise investors of information material to their investment and to inoculate issuer companies from fraud claims.

Issuer anti-fraud inoculation in VC-led offerings is usually accomplished through a Disclosure Schedule. As described in Chapter 11, such a document details all of a company's IP concerns, pending or threatened litigation, regulatory matters, significant HR matters, and any other negative information.

Issuers also sometimes protect themselves by providing investors with Risk Factor disclosures. Although these are more commonly found in formal disclosure documents, they can also be provided in a stand-alone document or included with an "Investor Letter" accompanying final offering documents. We look at Investor Letters briefly in Chapter 14.

When working with less sophisticated investors, I also sometimes include Risk Factors or Forward-looking Statement disclaimers as attachments or additional pages to the official Term Sheet.

In this discussion of deal docs, we are generally not talking about a company's pitch deck, written executive summary, or other pre-closing solicitation materials.

To be clear, those documents must always be truthful and accurate, and they are unavoidably part of the disclosure record for purposes of potential anti-fraud claims.

The only solicitation materials that might be included among a financing round's closing documents would be any form of detailed "Offering Circular," "Private Placement Memorandum," or other similar formal disclosure documents, which are rarely seen in VC-led financings or rounds with sophisticated angels.

<u>Offering Exemption Compliance.</u> A second purpose of deal documentation is to provide proof of regulatory compliance with applicable securities law exemptions. Future investors or acquirors will look back at each fundraising round for documentary assurance that it was conducted properly and poses no legal or regulatory risks.

As mentioned, every investor in every financing should sign an Investor Questionnaire, attesting to their accredited investor status and, if taking a 20%+ interest, to their non-"bad actor" status.

In Chapter 11, we learned that most securities law exemptions, including Rule 506(b), prohibit the presence or involvement of any bad-actor officers, directors, or major investors.

A sample Investor Questionnaire can be found in the BLSG Data Room at *Finance > Equity Financing Documents > Misc Financing Docs*.

Transaction Authorization. A third purpose of deal documentation is authorizing the creation of the rights and obligations that are spelled out between the investors and the company.

This is accomplished through (i) board resolutions authorizing the transaction and all of the deal documentation and (ii) any shareholder or noteholder consent (vote) documents required from existing shareholders or noteholders approving and consenting to the transaction and all of its details.

Determining the authorizations required and properly obtaining and documenting them is an exercise where the carpentry mantra *"measure twice and cut once"* applies. When in doubt about the need for shareholder approval, obtain it.

Creating Rights and Obligations. A fourth fundamental purpose of deal documentation is establishing or creating the economic and control rights and obligations between and among the investors and the company outlined in the Term Sheet.

In an equity deal, this will involve amending the Certificate of Incorporation and signing documents such as a Stock Purchase and Sale Agreement, Shareholders Agreement, and Voting Agreement.

In Convertible Note financings, the parties sign Promissory Notes and Promissory Note Agreements.

Lastly, a SAFE is a contract between the company and the investor that must be fully executed, along with a SAFE Purchase and Sale Agreement.

Financing Approval Processes

Board Approval. Every financing transaction, whether debt or equity, must be approved by a corporation's board of directors. This includes binding commitments to issue debt or equity, including, for example, a SAFE.

This can be accomplished by approving detailed resolutions at an actual board meeting or, perhaps more commonly, using an equally detailed UWC (Unanimous Written Consent).

A board's resolutions authorizing a series seed preferred stock financing would need to cover at least the following:

- Amendment and Restatement of Certificate of Incorporation
    - increase the number of authorized common stock and preferred stock,
    - designate some number of the company's authorized preferred shares as Series Seed Preferred Stock,
    - set forth rights, privileges and preferences of the Series Seed Preferred,
    - acknowledge need for and authorize obtaining shareholder approval of the amendment and restatement.
- Approving the Series Seed Preferred Stock Financing
    - approve number of shares to be sold and price,
    - approve form of Stock Purchase Agreement,

- authorize management to sign and deliver documents, including any Side Letters, Management Rights Letters, Voting Agreement or Shareholders Agreement, and Right of First Refusal and Co-sale Agreement,

- authorize the issuance of the common shares into which the preferred can be converted and reserving common shares for those potential conversions,

- authorize issuance of Series Seed Preferred Stock certificates by management,

- statement that *"... the Series Seed Preferred shall be offered, sold and issued in reliance on applicable exemptions from registration provided by the Securities Act of 1933, as amended, and applicable exemptions under applicable state blue sky laws."*

- Filing a Form D with the SEC and all required state blue sky filings.

- Ratification, meaning that all prior acts of management toward closing the financing are ratified with very broad language.

- Approving all necessary acts through "Omnibus Resolutions" providing that management is empowered to take all necessary and appropriate acts to consummate and document the transaction, to complete all steps required by the deal document and to comply with applicable laws.

Find examples of Board Consent UWCs approving debt and equity financings in the BLSG Data Room under *Finance > Equity Financing Documents.*

Shareholder Approval. Every financing involving new issuances of equity must be approved by a company's shareholders. Whether or not a debt financing requires shareholder or unitholder approval will depend on the company's governing documents. Shareholder consents are similar in structure and content to board consents, whether approved in person or via documents called shareholder consents.

Find examples of shareholder consents (or stockholder consents) in the BLSG Data Room under *Finance > Equity Financing Documents.*

Deal Documents

Aside from certain deal-specific, ancillary documents and agreements discussed under *Ancillary Deal Documents* below, the following are typical closing documents by transaction type.

SAFEs

Documents for a SAFE financing would include the following:

- signed board resolutions or UWC authorizing the transaction,

- signed shareholder resolutions or consents authorizing the transaction,

- each investor's signed SAFE Purchase and Sale Agreement,

- each investor's signed SAFE,

- a Receipt or other evidence of payment by each investor,

- signed Investor Questionnaire from each investor,

- original Term Sheet,

- any Offering Memorandum or other disclosure document such as a Disclosure Statement or Risk Factors provided to investors.

Note that using a SAFE, which is merely a contract, defers any need to issue actual equity securities. While the SEC still deems SAFEs "securities" under the Howey Test, they do not represent current ownership interests in a company. SAFE holders, therefore, do not receive anything like a stock certificate.

Find examples of SAFEs and a SAFE Purchase and Sale Agreement in the BLSG Data Room under *Finance > Equity Financing Documents > SAFEs*.

Convertible Notes

Closing documents for a typical seed round Convertible Note financing include the following:

- Term Sheet,

- signed board resolutions or UWC authorizing the transaction,

- signed shareholder consents authorizing the transaction, if company documents require shareholder approval of the transaction,

- each investor's Convertible Note, signed by both the company and the investor,

- a Note Purchase Agreement, *if* a separate Note Purchase Agreement document is used, signed by the company and all investors,

- a Receipt or other evidence of payment by each investor,

- signed Investor Questionnaire from each investor,

- any Offering Memorandum or other disclosure documents such as a Disclosure Statement or Risk Factors provided to investors.

Security Interests/Collateral. On occasion, some early investors taking promissory notes will seek to have their investment collateralized by a security interest in the company's assets.

First of all, try to reject this. It is rare for companies to provide any security interests in early Convertible Note deals.

Any founder presented with a request for a security interest from an early investor should push back hard or immediately seek experienced counsel. Armed with a proper security interest, a lender owed money can liquidate the company on its own.

Deals involving a security interest will include a document called a "Security Agreement," "Loan and Security Agreement," or something similar. Once a Security Agreement or Loan and Security Agreement is being negotiated, counsel absolutely must be on point to try to limit the assets covered by the security interest and to narrow the borrower's rights in default.

Closing a collateralized deal will also likely require the filing of a UCC "Financing Statement" by the company with the Secretary of State where its headquarters is located. This easy filing provides public notice of the security interest.

The Company may also need to file a "Short Form Intellectual Property Security Agreement" with the USPTO if patent or trademark assets are involved.

The BLSG Data Room contains sample board resolutions, a sample Convertible Note, a sample Convertible Note Purchase Agreement, an IP Security Agreement, a UCC Financing Statement, and a Short Form IP Security Agreement at *Finance > Debt Financing Documents > Convertible Note Financing Docs.*

Series Seed Preferred

Documents for a series seed preferred stock financing would include the following:

- Term Sheet,

- signed board resolutions or UWC authorizing the transaction,

- signed shareholder consents authorizing the transaction,

- proof from the applicable Secretary of State that the Amended and Restated Articles of Incorporation authorizing the new series of stock were filed and accepted (usually done immediately before closing on an expedited basis for a higher processing fee),

- signed signature pages from each investor for the Series Seed Preferred Stock Purchase Agreement or Subscription Agreement,

- signed signature pages for any Shareholders Agreement, Right of First Refusal Agreement, and Voting Agreement applicable to the transaction, as agreed in the Term Sheet,

- a Receipt or other evidence of payment from each investor,

- signed Investor Questionnaire from each investor,

- Series Seed Preferred Stock Certificates or notices of electronic certificate issuance, called digital or electronic shares or certificates, and

- any Offering Memorandum or other disclosure document such as a Disclosure Statement or Risk Factors provided to investors.

The BLSG Data Room contains sample board resolutions, a sample Stock Purchase Agreement for a Series Seed financing, and other Series Seed deal documents at *Finance > Equity Financing Documents > Series Seed Preferred Stock Financing Docs.*

Deal documents listed above for a Series Seed Preferred Stock financing are generally just lighter versions of some of the documents required to document and close a series A Preferred Stock financing, discussed in the next chapter.

Common Stock

The simplicity of common stock deals makes them very easy to close. Closing documents for a common stock financing include the following:

- signed board resolutions or UWC authorizing the transaction,

- any signed shareholder consents required to authorize the transaction (less likely than in a preferred stock round, as there may be sufficient numbers of authorized but unissued shares still available under the Certificate of Incorporation),

- proposed Amended and Restated Articles of Incorporation if necessary to increase the number of authorized shares of common stock,

- signed signature pages from each investor for the Stock Purchase Agreement or Subscription Agreement,

- signed signature pages from each investor for any Shareholders Agreement or Voting Agreement,

- a Receipt or other evidence of payment by each investor,

- signed Investor Questionnaire from each investor,

- original Term Sheet,

- Common stock certificates or notices of electronic certificate issuance, called digital or electronic shares, and

- any Offering Memorandum or other disclosure document such as a Disclosure Statement or Risk Factors provided to investors.

The BLSG Data Room contains sample board resolutions, a sample Stock Purchase Agreement, and other docs for a common stock financing at *Finance > Equity Financing Documents > Common Stock Financing Docs.*

Ancillary Deal Documents

Financings with sophisticated investors can involve a number of ancillary documents, including more complex versions of the Shareholders Agreements and Voting Agreements described in Chapter 8, *Structuring and Managing Key Relationships.*

Other common ancillary documents often include Right of First Refusal and Co-sale Agreements, Investor Rights Agreements, Management Rights Letters, and Side Letters. These documents are discussed in Chapter 14 because they are more commonly associated with VC-led deals.

Post-Closing Administrative Steps

Form D Notice Filing and State Blue Sky Notice Filings. As discussed in Chapter 11, a Form D must be filed for any offering conducted under Reg D, including Rule 504, Rule 506(b) and Rule 506(c). The vast majority of exempt securities offerings are conducted under Rule 506(b).

The Form D must be filed <u>within fifteen days</u> of the first sale (binding, written commitment) of securities in the financing, whether a SAFE, Convertible Note, series seed preferred, or common stock, all of which constitute securities in the eyes of the SEC.

As soon as the Form D notice filing has been made with the SEC via EDGAR, the issuer uses the codes provided from that filing to make the state law filings with NASAA via its Electronic Filing Depository at this link - http://www.nasaa.org/efd/.

Closing Document Distribution. Immediately after closing any deal, send each investor a fully-executed set of closing documents and confirm that they received them.

The distribution of closing documents to a company's new investors is the first opportunity to demonstrate good communication. The package should include a cover letter from the founders or CEO thanking the investors for their participation in the round and support of the company and suggesting that they store their copies of the deal documents in a permanent, secure location.

The cover letter should also pledge that the company will keep them informed with quarterly reports on the company's progress and invite them to share feedback and helpful connections with the company.

Secure and Organize. The company should also immediately organize the closing documents in one or more permanent and secure locations. Ideally, one of these would be a robust virtual data room. In a company's virtual data room, each fundraising round should have its own separate folder, including a main folder with a complete set of the final, signed closing documents, and also, as applicable, separate sub-folders for every investor in the round, each containing all of the investor's separately executed documents.

Cap Table Entries. Another important administrative step following every deal closing is updating the company's cap table to reflect the new instruments and their terms.

Keep Investors Informed. As noted above, companies should strongly consider sending their investors quarterly updates, whether or not they are required to do so by the financing documents.

Investors who are kept up to date are always much happier than investors who are left in the dark.

They are also much more likely to invest in a subsequent round if asked to do so.

Startups that neglect their seed or pre-seed investors, assuming they will not need any more money from them, are taking a risky gamble. The transition from seed to series A is difficult for most startups, and unanticipated second and third seed rounds are common.

Each of my companies sends a quarterly report fifteen days after the end of each calendar quarter detailing financial results year-to-date and year-over-year, along with narrative descriptions of financial and operational wins and losses since the most recent report.

Other founders hold monthly video meetings with their investors, answering investor questions after providing a brief financial and operational update. Some investors prefer this interactive approach and say that they benefit from hearing other investors' questions and company responses.

CHAPTER FOURTEEN

VC Fundraising

This chapter is about laying the groundwork for a VC-led series A financing, getting a VC Term Sheet, closing the round, adjusting to new realities as a VC-funded startup, and anticipating what might come next, including B, C, D, E rounds and beyond.

As in any round of financing, the goal of a series A round should be to raise *the right amount of money, at the right time, from the right investors, and on the right terms.*

That is easier said than done. Setting out to raise VC funds is a major milestone for any company. Here are some key drivers of fundraising success with VCs:

- a great business model with rapidly growing revenues,

- strong product-market fit,

- solving an important problem,

- large addressable market and a big opportunity,

- great team,

- interesting IP,

- strong connections with the right investors,

- no major legal or regulatory issues,

- clean cap table, and

- money in the bank.

Companies that are strong in these areas have the best chances for VC funding. Proximity to Silicon Valley is also a major plus, based on funding statistics.

But less-than-perfect companies get VC funding too. They may just need to work harder and be more proactive about optimizing variables within their control. This means reaching more well-targeted VCs, being better prepared to make the right impression with them, and avoiding costly mistakes in negotiating deal terms, getting through due diligence, and closing a deal.

Successful Fundraising Overview

Fundraising is a numbers game. It takes a lot of well-targeted interactions to find the right investors and close an A round.

Rejection by VCs is the norm.

Founders who have established relationships with too few VCs at the launch of an A round or who waste their time and resources soliciting the wrong investors can find themselves in a stalled financing.

A VC financing round that takes too long can create the impression that something is wrong.

To avoid stalling out, a series A financing should be launched decisively with an aggressive plan and legions of warm prospects.

In addition to doing lots of prep work and having a good plan, attitude is key. There is no place for doubt or uncertainty in VC fundraising - only a 100% commitment to success.

Conveying confidence is critical. Words like "trying" or "hoping" have no place in talks with VCs:

- Incorrect: *"We are trying to raise an $8 million series A round."*
- Correct: *"We are raising an $8 million series A round."*

The goal should be to bank the round within three to six months, the faster, the better. Rounds that take much longer than six or eight months are more likely to fail, with odds of failure increasing as more time passes, unless, of course, the company starts to experience strong traction.

Case Study #41 – The Serial Meeter

One of my favorite founders also happened to be someone who struggled with fundraising. He was great at managing operations, motivating the team, and presenting a compelling vision. As a fundraiser, though, he focused too much on process and repetition, and he lacked the attitude and skills to force a deal to closure.

This case highlights the difficulty many founders face in assessing their strengths and weaknesses and breaking through their current mindsets and limitations. This founder was too willing to let others lead discussions in endless loops, and too submissive to use psychological techniques to assert a degree of dominance and play on investors' motivations and vanities.

This founder relied too heavily on the idea that holding lots of meetings in the same manner would eventually result in funding, rather than doubling down hard on his strongest prospects and exerting maximum effort and charm to convince them to present a Term Sheet.

Consequently, the company was chronically low on cash. The availability of less-than-ideal Convertible Note borrowings from a key investor undermined the sense of urgency necessary to accomplish the harder job of a larger financing. The result was an endless cycle of somewhat superficial VC calls and meetings that never produced a Term Sheet or lead investor.

Early in the process, when the company's numbers were less compelling, we could point to them as the problem. But the failure to find a lead investor, even after the company's sales numbers "hockey-sticked" into an impressive trajectory, highlighted that the problems had to do with the founder's passive approach.

The defects in that approach were subtle but pernicious. The founder was going through the motions of holding calls and meetings, but without using aggressive selling and closing techniques to make a deal happen. This left the company starved for capital at a time when that capital could have been used to substantially boost the company's trajectory and value. The impacts were real and long-lasting.

To close larger financings, founders need to feel like, and work like, they have a fire burning under them. Fundraising needs to be *the* priority, not just *a* priority. The process should include daily war-room type sessions to assess progress, evaluate and reevaluate investor prospects and strategies related to each, and determine next steps for the day and for the coming days.

And hard work, alone, is often not sufficient. Founders need to develop their own aggressive selling techniques and style. There are countless great books on closing deals. Founders who can close deals of all kinds, including financings, are huge assets to any startup.

Among other things, successful founders use company traction, pipeline opportunities, compelling socioeconomic trends, and social proof involving other potential investors, partners, and customers to position their company as the next great investment opportunity.

These founders also set firm deadlines for investors to commit and get in the deal. They also seem to use psychology on their preferred lead investors in each round, convincing each of them that they are the missing ingredient to help lead the company to greatness.

Understanding VCs

The VC world is not quite a parallel universe, but it is different, sometimes in counterintuitive ways. Here are some unique facts about VCs:

- VCs will *not* sign NDAs.

- When VCs sign Term Sheets, they close on those deals at very high rates.

- VCs generally only invest in companies they believe can return at least 10x the VC's investment.

- Cold calls and uninvited, spammy emails to VCs work poorly.

- VCs reject most companies and deals pitched to them. VCs generally invest in 10 to 15 companies per fund and generally have at most two active funds, yet they hear numerous pitches per week. Rejection is part of their job, and it can make them seem cold and arrogant. Founders should avoid taking VC rejection personally. It is simply a numbers game. Ignore rejections and move on.

- Related to the above, some VCs that are not actively investing continue to take founder meetings without disclosing the futility of meeting with them. These "zombie VCs" are simply trying to remain relevant between their fundraising activities.

- Some VCs will stop communicating without comment or explanation. This usually means "not interested," but not always. It could mean the VC does not want to say "no" yet and wants to keep options open if other VCs jump in and validate the opportunity.

- The vast majority of VC funding comes from one place, Silicon Valley, with Boston a distant second.

- VCs have their own investors to court and answer to.

- Most VCs naturally focus more on the few companies in their portfolios that are headed for big exits. Poorly or even reasonably well-performing companies that lose the financial support of their original VCs can find it difficult to convince other VCs to invest.

- Any breach of trust between a company or founder and a VC can cause irreparable damage to the relationship – e.g., renegotiating something in a Term Sheet, secretly shopping a Term Sheet to other VCs, or lying about a disclosure matter.

- VCs talk to each other about companies, and they also take signals from each other. If a deal takes too long to get a lead VC, it starts to look like a house that has been on the market for too long.

- On the other hand, a deal with a big name lead VC will quickly attract other VC interest.

- All VCs seem to have different opinions about little things like what should be in a pitch deck and which metrics should be emphasized. Rarely does the same pitch deck work for everybody.

- VCs usually have little or no interest at all in funding the repayment of accumulated debts, particularly those owed to founders as deferred salary. One founder team experienced months of rejection before I pointed out a possible culprit – more than $700,000 on their balance sheet in deferred salary owed to them. As I heard a VC say in a meeting, "*You don't always know why an investor passes on a deal….*" A huge payable going to founders from offering proceeds instead of toward future growth could certainly cause VCs to quietly pass.

- VCs are in the business of judging character. Founders should exemplify standards of good character – humility, openness to new ideas and information, self-awareness of personal strengths and weaknesses, ability to see other perspectives, interest in others, lack of self-absorption, and lack of hubris.

- VCs have been criticized for being dominated by white males and investing mostly in white male-dominated companies. Diverse founder and executive teams are very appealing to VCs as they strive to address these concerns. Related to this trend, female founders can capitalize on the increasing numbers of female-led VCs that focus on female-led startups.

Aligned and Misaligned VC Financial Incentives

Understanding these and other VC traits can help in successfully approaching and interacting with VCs. A deeper dive into VC financial incentives can also help to explain another curious phenomenon – how is it that such smart people end up investing round after round in companies that fail spectacularly?

Anybody paying attention to the world of VC-funded companies can't help but notice that, almost weekly, companies that have received massive amounts of VC funding over multiple rounds fail spectacularly.

Given that many of the folks behind these failures, both on the VC side and the startup side, are Stanford graduates, one cannot help but wonder – *"Didn't they see that coming?"* This phenomenon of doubling-down on losing business models - throwing good money after bad – can sometimes be explained by how VCs make money.

VCs have two primary sources of income and profits – they charge a 2% annual management fee on all funds raised and they typically also receive between 20% to 30% of a fund's ultimate investment gains – a concept called carried interest, or "carry."

VCs make the most money when their portfolio companies are successful because they earn both the management fee *and* their 20% to 30% of the fund's ultimate gains from successful exits.

But note, even when a fund is doing very poorly, and the VCs are unlikely to earn anything from actual gains, during the entire life of a fund, the VCs will continue to earn a 2% management fee against the value of each fund for ten to twelve years. On a $300M fund, that is $6M per year.

To maintain a consistent business model, VCs tend to raise new investment funds every three to five years. They do this by going out to existing fund limited partners and to potential new investors. In doing so, they have an incentive to tout strong returns in their existing funds.

This almost continual need to raise funds to maintain healthy management fees creates an incentive to keep failing portfolio companies alive by investing more money in them at ever-higher valuations. Failing to do so, and allowing portfolio company valuations to drop, would require the VC to record those reductions in value in the overall fund value, harming the currently stated returns for the fund, thus harming fundraising for the next fund.

Thus, VCs have incentives to push their portfolio companies to raise higher and higher rounds. In addition to hopefully fueling more rapid growth for their companies, this enables VCs to mark up the value of their existing funds with paper gains. The paper gains, in turn, can be used to tout new VC funds in order to generate more VC management fees.

These misaligned financial incentives, and not pure stupidity, possibly explain why some VCs make seemingly illogical follow-on investments in money-losing portfolio companies that ultimately fail.

Finding VCs

Being able to choose your VCs is obviously an elusive goal, but it should be the goal. Founders should try to position themselves with a surplus of funding options. This requires having a very large list of viable and interested investor prospects.

Think back to List #1 from Chapter 13, under *Building Fundraising Connections*.

Well before launching a series A round, a startup should have a highly vetted and prioritized list of VC prospects list like List #1:

- 5 VCs that are the top prospects and most likely to lead a round,
- 20 VCs that are very good prospects, and
- 80 or more VCs that are viable prospects.

In Chapter 13, we learned how to use either Crunchbase or PitchBook to find VC prospects. Finding VC prospects is easier than prioritizing them. Prioritizing requires going to each VC's website and other resources to figure out exactly what kinds of investments a VC is making, in what amounts, and when.

Here are two other websites that cover VC investing activities and priorities:

- www.pehub.com
- www.techcrunch.com

PE Hub is a VC and private equity industry website that mostly carries deal press releases. TechCrunch, previously affiliated with Crunchbase, carries press releases too, but its writers also produce insightful articles on startups, VCs, deals, industry and investing trends, and other details behind the deal press releases.

And, as mentioned, virtually every VC also has a website. These are loaded with useful information. They usually describe the firm's investing objectives, areas of focus, team members, portfolio companies, successful exits, and other newsworthy events and insights. The portfolio company sections can be very useful for developing more networking connections.

The information is all out there. There's just a lot of it to sort through and assimilate.

Ranking VCs Based on Publicly Available Information

In prioritizing VCs, consider sorting them, in part, based on these factors:

- degree of focus on the company's space/category,
- investing approach, timing, and target sizes of investments,
- number and size of recent investments in the space,
- investing leadership in the category,
- age of the fund (<4 years old is best), and
- geographic location of the VC.

Ranking VCs Based on Reputation

Organizing and ranking VCs based on publicly available information is just a starting point.

These sources provide few clues about:

- the VC's reputation for working well with founders,

- the VC's reputation for handling crises or conflicting interests,

- the VC's expertise and connections in a company's space,

- how individual members of the firm are as board members,

- the VC's fund's remaining dollars for investment, and

- the VC's plans for those dollars.

Gathering information on these important questions takes time and generally requires networking and relationships.

Founders who have taken funds from a VC firm and who then worked closely with the VC firm through ups and downs are great sources of information. They will have the best insights on what kind of partner the firm has been in good times and bad, what its culture is like, the personalities of its key principals, and likely even the status of a firm's funds.

Founders should use all of these types of data points to update and fine-tune their rankings of potential VCs. Time invested in targeting optimal VCs is far better spent than time wasted meeting the wrong VCs.

Building Pre-Solicitation Relationships

Months before officially kicking off an A round, founders should be already receiving warm introductions to their top VC prospects and holding informational, "getting to know you" meetings with them.

Informational Meetings

VCs are generally very willing to hold informational meetings and calls.

These are a two-way street. VCs will be making initial judgments about whether a company and its team are potential candidates for the firm's series A deal pipeline. For founders, top objectives in VC meetings include:

- developing personal relationships,

- practicing and fine-tuning the company's story,

- getting comfortable talking with VCs,

- receiving free advice and feedback on the story, team, revenue model, go-to-market strategy, competitors, industry trends, and other business and fundraising insights,

- learning what individual VCs think is most interesting or important about the company or its pitch, and

- getting an early read on which VCs might be interested already, which VCs might be interested if certain milestones are achieved, and which might never be interested.

Warm Introductions

As discussed already, the best way in the door to any VC is through a warm introduction from another founder, preferably a founder the VC has already funded, and preferably one that made money for the VC.

Warm introductions from other VCs or investors can also be helpful, but introductions from any investor who has already passed on investing in the founder's company can be toxic and should be avoided. Warm introductions from VCs or other investors who simply do not invest in a company's space do not raise the same concerns.

An in-person warm introduction to a VC is best, but less likely and not necessary. Email introductions are probably most common these days and nothing to sneeze at.

Following Up on Warm Leads

Whenever someone sends a warm lead to a VC, the founder being introduced should follow up quickly and try to lock down a meeting or call.

A typical response to a warm lead email might look like this:

> *Susan, thank you for that nice introduction. Bill, it is very nice to meet you.*
>
> *As Susan said, we're in the XYZ space and getting some great traction. We are still working through some earlier seed funding and are not yet fundraising again, but we know you invest in our space, and we'd love to come in and say hello, tell you more about what we're up to and get any feedback you can share on our revenue model and go-to-market strategy.*
>
> *Please let us know if we can come in sometime soon. Looking forward to meeting you in person.*
> *Sincerely,*
> *Lisa*

This puts the ball into the VC's court. If the warm lead has a close relationship with the VC, the VC might respond quickly. The founder should be watching for that response and reply promptly and decisively.

Cold Calls and Cold Emails

Sometimes it is simply impossible to get a timely warm introduction to a VC that is high on a company's list. If unsolicited contacts must be made, they should be highly targeted, to the point, authentic, and compelling.

Do as much research as possible and tailor each communication carefully to its recipient. It might be worthwhile to call the VC's main phone number and ask to speak with that potential recipient's assistant or admin to figure out whether a call or email might be best.

If email is suggested, follow that advice, but try to get on a call as soon as possible to get past the "cold call" phase of the relationship.

Any cold email to a VC should be extremely short and to the point, with a specific request. A long, meandering, poorly focused email is likely to be ignored or to provoke a negative response.

Here is what a short, unsolicited email might look like:

> *Dear Ann,*
>
> *My apologies for the unsolicited email.*
>
> *I know you focus on fintech, and our company ABC has an outstanding fintech prototype that is getting great feedback from beta testers.*
>
> *We'd like to show you a quick demo and hear your thoughts on how we might enhance the product, plus any thoughts you might have on our go-to-market strategy.*
>
> *Below my signature you will find a link with more information about us and our mission.*
>
> *Please let me know if my co-founder Susan and I can stop in for a short meeting with you. That would be much appreciated.*
> *Sincerely, Tom Smith*

Responding to VCs

Again, whether from a warm lead or a cold email, when a founder gets a positive response from a VC, he or she should respond promptly and thoughtfully.

There may be an invitation to come in for a meeting or to schedule a call. In-person meetings are best and should be taken whenever offered.

The VC is also very likely to ask for either or both an executive summary and a pitch deck. These are both discussed below. Both need to be ready to be sent out immediately upon a VC's request. Immediately means the same day, not next week.

When a VC asks for these documents, they likely intend to share them with others internally, including with other key decision makers and other staff members who might be asked to do some research and evaluation.

Do not set in motion warm introductions or make cold calls if the company is not ready to send out a polished and compelling executive summary and pitch deck. VCs are busy and highly distracted. Sending materials days after a request is a recipe for being ignored.

When meetings require travel, it can get expensive. But if the founders have done their targeting correctly, it is money well spent. Prior to the COVID-19 pandemic, many VCs probably expected founders to travel readily. As of this writing in May of 2020, the extent to which those attitudes have changed permanently or not is still unknown. If and when travel to meet VCs becomes the norm again, suggesting a videoconference or phone call instead for a first meeting could send the wrong message.

Pitching and Pitching Materials

As mentioned in Chapter 13, the requirements for pitching angels and VCs are essentially the same. The core documents are an executive summary, a pitch deck, and a financial model. But before a founder is likely to be invited to share those with a VC, he or she will first have to give an elevator pitch.

Elevator Pitch

An elevator pitch is a short, persuasive speech intended to hook the listener on a product, company, project, or person.

In the startup context, founders should always be ready to hook a potential investor at a networking event, any other business or social context, or in the proverbial elevator.

An elevator pitch should be interesting, memorable, and succinct – 30 seconds or so, depending on the context.

As an example, when asked about one of my companies, Observa, I say something along these lines:

> *Retailers spend billions on in-store merchandising and have no cost-effective way to see how those dollars are working. Observa lets brands see their products on store shelves anytime and anywhere. They can check pricing, stocking levels, special promotions, and competitive products. Observa's 100,000+ and growing network of Observers can quickly perform audits across thousands of stores. Brands can also use Observa as a private, white-labeled solution, leveraging the platform's auditing and reporting capabilities with their own employees. Observa's use of Artificial Intelligence to provide rich information from store shelves is even being considered for use by some of our competitors that also photograph store shelves.*

It is tempting to try to cover too much in an elevator pitch. The above example quickly touches on only the following:

- the problem,
- the size of the problem,
- who has the problem,
- the company's solution to the problem,
- a little about the company's competitive "secret sauce," and
- the company's traction.

As with pitch decks, which we will look at next, there is no one-size-fits-all approach to elevator pitches. If one of the founders, for example, has already co-founded a very successful company, it might be best to emphasize team. If the company has extremely valuable IP, emphasize the key role of IP.

The goal is simply to convince the listener to schedule a longer meeting to learn more about the company.

One element every great elevator pitch needs is passion. Investors tend to invest in founders who exhibit messianic zeal for their "mission."

Founders should seek out other advice on crafting a perfect elevator pitch and practice different approaches on friendly audiences.

As a company moves through different milestones and financings, the elevator pitch should naturally evolve as well. Giving a good elevator pitch becomes second nature quickly for most founders.

Pitch Deck

Opinions vary on what decks should cover and how they should be organized, but most hit these points:

- the problem we solve,
- the size of the problem, and opportunity
- how we solve it,
- our traction,
- our go-to-market strategy,
- our team,
- our competitors and how we differentiate, and
- two or three years of projected revenues and expenses.

Examples of slides that some VCs like to see but others do not include:

- company overview,
- exit strategies,
- the "ask" - amount of any current raise and other deal terms,
- IP,
- technology, and
- summary.

There is no such thing as a perfect pitch deck template. Every company and business model is different, and every VC has different likes and dislikes when it comes to pitch decks.

Founders should delve into the extensive online commentary on what makes a perfect pitch deck and look at as many recent, strong examples as possible.

As in every method of communication, the focus must be on the audience and what information they need to become interested and engaged. A more complicated business model or technology may require greater explanation.

Keep the Deck in Check. There is general agreement that most startup decks should consist of 10 to 13 slides.

Most founders want to make long pitch decks, but short is best. VC meetings are usually only an hour or less. Founders need to get VCs talking and asking questions. Long decks can result in too much talking by founders instead of engaging meaningfully with the VCs.

VCs who are not talking are not investing.

No Pitch Deck is Perfect. No matter what approach you take, be prepared for the fact that some VCs will think your deck is great, and others will criticize it for including or not including one or more elements.

This is a battle you cannot win. Opinions are strong and often contradictory. Some VCs will tell you to take out "the ask," others will criticize a deck for not including it. Same thing with an "exit options" slide – some VCs love them, some hate them.

Do not get defensive or bother explaining that someone else told you to include or exclude the offending slide(s). Just say, "*That's good feedback, thank you.*" Try to get back to discussing the company and not the deck.

While much deck feedback is good, some is not. I calibrate how much credibility to assign to negative feedback based on the VC's experience, reputation, degree of familiarity with the specific space, and the extent to which any others present seem to agree.

Draft, Test, Revise, Repeat. Founders should test drafts of their pitch decks first with investors who are not prospects to understand what hooks them and what confuses or distracts them.

It is best if this can be done with active, sophisticated investors who are familiar with the space to limit the risk of misguided feedback.

In a one-hour VC meeting, every minute counts. Use practice runs with these other investors to maximize the deck's clarity and impact.

Encourage them to be as candid and direct as possible about the deck and the entire business model.

Common Pitch Deck Mistakes. The following are a few mistakes worth avoiding in creating pitch decks:

- _Ignoring Competition_. Some founders believe so strongly in their product or service or its novelty that they convince themselves they have no competition. Every company has competition in the form of other solutions or workarounds to whatever problem the company is solving. Failing to properly address competition is a rookie mistake that could signal lack of sophistication or poor judgment.

- _Too Many Words_. A pitch deck should not be overly dense with text. Each slide should probably have no more than ten or fifteen words total, and they should be in twenty or thirty point font or bigger.

- Poor Organization. Every pitch deck should have a logical flow, like the conversation it is intended to support.

- Poor Graphics. A pitch deck should not be all flash and no substance, but it should be attractive and professional, with a consistent look and some eye-catching graphics. There is no excuse for subjecting your audience to fuzzy, poorly-selected images. Others seeking VC dollars are using visually appealing pitch decks. Your deck needs to be in the same league – not way above the average deck, but not way below, either.

- Confusing Graphs and Charts. Some founders get carried away with complex charts that try to convey too much. This often results in charts that make no sense to anyone. It is better to use multiple clear charts than one or two utterly confusing charts.

- Incorrect or Exaggerated Information. I find incorrect or exaggerated information in almost every draft pitch deck I review. Any founder who thinks they are going to put one over on a room full of VCs is in for a surprise. Not only does every statement, fact, and statistic in a deck need to be correct, founders need to be able to quickly identify the source or other proof for every statement, fact, and statistic in a deck. VCs are great at spotting questionable information, and they will call it out without hesitation. Few things will turn off any investor faster than a sense that a founder cannot be trusted. Similar concerns are discussed later regarding unrealistic projections and financial models.

VCs frequently ask founders for a copy of their deck. Always send decks via email as PDF documents. Do not send links and make VCs or other investors download or "access" them via the latest, ultra-secure platform. Create no barriers that could slow or prevent VCs from accessing and easily sharing your deck with colleagues. Avoid being too clever, keep it simple.

Locking the shared deck down as a PDF eliminates any deck animations, but it also eliminates the possibility of ugly reformatting that can occur when a deck is converted by Google Docs or other cloud-based platforms.

Financial Modeling and Literacy

Be Realistic. The only certain thing about startup financial forecasts is that they are wrong, especially on the revenue side.

This next advice is a tough sell, but founders should avoid outlandish forecasts. Wildly aggressive projections can harm founders' credibility.

Revenue forecasts should be explainable to investors and achievable, so be realistic. Again, VCs generally only invest if they believe a company can return at least 10x their investment. If the revenue opportunity does not support VC funding, consider another source of funding.

Financial Literacy. For things to go well, every company seeking a VC-led series A round needs to have at least one financially literate team member or adviser who knows his or her way around a balance sheet and profit and loss statement. Ideally, this is also a co-founder with fundraising experience.

There is simply no way to fake financial literacy in front of VCs. They all have MBAs, and many have decades of experience.

And it is not enough simply to have a respectable three-year financial model to email around. Someone on the team must be able to talk about its inputs, assumptions, and uncertainties. That same person needs to be able to run different scenarios, called sensitivity analyses, to quickly explain how the model's financial outputs change with different inputs.

Being able to crush these kinds of questions on the spot in VC meetings is a huge advantage for any founder team. It can make the difference between funding and no funding.

A potential solution for startups with no strong finance and accounting person on the team is to explore some type of part-time or outsourced CFO relationship.

Core Financial Metrics

Unit Economics. In connection with developing financial forecasts and preparing to discuss a company's business model with VCs, founders need to deeply steep themselves in their "unit economics."

Unit economics is the study of the fundamental economic/financial building blocks, or "units of value," of any business model. A classic definition of unit economics is:

> *"direct revenues and costs associated with a particular business model,… specifically expressed on a per-unit basis."*

Focusing on unit economics means looking at the costs and revenues associated with a company's core product or service, versus looking at costs and revenues more generally across an entire company or industry.

- How much does it cost to produce each widget and sell it, including costs associated with acquiring a customer ("Customer Acquisition Cost" or "CAC"), and how much can the company charge for the widget?

- For a service-based model, how much does it cost to get a customer and then deliver the service, and how much will the company derive from the customer – i.e., what is the "lifetime value," or "LTV," of a customer?

Analyzing unit economics is critical for forecasting, understanding when a business will become profitable, and assessing a business's viability.

A SaaS company's "unit of value" is a single software subscription. For a company selling bottled CBD beverages, the unit of value might be each beverage sold. Many service-driven businesses and even sellers of retail products define a "customer account" as a unit.

Each unit of value has a sale price, cost of sale, and gross profit. To complicate matters, many companies have more than one unit of value.

As noted, LTV and CAC are common drivers of unit economics, because many companies calculate their unit economics at the customer level, versus at the product level.

Calculating lifetime value of a customer for a subscription-type product or service requires knowing (i) how much the average customer spends on the company's service each month, (ii) how many months the average customer stays active (churn), and (iii) the company's gross margin.

Customer acquisition cost is simply the fully loaded cost of acquiring each customer, including related advertising and sales costs. For many businesses, this is generally calculated by comparing marketing or sales costs over defined periods, whether monthly or yearly, with the numbers of new, active customer accounts obtained during that same period.

To succeed, a company must have positive unit economics and the ability to scale them up to generate substantial gross profits. A company that can scale up its unit economics sooner will invariably be worth more (and be more interesting to investors) than the same type of business on a slower trajectory.

Speed to profitability is important not only because of the time value of money (a dollar now is worth more than a dollar a year from now), but also because of risk. Investments that take longer to return value are always riskier, a negative factor for valuation.

Founders should look online for resources for building financial models, understanding their unit economics, and determining CAC and LTV, and master all of these subjects before meeting with any VCs.

Customer Unit Economics. VCs will sometimes even ask founders of B2B (business-to-business) startups to try to analyze the unit economics of their customers, an even trickier exercise. Be prepared to answer this question by considering how much it costs your customers to purchase your product or service, what other costs are built into their unit economics, and their resulting gross margin.

As an example, one of my companies sells services that help brands get the most from their in-store merchandising efforts. Given retail's very tight margins, VCs asked how purchasing our services would impact our customers' unit economics. We were able to explain how our customers' slight incremental cost per unit was greatly outweighed by the substantial increase in unit sales, a fact our customers corroborated.

Preparing for VC Meetings

A VC's willingness to meet or get on a call or video conference should generally put that VC at or near the top of a founder's priority list, at least temporarily.

An extra level of research is warranted for a company's top 3 to 5 VC prospects. Founders should go into every VC meeting knowing everything possible about the VC and its team.

This level of research is time-consuming but imperative. VCs see hundreds, if not thousands, of companies, founders, and pitches. Deep research is necessary to effectively articulate exactly why a specific VC firm and team is a great fit for your company and why your company is a great fit for the VC firm.

Assume that other startup teams competing for a VC's funds are doing the same level of research and articulating similar synergies.

VC Decision Makers

In dealing with VCs, it is important to understand who makes the decisions. VC titles can be confusing since most of them sound important.

In order of decision-making authority, the hierarchy tends to be:

- general partners ("GPs")
- managing directors ("MDs")
- partners
- senior associates
- associates

In scheduling a VC meeting, it is always best to try to ensure that at least one GP or MD will be present. If they are not, consider making a gentle suggestion - *"Do you know if Steve or Ellen will be able to join us? It would be great to meet them as well."*

Deep Research and Preparation

Founders should prepare for any call or meeting with VCs as they would for a job interview.

- name, title, and background of every attendee,
- identities of the VC firm's top decision makers,
- all publicly available information about each of the VC's current funds, especially the amount originally raised, date funded, focus of the fund, and investments made,
- most recent investments made,
- key (top performing) portfolio companies, and
- all recent press releases from and news stories about the VC firm.

VC firms tend to have at least some biographical information about their teams, but finding much on individual VCs on LinkedIn can be hit or miss.

As in any situation where it is important to build relationships, looking for points of connection or common interests never hurts, whether a common school, hometown, former employer, community or philanthropic interest, or hobby.

Arrive a few minutes early to every VC meeting. Doing so has two benefits. First, it might reduce the chances of arriving late – something founders do with surprising frequency. Second, someone will usually show you to the meeting room early, which allows you to connect to the firm's presentation technology and get the pitch deck on the screen before the other attendees arrive.

Every meeting between founders and VCs starts with a minute or two of getting situated where informal introductions and small talk happen. Try to make connections that can create memorable, positive associations in the minds of the VC attendees.

- *"Steve, I hear you have a great winery in Walla Walla. My family had property there. Are you enjoying it?"*

- *"Beth, I believe you know my friend Jim, from ABC, Co. We had lunch the other day. I told him we were meeting and he said to say hello."*

- *"Ellen, I noticed that you graduated from XYZ a few years ahead of me. Do you ever get back?"*

If nothing else, starting things off with some lively conversation fills the room with positive energy.

As mentioned already, the best sources of information about individual VCs are founders who know them well, either from meeting with them recently or, better yet, having them on a board as a VC board designee.

A founder who knows a VC well can sometimes tell you what issues he or she will focus on, the questions he or she will ask, and how to tweak the pitch to gain their interest quickly.

Most VC meetings go very well, but occasionally founders struggle to hook a VC's interest quickly enough and things can get awkward or simply off-track. A big part of preparation is knowing what parts of the story are most likely to hook each group.

Many individual VCs have their go-to questions and issues – things like:

- "Tell me about your unit economics."

- "How are you different than XYC company?"

- "What key metrics do you focus on?"

- "What is your customer acquisition cost?"

- "What's the lifetime value of a customer?"

- "How much cash do you have and what's your burn rate?"

Knowing in advance what a VC might ask is like getting the questions for a test in advance. Some questions can be tricky to answer under pressure, especially if they can be answered correctly in different ways. The request, *"Tell me about your unit economics,"* is a good example of this. As discussed, VCs sometimes take different approaches to looking at unit economics.

Search online for "questions VCs ask," and you will find plenty of helpful articles. Getting caught flat-footed on basic questions can suck the energy out of the room and also potentially derail the conversation.

Demos and Prototypes

Be prepared to do a product demo at every VC meeting. Even if it is a second meeting, there will almost always be one or more new persons who have not seen the demo or handled the prototype.

Do not try to "wing" the product demonstration. Even if you rehearse it ten times, it will still probably fail or glitch-up in front of the VCs. Not practicing will only increase the likelihood and magnitude of any failure.

For certain types of platforms, it is important to ensure that nobody back at the company is tinkering with it during the demonstration. VCs tend to be pretty gentle in person about these things, but having to announce that "... *Someone must be in the test environment or something...*" shows a lack of preparation and questionable ability to execute on a basic task.

Always try to have a backup way to "perform" the demo. I have been in numerous VC meetings where the only thing that worked was the backup plan. Screenshots of the customer experience are not ideal, but almost any form of vaporware is better than nothing.

Anticipate what might go wrong and have an alternative. From my experience, Murphy's law is alive and well in every VC conference room.

A final tip on demos and prototypes is to try to get the individual VCs to engage with the product.

Listen for feedback. Be positive, never defensive.

Lastly, founders should not cut each other off, contradict each other, or exhibit any other signs of discord or misalignment, since the strength and cohesiveness of the team will be paramount in the minds of most VCs.

Business Plans

Unlike investment bankers, virtually no VCs will ask a company for its "business plan." But creating an MBA-style business plan is great preparation for meeting with VCs. It also provides a strong foundation for a thoughtful pitch deck and executive summary.

Hashing out a business plan also prepares founders to address the granular types of questions VCs often ask about things like market size, go-to-market strategy, product-market fit, competition, customer acquisition costs, unit economics, and staffing plans.

Consequently, companies seeking VC funding should have a business plan. But nobody wants to see it, so do not try to force it on them.

VCs are more likely to be interested in seeing or receiving a copy of a company's two or three-year financial model supporting its revenue and expense assumptions.

Case Study #42 Demo Daze

One of my financially riskier business activities involves working with startups on a deferred fee basis. In these arrangements, I accrue but defer fees or salary until I have helped the company establish a solid legal foundation and a business plan, and raise some capital.

It's a lot like angel investing. Some companies perform well and I am rewarded professionally and financially, not to mention the personal satisfaction of knowing I have helped someone launch an interesting, innovative business.

But I am not always the best picker. Sometimes I devote lots of time and effort to companies that fail. When the entrepreneurs are smart, hard-working, and appreciative, I take my lumps and learn my lessons.

It is more annoying, though, when entrepreneurs fall far short of my expectations of them in terms of their diligence, commitment, or candor. One young entrepreneur played me quite badly.

The core problem with this entrepreneur was that he was a liar and a poser. He talked up his B2B professional services platform deceptively, suggesting that substantial functionality had been coded and that a large test group was providing glowing feedback on its revolutionary features. He told me he had raised $600K and that most of that money had been spent creating a platform that was nearly ready for the market.

He talked a great game, but always had reasons why it was inconvenient or not possible to give me a full demonstration of the platform. I told him he would certainly need to be prepared to give a full demonstration when I put him in front of VCs. He showed no concerns about that.

After spending countless hours with him creating a financial model and a pitch deck and fine-tuning his go-to-market strategy, I set up a meeting at a large and prestigious VC firm.

It was just us and a single Managing Director at the meeting. The pitch was challenging from the get-go, but not unusually so. His addressable market was not particularly large, but his potential revenues per customer looked very good, at least on paper.

The real issues struck when the VC asked for a demo of the platform. The pitch deck included several pages showing the platform, its features and functions, and a comprehensive navigation system. The entrepreneur balked and said it wasn't quite where he wanted it. The VC said, "*I don't mind, I want to see what you have.*"

The entrepreneur resisted and the VC became quite insistent. I remember him saying impatiently and with authority, "*Look, you've raised and spent $600K developing the platform, I want to see what you were able to do with that money.*"

This had quickly become the most awkward pitch I had ever witnessed. I was getting embarrassed by the entrepreneur's strange behavior and was losing patience myself. I kicked him discretely under the table.

Reluctantly, the entrepreneur finally brought the "platform" up on the big screen. For $600K, all he had developed was a log-in function to nothing – an "account backend." The platform shown in the pitch deck was non-existent vaporware.

The VC was fairly blunt, practically ridiculing him for producing nothing more than a pitch deck and a financial model for $600K. The VC thanked us and cut the meeting short saying something like, "*You've got work to do before we'd be interested.*"

After the meeting, I told the entrepreneur I was done and cutting my losses. I told him that it was one thing to lie to me about the platform's stage of development, but that his willingness to harm my reputation was unacceptable.

Lessons: Among other things, this instance highlights the types of risks that VCs associate with single founders – fewer checks and balances, less accountability, and a single point of failure.

415

Also, potential investors will be very interested in knowing how entrepreneurs have used any money raised to date, as those achievements or lack thereof will be viewed as predictive of future uses of investment dollars.

And it should go without saying that a founder's reputation is everything. There is little to be gained by exaggerating or lying to advisors, team members, and especially to potential investors.

Launching an A Round

Launching any financing round should be managed as any other important project having distinct phases of execution: (i) preparation, (ii) launch, (iii) execution/middle, and (iv) completion.

So far, we have only focused on the preparatory phase, including initial "getting to know you" meetings with VCs. Some pre-launch VC meetings no doubt result in VCs rushing to present term sheets. But, more often than not, it is probably best to hold pre-launch meetings with a good number of well-targeted VCs, making it clear that the A round has not yet started.

There are many benefits to this. Most importantly, learning which VCs seem like they would be the best to work with.

Socializing a company to numerous VCs over several months leading up to an A round launch increases the possibility of receiving more than one Term Sheet.

Seeking Competing Term Sheets

Receiving competitive term sheets is a good goal. For most non-Silicon Valley founders with no successful exits yet, the likelihood of being lavished with multiple competing term sheets is low. As in many aspects of life, though, aiming high and executing strongly almost always produces the best results.

One important caveat – do not announce that you are seeking multiple competitive term sheets. Courting VCs is not like buying a car. It is always fine to say you are talking to a number of VCs in the space, but do not name drop. If asked about other VCs, use your best judgment, but try to gently avoid disclosing that information by saying something like, "*We prefer to keep that information confidential at this point.*"

The VC world is much smaller than most think. If a founder tells VC "A" they are also talking to VC "B," VC A is likely to send an email to VC B and ask them what they think of the company. When this happens, VC B might provide an inaccurate and unhelpful perspective.

Keep in mind that financing discussions are generally considered private and highly sensitive.

Any VC who insists on learning the identities of other VCs being approached over a founder's objections is tipping his or her hand. He or she is likely going to insist on other things over the founder's reasonable objections before and after any investment is made.

Founders should be alert for any signs that a particular VC might be difficult to work with and factor those into the company's VC rankings.

Pre-Launch Checklist

Launching a series A financing is similar in many respects to listing a house. Everything has to be lined up for a quick, smooth sale because the longer a house sits on the market, the more skeptical potential buyers become, leading to price declines and greater conditions on closing.

Similarly, a company's first VC-led financing needs to be thoughtfully and diligently queued up and positioned for success. Taking too long to close a round is the opposite of social proof. An offering that drags on, as many do, telegraphs to potential investors, correctly or incorrectly, that something must be wrong with the company's business model or the deal terms.

Let's re-visit some key lessons from the preceding chapters about positioning a company for a successful series A. Many of these things may have no impact on a particular VC's impression of a company, but shortcomings in any area risk alienating a company's top VC prospects:

- build a complete, secure, well-organized virtual data room,

- check the data room against a good due diligence list and make sure nothing important is missing, like PIIAs, formation and governance documents, documents from early financings, key contracts, and so forth,

- create a thoughtful and realistic two or three-year financial plan/spreadsheet forecasting revenues and expenses,

- comply fully with state and federal securities laws in all financing rounds and do not become a "bad actor" or associate with one,

- know what to share and not to share with VCs in order to protect trade secrets without using NDAs,

- make sure the cap table is complete, accurate, and maintained on a platform recognized by most VCs,

- be prepared to fully and accurately explain the cap table and the pro forma impacts of any existing notes or SAFEs expected to convert in the financing,

- try to resolve any significant open litigation or regulatory matters,

- ensure that all contractual arrangements are correctly documented and well-managed, especially key sales and user templates, licensing agreements, distribution agreements, manufacturing agreements, and key vendor agreements,

- be ready to describe the terms of all material contracts and key customer relationships,

- have a comprehensive IP strategy in place and in progress,

- implement good HR practices to ensure the receipt of consistent onboarding documentation and to prevent unexpected, poorly-timed employee-related disputes or claims,

- know how much money you need and exactly how it will be used to achieve what operational and revenue milestones,

- have a staffing plan that supports achieving those operational and revenue milestones, including the timing of key hires,

- have in mind a tight range of acceptable pre-money and post-money valuations that are ambitious but achievable,

- have a plan for dealing with a demand that founder shares vest or "reverse vest" through a clawback mechanism,

- have a plan for discussing when to increase the option pool and how much,

- do not run out of money during the A round process,

- have sophisticated deal counsel in place to negotiate the Term Sheet, and

- make sure your entity is not an LLC; optimally it will be a Delaware corporation.

Due Diligence

Some founders are a little confused about "due diligence." I had a founder mistakenly tell me that a VC was committed to investing and was already conducting due diligence.

I was busy and took this statement at face value and assumed he meant "legal due diligence," as the words due diligence customarily imply. I pulled back on cajoling the founder to continue contacting, talking with, and meeting with VCs on his top-20 VC list.

Believing he had a lead investor lined up, the founder unfortunately pulled back on communications with other VCs and lost momentum. Four weeks later, the VC decided not to invest. Whatever the founder thought he had heard, the VC was in a very preliminary phase of due diligence that might be called "business due diligence." This is a phase just after what might loosely be called "screening due diligence."

Screening due diligence is the most basic assessment of whether a company's model is within the VC fund's stated objectives and criteria in terms of stage of development, geographic location, sector, and deal size.

Business due diligence involves an assessment of business fundamentals – the management team, business model, product-market fit, and market size, to name a few likely areas.

These first two phases of due diligence happen before a VC will issue a Term Sheet. These phases of due diligence imply no degree of commitment and should not be construed or misinterpreted otherwise.

Legal due diligence generally only starts after a Term Sheet has been proposed. Legal due diligence begins with the VC's law firm sending the company a due diligence list, or due diligence request list. When you receive a due diligence list, you are in due diligence, not before then.

As described earlier, responding to a proper due diligence list requires effort and organization. Due diligence lists are generally spreadsheets containing between 300 and 700 separate questions and document requests. The questions and requests are often grouped by category. Each question and request is usually assigned to a specific department and person (i.e., "Legal/Swegle") on the spreadsheet and there are boxes for checking and tracking completed items and indicating where in a company's data room responsive documents are located.

Having a well-established data room makes for a smooth showing in due diligence. If issues come up in due diligence, they need to be resolved as quickly as possible. VCs might be willing to take a pragmatic view of outstanding litigation, an HR issue, or bad early financing documentation, but delays of any kind can kill deals

Lawyering Up

Going toe-to-toe with VCs is generally best done with lawyers at your side who know the VCs, their term sheet templates, their negotiating style, and their deal counsel.

In my personal view, the best way to lawyer-up for Term Sheet negotiations is to use the launch of an A round to negotiate a contingent, fixed-fee arrangement with a big name law firm – preferably one of the top twenty firms in terms of VC deals.

I spread my other legal work around, often favoring smaller and medium-sized firms for commercial litigation, IP, employment law, and even regulatory matters. But when it comes to VC financing, I go with the big firms.

I could certainly handle all aspects of lawyering my own companies' series A financings, but there are several reasons for entrusting complex financings to large, sophisticated firms.

First and foremost, these firms do the most deals and are more likely to know the other players and how to negotiate with them.

Second, they are staffed to provide rapid document turns through and beyond deal-closing, even on weekends and sometimes on holidays.

Not long ago, I finished closing a challenging $22 million financing plagued by numerous last-minute demands from lead investor counsel and from separate counsel for a bridge loan investor. These frustrating last-minute changes required our outside counsel to work late into the evening many nights in a row, right up to the day before Christmas Eve. I was impressed and grateful. A smaller firm might not have been able to keep pace and close that deal on schedule.

Third, larger firms are also more likely to provide staffing continuity over many years and through multiple financings.

Fourth, selecting the right counsel is also about optics and social proof. A company's counsel is a reflection on the company. Working with a top-tier law firm validates that the company knows what it is doing. The fact that a highly respected law firm is willing to put its reputation behind the company and its founders is positive social proof.

Whichever firm is selected, it should be one that the startup intends to stick with through multiple rounds of financing. This greatly facilitates marking up evolving deal documents from one financing to the next and reduces the potential for errors as things get more complicated.

Additionally, as discovered in Chapter 12, *State and Federal Securities Law,* working with the same law firm through all of a company's financings will likely make it easier to get a comprehensive Legal Opinion when necessary.

Structuring Legal Fees. Law firms are usually very interested in working with startups on the verge of a series A financing. The likelihood of funding provides some validation that bills will be paid. And helping with a financing transaction is the best way to learn everything about a potential client and the full range of its current and future legal needs.

Additionally, in the legal industry, there are substantial marketing and reputational benefits to being involved in closing VC deals.

As a result, founders should be able to negotiate contingent, fixed-fee agreements with certain of these major law firms for complete deal representation. Although these numbers will vary by situation, a contingent, fixed fee arrangement of $20,000 to $30,000 should cover legal representation for the Term Sheet negotiations, due diligence assistance, and documenting a series A deal, assuming the company has a reasonably clean governance foundation, cap table and balance sheet, a complete data room, and few legal or regulatory problems.

Again, this should be a contingent, fixed-fee arrangement with the law firm. "Contingent" means that the obligation to pay any fees to the firm should be *entirely contingent upon closing the deal.* No matter how much work the firm does, no fees should be due unless and until the series A financing closes.

Making the fees contingent is important because it ensures that the firm will be focused on ensuring a successful closing and also because, if the financing falls apart, as many do, the startup may not be in a position to pay any fees without bankrupting itself.

To offer that kind of fee arrangement, these firms may also want the right to make an investment of around 1% in the company at a pre-offering price per share. This might bother some founders, and it certainly raises the possibility of conflicts of interest, but I have never heard of an instance of an actual conflict of interest arising or becoming an issue. On the contrary, I believe it is healthy for a company's most important legal advisors to have a stake in its prosperity.

Contingent fee arrangements are less likely to be offered to companies working on more complex series B and C transactions, but non-contingent fixed fees may still be an option.

While $20,000 to $30,000 for a series A financing may seem like a lot of money, deals are a lot of work and obtaining the very best counsel at this critical juncture is a wise investment. The guidance and representation a talented deal lawyer can provide through a startup's financings is generally worth much more than the fees charged, particularly over the long run.

And again, a company with substantial legal or regulatory mistakes and loose ends might have to pay a premium to have those cleaned up. In such cases, a fixed-fee arrangement may be more difficult to negotiate.

Founders should use the leverage of their A round financing to timely engage top-tier counsel well before a Term Sheet arrives. This will give counsel time to get to know the company and hopefully even help the company anticipate any due diligence issues.

VC Term Sheets

As mentioned earlier, a signed VC Term Sheet is a serious commitment. While founders should be careful to confirm that a VC fund's investment committee has approved the investment, a signed Term Sheet generally means that the VC is committed to investing on those terms, subject to legal due diligence and negotiating more than a hundred pages of deal documents.

The provisions of a signed Term Sheet are carried over and used to create the deal docs discussed below under *Customary Deal Documents*.

Founders need to understand that, once they sign a Term Sheet, they should not renegotiate any of the key terms in the course of negotiating final deal documents – not the valuation, liquidation preferences, board representation, anti-dilution, shareholder protective provisions, or anything else specifically covered in the Term Sheet.

Reneging on key points agreed to in a Term Sheet would likely be viewed as a breach of good faith and could result in the deal being killed.

This means that founders need to get their Term Sheet right the first time. The best way to do that is to have a very good understanding of what to expect before receiving a first Term Sheet and, as noted above, to have sophisticated legal counsel standing by to immediately review and provide feedback on any initial Term Sheet received from a VC.

Other high-level thoughts on negotiating VC term sheets:

- Focus on the big picture, not just the amount raised and the valuation. Play a "long game." A founder-VC relationship should be viewed as a long-term partnership. The relationship should be built on a strong foundation of mutual trust, respect, and admiration.

- Term sheet negotiations should not be unduly contentious. A VC that does not like a founder team will not be nearly as helpful as a VC that values his or her relationship with a founder team. Negotiate thoughtfully with the leverage you have, but always protect and grow the future relationship – the long game.

- Founders lucky enough to be presented with more than one Term Sheet should be careful about using them too aggressively as negotiating tools. It is probably fine to let a VC know that you are still in talks with others, but playing VCs against each other is likely to result in one or all of the VCs backing out. Avoid being unlikeable, especially by reducing the discussions to money and little else.

- Similarly, once a deal has been struck, whether or not there's a signed Term Sheet yet, a VC that hears you are still shopping for better terms is likely to view that as a breach of trust and might back out. Avoid all conduct that might foster mistrust.

- Founders usually underestimate their burn rate and fail to ask for enough money in early financings. Be realistic, especially about revenues. Get enough money to get through the next set of key milestones without running out of money. Founders too often obsess more over maintaining their equity position than they do over the company's actual financing needs. This short-sightedness often ends up costing more equity in the long run when a later cash crunch weakens the company's negotiating leverage with investors.

- Reasonableness in negotiations is a two-way street. Be alert for signals that a VC might be unhelpful or unreasonable in the inevitable ups and downs that every business experiences. A VC who sticks to unreasonable positions at the outset of the relationship is unlikely to become more reasonable over time, particularly if the company finds itself in a difficult situation.

With that introduction, we turn to a look at specific provisions commonly found in Term Sheets. Several sample series A Term Sheets can be found in the BLSG Data Room under *Finance > Equity Financing Documents > Series A Docs > Term Sheets.*

Offering Terms

Most Term Sheets have an introductory section that highlights basic aspects of the deal. The following are some of the more common deal points covered in the introduction.

Closing Date. Not all Term Sheets specify an estimated closing date. Some simply state that closing will occur when all closing conditions have been satisfied. Requesting an estimated date that is thirty days out might help to keep both sides focused and driving toward a timely closing.

If a "second closing" is not provided for, that might also be something to raise. Many financings have a first closing with investors who know the founders better and who are farther along in their internal review, followed weeks later by a second closing that brings in additional cash from one or more stragglers. The need to break a round into an initial closing and a second closing is often driven by a company's need to get money in the door quickly, although it probably does not help for founders to emphasize financial desperation unless necessary.

Language contemplating a potential second closing can provide flexibility to bring in more money as other VCs or strategic investors finish their internal review and approval processes.

Investors. The most important information in this section is the identity of the lead investor. Some Term Sheet templates seek to account for 100% of the shares to be acquired and by whom. Consider requesting flexibility when appropriate to allow for other investors, perhaps language along the lines of "and other investors acceptable to the company and the lead investor."

Amount of Financing. This number will usually include language clarifying the exact amount of the raise, including any amount that relates to notes and SAFEs converting in the round. The National Venture Capital Association ("NVCA") template reads this way:

$[_____], [including $[_____] from the conversion of principal [and interest] on bridge notes].

The amount of cash raised should be sufficient to meet the company's cash needs for at least 18 months and maybe longer, depending on the milestones being funded.

<u>Price Per Share and Valuation.</u> This section of a Term Sheet can be addressed several ways. A specific price per share might be stated, along with a reference to an attached cap table. A more cryptic approach simply describes the post-money valuation, with no reference to a price per share or even a cap table.

A third approach provides the price per share and the fully-diluted pre-money and post-money valuations, with the new investors' post-closing ownership stake stated separately under the "Amount of Financing" section. That approach seems clearest. The following is from the Foundry VC firm's template, found at www.askthevc.com:

> $_____ per share (the "Purchase Price"). The Purchase Price represents a fully-diluted pre-money valuation of $ million and a fully-diluted post-money valuation of $ million.

<u>Type of Security.</u> A typical security description might read like this:

> Series A Convertible Preferred Stock (the "Series A Preferred"), initially convertible on a 1:1 basis into shares of the Company's Common Stock (the "Common Stock"). The Series A Preferred shall be considered "restricted securities" and shall be subject to customary restrictions on transfer and shall bear appropriate legends.

The "initial" 1:1 "conversion ratio" in this passage relates to the optional and mandatory conversion features discussed later. A conversion ratio of 1:1 is the market standard – one share of common for each share of preferred.

<u>Capitalization.</u> Some Term Sheets require that a current cap table be attached. Founders need to be ready to provide a reliable cap table whenever a Term Sheet is proposed. Signing a Term Sheet with an inaccurate cap table is likely to lead to serious credibility issues. Closing a financing with a knowingly inaccurate cap table would generally constitute securities fraud, so cap table issues need to be ironed out well before the Term Sheet stage.

Board of Directors

Each series of preferred stock that involves significant new investors usually results in the creation of a new board seat. In a series A round, this person would subsequently be referred to as the Series A Designee or the Series A Director.

In later rounds where only existing investors participate, there may or may not be interest in creating a new board seat, depending on the facts and any negotiations among the investors and founders. There is often logical and valid resistance to growing startup boards beyond five members, as larger boards usually result in more scheduling and quorum problems, delays in obtaining signatures on governance documents, and greater challenges in reaching consensus on important decisions.

Later rounds may also involve negotiations to remove an earlier board designee to make room for a series B or C designee. Seed shareholder classes are sometimes asked to give up their right to designate a board designee if key investors in the class are not participating in the current round.

The allocation of seats to be elected by each class of security holders is found in a company's Certificate of Incorporation. The mechanics for selecting or nominating the individual designees for each such seat, such as the Series A Director, are generally covered in a new or amended Voting Agreement.

However documented, the "lead investor" in a round often has the privilege of selecting the board designee, and the other members of the share class are obligated to vote for the lead investor's choice. In many VC financings, the lead VC in the round will appoint as designee the individual in the firm most familiar with and most involved with the company.

When faced with multiple Term Sheets, founders should carefully consider which VC firm is likely to put forward the strongest, most advantageous board designee. Founders should watch carefully for signs that a potential designee could be difficult, unsupportive, or unreliable as a board member.

The following is a typical Term Sheet clause on board representation:

> *The size of the Company's Board of Directors shall be set at five. At each meeting for the election of directors, the holders of the Series A Preferred, voting as a separate class, shall be entitled to elect one member of the Company's Board of Directors, which director shall be designated by the Lead Investor; the holders of the Common Stock, voting as a separate class, shall be entitled to elect four members of the Board of Directors.*

The Y Combinator Series A Term Sheet template is less wordy but leads to a similar result:

> *[Lead Investor designates 1 director. Common Majority designates 2 directors.]*

The Foundry Group Term Sheet template varies depending on Foundry's anticipated ownership stake:

> *The size of the Company's Board of Directors shall be set at Closing at [___] persons. The Board shall initially be comprised of _____, as the Foundry representative[s], _____, _____, and _____. The holders of Series A Preferred shall be entitled to elect [one] member[s] of the Company's Board of Directors, which director shall be designated by Foundry (the "Series A Director[s]"), the holders of Common Stock shall be entitled to elect [one] member[s] [who] [one of whom] shall be the person serving as Chief Executive Officer and the remaining directors will be [Option 1 (if Foundry to control more than 50% of the capital stock): mutually agreed upon by the Common and Preferred, voting together as a single class.] [or Option 2 (if Foundry controls less than 50%): chosen by the mutual consent of the Board of Directors].*

While the balance of board power will eventually tip away from a company's founders following a series of VC-led financings, that should never happen in a series A financing.

As a board grows in size through successive financings, founders should push for the inclusion of thoughtfully selected, truly independent directors. These should be experienced persons who know the important role they play in balancing the competing interests of founders and VCs for the overall good of the company and its shareholders. The presence of one or more independent directors can be instrumental (and inoculating) in approving transactions where all of the other directors have conflicts of interest.

Dividends

The following Term Sheet language is typical. An unsophisticated investor might believe the shares are entitled to dividends, but, as we know, the word "noncumulative" combined with the phrase "when and as declared" undercuts any such expectation and makes any suggestion of dividends largely illusory.

> *The holders of the Series A Preferred shall be entitled to receive noncumulative dividends in preference to any dividend on the Common Stock at the rate of 6% of the Original Purchase Price per annum when and as declared by the Board of Directors.*

This language means that no dividends will be owed or paid and no time or effort should be devoted to debating it. Any Term Sheet dividends clause that excludes the words "noncumulative" or "when and as declared" would be very non-standard and must be fixed.

Pro Rata Rights

Every VC Term Sheet will include rights that go by various names, including pro rata rights, pre-emptive rights, rights of first offer, and rights to participate pro rata in future rounds. These are rights, but not obligations, to maintain an investor's proportional ownership position in a company by participating in future rounds.

The following is a typical clause:

> *The Major Holders will have a right, but not an obligation, to purchase their pro rata share of any offering of new securities by the Company, subject to customary exceptions. The pro rata share will be based on the ratio of (x) the number of shares of Preferred Stock held by such holder (on an as-converted basis) to (y) the Company's fully-diluted capitalization (on an as-converted and as exercised basis). Participating holders will have the right to purchase, on a pro rata basis, any shares as to which eligible holders do not exercise their rights. The right of first offer will terminate on an initial public offering or change of control transaction.*

While there are not too many issues to consider regarding pro rata rights clauses, the following clause from the NVCA Term Sheet template suggests two worth considering – non-financing stock issuances that do not trigger pro rata rights and what I will call rights to "leftovers."

> *All [Major] Investors shall have a pro rata right, based on their percentage equity ownership in the Company (assuming the conversion of all outstanding Preferred Stock into Common Stock and the exercise of all options outstanding under the Company's stock plans), to participate in subsequent issuances of equity securities of the Company (excluding those issuances listed at the end of the "Anti-dilution Provisions" section of this Term Sheet.) In addition, should any [Major] Investor choose not to purchase its full pro rata share, the remaining [Major] Investors shall have the right to purchase the remaining pro rata shares.*

The phrase "excluding those issuances listed at the end of the 'Anti-dilution Provisions' section of this Term Sheet" is a reference to a list of stock issuances that don't trigger anti-dilution. By this language, those same types of issuances are also to be exempted from triggering investor pro rata rights. That list includes stock issued from the conversion of notes, preferred stock, and other instruments, and stock issued from the exercise of compensation stock options.

The previous example covered these exclusions with the more opaque phrase, "subject to customary exceptions."

An exception worth adding would explicitly cover "strategic transactions" – i.e., language such as "shares issued in connection with a strategic or commercial relationship."

As discussed later regarding Term Sheet Anti-dilution Provisions, suggesting a similar exemption to avoid triggering anti-dilution rights in the event of a strategic transaction, this language can provide a clever back door for a struggling company to bring in some quick cash from a strategic investor at a lower valuation and without offering the same shares to existing investors.

Also of interest in this sample clause is the right of Major Investors to pick up the "leftover" pro rata rights not exercised by other Major Investors. I would urge striking such a clause.

This "leftover" clause is a little like the much-derided supermajority pro rata rights that occasionally rear their heads in VC Term Sheets – i.e., that an investor has a right to participate at the rate of 1.5 times or 2 times their existing proportional ownership in future rounds.

These leftover and supermajority pro rata rights can generally only be harmful to companies. If a company is performing poorly, and they are not exercised by an existing investor, the lack of confidence shown by the investor could reflect poorly and spook new investors.

Worse yet, if a company is performing well, supermajority rights can drive away important new investors. Keep in mind that VC firms often have internal guidelines or even requirements that they must receive an ownership interest of 10%, 15%, or even 20% in a company to participate in a financing. Super-majority pro rata rights held by earlier investors can prevent new investors from investing if they cannot acquire a meaningful stake. This limits the number of potential investors for a round, and thus also can hurt the company's efforts to negotiate a fair valuation and other key financing terms.

Liquidation Preference

Fortunately, we wrestled through liquidation preferences and the significant differences between participating and non-participating preferred in Chapter 12, *Startup Finance Overview*.

In that discussion, we noted that the current standard of "1x non-participating" is perfectly reasonable from a founder perspective. Founders should resist more onerous proposals.

Different Term Sheet templates take more or less detailed approaches to liquidation preferences, with the Y Combinator template providing the most basic language:

> *1x non-participating preference. A sale of all or substantially all of the Company's assets, or a merger (collectively, a "Company Sale"), will be treated as a liquidation.*

The NVCA template, on the other hand, provides alternative language covering every potential liquidation preference and participation right combination, along with additional clarifying text on what constitutes a liquidation event:

In the event of any liquidation, dissolution or winding up of the Company, the proceeds shall be paid as follows:

[Alternative 1 (non-participating Preferred Stock): First pay [one] times the Original Purchase Price [plus accrued dividends] [plus declared and unpaid dividends] on each share of Series A Preferred (or, if greater, the amount that the Series A Preferred would receive on an as-converted basis). The balance of any proceeds shall be distributed pro rata to holders of Common Stock.]

[Alternative 2 (full participating Preferred Stock): First pay [one] times the Original Purchase Price [plus accrued dividends] [plus declared and unpaid dividends] on each share of Series A Preferred. Thereafter, the Series A Preferred participates with the Common Stock pro rata on an as-converted basis.]

[Alternative 3 (cap on Preferred Stock participation rights): First pay [one] times the Original Purchase Price [plus accrued dividends] [plus declared and unpaid dividends] on each share of Series A Preferred. Thereafter, Series A Preferred participates with Common Stock pro rata on an as-converted basis until the holders of Series A Preferred receive an aggregate of [_____] times the Original Purchase Price (including the amount paid pursuant to the preceding sentence).]

A merger or consolidation (other than one in which stockholders of the Company own a majority by voting power of the outstanding shares of the surviving or acquiring corporation) and a sale, lease, transfer, exclusive license or other disposition of all or substantially all of the assets of the Company will be treated as a liquidation event (a "Deemed Liquidation Event"), thereby triggering payment of the liquidation preferences described above [unless the holders of [_____]% of the Series A Preferred elect otherwise]. [The Investors' entitlement to their liquidation preference shall not be abrogated or diminished in the event part of the consideration is subject to escrow in connection with a Deemed Liquidation Event.]

Again, 1x non-participating is most common. Founders facing less favorable terms should negotiate as best they can at the margins for incremental improvements – perhaps asking for preference of 1.2x instead of 1.5x, or seeking a 1.5x participation cap instead of a 2x participation cap.

Term Sheet negotiations headed toward an unexpectedly low valuation or excessively high liquidation preferences could be a sign that the founders should consider other funding options that are less potentially harmful to the common holders. In such cases, founders often opt to extend their runway with additional seed rounds, hoping to use those funds to get the traction needed to enhance their leverage with potential VCs.

Voting Rights

Term Sheet language on voting rights can take many forms. Sometimes board composition clauses and protective rights are included, other times those concepts are addressed individually.

The following is a basic example of class voting language, with board representation and protective rights addressed separately elsewhere.

> *The Series A Preferred will vote together with the Common Stock and not as a separate class, except as specifically provided herein or as otherwise required by law. The Common Stock may be increased or decreased by the vote of holders of a majority of the Common Stock and Series A Preferred voting together on an as-if-converted basis, and without a separate class vote. Each share of Series A Preferred shall have a number of votes equal to the number of shares of Common Stock then issuable upon conversion of such share of Series A Preferred.*

The only notable aspect of that example is that the series A preferred have no class blocking rights for the authorization of additional common stock. This could make it easier for the company to add more common stock to a depleted stock option plan.

Here is an example where series seed shares have also been issued:

> *The Series A Preferred will vote together with the Series Seed Preferred Stock and Common Stock and not as a separate class except as specifically provided herein or as otherwise required by law.*

> *Each share of Series A Preferred shall have a number of votes equal to the number of shares of Common Stock then issuable upon conversion of such share of Series A Preferred.*

Like the other example, this voting language mostly states the obvious – that all classes vote together except as otherwise provided. Protective voting provisions often come later in a Term Sheet and specify situations where individual classes have separate rights of approval that serve as veto or blocking rights.

Protective Provisions

In Chapter 12, *Startup Finance Overview*, we discussed that protective provisions are essentially voting rights to block certain types of transactions.

They are written various ways in Term Sheet templates, and they warrant close attention to ensure that excessive control rights are not being sought by the VCs. Founders are at risk of losing substantial control and flexibility in the management of the company if they focus too much on valuation and too little on the details buried in protective rights clauses.

> *Approval of the holders of at least 66% of the Preferred Stock, voting together as a single class, will be required on (i) the creation of any senior or pari passu equity security, (ii) payment of any dividends on any class of stock, (iii) redemptions, repurchases (other than at cost in connection with cessation of employee/consultant services) of any class of stock or options, and any increase or decrease in the number of authorized shares of Preferred Stock or Common Stock; (iv) consummation of any sale of all or substantially all of the assets of the Company or any other liquidation event, (v) any amendment of the Certificate of Incorporation or Bylaws of the Company or any adverse change to the rights, preferences, and privileges of the Preferred Stock, (vi) any change in the size of the Board of Directors, and (vii) consummation of any liquidation, dissolution, merger, or sale of the Company.*

In addition, approval of the holders of a majority of the Series A Preferred Stock will be required on (i) any increase in the number of authorized shares of Series A Preferred Stock and (ii) any change to the rights or preferences of the Series A Preferred Stock so as to affect them adversely but not so affect all of the other series of Preferred Stock (provided that the authorization or issuance of a new series of preferred stock, on its own, is not deemed to have an adverse effect).

The 66% approval threshold in this example would be worthy of a founder's attention. Shareholders generally only vote on transactions that have been vetted and recommended by both management and the board. Giving a class of preferred shareholders a supermajority voting threshold to approve any kind of transaction can serve to limit management's and the board's flexibility.

Here is another example of a Term Sheet protective rights clause:

For so long as any shares of the Series A Preferred remain outstanding, consent of the holders of at least a majority of the Series A Preferred shall be required for any action, whether directly or through any merger, recapitalization, or similar event, that (i) alters or changes the rights, preferences, or privileges of the Series A Preferred; (ii) increases or decreases the authorized number of Preferred Stock; (iii) creates (by reclassification or otherwise) any new class or series of shares having rights, preferences, or privileges senior to or on a parity with the Series A Preferred; (iv) results in the redemption or repurchase of any shares of Common Stock (other than pursuant to equity incentive agreements with employees or service providers giving the Company the right to repurchase shares upon the termination of services); (v) results in any merger, other corporate reorganization, sale of control, or any transaction in which all or substantially all of the assets of the Company are sold; (vi) amends or waives any material provision of the Company's Certificate of Incorporation; or (vii) results in the payment or declaration of any dividend on shares of Common or Preferred Stock.

Although high voting thresholds for approving transactions are generally more constricting than beneficial, predicting how such control provisions will play out is an imperfect art. A high approval threshold, for example, might provide founders with strong negotiating leverage to increase the valuation in a later stage financing by giving them the ability to say credibly, "*I don't think we'll be able to get approval of our Series A holders at that valuation.*"

Drag Along

As we know, drag-along rights often allow the preferred stockholders to force a sale of the company. These rights allow VCs to timely wind down their investment funds.

Drag-along rights can also be used to force the sale of what VC's call "zombie companies." These are companies that may be providing a regular income for their founders and even many employees, but that are unlikely to provide any meaningful return for their investors.

In those cases, VCs sometimes force a sale to merely take a tax loss or, better yet, to get all or some of their investment back and use those funds to invest in a new and more promising company. VCs refer to this as "recycling" a fund's capital.

Here is an example of a Term Sheet drag-along clause:

> *The holders of the Common Stock and the Series A Preferred shall enter into a drag-along agreement whereby if, the Board of Directors and a majority of the holders of the Series A Preferred agree to a sale or liquidation of the Company, the holders of the remaining Series A Preferred and Common Stock shall consent to and raise no objections to such sale or liquidation.*

Even though an asset sale can often be approved by a simple majority shareholder vote, drag-along rights are necessary to facilitate a transaction with a buyer that wants to acquire 100% of a company's stock and also avoid fights with litigious holdouts.

It is always important to provide that board approval is required to trigger drag-along rights. Board approval provides a degree of minority shareholder protection by requiring the transaction to be approved by persons whose self-interest is constrained by fiduciary duties.

Optional Conversion

Optional conversion simply refers to the nearly universal right of preferred stockholders to convert their preferred stock into common stock. Preferred stockholders do that when, for example, they will do better in a sale by taking their pro rata consideration versus their liquidation preferences.

Preferred stockholders also have the option of converting to common on those rare occasions when doing so will help them control an important vote of the common stockholders, such as to approve a financing or a company sale.

The NVCA Term Sheet template contains this optional conversion language clause:

> *The Series A Preferred initially converts 1:1 to Common Stock at any time at option of holder, subject to adjustments for stock dividends, splits, combinations and similar events and as described below under "Anti-dilution Provisions."*

Mandatory Conversion

A Term Sheet's mandatory conversion clause describes when a series of preferred is automatically converted, whether or not approved by all or any of the preferred stockholders. The triggers for automatic or mandatory conversion generally include an IPO above a stated amount of proceeds and also a supermajority vote of the shareholders of the class. The following example is typical:

> *Preferred Stock automatically converts into Common Stock upon (i) the election of at least [66%] of the outstanding shares of Preferred Stock, voting together as a single class on as-converted to Common Stock basis or (ii) the consummation of an underwritten public offering with aggregate gross proceeds in excess of $50,000,000 (a "Qualified Public Offering").*

Regarding supermajority voting thresholds for mandatory conversion, it is almost always in founders' best interests to keep the number as low as possible, with 66% being about as low as is likely to be acceptable to VCs.

This allows for management and a board to more successfully push for conversion in the event of difficult circumstances. Mandatory conversion might be necessary, for example, where existing investors are not willing to fund an insolvent company and a new investor is only willing to come in if all of the existing preferred shares are converted to common stock in order to "clean up the cap table."

It is also important to ensure that the IPO proceeds threshold is not set unreasonably high. Founders enjoy greater flexibility and leverage with a lower conversion threshold. That said, the $50,000,000 figure in the above clause suggests a very small and barely viable IPO and is lower than most VCs would be willing to go.

By way of example, a $50,000,000 IPO threshold was carried over recently from a B round into a C round Term Sheet. The lead investor's counsel objected to it repeatedly in a call among company management and representatives from the lead investor. He argued that it was too low, bore no relation to the company's current price per share, and gave the company the ability to force a conversion of the preferred shares in a transaction that might not provide meaningful liquidity to the preferred investors.

The founder held firm to the $50,000,000 number, prompting the lead investor representatives to say to the founder, *"You don't always know why an investor passes on a deal, but I'm telling you I don't like the idea of an IPO at that level forcing a conversion."*

Anti-Dilution Provisions

As we learned in Chapter 12 under *Preferred Stock Key Provisions*, anti-dilution provisions are generally either full ratchet or weighted-average, with the latter being the most common and certainly the most reasonable option for founders and other holders of common stock. Anti-dilution works by adjusting the price at which preferred stock converts into common stock, with a lower (reduced) conversion price providing more shares upon conversion.

The following is a weighted-average anti-dilution description from a Term Sheet – watered down from the actual template:

> *The Conversion Price of the series A Preferred will be subject to a weighted average adjustment to reduce dilution in the event that the Company issues additional equity securities (other than shares (i) reserved as employee or service provider shares described under the Company's employee and service provider equity incentive plan; (ii) shares issued for consideration other than cash pursuant to a merger, consolidation, acquisition, or similar business combination approved by the Board of Directors; (iii) shares issued pursuant to any equipment loan or leasing arrangement, real property leasing arrangement, or debt financing from a bank or similar financial institution approved by the Board of Directors; and (iv) shares with respect to which the holders of a majority of the outstanding Series A Preferred waive their anti-dilution rights) at a purchase price less than the applicable Conversion Price. In the event of an issuance of stock involving tranches or multiple closings, the anti-dilution adjustment shall be calculated as if all stock was issued at the first closing. The Conversion Price will also be subject to proportional adjustment for stock splits, stock dividends, combinations, recapitalizations, and the like.*

This example includes some very common issuances that are excluded from triggering anti-dilution. As mentioned earlier regarding preemptive rights, another exclusion that founders might propose is one for "strategic transactions" – i.e., "*shares issued in connection with a strategic or commercial relationship.*" Again, this language can provide a clever back door, allowing a struggling company to bring in some cash from a strategic investor at a lower valuation.

As ubiquitous as they are, anti-dilution provisions are worth pushing back against in pre-A round financings, where they are less common. Further, only distressed companies or those with very limited financing options should accept full-ratchet anti-dilution.

Not only does the triggering of an anti-dilution clause in a down round harm founders, employees, and other common stockholders, anti-dilution clauses generally only add to the already very difficult challenge of closing a down round.

Redemption Rights

Redemption rights give investors the right, at least in theory, to force the company to buy back their shares after a certain number of years. Redemption rights are not common in series A Term Sheets, and founders would be wise to push back on them when they show up.

At a minimum, the redemption rights should not kick in for at least five or six years, triggering them should require an affirmative, supermajority vote by the holders of the class of shares involved, and the company should have at least three years to pay back the purchase price of the shares in question.

Redemption rights can be difficult or even impossible to enforce when they are most likely to be invoked since state laws limit the ability of insolvent companies to redeem their shares.

The Delaware Court of Chancery addressed these issues in a seminal case called *SV Investment Partners v. Thoughtworks, Inc.*, 7 A.3d 973 (Del.Ch. 2010). In that case, the court sided with the Thoughtworks board's determination that there were insufficient funds "legally available" to honor the redemption demanded by SV Investment Partners.

The court based its decision, in part, on the following:

> *Since at least 1914, this Court has recognized that, in addition to the strictures of Section 160, "[t]he undoubted weight of authority" teaches that a "corporation cannot purchase its own shares of stock when the purchase diminishes the ability of the company to pay its debts, or lessens the security of its creditors." Int'l Radiator, 92 A. at 255. In Farland v. Wills, 1975 WL 1960 (Del. Ch. Nov. 12, 1975), this Court enjoined payments by a corporation to its sole stockholder, including a repurchase of stock. The Court held that it was not necessary " to conclude preliminarily that there was an actual impairment of capital" under Section 160 of the DGCL.... Rather, the Court enjoined the repurchase on the legal principle that "[a] corporation should not be able to become a purchaser of its own stock when it results in a fraud upon the rights of or injury to the creditors."*

In finding against the plaintiffs, the court pointed out that, among other alternatives, they could have opted for a debt instrument providing the right to a specific payment at a specific time.

The Thoughtworks case analyzes several issues likely to arise in any redemption rights dispute. It would be worth reading in its entirety whenever debating redemption rights provisions or other rights designed to produce similar results.

The following redemption rights provision is from the NVCA template Term Sheet:

> *Unless prohibited by Delaware law governing distributions to stockholders, the Series A Preferred shall be redeemable at the option of holders of at least [_]% of the Series A Preferred commencing any time after [_____] at a price equal to the Original Purchase Price [plus all accrued but unpaid dividends]. Redemption shall occur in three equal annual portions. Upon a redemption request from the holders of the required percentage of the Series A Preferred, all Series A Preferred shares shall be redeemed [(except for any Series A holders who affirmatively opt-out)]*

Representations and Warranties

All properly drafted stock purchase and sale agreements require the parties to make fairly extensive, mutual "representations and warranties." Some Term Sheets, but not all, have a clause merely highlighting the fact that representations and warranties will be required.

The NVCA Term Sheet template contains this brief clause and optional, bracketed language:

> *Standard representations and warranties by the Company. [Representations and warranties by Founders regarding technology ownership, etc.]*

"*Standard representations by the Company*" suggests more agreement on that topic than I usually experience with deal attorneys, but the optimistic tone here is fine.

Conditions to Closing

Any "Conditions to Closing" clause should recite only that closing is subject to due diligence and the negotiation and signing of customary deal documentation.

The following is typical:

> *Any obligation on the part of the Lead Investor is subject to the following conditions precedent:*
>
> 1. *Completion of legal documentation satisfactory to the Lead Investor, including all necessary consents and approvals from existing stockholders of the Company.*
>
> 2. *Completion of legal due diligence by the Lead Investor.*

The NVCA Term Sheet template has slightly more specific language:

> *Standard conditions to Closing, which shall include, among other things, satisfactory completion of financial and legal due diligence, qualification of the shares under applicable Blue Sky laws, the filing of a Certificate of Incorporation establishing the rights and preferences of the Series A Preferred, and an opinion of counsel to the Company.*

In the NVCA example, the requirement of an Opinion of Counsel, or Legal Opinion, would add thousands of dollars in additional expense and could also add to overall deal risk, if not deal anxiety.

Lawyers don't sign opinions loosely, and getting agreement on scope and other specifics can be difficult, time-consuming, and uncertain if there are legal or regulatory issues.

A company with a clean, well-managed cap table and a confidence-inspiring data room might be able to successfully push back on providing a Legal Opinion.

We will look at Legal Opinions again when we discuss Customary Deal Documents.

Counsel and Expenses

Invariably, companies are expected to pay the lead VC's legal expenses. However this self-serving requirement originated, all a company can usually hope to do is cap the expenses at $20,000 or $30,000.

A typical Term Sheet clause on counsel expenses reads like this:

> *At the Initial Closing, the Company shall pay the Lead Investor's reasonable and documented legal fees and expenses to the Lead Investor (not to exceed $25,000 in the aggregate).*

Note that this clause says, "*At the Initial Closing.*" Under this language, the company would not be required to pay the lead VC's legal expenses if the deal does not close. This is very favorable language, but it is probably also rare.

Cooley's Series A Term Sheet template contains this clause on attorneys' fees:

> *Company to reimburse counsel to Purchasers for a flat fee of $10,000.*

This language gives the investors only $10,000, but the presumption seems to be that it must be paid whether or not the deal closes.

The NVCA Term Sheet template takes a slightly different approach with this language:

> *[Investor/Company] counsel to draft Closing documents. Company to pay all legal and administrative costs of the financing [at Closing], including reasonable fees (not to exceed $[___]) and expenses of Investor counsel [, unless the transaction is not completed because the Investors withdraw their commitment without cause].*

Founders should not draw much comfort from a "without cause" language in a clause like this. In most cases, investors will have one or more issues to raise in good faith or otherwise following due diligence as a basis for withdrawing a funding commitment.

Founders negotiating a legal fees clause should always push for a cap, starting as low as $10,000 and consider inserting "at the Initial Closing" language.

Barring success with the "initial closing" addition, founders might consider adding language that the company's obligation to pay legal expenses goes away if the lead investor withdraws its commitment for any reason.

One or more of these tactics might succeed if the lead investor knows the company still has other funding options, but founders should use good judgment and not allow a financing to fall apart over a $20,000 issue, or even a $30,000 issue. For any company having trouble getting a signed Term Sheet, this is not the right issue to take a stand over.

Registration Rights

Registration rights clauses frequently receive more legal and management attention than they warrant. They spell out company obligations to ensure that investors' shares do not remain unregistered, "restricted" securities following a company's IPO.

Registration rights are necessary because many IPOs only cover the issuance of new shares by a company and do not include registration of insiders' shares, for which the company would receive no proceeds.

Registration rights obligate the company to conduct and pay for registered "secondary offerings" of the investors' shares on a special SEC form called Form S-3.

These are relatively complex issues, but fortunately the registration rights clauses in most Term Sheets are relatively standard and the obligations they describe are relatively high-class problems for a company to have – and generally many years from being triggered, if ever.

Another thing worth noting is that, in the end, a company's investment bankers and the markets themselves often dictate when and how secondary offerings of insider shares are registered and offered to the public.

The following is a very brief and perfectly acceptable registration rights clause:

> *The Preferred Stock will be granted standard registration rights, including without limitation demand rights, piggyback rights and S-3 rights.*

Other Term Sheets, including the NVCA template, include lengthy provisions and sub-provisions regarding "demand registration rights" and "piggyback registration rights."

Piggyback registration rights require a company to include investors' shares in certain of the company's SEC registration statements so the investors' shares can be sold alongside the company's shares. Demand registration rights are superior because they allow investors to make a certain number of demands on the company to file SEC Form S-3 registration statements solely to cover sales of the investors' shares.

Given the complexity of these issues, founders should rely on sophisticated company counsel to guide the company's response to Term Sheet registration rights issues, but also be wary of counsel who suggest sweeping edits that could trigger a costly back-and-forth with investor counsel on a largely theoretical issue.

Lock-Up

In this context, the term "lock-up" refers to a future restriction prohibiting shareholders from selling into the market for six months after an IPO.

Again, no matter what terms are agreed upon prior to an IPO, the parameters of any IPO lock-up are likely to be dictated solely by company's IPO investment bankers. Lock-ups are found in most Stock Purchase Agreements, Stock Option Agreements and other equity issuance documents. Lockups prevent selling shareholders from dumping shares on the market too quickly after an IPO and depressing the stock's trading price.

Barring highly unusual language, it is generally best to leave this section of a proposed Term Sheet as is. Keep in mind that, ultimately, the investment bankers will negotiate for sole discretion over the nature and duration of insider lock-ups as part of any IPO "underwriting agreement." Rarely do investors interfere with the prerogatives and dictates of lead underwriters hired to run an IPO.

The following lock-up clause comes from the NVCA Term Sheet template and contains nothing out of the ordinary:

> *Investors shall agree in connection with the IPO, if requested by the managing underwriter, not to sell or transfer any shares of Common Stock of the Company [(including/excluding shares acquired in or following the IPO)] for a period of up to 180 days [plus up to an additional 18 days to the extent necessary to comply with applicable regulatory requirements] following the IPO (provided all directors and officers of the Company [and [1 – 5]% stockholders] agree to the same lock-up). [Such lock-up agreement shall provide that any discretionary waiver or termination of the restrictions of such agreements by the Company or representatives of the underwriters shall apply to Investors, pro rata, based on the number of shares held.*

Information Rights

Investors in any series A offering will require the company to provide regular reports and financial information, as well as rights to visit the company and inspect its books. These rights should be limited to investors with holdings over a certain threshold, as in this example:

> *The Company will deliver to any holder of at least [500,000] shares of Preferred Stock (a "Major Holder") (i) audited annual financial statements within 75 days following year-end and (ii) unaudited quarterly financial statements, capitalization table and stock option schedule within 45 days following quarter-end. Each Major Holder shall also be entitled to inspection and visitation rights.*

The NVCA Term Sheet template information rights clause is more detailed and, among other things, suggests optional language denying inspection rights to company competitors:

> *Any [Major] Investor [(who is not a competitor)] will be granted access to Company facilities and personnel during normal business hours and with reasonable advance notification. The Company*

will deliver to such Major Investor (i) annual, quarterly, [and monthly] financial statements, and other information as determined by the Board; (ii) thirty days prior to the end of each fiscal year, a comprehensive operating budget forecasting the Company's revenues, expenses, and cash position on a month-to-month basis for the upcoming fiscal year; and (iii) promptly following the end of each quarter an up-to-date capitalization table. A "Major Investor" means any Investor who purchases at least $[_____] of Series A Preferred.

Management Rights Letter

Management Rights Letters are discussed more fully later under *Customary Deal Documents* but are generally two-page documents that provide VCs with certain rights, including among others, rights to receive information, inspect company records, and consult with and advise management of the company on significant business issues, including management's proposed annual operating plans.

Management Rights Letters are less important than they sound, and Term Sheet language relating to them is generally not worth any expensive back-and-forth with investor counsel. Because management rights letters are largely driven by "ERISA" issues, as discussed later, VCs are highly unlikely to accept the deletion or modification of typical management rights clauses, most of which are similar to this:

The Company shall execute a Management Rights Letter in favor of Investor prior to Closing.

Special Board Approval Requirements

State corporate governance laws, together with case law, dictate a range of corporate actions requiring board approval, as discussed earlier. Some Term Sheets go further and enumerate other actions requiring board approval.

While many corporate attorneys likely view such terms as unnecessary, and even an infringement upon the flexibility of company management, these provisions, when properly tailored, can facilitate financial transparency and better governance.

Term Sheet provisions on board voting might also require not only board approval for certain transactions, but also approval by one or more shareholder designees. This is another form of blocking right.

The NVCA Term Sheet template contains these director blocking rights:

[So long as the holders of Series A Preferred are entitled to elect a Series A Director, the Company will not, without Board approval, which approval must include the affirmative vote of [one/both] of the Series A Director(s):

(j) make any loan or advance to, or own any stock or other securities of, any subsidiary or other corporation, partnership, or other entity unless it is wholly owned by the Company; (ii) make any loan or advance to any person, including, any employee or director, except advances and similar expenditures in the ordinary course of business or under the terms of a employee stock or option plan approved by the Board of Directors; (iii) guarantee any indebtedness except for trade accounts of the

Company or any subsidiary arising in the ordinary course of business; (iv) make any investment inconsistent with any investment policy approved by the Board; (v) incur any aggregate indebtedness in excess of $[___] that is not already included in a Board-approved budget, other than trade credit incurred in the ordinary course of business; enter into or be a party to any transaction with any director, officer or employee of the Company or any "associate" (as defined in Rule 12b-2 promulgated under the Exchange Act) of any such person [except transactions resulting in payments to or by the Company in an amount less than $[60,000] per year], [or transactions made in the ordinary course of business and pursuant to reasonable requirements of the Company's business and upon fair and reasonable terms that are approved by a majority of the Board of Directors]; (vii) hire, fire, or change the compensation of the executive officers, including approving any option grants; (viii) change the principal business of the Company, enter new lines of business, or exit the current line of business; (ix) sell, assign, license, pledge or encumber material technology or intellectual property, other than licenses granted in the ordinary course of business; or (x) enter into any corporate strategic relationship involving the payment, contribution or assignment by the Company or to the Company of assets greater than [$100,000.00].

Board voting provisions like these are not found in every series A Term Sheet and should be negotiated diligently. This example would allow one or more directors to veto any (i) change in executive compensation, (ii) new line of business, and (iii) various types of strategic relationships.

Founders should use what leverage they have to resist overreaching board approval requirements that could interfere with sound governance and management.

Non-Competition and Non-Solicitation

A Term Sheet clause on non-competition might read like this:

Each Founder and key employee will enter into a [one] year non-competition and non-solicitation agreement in a form reasonably acceptable to the Investors.

The law involving non-competition clauses is changing rapidly, putting such clauses under significant legal pressure. The above clause would no longer be legally enforceable in California and would be subject to substantial restrictions in Washington state. Public policy favors competition, commerce, employment, and employee flexibility.

Any clause purporting to reduce or possibly having the effect of reducing competition, commerce, employment, or employee flexibility should be reviewed closely for legality.

Employee Stock Options

There is often a clause in Term Sheets that requires the company to replenish its option pool to at least 15% of the company's total outstanding shares on a "fully-diluted" basis. As we have discussed, the reason for this is that, by replenishing the option pool before closing a financing, the additional dilution impacts the pre-financing investors and not the new investors.

This is a hard request to fight. Recent tradition favors the VCs on this one. Founders with no intention to use more than a 10% option pool in the coming twenty-four months might try to push the number down to 12% or even 10%.

Right of First Refusal

As discussed earlier regarding preemptive rights, series A investors and beyond will all receive the right to maintain their proportionate interest through future financing rounds. This is not something that should be resisted. Similarly, sophisticated investors will require that founders and other significant shareholders be required to offer shares for sale to them first before selling to outsiders. These are also terms that are not worth fighting over unless the mechanics are somehow unfair or illogical.

Right of Co-Sale

As we know, co-sale rights require founders and other shareholders to let others participate pro rata in opportunities for liquidity – i.e., to sell shares.

The following is one example of how co-sale language might appear in a VC Term Sheet:

> *The shares of the Company's securities held by the Founders shall be made subject to a co-sale agreement (with certain reasonable exceptions) with the Investors such that the Founders may not sell, transfer, or exchange their stock unless each Investor has an opportunity to participate in the sale on a pro rata basis. This right of co-sale shall not apply to and shall terminate upon a Qualified IPO.*

Co-sale rights are likewise very common and not worth arguing over.

Founders Stock Vesting

Discussions of founder shares are among some of the most uncomfortable discussions that can arise in Term Sheet negotiations.

Founders who have already earned all of their founder stock can suddenly find themselves re-negotiating their ownership interests and putting those interests in jeopardy.

If they had their way, VCs would always tell founders that all of their shares are subject to a four-year reverse vesting program, under which the founders allow their shares to be clawed back by the company if they leave or are fired for cause during the four year "reverse vesting" period.

From their perspective, VCs feel justified imposing "do-over" vesting. Their argument to founders is, *"We're investing in you, founders. Stick around or we'll give your stock to someone who will."*

These negotiations come down to pure leverage. Founders with several Term Sheets can afford to say, *"Go pound sand."* Founders struggling to get a single Term Sheet might find themselves earning their stock all over again. Pushing back and asking for two-year reverse vesting is a good strategy for founders.

Founders Activities

A small percentage of Term Sheets specify that the founders are expected to commit themselves 100% to the startup and will not engage in other work that either conflicts with or detracts from their commitment to the company.

These provisions all warrant careful negotiation. Founders should not unduly limit their ability to serve on boards or advisory boards that expand their abilities, connections, or expertise.

As a general rule, founders with leverage should try to strike such clauses. At a minimum, they should not prohibit participation on boards or advisory boards of companies with no obvious conflicts of interest. Companies can benefit greatly from founders' engagement with others in adjacent or complementary industries.

No Shop and Confidentiality

No shop clauses might be more common on the East Coast than on the West Coast. This is driven, in part, by the popularity of the NVCA templates in the East. The NVCA Term Sheet template includes this "no shop" clause:

> *The Company agrees to work in good faith expeditiously towards a closing. The Company and the Founders agree that they will not, for a period of [_____] weeks from the date these terms are accepted, take any action to solicit, initiate, encourage or assist the submission of any proposal, negotiation or offer from any person or entity other than the Investors relating to the sale or issuance, of any of the capital stock of the Company [or the acquisition, sale, lease, license or other disposition of the Company or any material part of the stock or assets of the Company] and shall notify the Investors promptly of any inquiries by any third parties in regards to the foregoing. [In the event that the Company breaches this no-shop obligation and, prior to [_], closes any of the above-referenced transactions [without providing the Investors the opportunity to invest on the same terms as the other parties to such transaction], then the Company shall pay to the Investors $[_] upon the closing of any such transaction as liquidated damages.] The Company will not disclose the terms of this Term Sheet to any person other than officers, members of the Board of Directors and the Company's accountants and attorneys and other potential Investors acceptable to [_____], as lead Investor, without the written consent of the Investors.*

In general, as long as a financing no-shop clause is reasonable in length, they are generally less concerning that no-shop clauses in M&A deals where much more is at stake and timing concerns are often even more critical. M&A no-shop clauses are discussed in Chapter 16, *The Exit*.

Summary - VC Term Sheets

Again, when faced with their first VC term sheet, founders need to "lawyer up" or risk committing mistakes that could be costly to themselves, the company, and the company's other investors.

Founders should generally trust their deal counsel to ensure a Term Sheet's provisions are not over-reaching, and focus their efforts on bigger concerns such as valuation, liquidation preferences, protective provisions and other clauses that impact management and decision-making, and board composition:

- Do any protective provisions overreach into areas that should be left to the board? Or do they require unreasonable supermajority voting thresholds that could interfere with the board's flexibility?

- What does this deal mean for the makeup of the board, and how is decision making likely to change?

- It is rare for a financing round to result in two board seats. If a deal is headed in that direction, can the company push for one of those to be merely a board observer?

- From the outset of any discussions involving a potential new board seat, identify and push for the best available individual candidate to occupy that board seat in terms of expertise, industry profile, credibility, connections, temperament, people skills, and chemistry with the founders.

- If the company has leverage and the potential board seat candidates are either weak or unknown, consider pushing for rights in the Shareholders Agreement or Voting Agreement to force the investor(s) with a board seat right to appoint a new designee if the founders find a particular designee adds little value or is disruptive.

- Consider adding "stock issuances in strategic transactions" to the list of future stock issuances that do not trigger preemptive rights or anti-dilution.

- Be sure the Term Sheet contemplates and permits a second closing to ensure that the entire round can be filled out by any stragglers.

Customary VC Deal Documents

Term Sheets can be fairly long and detailed, but for the most part, they are non-binding outlines of key concepts. Their only legally binding provisions tend to be "Confidentiality" and, if included, the liquidated damages provisions of a "No Shop" clause.

Once a Term Sheet is signed, the founders and their deal team will hit a busy phase requiring focus and discipline to close the deal as quickly as possible. If the round hasn't already been "fully subscribed," the founders should also be marketing the now well-defined deal to any other investors who were "waiting to see a term sheet."

Simultaneously with this furious marketing push to "fill out" the round, legal due diligence needs to go into high gear and company counsel should waste no time circulating initial deal documents.

The following overview of the types of documents common to VC-led financings is general and is provided primarily for context and high-level tips. No founder or new attorney will be completely comfortable working with many of these types of documents until completing multiple VC-led financings and experiencing how these documents are drafted and operate in the real world.

Closing Checklist

A Closing Checklist provides a road map of everything that will be required to close a financing.

Closing Checklists are used solely for internal purposes by the company and its counsel to ensure that key steps aren't missed and that the closing process goes smoothly. In any deal, the absence of a single document or signature can hold up a financing. Closing Checklists are present in every well-run major financing, particularly series A and beyond.

Closing Checklists generally run several pages and serve the following functions:

- detailing all of the documents that need to be circulated, signed, and filed pre-closing and post-closing,

- assigning responsibility to specific individuals or entities for the completion of each task,

- detailing whose signatures, if any, are required for each document, and

- tracking the status of each such task.

A sample series C Closing Checklist can be found in the BLSG Data Room at *Finance > Equity Financing Documents > Series A Docs.*

Investor Questionnaire

Completed and signed Investor Questionnaires should be collected from every investor prior to closing. They are often circulated with the first near-final draft of the Stock Purchase Agreement, or SPA.

Unlike other documents collected prior to closing, Investor Questionnaires are not included with the fully executed documents distributed post-closing to investors. Instead, they are retained by the company as compliance records.

It would be reasonable to assume that most VCs or institutional investors should not be forced to sign Investor Questionnaires. After all, these professional investors are the epitome of accredited investors. But as has been discussed already, Investor Questionnaires also usually require attestation that the investor is not a "bad actor" and is not associated with any bad actors. For this reason alone, it is likely common practice to obtain signed questionnaires from *all* investors.

Stock Purchase Agreement

The SPA in a VC-led round will be longer and more detailed than a Founder SPA or an SPA for a common stock financing or a series seed financing, although the latter is closer in length and complexity.

A sample Series A SPA can be found in the BLSG Data Room at *Finance > Equity Financing Documents > Series A Docs.*

As discussed earlier, an SPA is a contract. In this case, the parties are the company and its new investors. Many of the terms of the contract are intended to formalize the understandings from the VC Term Sheet, including:

- the per-share purchase price,

- the series of preferred stock being offered,

- the company's obligation to file an Amended and Restated Certificate of Incorporation to create the new shares and define their rights and preferences,

- reps and warranties by both the company and the investor;

- timing and conditions of closing, such conditions being, for example, that the reps and warranties are still true and that the Amended and Restated Certificate of Incorporation has been filed,

- uses of proceeds,

- obligations of the parties to enter into collateral agreements, often including a Stockholders Agreement, Investor Rights Agreement, and a Right of First Refusal Agreement, and

- general or miscellaneous provisions such as survival of warranties, successors and assigns, governing law, notices, severability, dispute resolution, and so forth.

VC SPAs are particularly bloated in a section captioned "Company's Representations," or "Representations and Warranties of Company." In a recent series C financing, the company's representations and warranties filled fifteen pages.

Although it is even more important in M&A deals to ensure that reps and warranties are reasonable, founders should be sure to scrutinize them in any financing and take counsel's advice on where and how to limit them. In any event, founders will be forced to scrutinize all of the reps and warranties in preparing a proper Disclosure Schedule. Management needs to take the lead in preparing the Disclosure Schedule.

Amended and Restated Certificate of Incorporation

Well in advance of closing, investors will be permitted to review the company's draft Amended and Restated Certificate of Incorporation, which must be filed and confirmed by the Secretary of State where the company is incorporated immediately prior to closing.

Examples of highly evolved Articles of Incorporation can be found in the BLSG Data Room at *Company Formation and Governance > Corporations > Articles of Incorporation.*

Investor Letter

Investor Letter or Investor Disclosure Package Letter is just one possible name for an optional, high-level disclosure document that can be sent to investors just prior to closing to provide an overview of the offering and the steps needed to close, and it might also serve as a final opportunity to list some key risk factors.

In every securities offering, there should be at least one prominent "belt and suspenders" disclosure document that the company can later point to as evidence that the investors were clearly apprised of the company's and the offering's key risk factors. The Disclosure Schedule serves this purpose in a VC-led financing, but they are usually lengthy and legalistic. A Disclosure Package Letter can more clearly highlight key risks.

Some attorneys also like to attach a copy of the company's Disclosure Schedule and reference it in the Investor Letter, although it is also perfectly fine to attach the Disclosure Schedule solely to the Stock Purchase Agreement, the document of which it is a schedule.

Disclosure Schedule/Schedule of Exceptions

Again, the many pages of representations and warranties in a VC SPA (or an M&A SPA or APA) will tie directly to a key disclosure document called the Disclosure Schedule or Schedule of Exceptions.

It is essentially impossible for any company to make all of the required reps and warranties in a VC financing without some caveats, explanations, or outright "exceptions." These and other disclosures of caveats, exceptions, requested items, and outright corrections against the reps and warranties in the Purchase and Sale Agreement make up the Disclosure Schedule.

Shareholders Agreement

In Chapter 8, *Structuring and Managing Key Relationships*, we looked at Shareholders Agreements. Early in a company's development, they are primarily for ensuring the continuity of the company's management and ownership. Typical provisions can include:

- transfer restrictions and legends,
- rights of first refusal,
- share voting requirements relating to board seats and composition,
- preemptive rights, and
- co-sale rights.

In a VC-led financing, the purpose shifts a bit the other way, including with drag-along rights allowing the VCs to force a sale, among other things.

Interestingly, it seems more common in VC-led deals to *not* have a Shareholders Agreement or Stockholders Agreement, but rather to accomplish the same "control" objectives through a Voting Agreement, Right of First Refusal and Co-Sale Agreement, and sometimes also a Preemptive Rights Agreement.

While there are no hard and fast rules, it seems that Shareholders Agreements are more common in pre-VC financings, but are less common among companies that have been through their first VC-led financing. An advantage of this multi-document approach is that it is easier to split up which shareholders receive certain rights, such as preemptive rights.

Voting Agreement

As we just learned, at the time of a first VC-led financing, a company previously operating under a Stockholders Agreement or Shareholders Agreement might find that document replaced with one or more documents, including a Voting Agreement, a Right of First Refusal and Co-Sale Agreement, and possibly a Preemptive Rights Agreement.

A VC Voting Agreement is an agreement under which the parties agree to vote their shares of stock in certain ways regarding the following types of matters:

- election of directors/board composition,
- removal of directors,
- approving financing transactions, and
- approving sale transactions.

Board composition provisions are central to every Voting Agreement. They ensure that the lead VC's designee will be elected to the board and that only certain shareholders can vote to remove that person from the board.

Through sequential VC-led funding rounds, the same Voting Agreement is often amended to provide for the election of a series A board designee, a series B board designee, a series C board designee, and so forth, unless and until investors in an earlier round do not invest in a subsequent round and lose their board seat rights.

Drag-along rights are also common in Voting Agreements. The language used in these provisions is often highly negotiable, particularly regarding the dollar thresholds and other aspects of the transactions deemed to be covered. This is an area where founders and their advisors should pay close attention.

As an example, it is reasonable to negotiate for drag-along provisions to only cover financing and M&A transactions that benefit all classes of shareholders. Thus, regarding a sale of business drag-along clause, a founder might push for a minimum dollar threshold that exceeds (i) the total liquidation preferences owed to preferred stockholders plus (ii) the amount of any debt in order to ensure the drag-along only covers sales that would also provide some payout to the common stockholders.

Find sample Voting Agreements in the BLSG Data Room under *Company Formation and Governance > Corporations > Voting Agreements.*

Right of First Refusal and Co-Sale Agreement

As we learned in Chapter 8, *Structuring and Managing Key Relationships,* ROFR provisions are intended to prevent a company's shares from being sold to persons not already on the cap table, to keep shares out of the hands of potentially hostile or adverse parties, and to prevent voting control from being transferred to persons not subject to any applicable Voting Agreement.

And again, co-sale rights allow their holders to include some or all of their shares in any sale of shares by another shareholder. These provisions are intended to allow certain shareholders the right to participate in any "liquidity" opportunities that may come up.

Find sample Right of First Refusal and Co-Sale Agreements in the BLSG Data Room under *Company Formation and Governance > Corporations > Right of First Refusal and Co-Sale Agreements.*

Investor Rights Agreement

Investor Rights Agreements, or Investors' Rights Agreements, are rarely if ever part of any financing transaction unless VCs are involved, but they are part of every VC transaction.

A typical Investor Rights Agreement covers three topics – information rights, inspection rights, and registration rights. We have already discussed registration rights extensively.

Information Rights/Delivery of Financial Statements. These clauses usually require a company to deliver to each "Major Investor" unaudited quarterly financial statements and audited annual financial statements, as well as an annual budget and business plan.

Inspection Rights. This clause typically grants each "Major Investor" the right to visit company facilities and ask questions. Here is a typical clause:

> *"The Company shall permit each Major Investor, at its own expense and upon written request, to visit and inspect the Company's properties; examine its books of account and records; and discuss the Company's affairs, finances, and accounts with its officers, during normal business hours…, provided… the Company shall not be obligated… to provide access to any information that it reasonably and in good faith considers to be confidential information, a trade secret or the disclosure of which would adversely affect the attorney-client privilege between the Company and its counsel."*

Registration Rights. While information rights and inspection rights might take up two pages in an Investor Rights Agreement, clauses on registration rights may go on for another ten or more pages.

Registration rights are generally only negotiable around the edges, i.e., the number of "demand registrations" and the time intervals between them. Founders should follow the advice of experienced counsel and not let haggling over registration rights minutia become a deal hindrance.

In the rare event that registration rights are going to cause problems, that will likely be far off in the future, and it will probably be someone else's problem.

That said, I did once serve as an expert witness in securities litigation focused entirely on registration rights.

Compliance Certificate

In most VC-led financings, a senior company officer, usually the Chief Executive Officer or the Chief Financial Officer, is required to deliver to the purchasers at closing a Compliance Certificate, also sometimes called an Officer's Certificate, certifying that certain specified conditions to closing have been fulfilled.

These conditions are usually (i) that the company's representations and warranties remain true at closing (any last-minute affirmation of specific facts is often called a "bring down") and (ii) that the company has performed and complied with all covenants, agreements, obligations, and conditions contained in the SPA required to be performed or complied with by the company on or before closing.

Indemnification Agreement

An Indemnification Agreement in a VC-led financing is a document that contractually obligates the company to provide full and timely indemnification to the Lead VC's board designee.

Until a VC-led financing, most board members derive a certain degree of comfort from hold-harmless and indemnification clauses commonly found in their companies' Certificates of Incorporation and Bylaws.

Here is a typical set of clauses from a Certificate of Incorporation:

> *To the fullest extent permitted by the Delaware General Corporation Law,… a director of the Company shall not be personally liable to the Company or its stockholders for monetary damages for breach of fiduciary duty as a director. If the Delaware General Corporation Law is amended to authorize corporate action further eliminating or limiting the personal liability of directors, then the liability of a director of the Company shall be eliminated or limited to the fullest extent permitted by the Delaware General Corporation Law, as so amended.*

> *The Company shall indemnify, to the fullest extent permitted by applicable law, any director or officer of the Company who was or is a party or is threatened to be made a party to any threatened, pending or completed action, suit or proceeding, whether civil, criminal, administrative or investigative (a "Proceeding") by reason of the fact that he or she is or was a director, officer, employee or agent of the Company or is or was serving at the request of the Company as a director, officer, employee or agent… against expenses (including attorneys' fees), judgments, fines and amounts paid in settlement actually and reasonably incurred by such person in connection with any such Proceeding….*

Company Bylaws frequently contain similar requirements and go even further, mandating how indemnification is to be provided and also permitting or even requiring the company to maintain director and officer insurance coverage ("D&O"), as in this language:

> *…The expenses of officers and directors incurred in defending a civil or criminal action, suit or proceeding must be paid by the corporation as they are incurred and in advance of the final disposition of the action, suit or proceeding upon receipt of an undertaking by or on behalf of the director or officer to repay the amount if it is ultimately determined by a court of competent jurisdiction that he is not entitled to be indemnified by the corporation. Such right of indemnification shall be a contract right which may be enforced in any manner desired by such person. Such right of indemnification shall not be exclusive of any other right which such directors, officers or representatives may have or hereafter acquire and, without limiting the generality of such statement, they shall be entitled to their respective rights of indemnification under any bylaw,*

agreement, vote of stockholders, provision of law or otherwise, as well as their rights under this Article.

The Board of Directors may cause the corporation to purchase and maintain insurance on behalf of any person who is or was a director or officer of the corporation or is or was serving at the request of the corporation as a director or officer of another corporation, or as its representative in a partnership, joint venture, trust or other enterprise against any liability asserted against such person and incurred in any such capacity or arising out of such status, whether or not the corporation would have the power to indemnify such person....

Notwithstanding the existence of these types of limitations on liability and affirmative indemnification obligations, most VCs will require that the company sign an Indemnification Agreement, providing an enforceable contractual obligation between the company and the VC director designee.

Indemnification Agreements vary, but they can expand and clarify indemnification obligations in several ways, including the following:

- extending indemnification to the VC firm that appoints a director designee;

- clarifying that any insurance carried by the director or by the VC firm that designated the director is secondary to D&O coverage carried by the company,

- clarifying rights to indemnification when the indemnitee's defense is successful as to some claims but not others, and defining what constitutes success, including dismissal of a claim, with or without prejudice,

- providing indemnification for expenses even if an indemnitee is only "threatened" with a claim or action,

- requiring indemnification of the director for expenses incurred merely in the capacity of a witness in a claim or action; and

- establishing criteria and processes for selecting an "Independent Counsel" when necessary to determine entitlement to indemnification.

A sample Indemnification Agreement can be found in the BLSG Data Room under *Company Formation and Governance > Indemnification Agreements*.

Legal Opinion

A VC-led financing is generally the first time most companies find themselves paying for a Legal Opinion and seeing the types of issues they can raise. In a financing, a Legal Opinion is intended to assure the investors that the company's external legal counsel have looked closely at the company, its organization and standing, the facts underlying the cap table, and also the soon-to-be-issued shares, and that the attorneys are willing to state in writing that they found no irregularities with any of the foregoing.

A financing Legal Opinion generally covers the following specific items:

- that the company is incorporated, validly existing and in good standing,

- that the company has the power and authority required to conduct its business and to execute, deliver, and perform its obligations under the financing documents,

- the numbers and classes of shares that are outstanding immediately prior to the closing of the financing transaction,

- that the company's board and stockholders have taken all necessary steps to execute, deliver, and comply with the financing documents and to authorize the sale and issuance of the shares to be issued in the financing,

- that the shares to be issued will be validly issued, fully paid, and nonassessable,

- that the company will have sufficient authorized shares of common stock to accommodate conversion of the preferred following the closing of the financing, and

- that no other consent, approval, or authorization of, or filing with, any governmental authority is required.

The Legal Opinion might also confirm that counsel is unaware of any preemptive rights, rights of first refusal, or other prior or superior rights to acquire the shares in question, and it might also confirm that counsel is unaware of any undisclosed litigation or regulatory actions.

These are all great things to have covered in a Legal Opinion. The problem with Legal Opinions, though, is that an eleven-page Legal Opinion is usually composed of about seven pages of qualifiers, caveats, hedging language, and other "weasel words" masquerading as important legalese. And legal opinions are not cheap, usually averaging between $5,000 and $10,000.

Company counsel should be asked to produce a draft of their proposed Legal Opinion relatively early in the process, in case any difficult issues come up, particularly relating to prior financings, cap table issues, or other matters that might take time to work through.

Waiting for a law firm to produce a Legal Opinion when a deal is almost closed can be stressful, particularly given that they generally must be approved by the firm's "Opinion Committee."

As a cautionary note, any company with one or more poorly documented equity offerings can have difficulty getting a clean Legal Opinion. Opinions that specifically disclaim covering certain earlier offerings are less than ideal.

The NVCA Model Forms website includes a downloadable Model Legal Opinion at:
https://nvca.org/model-legal-documents/.

Management Rights Letter

As we discussed earlier, Management Rights Letters are fairly inconsequential documents, particularly given the information and inspection rights often found already in most Investor Rights Agreements.

Their presence in VC deals is driven primarily by the desire of VCs to not become subject to certain requirements of the Employee Retirement Income Security Act of 1974 (ERISA) and related regulations.

The ERISA issue stems from the fact that pension funds frequently invest in VC funds, creating the possibility that the VC fund will be deemed "ERISA plan assets" and that the VC managers then would be deemed ERISA plan fiduciaries.

A Management Letter in favor of a VC fund makes the fund a "venture capital operating company," and thus exempt from being deemed to hold ERISA plan assets.

Founders and other startup advisers should simply view Management Letters as a bit of a formality. It is certainly possible that a VC firm might misuse its rights to unreasonably pester company management and no doubt that has occurred, but that problem could happen with or without a Management Letter.

The BLSG Data Room has a sample Management Rights Letter under *Finance > Equity Financing Documents > Misc Financing Documents*.

Side Letters

Side Letters are another common feature of VC deals, and perhaps the murkiest type of document in financing deals. The idea behind a Side Letter in a VC financing is to create or define special rights and privileges outside of the main transactional documents.

These special rights or privileges often go to a significant investor, if not the lead investor. Sometimes they go to a strategic investor.

Side Letters can involve:

- providing a VC firm with a board observation right,
- detailing the terms and mechanics of "board seat rights" to be implemented and maintained in a Voting Agreement, including conditions upon which the investor agrees to give up its right to designate a board member,
- providing preemptive rights,
- describing a potential commercial arrangement with a strategic investor, or
- providing for other contractual rights.

In one Side Letter, an investor with rights to designate a board member under a Voting Agreement agreed that, in the event it did not invest more than $2 million and another "New Investor" did invest more than $2 million, the investor would forfeit its right to designate a board member and sign an amendment to the Voting Agreement allowing the New Investor to have that board seat designation right.

Side Letters, no doubt, sometimes stray into more unusual areas. The language below is taken directly from a fairly aggressive Side Letter, underlining added:

> *"This letter will confirm our agreement that effective as of the date hereof, [REDACTED], Inc., a Delaware corporation (the "Company"), hereby agrees that the confidentiality and non-use obligations of [VC NAME REDACTED], a Delaware limited partnership (the "Investor"), contained in Section 2.3 of the Amended and Restated Investors' Rights Agreement among*

the Company, the Investor and the other parties thereto, dated as of the date hereof (as may be amended from time to time, the "IRA"), shall not apply to Investor, and such confidentiality and non-use obligations of the IRA are null and void ab initio, and of no force or effect in relation to Investor. The Company further explicitly acknowledges and agrees that no fiduciary relationship or obligations are created or exist between the Investor and the Company pursuant to such confidentiality and non-use obligations contained in the IRA.

Investor acknowledges that, notwithstanding the terms of the IRA, the Company shall not be obligated to provide access to any information that it considers to be a trade secret or confidential information or the disclosure of which would adversely affect the attorney-client privilege between the Company and its counsel."

What this Side Letter says is that the VC firm in question has no obligations to keep company information confidential and no obligation to not use company confidential information for its own competitive or financial advantage. It could use the information, for example, to help another of its portfolio companies in which it had a bigger investment.

As discussed earlier, VCs never sign NDAs. Off-putting as that may be, it is notably worse for an investor to have broad rights to regularly receive confidential company information under an Investor Rights Agreement and then have a Side Letter disclaiming all confidentiality and non-misuse obligations.

It is not clear how a company officer can sign such a letter without violating his or her fiduciary duties to the company.

And at least one major case has found a Side Letter invalid, *ESG Capital Partners v. Passport Special Opportunities Fund*. In this 2015 case, the Delaware Court of Chancery found that the Side Letter in question was invalid because it had been nullified by an "integration clause" in the Subscription Agreement, as to which the Court said:

"… the integration clause in the Subscription Agreement rendered the Side Letter a nullity. It stated that the Subscription Agreement constitutes the entire understanding among the parties with respect to the subject matter hereof, and supersedes any prior understanding and/or written or oral agreements among them…. Passport Capital and the Original GP signed the Side Letter on March 4, 2012. On March 5, the next day, Passport Capital signed the Subscription Agreement. The Side Letter was a prior agreement relating to the subject matter of the Subscription Agreement. The subsequent agreement therefore superseded its terms."

The case also highlights the risks that company officers might commit to terms beyond their authority in Side Letters to induce a major investor to participate. Officers and others can exceed their authority by making promises that contradict or violate underlying deal documents or by making promises contrary to the officers' fiduciary duties to the company or to other shareholders.

Other concerns raised by this case are the possibility of committing fraud or other wrongdoing by secretly promising benefits to certain investors without telling the others. If it is later determined that the withheld information would have been material the other investors, those omissions might violate state and federal securities antifraud rules.

Previously, it seemed to be the case that Side Letters were tacitly accepted by other investors as confidential between the company and the counterparty. More recently, some VC SPAs are requiring that all Side Letters be listed and described in a company's Disclosure Schedule or Schedule of Exceptions. This trend should dispel expectations that Side Letters will remain "on the side."

In summary, company officers being asked to sign Side Letters should be sure to seek the assistance of competent deal counsel. More routine Side Letters that are fully disclosed to all other investors are unlikely to cause any problems. Secret Side Letters promising non-routine preferences may be worth pushing back on for risk management reasons.

CHAPTER FIFTEEN

Venture Capital Alternatives

In Chapter 12, *Startup Finance Overview,* we looked at some debt financing options that might also be viewed as falling into the alternative fundraising bucket.

"Venture debt" is arguably an alternative fundraising method, but, unlike equity, there are natural limits to how much debt a company can take on. Most venture debt is based on projected revenues. Once those revenues are no longer sufficient to service (repay) additional borrowing, debt alternatives are tapped out.

Venture debt is also secured against a company's assets, and there's only one true "first position" security interest. Depending on the value of a company's assets, second and third position security interests generally support increasingly smaller loans.

Thus, while debt fundraising is important, its natural limits for startups are fairly obvious. In general, companies spending more than they're making need to find equity investors.

Thus, rather than exploring any debt options in this chapter, we will focus on three equity fundraising methods that are potential substitutes for venture capital:

- Crowdfunding for Accredited Investors under Rule 506(b) and (c)

- Crowdfunding under Regulation CF

- Mini IPOs under Regulation A, Tier 2

We will discuss these alternatives in that order because that is how I rank them based on various pros and cons. At a high level, those pros and cons can be summarized as follows:

- **Rule 506 Crowdfunding** offerings can be conducted the least expensively. When limited to accredited investors, 506(b) requires very little documentation. Rule 506(c) requires verifying every investor, but that's easier and cheaper than creating a formal disclosure document. Rule 506 is also totally flexible as to offering amount. The only filings are SEC Form D and equally simple state "offering notice" filings.

- **Reg CF** offerings are the smallest, but they are lower cost than Mini IPOs, and the post-offering requirements are much less onerous than Mini IPOs. Reg CF crowdfunding also has not yet generated nearly as much negative press as Mini IPOs.

- **Mini IPOs** serve an interesting niche – providing freely tradeable shares that offer not only investor liquidity, but also the ability to use those shares as "acquisition currency" to acquire or merge with other companies. Mini IPOs, however, have suffered high profile legal, regulatory, and financial black eyes, as discussed earlier. Lastly, Mini IPOs are the most expensive alternative, costing a minimum of $100,000 and triggering public company reporting.

The term "alternative" is not meant in a bad way. These methods are "alternative" only in the sense that they are newer and edgier than typical VC funding paths.

They also help to reduce geographic barriers and provide funding to greater varieties of companies, projects, and teams. Only a small percentage of companies that seek VC funding receive it. Other companies need options and need to make the best of them. Any of these methods can be used to raise millions of dollars.

But alternative types of financings are also risky for companies hoping to later raise VC funds.

And as always, whatever financing strategy is used, it is important to always strive to raise *the right amount of money from the best investors on the best terms.*

Why Some Entrepreneurs Avoid VC Money

As Chapter 14, *VC Fundraising*, made clear, there are pros and cons to taking venture capital. The pros include the ability to raise a lot of money and get mentoring, introductions, and other support from knowledgeable and influential persons.

The actual and perceived negatives around VC funding are also significant and can drive some entrepreneurs to explore alternatives.

These *can* include:

- difficulties attracting VC interest in many industries and geographies,
- loss of control by founders,
- being forced to raise too much money, too quickly,
- the risk of legal, regulatory, and business mistakes from growing too quickly,
- conflicts of interest around exit timing and strategies,
- inability to easily raise money from other sources if a company's VCs lose interest, and
- myriad other potential power dynamics between VCs and founders.

Stories of great relationships between startups and their VCs abound. Unfortunately, stories of very bad relationships also abound. Some founders decide to avoid VC funding simply based on third-party horror stories. Others decide "never again" after personal experiences. Common complaints include:

- power struggles,
- poor financial support in difficult times,
- inadequate or even bad guidance,
- ineffective or annoying VC-appointed board members, and
- poor financial outcomes for founders and other holders of common stock after debt obligations and VC liquidation preferences are paid out in an exit.

Whatever the reasons, many founders are happy to have non-VC financing alternatives like those created by the JOBS Act.

Cap Table Implications

As we will discuss, crowdfunding for accredited investors under Rule 506(b) and (c) is compatible with later seeking VC funding if the number of investors is kept small.

But crowdfunding rounds under Reg CF or Mini IPOs under Reg A+ that cause a company's cap table to bloat with hundreds or thousands of small, non-accredited investors, will likely harm any chances of VC funding.

Some of the crowdfunding platforms are using investment instruments designed to address these concerns by combining all investors into a single entry on a company's cap table. Crowdfunding platforms have done this through "special purpose vehicles" ("SPV") and through what are called "Crowd SAFEs."

Although the *legal* structures and concepts for SPVs under Reg CF are clear enough, there is little *regulatory* guidance indicating that the SEC is on-board with Reg CF SPVs, given how SPVs defeat individual shareholder ownership and voting rights. That said, the SEC does not appear to have taken any adverse actions yet against crowdfunding portals that use SPVs or Crowd SAFEs. As discussed later though, new SEC rules could be coming.

Initial Coin Offerings

Few financial innovations have made a bigger splash in the startup fundraising realm than the fantastic rise and even more fantastic implosion of initial coin offerings, or ICOs.

ICOs were intended to be the financing method of choice for companies leveraging blockchain-based technologies to replace traditional technologies across myriad areas of commerce, government, and other human activity. We look at ICOs here for regulatory context and insights.

Blockchain

Blockchain, in short, is described as a software-based, non-centralized ledger that transparently and irreversibly records any kind of transaction, including multi-step transactions. Because blockchain is largely self-executing, it is considered to not require any degree of "trust," and hence it enables transactions of all kinds to be conducted and recorded without any kind of intermediary.

Tokens

Blockchain also facilitates the creation and use of "cryptographic tokens" that can record transactions, contracts, property rights, and all manner of other asset values and attributes.

Such tokens can be used to represent, for example, rights to purchase specific products or services, rights to use specific assets, such as photographs, interests in real property, and all manner of other exchanges of value.

Token Offerings

The first ICO occurred in 2013. It was called "Mastercoin." This project was built on the Bitcoin Blockchain platform, which has very limited functionality. The Bitcoin Blockchain, for example, does not allow *"if this, then that"* coding logic, necessary to support what came to be called "smart contracts."

The 2013 Mastercoin ICO raised $500,000, and the issued tokens rose in value to around $5.5 million, ushering in the brief era of the ICO.

The Etherium Blockchain was launched in 2014, enabling the deployment of smart contracts, greatly expanding the types of cryptographic tokens that could be created and the tasks those tokens could perform.

By the end of 2016, ICOs had raised around $300 million. In 2017, ICOs raised around $10 billion, and in 2018, ICOs raised around $11.4 billion. In the first quarter of 2019, ICOs raised only $118 million, an incredible drop from the $6.9 billion raised in the first quarter of 2018.

A primary driver of this epic collapse was regulatory pressure from the SEC, which brought several major enforcement actions.

The SEC refused to ignore that the ICO market was frothy with hype and fraud and that virtually none of the lavishly funded projects came close to meeting the hype, let alone even launching a meaningful, functioning Blockchain project.

SEC Clamps Down on ICOs

Many operating in the ICO space had hoped the SEC and other regulators would ultimately conclude that ICO tokens were not securities, and hence not subject to SEC regulation.

A key argument was that tokens were not securities, but rather stand-alone assets, the value of which was dictated and driven by their ability to do certain things already at the time they were sold and issued.

The term "utility token" was coined to capture this idea.

The Howey Test. These arguments were intended to get around the SEC's "Howey Test," arising out of the U.S. Supreme Court Case, *S.E.C. v. Howey Co.*, 328 U.S. 293 (1946).

Under the Howey four-factor test, a security exists wherever there is.

- an investment,
- in a common enterprise,
- made with an expectation of profits,
- from the efforts of others.

When all four factors are present, the investment is deemed an "investment contract," and hence a security.

ICO proponents made valiant arguments that there was no common enterprise or that any expectation of profits had nothing to do with the efforts of others.

Attempts to avoid tripping the common enterprise element included operating in loose, communal governance structures, including cooperatives.

Proponents also argued that the "efforts of others" element was not met in cases where utility tokens were sold after their full functionality had been achieved. A series of enforcement actions beginning in 2017 undercut these arguments, culminating in a case called <u>Munchee</u>, which drove a big nail into the ICO regulatory coffin.

<u>Munchee.</u> Munchee had good advisors and seemed to be doing most things correctly toward creating a "utility token," the value of which was to be derived largely from its utility. The founders of Munchee sought to develop a payment rewards system around restaurant reviews, using its MUN coin.

Munchee received a cease and desist from the SEC on December 11, 2017. The SEC's <u>Howey</u> analysis is neatly summed up in this paragraph from the <u>Munchee</u> cease and desist order.

> *"MUN token purchasers had a reasonable expectation of profits from their investment in the Munchee enterprise. The proceeds of the MUN token offering were intended to be used by Munchee to build an "ecosystem" that would create demand for MUN tokens and make MUN tokens more valuable.'*

This excerpt supported the SEC's views that the "efforts of others" element of <u>Howey</u> was met:

> *"Investors' profits were to be derived from the significant entrepreneurial and managerial efforts of others – specifically Munchee and its agents – who were to revise the Munchee App, create the "ecosystem" that would increase the value of MUN (through both an increased demand for MUN tokens by users and Munchee's specific efforts to cause appreciation in value, such as by burning MUN tokens), and support secondary markets."*

To rebut arguments that the MUN coin had "full utility" when sold to investors, the SEC said:

> *"While Munchee told potential purchasers that they would be able to use MUN tokens to buy goods or services in the future after Munchee created an "ecosystem," no one was able to buy any good or service with MUN throughout the relevant period."*

And these excerpts from the cease and desist order highlighted the pivotal role Munchee's statements played in proving the "expectation of profits" element of the <u>Howey</u> test:

> *"In the MUN White Paper, on the Munchee Website and elsewhere, Munchee and its agents further emphasized that the company would run its business in ways that would cause MUN tokens to rise in value. First, Munchee described a "tier" plan in which the amount it would pay for a Munchee App review would depend on the amount of the author's holdings of MUN tokens...."*

> *"Munchee emphasized to potential purchasers how they could profit from those efforts: Munchee could potentially choose to [sic] burn (take out of circulation) a small fraction of MUN tokens everytime [sic] a restaurant pays Munchee as [sic] advertising fee. This, along with our tiered membership*

plan could potentially increase the appreciation of the remaining MUN tokens as the total supply in circulation reduces and as users would prefer holding their MUN tokens...."

"Munchee intended for MUN tokens to trade on a secondary market. In the MUN White Paper, Munchee stated that it would work to ensure that MUN holders would be able to sell their MUN tokens on secondary markets, saying that "Munchee will ensure that MUN token is available on a number of exchanges in varying jurisdictions to ensure that this is an option for all token-holders." Munchee represented that MUN tokens would be available for trading on at least one U.S.-based exchange within 30 days of the conclusion of the offering. It also stated that Munchee would buy or sell MUN tokens using its retained holdings in order to ensure there was a liquid secondary market in MUN tokens...."

https://www.sec.gov/litigation/admin/2017/33-10445.pdf

After a series of SEC enforcement actions, including the Munchee case, cryptocurrency and blockchain proponents spent all of 2018 and the first part of 2019 trying to pick up the pieces and make sense of the regulatory environment.

I and others involved in trying to protect certain types of token sales argued that no security should be found where (i) a utility token with "full utility" within an ecosystem is sold for use purely within that system and (ii) prominent disclaimers state that the tokens should only be purchased for use in the ecosystem and not with any expectation of profits.

Concurrently, others conceded that many tokens would be securities under Howey and pushed to register them with the SEC in Mini IPOs under Regulation A+.

As of mid-2019, both of these have come to pass – the SEC has recognized "utility tokens," and the SEC has allowed security token offerings under Reg A+.

SEC No Action Letter Acknowledging Utility Token

On April 3, 2019, the SEC issued a No Action Letter to TurnKey Jet, Inc. ("TKJ"), agreeing that its "tokenized" "jet cards" used to facilitate charter services via a private blockchain network would not be deemed securities under Howey.

In reaching that position, the SEC emphasized the following:

- "TKJ will not use any funds from Token sales to develop the TKJ Platform, Network, or App, and each of these will be fully developed and operational at the time any Tokens are sold;

- the Tokens will be immediately usable for their intended functionality (purchasing air charter services) at the time they are sold;

- TKJ will restrict transfers of Tokens to TKJ Wallets only, and not to wallets external to the Platform;

458

- TKJ will sell Tokens at a price of one USD per Token throughout the life of the Program, and each Token will represent a TKJ obligation to supply air charter services at a value of one USD per Token;

- If TKJ offers to repurchase Tokens, it will only do so at a discount to the face value of the Tokens (one USD per Token) that the holder seeks to resell to TKJ, unless a court within the United States orders TKJ to liquidate the Tokens; and

- The Token is marketed in a manner that emphasizes the functionality of the Token, and not the potential for the increase in the market value of the Token."

https://www.sec.gov/divisions/corpfin/cf-noaction/2019/turnkey-jet-040219-2a1.htm

While an SEC No Action Letter provides protection only to the recipient, Turnkey Jet in this instance, companies that observe identical requirements and restrictions have near immunity from SEC enforcement action.

These conditions allow a company to sell tokens and use them to conduct a Blockchain-based business model. Limiting the use and transfer of the Turnkey Jet tokens within a closed ecosystem prevents them from increasing in value and eliminates any possibility that they could be used to generate investment-like profits.

In essence, sales of Turnkey Jet tokens are simply "pre-sales" of flight capacity – not unlike rewards-based crowdfunding.

These conditions and limitations make it clear that fully financing an endeavor like Turnkey Jet would need to come from sources other than an ICO, such as a more typical debt or equity financing.

Interestingly, although Turnkey Jet seemed to go dormant, a company called Jet Token adopted a nearly identical business model, raised $1.13M under Reg CF in late 2019, and filed a Reg A+ offering for $10M with the SEC in 2020. The original Jet Token Reg A+ Offering Circular can be found in the BLSG Data Room under *Finance > Equity Financing Documents > Reg A and Reg A+*.

At about the same time as the Turnkey Jet No Action Letter, the SEC's Division of Corporation Finance issued guidance on the application of the Howey Test to cryptocurrencies, captioned *"Framework for "Investment Contract" Analysis of Digital Assets."*

https://www.sec.gov/corpfin/framework-investment-contract-analysis-digital-assets

In July of 2019, the SEC offered further guidance in another utility token no action letter, this time issued to Pocketful of Quarters, Inc.

The Pocketful of Quarters No Action Letter is slightly different and perhaps broader than the Turnkey Jet No Action Letter. First, the price of the Pocketful of Quarters token is not required to remain at a single price, unlike the Turnkey Jet token.

Second, use of Pocketful of Quarters tokens across a wide gaming platform offers greater flexibility and functionality than simply purchasing charter air services.

Here are some of the conditions imposed by the <u>Pocketful of Quarters</u> No Action Letter:

- *gamers will only be able to transfer Quarters from their Quarters Hot Wallets for gameplay to addresses of Developers with Approved Accounts or to PoQ in connection with participation in e-sports tournaments;*

- *only Developers and Influencers with Approved Accounts will be capable of exchanging Quarters for ETH at pre-determined exchange rates by transferring their Quarters to the Quarters Smart Contract;*

- *to create an Approved Account, Developers and Influencers will be subject to KYC / AML checks at account initiation as well as on an ongoing basis;*

- *Quarters will be made continuously available to gamers in unlimited quantities at a fixed price;*

- *there will be a correlation between the purchase price of Quarters and the market price of accessing and interacting with Participating Games;...."*

https://www.sec.gov/corpfin/pocketful-quarters-inc-072519-2a1

Again, the <u>Pocketful of Quarters</u> No Action Letter is significant in terms of that company's business model, but it does not represent any kind of breakthrough toward legitimizing ICOs or any other reliable means of raising money through cryptocurrency sales.

Cryptocurrency Mini IPOs Receive SEC Approval

The second major securities law development for cryptocurrency in 2019 was the approval of the first two cryptocurrency Mini IPOs under Reg A+. The first company to obtain approval was Blockstack. Blockstack's Mini IPO Offering Circular gives this overview of the company and its offering:

> *"We are a technology company that, together with our affiliates is developing, sponsoring and commercializing an open-source peer-to-peer network using blockchain technologies to ultimately build a new network for decentralized applications, which we refer to in this offering circular as the "Blockstack network." The Blockstack network can be accessed using our open-source Blockstack Browser available at blockstack.org. Examples of decentralized applications that have already been built and are being used on the Blockstack network include: Dmail, a secure, encrypted email solution with no corporate intermediaries; Graphite, a decentralized alternative to Google Docs; Sigle, a decentralized and open-source blogging application; and BitPatron, a subscription content service for creatives.*

> *The ultimate goal in creating the Blockstack network is to enable application developers to build and publish decentralized applications without the need to maintain central databases, and for users of these decentralized applications to retain control over their own data. Over 115,780 user accounts have been registered on the Blockstack network and over 7,000 enthusiasts and developers currently participate in our open-source community (including through our Slack group and online forum)."*

Blockstack's complete Offering Circular can be viewed on the SEC's EDGAR platform here:

https://www.sec.gov/Archives/edgar/data/1693656/000110465919039908/a18-15736_1253g2.htm

The second cryptocurrency Mini IPO to received SEC approval to go forward was "Props." The Props Mini IPO Offering Circular gives this overview of the company and its offering:

> We are creating a network of consumer-facing digital media apps (collectively, "Props Apps"). We expect Props Apps to operate, in some regards, as traditional apps that may be downloaded and accessed by users in a manner similar to any other mass market app—but Props Apps will share a common, special feature: the ability to provide an extra level of premium, built-in functionality to users who hold Props Tokens.
>
> There are currently two apps that are designed to give Props Tokens holders these premium in-app experiences. Each of these apps was created by YouNow. The first is Rize, a many-to-many livestreaming application, which we intend to merge into our YouNow live streaming app. We refer to this app as our 'Props Live Video App.' The second is 'WTF,' an interactive game show application, which we refer to as the "Game Show App." We expect that these Props Apps, as well as Props Apps we anticipate will be developed by third parties in the future, will provide the types of functionalities described below, subject to each app's terms and conditions:

- Application-Specific Premium Features. *Props Tokens may entitle holders to enjoy key features, including, for example, the power to "upvote" or recommend content to other users, increased sharing of certain app revenues, discounts for the purchase of in-app virtual goods, and additional gameplay features like extra games or videos only available to Props Token holders.*

- Tipping. *Props Token holders may be able to send each other Props Tokens directly, from one user's wallet to another—thereby allowing Props App users to send each other gifts and share the other benefits of holding Props Tokens in these apps.*

- Voting. *Props Token may allow holders to influence potential changes to the rules of a Props App, its content, or desired features by voting. In addition, in the future, Props Token holders may be able to provide votes on key issues affecting the network.*

- Network Reputation and Status. *Props Tokens may enable users to enjoy a network-wide elevated status. Because the Props Tokens earned in any single Props App are fungible and the same as those that can be earned in any other Props App, this feature allows users to, effectively, "port" their reputation and status across Props Apps and maintain a network-wide reputation and status.*

Props' complete Offering Circular can be viewed on the SEC's EDGAR platform here: https://www.sec.gov/Archives/edgar/data/1725129/000162827918000249/filename2.htm

These and other cryptocurrency Mini IPOs were stuck in SEC regulatory review for months, and in some cases, longer than a year, before these signs of regulatory loosening. There now seem to be evolving paths for legally offering cryptographic securities using Reg A+.

Unregulated ICOs have effectively come and gone, leaving much to be desired in their wake. But those issues should not hang as a permanent cloud over the many positive innovations that have been and continue to be pursued involving Blockchain technology and cryptographic tokens.

Seeing these first crypto Mini IPOs finally come to market offers hope of better days to come for many pursuing cryptocurrency and Blockchain entrepreneurial dreams, even if they're not as easily funded as they were during the brief ICO era.

While embracing approaches treating tokens as regulated securities, the SEC has continued its drive to extinguish unregulated ICOs. As late as February 2020, the SEC was still pursuing enforcement actions against ICOs from 2017. The SEC's February 19, 2020 press release announcing a settlement with ICO issuer Enigma included the following:

> *"…Enigma, based in San Francisco and Israel, has agreed to return funds to harmed investors via a claims process, register its tokens as securities, file periodic reports with the SEC, and pay a $500,000 penalty.*
>
> *According to the SEC's order, Enigma raised approximately $45 million from sales of its digital assets (called ENG Tokens) in 2017. The SEC's order finds that ENG Tokens are securities and that Enigma did not register its ICO as a securities offering pursuant to the federal securities laws and its ICO did not qualify for an exemption from the registration requirements…."*

https://www.sec.gov/news/press-release/2020-37

Crowdfunding for Accredited Investors

Regulatory Framework

Modern equity crowdfunding originated as "matchmaking networks" that were strictly limited to accredited investors.

Industry pioneers EquityNet launched in 2005 and AngelList formed in 2010. Both are still limited to accredited investors, despite the JOBS Act.

While less showy than some of the newer crowdfunding platforms, AngelList is a quiet giant that has remained vibrant due to continued evolution and reinvention and a loyal network of angel investors.

On the other hand, EquityNet, while still active, falls outside of the top tier of platforms in terms of platform sophistication, deal flow, quality of deals, and funds raised.

As early matchmaking network innovators tested regulatory boundaries with new technologies and funding models, they created a legacy of SEC No Action Letters that laid the foundations for today's accredited investor crowdfunding platforms. Those No Action Letters can be found by searching the following names or going to the links shown:

- Lamp Technologies No Action Letter (May 29, 1997) (https://www.sec.gov/divisions/investment/noaction/1997/lamptechnologies052997.pdf)

- Funders Club No Action Letter (March 26, 2013) (https://www.sec.gov/divisions/marketreg/mr-noaction/2013/funders-club-032613-15a1.pdf)

- <u>AngelList</u> No Action Letter (March 28, 2013) (https://www.sec.gov/divisions/marketreg/mr-noaction/2013/angellist-15a1.pdf)

- <u>Citizen VC</u> No Action Letter (Aug 6, 2015) (https://www.sec.gov/divisions/corpfin/cf-noaction/2015/citizen-vc-inc-080615-502.htm)

Before these, the SEC issued its <u>IPOnet</u> No Action Letter (July 26, 1996). The <u>IPOnet</u> No Action Letter supports the proposition that providing password-protected access for accredited and sophisticated investors to certain investment opportunities should not be deemed to involve "general solicitation" or "general advertising."

Passive Versus Active Fundraising Support

The issue of general solicitation is just one of several regulatory challenges for these early platforms. Another involved broker-dealer registration. Platforms that involve themselves in securities transaction activities, receive "success-based compensation," or that even recommend or promote specific offerings still need to register as broker-dealers under the 1934 Act.

SeedInvest, MircroVentures, and, more recently, StartEngine, all have affiliated broker-dealers, allowing them to recommend specific companies to their registered users and to have "skin in the game" by earning success-based fees for successful fundraisings.

Additionally, platforms that create special purpose vehicles, or SPVs, to invest in pools of startups also need to register as investment advisors, as the SPVs constitute "funds" that they are "advising."

AngelList is an example of a platform that has a registered investment advisor affiliate for this reason. Syndicate leads on AngelList play a very direct role in recommending and encouraging investments in deals they have decided to support, and the AngelList platform also helps drive investors into supported deals.

At the lowest level of regulation, platforms that merely allow companies to post profiles and offering materials and permit accredited investors to interact with those materials and companies do not need to become broker-dealers or registered investment advisors.

These general concepts regarding broker-dealer or investment advisor registration explain why some platforms are more involved in endorsing specific companies or effecting transactions, while others are not.

Platforms that are not registered as, or affiliated with, registered broker-dealers or investment advisors are limited to passively bringing companies and investors together on platforms that provide only marketing and communication services.

Platforms with very basic services tend to have the lowest fees, and platforms that are more involved in transactional activity tend to charge higher fees.

Rule 506(b) Versus Rule 506(c)

Once Rule 506(c) was adopted, accredited-investors-only platforms could offer Rule 506(c) deals with full offering details right on the platform homepage and still also offer Rule 506(b) deals behind a password-protected wall that only accredited investors could see.

As a result of these changes, on some of the crowdfunding platforms it is almost impossible to tell the difference between offerings under Rule 506(c), Reg CF, or even Reg A+, all of which allow general solicitation.

Unless the platform identifies the applicable exemption, as some do, an investor can generally identify non-Reg CF deals because the offering amounts are usually higher than $1.07 million.

Interestingly, while some platforms specifically identify Rule 506(c) deals, others tend to lump Rule 506(b) and Rule 506(c) deals together simply as Rule 506 offerings.

Some platforms even bump dangerously against the general solicitation prohibition still applicable to Rule 506(b) offerings. They do so by showing teasers of those offerings in front of the accredited-investor-only, password-protected sections of the platforms.

Any general solicitation of a 506(b) offering invalidates the exemption. General solicitation is not cured simply by preventing non-accredited investors from investing. General solicitation violations, however, can be quietly addressed by converting a 506(b) offering to a 506(c) and simply obtaining accredited investor verifications from all participating investors.

Again, the issue is not so much about getting "caught" by the SEC for a general solicitation violation, but having a later investor or acquiror raise the issue as a potential "rescission" concern in due diligence.

To Generally Solicit or Not

Relative to Reg CF and Reg A+ offerings, in general, Rule 506 offerings are likely to be perceived as "higher quality" companies and deals. And between 506(b) and (c), Rule 506(b) deals are likely to be perceived as higher quality than 506(c) deals.

The attorney survey results we discussed in Chapter 11 indicated a degree of stigma attached to Rule 506(c) and a company's perceived "need" to advertise an offering broadly since not enough wealthy, sophisticated investors are interested in it.

As we also discussed in Chapter 11, Rule 506(c) is used about 1/10th as often as Rule 506(b), according to reviews of SEC Form D filings.

Assumptions about exclusivity and "deal quality" are not accurate in every case, but, as in many aspects of life, perception is reality, and general solicitation could very well turn away some of a company's most promising potential investors.

Consequently, any company that believes it can get its deal done in a more discreet, behind-the-scenes manner with a smaller handful of investors should probably do so, perhaps only using general solicitation very selectively if necessary.

If a completely discreet approach does not work, it is always easier to switch from a quiet Rule 506(b) offering to a splashier Rule 506(c) offering than it is to go the other way, from splashy to discreet.

Note that, once *any* general solicitation has occurred, Rule 506(b) may not be available for use again until after a 6-month break in offering activities. This has to do with the offering integration rules we looked at in Chapter 11, *State and Federal Securities Laws.*

Despite this relatively low usage, there are several online investing platforms supporting high-profile, crowdfunding-like fundraising efforts.

Choosing from Among the Top Rule 506 Platforms

As we know, entrepreneurs should always try to raise the right amount of money from the right investors on the right terms. They should also try to do this with the least wasted time and effort so they can quickly get back to running their businesses.

If this can be done with a single call to a wealthy, trusted, industry icon, by all means, place that call and be done with it. If instead, the reach and resources of a modern fundraising platform seems like the way to go, pick the very best platform for your company, deal, and other circumstances.

While I refer to these as Rule 506 platforms, as they sometimes call themselves (instead of Reg CF platforms), it might be better to call them Accredited Investor Only platforms, since there do not seem to be any crowdfunding-type platforms outside of Reg CF or Reg A+ platforms that accept non-accredited investors.

As we know, non-accredited investors can participate in a Rule 506(b) offering as long as the company provides a full-scale (expensive) disclosure document. Even where a company chooses to use a platform that only allows accredited investors, the company can still extend the same offering to non-accredited investors outside of the platform if it provides those investors and all others with the type of full disclosure document required.

To choose the best Rule 506 platform, consider doing the following:

- study the top four or five platforms carefully, including their current offerings, approaches to fundraising, and recent funding successes,

- figure out which of the top platforms are strongest in your sector,

- figure out which platforms have the largest network of accredited investors who are likely to be interested in your sector, idea, and stage of development,

- talk to platform representatives to fully understand the role they and others will play, if any, to ensure the success of your offering,

- consider which of the platforms are better positioned to successfully facilitate more discreet offerings not reliant on broad advertising and general solicitation, and

- talk with founders currently conducting offerings on your top platform choices to challenge and validate your assumptions and understandings about the platforms and how well they perform.

The last of these is most important, as I have found some of the platforms exaggerate the level of engagement of their investor networks, the traffic on their platforms, the effectiveness of their offering marketing efforts, and their offering success rates.

The platforms discussed next are currently the leaders in fundraising metrics under Rule 506(b) and (c).

AngelList. (www.angellist.com)

Except for its popular job posting site, which is open to the public, AngelList is a relatively exclusive platform. Investment opportunities are limited to accredited investors, and all current offerings are completely hidden behind a password-protected login.

Potential investors cannot see any deal offerings until after applying to the platform as an accredited investor. After that, the platform allows a potential investor to "browse by recent deals" *by syndicate.* These are sorted by (i) date of last syndicated deal, (ii) number of deals closed in the last year, or (iii) by "follow on rate," meaning syndicates "where at least 50% of their investments over 18 months old have raised another round of funding at a higher valuation."

AngelList's use of syndicates structured as separate venture funds that are led by specific lead angel investors is more sophisticated than anything offered by the other top platforms, with the possible exception of MicroVentures.

AngelList is a registered investment advisor and uses that status to offer a sophisticated approach to platform-driven fundraising.

AngelList also provides a high degree of transparency regarding the investors on the platform. It facilitates networking with them similarly to networking on LinkedIn.

In this regard, unlike other platforms, AngelList has attributes of Crunchbase built-in, particularly the ability to see who is investing and in what companies. Combining this degree of transparency with a degree of networking sets AngelList apart from the other platforms.

On the other hand, AngelList does not accept every company for fundraising, unlike passive match-making platforms like Crowdfunder and Fundable.

To raise on AngelList, a founder needs to gain the interest and support of a syndicate "lead" and agree to mutually acceptable terms of investment. The lead then uses his or her relationships on the platform to encourage others to join the investment.

The role of the lead is pivotal to fundraising on AngelList. As the platform discloses, "*Syndicate leads earn carried interest on the additional capital that follows them. This increases their stake in your company's success.*" As mentioned earlier, carried interest, or carry, is common to all VC deals. In this case, it means that each AngelList lead earns a larger share of the profits on a successful deal compared to others in the syndicate, ranging from about 10% to 20% of the syndicate's gains.

This also inspires syndicate leads to select great companies and encourage others to invest. Strong syndicate leads seem to develop a reputation as deal pickers and, in the right circumstances, seem able to close rounds faster than passive accredited investor crowdfunding platforms.

Because of the role of sophisticated leads on AngelList, founders should expect to have to "sell" a lead on their company and deal much in the way they would a seed-stage VC.

The following excerpts from AngelList's "2019 AngelList Year in Review" highlight the unique place it occupies in startup finance:

> *"In 2019, we reached nearly $1.8 billion in assets under management, supported over 3.5 million candidates in their job search, and helped makers launch over 25,000 products that will define the future of tech."*
>
> *"Angels and VCs rely on AngelList for capital and fund infrastructure. We eliminate the hassles of investing so they can focus on helping founders. In 2019, assets under management grew nearly 80%, with 36% of all top-tier U.S. VC deals in our portfolio."*
>
> *"Over 62% of 2019 investments came from full-fledged venture funds managed on AngelList."*

As a final point, closing a round through AngelList will generally have more favorable cap table implications than a round closed on certain other platforms. An AngelList round will show two investors – the lead investor, likely an individual with many investments to his or her credit, plus the separate entity through which the syndicate invested.

This outcome is generally more favorable than a funding round that puts twenty or more new, individual investors on a company's cap table.

On the other hand, because AngelList itself is not an investor, founders are unable to easily research AngelList-supported investments by company, industry, or size/nature of investment using sites like Crunchbase. This opaqueness is a barrier for many founders in finding and assessing AngelList as a funding option.

SeedInvest. (www.seedinvest.com)

As of this writing, SeedInvest had raised $150M+ for over 150 startups. SeedInvest runs all of its Rule 506, Reg A+, and Reg CF fundraisings through its affiliated registered broker-dealer, SI Securities, LLC.

Offerings on SeedInvest seem about evenly split between Rule 506 and Reg A, with fewer Reg CF offerings.

SeedInvest holds itself out as highly exclusive and claims to approve only 1% of all companies seeking to fundraise on its platform, referring to its offerings as "vetted."

SeedInvest says this about the types of companies it works with:

> *"Investors on SeedInvest are typically not interested in financing ideas or projects, but in funding companies and businesses. Therefore, we recommend that companies meet the following **minimum requirements**:*
>
> - *At least a minimum viable product or prototype*
> - *Proof of concept (includes customer traction or partnerships)*
> - *At least two full-time team members*

There is no typical company on SeedInvest, but companies which have been successful thus far generally share the following characteristics:

- *Technology, 'technology-oriented,' and consumer-focused businesses*

- *Startups raising between $500,000 - $50,000,000 (including offline)*

- *Companies looking to raise Seed Rounds, Series A Rounds, Bridge Rounds, and Growth Rounds*

- *Companies which already have funding terms and have attracted a lead investor."*

The last bullet raises questions about the usefulness of the platform to companies who do not already have a lead investor. Virtually all crowdfunding platforms admit that founders generally need to get substantial initial commitments on their own first to be successful.

But this begs the question of whether a company with a lead investor even needs a platform like SeedInvest to fill out the round.

To initiate the funding review process, founders create a personal SeedInvest account and then "apply to raise funds" at www.seedinvest.com/apply.

If the SeedInvest team then decides the company is a good fit, SeedInvest will initiate due diligence.

As part of the application process, each company states its preferred terms for the offering, and SeedInvest's Investment Committee reviews the suggested terms and provides feedback, accepting the suggested terms or proposing different terms for the raise.

Existing fundraising traction with specific terms can serve as the basis for the valuation and terms offered through SeedInvest.

Companies must reach their minimum funding target before investments are finalized and funds are released from an independent escrow account.

As of this writing, SeedInvest says this about costs:

"COST HIGHLIGHTS

- *Placement fee: 7.5% of what you raise on SeedInvest.*

- *Equity fee: 5.0% of what you raise on SeedInvest.*

- *Only pay if your fundraise is successful.*

- *Up to $3,000 of accounting fees reimbursed upon campaign launch*

SeedInvest will cover up-front costs including escrow account setup, legal review and filing fees. Upon a successful raise, SeedInvest is reimbursed at closing. Otherwise, SeedInvest will eat the costs."

An earlier description of costs from the SeedInvest website discussed these fees and costs a little differently and also mentioned a flat $10,000 fee for "costs" at closing. It's hard to say, but that fee seems to have been adjusted or eliminated. Here is the earlier fees and costs description:

- *"SeedInvest will pay certain upfront costs related to escrow, operational, due diligence, and legal fees (reimbursed at closing). We only make money if your fundraise is successful:*

- *$0 retainer*

- *SeedInvest will pay upfront costs related to escrow set up, legal review, due diligence, and filing fees. SeedInvest will be reimbursed with a flat $10,000 for these costs at closing. In the event the raise is unsuccessful, SeedInvest will eat these costs.*

- *SeedInvest will reimburse up to $3,000 of accounting fees (if applicable) upon campaign launch.*

- *7.5% placement fee on funds raised through SeedInvest ($37,500 assuming $500,000 raised).*

- *5% equity fee (on the same terms as the round) on funds raised through SeedInvest ($25,000 assuming $500,000 raised).*

SeedInvest's careful vetting, exclusivity, and broker-dealer-backed credibility make it a potentially attractive alternative for companies that fit the platform's standards and sector preferences, generally tech and consumer-facing companies versus non-tech or B2B.

As SeedInvest is a registered broker-dealer, it can actively promote vetted deals to its network of accredited investors and is strongly incented to do so by a 5% kicker on all funds raised. This looks like a fundamental advantage compared to platforms that are not registered as broker-dealers or investment advisors and possibly one that could mean the difference between fundraising success or failure.

MicroVentures. (www.microventures.com)

MicroVentures has an affiliated registered broker-dealer, purportedly only accepts about 5% of companies that apply to raise funds, and currently supports only Rule 506 and Reg CF offerings, not Reg A offerings.

It describes its funding "sweet spot" as between $150K and $1M. As of this writing, MicroVentures had raised $220M+ from 125K investors for over 400 startups. It positions itself this way:

> *"What makes MicroVentures different is that we are a full service online platform for venture capital investments that is open to the public. We take the best parts of Venture Capital (connections, research, deal flow, mentoring) and combine it with the best aspects of Equity Crowdfunding (open access, ease of use, diversification) to give investors the best of both worlds."*

The MicroVentures website also provides this information:

> *"Founded in 2009, MicroVentures built a platform that gives both accredited and non-accredited investors access to invest in startups. Over $200M has been raised on our platform to date.*
>
> *MicroVentures is one of the financial industry's first organizations which merges crowdfunding with the venture capital industry. The San Francisco, CA and Austin, TX based firm provides an opportunity for angel investors to invest in startups alongside Venture Capitalists, often at the same terms. We conduct detailed due diligence on startups and if approved we help them raise capital from angel investors."*

As noted earlier, MicroVentures also has a registered broker-dealer, called MicroVentures Marketplace, that it describes this way:

> *"MicroVenture Marketplace is a FINRA registered broker-dealer, offering both primary and secondary investment opportunities through special purpose vehicles or directly into issuers."*

The MicroVentures website is opaque regarding fees, which have been described by various online commenters as including a $99 application fee, $250 due diligence fee, and 10% of the amount raised.

Others have suggested the MicroVentures also takes 5% carried interest, but this would only seem to be possible in cases involving investment through a single special purpose entity in which MicroVentures is also an investor.

In applying to raise funds, founders are told, *"We raise capital for startups and small businesses through Regulation D, Regulation A, and Regulation Crowdfunding. Once you apply, we can discuss which option might be right for you."* Presumably, founders can learn more about fees in those discussions.

Given its stated "sweet spot" ranging up to $1 million, it may not have the same 506 deal-closing horsepower as AngelList. That said, MicroVentures has been involved in funding highly successful startups and has a strong reputation.

Crowdfunder. (www.crowdfunder.com)

Crowdfunder supports Rule 506 and Reg A deals, but not Reg CF deals, and says this about accredited status:

> *"Non-Accredited Investors may still be eligible to invest in Title IV (Regulation A) and Title III (Regulation CF) offerings. Unfortunately, Crowdfunder does not support Regulation CF deals at this time. Most of the Crowdfunder deal flow is for Rule 506(b) and 506(c) under Regulation D, which is mostly limited to Accredited Investors. You can still sign up and be notified when we have offerings available for Non-Accredited Investors."*

Crowdfunder claims to have raised more than $160 million and says this about itself:

> *"Crowdfunder is the leader in equity crowdfunding and has helped raise capital for thousands of companies from our network of 12,000 VCs and angel investors. We've helped startups at all stages raise money from Pre Seed to Series A."*

Unlike AngelList, SeedInvest, StartEngine, and Microventures, Crowdfunder has no affiliated broker-dealer or investment advisor and merely serves as a matchmaking platform. Although the company has an email list of some 12,000 accredited investors, companies should assume that all fundraising success is directly dependent upon their own efforts.

As a result, costs on Crowdfunder, although fixed, are among the lowest. As of this writing, Crowdfunder describes costs this way:

> *"You can create a private deal room with all your company information and documents for free. Fundraising plans start at $299/month. Premium plans with additional services are available for purchase."*

Crowdfunder may be a good option for startups (i) that are not accepted on one of the more exclusive "vetted" platforms or (ii) that expect to be so appealing to potential investors that they can raise their desired level of funding from accredited investors based on low, fixed platform fees and without sharing any percentage of the funds raised with a broker-dealer.

Fundable. (www.fundable.com)

Fundable says it has "*helped startups raise over $563 million in funding commitments.*" What this means is unclear. As discussed earlier, investment "commitments" mean nothing, since they are not binding. Only funded amounts matter.

Like Crowdfunder, Fundable has no affiliated broker-dealer or investment advisor. It functions solely as a deal marketing platform, and companies and investors handle all investment-related activities off of the platform.

The Fundable website explains those limitations this way:

> "*Fundable is not a broker dealer, so legally we cannot charge fees after funding for equity. All funds transfers, final deal terms and legal documentation are worked out between the investor and company directly after the end of the fundraise off-site.*
>
> *Any fees charged are up to the discretion of both you and the individual investor, and you can investigate methods of transferring the money between yourselves.*"

Without a broker-dealer or investment advisor, Fundable cannot "recommend" the companies on its platform, nor can it say it has "vetted" them.

On the other hand, the platform is limited exclusively to accredited investors. Investors signing up to review deal documentation must self-attest that they are accredited. Each company has a public profile about its product, team, opportunity, press accolades, and so forth, but "Business Plan" information can only be seen after requesting access. This includes all financial information and offering details.

As an aside, not knowing which offerings shown in Fundable's public profiles are 506(b) versus 506(c), it is difficult to tell whether Fundable is inadvertently allowing its listed companies to violate the prohibition against general solicitation. Rule 506(b) offerings should not be shown *at all* in public-facing sections of any website. Presumably, Fundable is not doing that.

Restricting use of the platform to accredited investors and limiting access to company information to investors who specifically request access to a company's deal information make those investor prospects more valuable and compelling to founders.

Fundable is the only top-tier equity crowdfunding platform that also supports rewards-based crowdfunding too. Fundable describes this unique pairing this way:

> "*Fundable offers unparalleled flexibility for startups' specific needs — allowing them to fund their companies through Rewards or Equity campaigns. Rewards campaigns are a great fit for startups raising smaller amounts of capital that have something of value (a compelling reward) that they can offer in exchange for funding. Equity campaigns are best for companies seeking larger amounts*

of capital and have gained enough traction to incentivize accredited investors with the opportunity to own a piece of the company."

Like Crowdfunder, Fundable charges a flat monthly fee, currently described to be *"as little as $179"* per month and no success fee. Companies can pay more for additional services, including help setting up a profile and assistance with PR and marketing, including an email to Fundable's base of accredited investors.

Like Crowdfunder, Fundable may be a good option for startups that either are not accepted on one of the more exclusive "vetted" platforms or that expect to be so appealing to potential investors that they can raise funds based on low, fixed platform fees and without sharing any percentage of the funds raised with a broker-dealer.

Rewards-Based Crowdfunding Plus Equity Crowdfunding. The discussion of Fundable should serve as a reminder that any company pursuing an equity crowdfunding for accredited investors under Rule 506 can pair that with a rewards-based crowdfunding on any number of other platforms, leveraging some of the same non-investment related marketing content used for the equity crowdfunding. Based on the review of Kickstarter's stats earlier, this could be a promising two-track approach for game developers, creators of viral consumer products, and inventors of interesting new technologies.

Rewards-based crowdfundings are less complex, less expensive, and pose little or no legal or regulatory risk absent intentional fraud. The only thing to be mindful of in simultaneously conducting a Rule 506(b) offering and a rewards-based crowdfunding effort is to keep them separate. Participants in the Rule 506(b) offering can see information about the rewards-based crowdfunding, but the Rule 506(b) offering should *not* be shown to participants in the rewards-based offering. Doing so would constitute general solicitation and blow the Rule 506(b) exemption.

Matchmaking Platforms Generate Little Organic Traction

Anecdotally, I have not been impressed by fundraising results from purely matchmaking platforms like Crowdfunder and Fundable. Merely posting a compelling company profile on two top matchmaking sites did not generate meaningful accredited investor interest, and even email blasts by the platforms to their accredited investors did not generate meaningful leads in our offerings.

Two of my companies have gone down this path without success, despite devoting substantial time and money putting together videos, solid pitch decks, and other professional looking content. Neither platform we tried drove significant numbers of investor leads for either company. We pulled those campaigns and went back to more traditional offline fundraising – successfully in one case and unsuccessfully in the other.

The matchmaking platforms look great, they have lots of deals on them, they are staffed by knowledgeable people, and they say they have lots of accredited investors visiting the platforms and opting into their email lists.

But getting traction with actual accredited investors does not seem much easier than using old school methods.

Whatever the reasons, founders using these matchmaking platforms are still likely to find themselves working just as hard as ever seeking out warm introductions, emailing around executive summaries and pitch decks, and holding in-person or videoconference meetings to close deals.

If there are exceptions to this paucity of investor traction on matchmaking platforms, they might be limited to certain types of products. Catchy consumer products, for example, likely do much better than commercial, B2B, or industrial products or services. Support may also be stronger for alcoholic beverage companies and commercial real estate projects.

Rule 506 Crowdfunding Summary

Working with the limited known data, and looking at the pros and cons of the platforms just considered, I suggest founders focus on accredited investor crowdfunding platforms that have a high degree of exclusivity, truly strong investor networks, financial skin in the game, and that provide real support for circling up deals and getting them closed.

Based on these criteria, AngelList might come out on top, followed by either SeedInvest or MicroVentures.

Note that I have not included StartEngine in the top Rule 506 platforms, even though it, too, recently registered a broker-dealer affiliate. Despite its stated willingness to do Rule 506 offerings, a quick view of StartEngine's nicely transparent website reveals that it is focused on Reg CF offerings and Reg A+ offerings. This is likely driven by StartEngine's bias toward including non-accredited investors in its deals.

Crowdfunding under Reg CF

As a refresher, let us revisit some basic Reg CF requirements and stats. These include:

- offerings must be conducted through SEC-registered, FINRA-regulated portals,

- maximum offering amount of $1.07 million within a 12-month period, meaning, a company can raise $1.07 million per year under Reg CF – every year,

- companies must complete an SEC Form C describing the company and offering (https://www.sec.gov/files/formc.pdf),

- companies must provide financials prepared in accordance with GAAP and reviewed by a CPA, but audited financials are required for issuers that have previously raised funds under Reg CF and are proposing to raise more than $530K in a subsequent Reg CF offering,

- investors are limited in how much they can invest in Reg CF offerings per twelve-month period as follows: the higher of (i) $2,200 or (ii) 5% of net worth or annual income, for investors who make less than $107,000 per year, and the lesser of (i) $107,000 or (ii) 10% of the lesser of annual income or net worth for investors whose income and net worth both exceed $107,000.

- securities purchased by investors generally cannot be transferred for one year, and

- issuers that complete a Reg CF offering must file annual reports with the SEC and post them on their websites within 120 days of financial year-end.

Funding trends in Reg CF offerings have remained positive from inception, albeit at comparatively modest levels relative to Rule 506. As of mid-2019, *monthly* funding totals appear to be coming in at around $11 million nationwide.

The following are some approximated statistics for Reg CF offerings based on data collected by the SEC and others,

- number of offerings: 474 in 2017, 680 in 2018, and 735 in 2019,

- amount raised: $71.2 million in 2017, $109.3 million in 2018, and $137 million in 2019,

- average Reg CF raise per offering in 2019 - $270,000,

- total number of investors: 77,558 in 2017, 147,448 in 2018,

- campaigns are lasting around 113 days, and

- about 60% of fundraising efforts are deemed successful, meaning they achieved their stated minimum fundraising goal.

The primary pros and cons of Crowdfunding include:

Pros:

- companies with modest capital needs can develop viable strategies around raising roughly $1 million per year for a few years,

- crowdfunding offers the potential to turn investors into customers and customers into investors,

- crowdfunding is a relatively cost-effective form of advertising and brand-building,

- crowdfunding creates a positive association in that it "democratizes investing,"

- properly conducted Reg CF offerings are not aggregated or integrated with Reg A or Reg D offerings and can be conducted simultaneously,

- the top crowdfunding platforms are well designed and professional looking and seem to be staffed by knowledgeable, dedicated persons, and

- being under the SEC/FINRA regulatory tent helps companies stay on the right side of the line regarding compliance, regulatory, and legal matters.

Cons:

- even the best platforms likely produce few organic investor leads for most companies,

- crowded cap tables with unaccredited investors are not ideal,

- Reg CF's $1.07 million annual cap will not work for companies with more capital-intensive needs – average seed rounds are higher than $1 million these days,

- crowdfunding involves high up-front costs of at least $10,000 to $20,000,

- Reg CF is a lot like a registered offering, but without the advantages of freely tradeable stock, unlike Reg A, and

- completing a Reg CF campaign takes just over four months on average, not including pre-launch efforts shooting a video and creating a company profile on the platform, as well as a pitch deck and other offering materials.

In summary, Reg CF works for raising small amounts of money, $271,000 on average, but upfront costs are high, and virtually all of the work to get investors falls to the founders themselves. The platforms rarely drive substantial investments apart from those founder efforts. Closing a Reg CF offering is also slower than a typical Rule 506(b) angel round, and it results in post-closing SEC annual reporting obligations.

The biggest plus about crowdfunding is simply that it is happening. This innovative loosening of the federal securities laws is funding new companies, supporting entrepreneurial dreams, creating jobs, and stimulating innovation.

The platforms and ecosystems are still just a few years old. Current experiences and results are relevant, but not dispositive of where crowdfunding could be just a few years from now.

SAFEs and SPVs in Crowdfunding

While SPVs (grouping all investors into a single newly-created partnership or LLC) and Crowd SAFEs may solve the issue of messy cap tables and other VC turnoffs, they seem contrary to the fundamental goal of democratizing investing and allowing the little guy into the game on a level playing field.

Most importantly, these indirect investment vehicles seem to offer crowdfunding investors significantly inferior rights and opportunities compared to traditional startup investments like Convertible Notes, series seed preferred, or even common stock.

The SEC expressed very similar concerns and skepticism in a May 9, 2017 publication captioned "Investor Bulletin: Be Cautious of SAFEs in Crowdfunding."

https://www.sec.gov/oiea/investor-alerts-and-bulletins/ib_safes

Ironically, some of the very individuals who championed crowdfunding to Congress and the SEC have invented these investor-unfriendly cures to what might be called "the VC problem" – i.e., VC concerns about crowded cap tables.

Like any business, the platforms need volume. Rather than accept crowdfunding as an alternative to VC funding, these platforms are trying to pound a square peg into a round hole to drive deal volume, pretending that crowdfunding is a great path toward VC funding.

Most companies that pursue crowdfunding do so probably because they are not good candidates for VC funding, and hence also not as appealing to sophisticated angel investors. Sophisticated angels generally want to get in early, before VCs, but then ride VC funding coattails to big exits.

In trying to drive deal traffic with investor-unfriendly terms, these platforms may be doing a disservice to the constituency they fought to champion.

The SEC's concerns with SAFEs in Reg CF offerings arose again in March 2020, with SEC Release Nos. 33-10763, in which the SEC proposed rules banning the use of SAFEs in Reg CF offerings. https://www.sec.gov/rules/proposed/2020/33-10763.pdf

Crowdfunding Research

As in almost any endeavor, the only way for a founder team to decide whether and how to approach crowdfunding is to see what is currently going on in the world of crowdfunding.

- Which platforms currently have the best deal traffic?
- Which are raising the most money for the most companies?
- What sectors are most popular on which platforms?
- How do the top platforms differ in services, platform features, transactions supported, and fees?

The Reg CF ecosystem seems a lot more defined and transparent than the more complex and diffuse world of venture capital, but this is only partly true.

Fortunately, most of the successful Reg CF fundraisings happen on just a small handful of sites and not across all 51 FINRA-registered crowdfunding portals. So, at any given time, it is easy to see which companies are trying to raise funds on which platforms.

Unfortunately, every site reports its pending and completed deals differently, complicating comparisons among the platforms.

For any company considering Reg CF crowdfunding, the goal should be to find the site that is going to position it the best and help draw the most potentially interested investors.

A good first step is to look at several months of statistical reports from the "StartEngine Index." Search for it online or go to this link:

https://www.startengine.com/blog/category/equity-crowdfunding-index/

These monthly reports vary, but they always discuss recent deal traffic and fundraising statistics in great detail, often by industry sector, state, county, entity type, and sometimes by crowdfunding platform.

Crowdfund Insider is another source of crowdfunding information. It covers Reg CF deals, Rule 506 deals and Reg A+ deals, and can be found at this link: https://www.crowdfundinsider.com/.

Crowdwise is another good source for crowdfunding statistics, comparative information regarding the top platforms, and other useful crowdfunding information for founders. Their website is found at www.crowdwise.org.

Top Reg CF Platforms

More than 90% of all Reg CF offerings currently happen on just six platforms: StartEngine, Wefunder, SeedInvest, Republic, Microventures, and Net Capital Funding. There are some other platforms handling offerings, like NextSeed, but founders are best off sticking with the largest, most successful platforms.

This discussion reviews the platforms in order of their general rankings based on the number of Reg CF offerings completed and amounts of funds raised, although these stats change from month-to-month, quarter-to-quarter, and year-to-year.

StartEngine. (www.startengine.com)

As already mentioned, StartEngine supports Reg CF, Reg A+, and Rule 506 deals. The company currently says it has helped over 300 companies raise more than $125 million from a community of over 200,000 prospective investors. StartEngine has an affiliated registered broker-dealer called StartEngine Primary, LLC.

StartEngine provided this description of itself in connection with its own Reg A+ offering.

> *"Founded in 2014, StartEngine is an equity crowdfunding and security token offering platform that seeks to help entrepreneurs achieve their dreams by democratizing access to capital. This is our second public offering, for a maximum of $1.07 Million. In June 2018, StartEngine closed its first Reg A+ round, raising nearly $5 Million from 3,425 investors."*

StartEngine's website Terms and Conditions contain this description of its offering capabilities:

> *"Investment opportunities posted and accessible through the site are of three types:*
>
> *1) Regulation A offerings (JOBS Act Title IV; known as Regulation A+), which are offered to non-accredited and accredited investors alike. These offerings are made through StartEngine Primary, LLC (unless otherwise indicated). 2) Regulation D offerings (Rule 506(c)), which are offered only to accredited investors. These offerings are made through StartEngine Primary, LLC. 3) Regulation Crowdfunding offerings (JOBS Act Title III), which are offered to non-accredited and accredited investors alike. These offerings are made through StartEngine Capital, LLC. Some of these offerings are open to the general public, however there are important differences and risks."*

A review of the offerings on the StartEngine website suggests that it is mostly focused on Reg CF offerings, followed by Reg A+ offerings, and few Rule 506 offerings. Out of 73 offerings posted on the main offerings page, 66 were Reg CF offerings, 7 were Reg A+ offerings, and 1 was a Reg D (Rule 506) offering.

StartEngine does not publish its fees, but as of May 2019, it appeared StartEngine was charging companies the following fees to use its platform:

- 7% of the amount raised via domestic ACH transfers and wires (11% on amounts paid via credit card),

- 9% of the amount raised from international investors (12% on amounts paid via international credit card),

- 50 basis points (.5%) of funds committed as a cash management fee taken by the escrow agent, and

- a $10,000 service fee for account management and campaign strategist support, which is taken out of the campaign's first disbursement.

StartEngine seems to lead the pack in terms of deal flow and most dollars raised, but Wefunder is generally very close.

Wefunder. (www.wefunder.com)

Wefunder claims to have funded 357 startups with a total of $125.5 million. In one fairly bold founder FAQ, the company makes this claim:

> *"How are you better than your competitors?*
>
> *We're the largest funding portal by dollars raised, number of companies funded, and number of investors."*

Wefunder supports Reg CF, Rule 506 offerings, and Reg A offerings. Wefunder has no registered broker-dealer and hence makes no recommendations regarding its companies and is not at all involved in the transactions between investors and issuers.

Wefunder seems to compete largely on price and pricing simplicity, charging companies a fee of 7.5% of the amount raised. Regarding its involvement in setting up companies on the site, Wefunder says this:

> *"Also, while we may sometimes help companies "make their profiles look pretty", all of this information is provided and fact-checked as true by the companies, not us."*

As with all Reg CF offerings, the minimum offering amount must be raised before funds are released. Wefunder describes this process as follows:

> *"When you invest, your funds are transferred to an escrow account, in custody of Boston Private Bank. If the fundraise succeeds, your money will be released to the startup. Otherwise, it will be refunded to you."*

Wefunder also seems to either direct or strongly suggest the use of certain investment instruments, perhaps for ease of comparison purposes and to prevent companies from making mistakes, like blowing up their cap tables with 1,200 investors. The following Wefunder FAQ suggests as much:

> *"It's rare for an investment on Wefunder to offer voting rights directly to smaller investors because founders fear it can scare off venture capitalists who invest in later rounds. They are concerned with the hassle of collecting thousands of signatures to make any major decision. You should assume your investment does not include voting rights unless specified otherwise."*

> *"The Wefunder SAFE treats Major Investors (typically defined as investing between $10,000 and $25,000) much like the Y Combinator variation, but it has no voting rights for Minor Shareholders.*
>
> *Except for Major Shareholders, the company may opt to repurchase an investor's SAFE at any time prior to conversion at the greater of the purchase amount or the Fair Market Value, as determined by an appraiser the company chooses. Startups want this because they are scared that venture capitalists may not fund their companies at a later date because they have a "messy cap table"."*
>
> *"... Grants CEO Power of Attorney for Minor Shareholders. Once the SAFE converts into equity, investors who are not Major Shareholders grant the current CEO a power of attorney to vote all shares and execute any documents on their behalf. This mitigates the potential problem of hundreds of minor shareholders slowing down further follow-on financings."*

Again, the SEC proposed new rules in March of 2020 that might ultimately force companies using Reg CF to provide stronger rights to investors than what platforms like Wefunder are promoting.

Republic. (https://republic.co/)

Republic, founded by alumni of AngelList, exclusively offers Reg CF offerings and raised the third highest amount of funds in Reg CF offerings in 2019, behind Wefunder and StartEngine.

And although Republic does not have a broker-dealer affiliate, it does screen companies before approving them for listing. In its own words, *"All companies are rigorously screened & pass due diligence."*

I know of at least one company that did not make the cut with Republic because one of the company's founders had previously gone through a bankruptcy.

Ostensibly because companies are so carefully vetted, Republic claims that 89% of the campaigns on Republic to date have been successful. Republic also extols other benefits companies experience from the Republic platform:

> *"A Republic campaign is much more than fundraising. Our companies tripled user bases, sold millions worth of product, gained press coverage, connected with VCs, and raised follow on rounds at great terms—all because of their Republic campaigns."*

In addition to its strict vetting processes, another unique aspect of Republic's approach to Reg CF is that it seems to drive most of the companies on its platform to use the "Republic Crowd SAFE."

As discussed earlier, SAFEs are highly company-favorable, as they have none of the true investor protections of debt or equity. Republic describes some of these company benefits (and investor drawbacks) as follows:

> *"Holders of Crowd Safe instruments have no information or voting rights, meaning until there is a conversion event, your client will have no duties beyond publishing an annual report. Republic helps you maintain a list of investors, including their investment amount and contact information. Through the Republic portal, your client can update their investors as a group privately, individually or post company updates for anyone following the company on the portal."*

"The Republic Crowd SAFE bundles all investors into a single pool of investors."

"Crowd SAFE is an investment agreement between founders and investors that most companies use on Republic. It's simple and super founder-friendly, allowing founders to maintain control while bringing in the funds needed to achieve their growth milestones.

The Crowd SAFE allows all investors in your Republic campaign to be represented as one line item on your cap table. It helps startups fundraising under Reg CF avoid "messy cap table" concerns, save legal fees, and reduce the time spent structuring the terms of their financing.

With the Crowd SAFE, investors only convert at a liquidity event—an acquisition, IPO, or change of control. Unlike a traditional SAFE, they don't automatically convert at subsequent equity financing. This ensures investors are never on the cap table as individuals. (That is, unless you'd like them to be—we can make that work, too.)"

Republic also offers a "traditional" SAFE, a "Crowd Simple Debt Agreement," or "SDA," as well as a token-based equity instrument and a token-based debt instrument. These token-based instruments seem a little gimmicky and are likely seldom used by companies.

Republic says this about its SDA instrument:

"A Crowd SDA is an investment contract between lenders (investors) and companies looking to raise capital. Individuals make investments in exchange for the chance to earn a return in the form of cash interest payments.

The Crowd SDA was created by Republic and is a debt crowdfunding-specific version of a typical debt agreement, a financial instrument widely used by angels, VCs and other accredited investors investing in startups.

Under the terms of the Crowd SDA, investors lend money to the company in exchange for annual interest payments during the term of the agreement. The company has the right to accelerate repayment of interest and/or principal, subject to a minimum return multiple (e.g. 1.5x the principal). If the company makes all interest payments due under the Crowd SDA, the minimum return multiple will be satisfied.

RISK NOTE: payments are not guaranteed. The company may not have sufficient capital available to meet its payment obligations under the Crowd SDA, and the Crowd SDA is unsecured, meaning there is no collateral to which investors would have recourse in the event that the company is unable to meet its payment obligations."

As of this writing, Republic charges companies the following fees to raise funds on its platform:

- 6% of the total amount raised and 2% of securities offered in a successful financing,
- $1,500 for use of iDisclose to prepare SEC Form C.

It's clear Republic is a top player in the Reg CF space. The jury may still be out on the crowd SAFE, though, given the SEC's rule proposals.

SeedInvest. (www.seedinvest.com)

We have already discussed SeedInvest in the context of Rule 506 offerings and noted that the company is primarily focused on those and Reg A offerings, and less on Reg CF offerings. But that said, SeedInvest helped raise the fourth largest amount of Reg CF funding in 2019 - $7.23M.

SeedInvest's reputation for being picky about who gets to raise on its platform is clear. Any company considering a Reg CF offering needs to keep that in mind – i.e., how much effort to expend convincing the 4th place Reg CF portal to do the deal.

The difficult element to factor in may be SeedInvest's purported high success rate of almost 90%.

Should a highly confident founder team go the more exclusive route with SeedInvest?

MicroVentures. (www.microventures.com)

As noted above, MicroVentures seems to focus more on Rule 506 and Reg A+ offerings than it does on Reg CF offerings. As of this writing, there appeared to be only seven Reg CF offerings on the MicroVentures site, far fewer than one finds on StartEngine or Wefunder.

In 2019, MicroVentures helped companies raise a total of $3.34M in Reg CF offerings, positioning it in sixth place among Reg CF platforms in terms of dollars raised.

Because MicroVentures has a broker-dealer, it may be more interested in earning larger commissions from higher transaction amounts than the smaller fees it can charge companies for Reg CF services. If true, MicroVentures might maintain the Reg CF business simply as a feeder for larger Rule 506 and Reg A deals.

This theory, though, is in conflict with the company's prominent statement that *"The sweet spot for our platform is companies or startups that need at least $150,000 to $1,000,000 in capital."*

The company's low volume of Reg CF offerings might raise questions for any company considering such an offering on the platform, but that may be a conscious choice by MicroVentures and may have no bearing on the platform's ability to help drive a maximum Reg CF raise.

Net Capital Funding. (https://netcapital.com/)

Outside of the top three or four portals, rankings are more in flux. Net Capital Funding always seems to be in the top six but often fluctuates in a range between fourth place and sixth place on a quarter-to-quarter and year-to-year basis.

Even though Net Capital Funding is sometimes ahead of MicroVentures in Reg CF deals, the momentum seems to be with MicroVentures, or another portal called truCrowd (https://us.trucrowd.com).

Net Capital Funding's website is not flashy or exciting, and there appear to be only a handful of live deals on the website at any given time. The pitch to founders is essentially, *"You will need to bring the investors and we'll help you with your pitch materials and some administrative tasks."*

Reg A+ Mini IPOs

Pros and Cons Overview

Despite the fact that 51 companies raised a total of $1 billion under Reg A+ in 2019, the most important thing founders should keep in mind about Reg A+ is the fact that it is truly an "alternative fundraising method." It is way less popular than Rule 506 fundraising. VC investments totaled $136.5 billion in 2019, according to PitchBook.

Reg A+ offerings are also more difficult, expensive, and risky.

An SEC report from March 4, 2020, called *"Report to the Commission - Regulation A Lookback Study and Offering Limit Review Analysis,"* ("2020 Reg A Report") provides detailed metrics and trends regarding Reg A offerings through 2019. This report describes Reg A's alternative status in clear terms:

> *"…However, aggregate Regulation A financing levels remain modest relative to registered offerings or Regulation D offerings. Financing levels are likely related to a combination of factors, including the pool of issuers and investors drawn to the market under existing conditions; the availability to issuers of attractive private placement alternatives without an offering limit; the availability to investors of attractive investment alternatives with a more diversified pool of issuers; limited intermediary participation and a lack of traditional underwriting, which limits certification (i.e., signaling of an issuer's growth potential to the market through an underwriter's reputation, which mitigates the information asymmetry about an issuer's potential); and a lack of secondary market liquidity."*

https://www.sec.gov/files/regulationa-2020.pdf

Launching a Reg A+ offering requires spending a *minimum* of $50,000 to $100,000 before it has even cleared SEC review, and then spending even more afterward complying with public company reporting requirements.

Plan on about 60 days to prepare and submit a filing on SEC Form 1-A and plan on another 90 to 120 days before the offering can be declared effective by the SEC. Reg A+ is the wrong solution to fill immediate cash needs.

To better understand Reg A+ costs, complexity and timing, simply review a few Reg A+ Form 1-A SEC filings. These documents look a lot like full-blown IPO registration statements because, essentially, they are.

See examples of Form 1-A filings in the BLSG Data Room at *Finance > Equity Financing Documents > Reg A and Reg A+.*

Two goals founders often cite in pursuing Reg A+ offerings is growing their community of customers, both accredited investors and non-accredited, and providing liquidity for those investors.

A closely related motivation is to use the liquidity of publicly tradeable stock as "acquisition currency" – stock used to purchase other companies.

Some companies even see Reg A+ as a tool for executing a "roll-up" strategy, which means acquiring a number of related companies. The idea of a roll-up strategy is to dominate an emerging or even mature market, rapidly expand geographically, and rapidly grow revenues and achieve efficiencies through consolidation of administrative, financial, and operational functions and systems among the rolled-up companies.

Again, virtually every stock offered through Reg A+ to date has plummeted in value to almost nothing due to poor fundamentals and lack of liquidity in the backwater OTC market. Companies that cannot meet the Nasdaq's new two-year operating history requirement and that fail to achieve impressive financial results are likely to suffer the same fate.

Shares that plummet in value after an expensive Mini IPO may not provide meaningful liquidity for insiders or serve effectively as acquisition currency.

Another suggested advantage of Reg A+ for founders is the ability to potentially raise VC-levels of funding, but with less risk of losing control over the company or being forced into a premature sale. A successful Reg A+ offering might offer sustainable independence, but the substantial costs and distractions of a Reg A+ offering and of the resulting public company reporting obligations could have the opposite effect, by forcing some companies into financial distress.

Broker Network, Crowdfunding Platform, or Both

As with Rule 506 offerings and Reg CF offerings, selecting the right platform and partners to pursue a Reg A+ offering is critical – even more so, given the greater costs and complexity involved.

An initial question for founders looking at Reg A+ is whether to (i) simply list on one of the high profile crowdfunding platforms, (ii) try something more akin to a traditional "investment banking" approach, or (iii) explore some combination of the two – i.e., crowdfunding platform plus assistance from one or more registered broker-dealers.

As a quick caveat, even though the portals SeedInvest, StartEngine, and Banq, discussed soon, have affiliated, registered broker-dealers, it is unlikely that these newer entities have extensive retail brokerage customer bases like those of more established, traditional, full-service broker-dealers. Those platforms primarily created registered broker-dealers so they can receive success-based fees and recommend investment in their companies.

Here is a list of registered broker-dealers holding themselves out supporting Reg A+ offerings:

- Cambria Capital (http://www.cambriacapital.com/)

- TriPoint Global Equities (https://www.tripointglobalequities.com/)

- TruCapital Financial Partners (https://www.truecapitalfp.com/)

- Dalmore Group (https://www.dalmorefg.com/)

These are smaller, less well-known broker-dealers than one finds in other investment banking contexts. If I were considering hiring any of them for a Reg A+ offering, my information requests would be:

- Tell me about all of your Reg A+ offerings.

- Tell me about the other broker-dealers in your retail distribution network.

- Let me see your engagement letter.

The 2020 Reg A Report directly addresses the possible reasons that more sophisticated, higher-end broker-dealers or investment banking firms have shown little or no interest in supporting Reg A offerings.

The report specifically states that few registered broker-dealers are getting involved with Reg A offerings because the potential fees are low relative to the potential risks, and that those that do take fees and commissions in Reg A offerings tend to have a greater likelihood of regulatory blemishes.

The SEC put it this way, with *"registered intermediaries"* referring primarily to registered broker-dealers and possibly also to registered investment advisors:

> *"Some registered intermediaries engaged in Regulation A offerings make disclosures of prior actions, including, in some instances, violations of FINRA or other rules. With the caveat about data availability, among offerings where the use of a registered intermediary was disclosed, the intermediary had at least one disclosure on FINRA's BrokerCheck website in approximately 36% of cases."*

A "disclosure" in this context is regulatory-speak for a prior securities regulatory violation.

The SEC would like to see more reputable broker-dealers and investment bankers involved in Reg A offerings to enhance regulatory compliance and investor protections. For companies, having established broker-dealers supporting a Reg A offering can help to ensure that the financial goals of the offering are achieved.

Assuming all of the platform-plus-brokerage fees and other costs are not driven too high, using a combination of the best possible platform and the best possible registered broker might be worth exploring.

Broker-Dealers Versus Unregistered Service Providers

Founders should be somewhat cautious about working with firms that are neither major Reg A+ platforms or true registered broker-dealers with substantial Reg A+ experience and a demonstrated ability to sell shares through an existing retail investor base.

In addition to possibly not providing value for fees charged, "unregistered intermediaries" might also lead issuers into regulatory problems. In its 2020 Reg A Report, the SEC expressed concern about the number of unregistered intermediaries touting Reg A+ services:

> *"Regulation A offerings are not required to be conducted via registered intermediaries, and various Regulation A issuers have solicited prospective investors via unregistered entities, such as finders, promoters, marketing platforms, and other third parties that are not registered with the Commission or FINRA. The use of unregistered intermediaries poses potential investor protection concerns because of the absence of regulatory framework for such intermediaries' practices and involvement in offerings."*

Top Mini IPO Crowdfunding Platforms

These are the top platforms for Reg A+ offerings:

- SeedInvest (https://www.seedinvest.com/)
- StartEngine (https://www.startengine.com/)
- Manhattan Street Capital (https://www.manhattanstreetcapital.com/)
- Crowdfunder (https://www.crowdfunder.com/)
- Wefunder (https://wefunder.com/)
- Banq (https://banq.co/)
- Republic (https://republic.co/)

SeedInvest, StartEngine, Republic and Banq each have an affiliated broker-dealer, although, as noted below, Republic does not seem to focus on Reg A+ offerings.

The best way to research what is currently happening under Reg A+ is to review the offerings on the top plaforms. SeedInvest and StartEngine make that easiest by clearly identifying all Reg A+ offerings on their platforms. On other platforms, it can be challenging to distinguish Reg A+ offerings from Rule 506(c) offerings without requesting information or searching EDGAR for Reg A+ offering filings on Form 1-A.

Anecdotally, as of this writing, SeedInvest had 5 live Reg A+ offerings, StartEngine had 2, Manhattan Street Capital had 4, Banq had 1, and Republic had 0. Because Crowdfunder and Wefunder provide little assistance to their listing companies, information presented on their platforms is less clear and more suspect. Crowdfunder seemed to have 2 or 3 active Reg A+ offerings and Wefunder seemed to have none.

Despite not having an affiliated broker-dealer, Manhattan Street Capital might be the platform most focused on Reg A+ offerings and possibly among the most sophisticated on how to conduct them effectively.

Manhattan Street Capital has been involved in some of the more significant Reg A+ offerings to date and seems to have Reg A+ deal flow equal to or greater than that found on the other top platforms, despite being less flashy and seemingly less social media-savvy.

At the other end of the spectrum, Republic holds itself out as supporting Reg A+ offerings, and it has conducted its own Reg A+ financing, but all or virtually all of the offerings on its platform appear to be Reg CF offerings.

Strategies for a Successful Reg A+ Mini IPO

Based on the statistics, anecdotal evidence, and commentary from those in the Reg A+ trenches, success under Reg A+ requires four elements:

- a product or service with exceptionally strong consumer interest or appeal,
- a substantial budget for marketing and fees,

- a very well-designed and executed offering strategy, and

- support from an established broker-dealer network in addition to a strong platform presence.

As mentioned earlier, Reg A+ is also popular with real estate development companies.

The requirement of strong consumer interest means fewer SaaS products or B2B plays, and more restaurants, microbrews, cool gadgets, consumer health and wellness plays, electric vehicles, or other innovative products and services capable of generating a consumer frenzy or tapping into trending issues or concerns.

High consumer interest is vital for getting an offering off to a fast start and generating a level of validation and social proof capable of drawing in more sophisticated, skeptical investors with bigger checks.

Commentators in the space say that any offering that takes weeks to get investor traction will likely fail.

Commentators also say that registered broker-dealers are critical for filling out most rounds. The same commentators also say, though, that broker-dealers will not begin recommending a Reg A+ offering to their retail investor clients until an offering reaches a convincing critical mass demonstrating strong consumer support.

A final element of a successful Reg A+ strategy involves successfully raising funds first under either Rule 506 or Reg CF. This not only provides the substantial budget necessary for a successful Reg A+ offering, but successful earlier offerings also provide additional validation/social proof, not to mention critical fundraising experience for the founder team.

PART III – LIQUIDITY OR LIQUIDATION

CHAPTER SIXTEEN

The Exit

This chapter is about understanding and planning for a successful exit.

Exits generally come in two forms: (i) a sale of the company or (ii) an IPO. Some would also add mergers to this list. While it is true that many sales are *structured* as mergers for tax and legal reasons, a simple merger of privately held companies that involves no cash compensation or freely tradeable securities is not an exit of the type that professional investors have in mind.

As a caveat to calibrate expectations, this chapter's discussion of IPOs and sale transactions is intended to provide a high-level overview.

The value of this information is in (i) understanding generally how exits come together and how to plan and drive toward them and (ii) knowing the types of mistakes in the formation, development, and growth of a company that come back to haunt efforts to raise capital and ultimately provide a return to investors.

In M&A deals, the company for sale is often referred to interchangeably as the "seller" and the "target." The acquiring company is often referred to interchangeably as the "acquiror" or "buyer," and sometimes as the "suitor." Here we will use buyer/acquiror and seller/target.

Financing Choices Determine Exit Flexibility

As discussed earlier, some types of companies do not need to concern themselves with an exit. These include (i) self-funded lifestyle companies, (ii) other businesses grown organically through revenues and borrowings, and (iii) any other company that has not taken equity capital from VCs, angels, or other investors with negotiated rights to force a sale or IPO.

Founders of these companies can exit if and when they want to.

As indicated here, borrowings not convertible into equity create no expectation of an exit. Borrowings often do include rights to force a sale in the event of default, but forced liquidations and exits are legal cousins at best.

Additionally, some founders offer investors rights to receive a portion of future revenues, called revenue participation interests. These investments also rarely involve expectations of an exit or rights to force one.

But all companies that take *equity* investments from third parties will eventually be expected to provide a financial return to those investors. And companies that take money from VCs or other sophisticated investors will find themselves on a fixed time frame for doing so.

This is usually within ten years or less. Exit deadlines are often dictated by the shortest timeframe within which one or more of a company's lead VCs must wind up the fund that wrote the company a check. As previously discussed, VCs write drag-along rights into their investment documents that allow them to force an exit.

As fiduciaries, the leaders of any startup inescapably heading toward an exit are obligated to position their company for its highest value exit, whether by IPO or sale.

Defining Success

Like everything else, exits vary in quality. Some produce fantastic returns for shareholders, plus financial and other benefits for employees and other stakeholders.

At the other end of the spectrum, some exits offer shareholders only a clear date by which they can completely write off their investment.

While "success" is always a relative term, any sale or IPO that generates a positive return on investment for investors is arguably a success. An exit that provides substantial financial benefits for a company's founders and option-holding employees is even more successful.

In general, exit success is correlated directly with the size of the financial return provided to a company's investors. VCs tend to celebrate their 10x exits most loudly, but any founder producing 2x or better returns is probably still welcome around their VCs' offices.

Successful exits reflect well on founders and their teams. Founders with successful exits find it much easier to raise funds and assemble new teams for future startups. VCs, angels, and other investors view them as having proven that they are capable of executing on a business plan and returning value to investors.

Additionally, a founder's successful exit may well generate a financial windfall that enables them to help finance later startups.

An Awkward but Necessary Topic

For many founders, the entire subject of exiting someday *is* awkward, if not annoying. Founders often say commendable things like, *"This isn't about money, we're building something special here"* or *"It's way too early to think about that, let's focus on building something first."*

It is natural for founders to want to focus their time, resources, and creativity on growing their company and changing the world with their incredible idea, not on simply growing their company to "flip it."

But for founders who have taken exit-required cash, that laudable world-view must be balanced with the ultimate objective of producing the best possible returns for those investors. That is the deal, and that is the fiduciary obligation that has been accepted.

Whether a founder team wants to go the IPO route or perhaps be bought out on a faster track by a big strategic player, envisioning those possibilities from a startup's earliest days can sharpen focus on value creation and guide key decisions along the way: the team to build, the investors to seek out, the types of strategic relationships to develop and maintain, and the products and services to focus on.

The more innovative and groundbreaking a company's vision, the more difficult it may be to accurately foresee the optimal exit. But rather than being an excuse for ignoring the subject, charting unknown territory just means those founders have to think even harder about shaping and creating their ultimate destination.

IPO Slowdown

Going public used to be the exit strategy of choice, the "brass ring." Through the late 1990s, investors, founders, and employees alike defined success as achieving riches and maybe even a certain amount of fame through the public markets.

But beginning in about 2000, several factors conspired to make going public less viable and less attractive than seeking capital in private markets and exiting through M&A events.

Publicly available data clearly illustrate the IPO decline that started in 2000 and continues today.

Between 1980 and 1999, about 311 companies went public in the U.S. each year. Problems began with the steep market drops of 2000. After seeing 486 and 406 IPOs in 1999 and 2000, respectively, IPOs slid to fewer than 85 per year in each of 2001, 2002, and 2003.

Despite spikes of 222 and 275 IPOs in 2013 and 2014, respectively, there are generally fewer than 200 IPOs per year in U.S. markets, with 2017, 2018 and 2019 seeing 160, 192, and 160 IPOs, respectively.

Private Capital

One factor for the decline in IPOs has been the explosive growth in capital available in private markets from VCs, angels, corporate strategic investors, private equity firms, and other sources. These sources of private capital are far less regulated than the public markets, and therefore frequently offer advantages in both speed and cost over raising capital in public markets.

Simultaneously with the rapid growth in private capital markets during that same period, costs and regulatory burdens associated with public markets have steadily risen as a result of congressional and regulatory responses to actual and perceived financial disclosure and accounting issues in the public markets.

Sarbanes-Oxley (2002)

Substantial increases in regulatory burdens for public companies and companies seeking to go public began in 2002, with the adoption of the Sarbanes-Oxley Act ("SOX"). SOX was a congressional response to accounting and financial disclosure frauds and irregularities by Enron and other companies. SOX created numerous enhanced accounting and disclosure requirements:

- strengthened accounting practices and corporate governance rules,

- heightened accountability and disclosure requirements for corporations, company officers and directors, public accountants, and auditors,

- increased corporate disclosure requirements,

- new whistle-blower regulations,

- increased penalties for corporate or executive misconduct,

- creation of the Public Company Accounting Oversight Board (PCAOB) to monitor corporate behavior and accounting practices, and

- new obligations for companies to provide a year-end report detailing internal controls and the effectiveness of those internal controls.

The changes ushered in by SOX added to the already substantial burdens facing any company wanting to go public and comply with rigorous SEC disclosure and GAAP accounting requirements. The costs and administrative burdens required to establish detailed and exacting internal controls under SOX, and to annually certify their effectiveness, has often been identified as a key deterrent to companies that might otherwise consider going public.

Dodd-Frank (2010)

Markets again melted down in 2008, and once again, Congress stepped in to enact new laws. Enacted in 2010, the Dodd-Frank Act included many laws requiring rulemaking by the SEC, but adverse impacts on the IPO market were not as obvious as from SOX.

Regulatory changes from Dodd-Frank directly impacting public companies included:

- requirement to disclose median annual compensation of all employees except the principal executive officer and, separately, annual compensation of the principal executive officer, and the ratio of the two amounts,

- requirement to allow stockholder advisory votes on executive compensation, and

- requirement that stock exchanges and markets adopt rules for three-year clawback provisions to recover incentive compensation from executives after any restatement of financial statements stemming from a material error.

The reasons for the substantial reduction in IPOs since 2001 are varied, but in general, they have to do with (i) increased legal, regulatory, and financial burdens associated with becoming a public company and (ii) the great expansion of private capital.

And in addition to there being generally at least one-third fewer IPOs per year, on average, the number of small IPOs has also greatly diminished. In the 1980s and 1990s, IPOs producing offering proceeds of $30 million to $50 million were quite common, but they are almost unheard of now.

Despite these trends, going public still has certain advantages, so many VC-funded companies still wisely keep the prospect of an IPO an open possibility.

Continuing Relevance of IPOs

Here are numerous reasons that companies with the potential to go public should keep that option open:

- for a company with a bright future under the same leadership team pursuing the same mission and vision, an IPO may be the best way to fully finance that future and ensure that continuity,

- boards and executive teams that have a potential IPO in mind are likely to be more rigorous in designing and operating key accounting, financial reporting, and administrative systems and controls,

- driving toward an IPO also helps focus company resources and attention on key financial goals,

- companies scaling toward an IPO may have less difficulty raising funds and tend to draw out more potential acquirors and competing liquidity opportunities,

- IPOs almost always cause all of a company's preferred stock to automatically convert to common, greatly cleaning up a company's cap table and eliminating liquidation preference overhang,

- company officers and employees often continue in their roles following an IPO and gain valuable experience, and

- taking a company public is still probably viewed as the most successful form of exit, provided the process goes well for the company and its stock doesn't tank in the aftermarket.

In summary, the effort required to become a public company is significant, but any company on that path is likely to be better and stronger because of it.

Signs that a company is considering an IPO include increased finance and accounting staff recruitment, especially the hiring of a high-powered CFO. Rumors always fly when a successful startup hires a CFO with public company experience. Those rumors can make a company more appealing to investors and acquirors alike, potentially stirring up new financing and exit opportunities.

Downsides of IPOs

The downsides of IPOs are noteworthy as well:

- for accounting, finance, legal, and leadership teams, life in a public company becomes much more bureaucratic and less about business, creativity, and innovation,

- as WeWork found out in 2019, the SEC's review process for IPOs can cause substantial uncertainty, sometimes destroying any chances for completing an IPO, despite expenditures of hundreds of thousands of dollars and countless hours of distraction,

- the costs and distractions associated with being a public company are substantial and company-changing,

- officers and directors of publicly traded companies are subjected to increased legal and regulatory risks,

- company officers, employees, and most pre-IPO investors have to wait at least six months to sell any stock after an IPO due to underwriter-imposed lock-up restrictions. Six months is often long after an initial IPO price spike has faded.

IPO Positioning

Regardless of where a management team's ego might lead them, there are key requirements for joining the IPO club successfully.

Annual sales of at least $100 million to $250 million are commonly suggested as minimum revenue thresholds for contemplating an IPO. But, as I learned in my almost three years of reviewing IPO filings at the SEC, the real ingredients for success are trickier.

Among other things, to succeed in the public markets, a company must demonstrate: (i) that it is operating in a very large market, (ii) that its business model is highly scalable with healthy profit margins, and (iii) that it is positioned for sustained, continuous growth for years to come.

If those conditions are not present, stay out of the public markets. Life in an underperforming public company means enjoying few, if any, of the benefits described earlier, while suffering all of the downsides of public company life.

Case Study #43 – WeFail

WeWork's withdrawn IPO in 2019 was one of the most epic IPO fails in history. While it was true that WeWork generated annual revenues much larger than $250 million and that it operated in a very large market, Wall Street quickly figured out that its model was not truly scalable at its current growth rate. WeWork's economics were upside down due to extreme debt loads tied to rapid expansion. These factors did not bode well for sustained, continuous growth in the years ahead.

WeWork offers a very good product, it grew at an incredibly impressive pace, and much of its execution has been excellent, particularly from a customer or outsider's perspective. I have worked in and visited many WeWork locations. I am always impressed and have enjoyed the working environment at every location.

But Wall Street wasn't keen on the wall of debt. WeWork's $47 billion valuation evaporated almost overnight after it filed its Form S-1 registration statement with the SEC.

Even if the math regarding WeWork's debt obligations had not been quite as severe as it was, the company's SEC filings revealed numerous other facts that investors found troubling, including (i) founder Adam Neumann buying up property and then leasing it to WeWork for many millions and creating huge conflicts of interest, (ii) Neumann forcing WeWork to pay him $5 million for the We trademark, and (iii) Neumann's 65% voting control over the company, particularly when paired with information regarding conflicts of interest and self-dealing.

<u>Lessons:</u> See the requirements above again for what makes a company a good IPO candidate. A pre-IPO company's financial future should look exceptionally bright, even under close scrutiny. Skeletons in the closet such as looming walls of crushing debt are unlikely to pass unnoticed either by the SEC or Wall Street.

Additionally, success in public markets generally requires confidence in management's competence and integrity. Self-dealing and conflicts of interest send the wrong signals and will likely doom any company's foray into the public markets.

Optimizing for a Sale

With fewer IPOs, the natural trend has been for VC-backed startups to primarily exit via the M&A route, either by asset sale or stock sale. Statistically speaking, at least 90% of exits are sales or mergers. But, as we have discussed, one way to optimize for the best M&A outcome is to build the company like it's eventually "going IPO."

First and foremost, this means finding a scalable business model in an area of huge opportunity, with many years of untapped growth ahead. The same financial strengths that make a company a great IPO candidate also drive acquisition interest, which in turn drives higher valuation in a sale.

Other keys to M&A success include (i) strong leadership, (ii) a high-functioning technology team, (iii) valuable and protectable IP, and (iv) a big market position backed by identifiable competitive advantages. And again, a strong legal and regulatory foundation supports maximizing enterprise value by creating a reliable platform for growth and innovation while reducing unnecessary costs and distractions that slow growth and innovation and frighten away potential investors and acquirors.

Due Diligence and Disclosure Schedules

Like an IPO, M&A transactions shine a very bright light into all business, financial, legal, and regulatory corners.

This is done first in the due diligence process, in which the acquiror sends the target company a due diligence list. As we have learned, this is a comprehensive list of questions and document requests designed to understand absolutely everything about a company's business, finances, ownership, governance structure, assets, and legal and regulatory matters.

The second phase of this process is the dreaded "Disclosure Schedule," a document in which a company must disclose in excruciating and embarrassing detail all of the things that are imperfect about it – liens, loans, lawsuits, disputes, IP weaknesses, defaults, regulatory issues, and myriad other issues, in addition to attesting about more ordinary matters such as subsidiaries, leases, material contracts, key IP licenses granted or held, and so forth.

In the first chapters, we described all the ways that M&A transactions and financings can be harmed by legal and regulatory mistakes and other problems that come out in due diligence, or that are highlighted in a company's Disclosure Schedule.

These harms include, among others:

- scaring aware potential acquirors,
- valuation reductions,
- deal delays that increase the risk of deal failure,
- lower initial cash payments and greater deferred and contingent compensation in the form of earnouts, and
- larger cash escrows to account for legal and regulatory risks.

A complete and well-organized virtual data room is key to getting through a potential acquiror's due diligence reasonably quickly without any major issues. Checking it against a due diligence list is the best way to ensure nothing is missing.

Companies that are serious about maximizing value in an M&A transaction should consider working with outside M&A counsel well before the deal is presented to create a full-blown Disclosure Schedule. Doing so could help a company prioritize cleaning up issues that would be concerning to a potential acquiror, or that might be used to drive down the company's valuation.

M&A Cleanup

Companies on the verge of an M&A exit process should do what they can to clean up obvious problems, like incomplete equity transaction paperwork, cap table discrepancies, employee issues, IP gaps or clouds, and any litigation.

Pending litigation can become particularly difficult in an M&A deal. Litigation can drive away many potential buyers and will certainly result in risk shifting to the seller in the form of reduced valuation, a larger escrow fund, and possibly other compensation delays, such as larger earnouts.

As we learned in Case Study #8, *Taking on the Troll*, dealing with litigation during an M&A deal can be difficult. When litigants think they can hold up a sale, the cost of settlement goes up.

A final consideration before entering an M&A process is ensuring that the company has sufficient financial resources to get through the process without running out of money. Whether accomplished through equity sales or borrowings, avoiding insolvency during a sale is key.

No seller can hide or obscure its financial condition from a buyer and, as discussed below, most buyers that sense near-term insolvency will simply drag their feet to ensure that the seller is forced into a fire sale at a much lower valuation.

I once saw a target receive a formal Notice of Termination because of its financial difficulties, killing a $20 million strategic deal. This happened the same day the target's accounting department sent a notice to one of the acquiror's subsidiaries saying it was unable to pay a delinquent $200K+ invoice.

Insolvency kills all kinds of deals, including strategic deals, M&A deals, and financings.

Financial Statements - Audited versus Unaudited

Many startups go for several years before paying the high costs of a full financial audit, and this certainly makes sense in the early years. Audits are extremely expensive, costing more than $30,000 even for the most basic financials. Costs grow quickly from there. Audits are also hugely distracting.

For these reasons, most startups put off having their financials audited until potential investors demand an audit. This might occur at a series A round, or it might be put off until a series B round.

But founders and boards positioning any startup for a meaningful sale – something other than a fire sale – might consider an audit well in advance if the company has the resources. Doing so could be helpful for a couple of reasons.

The first is simply that an acquiror may lack confidence in the accuracy of the company's financials without an audit – or may at least feign lack of confidence to drive down the company's valuation.

Secondly, and perhaps more importantly, potential acquirors that are public companies, or that want to become public companies, know that they will need to "consolidate" the financials of significant acquired entities into their own financial statements and that doing so *requires* those acquired entity financials to be audited.

For many companies going public, completing financial audits of previously acquired entities and consolidating them into the company's financials to the SEC's satisfaction is a top hold-up in clearing SEC review.

Thus, having audited financial statements not only makes a company's financial statements completely credible, it also enhances the possibility that desirable acquirors will be able to consider acquiring the company.

Despite their cost and inconvenience, the benefits of audited financial statements are significant: (i) they sometimes uncover important issues, (ii) having them can greatly speed up deals by removing legitimate and feigned issues regarding a company's actual financial picture, (iii) they expand the field of potential acquirors with greater resources to close a deal quickly, and (iv) expanding the field of potential acquirors increases the chances of creating a value-enhancing bidding contest for the company, which is the next topic.

Using Investment Bankers to Attract Multiple Bidders

Just as it helps to have multiple bidders when selling a house, so it is in selling a company.

And the best way to attract multiple bidders to an M&A exit is to engage the best investment banking team possible. Deals of at least $100 million tend to attract the A-list bankers, but potential deals over $10 million or $20 million should be able to attract competent mid-level bankers. Even though A-list bankers usually command higher fees, their greater expertise, influence, reach, and social proof likely offset those costs in the form of higher valuations.

Despite noting earlier that VCs can be wary of and even put off by companies using investment bankers to raise funds in typical VC rounds, VCs and other investors generally welcome working with investment bankers to optimize an exit.

Having great bankers help lead a sale effort offers numerous benefits, including:

- helping to identify and prioritize likely acquirers,

- guiding management and the board through the process,

- helping prepare presentation materials,

- coordinating and bringing structure and discipline to a complex and somewhat unfamiliar process,

- serving as a sophisticated buffer between potential bidders and the company on due diligence issues and other tactical matters,

- advising management and the board on valuation and other key terms, particularly when comparing competing bids, and

- advising management and legal counsel on key terms of a purchase and sale agreement.

As with any significant relationship, hiring an investment banking firm is not a matter to take lightly. The first draft of any investment banking engagement letter invariably requires substantial push back and negotiation. These documents are practically "contracts of adhesion" – meaning "take it or leave it."

Given the stakes, effectively identifying and fixing key issues to the limited extent that may be possible is best left to experienced M&A legal counsel.

A notable percentage of investment banking relationships seem to end in disputes and hardships caused by investment bankers' "fee tails." As discussed earlier, those provisions warrant particular focus.

Fee tail provisions allow investment bankers to receive compensation for transactions after the termination of the investment banking engagement letter.

Generally speaking, though, the only reason for a company to terminate an investment banking engagement letter is the investment bankers' failure to deliver on a desired financing or M&A deal.

When investment bankers are unable to deliver on a financing or sale, the company client is frequently left in a difficult, if not distressed, situation, sometimes direly in need of a financing. In these situations, the fee tail can become an anchor around the neck of the company, making it difficult, if not impossible, to attract financing on any terms.

These situations reveal an ugly side of investment banking, as most investment banking firms will let a company go into insolvency rather than throw it a life preserver by waiving or modifying fee tail rights.

The only way to avoid ugly fee tail problems is to not sign engagement letters with long fee tails. It is very difficult, though, to limit fee tails to a reasonable period, like six months. A six-month tail effectively rules out working with many top firms, as they routinely require tails of at least one to two years. Again, "contract of adhesion" is the reality – take it or leave it.

Letters of Intent/Term Sheets

Virtually every M&A deal starts with a document captioned Letter of Intent or Term Sheet. Even though many of the terms in an LOI are explicitly non-binding, including the requirement to consummate a deal, it would be a terrible mistake for a target company to not work with experienced M&A counsel to ensure that the LOI anticipates and covers at a high level all of the key provisions the target company wants to see in the final PSA.

This is because the target company's leverage is at its greatest before the LOI is signed, after which, through the due diligence process and drafting of the PSA, the negotiating advantage generally shifts to the acquiror.

Thus, it is usually in the target company's best interest to ensure that the LOI is as complete as possible, rather than hope to save key asks for the final document drafting process.

Lock-up Provisions

A tricky LOI term acquirors typically demand is called a lock-up. A lock-up is a period of exclusivity during which the seller cannot solicit or consider offers from any other acquiror and agrees to pay a substantial "break-up fee" in the event the seller takes an offer from another acquiror.

Agreeing to a lock-up suspends the competitive bidding process and may permanently harm a target company's ability to re-start it. If there is a competitive process underway, it would generally be best for the seller to avoid agreeing to any lock-ups until all bids are in and the seller has done some due diligence of its own to determine which buyer is most likely to get through the process and consummate the acquisition with the highest cash purchase price.

Additionally, any lock-up should be for the shortest period possible. Ideally this would be two weeks, but thirty days is more typical. Forty-five days is unnecessarily long, unless the company has an inadequate virtual data room or a messy Disclosure Schedule.

Again, being highly prepared for an M&A deal has numerous benefits, including possible leverage to shorten lock-up periods.

Acquiror Delay Tactics – Move Deals Quickly

As discussed below, acquirors can play a game of dragging out due diligence and document negotiation if they suspect they can run out a target company's financial resources and then force a sale at a lower valuation.

Being extremely well-prepared for due diligence and having audited financials before any potential acquiror comes calling are strong deterrents to these tactics.

Fortunately, VC financings, particularly series B, C and later rounds, can be very good preparation for M&A due diligence and also for forcing a company to maintain audited financials.

Whether or not an acquiror is playing delay games, time is *never* the friend of any deal. Allowing a deal to drag out increases the chances of negative factors arising and killing the deal. Teams and priorities can change without warning, and acquiring company boards can abruptly call off or delay M&A deals if their own quarterly financial results come in below expectations.

I was in the deal documentation phase of a substantial M&A deal when the COVID-19 pandemic struck. Had certain parties on each side of the deal moved faster, the deal could have been completed before the global lockdowns started. Fortunately, the buyer was highly motivated and kept the deal moving, despite everyone, including the lawyers, having to work remotely from home.

Additionally, being in deal mode diverts the attention of an executive team from the day-today business of executing on its business plan, possibly harming operating results. A seller should expect that any poor results during a prolonged deal process will negatively impact the valuation or holdbacks.

For these reasons, target companies should comply with all due diligence requests as quickly and fully as possible to enable deal principals to focus on big-picture value questions instead of legal and regulatory distractions. The best pace for an M&A deal is the fastest pace the target can support without seeming desperate.

Managing a Distress Sale

Some M&A transactions come out of the blue organically, with a competitor or strategic player making an overture. Other M&A transactions arise out of well-executed initiatives to identify and reach out to potential acquirors, often through investment bankers or other strategic advisors.

Other times, as discussed in the next and final chapter, *The Zone of Insolvency*, companies belatedly realize that sources of capital have dried up and that they are facing insolvency four to six months out.

Hastily structured sales in the weeks or months leading up to insolvency are never ideal, but they are common, and they are certainly better than sales amid full-blown financial crises once staff have been laid off and loans and leases are in default.

Being prepared to take advantage of a sale opportunity on short notice, whether by choice or necessity, is another reason for maintaining a deal-ready data room from a company's earliest days. If cash runs short and layoffs are required before a sale closes, tracking down missing due diligence documents can become progressively more difficult.

As in all negotiations, weakness should not be revealed unnecessarily. Even a distressed company seeking a rushed sale should find leverage wherever it can, whether by seeking competitive offers, pursuing bridge financing, or playing other actors against an acquiror to increase the amount of any offer, e.g., *"that offer doesn't cover our senior debt plus our liquidation preferences, so I don't think I can get the preferred stockholders' consent."*

Advantages of a Stock-Based Deal Structure

When an acquiror is buying an entire company, documenting and closing the deal is generally easier if structured as a purchase of the target's stock instead of the target's assets.

The following are some of the reasons why a stock deal can be "cleaner" than an asset deal:

Avoiding Need for Asset Assignments. In a stock deal, there is no need for the seller to "assign" any of its assets or for the buyer to "assume" any of the seller's assets. By simply changing who owns the company (i.e., all of its stock), all assets go with the sale, including but not limited to all contracts, licenses, IP, regulatory permits and registrations, and employee relationships.

The only exceptions to this are situations where contracts, licenses, permits or other assets are subject to "change of control" restrictions or prohibitions. Change of control clauses are common in certain types of agreements, including leases, banking and loan agreements, and large commercial agreements where one or both parties do not want to be forced into a critical or sensitive relationship with a competitor or other potentially undesirable party.

Contracts that are subject to change of control provisions include specific clauses that, after stating that the agreement may not be assigned without the permission of the other party, go on to state something like:

> *"... any change of control involving more than 50% of the Seller's assets or capital stock shall be deemed an assignment requiring the permission of the other party."*

Because non-assignment and change of control language in a company's agreements and other key documents can greatly complicate closing M&A deals, it is extremely helpful to keep future M&A possibilities in mind from a company's inception. Best practices include (i) always protecting the right to assign agreements and relationships *"in the event of any merger, sale, or reorganization involving all or substantially all of Party A's assets or capital stock"* and also (ii) resisting whenever possible contractual language that deems your company's change of control an assignment requiring the other party's permission.

Negotiating flexibility for future M&A deals is a two-way street. Sometimes a party in a dominant negotiating position can demand total flexibility to assign while denying the other party that same privilege. In other situations, such clauses need to be mutual in order to be accepted. Having been in many situations where the lack of contract assignability caused issues, the better practice seems to be allowing for mutual assignability, except where risks of assignment to a hostile or aggressive competitor exist.

Regulatory Licenses and Approvals. Regulatory licenses and approvals are rarely subject to easy assignment or sale, and their effectiveness is sometimes conditioned upon the absence of any change of control. But for the most part, it is far more likely that a regulatory license or approval will carry forward for the benefit of an acquiror in a stock deal than in an asset deal.

Net Operating Losses, or NOLs. The question of whether an acquiror can use a selling company's accumulated operating losses to offset any of the acquiror's future taxable income is frequently a factor in determining whether a deal should be a stock deal or an asset deal.

While it seems rare that NOLs have sufficient value to an acquiror to swing the decision either way, when NOLs do have substantial value to an acquiror, the deal must be structured as a stock deal.

Advantages of an Asset-Based Deal Structure

Asset deal structures can offer specific advantages for acquirors, including the following.

Avoiding Liabilities. M&A deals are frequently structured as asset sales when the seller has substantial liabilities that the acquiror wishes to leave with the seller. These can include unsecured debts, litigation, regulatory matters, environmental risks, employee claims, and so forth.

While certain types of liabilities, such as certain tax claims, can follow closely related assets, for the most part, they do not in bona fide sales for fair value.

Step-Up in Tax Basis. Tax considerations beyond NOLs are often very important in determining structure. A major consideration for many acquirors is obtaining what is called a "step-up in basis" of acquired assets. A step-up in basis of acquired assets means the buyer will pay less capital gains tax if it later sells those same assets.

Buyer Attributes and Deal Structure

The attributes and motivations of the buyer will also drive a range of factors involving deal structure, terms, and complexity. The overarching question here is whether the buyer is a "financial buyer" or a "strategic buyer."

Financial Buyers

Financial buyers are primarily focused on generating a financial return directly from the investment, either (i) by making the target company more profitable and holding on to it for cash flows or (ii) by improving the company's profitability and taking it public or selling it. Financial buyers also sometimes look to acquire several companies in the same industry to create economies of scale. As discussed in Chapter 15, this is called a roll-up strategy.

Financial buyers often consider themselves business savvy and will focus closely on a company's historical financials. They are usually looking for well-managed companies with a history of good earnings and earnings growth.

Acquisitions by financial buyers are also more likely to be largely financed by debt – often as much as 80% of the purchase price.

Private Equity Firms. A private equity, or PE, firm is a classic financial buyer. As mentioned earlier, some of the most famous PE firms are The Carlyle Group, Kohlberg Kravis Roberts (KKR), and The Blackstone Group. There are more than 2,000 PE firms in North America.

When a PE firm buys a company, it may or may not keep the senior team intact. The PE firm may view the senior team as expensive or ineffective and replace it, or it may keep the senior team and tap key persons from the PE firm to become active managers of the business, alongside or over the existing team.

A PE firm may leave operations largely intact and merely fine-tune things around the edges to improve profitability, or it might introduce substantial restructurings to fix perceived problems with the company's cost structure or operations.

Strategic Buyers

Strategic buyers also focus on a target's historical and forward-looking financial performance, particularly since an acquired entity's financial results are likely to be consolidated with and into the acquiror's financial statements.

But strategics are *more* focused on the potential business synergies of an acquisition. These strategic synergies often relate to (i) adding acquired products to an existing line, (ii) acquiring operations, technology or IP that can be leveraged to support or improve existing or anticipated products or services, or (iii) gaining access to new markets or customers.

The majority of M&A exits by VC-funded companies tend to involve strategic acquirors. Any acquisition you read about by Google, Amazon, Apple, Facebook, or Microsoft is a strategic acquisition. And while acquisitions by these tech giants are the ones that grab the headlines, many other lower-profile strategic acquisitions occur almost daily.

Case Studies #38, #45, and #46 all involve examples of strategic acquisitions.

Reasons for Preferring Strategic Acquirors

Strategic Buyers Often Bid Higher. Again, financial buyers look solely at the company's historical operating and financial results to value a business, and they often plan to operate the business as is, albeit with operational improvements and greater financial resources.

Strategic acquirors, on the other hand, often hope to do one or both of the following: (i) *leverage* the target's products, technology, IP, or existing customer base to drive improved revenue growth and profitability from the acquiror's existing businesses and (ii) generate improved revenue growth and profitability from the target's existing products and services by selling them across the acquiror's existing markets and customer base.

Thus, the ideal strategic acquiror has the potential for generating much greater financial returns using the target's assets than does the target operating on its own.

For this reason, the bids of strategic buyers tend to be higher than those of financial buyers – often much higher.

Acquiror Stock as Acquisition Capital. Another advantage many strategic acquirors have over financial buyers is the ability to add some of the acquiror's stock to the mix of consideration offered to the target company's shareholders. When the acquiror is a publicly-traded company, the ability to use stock as acquisition currency is a significant advantage over financial purchasers.

As an aside, sellers should be very cautious in valuing the stock of a privately held acquiror in any deal, as those valuations are often overstated and far more speculative than the shares of a publicly-traded company with an established operating history, current and highly transparent financial statements, and a trading price established by efficient markets.

As virtually every company acquired by WeWork learned, private company valuations can vanish overnight.

In summary, founders and investors alike often do better in transactions with strategic buyers than with financial buyers due to the higher prices generally offered by strategic investors and the potential for a strategic to sweeten its bid with valuable acquiror stock. This likely explains why strategic acquisitions outnumber financial buyer acquisitions. This also reinforces the earlier advice that founders connect with a wide range of potential strategic buyers from a company's earliest days.

Typical M&A Deal Documents

No two M&A deals are exactly alike. There will always be documentation similarities and differences.

Examples of documents not described below that might also be found in an M&A deal include key person employment agreements, an agreement requiring a seller of assets to provide various types of transition services to the buyer, IP cross-licensing provisions in asset deals where less than all of a seller's IP is transferred, insurance certificates evidencing fee tail insurance coverage protecting a buyer, myriad documents relating to selling shareholders receiving buyer's stock in a cash and stock deal, and asset pushdown or assignment agreements where a seller in a stock deal needs to move assets from one or more subsidiaries into the entity being sold.

With those caveats, the following is a somewhat typical document set for an asset sale. The descriptions of these documents are necessarily brief, but examples of each, except for a Disclosure Schedule, can be found in the BLSG Data Room under *Finance > Merger and Acquisition Documents.*

Letter of Intent

We discussed Letters of Intent earlier. These are also often called Term Sheets. Either way, it is important that the document capture all of the key provisions of the deal.

Stock/Asset Purchase and Sale Agreement

In a stock deal, there will be a document likely captioned "Stock Purchase and Sale Agreement." In an asset deal, there will be a document likely captioned "Asset Purchase and Sale Agreement." Again, we can refer to these as SPAs and APAs, respectively. Whether stock deal or asset deal, this is the central deal document that captures all or most of the terms detailed in the Letter of Intent or Term Sheet.

Assignment and Assumption of IP Agreement

Assignment and Assumption of IP Agreements are only found in asset deals. These documents are necessitated by the fact that the legalese and mechanics of transferring IP are highly specialized.

Additionally, addressing IP conveyances in a separate document from the APA can be helpful if that document needs to be filed with one or more agencies, like the USPTO, to effect IP assignments.

Lastly, an Assignment and Assumption of IP Agreement can be used to address in detail (i) IP that is transferring in a deal, (ii) IP that is not transferring in a deal, and (iii) IP that will be subject to cross-licenses between the buyer and seller.

Disclosure Schedule/Schedule of Exceptions

As we have learned, Disclosure Schedules are loaded up with all kinds of things, including:

- cap table,

- financial statements,

- material changes since the date of the most recent financials,

- caveats and exceptions to the seller's representations and warranties,

- lists of leased premises,

- equipment leases,

- any licensed IP necessary for the conduct of the business being sold, including detailed lists of all open source IP licenses,

- lists of material contracts,

- lists of employees and their compensation,

- special bonuses or other compensation being paid out in the sale transaction,

- lists of independent contractors and consultants,

- any union/labor contracts or issues,

- any IP of the seller that has been licensed to or from others,

- pending or potential litigation matters,

- pending or potential regulatory matters,

- potential environmental liabilities,

- any potential tax liabilities, and

- any other liabilities not in the ordinary course of business.

Seller Board Consents

Every M&A transaction requires board approval, whether the deal is a stock deal or an asset deal. While approaches vary, board consents of this type are sometimes lengthy and detailed, incorporating by reference and approving as "in the Company's best interests" each of the applicable transaction documents and also identifying and approving many of the key deal terms.

Other key elements of M&A board resolutions include (i) identifying and approving as in the company's best interests any special interests of board members or senior management in the proposed transaction and (ii) mandating, where appropriate, that management also seek and obtain requisite shareholder approval.

Seller Shareholder Consents

As just alluded to, it is generally necessary to obtain both board and shareholder approval to sell all or substantially all of a company's equity or assets. Fortunately, the resolutions drafted for board approval can generally be easily redrafted as Shareholder Consent documents. Shareholder Consents must be solicited in accordance with a Company's Certificate of Incorporation and Bylaws.

Seller Secretary's Certificate/Officer's Certificate

At the closing of virtually every M&A deal, an officer of the selling company will be required to attest to a number of things in the form of a signed Officer's Certificate or Secretary's Certificate. The requirement for such a certificate generally appears in a section of the PSA captioned "Conditions to Closing," "Buyer's Conditions to Closing," or "Conditions to Obligations of Buyer."

The requirements for Officer's Certificates to be delivered at Closing vary, but the language in a PSA might read like this:

> *"Buyer shall have received a certificate, dated the Closing Date and signed by a duly authorized officer of Seller, (i) stating that each of the representations and warranties of the Seller remains true and correct at and as of the Closing Date, (ii) stating that Seller has duly performed and complied in all respects with all agreements, covenants and conditions required by this Agreement and each of the other Transaction Documents to be performed or complied with prior to or on the Closing Date, (iii) certifying that attached thereto are true and complete copies of all resolutions adopted by the board of directors of Seller authorizing the execution, delivery and performance of this Agreement and the other Transaction Documents and the consummation of the transactions contemplated hereby and thereby, and that all such resolutions are in full force and effect and are all the resolutions adopted in connection with the transactions contemplated hereby, and (iv) certifying the names and signatures of the officers of Seller authorized to sign this Agreement, the Transaction Documents and the other documents to be delivered hereunder and thereunder.*

Escrow Agreement

Sale proceeds subject to any kind of holdback can be held by the buyer or in an escrow account.

When held by the buyer, it's called a holdback, and when held in escrow, it's called an escrow.

Holdbacks and escrows are usually one or two years, sometimes longer. They are a buyer's insurance against third-party claims the seller said wouldn't happen in its reps and warranties.

These claims can include unexpected tax or environmental liabilities, IP infringement claims, claims of unpaid bonuses or other compensation relating to work performed pre-closing, claims from aggrieved shareholders, or almost any other matter arising out of the seller's reps and warranties.

When a holdback is escrowed, an Escrow Agreement provides for the establishment of the escrow account to be managed by a neutral third party, called the Escrow Agent. The Escrow Agreement details the fees related to the escrow account. The parties generally agree to not sue the Escrow Agent and agree to indemnify the Escrow Agent in the event of any such suits.

Most importantly, though, the Escrow Agreement details all of the mechanics and standards regarding (i) how claims against the escrow are to be made, processed, paid out, or rejected, (ii) when and how the escrow account is to be closed at the end of the escrow period, (iii) to whom the remaining funds should be directed, and (iv) how any disputes are to be handled.

Find an *Escrow Agreement Example* in the BLSG Data Room at *Finance > Merger and Acquisition Documents > Escrow Agreement Example.*

Notices of Assignment and Consents to Assignment

In any asset deal, there are likely to be one or more contracts that need to be assigned from the seller to the buyer. If the seller has a manufacturing agreement, for example, and the buyer wants to continue operating under that manufacturing agreement, that agreement by its terms might require the seller to simply give the manufacturer formal notice of the assignment.

In that case, the seller will prepare, sign and execute the required Notices of Assignment and provide them to buyer at closing.

Under many contracts, simple notice is insufficient and the counterparty must agree to any assignment of the agreement. In the case of the manufacturing agreement, for example, the manufacturer would need to be contacted in advance of closing and convinced to sign an "Assignment Agreement" that is contingent upon the closing of the M&A deal. That Assignment Agreement would be delivered to the buyer at closing, fully executed by the seller and the manufacturing company, but would only become effective upon closing.

Where a buyer is a publicly-traded company, information about the deal likely must be kept completely confidential, and the buyer must be consulted about when and how to deal with assignment notices and consents.

When deal confidentiality is critical and the buyer is a large, reputable company, the buyer may simply take its chances and only provide notice of assignment or seek consent to assignment after closing, as happened in one of my recent deals.

Bill of Sale

Oddly enough, even very large asset-based M&A deals require a Bill of Sale at closing. This is primarily for tax reasons.

Bills of Sale are usually a single page of text describing the assets conveyed, the amount being paid, other applicable terms, and the date of Closing, followed by a signature page that is signed only by the Seller. A Bill of Sale is not required in stock-based deals.

Find a Bill of Sale example in the *BLSG Data Room at Finance > Merger and Acquisition Documents > Asset Sale Bill of Sale Example.*

Case Study #44 – Good Is Not Enough

Sales and sales growth are critical for every startup. And as we know, once a startup takes VC money, sales growth expectations skyrocket.

Companies that would otherwise be viewed as experiencing acceptable sales growth, even 20% to 40% annually, can find themselves pressed by their VCs for faster sales increases than the market and opportunity can support. VCs expect exceptional growth, not reasonable growth.

When exceptional growth fails to materialize after one or two financing rounds, a company's VCs can lose interest and stop supporting a company. This can usher in a painful decline, especially if the company comes to be viewed as damaged goods. Costs of capital can rise, and sometimes capital can dry up completely.

While there are various definitions for the term "zombie company," companies that have been abandoned by their VCs seem like the true zombies. They are often unattractive to other investors given (i) their shunning by supposedly "smart money" and (ii) the often substantial liquidation preferences that have accumulated.

In a poorly performing company, these liquidation preferences are often only part of the cap table issues. There may also be a variety of outstanding highly-discounted warrants, not to mention other special rights negotiated by VC investors during earlier troubled financing rounds.

A potential investor in a struggling company with two or three prior VC rounds will invariably have much negotiating to do to arrive at an economically logical down round or recapitalization financing. Existing investors may have little incentive to negotiate, aside from reputation and founder goodwill. If existing investors don't believe new money will finally produce a scalable revenue spike, self-interest and their own fiduciary considerations to VC fund investors may cause them to opt for keeping their liquidation preferences intact, forcing a sale, and writing off any losses.

These zombie companies are generally headed for disappointing exits.

I have witnessed these challenges a few times. One involved a company I thought looked very promising.

Imagine a small company of maybe 30 employees that has developed a "social listening" platform that tells client companies in real-time what customers are doing and saying online from their retail locations.

By all accounts, this company executed well. It had an impressive roster of big brand clients. The company was operated in a competent, cost-conscious manner.

And then it produced only modest sales growth, likely no more than 30% to 40% annually. The company was originally funded by angels and a high-profile strategic investor. VC interest never materialized due to the company's moderate sales growth trajectory. This created financing difficulties that no-doubt fed a vicious cycle of insufficient investment in growth and experimentation.

Insufficient funding eventually forced the company to accept what was probably a low-priced acquisition offer by a publicly-traded strategic acquiror. Given the company's condition, this may have even been an "acquihire" – i.e., an acquisition where the purchase price covers outstanding debts and little more, but which also involves offers of employment to the founders and part or all of the rest of the team.

While not a financial home run by any means, as discussed in Chapter 17, an acquihire is a clean, respectable ending. Liabilities are usually addressed, and the target's products and teams might thrive with the new parent's greater resources and structure.

> Lessons: Rapid revenue growth is critical for the success of most startups, particularly between VC funding rounds.

Case Study #45 – Out of the Ashes

Following a common pattern in the world of startups, after years of driving hard to hockey-stick revenues, the dominant shareholder of one of my companies decided it was time to at least partially exit and sell off a line of business.

We had great technology and a strong go-to-market strategy, but our limited size and financial resources compounded some manufacturing, distribution, and working capital challenges. With little margin for error, even minor manufacturing problems became huge headaches.

After retaining an investment banker and soliciting potential suitors, a strong candidate stepped forward. We had an excellent data room, and few issues were raised in due diligence. Things slowed down precipitously, though, during the drafting phase as the holidays approached. Our team was ready to work right on through and close early in the new year, but the other team, a publicly-traded company, was less focused and essentially took two or three weeks off.

Then the deal hit the rocks – completely unrelated to anything having to do with its merits or our showing in due diligence. The board of this publicly-traded company was unhappy with their company's performance in completely unrelated divisions and essentially called off all M&A activity.

The deal was dead. The acquiror walked, expressing no hope of or interest in reviving the deal at a later date.

As is always the case, pursuing the deal aggressively for almost three months had completely distracted the company and taken its toll on business plan execution. We had a great team, though, and we dusted ourselves off and got back to business.

And then, a few months later, our CEO announced that the deal was back on. Like the proverbial hot dog that had fallen into the campfire, this one was cleaned off and back in the bun. Our CEO had given the other company some time to deal with their own issues and then re-kindled the conversation through back channels.

Lessons: This case study highlights the importance of perseverance in deal-making. I learn this time and time again from best-in-class CEOs. They see opportunity through chaos and conflicting signals. And they are true "closers." I have learned never to believe early negative signals in any deal and to make at least two or three runs at saving any important deal or relationship, even if others have given up.

This case study also demonstrates that time is the enemy of all deals.

Case Study #46 – The Triple-Rainbow

Exiting a company twice is one of the more unlikely wins, but it is possible if a founding team is integral to a company's success, no matter who owns it. Companies often change hands more than once. Few team members stay on with, or rejoin, a business through three sales. But it happened to me and a few others.

I became general counsel of startup Netstock in May of 2000. Following the ".com bust" of 2000, when the term "net" was out of style, we renamed the company ShareBuilder.

ShareBuilder opened more than 1,000 brokerage accounts per day for years and was recognized as one of the fastest-growing online brokerages in the world. The company was well-managed and struck a great balance between entrepreneurialism and sound legal, governance and regulatory practices.

ShareBuilder raised $60 million over the course of several financings, including series A, B, C, C+, and D financing rounds.

The market collapse of May 2000 severely tightened up financing for startups. Closing our series C+ bridge financing was difficult. In a board meeting, a senior officer slid a set of keys across the table to the investor board-designees, saying with a dead-pan seriousness, "*If you don't want to fund it, maybe you would like to run it, because the team and I will just leave.*"

Although we struggled a little to close that financing, our investors stepped up. Meanwhile, other startups were collapsing left and right as VC capital dried up.

In about 2006, our major investors began pushing for an exit.

We hired investment bankers and found an ideal acquiror, ING Direct, which acquired ShareBuilder in 2007. ING Direct was then one of the largest online banks in the world, with 7.5 million active online banking customers. ShareBuilder then had more than 1.5 million active online brokerage customers.

Although this was technically an acquisition, ShareBuilder retained its corporate and management structure and operated fairly autonomously from the banking side. The brokerage and banking teams cooperated closely on creatively integrating customer accounts and user experiences.

The success of ShareBuilder is worth noting. We built ShareBuilder for an IPO. We did not cut corners, and we did not accumulate a closet of legal or regulatory skeletons.

In a political twist of fate, the European Commission forced behemoth ING Group to restructure globally, including forcing the sale of ING Direct in the U.S.

https://www.ing.com/Newsroom/PBOld/ING-restructuring-plan-approved-by-European-Commission.htm

This put ING Direct and ShareBuilder into an auction-sale process. The auction resulted in Capital One buying ING Direct and ShareBuilder for $9.5 billion in 2012.

Once again, it was clear that maintaining the ShareBuilder team was critical for the continued success and operational viability of the brokerage business and its related technology. Although working on this double-rainbow transaction was intellectually interesting and professionally rewarding for virtually all who stayed on with Capital One, the sale ultimately resulted in the demise of ShareBuilder.

In the M&A world, when a large company acquires a smaller, leaner, and more innovative company and then accidentally suffocates it with costs and bureaucracy, we say the larger company *"crushed the butterfly,"* or *"smothered the kitten."*

While general counsel of ShareBuilder, I had helped establish a registered investment advisory subsidiary called ShareBuilder Advisors, LLC, to launch a cool 401k offering for small and medium-sized businesses. We named that offering ShareBuilder 401K.

In late 2019, the remaining officer of ShareBuilder 401K, a former colleague, pulled together investors, including other former ShareBuilder colleagues, to buy the ShareBuilder 401k business, operations, and IP from Capital One.

In a bit of a triple-rainbow development, I am once again providing legal and regulatory counsel to ShareBuilder 401k.

ShareBuilder 401k is a very cost-effective and user-friendly 401k option. I highly recommend it to all small and medium-sized businesses. Go here - https://www.sharebuilder401k.com/ - and tell them Paul sent you.

> Lessons: Both the ING Direct and the Capital One acquisitions of ShareBuilder went smoothly because the company was built on a strong legal, governance, and regulatory foundation and had few skeletons in the closet.
>
> For in-house counsel who stay on with an acquiror after an acquisition, the absence of legal and regulatory skeletons in the closet is critical for avoiding post-acquisition conflicts of interest. Substantial conflicts can arise, for example, when an acquiring entity makes a claim against an acquisition escrow account due to an alleged rep or warranty breach. Any attorney caught in the middle of that kind of dispute will need to handle the conflict with great care – likely by recusing himself or herself.
>
> Many states have a rule of professional conduct similar to Washington's RPC 1.9, that imposes this restriction on attorneys:
>
> *RULE 1.9 – DUTIES TO FORMER CLIENTS*
>
> *(a)A lawyer who has formerly represented a client in a matter shall not thereafter represent another person in the same or a substantially related matter in which that person's interests are*

materially adverse to the interests of the former client unless the former client gives informed consent, confirmed in writing.

Professional risks would be even greater to the extent any claims related to potential acts, omissions, or non-disclosures involved the attorney. In such cases, the attorney's self-interests conflict with the acquiror's interests, thereby interfering with the attorney's ability to effectively represent the new client.

The possibilities of such conflicts deter some in-house attorneys from accepting employment with acquirors.

Case Study #47 – Graceful Exit Under Pressure

Companies with good legal representation from beginning to end are often able to raise more money and, anecdotally at least, they may have certain advantages if insolvency looms.

In one situation, I was asked to help develop and launch an innovative financial services company. I helped it raise $25M of the total $50M raised.

This company was building a highly innovative product in the financial services space that required regulatory approval. Getting that approval was never guaranteed. But the company's product was so helpful and appealing that all of us were confident we could ultimately get the regulators on board. Key state financial regulators were already among our champions.

We made pitches to dozens of federal regulators and felt we had good answers to all of their questions. And then weeks stretched into months without a clear signal from the regulators. The team worked on a range of revenue-producing ideas for sustaining the company through its period of regulatory uncertainty.

During that period, the company was approached by a large strategic buyer that paid $100 million for the company. This was enough to cover the company's debts, provide a decent return to investors, and support a modest payout to the team.

Though I had left the project before the acquisition, I know the decision to pull the plug on this project must have been difficult for the founder.

In fact, within months after the acquisition, the federal banking regulator that had stymied the project through inaction suddenly announced that it would consider more flexible rules for approving similar innovative financial services products.

But the company's financial runway would have run out before this regulatory change of heart could be implemented. Had the founder passed on the sale, the exit reported favorably in the media could have been replaced by a much different story of investors losing everything in a messy shutdown. The likelihood of this outcome is supported by the fact that the acquiror eventually gave up on launching the product as well.

<u>Lessons:</u> Knowing when to throw in the towel on a startup requires judgment, objectivity, good advisors, and a strong moral compass. This experienced founder surrounded himself with and listened to a well-rounded team of executive leaders, board members, external advisors, and investors in making this decision. The facts bear out that it was the right one, leading to a graceful exit instead of an embarrassing financial calamity.

Case Study #48 – Fishing in Jersey

Any company that is for sale, whether as part of an orderly exit or a hasty fire sale, may find itself the subject of one or more fishing expeditions. Here, fishing expedition means feigned interest by an acquiror, usually a competitor, that is a ruse for gathering business intelligence and possibly even stealing IP.

My companies have been on the receiving end of fishing expeditions, and I have even unintentionally gone fishing once myself, in a nondescript office park in New Jersey.

To be clear, nobody outright admitted that we were fishing for business intelligence from our struggling competitor. But the colleague leading this process at the time wasn't exactly the best at disguising his intentions either.

Toiling away over stacks of documents in a cramped office in a New Jersey office park, I recall asking, *"The fact that they are failing means that their accounts are lower value than ours; and converting bad accounts is probably even harder than converting good accounts, so why would we consider buying this dog?"* To which my colleague replied, *"We probably aren't, but you never know what you'll learn."*

I could tell from that reply that there was no interest in buying the company. We were simply gathering business intelligence on things like marketing strategies and costs, customer behavior based on different account features and pricing models, and possibly selected IP assets that might be worth acquiring apart from the primary assets.

> <u>Lessons:</u> M&A activity always carries risks of competitive espionage. And, unfortunately, NDAs offer little real protection when a direct competitor's business, finance, tax, legal, and IP teams are allowed unfettered access to a company's data room.
>
> Consider holding back critical business strategies and metrics, trade secrets, and other IP in the initial phases of due diligence to allow for more time to gauge a potential acquiror's true motives.

CHAPTER SEVENTEEN

The Zone of Insolvency

This chapter is about saving insolvent startups when possible and putting them down responsibly when it is not.

Great startup founders and teams frequently persevere through extreme financial challenges and emerge on the other side stronger, smarter, and better positioned.

But not always. Startups shut down every day.

Earlier I mentioned that penny warrants are the equivalent of smoke in the cockpit, meaning that, absent quick, effective action, the company could be in for an imminent crash landing.

The only thing worse than a metaphorical smoky cockpit situation is what I think of as "*company down*" – total financial collapse. Company Down is also the title of the final case study.

Unfortunately, I've endured several smoky cockpit episodes. Some work out, and some don't.

As noted from the outset, the goal of this book is to help keep companies out of trouble and help them *raise the right amounts of capital at the right time, and on the right terms.* Following best practices will reduce the risks of failure, but not eliminate them. A well-run and well-funded company making a product nobody wants will eventually die if it cannot pivot to a product the market does want.

The more money a company has raised and the more complicated the cap table and balance sheet, the more unnerving these situations can be.

The next case study presents facts that probably seem extreme. But similar facts are taking place in many companies around the U.S. and around the globe at any given time.

When cash reserves are down to months or even weeks, some officers, directors, and advisors quit or step away to get out of harm's way. I recently observed a VC board designee refuse to take the board seat she had committed to in a financing Term Sheet due to the company's deteriorating financial situation.

But, commendably, many directors, officers, employees, and advisors stay in their roles through difficult situations for the good of the enterprise and its stakeholders.

Case Study #49 – Smoke in the Cockpit

There are several types of events that I equate with "*smoke in the cockpit,*" including:

- Insufficient funds to cover payroll within 30 days.
- Defaulting on a payment obligation to a landlord.

- Skirting at or below secured lender cash covenants.

- Deferring all A/P payments for 60 days.

- Issuing debt with 2x liquidation preferences.

- Issuing debt with penny warrants.

- Maxing out the last available borrowing resources.

Any of these would be cause for concern by itself. In one situation, all were present.

This was mostly a case of a company still trying to perfect its business model at a point of scale where it needed to substantially slow its burn rate or raise a lot more capital.

The company's too-high monthly burn rate, combined with founder reluctance to raise substantial equity capital in a dilutive down round, put the company in a difficult situation. The founder was bright and had his own ideas about getting through the challenges, but they required an adventurous spirit.

The company had been working on a financing for a couple months, but it wasn't coming together, despite a lot of well-placed and well-executed pitches. Cash was getting low, and the company had been deferring non-critical payables for months.

Ideas for asset sales and cost reduction efforts were percolating at the board level, and overtures were being made to the likely buyers of the company's non-core business lines.

As frequently happens, financing efforts continued to struggle. The monthly burn rate was too high and, as often goes left unspoken, the company's valuation was likely too high. The company was ultimately forced to accept a weak lead investor - a small, inexperienced VC firm with a small checkbook.

We pulled together an onerous bridge loan, penny warrants and all, and then closed a smallish but adequate equity financing.

Things looked like they were going well, like we might have enough in the bank to get through some significant asset sales in the works.

And then, external market factors turned negative. Funding turned off and M&A deals were put on hold. In holding out for a home run, the founder had played it too close. The down round I was advocating six months earlier was probably the correct path, but it was no longer an option.

> Lessons: The founder in the earlier Case Study #47, *Graceful Exit Under Pressure*, managed his challenges more successfully than this founder. He assessed his burn rate, conceded that more money probably wasn't coming in, and found a buyer. Although the exit was not the home run he was hoping for, he and the board preserved substantial value.

Managing through an impending financial collapse is one of the most challenging battles a startup team can face. There are important reasons for not giving up too easily. But poorly funded companies pose legal, financial, and regulatory dangers to those who continue to work with them.

Officers and directors must understand and observe their fundamental legal and fiduciary obligations in the zone of insolvency. Directors must be particularly mindful of the boundaries of the business judgment rule and the more exacting requirements of the entire fairness standard, which we looked at in Chapter 8.

Founders and other officers and directors should retain specialized counsel for this leg of the journey and make sure that D&O insurance coverage, including "tail insurance" is prepaid as far out as possible or that cash has been set aside for those coverages. We will discuss tail insurance coverage later in the chapter.

Insolvency Defined

Insolvency is an important legal and financial status:

- insolvency makes it hard to raise new capital,

- insolvency trips debt, loan, lease, and contractual covenants, including creditors' rights to "accelerate" (declare due) loan repayments and rights in other parties to terminate contracts, including leases,

- insolvency provides a lookback date for invalidating both "fraudulent conveyances" and "preference" payments, and

- insolvency impacts governance obligations.

The U.S. Bankruptcy Code (Section 101(32)(A)) defines insolvency for corporations as:

> "… *financial condition such that the sum of such entity's debts is greater than all of such entity's property, at fair valuation.*'

The phrase "fair valuation" has been heavily litigated by parties arguing over an entity's solvency or insolvency as of a given moment. Two guideposts that have emerged are that a valuation under Section 101(32)(A) cannot be based on (i) estimated net proceeds from a rushed sale or (ii) after-the-fact information.

In re Heilig-Meyers Co, 319 B.R. 447 (2004) is an influential and instructive case on valuing insolvent companies.

https://www.courtlistener.com/opinion/1521985/in-re-heilig-meyers-co/

We'll see that state creditor-debtor laws also help to define insolvency.

Leading through Insolvency

Although an exaggerated analogy, in guiding nearly insolvent startups, I view the team's role like that of a crew flying a shot-up Flying Fortress B-17 bomber.

For historical context, B-17s could take unbelievable damage and still make it to safety if the crew kept their wits, followed their training, and exhibited courage and resourcefulness.

Like these bombers, startups can get into seemingly hopeless financial and legal predicaments, yet still survive and thrive.

Leading up to and even through dire financial situations, officers and directors should look for potential solutions and paths to success everywhere and anywhere, including:

- cutting expenses to extend runway,

- pivoting the revenue model,

- cajoling existing or new investors to help continue the fight, in a down round if necessary,

- seeking concessions from creditors, and

- exploring opportunities for strategic sales or mergers.

Identifying and executing on viable strategies at the earliest time possible is key, as options rapidly and dangerously narrow on the approach to insolvency, like crossing the "event horizon" of a black hole.

In the zone of insolvency, keep stakeholders engaged and talking. Positions can harden when key stakeholders feel left out, ignored, or taken for granted. They can also start scheming among themselves behind the scenes. Look for creative solutions that give everybody something and that seek to focus all stakeholders on meaningful common interests in supporting the company and its mission.

Wage Theft and Officer Liabilities

Managing employees correctly in the zone of insolvency is very important. Employees have only modest priority in federal bankruptcy, but the failure to pay wages violates "wage theft" laws in many states and can result in civil and sometimes criminal liability for officers and directors.

In the 9th Circuit Court of Appeals case _Boucher v. Shaw_, the Court held corporate officers liable for unpaid wages under FLSA and also held that their liabilities were unchanged by the company's later bankruptcy filing.

The officers were each deemed independently to be an "employer," jointly and severally liable with the company, as emphasized in footnote 10 of the decision:

> _To the contrary, the managers are independently liable under the FLSA, and the automatic [bankruptcy] stay has no effect on that liability. The defendants in their supplementary briefing repeatedly assert that they were unable to find any authority in support of this proposition. We have found at least two cases holding that individual managers can be held liable under the FLSA even after the corporation has filed for bankruptcy. See Donovan v. Agnew, 712 F.2d 1509, 1511, 1514 (1st Cir. 1983) (finding managers of bankrupt corporation individually liable under FLSA and noting, "The overwhelming weight of authority is that a corporate officer with operational control of a corporation's covered enterprise is an employer along with the corporation, jointly and severally liable under the FLSA for unpaid wages."); Chung v. New Silver Palace, 246 F. Supp. 2d 220, 226 (S.D.N.Y. 2002) ("The automatic stay... affects only [the debtor]; it does not apply to plaintiff's [FLSA] claims against the [debtor]'s non-debtor co-defendants.")._
>
> _(http://cdn.ca9.uscourts.gov/datastore/opinions/2009/07/27/05-15454.pdf)_

State laws vary, with Washington, Illinois, and New York holding officers personally liable for unpaid wages, but California and Nevada not.

In the interest of risk mitigation, no company with employees and payroll obligations should be allowed to run out of money and miss payroll, however state law leans. Well before payroll cannot be made, or at least the period before, employees should be furloughed or terminated.

Under state and federal law, employees cannot work for free – even voluntarily. As we discussed in Chapter 10, *Common Regulatory Mistakes*, the law regarding who can work without compensation is extremely unclear from state to state, and it is best to assume that everyone needs to be paid at least minimum wage, including officers.

Officers and directors can also be held liable for a company's failure to remit any withheld payroll taxes.

Voidable Preferences and Fraudulent Conveyances

Under state and federal law, creditors and bankruptcy trustees have powerful tools to claw back all kinds of payments and asset transfers that occur during and before a company's insolvency. Payments and transfers that can be clawed back include "fraudulent conveyances," "voidable preferences," and "fraudulent transfers."

Transfers of payments or assets to insiders during insolvency are particularly vulnerable to challenge and can result in personal liability for officers and directors.

<u>Uniform Fraudulent Transfer Act.</u> Virtually every state has adopted a version of what is called the Uniform Fraudulent Transfer Act ("UFTA"), also called the Uniform Voidable Transactions Act. The UFTA provides powerful remedies to creditors who believe a debtor has attempted to make itself judgment-proof against its debts or obligations by transferring assets or incurring liabilities.

The UFTA is the state-law equivalent to the federal bankruptcy code except that it gives both bankruptcy trustees and ordinary creditors the ability to go after two types of "fraudulent transfers" by a debtor/company:

- "Actual Fraud" - transfers made with "actual intent to hinder, delay or defraud any creditor."

- "Constructive Fraud" - transfers made while a debtor is insolvent (or which make the debtor insolvent) for which the debtor did not receive "reasonably equivalent value in exchange for the transfer or obligation."

Under the UFTA, creditors can unwind transactions, recover transferred funds or assets, and obtain money judgments against transferees.

Since proving "intent" to hinder, delay, or defraud could be difficult, the UFTA lists factors to be considered. These "badges of fraud," as they are called, include, among others:

- whether the transfer was to an "insider," such as a family member,

- whether the debtor kept possession or control of the property after the transfer,

- whether the transfer was concealed or hidden, and

- whether the debtor received "reasonably equivalent value" in exchange for the property transferred.

The UFTA defines insolvency very broadly. A debtor is insolvent if (i) the sum of its debts is greater than the sum of the its assets or (ii) the debtor is "generally not paying the debtor's debts as they become due."

When creditors are unable to recover fraudulently transferred funds or assets from the debtor or the transferee, they sometimes go after the officers and directors who approved or allowed the transfers. Those are probably the exceptional cases, though, likely involving claims of egregious self-dealing, fraud, or corporate looting.

But officers and directors should never underestimate the willingness of creditors to sue them personally.

Voidable Preference. Under federal bankruptcy law, a "voidable preference" is a transaction the trustee or debtor in possession can "avoid," i.e., not pay, unwind, or otherwise claw back. We discuss debtors in possession again when we look at Chapter 11 bankruptcy.

A voidable preference under the bankruptcy code is defined as: (i) a transfer of assets to a creditor, relating to an existing debt, (iii) not in exchange for new value, (iv) shortly before a debtor files for bankruptcy protection, and (v) the asset transfer allowed the creditor to receive more than would have been the case if the debtor had been liquidated.

The "look back" timeframe is 90 days from the date of a bankruptcy petition date or, as to payments to insiders, one year from the date of a bankruptcy petition.

Bankruptcy trustees will look at every payment made by a company looking back two years and will require many payees and transferees to justify every transaction with the company.

Even compensation to insiders can be claimed back by a trustee if not structured carefully, particularly severance payments. And again, the look back for insiders is one year from the date of the petition.

Fraudulent Conveyance. Section 548(a)(1)(A) of the Bankruptcy Code allows a trustee or debtor in possession to avoid any transfer made or obligation incurred by a debtor within two years of a bankruptcy filing if effected with the "actual intent to hinder, delay, or defraud" creditors.

But even non-fraudulent transfers can be challenged.

Section 548(a)(1)(B) allows a trustee or debtor in possession to avoid any transfer made or obligation incurred by a debtor within two years of bankruptcy if the debtor received "less than a reasonably equivalent value in exchange" and was, or became because of the transaction, (i) insolvent, (ii) undercapitalized, or (iii) unable to pay its debts generally as they matured.

Additionally, under Section 544(b) of the Bankruptcy Code, a bankruptcy trustee or debtor in possession can potentially leverage longer state law look back periods to avoid or reclaim similar types of payments under a state UFTA.

Payments to Insiders. Any payments or asset transfers to company insiders, including officers, directors, or major shareholders, made during or shortly before insolvency, are subject to challenge by creditors, bankruptcy trustees, and debtors in possession.

Payments or transfers that could raise concerns include:

- severance payments,

- loan repayments to insiders, or payments for other liabilities or obligations,

- increased salaries, bonuses, commissions, or other payments to insiders,

- repurchases of stock from insiders,

- any other transfer of assets to insiders, or

- the forgiveness of debts or liabilities of insiders.

Officers and directors need to be careful regarding any transactions involving conflicts of interest during or leading up to insolvency.

It is prudent to tie any special payments to insiders to obligations of continuing performance. Other consideration to support such payments can include a waiver and release, covenant not to sue, noncompetition agreement, and similar meaningful obligations.

Specific legal advice should be obtained regarding any payments that might trigger concerns under the UFTA or the bankruptcy code.

Two important cases relevant to these issues are In re TransTexas Gas Corp., 597 F.3d 298 (5th Cir. 2010) https://casetext.com/case/in-re-transtexas-gas-corp and In re Munford, Inc., 98 F.3d 604 (11th Cir. 1996) https://casetext.com/case/matter-of-munford-inc.

Stakeholder Dynamics

Another threshold issue worth discussing is stakeholder dynamics. They are usually at their most extreme in the zone of insolvency:

- notes and loans will likely be in default or nearing default, causing those stakeholders to begin clamoring to be paid off,

- unpaid creditors and landlords can be highly aggressive, delaying or denying rational concessions and making financings and sale transactions difficult or impossible to close,

- VCs may lean toward a more immediate resolution, like a quick sale, and will also be keenly aware of their place in the liquidation preference waterfall in any sale, merger, or restructuring, and

- founders will often focus on avoiding outcomes in which they and other common stockholders and employees may end up with little or nothing.

On this last point, structuring any deal that offers any cash to common stockholders is difficult in the zone of insolvency. Schemes involving stock repurchases, cash bonuses, or other payments intended to do so could come back to haunt those involved.

Divided Loyalties in Insolvency

When acting as board members, VC designees must always observe their fiduciary duties, including their duty of loyalty and duty of good faith.

But in a VC firm's capacity as a shareholder, VCs can and generally do "vote their shares" in their pure economic self-interest. They are obligated to do so as fiduciaries for their own VC fund limited partners.

Thus, while a VC board member might vote yes, approving a down round and waiving anti-dilution rights for its share class, the VC firm itself has no obligation to approve the transaction and waive its anti-dilution rights.

Some startups that enter insolvency do so, in part, because their VCs lost interest in them. For better or for worse, VCs focus their interest, energy, and financial resources on companies in the top 30% of their portfolio.

Despite this, VCs generally do a good job of staying positive and constructive in distressed situations. But reality is reality. Even a highly enthusiastic VC board designee can only have so much influence on the votes of his or her VC partners to cajole investment in another round when there are better uses for limited capital.

VCs tend to have good legal counsel, so their board designees' conduct in the zone of insolvency will generally track good governance principles, including a willingness to explore and support all reasonable avenues for a turnaround that maximizes enterprise value.

Working with Lenders

Banks and other lenders or creditors with security interests must be communicated with regularly and openly when insolvency looms. Secured creditors have the strongest legal claims and protections in insolvency.

They are also usually very sophisticated and diligent about protecting their secured interests. Attempts to deceive them or keep them in the dark can backfire in the form of accelerated steps to foreclose on secured assets, which can cut off or complicate other plans for maximizing value.

On the other hand, *some* banks and other creditors show commendable patience and flexibility when they are kept informed of alternative strategies and the dynamics that could help or hurt those strategies. Weekly calls with such creditors will go a long way toward preventing unnecessary anxiety.

Running out the Clock

As insolvency nears, issues involving founders can get more complex. On a board, founders are often viewed as representing a company's most vulnerable stakeholders, its common stockholders.

Even though common stockholders are generally last in line for liquidation proceeds, they are entitled to *procedural fairness*. Common stockholders must also be protected from abuses in transactions that are subject to the entire fairness standard discussed earlier.

A founder's mix of motivations are often both financial and personal. On the financial side, founders often have all or most of their financial eggs in one basket – the startup.

On the personal side, there can be what might be called "attachment issues." It is hard for many founders to "give up on the dream" or to "let their baby die."

Always the most optimistic players around the table to the bitter end, founders rarely give up on the idea that one more round of financing will bridge their company to profitability and greater success.

This mix of financial and personal motivations, combined with genuine concerns for early common stock investors, can lead founders to advocate for risky behavior. In particular, founders are sometimes more willing than other board members, professional investors, or company creditors to run out the clock – meaning the bank account – before agreeing to either wind up or reorganize.

And because founders are viewed as representing the common, board members representing preferred stockholders in the board room sometimes defer to founders' requests to keep working on a troubled financing or other strategic deal, even as bank balances dwindle.

A reasonable game of chicken has its place in the mix of strategies to be considered, but directors should not allow themselves to be blinded or deceived by a founder's unduly optimistic thinking in the face of other credible alternatives.

Employee Considerations

In any company shutdown or restructuring, employee issues and claims can be distracting wild cards. Avoid stumbling into wage theft claims and make every effort to avoid needlessly antagonizing or annoying employees at any level.

Work with an HR specialist on messaging. Never miss payroll. And make sure no mistakes are made in calculating PTO obligations or earned bonuses, or in honoring other obligations to employees.

If employees cannot be made whole, winding down informally may not be the right choice.

Employees cannot be made to sign a waiver and release unless *additional* compensation is paid to them. Winding up early so that each employee can be offered a week or two of severance will put the company in a position to request full waivers and releases, capping off one of the more likely sources of claims.

Preserving a Cash Cushion

There is no free "emergency room" where good Samaritans or the government help destitute startups structure fire sales or wind down. Winding down correctly *always* costs money.

- Chapter 7s require roughly $15,000 to $20,000 in upfront legal fees, with the trustee receiving compensation from available assets and asset sales.

- Initiating an ABC (Assignment for the Benefit of Creditors) will require at least $30,000, with the ABC firm taking other fees from asset sale proceeds.

- Chapter 11 reorganizations for most startups probably cost at least $200,000 in total, with upfront legal retainers of $20,000 or more.

When companies run their bank accounts to zero hoping for a miracle, all they usually find are vultures – and sometimes disgruntled stakeholders. The game of chicken that founders sometimes play with boards and VCs can cause a company to miss its last and best opportunities for maximizing enterprise value in some kind of sale or merger, Chapter 11 reorganization, or ABC.

Sometimes, the only thing worse than holding a fire sale is losing out on the opportunity to hold a fire sale.

Any board entering the zone of insolvency should seek expert advice, start mapping out possible scenarios, and consider establishing an absolute minimum threshold of available cash that triggers definitive action, possibly somewhere between $100K and $250K, depending on the facts.

Adding Runway by Negotiating Down Debts

When no new cash is coming in, and bank balances are dropping, management should develop and execute a plan for reaching out to creditors and trying to negotiate down outstanding payables.

This is most likely to be effective with unsecured creditors, such as vendors and service providers who may be at risk of receiving nothing in a winding down.

These efforts should never involve fraud or deception, but rather appeals to goodwill and reason, particularly the logic that concessions will help keep the company alive and able to buy services or supplies again in the future.

A common line I use is:

> *"We are having trouble financing the company with the current debt and payables on the balance sheet, and we are asking all of our creditors to take a [50-90]% haircut on their payables."*

But exercise extreme discretion in all communications with creditors. Actual breach or "anticipatory breach" can cause some creditors to quickly file suit to compel payment, seek writs of attachment, and take other actions "to get in line" that complicate financings, M&A transactions, and other transactions a board may want to pursue.

And note, this strategy of asking creditors to take "haircuts" on what is owed to them does *not* work with banks, other secured institutional lenders, or landlords. Those types of creditors do not take haircuts and usually treat such communications as notice of breach or impending breach. They are likely to respond by fully escalating the situation and declaring all obligations immediately due and payable, including any fees and penalties.

Banks and other secured lenders and landlords have powerful remedies to protect themselves. Care should be taken to avoid provoking them without a good plan. The most they'll usually agree to is temporary forbearance from legal action and possibly waiving or reducing some late fees or default fees.

D&O Coverage with Tail Insurance Coverage

In addition to maintaining a cash cushion, boards guiding their companies in and around the zone of insolvency need to prioritize the maintenance of all applicable insurance policies through insolvency and beyond.

This is important because D&O insurance is what's called a "claims made" type of coverage, meaning that only claims made during the life of the policy are covered. Claims made after the policy expires are not covered, even if related to conduct that occurred during the term of the policy.

That is why officers and directors of a struggling company should make sure there is a tail on the company's D&O insurance coverage.

"Tail" or "Run-off" Policies. Insurance that continues beyond a normal policy period is called a "tail." This is short for "tail insurance," or an "insurance coverage tail." They are also called "run-off" policies.

Tail policies respond to claims against former officers and directors for a stated period of time after the underlying policies have expired, usually following a sale of a company or its insolvency and winding down.

Tail coverage can be acquired for D&O insurance, employment practices insurance, professional services errors and omissions insurance, product liability insurance, and any other insurance relevant to a company's risk management profile.

The price for tail coverage varies, but expect to pay up to 200% of the usual annual premium for three to six years of coverage after a company is sold or winds down.

Six years is a common coverage period for tail policies in the U.S. And tail policies are almost always non-cancellable. This prevents an acquiror from trying to cancel a tail policy and reclaim the premiums for itself to the detriment of an acquired entity's former officers and directors.

Many providers of D&O tail coverage only provide it to companies that currently have D&O coverage, which is another incentive for ensuring all applicable insurance coverages are in place well before insolvency or a sale in the face of potential insolvency.

I recently paid $34,000 for six years of D&O tail coverage related to the sale of a completely solvent $20 million company with no issues. Insurance premiums go up in insolvency, and tail coverage may not even be available, depending on the situation.

Most companies obligate themselves to indemnify their officers and directors in their Certificate of Incorporation, so acquiring and maintaining insurance coverages, including tails, is appropriate and advised.

D&O Coverage Basics. D&O and tail policies and carriers vary. As with most things in life, you get what you pay for.

D&O policies are generally broken out into three types of coverage: side A, side B, and side C coverage. Side A covers officers and directors when the company cannot or will not indemnify them, like when it is insolvent. Side B and side C coverages protect the entity, with side B responding to a company's officer and director indemnification obligations. Side C coverage protects the entity itself if it is sued directly.

Work with a trusted broker to ensure appropriate protection.

Having insurance coverage is great, but, like a Kevlar vest, D&O coverage is a product you never want to test for effectiveness. The following section on governance standards offers guidance for avoiding shareholder and creditor claims against officers and directors.

Delaware Governance Standards

Two leading Delaware cases define and explain the governance duties of directors of insolvent and nearly insolvent Delaware corporations:

- *North American Catholic Educational Programming Foundation, Inc. v. Gheewalla,* 930 A.2d 92, 99 (Del. 2007) and

- *Trenwick America Litigation Trust v. Ernst & Young*, 906 A.2d 168 (Del. Ch. 2006).

While these cases are not binding on other states, they could be viewed by other state supreme courts as providing compelling guidance. It is likely many states do not have well-developed case law in this delicate area, further validating why companies choose to incorporate in Delaware.

Regarding solvent companies, the *Gheewalla* court summarized board member duties in this passage:

> *It is well established that the directors owe their fiduciary obligations to the corporation and its shareholders. While shareholders rely on directors acting as fiduciaries to protect their interests, creditors are afforded protection through contractual agreements, fraud and fraudulent conveyance law, implied covenants of good faith and fair dealing, bankruptcy law, general commercial law and other sources of creditor rights. Delaware courts have traditionally been reluctant to expand existing fiduciary duties. Accordingly, "the general rule is that directors do not owe creditors duties beyond the relevant contractual terms."*

Regarding insolvent companies, the *Gheewalla* court further held:

> *The corporation's insolvency "makes the creditors the principal constituency injured by any fiduciary breaches that diminish the firm's value." Therefore, equitable considerations give creditors standing to pursue derivative claims against the directors of an insolvent corporation. Individual creditors of an insolvent corporation have the same incentive to pursue valid derivative claims on its behalf that shareholders have when the corporation is solvent.*

A key nuance in the above passage is that a company's creditors have the right to pursue derivative claims against directors. The opinion goes on to make clear that there is no direct fiduciary obligation to creditors and hence no right of direct claims against directors, merely derivative actions.

Value-Maximization and the Business Judgment Rule

Even when the firm is insolvent, directors are free to pursue value-maximizing strategies, while recognizing that the firm's creditors have become its residual claimants and the advancement of their best interests has become the firm's principal objective.

On this point, the *Trenwick* court further noted:

> *The incantation of the word insolvency, or even more amorphously, the words zone of insolvency should not declare open season on corporate fiduciaries. Directors are expected to seek profit for stockholders, even at risk of failure. With the prospect of profit often comes the potential for defeat.*

The *Trenwick* court also helpfully held that the business judgment rule continues to apply in insolvency. Pursuant to that rule, well-considered decisions of independent board members will not be second-guessed by the courts:

> *If the board of an insolvent corporation, acting with due diligence and good faith, pursues a business strategy that it believes will increase the corporation's value, but that also involves the incurrence of additional debt, it does not become a guarantor of that strategy's success. That the strategy results in continued insolvency and an even more insolvent entity does not in itself give rise to a cause of action. Rather, in such a scenario the directors are protected by the business judgment rule. To conclude otherwise would fundamentally transform Delaware law.*

The preceding excerpts from *Trenwick* and *Gheewalla* acknowledge that insolvency makes the creditors the principal constituency injured by any *fiduciary breaches* that diminish the firm's value, providing those creditors an indirect right of action via derivative suit.

But both decisions guide directors to focus on the goal of maximizing value for the corporation, with the underlying premise that such a course will always serve the appropriate beneficiaries.

The courts helpfully note that, even during insolvency, a board of directors retains substantial latitude to explore and to pursue risky strategies that may ultimately fail, without losing the protections of the business judgment rule.

While this latitude doesn't mean much if creditors have already obtained *writs of attachment* or other judicial relief making it impossible to raise necessary funding or sell non-critical assets, to the extent breathing room can be negotiated with creditors, the board of an insolvent company can and should continue to consider strategies other than winding up if those strategies hold the promise of increasing enterprise value.

Strategic Transactions

The board of a financially troubled company approaching insolvency should always look for opportunities to sell or merge the company, or to sell all or some of its assets, to maximize value.

In less dire situations, selling off only certain underperforming assets or operations is a common strategy to "keep the lights on" long enough to support a pivot to higher growth and higher-margin products or services.

Selling the entire company well before insolvency is arguably the cleanest, safest, and most dignified solution for any otherwise doomed company. On balance, founders and VCs probably prefer to be able to say, "*We sold the company to XYZ company*" instead of "*We put the company into Chapter 7 bankruptcy.*"

A timely sale or merger will *always* generate more sale proceeds than a fire sale after insolvency or asset sales by a bankruptcy trustee. Negotiating an orderly sale and obtaining creditor support for it also gives management control over obtaining concessions and releases from creditors. Chapter 7 bankruptcy offers no such releases.

Soliciting acquisition interest and evaluating proposals can preserve protections under the business judgment rule, which requires proof that the board has considered all available alternatives before deciding on a particular course of action.

Efforts to pull together strategic transactions should be well documented. The absence of any buyer at almost any price is very compelling evidence under the business judgment rule supporting the need for more dire alternatives, including cramdown financings, an upcoming topic.

The Acquihire Exit

As mentioned in Case Study #44, acquihire is an informal and somewhat pejorative term that refers to deals at the less successful end of the M&A spectrum.

These are essentially low or no-consideration deals in which the only asset the buyer wants is the target company's team, often its technology/development team.

The upfront acquisition price in an acquihire is usually only one or two-times annual earnings at most, sometimes with earnouts of one to three years based on revenue milestones. An acquihire is an exit-of-last-resort, as shareholders are likely to receive little or no consideration.

A key feature of the acquihire model is that many employees are offered continued at-will employment with the acquiror, and key individuals, including founders, may receive employment contracts for one to three years.

Acquirors in acquihires often sweeten the deal (mostly to clear any existing liens and cut off voidable preference claims) by agreeing to pay off or assume the target's debts and vendor payables.

Any proposed exit that looks like an acquihire is bound to be disappointing to a company's non-employee shareholders, who may receive little or no consideration in the deal. Founders who expect to receive any consideration not enjoyed by other shareholders, including employment compensation, should recuse themselves from any board vote approving the transaction, due to the conflict of interest.

Additionally, those same founder conflicts must also be identified in any shareholder consent resolutions used to approve the transaction.

Cramdown Financings

The financing of last resort for a startup is a cramdown. A cramdown is a down round on steroids.

Cramdown Mechanics

Existing investors who do not participate by putting in new money to save the company get "crammed down." Their equity ownership percentage can be reduced to virtually nothing and its value wiped out.

The basic mechanics involve raising new money at a much lower valuation and causing substantial dilution to all existing shareholders who do not invest new money. The investors putting in new money force this dilution by requiring existing investors who do not participate to waive their rights to anti-dilution in the down round or, more severely, to convert their preferred shares to common.

The leverage the new investors have is simply, "*take it, or leave it.*" Without the financial infusion, the company is likely facing bankruptcy and the shareholders would receive nothing.

Cramdowns are sometimes described as necessary to "clean up a cap table." Cap tables of distressed companies that have raised lots of money over the course of many financings can be so crowded, bloated, and complex that nothing short of a severe cramdown followed by a reverse stock split will work to encourage new investment.

This is particularly true when a cap table with massive accumulated liquidation preferences is paired with a debt-heavy balance sheet.

In a cramdown, after a highly dilutive transaction involving the issuance of hundreds of millions or even billions of new shares, the company's shares will go through a reverse split, meaning, for example, that every 1,000 shares will be pro rata reduced to one share. Shareholders with fewer than 1,000 shares would be entitled to only a fraction of a share, and that usually allows a company to cash out the shareholder and remove them from the cap table.

New money investors will also usually require debt holders to convert some or all amounts owed to them into new equity in the deal.

Required Consents and Approvals

There are myriad challenges and risks in negotiating and closing a cramdown:

- A cramdown must be approved by the board, by the shareholders, and by any impacted noteholders. Preferred shareholders often have blocking rights and rights to anti-dilution that must be waived.

- Conflicts of interest in cramdowns often push sketchy boundaries. The potential cramdown investors are frequently VCs with board seats and substantial preferred stock positions and voting rights. This often leads to one or two non-conflicted, independent board members being appointed to a special committee to approve the transaction, a relatively unappealing role from the perspective of most independent directors.

- Even if any shareholder or noteholder could be contractually "dragged along" on a cramdown, smart investors insist upon 100% consent by equity holders and impacted debt holders to mitigate the extreme conflicts of interest that are usually involved.

- Secured noteholders sitting in first position can be difficult to negotiate concessions from, particularly if net asset sale proceeds would cover most of what is owed to them.

- In one deal, I also had to negotiate with a manufacturing vendor that had a $1.1 million "writ of attachment," perhaps the most difficult creditor of all time.

- Other creditors may refuse to negotiate down debts and payables sufficiently to the satisfaction of the investors. Most debts, if not all, usually need to be cleaned up before new-money investors will proceed.

- An uncooperative founder with a large common stock position can derail a cramdown by withholding consent if common stockholders will do poorly in a proposed deal.

- Key staff may have already departed before a cramdown is considered, gutting administrative support for pro forma cap tables reflecting evolving deal structures, updated financials and financial forecasts, and other basic deal-closing assistance.

Unsecured creditors, including suppliers, manufacturers, or other vendors, may also have substantial claims that need to be negotiated down to clean up the balance sheet.

Another group that needs to be encouraged to support a cramdown are officers and key employees. Any cramdown will substantially dilute the holdings of existing common stockholders. At the point a cramdown is being considered, many employees may have already left. Obtaining new investment dollars may require holding onto remaining key talent. As a result, cramdowns usually "top-up" the post-transaction option pool.

Managing Fiduciary Risks - Entire Fairness Standard

A cramdown financing is one of the most difficult and legally fraught transactions in all of corporate finance. Officers and directors may face allegations of breaching their fiduciary duties for personal gain.

Directors are obligated to exercise due care and observe the duty of loyalty to the corporation and are prohibited from acting in their own self-interest to the detriment of other shareholders.

A cramdown, on the other hand, often involves VC directors who are investing in the financing, for self-interest, and other investors may well feel harmed.

As discussed in Chapter 8, any self-interest in a transaction approved by a board takes it out from under the protection of the business judgment rule and subjects it to the entire fairness standard.

Aggrieved shareholders can raise their objections later, if and when the company is considering a lucrative exit within the timeframe of the applicable statute of limitations.

For these reasons, cramdown financings require the highest level of legal and financial expertise and guidance. Paying for that expertise and guidance when cash levels are critically low is usually just one of many other challenges.

Here are some tips for minimizing litigation risks in a cramdown or other severe recapitalization:

- As noted earlier, consent by 100% of a company's shareholders and debt holders is the best inoculation.

- Let all existing investors participate pro rata to their existing ownership levels, often called a "rights offering."

- The company's disclosures to all investors and debt holders in a cramdown must be extremely transparent, including prominent disclosure of all conflicts of interest, by firm name, individual name, and including each person or firm's capacity as a board member, shareholder, and debt holder, as applicable.

- The board should meet at least weekly, if not twice a week, during a financial crisis. The board's minutes should reflect diligent and thoughtful efforts to preserve assets, manage costs, and finance the company on the best terms possible.

- The board should also engage in parallel efforts to sell or merge the company, so it has another value-creating option to compare to the cramdown financing.

- Any directors participating in the financing as interested parties should recuse themselves from voting on the transaction.

- If a majority of the board are interested parties, the board should appoint a special committee consisting of one or more non-interested directors to evaluate the fairness of the transaction.

- If that is not possible, the board should consider paying a reputable investment banker for a "fairness opinion" if the company can afford the $20,000 to $30,000 or greater price tag.

During any major financial crisis, the board should consult regularly with the company's D&O insurance broker to ensure that coverage-cancelling omissions or missteps are avoided and to explore possible options for enhancing coverages or coverage amounts.

Case Study #50 – Wonderful Day for a Recap

A CEO of a client company emailed me late on a Friday and asked if I could review some loan documents ASAP. He "*...wanted to sign them in the morning.*" Without letting on that his request struck me as a giant red flag, I said I'd review the documents early in the morning and report back.

First, a little background. This company has great products and a potentially very bright future, but, in its early days, it made terrible financing mistakes, compounded by numerous other governance and leadership errors. I had been retained to clean things up. My first week as outside counsel, I wrote a General Counsel Audit memorandum with numerous recommendations. Some of my recommendations were implemented, but most were not.

The board was compromised in its judgment and conflicted in its flexibility by early financing mistakes that I called out for correction. Specifically, for relatively small investments, one investor group (the "Early Investors") received (i) special voting LLC units with broad veto authority over equity financings and other corporate actions, (ii) 2x liquidation preferences, and (iii) two of five authorized board seats.

For the amount invested, I noted that the Early Investors should have received (i) common LLC units, (ii) a 24-month Convertible Note, or, at best, (iii) series seed preferred LLC units with a 1x liquidation, non-participating preference, limited blocking rights, and a single board seat.

Most importantly, I pointed out that a company's early investors should never receive rights to vote separately as a class to approve or veto future financings, as happened here, unfortunately. Those rights should only come with much larger investments – not small, seed investments.

The Early Investors were purely financial investors with no relevant experience or involvement in the company's industry. The persons they appointed to the board had no prior board or company leadership experience.

The company's early financing, governance, and leadership mistakes flowed directly from the founder's aversion to spending any money on legal advice. That short-sightedness had come home to roost yet again (this was not the first financial crisis) and was causing substantial harm to the enterprise. The CEO was hired years later, but his hands were tied by the errors of the past.

With that checkered background, the CEO's request for a hasty review of loan documents made me suspect the worst. My suspicions were confirmed:

- the loan agreement and promissory note were for a total of $50,000, or just a few weeks of operating capital,
- the tiny loan would be secured against all of the company's assets,
- it included expedited, easy rights of foreclosure, allowing the lenders to seize and sell all assets upon any default,
- the loan agreement prohibited the company from borrowing any further amounts unless approved by the lender, and
- the loan covenants were drafted such that the company would be in breach as soon as it signed the loan documents.

And those were just *some* of the bad things in the loan documents.

After writing a lengthy email to the CEO documenting all of my concerns, I followed up with a call. Asking a few questions first, I learned the following:

- this loan agreement was from the Early Investors,
- despite revenues of $2M in the 12 month period, the company had only 3 weeks of cash, including payroll,
- the company owed $200K in A/P to vendors, and
- capital constraints were preventing the company from scaling quickly to profitability.

This was no bridge loan to a better tomorrow. Coming from the Early Investors, it looked like a cynical attempt to take over the company after having put it in a position where arms-length, third-party financing was nearly impossible. With their original investment, the Early Investors obtained a veto right to disapprove any equity financings, which they had used to block prior equity financing proposals. The loan agreement would then give the same group the right to approve or veto future borrowings, and hence the ability to force the company into foreclosure and immediately seize and sell all of the company's assets.

Among other things, I advised the CEO as follows:

- Do not sign the loan.

- For a paltry $50K, the lenders should receive only the most basic, unsecured promissory note, with few, if any, covenants aside from a promise to be paid in full at maturity.

- I told him that, as an officer and a director, he should immediately work with the board to ensure that the company was recapitalized to fix the terms of the early financing that were harming the company's ability to raise funds and subjecting it to extortionate loan terms.

- The CEO had informed me that a friendly investor was willing to put in $600K if appropriate terms could be reached. I told him the board should put as much pressure as necessary on the Early Investors to accept a down round recap, with that $600K possibly constituting the lead investment for a roughly $2M common unit financing.

- I advised that the board seek to clean up the cap table and control problems by structuring the financing to (i) convert all existing preferred units to common units, (ii) force the Early Investors to give up one of their board seats, and (iii) grant that seat to a designee appointed by majority vote of the new-money investors.

- I advised that the new equity financing should be conducted at a new valuation reflecting the company's insolvency; although this would be dilutive to all current shareholders, the company was in desperate need of funds and a fair valuation would be required to attract those funds – whether from the existing investors up to their pro rata interests or from new investors.

- I also advised that if the Early Investors were not willing to cooperate, rather than take their "hard money" loan, the board should consider furloughing the company's employees and shutting down operations until the Early Investors came to their senses that they could no longer use their dysfunctional blocking rights to dictate the financing alternatives of an insolvent company.

The CEO was concerned about his and the board's fiduciary duties. I informed him that between (i) signing the $50K loan with no guarantee of any future debt or equity financing because of the Early Investors' blocking rights and (ii) letting the company shut down until a re-cap could be negotiated, the latter was certainly a very reasonable position for the board and for management to take.

As additional comfort, I advised him that, before running out of money for payroll, shutting the company down and furloughing its few workers was the course dictated by law, barring receipt of a bridge loan or other cash on reasonable terms.

Shutting down the company wasn't simply a negotiating tactic between the board and the Early Investors, but a legal necessity, until funding could be obtained on terms that served the company's and its owners' best interests. There was no legal obligation for the board to accept the extortionate bridge loan terms just to keep the doors open and the lights on.

> Lesson: Most founders should never handle financing rounds without sophisticated legal advice, even early financing rounds that seem "simple." There is no such thing as a simple financing.

> This case study is just one example of a recurring pattern - ill-conceived early financings that harm companies by preventing an orderly progression of future financings on reasonable terms. When access to capital is restricted, insolvency and the stresses of leading through insolvency may be in the future.

Closing the Company

For every highly distressed company running out of strategic options, an insolvency "event horizon" looms. Like the inescapable threshold of a black hole, it is the point where a company must shut down or risk causing unjustifiable harm to employees, creditors, taxing authorities, and other stakeholders.

Boards should understand the timing and nature of their insolvency event horizon and try to maximize value well away from it. As soon as insolvency has become a real possibility, founders, officers, directors, creditors, and investors should begin exploring and debating alternatives for maximizing enterprise value before opportunities slip away.

Knowing where everyone stands and hearing potential solutions from all stakeholders often helps shape the best approach.

The five paths through unavoidable insolvency are:

- informal winding down,
- formal dissolution under state law,
- Chapter 7 liquidation,
- Chapter 11 reorganization (or 363 asset sale),
- assignment for the benefit of creditors, or ABC.

Each of these options has pros and cons, depending on the facts and circumstances. Key factors include:

- remaining funds,
- amounts owed to creditors, and whether those creditors are secured or unsecured,
- costs versus benefits,

- what shareholders will be willing to approve,

- the preferences of a prospective buyer in a possible pre-packaged bankruptcy or ABC,

- timing concerns,

- current or potential legal or regulatory claims and the need to cap them off,

- the specific board's tolerance for risk, and

- the overall complexity of the situation.

This overview of options for winding down is just that – an overview. Every situation is different. Every startup drifting toward insolvency must work closely with experts to map out and execute the right strategy, including a back-up strategy or two.

Informal Winding Down

As the name suggests, this is the least formal approach to dealing with insolvency. It works best when, and perhaps only when, a company has no unpaid obligations to creditors, taxing authorities, or employees, no outstanding or potential legal or regulatory claims, and a relatively simple cap table.

The idea is to maximize value in a deteriorating situation by quickly capping off additional liabilities, keeping wind-down expenses low, and otherwise following good processes to approve an asset sale, market and sell the assets in a defensible process, and allocate the proceeds consistent with legal obligations and priorities.

There is no legally mandated formula for winding down, but here is a list of prudent steps to consider:

- the board meets and approves winding down after careful review of the company's current financial status, including current financial statements, and after careful evaluation of all other alternatives,

- the board approves terminating all employees except for those needed to help sell the assets and otherwise support the winding down,

- management promptly handles the employee terminations and pays all wages, leave, and commissions due,

- the company gives notice of the winding down to all potentially impacted parties, including employees, creditors, vendors, suppliers, landlords, regulators, and others,

- the company also gives notice of termination due to insolvency under all agreements that should be terminated immediately,

- the board's resolutions approve marketing and selling all of the company's assets,

- the board follows all procedures required under the company's Bylaws and Articles of Incorporation for obtaining shareholder approval to sell the company's assets,

- the board identifies any assets that secure loans or other obligations and seeks creditor approval before selling those assets,

- the company sells the assets in one or more arms-length transactions and in a manner designed to get the best price for the assets under the circumstances,

- the company follows advice of counsel on the order of payments to be made to secured and unsecured creditors, both before and after assets are sold,

- prior to tendering a final payment to creditors, vendors, suppliers and others, the company requests a signed Waiver and Release from each stating that they agree that the amount being tendered is the total amount owed and they waive all claims,

- after paying all known obligations to employees, taxing entities, and creditors, the board should allow three to six months to pass to see whether any additional invoices or other claims come in,

- following this wait-and-see period, the board should establish a level of reserves deemed necessary to pay one or more persons to respond to any potential claims from creditors or tax authorities, and to keep the entity alive for a few years to allow for most statutes of limitation to expire,

- at this point, it is probably safe to distribute any remaining funds except for the amount deemed necessary as reserves, keeping in mind that shareholders are generally liable to creditors and claimants of dissolved corporations up to the amount of any assets distributed to the shareholders,

- without terminating the entity's existence, management should cancel state and local registrations, permits, and licenses,

- after the relevant statutes of limitation have lapsed without further claims, affirmatively terminate the entity's existence or allow it to be administratively terminated by failing to file mandatory annual reports.

One of the bullet points above mentions requesting waivers and releases from creditors. The enforceability of these is a case-by-case question, but asking for them, and receiving them or not, provides useful information about potential future claims. The presence of potential claims may indicate that informal winding down is not the best path.

Lastly, closing out all tax obligations properly is very important. The IRS has a helpful webpage called "*Closing a Business Checklist*" that can be found by searching that title or by going to this link: https://www.irs.gov/businesses/small-businesses-self-employed/closing-a-business-checklist.

Formal Dissolution

Formal dissolution is a state law process governed by the laws of the state of incorporation. It is used to formally wind up a company's affairs, liquidate its assets, and dissolve the entity.

Like an informal wind-down, formal dissolution provides none of the protections of bankruptcy, so it may not be a good option where funds are insufficient to pay off all creditors or resolve other legal or regulatory issues.

Another key issue with dissolution is that it requires at least one director to stay engaged to oversee the process and at least one officer to manage the process. Avoiding this is one benefit of Chapter 7 bankruptcy, in which a trustee takes over everything.

Another thing worth highlighting is that companies remain subject to suit under state law long after being dissolved. Formal dissolution does not make claims go away.

As noted above, formal dissolution is governed by the laws of the state of incorporation. The following is a summary of how dissolution works under Delaware law.

Certificate of Dissolution. Dissolution is initiated by the filing of a "Certificate of Dissolution," but that filing must be preceded by obtaining board approval and shareholder approval and payment of all Delaware franchise taxes, among other requirements described in Delaware's certificate of dissolution template instructions. Delaware's template certificate of dissolution is barely a page.

Plan of Liquidation. The board and the company's shareholders must approve a plan of liquidation, which is usually a document called a "Plan of Liquidation and Dissolution." Examples of these plans can be found by searching online.

Find a template Plan of Liquidation and Dissolution in the BLSG Data Room under *Zone of Insolvency > Formal Dissolution > Plan of Liquidation and Dissolution.*

The following is a summary of key terms from a Plan of Liquidation and Dissolution:

- Adoption of Plan. States details of board and shareholder approvals.

- Cessation of Business Activities. Describes limits on the company's ability to engage in routine business and details what activities it can and will engage in to wind up the entity.

- Certificate of Dissolution. Describes how officers will obtain things like tax closing certificates from taxing authorities, pay those taxes, and then file a Certificate of Dissolution.

- Liquidation Process. Covers how each of these will be effected:

  - Sale of all or substantially all of the non-cash assets.

  - Payment of obligations.

  - Distributions to stockholders.

- Cancellation of Stock. States that outstanding shares of stock will be cancelled following appropriate distributions to shareholders.

- Liquidating Trust. Describes the board's authority to set up a "liquidating trust" and contribute funds or assets to the trust for the benefit of shareholders and creditors in furtherance of the plan of liquidation.

- Abandoned Property. Describes the board's authority to deal with any shareholders who cannot be located or who have failed to surrender their shares in the liquidation by transferring the shareholder's cash distribution to the official of the state authorized by applicable law to receive the proceeds of such distribution as abandoned property.

- <u>Final Liquidating Distribution</u>. Provides for transferring all remaining assets to a trust if final liquidating distributions of the company's assets have not been completed within three years.

- <u>Shareholder Approval of Sale of Assets</u>. States that shareholder approval of the plan of dissolution constitutes approval by the shareholders of the sale of all company assets, whether in one or more transactions, and ratification of any agreements for the sale of assets contingent upon adoption of the plan of dissolution.

- <u>Expenses of Dissolution</u>. States that the company is allowed to pay brokerage, agency, legal, and other professional fees in connection with the sale, exchange, or other disposition of the assets.

- <u>Employees and Independent Contractors</u>. States that the board may hire or retain any employees, consultants, independent contractors, agents and advisors as it deems necessary or desirable to supervise or facilitate the dissolution and liquidation.

- <u>Indemnification</u>. States that the company must continue to indemnify officers, directors, employees, agents, and any liquidation trustee, including in connection with the plan of dissolution, and also authorizes the board and any trustee to obtain and pay for such insurance as deemed necessary.

- <u>Amendment, Modification or Abandonment of Plan</u>. States that the board may, to the extent permitted by applicable state law, revoke the plan of dissolution without shareholder approval.

Cessation of Business Activities. Once a certificate of dissolution has been filed, all regular business activities must cease. Delaware law prescribes the permitted activities as:

> *"gradually to settle and close their business, to dispose of and convey their property, to discharge their liabilities and to distribute to their stockholders any remaining assets, but not for the purpose of continuing the business for which the corporation was organized."*

Creditor Notice Requirements. State laws regarding formal dissolution address creditor rights and creditor notifications in different ways. Some require certain forms of notice to creditors, along with a formal claims process, while other state laws simply bar creditor claims not timely submitted after a company goes through a specified notice and claims process.

Washington's statute, RCW 23B.14.030, mandates notice to creditors with the following provisions:

> *"A dissolved corporation shall, within thirty days after the effective date of its articles of dissolution, publish notice of its dissolution and request that persons with claims against the dissolved corporation present them in accordance with the notice. The notice must be published once a week for three consecutive weeks in a newspaper of general circulation in the county where the dissolved corporation's principal office (or, if none in this state, its registered office) is or was last located. The notice must also*

describe the information that must be included in a claim, provide a mailing address where a claim may be sent, and state that claims against the dissolved corporation may be barred in accordance with the provisions of this chapter if not timely asserted. A dissolved corporation's failure to publish notice in accordance with this subsection does not affect the validity or the effective date of its dissolution."

New York's statute, on the other hand, is permissive, based on the word "may" versus "shall" in the first line of the statute. But if a company initiates the described process, claims must be submitted as described or they will be deemed barred:

"At any time after dissolution, the corporation may give a notice requiring all creditors and claimants, including any with unliquidated or contingent claims and any with whom the corporation has unfulfilled contracts, to present their claims in writing and in detail at a specified place and by a specified day, which shall not be less than six months after the first publication of such notice. Such notice shall be published at least once a week for two successive weeks in a newspaper of general circulation in the county in which the office of the corporation was located at the date of dissolution. On or before the date of the first publication of such notice, the corporation shall mail a copy thereof, postage prepaid and addressed to his last known address, to each person believed to be a creditor of or claimant against the corporation whose name and address are known to or can with due diligence be ascertained by the corporation."

Under these statutes, including Delaware's, failure by a creditor to submit a formal claim by the appropriate deadline results in the claim being formally barred.

Chapter 7 Liquidation

Chapter 7 bankruptcy is sometimes the simplest, cleanest, easiest and safest way to wind up an insolvent company:

- the board and management walk away, and a trustee takes over,

- actions by creditors are automatically stayed,

- up-front costs are relatively low; most fees are paid from asset sales,

- shareholder approval is not required, and

- Chapter 7 provides a high degree of transparency regarding asset sales and the distribution of liquidation proceeds to creditors and other claimants.

Chapter 7 is a tempting option for boards with contentious creditors or shareholders, or any outstanding litigation or regulatory actions. But there are also downsides:

- costs of at least $15K up front and more on the back end from the asset sales,

- complete loss of control to a bankruptcy trustee,

- low fire-sale asset sale pricing,

- earlier transactions can be unwound as preferential or fraudulent,

- business debts are non-dischargeable,

- bankruptcy is a highly visible public process, and

- insiders can still be sued based on personal guarantees or suits alleging alter ego/piercing the corporate veil theories.

Because of these downsides, Chapter 7 should only be considered after efforts to sell assets in a more orderly fashion have failed, a major financing has unexpectedly fallen through, or substantial legal or regulatory problems strike. A Chapter 7 petition can also be prompted by the need to prevent junior creditors from taking actions to seize assets to the detriment of creditors with senior claims.

No Debt Discharge, but Lease Relief. While the debts of individuals are dischargeable under Chapter 7, business debts are not.

Investors and creditors can still sue insiders based on fraud, personal guarantees, and piercing the corporate veil/alter ego legal theories. Insiders subject to such claims may need to seek personal protection under Chapter 7.

In general, however, many believe that Chapter 7's highly transparent processes are a deterrent to less serious "nuisance" litigation from aggrieved vendors, commercial partners, or other claimants.

Interestingly, however, federal bankruptcy laws cap future lease obligations at one year's rent or 15 percent of the remaining lease term (not to exceed three years).

Costs. Bankruptcy court costs include a $245 case filing fee, a $75 miscellaneous administrative fee, and a $15 trustee surcharge. Competent legal counsel are often willing to take on Chapter 7 filings for as little as $15,000 down. For a board seeking a relatively definitive way out of a bad insolvency situation, the costs of a Chapter 7 filing are reasonable.

Although total costs can be significant, legal fees in a Chapter 7 bankruptcy are a fraction of the fees in a Chapter 11 reorganization, and the trustee is compensated almost entirely from asset sale commissions.

Initiating Chapter 7 Bankruptcy. A Chapter 7 bankruptcy begins with board deliberation and approval. The board or key officers should be working closely with bankruptcy counsel to ensure a full understanding of costs, processes, and potential outcomes.

This may be followed by seeking shareholder approval. Shareholder approval should probably be sought whenever possible to ensure a smoother and more easily defended process, but it is not necessary, as discussed below.

The next step is that bankruptcy counsel prepares and files a bankruptcy petition with the bankruptcy court, along with the following:

- schedules of assets and liabilities,

- a schedule of current income and expenditures,

- a statement of financial affairs, and

- a schedule of executory contracts and unexpired leases.

The court will appoint a trustee, who takes complete control over the company and all of its assets. Debtors must also provide the assigned trustee with a copy of the tax return or transcripts for the most recent tax year and any returns filed during the bankruptcy "case."

Shareholder Vote Not Required. Interestingly, few business lawyers can confidently and correctly answer the question of whether shareholders must approve a Chapter 7 bankruptcy.

The logical answer would seem to be yes. After all, under state corporate law, shareholders must approve dissolutions, liquidations and substantial asset sales.

Title 8 of the Delaware Corporate Law, Section 271(a) captioned *Sale of Assets, Dissolution and Winding Up*, for example, provides that a board of a company may "*sell, lease or exchange all or substantially all of its property and assets*" subject to the "*...approval of a majority of the outstanding stock of the corporation entitled to vote thereon....*"

And preferred stockholders always receive blocking rights to approve significant transactions, including liquidating transactions.

Common and preferred stockholders can clearly block an informal winding up liquidation or a formal state-law dissolution. As discussed below, they can also block an assignment for the benefit of creditors.

But the answer is different regarding Chapter 7. Shareholder approval is not required. A board, acting alone, can approve the filing of a petition for bankruptcy under Chapter 7 for a *truly insolvent entity.*

This is not an answer one finds in the bankruptcy code, although nothing in the code contradicts it, either. The answer lies in corporate governance concepts discussed earlier regarding the status of a creditor in insolvency.

Case law on this question is scarce in most states, but Delaware case law makes clear that, as to insolvent entities, shareholders cannot block a Chapter 7 bankruptcy petition filed to protect a company's creditors.

A key Delaware Court of Chancery decision, *Esopus Creek Value LP v. Hauf*, 913 A.2d 593 (Del. Ch. 2006), analyzes this question directly. In that case, the defendants were trying to push an asset sale by a non-insolvent corporation through Chapter 11. The court made this finding, which is equally applicable to petitions under Chapter 7:

> *"The primary interests protected by the bankruptcy process are those of creditors. Because of this simple fact, the bankruptcy code does not contemplate a freestanding right to vote by the holders of common equity. Were such a vote available, the legal rights of the creditors to the remaining assets of the entity would take a subsidiary position to the interests of the residual owners who, at least where a company is insolvent, no longer have any cognizable financial interest to protect.*

In this case, however, the company in question, Metromedia, was not insolvent, and hence the court also found as follows:

> *In sum, the actions of Metromedia's directors in structuring the proposed transaction as they did resulted in a theoretically legal, yet undeniably inequitable, reallocation of control over the corporate enterprise.*

The court focuses on the "good faith" requirement for bankruptcy petitions, making this finding (footnotes omitted):

> *The defendants correctly observe that the bankruptcy code imposes no "insolvency" requirement for a debtor to voluntarily file a petition for relief. However, bankruptcy courts typically dismiss a voluntary petition under 11 U.S.C. § 1112(b) unless that petition was filed in "good faith." While this court does not presume to determine the presence or absence of "good faith" in that context, the inquiries relevant to that "good faith" standard provide ample support for the notion that the board's conduct here inequitably abridged the justified expectations of the common stockholders.*

As noted above, though, allowing shareholders to vote on a Chapter 7 filing is probably the safer and more efficient practice when approval is likely.

Automatic Stay. The filing of a petition in bankruptcy triggers a complete "stay" of all attempts by creditors to foreclose on assets and all litigation by creditors. Chapter 7 imposes order on (i) liquidating an entity and (ii) distributing proceeds according to clear priorities.

Trustee powers are substantial. Trustees can pursue recovery of fraudulent conveyances and other preferential transfers, and they can also go after directors for breaches of fiduciary duties.

The trustee also assumes complete control over all pending litigation.

Chapter 11 Reorganization or Sale

Chapter 11 is a bankruptcy process for restructuring a company's debts so it can make another run at profitability.

Chapter 11 restructurings are long, complex, and expensive, generally costing a minimum of several hundred thousand dollars. Much of that money is spent before a company knows whether or not a plan of reorganization will be approved or the company liquidated in a conversion to Chapter 7.

Chapter 11 petitions are more common for large publicly traded companies than they are for smaller companies like early-stage startups, given the high costs and long timelines involved. Most startups that seek protection under Chapter 11 have raised $60 million or more.

Sometimes companies emerge from Chapter 11 with a plan to return to profitability, but most Chapter 11 cases are dismissed or converted to Chapter 7 liquidations.

Debtor in Possession. A key potential advantage of Chapter 11 is that management continues to run the business, which becomes a "debtor in possession," or "DIP." As a debtor in possession, the debtor-company performs many of the functions that a trustee performs in a Chapter 7.

Debtor in possession duties include accounting for property, examining and objecting to creditor claims, and filing informational reports. With the court's approval, a debtor in possession can also employ attorneys, accountants, appraisers, auctioneers, or other professionals to assist in the bankruptcy case.

The debtor in possession owes fiduciary duties to the creditors, but is free to pursue either a restructuring or a sale, subject to creditor, shareholder and court approval.

The trustee supervises the debtor in possession in performing its duties, and all major decisions must be approved by the court.

Creditor Involvement. In Chapter 11, one or more committees are appointed to represent the interests of creditors and stockholders and work with the company to develop a plan of reorganization to lower its debt. Both the company and its creditors have the right to propose a plan of reorganization.

This process enables unsecured creditors to challenge proposed restructuring plans, the company's bankruptcy financing, sale procedures, and the speed of proposed asset sales, all to negotiate a higher recovery against unsecured debts.

Frequently, creditors would rather see the company liquidated and will urge the court to reject a plan of reorganization and instead convert the case to a Chapter 7.

A Chapter 11 plan of reorganization must be confirmed by the court. Confirmation requires the court to find that the plan of reorganization is "in the best interests of its creditors." What is in the best interests of a company's creditors is generally a function of what the creditors would be expected to receive in a Chapter 7 liquidation.

In confirming a plan of reorganization, the court can disregard a vote of the creditors rejecting the plan of reorganization, but to do so, the court must find that the plan of reorganization is "fair and equitable."

Prepackaged Bankruptcy. A common strategy under Chapter 11 is to work on a plan of reorganization with creditors before filing, to reduce costs, delays, and disruptions. The court then blesses the plan, enabling the company to get back to focusing on business. This is called a "pre-packaged bankruptcy."

Completing a pre-packaged bankruptcy is still complex and expensive, but it can cut the process to a matter of months instead of years.

363 Asset Sale

Another common Chapter 11 strategy is called a "363 asset sale," named for Section 363 of the bankruptcy code, which governs any kind of asset sale under Chapter 7 or Chapter 11.

When bankruptcy lawyers use the term 363 asset sale, they mean specifically a sale of substantially all of a debtor's assets under Chapter 11.

In a 363 asset sale, a debtor will enter into a contingent asset purchase agreement, or APA, with a potential purchaser. This bidder becomes the "stalking horse" bidder. The debtor in possession takes the bid to the court and requests to sell the assets in a Section 363 auction.

If the 363 sale processes are approved by the court, the debtor in possession will send notices to potential bidders for the assets and provide approximately 30 days for bidders to submit bids.

Because stalking horse bidders may be outbid, they often push for breakup fees and transaction expenses as part of the deal, which the court is free to accept or reject, depending on the circumstances.

After the auction, the bankruptcy court still conducts a hearing to determine whether or not to approve the sale to the winning bidder.

363 asset sales are conducted outside of the usual "plan of reorganization" process under Chapter 11 and are relatively new. While bankruptcy judges still vary in their approaches to approving them and in dealing with things like breakup fees, the 363 asset sale process is well established.

A 363 asset sale is a much faster and more streamlined approach to selling debtor assets than a traditional Chapter 11 sale and is generally viewed as a better approach for maximizing value.

Assignment for the Benefit of Creditors

An ABC is a state law bankruptcy-like process that is similar to Chapter 7. In an ABC, the insolvent company's assets are sold off by an "assignee," rather than a bankruptcy trustee.

Specialized firms fill this assignee role and also serve as fiduciaries in distributing the proceeds from asset sales to creditors, investors and taxing authorities.

ABCs are common in California, where the ABC legal framework is well-known and trusted.

Delaware's ABC statute, Title 10, Chapter 73, Subchapter VI, "Voluntary Assignments," also works well for companies incorporated in Delaware.

The laws of other states vary widely in scope and requirements. Some states require filing with a court, for example, or the posting of a fiduciary bond.

Investors, creditors, or other insiders sometimes try to use the ABC process to assume control over a company's assets through what is called a "pre-packaged ABC." Success in doing so, however, requires that they be the highest bidder for the assets when auctioned off by the assignee.

Key pros and cons of the ABC process compared to the other insolvency alternatives include the following:

Pros:

- the board chooses the specific assignee, unlike Chapter 7, in which an unknown trustee is appointed,
- leading up to the actual asset "assignment," the board and management can play a large role in helping the ABC firm market the assets to ensure maximum value,
- ABCs are faster and less public than Chapter 11 bankruptcies,

- a neutral third party conducts the asset sale to reduce the appearance of any unfairness to creditors or shareholders, and

- court approval of the asset sale is not required.

Cons:

- shareholder approval is required, unlike a Chapter 7 liquidation,

- no automatic stay to stop creditor foreclosure efforts,

- no cap on landlord claims, unlike the real property lease cap in federal bankruptcy,

- assets are not sold free and clear, and contracts and leases cannot be assigned without consent, and

- creditors with secured claims will need to cooperate and consent.

The choice of an ABC versus a 363 asset sale under Chapter 11 is often driven by the preferences of a known potential buyer, but creditors and shareholders need to be on board, too.

Two-Part Process. An ABC is often a two-part process involving two different agreements between the company and the ABC firm.

The company and the ABC firm first sign an agreement to conduct a three to five-week sales and marketing process designed to identify all potential buyers of the assets and to collect bids.

After this, assuming there is some interest in the assets, the company will sign a General Assignment, initiating the ABC process by causing the ABC firm to become the assignee of all of the company's assets to conduct the ABC, including selling the assets, distributing the sale proceeds, and dissolving the company.

Pre-pack ABC. In a pre-pack ABC, the ABC firm conducts a roughly four-week sales and marketing process while the board seeks shareholder and lender approval for an ABC with a stalking horse bidder.

Creditor Security Interests. To make the assets more attractive to prospective buyers, the ABC firm will likely seek agreements from secured creditors releasing their security interests in the assets in exchange for similar priority security interests in the asset sale proceeds.

Asset Sale Process. The ABC process involves an orderly sale of the company's assets through a process that must be fair and equitable.

The company continues to operate under its existing board during the sales and marketing process to oversee and support the sales and marketing effort.

Powers of the ABC Firm. When the marketing process is complete, the ABC process is formally initiated. A general assignment is made to the ABC firm, the board resigns, and the ABC firm assumes all further responsibilities to shareholders, creditors, and other stakeholders.

The ABC firm has sole discretion to determine which bid(s) to accept, including whether all of the assets go to one buyer or are split up in two or more transactions to maximize value.

Distribution of Sale Proceeds. Following the sale of all of the company's assets, the ABC firm is solely responsible for paying off the company's creditors according to a priority "waterfall" that mirrors federal bankruptcy priorities.

Any funds remaining after satisfaction of all valid secured and unsecured creditor claims and other enforceable obligations are distributed to shareholders, consistent with any liquidation preferences found in the company's Articles of Incorporation.

Corporate Dissolution. Following the asset sale and distribution of the sale proceeds, the company would enter a dissolution process, which might last a year or so as the ABC firm fully winds up the company's affairs and corporate existence.

Insider Participation and the Entire Fairness Standard. Any insiders considering acquiring assets in an ABC should be aware that they could be subject to self-dealing or breach of fiduciary duty claims from shareholders. The protections of the business judgment rule do not apply to board members or their affiliates buying assets through the ABC. In such cases, the legal standard likely becomes the entire fairness standard.

Fees. A typical ABC firm will charge (i) up-front fees for the sales and marketing effort of at least $30,000, plus expenses, (ii) an assignment fee of at least $100,000, and (iii) a percentage-based success fee of approximately 10% of the asset sale proceeds.

Case Study #51 – Company Down

Occasionally I am asked to help companies that are down for the count, with little, if any, discernable corporate pulse.

Prospects for getting paid in such situations are uncertain, so I occasionally pass. But like a doctor with a sense of professional duty, and having a minor interest in corporate pathology, I still join efforts to resuscitate corporate roadkill if there's a potentially interesting business opportunity and a team to execute on it.

In one instance years ago, a recently hired turn-around CEO asked me to help revive a company that was flat on its back. A series C financing had recently failed, and all employees and officers were gone except one, the controller. The bank account was nearly empty.

The company's backstory and IP were interesting, so I agreed to help.

The company had been laid low by a combination of manufacturing execution errors, advertising "issues," and a regulatory action. The straw that broke the camel's back was a consent judgment from a federal regulator issuing a recall and forcing consumer refunds.

When I arrived, the regulatory action was still open, since the company had collapsed just before fully paying out thousands of consumer refunds and documenting the payments.

The CEO and I were the only officers. The controller stayed on, and several former employees worked on a consulting basis as needed, or *mostly* as needed. Support in shutdown mode is scarce and unreliable.

The board consisted of the founder, an independent director, and three VC designees. There were also several board observers representing other investors. We held weekly board meetings to ensure we were living up to our fiduciary obligations. Tensions were high after many months of failure and disappointment.

When I arrived, there was $300K of cash in the bank. The company's debts included $1.1M of A/P, another $1.2M owed to a cranky manufacturer, $450K in secured bank debt, and $850K of Convertible Notes due a year later.

The CEO was a master fundraiser and deal maker. His first priority was structuring an acceptable cramdown financing that would (i) bring in $4M to $5M of new money, (ii) convert all existing preferred shares to common, and (iii) convert the notes and one-half of the manufacturing vendor payable to common stock.

That structure would clean up both the cap table (eliminating all liquidation preferences) and the balance sheet (reducing debt to an amount that could be paid off with the new money).

The CEO's second priority was negotiating an opportunitic licensing deal for the company's IP.

While he socialized proposed financing structures with the various stakeholders and worked on the licensing deal, I focused on debt reduction. Within a few weeks, I had lowered A/P from $1.1M to $350K. I did this by negotiating with each vendor, getting most of them to take an immediate payment of about $.12 for every dollar owed in exchange for a full release.

Our next big break also came fairly quickly. The CEO worked out a licensing deal for $1.1 million in cash in exchange for a technology license. This was a lucky break for the company.

With the $1.1 million licensing fee, we immediately paid off the $450K secured bank loan. That loan was already in default and the subject of awkward weekly calls with the bank.

Another $300K of the $1.1M went out the door immediately to pay off an agitated landlord and other creditors credibly threatening litigation.

In another win, after many weeks of negotiations, I convinced the federal regulator to state in writing that the company had satisfied its obligations under "the Order." That was a big regulatory win. Fundraising under an open federal investigation is always challenging.

This all took many months, during which the company was still burning a little cash. But things were starting to look much better. The final hurdles standing in the way of a successful turnaround were (i) working out terms with the manufacturer, which had a writ of attachment for $1.2M, (ii) obtaining support of the $850K of noteholders to convert into common stock in the cramdown, (iii) obtaining board and shareholder consent for the cramdown financing package, and (iv) bringing in the $3.5M to $4M million needed to execute on a revised business plan.

We lost months dealing with the intractable manufacturer and again ran out of money, after which we lost our controller. The CEO and I worked without pay for months.

Ultimately, though, the CEO and I devised a financing package that seemed to have everybody's cooperation. We found a new lead investor willing to put in $2M. Other prior investors seemed willing to help round the new money number up to between $3.5M and $4M. The shareholder representatives were supportive of converting their existing preferred stock into common stock. And eventually, the cranky manufacturer agreed to take half of its $1.2M receivable in common stock in the cramdown.

The last holdout group was the $850K of noteholders. That group rejected the proposal to convert the notes to common stock, tipping over the entire financing deal.

Adding insult to injury, the representative of the noteholder group was a condescending jerk. I had worked for months without pay, and promptly resigned. The CEO resigned days later. Ultimately, nobody received anything, including the representative of the noteholder group.

> <u>Lesson:</u> Insolvent companies cannot always be saved, and sometimes it is difficult to obtain the cooperation necessary from divergent stakeholders to even wind them up properly. Difficulties in balancing and accommodating divergent stakeholder interests elevate the legal, financial, and professional risks associated with trying to help insolvent companies.

Zone of Insolvency Summary

As a company gets deeper into insolvency, options tend to narrow. When outcomes narrow, the quality and value of the potential outcomes are reduced and risks go up.

A startup team always has to deal with the hand of cards it has, but managers should take an expansive view of opportunities for maximizing value well before options have been reduced to a cramdown, bankruptcy, 363 asset sale, or assignment for the benefit of creditors.

A timely down round or strategic sale when a company still has resources and some alternatives may not be considered ideal at the time, but those are much cleaner options than a cramdown or *"controlled flight into terrain"* by way of bankruptcy or ABC.

Leading through financial difficulty requires seeking consensus with multiple stakeholders with different interests and aligning all of them toward a common goal. This always requires actively soliciting stakeholder input.

Striking deals amid financial distress requires founders and CEOs to use personal relationships adeptly and to exert whatever pressures are reasonably available to get investors and creditors on board with the best plan at any given moment.

The key is acting decisively while there are still options.

Sometimes all it takes is for the CEO to timely slide a set of keys across the conference room table in a board room and say to his or her investors, *"If you're not stepping up, the team and I are done. Don't forget to lock up behind you."*

It might be a bluff, and it might not. But investors are rarely keen on taking the captain's chair of a burning startup, so it might be worth a try.

Author's Note

Hello Reader,

I know *Startup Law and Fundraising* was long and challenging. Congrats!

You are now better prepared to lead or counsel your startup(s) as a founder, board member, employee, attorney, or other advisor.

Please send any suggestions for improving this book to my attention at businesslawseminargroup@ gmail.com. All submissions become the property of BLSG, including all IP rights, and all will be carefully considered by me.

If you liked this book, please help others find it by writing a thoughtful review on Amazon. That would be greatly appreciated.

Please also check out my best-selling (and much shorter) book, *Contract Drafting and Negotiation for Entrepreneurs and Business Professionals.*

https://www.amazon.com/dp/0692138307

In 2021, I will publish my third book, *Careers in the Law.*

In *Careers in the Law*, I profile every way to use a law degree, conventional and non-conventional, with insights on every area of practice and many uses for law degrees you probably didn't know about.

Thank you and best wishes in your entrepreneurial adventures!

Paul A. Swegle

https://twitter.com/pswegle

https://www.facebook.com/lawtalks/

https://www.startupgc.us/

Case Studies Plotted on the L&M Matrix

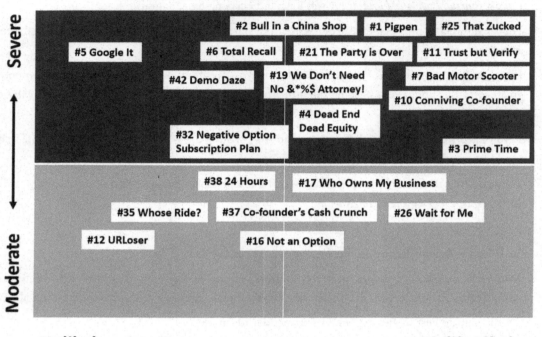

Index of Terms, Laws, Rules and Acronyms